# MORE PRAISE FROM ACROSS THE NATION FOR THE JOBBANK SERIES...

"If you are looking for a job ... before you go to the newspapers and the help-wanted ads, listen to Bob Adams, publisher of *The Metropolitan New York JobBank*."
**-Tom Brokaw, *NBC***

"For those graduates whose parents are pacing the floor, conspicuously placing circled want ads around the house and typing up resumes, [*The Carolina JobBank*] answers job-search questions."
***-Greensboro News and Record***

"A timely book for Chicago job hunters follows books from the same publisher that were well received in New York and Boston ... [*The Chicago JobBank* is] a fine tool for job hunters ..."
**-Clarence Peterson, *Chicago Tribune***

"Job hunters can't afford to waste time. *The Minneapolis-St. Paul JobBank* contains information that used to require hours of research in the library."
**-Carmella Zagone**
**Minneapolis-based Human Resources Administrator**

"*The Boston JobBank* provides a handy map of employment possibilities in greater Boston. This book can help in the initial steps of a job search by locating major employers, describing their business activities, and for most firms, by naming the contact person and listing typical professional positions. For recent college graduates, as well as experienced professionals, *The Boston JobBank* is an excellent place to begin a job search."
**-Juliet F. Brudney, Career Columnist**
***Boston Globe***

"No longer can jobseekers feel secure about finding employment just through want ads. With the tough competition in the job market, particularly in the Boston area, they need much more help. For this reason, *The Boston JobBank* will have a wide and appreciative audience of new graduates, job changers, and people relocating to Boston. It provides a good place to start a search for entry-level professional positions."
***-Journal of College Placement***

"*The Seattle JobBank* is an essential resource for job hunters."
**-Gil Lopez, Staffing Team Manager**
**Battelle Pacific Northwest Laboratories**

"*The Phoenix JobBank* is a first-class publication. The information provided is useful and current."

**-Lyndon Denton**
**Director of Human Resources and Materials Management**
**Apache Nitrogen Products, Inc.**

"Through *The Dallas-Fort Worth JobBank,* we've been able to attract high-quality candidates for several positions."

**-Rob Bertino, Southern States Sales Manager**
**CompuServe**

"Packed with helpful contacts, *The Houston JobBank* empowers its reader to launch an effective, strategic job search in the Houston metropolitan area."

**-Andrew Ceperley, Director**
**College of Communication Career Services**
**The University of Texas at Austin**

"*The San Francisco Bay Area JobBank ...* is a highly useful guide, with plenty of how-to's ranging from resume tips to interview dress codes and research shortcuts."

**-A.S. Ross, *San Francisco Examiner***

"[*The Atlanta JobBank* is] one of the best sources for finding a job in Atlanta!"

**-Luann Miller, Human Resources Manager**
**Prudential Preferred Financial Services**

"This well-researched, well-edited, job hunter's aid includes most major businesses and institutional entities in the New York metropolitan area ... [*The Metropolitan New York JobBank* is] highly recommended."

**Cheryl Gregory-Pindell, *Library Journal***

"*The Chicago JobBank* has proven to be an extremely useful resource for finding a job in the Chicagoland area."

**-George Pinder, Sr., VP/Human Resources**
**John Crane, Inc.**

"Thanks to our listing in *The Detroit JobBank,* we have received a large number of professional referrals."

**-Michael A. Solonika, Human Resources Manager**
**Prestige Stamping, Inc.**

"*The Florida JobBank* is the key to networking successfully in today's competitive job market."

**-Anthony LaMorte, Placement Specialist**
**City of Hialeah Adult and Youth Service**

# What makes the
# JobBank series
# the nation's premier
# line of employment guides?

With vital employment information on thousands of employers across the nation, the JobBank series is the most comprehensive and authoritative set of career directories available today.

Each book in the series provides information on **dozens of different industries** in a given city or area, with the primary employer listings providing contact information, telephone and fax numbers, addresses, Websites, a summary of the firm's business, and in many cases descriptions of the firm's typical professional job categories, the principal educational backgrounds sought, internships, and the fringe benefits offered.

In addition to the **detailed primary employer listings,** JobBank books give telephone numbers and addresses for **thousands of additional employers,** as well as information about executive search firms, placement agencies, and professional associations.

All of the reference information in the JobBank series is as up-to-date and accurate as possible. Every year, the entire database is thoroughly researched and verified by mail and by telephone. Adams Media Corporation publishes **more local employment guides more often** than any other publisher of career directories.

In addition, the JobBank series features current information about the local job scene -- **forecasts on which industries are the hottest** and **lists of regional professional associations,** so you can get your job hunt started off right.

The JobBank series offers **33 regional titles**, from Minneapolis to Houston, and from Boston to San Francisco. All of the information is organized geographically, because most people look for jobs in specific areas of the country.

A condensed, but thorough, review of the entire job search process is presented in the chapter **The Basics of Job Winning**, a feature which has received many compliments from career counselors. In addition, each JobBank directory includes a section on **resumes and cover letters** the *New York Times* has acclaimed as "excellent."

The JobBank series gives job hunters the most comprehensive, timely, and accurate career information, organized and indexed to facilitate the job search. An entire career reference library, JobBank books are the consummate employment guides.

# Top career publications from Adams Media Corporation

**The JobBank Series:**
*each JobBank book is $16.95*

The Atlanta JobBank, 1999
The Austin/San Antonio JobBank, 2nd Ed.
The Boston JobBank, 1999
The Carolina JobBank, 5th Ed.
The Chicago JobBank, 1999
The Connecticut JobBank, 1st Ed.
The Dallas-Fort Worth JobBank, 1999
The Denver JobBank, 11th Ed.
The Detroit JobBank, 8th Ed.
The Florida JobBank, 1999
The Houston JobBank, 10th Ed.
The Indiana JobBank, 2nd Ed.
The Las Vegas JobBank, 2nd Ed.
The Los Angeles JobBank, 1999
The Minneapolis-St. Paul JobBank, 10th Ed.
The Missouri JobBank, 2nd Ed.
The Northern New England JobBank, 1st Ed.
The New Jersey JobBank, 1st Ed.
The New Mexico JobBank, 1st Ed.
The Metropolitan New York JobBank, 1999
The Upstate New York JobBank, 1st Ed.
The Ohio JobBank, 1999
The Greater Philadelphia JobBank, 1999
The Phoenix JobBank, 7th Ed.
The Pittsburgh JobBank, 2nd Ed.
The Portland JobBank, 2nd Ed.
The Salt Lake City JobBank, 1st Ed.
The San Francisco Bay Area JobBank, 1999
The Seattle JobBank, 1999
The Tennessee JobBank, 4th Ed.
The Virginia JobBank, 2nd Ed.
The Metropolitan Washington DC JobBank, 1999
The Wisconsin JobBank, 1st Ed.

The JobBank Guide to Computer & High-Tech
    Companies, 2nd Ed. ($16.95)

The JobBank Guide to Health Care Companies,
    1st Ed. ($16.95)

The National JobBank, 1999
    (Covers the entire U.S.: $350.00 hc)

The JobBank Guide to Employment Services,
    1998 -1999
    (Covers the entire U.S.: $199.00 hc)

**Other Career Titles:**

The Adams Cover Letter Almanac ($10.95)
The Adams Electronic Job Search Almanac, 1999
    ($10.95)
The Adams Executive Recruiters Almanac
    ($16.95)
The Adams Job Interview Almanac ($12.95)
The Adams Jobs Almanac, 1999 ($16.95)
The Adams Resume Almanac ($10.95)
America's Fastest Growing Employers, 2nd Ed.
    ($16.00)
Career Shifting ($9.95)
Cold Calling Techniques, 3rd Ed. ($7.95)
College Grad Job Hunter, 4th Ed. ($14.95)
The Complete Resume & Job Search Book for
    College Students ($10.95)
Cover Letters That Knock 'em Dead, 3rd Ed.
    ($10.95)
Every Woman's Essential Job Hunting & Resume
    Book ($10.95)
The Harvard Guide to Careers in the Mass Media
    ($7.95)
High Impact Telephone Networking for Job
    Hunters ($6.95)
How to Become Successfully Self-Employed, 2nd
    Ed. ($9.95)
How to Get a Job in Education, 2nd Ed. ($15.95)
The Job Hunter's Checklist ($5.95)
The Job Search Handbook ($6.95)
Knock 'em Dead, 1999 ($12.95)
The Lifetime Career Manager ($20.00 hc)
The MBA Advantage ($12.95)
The Minority Career Book ($9.95)
The National Jobline Directory ($7.95)
The New Rules of the Job Search Game ($10.95)
Outplace Yourself ($15.95)
Over 40 and Looking for Work? ($7.95)
Reengineering Yourself ($12.95)
The Resume Handbook, 3rd Ed. ($7.95)
Resumes That Knock 'em Dead, 3rd Ed. ($10.95)
Richard Beatty's Job Search Networking ($9.95)
300 New Ways to Get a Better Job ($7.95)

Adams JobBank FastResume Suite (CD-ROM)
(Please call for details.)

If you are interested in variations of JobBank company profiles in electronic format for job search or sales mailings,
please call **800/872-5627x5304** or e-mail us at **jobbank@adamsonline.com.**

To order books, please send check or money order (including $4.95 for postage) to:
Adams Media Corporation, 260 Center Street, Holbrook MA 02343.
(Foreign orders please call for shipping rates.) Discounts available for standing orders.

Ordering by credit card? Just call **800/USA-JOBS** (In Massachusetts, call 781/767-8100). Fax: **800/872-5687.**
*Please check your favorite retail outlet first.*

——VISIT OUR WEBSITE——
**http://www.careercity.com**

# THE New Jersey JobBank

| | |
|---:|:---|
| *Managing Editor:* | Steven Graber |
| *Assistant Managing Editor:* | Marcie DiPietro |
| *Senior Editor:* | Michelle Roy Kelly |
| *Senior Associate Editor:* | Heidi E. Sampson |
| *Associate Editor:* | Jayna S. Stafford |
| *Editorial Assistants:* | Thom Blackett |
| | Heather L. Vinhateiro |
| | Jennifer M. Wood |

Adams Media Corporation
HOLBROOK, MASSACHUSETTS

Published by Adams Media Corporation
260 Center Street, Holbrook, MA 02343

Manufactured in the United States of America.

Because addresses and telephone numbers of smaller companies change rapidly, we recommend you call each company and verify the information before mailing to the employers listed in this book. Mass mailings are not recommended.

While the publisher has made every reasonable effort to obtain and verify accurate information, occasional errors are inevitable due to the magnitude of the database. Should you discover an error, or if a company is missing, please write the editors at the above address so that we may update future editions.

"This publication is designed to provide accurate and authoritative information with regard to the subject matter covered. It is sold with the understanding that the publisher is not engaged in rendering legal, accounting, or other professional advice. If legal advice or other expert assistance is required, the services of a competent professional person should be sought."
--From a *Declaration of Principles* jointly adopted by a Committee of the American Bar Association and a Committee of Publishers and Associations

The appearance of a listing in the book does not constitute an endorsement from the publisher.

ISBN: 1-58062-140-6

*This book is available at quantity discounts for bulk purchases.*
*For information, call 800/872-5627.*

**Visit our exciting job and career site at http://www.careercity.com**

# TABLE OF CONTENTS

## SECTION FOUR: EMPLOYMENT SERVICES

### Temporary Employment Agencies/302
*Includes addresses, phone numbers, and descriptions of companies specializing in temporary placement of clients. Also includes contact names, specializations, and a list of positions commonly filled.*

### Permanent Employment Agencies/306
*Includes addresses, phone numbers, and descriptions of companies specializing in permanent placement of clients. Also includes contact names, specializations, and a list of positions commonly filled.*

### Executive Search Firms/316
*Includes addresses, phone numbers, and descriptions of companies specializing in permanent placement of executive-level clients. Also includes contact names, specializations, and a list of positions commonly filled.*

### Contract Services Firms/335
*Includes addresses, phone numbers, and descriptions of companies specializing in contract services.*

### Resume/Career Counseling Services/336
*Includes addresses, phone numbers, and descriptions of companies providing resume writing services and/or career counseling services.*

## SECTION FIVE: INDEX

### Alphabetical Index of Primary Employers/340
*Includes larger employer listings only. Does not include employers that fall under the headings "Additional Employers."*

# HOW TO USE THIS BOOK

Right now, you hold in your hands one of the most effective job-hunting tools available anywhere. In *The New Jersey JobBank*, you will find a wide array of valuable information to help you launch or continue a rewarding career. But before you open to the book's employer listings and start calling about current job openings, take a few minutes to learn how best to use the resources presented in *The New Jersey JobBank*.

*The New Jersey JobBank* will help you to stand out from other jobseekers. While many people looking for a new job rely solely on newspaper help-wanted ads, this book offers you a much more effective job-search method -- direct contact. The direct contact method has been proven twice as effective as scanning the help-wanted ads. Instead of waiting for employers to come looking for you, you'll be far more effective going to them. While many of your competitors will use trial and error methods in trying to set up interviews, you'll learn not only how to get interviews, but what to expect once you've got them.

In the next few pages, we'll take you through each section of the book so you'll be prepared to get a jump-start on your competition.

## Basics of Job Winning

Preparation. Strategy. Time-management. These are three of the most important elements of a successful job search. *Basics of Job Winning* helps you address these and all the other elements needed to find the right job.

One of your first priorities should be to define your personal career objectives. What qualities make a job desirable to you? Creativity? High pay? Prestige? Use *Basics of Job Winning* to weigh these questions. Then use the rest of the chapter to design a strategy to find a job that matches your criteria.

In *Basics of Job Winning,* you'll learn which job-hunting techniques work, and which don't. We've reviewed the pros and cons of mass mailings, help-wanted ads, and direct contact. We'll show you how to develop and approach contacts in your field; how to research a prospective employer; and how to use that information to get an interview and the job.

Also included in *Basics of Job Winning*: interview dress code and etiquette, the "do's and don'ts" of interviewing, sample interview questions, and more. We also deal with some of the unique problems faced by those jobseekers who are currently employed, those who have lost a job, and college students conducting their first job search.

## Resumes and Cover Letters

The approach you take to writing your resume and cover letter can often mean the difference between getting an interview and never being noticed. In this section, we discuss different formats, as well as what to put on (and what to leave off) your resume. We review the benefits and drawbacks of professional resume writers, and the importance of a follow-up letter. Also included in this section are sample resumes and cover letters which you can use as models.

## CD-ROM Job Search

Jobseekers who are looking for an edge against the competition may want to check out these CD-ROM products.

## The Employer Listings

Employers are listed alphabetically by industry, and within each industry, by company names. When a company does business under a person's name, like "John Smith & Co.," the company is usually listed by the surname's spelling (in this case "S"). Exceptions occur when a company's name is widely recognized, like "JCPenney" or "Howard Johnson Motor Lodge." In those cases, the company's first name is the key ("J" and "H" respectively).

*The New Jersey JobBank* covers a very wide range of industries. Each company profile is assigned to one of the industry chapters listed below.

*Accounting and Management Consulting*
*Advertising, Marketing, and Public Relations*
*Aerospace*
*Apparel, Fashion, and Textiles*
*Architecture, Construction, and Engineering*
*Arts and Entertainment/Recreation*
*Automotive*
*Banking/Savings and Loans*
*Biotechnology, Pharmaceuticals, and Scientific R&D*
*Business Services and Non-Scientific Research*
*Charities and Social Services*
*Chemicals/Rubber and Plastics*
*Communications: Telecommunications and Broadcasting*
*Computer Hardware, Software, and Services*
*Educational Services*
*Electronic/Industrial Electrical Equipment*

*Environmental and Waste Management Services*
*Fabricated/Primary Metals and Products*
*Financial Services*
*Food and Beverages/Agriculture*
*Government*
*Health Care: Services, Equipment, and Products*
*Hotels and Restaurants*
*Insurance*
*Legal Services*
*Manufacturing: Miscellaneous Consumer*
*Manufacturing: Miscellaneous Industrial*
*Mining/Gas/Petroleum/Energy Related*
*Paper and Wood Products*
*Printing and Publishing*
*Real Estate*
*Retail*
*Stone, Clay, Glass, and Concrete Products*
*Transportation/Travel*
*Utilities: Electric/Gas/Water*
*Miscellaneous Wholesaling*

Many of the company listings offer detailed company profiles. In addition to company names, addresses, and phone numbers, these listings also include contact names or hiring departments, and descriptions of each company's products and/or services. Many of these listings also feature a variety of additional information including:

**Common positions** - A list of job titles that the company commonly fills when it is hiring, organized in alphabetical order from Accountant to X-ray Technician. Note: Keep in mind that *The New Jersey JobBank* is a directory of major employers in the area, not a directory of openings currently available. Many of the companies listed will be hiring, others will not. However, since most professional job openings are filled without the placement of help-wanted ads, contacting the employers in this book directly is still a more effective method than browsing the Sunday papers.

**Educational backgrounds sought** - A list of educational backgrounds that companies seek when hiring.

**Benefits** - What kind of benefits packages are available from these employers? Here you'll find a broad range of benefits, from the relatively common (medical insurance) to those that are much more rare (health club membership; child daycare assistance).

**Special programs** - Does the company offer training programs, internships, or apprenticeships? These programs can be important to first time jobseekers and college students looking for practical work experience. Many employer profiles will include information on these programs.

**Parent company** - If an employer is a subsidiary of a larger company, the name of that parent company will often be listed here. Use this information to supplement your company research before contacting the employer.

**Number of employees** - The number of workers a company employs.

Company listings may also include information on other U.S. locations and any stock exchanges the firm may be listed on.

Because so many job openings are with small and mid-sized employers, we've also included the addresses and phone numbers of such employers. While none of these listings include any additional hiring information, many of them do offer rewarding career opportunities. These companies are found under each industry heading. Within each industry, they are organized by the type of product or service offered.

A note on all employer listings that appear in *The New Jersey JobBank*: This book is intended as a starting point. It is not intended to replace any effort that you, the jobseeker, should devote to your job hunt. Keep in mind that while a great deal of effort has been put into collecting and verifying the company profiles provided in this book, addresses and contact names change regularly. Inevitably, some contact names listed herein have changed even before you read this. We recommend you contact a company before mailing your resume to ensure nothing has changed.

At the end of each industry section, we have included a directory of other industry-specific resources to help you in your job search. These include: professional and industrial associations, many of which can provide employment advice and job-search help; magazines that cover the industry; and additional directories that may supplement the employer listings in this book.

**Employment Services**

Immediately following the employer listings section of this book are listings of local employment services firms. Many jobseekers supplement their own efforts by contracting "temp" services, headhunters, and other employment search firms to generate potential job opportunities.

This section is a comprehensive listing of such firms, arranged alphabetically under the headings Temporary Employment Agencies, Permanent Employment Agencies, and Executive Search Firms. Each listing includes the firm's name, address, telephone number, and contact person. Most listings also include the industries the firm specializes in, the type of positions commonly filled, and the number of jobs filled annually.

**Index**

*The New Jersey JobBank* index is a straight alphabetical listing.

# THE JOB SEARCH

# THE BASICS OF JOB WINNING:
# A CONDENSED REVIEW

This chapter is divided into four sections. The first section explains the fundamentals that every jobseeker should know, especially first-time jobseekers. The following three sections deal with special situations faced by specific types of jobseekers: those who are currently employed, those who have lost a job, and college students.

## THE BASICS:
### Things Everyone Needs to Know

**Career Planning**
The first step to finding your ideal job is to clearly define your objectives. This is better known as career planning (or life planning if you wish to emphasize the importance of combining the two). Career planning has become a field of study in and of itself.

If you are thinking of choosing or switching careers, we particularly emphasize two things. First, choose a career where you will enjoy most of the day-to-day tasks. This sounds obvious, but most of us have at one point or another been attracted by a glamour industry or a prestigious job title without thinking of the most important consideration: Would we enjoy performing the everyday tasks the position entails?

The second key consideration is that you are not merely choosing a career, but also a lifestyle. Career counselors indicate that one of the most common problems people encounter in job-seeking is that they fail to consider how well-suited they are for a particular position or career. For example, some people, attracted to management consulting by good salaries, early responsibility, and high-level corporate exposure, do not adapt well to the long hours, heavy travel demands, and constant pressure to produce. Be sure to ask yourself how you might adapt to not only the day-to-day duties and working environment that a specific position entails, but also how you might adapt to the demands of that career or industry choice as a whole.

**Choosing Your Strategy**
Assuming that you've established your career objectives, the next step of the job search is to develop a strategy. If you don't take the time to develop a strategy and lay out a plan, you may find yourself going in circles after several weeks of randomly searching for opportunities that always seem just beyond your reach.

The most common job-seeking techniques are:

- following up on help-wanted advertisements
- using employment services
- relying on personal contacts
- contacting employers directly (the Direct Contact method)

Many professionals have been successful in finding better jobs using each one of these approaches. However, the Direct Contact method boasts twice the success rate of the others. So unless you have specific reasons to believe that other strategies would work best for you, Direct Contact should form the foundation of your job search.

If you prefer to use other methods as well, try to expend at least half your effort on Direct Contact, spending the rest on all of the other methods combined. Millions of other jobseekers have already proven that Direct Contact has been twice as effective in obtaining employment, so why not benefit from their experience?

With your strategy in mind, the next step is to work out the details of your search. The most important detail is setting up a schedule. Of course, since job searches aren't something most people do regularly, it may be hard to estimate how long each step will take. Nonetheless, it is important to have a plan so that you can monitor your progress. **Setting Your Schedule**

When outlining your job search schedule, have a realistic time frame in mind. If you will be job-searching full-time, your search could take at least two months or more. If you can only devote part-time effort, it will probably take at least four months.

You probably know a few currently employed people who seem to spend their whole lives searching for a better job in their spare time. Don't be one of them. If you are presently working and don't feel like devoting a lot of energy to job-seeking right now, then wait. Focus on enjoying your present position,

> **The first step in beginning your job search is to clearly define your objectives.**

performing your best on the job, and storing up energy for when you are really ready to begin your job search.

Those of you who are currently unemployed should remember that job-hunting is tough work physically and emotionally. It is also intellectually demanding work that requires you to be at your best. So don't tire yourself out by working on your job campaign around the clock. At the same time, be sure to discipline yourself. The most logical way to manage your time while looking for a job is to keep your regular working hours.

If you are searching full-time and have decided to choose several different contact methods, we recommend that you divide up each week, designating some time for each method. By trying several approaches at once, you can evaluate how promising each seems and alter your schedule accordingly. But be careful -- don't judge the success of a particular technique just by the sheer number of interviews you obtain. Positions advertised in the newspaper, for instance, are likely to generate many more interviews per opening than positions that are filled without being advertised.

If you are searching part-time and decide to try several different contact methods, we recommend that you try them sequentially. You simply won't have enough time to put a meaningful amount of effort into more than one method at once. Estimate the length of your job search, and then allocate so many weeks or months for each contact method, beginning with Direct Contact.

And remember that all schedules are meant to be broken. The purpose of setting a schedule is not to rush you to your goal but to help you periodically evaluate how you're progressing.

**The Direct Contact Method**

Once you have scheduled your time, you are ready to begin your search in earnest. If you decide to begin with the Direct Contact method, the first step is to develop a checklist for categorizing the types of firms for which you'd like to work. You might categorize firms by product line, size, customer type (such as industrial or consumer), growth prospects, or geographical location. Your list of important criteria might be very short. If it is, good! The shorter it is, the easier it will be to locate a company that is right for you.

Now you will want to use this *JobBank* book to assemble your list of potential employers. Choose firms where *you* are most likely to be able to find a job. Try matching your skills with those that a specific job demands. Consider where your skills might be in demand, the degree of competition for employment, and the employment outlook at each company.

Separate your prospect list into three groups. The first 25 percent will be your primary target group, the next 25 percent will be your secondary group, and the remaining names you can keep in reserve.

After you form your prospect list, begin work on your resume. Refer to the Resumes and Cover Letters section following this chapter to get ideas.

Once your resume is complete, begin researching your first batch of prospective employers. You will want to determine whether you would be happy working at the firms you are researching and to get a better idea of what their employment needs might be. You also need to obtain enough information to sound highly informed about the company during phone conversations and in mail correspondence. But don't go all out on your research yet! You probably won't be able to arrange interviews with some of these firms, so save your big research effort until you start to arrange interviews. Nevertheless, you should plan to spend several hours researching each firm. Do your research in batches to save time and energy. Start with this book, and find out what you can about each of the firms in your primary target group. Contact any pertinent professional associations that may be able to help you learn more about an employer. Read industry

> **The more you know about a company, the more likely you are to catch an interviewer's eye. (You'll also face fewer surprises once you get the job!)**

publications looking for articles on the firm. (Addresses of associations and names of important publications are listed after each industrial section of employer listings in this book.) Then try additional resources at your local library. Keep organized, and maintain a folder on each firm.

If you discover something that really disturbs you about the firm (they are about to close their only local office), or if you discover that your chances of getting a job there are practically nil (they have just instituted a hiring freeze), then cross them off your prospect list. If possible,

---

### DEVELOPING YOUR CONTACTS: NETWORKING

Some career counselors feel that the best route to a better job is through somebody you already know or through somebody to whom you can be introduced. These counselors recommend that you build your contact base beyond your current acquaintances by asking each one to introduce you, or refer you, to additional people in your field of interest.

The theory goes like this: You might start with 15 personal contacts, each of whom introduces you to three additional people, for a total of 45 additional contacts. Then each of these people introduces you to three additional people, which adds 135 additional contacts. Theoretically, you will soon know every person in the industry.

Of course, developing your personal contacts does not work quite as smoothly as the theory suggests because some people will not be able to introduce you to anyone. The further you stray from your initial contact base, the weaker your references may be. So, if you do try developing your own contacts, try to begin with as many people that you know personally as you can. Dig into your personal phone book and your holiday greeting card list and locate old classmates from school. Be particularly sure to approach people who perform your personal business such as your lawyer, accountant, banker, doctor, stockbroker, and insurance agent. These people develop a very broad contact base due to the nature of their professions.

---

supplement your research efforts by contacting individuals who know the firm well. Ideally you should make an informal contact with someone at that particular firm, but often a direct competitor, or a major supplier or customer, will be able to supply you with just as much information. At the very least, try to obtain whatever printed information the company has available -- not just annual reports, but product brochures and any other printed materials that the firm may have to offer, either about its operations or about career opportunities.

**Getting the Interview**

Now it is time to arrange an interview, time to make the Direct Contact. If you have read many books on job-searching, you may have noticed that most of these books tell you to avoid the personnel office like the plague. It is said that the personnel office never hires people; they screen candidates. Unfortunately, this is often the case. If you can identify the appropriate manager with the authority to hire you, you should try to contact that person directly. However, this will take a lot of time in each case, and often you'll be bounced back to personnel despite your efforts. So we suggest that initially you begin your Direct Contact campaign through personnel offices. If it seems that the firms on your prospect list do little hiring through personnel, you might consider some alternative courses of action.

The three obvious means of initiating Direct Contact are:

- Showing up unannounced
- Mail (postal or electronic)
- Phone calls

Cross out the first one right away. You should never show up to seek a professional position without an appointment. Even if you are somehow lucky enough to obtain an interview, you will appear so unprofessional that you will not be seriously considered.

Mail contact seems to be a good choice if you have not been in the job market for a while. You can take your time to prepare a letter, say exactly what you want, and of course include your resume. Remember that employers receive many resumes every day. Don't be surprised if you do not get a response to your inquiry, and don't spend weeks waiting for responses that may never come. If you do send a letter, follow it up (or precede it) with a phone call. This will increase your impact, and because of the initial research you did, will underscore both your familiarity with and your interest in the firm.

Another alternative is to make a "cover call." Your cover call should be just like your cover letter: concise. Your first statement should interest the employer in you. Then try to subtly mention your familiarity with the firm. Don't be overbearing; keep your introduction to three sentences or less. Be pleasant, self-confident, and relaxed. This will greatly increase the chances of the person at the other end of the line developing the conversation. But don't press. If you are asked to follow up with

> **Always include a cover letter if you are asked to send a resume.**

"something in the mail," this signals the conversation's natural end. Don't try to prolong the conversation once it has ended, and don't ask what they want to receive in the mail. Always send your resume and a highly personalized follow-up letter, reminding the addressee of the phone conversation. *Always* include a cover letter if you are asked to send a resume.

Unless you are in telephone sales, making smooth and relaxed cover calls will probably not come easily. Practice them on your own, and then with your friends or relatives.

If you obtain an interview as a result of a telephone conversation, be sure to send a thank-you note reiterating the points you made during the

## DON'T BOTHER WITH MASS MAILINGS OR BARRAGES OF PHONE CALLS

Direct Contact does not mean burying every firm within a hundred miles with mail and phone calls. Mass mailings rarely work in the job hunt. This also applies to those letters that are personalized -- but dehumanized -- on an automatic typewriter or computer. Don't waste your time or money on such a project; you will fool no one but yourself.

The worst part of sending out mass mailings, or making unplanned phone calls to companies you have not researched, is that you are likely to be remembered as someone with little genuine interest in the firm, who lacks sincerity -- somebody that nobody wants to hire.

### HELP WANTED ADVERTISEMENTS

Only a small fraction of professional job openings are advertised. Yet the majority of jobseekers -- and quite a few people not in the job market -- spend a lot of time studying the help wanted ads. As a result, the competition for advertised openings is often very severe.

A moderate-sized employer told us about their experience advertising in the help wanted section of a major Sunday newspaper:

*It was a disaster. We had over 500 responses from this relatively small ad in just one week. We have only two phone lines in this office and one was totally knocked out. We'll never advertise for professional help again.*

If you insist on following up on help wanted ads, then research a firm before you reply to an ad. Preliminary research might help to separate you from all of the other professionals responding to that ad, many of whom will have only a passing interest in the opportunity. It will also give you insight about a particular firm, to help you determine if it is potentially a good match. That said, your chances of obtaining a job through the want ads are still much smaller than they are with the Direct Contact method.

conversation. You will appear more professional and increase your impact. However, unless specifically requested, don't mail your resume once an interview has been arranged. Take it with you to the interview instead.

**Preparing for the Interview**

Once the interview has been arranged, begin your in-depth research. You should arrive at an interview knowing the company upside-down and inside-out. You need to know the company's products, types of customers, subsidiaries, parent company, principal locations, rank in the industry, sales and profit trends, type of ownership, size, current plans, and much more. By this time you have probably narrowed your job search to one industry. Even if you haven't, you should still be familiar with the trends in the firm's industry, the firm's principal competitors and their relative performance, and the direction in which the industry leaders are headed.

Dig into every resource you can! Read the company literature, the trade press, the business press, and if the company is public, call your stockbroker (if you have one) and ask for additional information. If possible, speak to someone at the firm before the interview, or if not, speak to someone at a competing firm. The more time you spend, the better. Even if you feel extremely pressed for time, you should set aside several hours for pre-interview research.

> **You should arrive at an interview knowing the company upside-down and inside-out.**

If you have been out of the job market for some time, don't be surprised if you find yourself tense during your first few interviews. It will probably happen every time you re-enter the market, not just when you seek your first job after getting out of school.

Tension is natural during an interview, but knowing you have done a thorough research job should put you more at ease. Make a list of questions that you think might be asked in each interview. Think out your answers carefully and practice them with a friend. Tape record your responses to the problem questions. If you feel particularly unsure of your interviewing skills, arrange your first interviews at firms you are not as interested in. (But remember it is common courtesy to seem enthusiastic about the possibility of working for any firm at which you interview.) Practice again on your own after these first few interviews. Go over the difficult questions that you were asked.

**Interview Attire**

How important is the proper dress for a job interview? Buying a complete wardrobe of Brooks Brothers pinstripes or Donna Karan suits, donning new wing tips or pumps, and having your hair styled every morning are not enough to guarantee you a career position as an investment banker. But on the other hand, if you can't find a clean, conservative suit or won't take the time to wash your hair, then you are just wasting your time by interviewing at all.

Top personal grooming is as important as finding appropriate clothes for a job interview. Careful grooming indicates both a sense of thoroughness and self-confidence. This is not the time to make a statement -- take out the extra earrings and avoid any garish hair colors not found in nature. Women should not wear excessive makeup, and both men and women should refrain from wearing any perfume or cologne (it only takes a small spritz to leave an allergic interviewer with a fit of sneezing and a bad impression of your meeting). Men should be freshly shaven, even if the interview is late in the day, and men with long hair should have it pulled back and neat.

Men applying for any professional position should wear a suit, preferably in a conservative color such as navy or charcoal gray. It is easy to get away with wearing the same dark suit to consecutive interviews at the same company; just be sure to wear a different shirt and tie for each interview.

Women should also wear a businesslike suit. Professionalism still dictates a suit with a skirt, rather than slacks, as proper interview garb for women. This is usually true even at companies where pants are acceptable attire for female employees. As much as you may disagree with this guideline, the more prudent time to fight this standard is after you land the job.

---

### SKIRT VS. PANTS:
### An Interview Dilemma

For those women who are still convinced that pants are acceptable interview attire, listen to the words of one career counselor from a prestigious New England college:

*I had a student who told me that since she knew women in her industry often wore pants to work, she was going to wear pants to her interviews. Almost every recruiter commented that her pants were "too casual," and even referred to her as "the one with the pants." The funny thing was that one of the recruiters who commented on her pants had been wearing jeans!*

---

The final selection of candidates for a job opening won't be determined by dress, of course. However, inappropriate dress can quickly eliminate a first-round candidate. So while you shouldn't spend a fortune on a new wardrobe, you should be sure that your clothes are adequate. The key is to dress at least as formally or slightly more formally and more conservatively than the position would suggest.

**What to**
**Bring**
Be complete. Everyone needs a watch, a pen, and a notepad. Finally, a briefcase or a leather-bound folder (containing extra, *unfolded*, copies of your resume) will help complete the look of professionalism.

Sometimes the interviewer will be running behind schedule. Don't be upset, be sympathetic. There is often pressure to interview a lot of candidates and to quickly fill a demanding position. So be sure to come to your interview with good reading material to keep yourself occupied and relaxed.

**The**
**Interview**
The very beginning of the interview is the most important part because it determines the tone for the rest of it. Those first few moments are especially crucial. Do you smile when you meet? Do you establish enough eye contact, but not too much? Do you walk into the office with a self-assured and confident stride? Do you shake hands firmly? Do you

---

### BE PREPARED:
#### Some Common Interview Questions

Tell me about yourself...

Why did you leave your last job?

What excites you in your current job?

Where would you like to be in five years?

How much overtime are you willing to work?

What would your previous/present employer tell me about you?

Tell me about a difficult situation that you
faced at your previous/present job.

What are your greatest strengths?

What are your greatest weaknesses?

Describe a work situation where you took initiative
and went beyond your normal responsibilities.

Why do you wish to work for this firm?

Why should we hire you?

---

make small talk easily without being garrulous? It is human nature to judge people by that first impression, so make sure it is a good one. But most of all, try to be yourself.

Often the interviewer will begin, after the small talk, by telling you about the company, the division, the department, or perhaps, the position. Because of your detailed research, the information about the company should be repetitive for you, and the interviewer would probably like nothing better than to avoid this regurgitation of the company biography. So if you can do so tactfully, indicate to the interviewer that you are very familiar with the firm. If he or she seems intent on providing you with background information, despite your hints, then acquiesce.

But be sure to remain attentive. If you can manage to generate a brief discussion of the company or the industry at this point, without being forceful, great. It will help to further build rapport, underscore your interest, and increase your impact.

Soon (if it didn't begin that way) the interviewer will begin the questions, many of which you will have already practiced. This period of the interview usually falls into one of two categories (or somewhere in between): either a structured interview, where the interviewer has a prescribed set of questions to ask; or an unstructured interview, where the interviewer will ask only leading questions to get you to talk about yourself, your experiences, and your goals. Try to sense as quickly as possible in which direction the interviewer wishes to proceed. This will make the interviewer feel more relaxed and in control of the situation.

> **The interviewer's job is to find a reason to turn you down; your job is to not provide that reason.**
>
> -John L. LaFevre, author,
> *How You Really Get Hired*
>
> Reprinted from the 1989/90 *CPC Annual,* with permission of the National Association of Colleges and Employers (formerly College Placement Council, Inc.), copyright holder.

Remember to keep attuned to the interviewer and make the length of your answers appropriate to the situation. If you are really unsure as to how detailed a response the interviewer is seeking, then ask.

As the interview progresses, the interviewer will probably mention some of the most important responsibilities of the position. If applicable, draw parallels between your experience and the demands of the position as detailed by the interviewer. Describe your past experience in the same manner that you do on your resume: emphasizing results and achievements and not merely describing activities. But don't exaggerate. Be on the level about your abilities.

The first interview is often the toughest, where many candidates are screened out. If you are interviewing for a very competitive position, you will have to make an impression that will last. Focus on a few of your greatest strengths that are relevant to the position. Develop these points carefully, state them again in different words, and then try to summarize them briefly at the end of the interview.

Often the interviewer will pause toward the end and ask if you have any questions. Particularly in a structured interview, this might be the one chance to really show your knowledge of and interest in the firm. Have a list prepared of specific questions that are of real interest to you. Let your questions subtly show your research and your knowledge of the firm's activities. It is wise to have an extensive list of questions, as several of them may be answered during the interview.

> **Getting a job offer is a lot like getting a marriage proposal. Someone is not going to offer it unless they're pretty sure you're going to accept it.**
>
> -Marilyn Hill,
> Associate Director,
> Career Center,
> Carleton College

Do not turn your opportunity to ask questions into an interrogation. Avoid reading directly from your list of questions, and ask questions that you are fairly certain the interviewer can answer (remember how you feel when you cannot answer a question during an interview).

Even if you are unable to determine the salary range beforehand, do not ask about it during the first interview. You can always ask about it later. Above all, don't ask about fringe benefits until you have been offered a position. (Then be sure to get all the details.)

Try not to be negative about anything during the interview (particularly any past employer or any previous job). Be cheerful. Everyone likes to work with someone who seems to be happy.

Don't let a tough question throw you off base. If you don't know the answer to a question, simply say so -- do not apologize. Just smile. Nobody can answer every question -- particularly some of the questions that are asked in job interviews.

Before your first interview, you may be able to determine how many rounds of interviews there usually are for positions at your level. (Of course it may differ quite a bit even within the different levels of one firm.) Usually you can count on attending at least two or three interviews, although some firms are known to give a minimum of six interviews for all professional positions. While you should be more relaxed as you return for subsequent interviews, the pressure will be on. The more prepared you are, the better.

Depending on what information you are able to obtain, you might want to vary your strategy quite a bit from interview to interview. For instance, if the first interview is a screening interview, then be sure a few of your strengths really stand out. On the other hand, if later interviews are primarily with people who are in a position to veto your hiring, but not to push it forward, then you should primarily focus on building rapport as opposed to reiterating and developing your key strengths.

If it looks as though your skills and background do not match the position the interviewer was hoping to fill, ask him or her if there is another division or subsidiary that perhaps could profit from your talents.

Write a follow-up letter immediately after the interview, while it is still fresh in the interviewer's mind (see the sample follow-up letter format found in the Resumes and Cover Letters chapter). Then, if you haven't heard from the interviewer within a week, call to stress your continued interest in the firm, and the position, and request a second interview. **After the Interview**

## THE BALANCING ACT:
### Looking for a New Job While Currently Employed

For those of you who are still employed, job-searching will be particularly tiring because it must be done in addition to your normal work responsibilities. So don't overwork yourself to the point where you show up to interviews looking exhausted and start to slip behind at your current job. On the other hand, don't be tempted to quit your present job! The long hours are worth it. Searching for a job while you have one puts you in a position of strength.

If you're expected to be in your office during the business day, then you have additional problems to deal with. How can you work interviews into the business day? And if you work in an open office, how can you even call to set up interviews? As much as possible you should keep up the effort and the appearances on your present job. So maximize your use of the lunch hour, early mornings, and late afternoons for calling. If you keep trying, you'll be surprised how often you will be able to reach the executive you are trying to contact during your out-of-office hours. You can catch people as early as 8 a.m. and as late as 6 p.m. on frequent occasions. **Making Contact**

Your inability to interview at any time other than lunch just might work to your advantage. If you can, try to set up as many interviews as possible for your lunch hour. This will go a long way to creating a relaxed atmosphere. But be sure the interviews don't stray too far from the agenda on hand. **Scheduling Interviews**

Lunchtime interviews are much easier to obtain if you have substantial career experience. People with less experience will often find no alternative to taking time off for interviews. If you have to take time off, you have to take time off. But try to do this as little as possible. Try to take the whole day off in order to avoid being blatantly obvious about your job search, and try to schedule two to three interviews for the same day. (It is

> **Try calling as early as 8 a.m. and as late as 6 p.m. You'll be surprised how often you will be able to reach the executive you want during these times of the day.**

very difficult to maintain an optimum level of energy at more than three interviews in one day.) Explain to the interviewer why you might have to juggle your interview schedule -- he/she should honor the respect you're showing your current employer by minimizing your days off and will probably appreciate the fact that another prospective employer is interested in you.

**References**     What do you tell an interviewer who asks for references? Just say that while you are happy to have your former employers contacted, you are trying to keep your job search confidential and would rather that your current employer not be contacted until you have been given a firm offer.

## IF YOU'RE FIRED OR LAID OFF:
### Picking Yourself Up and Dusting Yourself Off

If you've been fired or laid off, you are not the first and will not be the last to go through this traumatic experience. In today's changing economy, thousands of professionals lose their jobs every year. Even if you were terminated with just cause, do not lose heart. Remember, being fired is not a reflection on you as a person. It is usually a reflection of your company's staffing needs and its perception of your recent job performance and attitude. And if you were not performing up to par or enjoying your work, then you will probably be better off at another company anyway.

> **Be prepared for the question "Why were you fired?" during job interviews.**

A thorough job search could take months, so be sure to negotiate a reasonable severance package, if possible, and determine what benefits, such as health insurance, you are still legally entitled to. Also, register for unemployment compensation immediately. Don't be surprised to find other professionals collecting unemployment compensation -- it is for everyone who has lost their job.

Don't start your job search with a flurry of unplanned activity. Start by choosing a strategy and working out a plan. Now is not the time for major changes in your life. If possible, remain in the same career and in the same geographical location, at least until you have been working again for a while. On the other hand, if the only industry for which you are trained is leaving, or is severely depressed in your area, then you should give prompt consideration to moving or switching careers.

Avoid mentioning you were fired when arranging interviews, but be prepared for the question "Why were you fired?" during an interview. If you were laid off as a result of downsizing, briefly explain, being sure to reinforce that your job loss was not due to performance. If you were in fact fired, be honest, but try to detail the reason as favorably as possible and portray what you have learned from your mistakes. If you are confident one of your past managers will give you a good reference, tell the interviewer to contact that person. Do not to speak negatively of your past employer and try not to sound particularly worried about your status of being temporarily unemployed.

Finally, don't spend too much time reflecting on why you were let go or how you might have avoided it. Think positively, look to the future, and be sure to follow a careful plan during your job search.

## THE COLLEGE STUDENT:
### How to Conduct Your First Job Search

While you will be able to apply many of the basics covered earlier in this chapter to your job search, there are some situations unique to the college student's job search.

Perhaps the biggest problem college students face is lack of **Gaining** experience. Many schools have internship programs designed to give **Experience** students exposure to the field of their choice, as well as the opportunity to make valuable contacts. Check out your school's career services department to see what internships are available. If your school does not have a formal internship program, or if there are no available internships that appeal to you, try contacting local businesses and offering your services -- often, businesses will be more than willing to have any extra pair of hands (especially if those hands are unpaid!) for a day or two each week. Or try contacting school alumni to see if you can "shadow" them for a few days, and see what their day-to-day duties are like. Either way, try to begin building experience as early as possible in your college career.

### THE GPA QUESTION

You are interviewing for the job of your dreams. Everything is going well: You've established a good rapport, the interviewer seems impressed with your qualifications, and you're almost positive the job is yours. Then you're asked about your GPA, which is pitifully low. Do you tell the truth and watch your dream job fly out the window?

*Never* lie about your GPA (they may request your transcript, and no company will hire a liar). You can, however, explain if there is a reason you don't feel your grades reflect your abilities, and mention any other impressive statistics. For example, if you have a high GPA in your major, or in the last few semesters (as opposed to your cumulative college career), you can use that fact to your advantage.

What do you do if, for whatever reason, you weren't able to get experience directly related to your desired career? First, look at your previous jobs and see if there's anything you can highlight. Did you supervise or train other employees? Did you reorganize the accounting system, or boost productivity in some way? Accomplishments like these demonstrate leadership, responsibility, and innovation -- qualities that most companies look for in employees. And don't forget volunteer activities and school clubs, which can also showcase these traits.

**On-Campus**
**Recruiting**

Companies will often send recruiters to interview on-site at various colleges. This gives students a chance to get interviews at companies that may not have interviewed them otherwise, particularly if the company schedules "open" interviews, in which the only screening process is who is first in line at the sign-ups. Of course, since many more applicants gain interviews in this format, this also means that many more people are rejected. The on-campus interview is generally a screening interview, to see if it is worth the company's time to invite you in for a second interview. So do everything possible to make yourself stand out from the crowd.

The first step, of course, is to check out any and all information your school's career center has on the company. If the information seems out of date, call the company's headquarters and ask to be sent the latest annual report, or any other printed information.

Many companies will host an informational meeting for interviewees, often the evening before interviews are scheduled to take place. DO NOT MISS THIS MEETING. The recruiter will almost certainly ask if you attended. Make an effort to stay after the meeting and talk with the company's representatives. Not only does this give you an opportunity to find out more information about both the company and the position, it also makes you stand out in the recruiter's mind. If there's a particular company that you had your heart set on, but you weren't able to get an interview with them, attend the information session anyway. You may be able to convince the recruiter to squeeze you into the schedule. (Or you may discover that the company really isn't suited for you after all.)

Try to check out the interview site beforehand. Some colleges may conduct "mock" interviews that take place in one of the standard interview rooms. Or you may be able to convince a career counselor (or even a custodian) to let you sneak a peek during off-hours. Either way, having an idea of the room's setup will help you to mentally prepare.

Be sure to be at least 15 minutes early to the interview. The recruiter may be running ahead of schedule, and might like to take you early. But don't be surprised if previous interviews have run over, resulting in your 30-minute slot being reduced to 20 minutes (or less). Don't complain; just use whatever time you do have as efficiently as possible to showcase the reasons *you* are the ideal candidate.

## LAST WORDS

A parting word of advice. Again and again during your job search you will be rejected. You will be rejected when you apply for interviews. You will be rejected after interviews. For every job offer you finally receive, you probably will have been rejected a multitude of times. Don't let rejections slow you down. Keep reminding yourself that the sooner you go out and get started on your job search, and get those rejections flowing in, the closer you will be to obtaining the job you want.

# RESUMES AND COVER LETTERS

When filling a position, a recruiter will often have 100-plus applicants, but time to interview only a handful of the most promising ones. As a result, he or she will reject most applicants after only briefly skimming their resumes.

Unless you have phoned and talked to the recruiter -- which you should do whenever you can -- you will be chosen or rejected for an interview entirely on the basis of your resume and cover letter. Your cover letter must catch the recruiter's attention, and your resume must hold it. (But remember -- a resume is no substitute for a job search campaign. *You* must seek a job. Your resume is only one tool.)

## RESUME FORMAT:
### Mechanics of a First Impression

**The Basics**

Recruiters dislike long resumes, so unless you have an unusually strong background with many years of experience and a diversity of outstanding achievements, keep your resume length to one page. If you must squeeze in more information than would otherwise fit, try using a smaller typeface or changing the margins.

Keep your resume on standard 8-1/2" x 11" paper. Since recruiters often get resumes in batches of hundreds, a smaller-sized resume may get lost in the pile. Oversized resumes are likely to get crumpled at the edges, and won't fit easily in their files.

First impressions matter, so make sure the recruiter's first impression of your resume is a good one. Print your resume on quality paper that has weight and texture, in a conservative color such as white, ivory, or pale gray. Use matching paper and envelopes for both your resume and cover letter.

**Getting it on Paper**

Modern photocomposition typesetting gives you the clearest, sharpest image, a wide variety of type styles, and effects such as italics, bold-facing, and book-like justified margins. It is also much too expensive for many jobseekers. And improvements in laser printers mean that a computer-generated resume can look just as impressive as one that has been professionally typeset.

A computer or word processor is the most flexible way to type your resume. This will allow you to make changes almost instantly and to store different drafts on disk. Word processing and desktop publishing systems also offer many different fonts to choose from, each taking up different amounts of space. (It is generally best to stay between 9-point and 12-point font size.) Many other options are also available, such as bold-facing for emphasis, justified margins, and the ability to change and manipulate spacing.

The end result, however, will be largely determined by the quality of the printer you use. You need at least "letter quality" type for your resume. Do not use a "near letter quality" or dot matrix printer. Laser printers will generally provide the best quality.

Household typewriters and office typewriters with nylon or other cloth ribbons are *not* good enough for typing your resume. If you don't have access to a quality word processor, hire a professional who can prepare your resume with a word processor or typesetting machine.

*Don't* make your copies on an office photocopier. Only the personnel office may see the resume you mail. Everyone else may see only a copy of it, and copies of copies quickly become unreadable. Either print out each copy individually, or take your resume to a professional copy shop, which will generally offer professionally-maintained, extra-high-quality photocopiers and charge fairly reasonable prices.

**Proof with Care**

Whether you typed it yourself or paid to have it produced professionally, mistakes on resumes are not only embarrassing, but will usually remove you from further consideration (particularly if something obvious such as your name is misspelled). No matter how much you paid someone else to type, write, or typeset your resume, *you* lose if there is a mistake. So proofread it as carefully as possible. Get a friend to help you. Read your draft aloud as your friend checks the proof copy. Then have your friend read aloud while you check. Next, read it letter by letter to check spelling and punctuation.

> The one piece of advice I give to everyone about their resume is: Show it to people, show it to people, show it to people. Before you ever send out a resume, show it to at least a dozen people.
>
> -Cate Talbot Ashton,
> Associate Director,
> Career Services,
> Colby College

If you are having it typed or typeset by a resume service or a printer, and you can't bring a friend or take the time during the day to proof it, pay for it and take it home. Proof it there and bring it back later to get it corrected and printed.

If you wrote your resume on a word processing program, also use that program's built-in spell checker to double-check for spelling errors. But keep in mind that a spell checker will not find errors such as "to" for "two" or "wok" for "work." It's important that you still proofread your resume, even after it has been spell-checked.

**Types of Resumes**

The two most common resume formats are the functional resume and the chronological resume (examples of both types can be found at the end of this chapter). A functional resume focuses on skills and de-emphasizes job titles, employers, etc. A functional resume is best if you have been out of the work force for a long time and/or if you want to highlight specific skills and strengths that your most recent jobs don't necessarily reflect.

Choose a chronological format if you are currently working or were working recently, and if your most recent experiences relate to your desired field. Use reverse chronological order. To a recruiter your last job and your latest schooling are the most important, so put the last first and list the rest going back in time.

Your name, phone number, and a complete address should be at the **Organization** top of your resume. Try to make your name stand out by using a slightly larger font size or all capital letters. Be sure to spell out everything -- never abbreviate St. for Street or Rd. for Road. If you are a college student, you should also put your home address and phone number at the top.

Next, list your experience, then your education. If you are a recent graduate, list your education first, unless your experience is more important than your education. (For example, if you have just graduated from a teaching school, have some business experience, and are applying for a job in business, you would list your business experience first.)

Keep everything easy to find. Put the dates of your employment and education on the left of the page. Put the names of the companies you worked for and the schools you attended a few spaces to the right of the dates. Put the city and state, or the city and country, where you studied or worked to the right of the page.

This is just one suggestion that may work for you. The important thing is simply to break up the text in some way that makes your resume visually attractive and easy to scan, so experiment to see which layout works best for your resume. However you set it up, stay consistent. Inconsistencies in fonts, spacing, or tenses will make your resume look sloppy. Also, be sure to use tabs to keep your information vertically lined up, rather than the less precise space bar.

## RESUME CONTENT:
### Say it with Style

You are selling your skills and accomplishments in your resume, so it **Sell Yourself** is important to inventory yourself and know yourself. If you have achieved something, say so. Put it in the best possible light. But avoid subjective statements, such as "I am a hard worker" or "I get along well with my coworkers." Just stick to the facts.

While you shouldn't hold back or be modest, don't exaggerate your achievements to the point of misrepresentation. Be honest. Many companies will immediately drop an applicant from consideration (or fire a current employee) if inaccurate information is discovered on a resume or other application material.

**Keep it Brief**   Write down the important (and pertinent) things you have done, but do it in as few words as possible. Your resume will be scanned, not read, and short, concise phrases are much more effective than long-winded sentences. Avoid the use of "I" when emphasizing your accomplishments. Instead, use brief phrases beginning with action verbs.

While some technical terms will be unavoidable, you should try to avoid excessive "technicalese." Keep in mind that the first person to see your resume may be a human resources person who won't necessarily know all the jargon -- and how can they be impressed by something they don't understand?

Also, try to keep your paragraphs at six lines or shorter. If you have more than six lines of information about one job or school, put it in two or more paragraphs. The shorter your resume is, the more carefully it will be examined. Remember: Your resume usually has between eight and 45 seconds to catch an employer's eye. So make every second count.

**Job Objective**   A functional resume may require a job objective to give it focus. One or two sentences describing the job you are seeking can clarify in what capacity your skills will be best put to use.

> *Examples:*  An entry-level position in the publishing industry.
> A challenging position requiring analytical thought
> and excellent writing skills.

Don't include a job objective in a chronological resume. Even if you are certain of exactly what type of job you desire, the presence of a job objective might eliminate you from consideration for other positions that a recruiter feels are a better match for your qualifications. But even though you may not put an objective on paper, having a career goal in mind as you write can help give your resume a sense of direction.

**Work Experience**   Some jobseekers may choose to include both "Relevant Experience" and "Additional Experience" sections. This can be useful, as it allows the jobseeker to place more emphasis on certain experiences and to de-emphasize others.

Emphasize continued experience in a particular job area or continued interest in a particular industry. De-emphasize irrelevant positions. Delete positions that you held for less than four months (unless you are a very recent college grad or still in school). Stress your results, elaborating on how you contributed in your previous jobs. Did you increase sales, reduce costs, improve a product, implement a new program? Were you promoted? Use specific numbers (i.e., quantities, percentages, dollar amounts) whenever possible.

Mention all relevant responsibilities. Be specific, and slant your past accomplishments toward the position that you hope to obtain. For example, do you hope to supervise people? If so, then state how many people, performing what function, you have supervised.

Keep it brief if you have more than two years of career experience. **Education** Elaborate more if you have less experience. If you are a recent grad with two or more years of college, you may choose to include any high school activities that are directly relevant to your career. If you've been out of school for awhile, list post-secondary education only.

Mention degrees received and any honors or special awards. Note individual courses or research projects you participated in that might be relevant for employers. For example, if you are an English major applying for a position as a business writer, be sure to mention any business or economics courses.

## USE ACTION VERBS

*How* you write your resume is just as important as *what* you write. The strongest resumes use short phrases beginning with action verbs. Below are a few action verbs you may want to use. (This list is not all-inclusive.)

| | | | |
|---|---|---|---|
| achieved | developed | integrated | purchased |
| administered | devised | interpreted | reduced |
| advised | directed | interviewed | regulated |
| analyzed | discovered | invented | reorganized |
| arranged | distributed | launched | represented |
| assembled | eliminated | maintained | researched |
| assisted | established | managed | resolved |
| attained | evaluated | marketed | restored |
| budgeted | examined | mediated | restructured |
| built | executed | monitored | revised |
| calculated | expanded | negotiated | scheduled |
| collaborated | expedited | obtained | selected |
| collected | facilitated | operated | served |
| compiled | formulated | ordered | sold |
| completed | founded | organized | solved |
| computed | generated | participated | streamlined |
| conducted | headed | performed | studied |
| consolidated | identified | planned | supervised |
| constructed | implemented | prepared | supplied |
| consulted | improved | presented | supported |
| controlled | increased | processed | tested |
| coordinated | initiated | produced | trained |
| created | installed | proposed | updated |
| designed | instituted | provided | upgraded |
| determined | instructed | published | wrote |

**Highlight Impressive Skills** Be sure to mention any computer skills you may have. You may wish to include a section entitled "Additional Skills" or "Computer Skills," in which you list any software programs you know. An additional skills section is also an ideal place to mention fluency in a foreign language.

**Personal Data** This section is optional, but if you choose to include it, keep it very brief (two lines maximum). A one-word mention of hobbies such as fishing, chess, baseball, cooking, etc., can give the person who will interview you a good way to open up the conversation. It doesn't hurt to include activities that are unusual (fencing, bungee jumping, snake-charming) or that somehow relate to the position or the company you're applying to (for instance, if you are a member of a professional organization in your industry). Never include information about your age, health, physical characteristics, marital status, or religious affiliation.

**References** The most that is needed is the sentence, "References available upon request," at the bottom of your resume. If you choose to leave it out, that's fine.

## HIRING A RESUME WRITER:
### Is it the Right Choice for You?

If you write reasonably well, it is to your advantage to write your own resume. Writing your resume forces you to review your experience and figure out how to explain your accomplishments in clear, brief phrases. This will help you when you explain your work to interviewers.

If you write your resume, everything will be in your own words -- it will sound like you. It will say what you want it to say. If you are a good writer, know yourself well, and have a good idea of which parts of your background employers are looking for, you should be able to write your own resume better than anyone else can. If you decide to write your resume yourself, have as many people review and proofread it as possible. Welcome objective opinions and other perspectives.

> **Those things [marital status, church affiliations, etc.] have no place on a resume. Those are illegal questions, so why even put that information on your resume?**
>
> -Becky Hayes, Career Counselor
> Career Services, Rice University

**When to Get Help** If you have difficulty writing in "resume style" (which is quite unlike normal written language), if you are unsure of which parts of your background you should emphasize, or if you think your resume would make your case better if it did not follow one of the standard forms outlined either here or in a book on resumes, then you should consider having it professionally written.

There are two reasons even some professional resume writers we know have had their resumes written with the help of fellow professionals. First, they may need the help of someone who can be objective about their background, and second, they may want an experienced sounding board to help focus their thoughts.

The best way to choose a writer is by reputation -- the **If You Hire** recommendation of a friend, a personnel director, your school placement **a Pro** officer, or someone else knowledgeable in the field.

*Important questions:*
- "How long have you been writing resumes?"
- "If I'm not satisfied with what you write, will you go over it with me and change it?"
- "Do you charge by the hour or a flat rate?"

There is no sure relation between price and quality, except that you are unlikely to get a good writer for less than $50 for an uncomplicated resume and you shouldn't have to pay more than $300 unless your experience is very extensive or complicated. There will be additional charges for printing.

Few resume services will give you a firm price over the phone, simply because some resumes are too complicated and take too long to do for a predetermined price. Some services will quote you a price that applies to almost all of their customers. Once you decide to use a specific writer, you should insist on a firm price quote before engaging their services. Also, find out how expensive minor changes will be.

## COVER LETTERS:
### Quick, Clear, and Concise

*Always* mail a cover letter with your resume. In a cover letter you can show an interest in the company that you can't show in a resume. You can also point out one or two skills or accomplishments the company can put to good use.

The more personal you can get, the better. If someone known to the **Make it** person you are writing has recommended that you contact the company, **Personal** get permission to include his/her name in the letter. If you have the name of a person to send the letter to, address it directly to that person (after first calling the company to verify the spelling of the person's name, correct title, and mailing address). Be sure to put the person's name and title on both the letter and the envelope. This will ensure that your letter will get through to the proper person, even if a new person now occupies this position. But even if you don't have a contact name and are simply addressing it to the "Personnel Director" or the "Hiring Partner," definitely send a letter.

Type cover letters in full. Don't try the cheap and easy ways, like using a computer mail merge program, or photocopying the body of your letter and typing in the inside address and salutation. You will give the impression that you are mailing to a host of companies and have no particular interest in any one.

**Cover letter do's and don'ts**

- *Do* keep your cover letter brief and to the point.
- *Do* be sure it is error-free.
- *Don't* just repeat information verbatim from your resume.
- *Don't* overuse the personal pronoun "I."
- *Don't* send a generic cover letter -- show your personal knowledge of and interest in that particular company.
- *Do* accentuate what you can offer the company, not what you hope to gain from them.

# FUNCTIONAL RESUME
(Prepared on a word processor
and laser printed.)

## ELIZABETH HELEN LaFRANCE
129 Shoreline Drive
Harbor Point OH 45822
419/555-6652

### Objective
A position as a graphic designer commensurate with my acquired skills and expertise.

### Summary
Extensive experience in plate making, separations, color matching, background definition, printing, mechanicals, color corrections, and personnel supervision. A highly motivated manager and effective communicator. Proven ability to:

- **Create Commercial Graphics**
- **Produce Embossed Drawings**
- **Color Separate**
- **Control Quality**
- **Resolve Printing Problems**
- **Analyze Customer Satisfaction**

### Qualifications

**Printing:**
Knowledgeable in black and white as well as color printing. Excellent judgment in determining acceptability of color reproduction through comparison with original. Proficient at producing four- or five-color corrections on all media, as well as restyling previously reproduced four-color artwork.

**Customer Relations:**
Routinely work closely with customers to ensure specifications are met. Capable of striking a balance between technical printing capabilities and need for customer satisfaction through entire production process.

**Specialties:**
Practiced at creating silk screen overlays for a multitude of processes including velo bind, GBC bind, and perfect bind. Creative design and timely preparation of posters, flyers, and personalized stationery.

**Personnel Supervision:**
Skillful at fostering atmosphere that encourages highly talented artists to balance high-level creativity with maximum production. Consistently meet or beat production deadlines. Instruct new employees, apprentices, and students in both artistry and technical operations.

### Experience
Graphic Arts Professor, Ohio State University, Columbus OH (1987-1993).
Manager, Design Graphics, Lima OH (1993-present).

### Education
Massachusetts Conservatory of Art, Ph.D. 1987
University of Massachusetts, B.A. 1984

# CHRONOLOGICAL RESUME
(Prepared on a word processor
and laser printed.)

---

**RANDALL ELLIS**
557 Pine Street
Seattle, WA 98404
(206) 555-6584

## EXPERIENCE

THE CENTER COMPANY                                          Seattle, WA
*Systems Programmer*                                        1993-present
- Develop and maintain over 100 assembler modules.
- Create screen manager programs, using Assembler and Natural languages, to trace input and output to the VTAM buffer.
- Install and customize Omegamon 695 and 700 on IBM mainframes.
- Develop programs to monitor complete security control blocks, using Assembler and Natural.
- Produce stand-alone IPLs and create backrests on IBM 3380 DASD.

INFO TECH, INC.                                             Seattle, WA
*Technical Manager*                                         1991-1993
- Designed and managed the implementation of a network providing the legal community with a direct line to Supreme Court cases, using Clipper on IBM 386s.
- Developed a system which catalogued entire library inventory, using Turbo Pascal on IBM AT.
- Used C to create a registration system for university registrar on IBM AT.

## EDUCATION

SALEM STATE UNIVERSITY                                      Salem, OR
    B.S. in Computer Science.                      1989
    M.S. in Computer Science.                      1991

## COMPUTER SKILLS

- Programming Languages: C, C++, Assembler, COBOL, Natural, Turbo Pascal, dBASE III+, and Clipper.
- Software: VTAM, Complete, TSO, JES 2, ACF 2, Omegamon 695 and 700, and Adabas.
- Operating Systems: MVS/XA, MVS/SP, MS-DOS, and VMS.

# FUNCTIONAL RESUME

### (Prepared on an office-quality typewriter.)

**MEAGHAN O'LEARY**
703 Mulberry Avenue
Chicago, IL 60601
(312) 555-8841

**OBJECTIVE:**
To contribute over eight years of experience in promotion, communications, and administration to an entry-level position in advertising.

**SUMMARY OF QUALIFICATIONS:**
- Performed advertising duties for small business.
- Experience in business writing and communications skills.
- General knowledge of office management.
- Demonstrated ability to work well with others, in both supervisory and support staff roles.
- Type 75 words per minute.

**SELECTED ACHIEVEMENTS AND RESULTS:**
Promotion:
Composing, editing, and proofreading correspondence and PR materials for own catering service. Large-scale mailings.

Communication:
Instruction; curriculum and lesson planning; student evaluation; parent-teacher conferences; development of educational materials. Training and supervising clerks.

Computer Skills:
Proficient in MS Word, Lotus 1-2-3, Excel, and Filemaker Pro.

Administration:
Record-keeping and file maintenance. Data processing and computer operations, accounts receivable, accounts payable, inventory control, and customer relations. Scheduling, office management, and telephone reception.

**WORK HISTORY:**
Teacher; Self-Employed (owner of catering service); Floor Manager; Administrative Assistant; Accounting Clerk.

**EDUCATION:**
Beloit College, Beloit, WI, BA in Education, 1987

# CHRONOLOGICAL RESUME
### (Prepared on a word processor
### and laser printed.)

**PAUL K. NORTON**
16 Charles Street
Marlborough CT  06447
203/555-9641

**EDUCATION**

Keene State College, Keene NH
Bachelor of Arts in Elementary Education, 1995
• Graduated *magna cum laude*
• English minor
• Kappa Delta Pi member, inducted 1993

**EXPERIENCE**
September 1995-
Present

Elmer T. Thienes Elementary School, Marlborough CT
*Part-time Kindergarten Teacher*
• Instruct kindergartners in reading, spelling, language arts, and
   music.
• Participate in the selection of textbooks and learning aids.
• Organize and supervise class field trips and coordinate in-class
   presentations.

Summers
1993-1995

Keene YMCA, Youth Division, Keene NH
*Child-care Counselor*
• Oversaw summer program for low-income youth.
• Budgeted and coordinated special events and field trips,
   working with Program Director to initiate variations in the
   program.
• Served as Youth Advocate in cooperation with social worker to
   address the social needs and problems of participants.

Spring 1995

Wheelock Elementary School, Keene NH
*Student Teacher*
• Taught third-grade class in all elementary subjects
• Designed and implemented a two-week unit on Native
   Americans.
• Assisted in revision of third-grade curriculum.

Fall 1994

Child Development Center, Keene NH
*Daycare Worker*
• Supervised preschool children on the playground and during art
   activities.
• Created a "Wishbone Corner," where children could quietly
   look at books or take a voluntary "time-out."

**ADDITIONAL INTERESTS**
Martial arts, skiing, politics, reading, writing.

# GENERAL MODEL
# FOR A COVER LETTER

Your mailing address
Date

Contact's name
Contact's title
Company
Company's mailing address

Dear Mr./Ms. _____:

Immediately explain why your background makes you the best candidate for the position that you are applying for. Describe what prompted you to write (want ad, article you read about the company, networking contact, etc.). Keep the first paragraph short and hard-hitting.

Detail what you could contribute to this company. Show how your qualifications will benefit this firm. Describe your interest in the corporation. Subtly emphasizing your knowledge about this firm and your familiarity with the industry will set you apart from other candidates. Remember to keep this letter short; few recruiters will read a cover letter longer than half a page.

If possible, your closing paragraph should request specific action on the part of the reader. Include your phone number and the hours when you can be reached. Mention that if you do not hear from the reader by a specific date, you will follow up with a phone call. Lastly, thank the reader for their time, consideration, etc.

Sincerely,

(signature)

Your full name (typed)

Enclosure (use this if there are other materials, such as your resume,
             that are included in the same envelope)

## SAMPLE COVER LETTER

16 Charles Street
Marlborough CT 06447
March 16, 1999

Ms. Lia Marcusson
Assistant Principal
Jonathon Daniels Elementary School
43 Mayflower Drive
Keene NH 03431

Dear Ms. Marcusson:

Janet Newell recently informed me of a possible opening for a third grade teacher at Jonathon Daniels Elementary School. With my experience instructing third-graders, both in schools and in summer programs, I feel I would be an ideal candidate for the position. Please accept this letter and the enclosed resume as my application.

Jonathon Daniels' educational philosophy that every child can learn and succeed interests me, since it mirrors my own. My current position at Elmer T. Thienes Elementary has reinforced this philosophy, heightening my awareness of the different styles and paces of learning and increasing my sensitivity toward special needs children. Furthermore, as a direct result of my student teaching experience at Wheelock Elementary School, I am comfortable, confident, and knowledgeable working with third-graders.

I look forward to discussing the position and my qualifications for it in more detail. I can be reached at 203/555-9641 evenings or 203/555-0248 weekdays. If I do not hear from you before Tuesday of next week, I will call to see if we can schedule a time to meet. Thank you for your time and consideration.

Sincerely,

Paul Norton

Paul K. Norton

Enclosure

# GENERAL MODEL FOR A
# FOLLOW-UP LETTER

Your mailing address
Date

Contact's name
Contact's title
Company
Company's mailing address

Dear Mr./Ms._____:

Remind the interviewer of the reason (i.e., a specific opening, an informational interview, etc.) you were interviewed, as well as the date. Thank him/her for the interview, and try to personalize your thanks by mentioning some specific aspect of the interview.

Confirm your interest in the organization (and in the opening, if you were interviewing for a particular position). Use specifics to re-emphasize that you have researched the firm in detail and have considered how you would fit into the company and the position. This is a good time to say anything you wish you had said in the initial meeting. Be sure to keep this letter brief; a half-page is plenty.

If appropriate, close with a suggestion for further action, such as a desire to have an additional interview, if possible. Mention your phone number and the hours that you can be reached. Alternatively, you may prefer to mention that you will follow up with a phone call in several days. Once again, thank the person for meeting with you, and state that you would be happy to provide any additional information about your qualifications.

Sincerely,

(signature)

Your full name (typed)

# CD-ROM JOB SEARCH

*Jobseekers who are looking for any edge they can find may want to check out the following selected CD-ROM products. Since most of these databases cost upwards of $500, and are designed for use by other businesses or libraries, don't expect to find these at your local software store. Of course, not all libraries will have all of these resources. Depending on how technologically advanced your library is, you may find only one or two of these electronic databases. Call your library to find out what electronic resources it has available. Many of these databases can also be found in the offices of career counselors or outplacement specialists, and are used as part of your service.*

**ADAMS JOBBANK FASTRESUME SUITE**
260 Center Street
Holbrook MA 02343
800/872-5627
The CD-ROM version of the best-selling *JobBank* series contains 22,000 detailed profiles of companies in all industries, 1,800 executive search firms, and 1,100 employment agencies. For most companies, you will find the name, address, company description, and key contact name. The database also lists common professional positions and information on benefits for most companies. You can search the database by company name, state, industry, and job title. Calling itself a "total job search package," the CD-ROM also creates personalized resumes and cover letters and offers advice on job interviews, including over 100 sample interview questions and answers. *Adams JobBank FastResume Suite* CD-ROM is for Windows®98, Windows®95, and Windows®3.1.

**AMERICAN BIG BUSINESS DIRECTORY**
5711 South 86th Circle
P.O. Box 27347
Omaha NE 68127
800/555-5211
Provides profiles of 160,000 privately and publicly held companies employing over 100 people. The CD-ROM contains company descriptions which include company type, industry, products, and sales information. Also included are contact names for each company, with a total of over 340,000. You can search the database by industry, SIC code, sales volume, employee size, or zip code.

**AMERICAN MANUFACTURER'S DIRECTORY**
5711 South 86th Circle
P.O. Box 27347
Omaha NE 68127
800/555-5211
Made by the same company that created *American Big Business Directory*, *American Manufacturer's Directory* lists over 531,000 manufacturing

companies of all sizes and industries. The directory contains product and sales information, company size, and a key contact name for each company. The user can search by region, SIC code, sales volume, employee size, or zip code.

**BUSINESS U.S.A.**
5711 South 86th Circle
P.O. Box 27347
Omaha NE 68127
800/555-5211
Also from the makers of *American Big Business Directory* and *American Manufacturer's Directory*, this CD-ROM contains information on 10 million U.S. companies. The profiles provide contact information, industry type, number of employees, and sales volume. Each listing also indicates whether the company is public or private, as well as providing information about the company's products. There are a number of different search methods available, including key words, SIC code, geographic location, and number of employees.

**CAREER SEARCH - INTEGRATED RESOURCE SYSTEM**
21 Highland Circle
Needham MA 02194-3075
617/449-0312
*Career Search* is a database which contains listings for over 490,000 privately and publicly held companies. It has contact information, including names of human resources professionals or other executives, for companies of virtually all sizes, types, and industries. The database can be searched by industry, company size, or region. This product is updated monthly.

**COMPANIES INTERNATIONAL**
835 Penobscot Building
645 Griswald Street
Detroit MI 48226
800/877-GALE
Produced by Gale Research Inc., this CD-ROM is compiled from *Ward's Business Directory* and the *World's Business Directory*, and contains information on more than 300,000 companies worldwide. You can find industry information, contact names, and number of employees. Also included is information on the company's products and revenues. The database can be searched by industry, company products, or geographic location.

**CORPTECH DIRECTORY**
12 Alfred Street, Suite 200
Woburn MA 01801-1915
800/333-8036
The *CorpTech Directory* on CD-ROM contains detailed descriptions of over 45,000 technology companies. It also lists the names and titles of nearly 155,000 executives -- CEOs, sales managers, R&D managers, and human resource professionals. World Wide Web and e-mail addresses are also available. In

addition to contact information, you can find detailed information about each company's products or services and annual revenues. The *CorpTech Directory* also lists both the number of current employees, and the number of employees one year ago. Some companies also list the number of employees they project having in one year. You can search the database by type of company, geographic location, or sales revenue. This product is updated quarterly.

## DISCOVERING CAREERS & JOBS
835 Penobscot Building
645 Griswald Street
Detroit MI 48226
800/877-GALE
Provides overviews on 1,200 careers, 1,000 articles from trade publications, and contact information for professional associations. This CD-ROM also contains self-assessment tests, college profiles, and financial aid data.

## DISCOVERING CAREERS & JOBS PLUS
835 Penobscot Building
645 Griswald Street
Detroit MI 48226
800/877-GALE
This CD-ROM gives users contact information on more than 45,000 companies, with 15,000 in-depth profiles and 1,000 company history essays. In addition, the product also provides profiles and application procedures for all major two- and four-year U.S. colleges and universities.

## DUN & BRADSTREET MILLION DOLLAR DISC PLUS
3 Sylvan Way
Parsippany NJ 07054
800/526-0651
This CD-ROM provides information on over 400,000 companies in virtually every industry. About 90 percent of the companies listed are privately held, and all have at least $3 million in annual sales or at least 50 employees. Each company's listing includes the number of employees, sales volume, name of the parent company, and corporate headquarters or branch locations. The *Million Dollar Disc Plus* also provides the names and titles of top executives, as well as biographical information on those executives, including education and career background. Searches can be done by location, industry, SIC code, executive names, or key words in the executive biographies. This directory is updated quarterly.

## ENCYCLOPEDIA OF ASSOCIATIONS:
## NATIONAL ORGANIZATIONS OF THE U.S.
835 Penobscot Building
645 Griswald Street
Detroit MI 48226
800/877-GALE

Contains descriptions and contact information for nearly 23,000 national organizations. You can search by association name, geographic location, and key words. This CD-ROM is available in both single- and multi-user formats.

## GALE BUSINESS RESOURCES CD-ROM
835 Penobscot Building
645 Griswald Street
Detroit MI 48226
800/877-GALE
This two CD-ROM set contains detailed profiles on certain industries and covers the major companies in each industry, with statistics on over 200,000 businesses nationwide. You can search by company name, industry type, products, and more. This product is available in both single- and multi-user formats.

## HARRIS INFOSOURCE NATIONAL
2057 East Aurora Road
Twinsburg OH 44087
800/888-5900
This directory of manufacturers profiles thousands of companies. Although the majority of the companies listed are located in the United States, there are also listings for some Canadian businesses. The listings include the number of employees, plant size, and sales revenue, as well as the names and titles of top executives. This CD-ROM is updated annually and can be purchased in smaller regional or state editions.

## MOODY'S COMPANY DATA
99 Church Street
New York NY 10007
800/342-5647
*Moody's Company Data* is a CD-ROM which has detailed listings for over 10,000 publicly traded companies. In addition to information such as industry, company address, and phone and fax numbers, each listing includes the names and titles of its top officers, including the CEO, president, and vice president; company size; number of shareholders; corporate history; subsidiaries; and financial statements. Users can conduct searches by region, SIC codes, industry, or earnings. This CD-ROM is updated monthly.

## STANDARD & POOR'S REGISTER
65 Broadway
8th Floor
New York NY 10004
800/221-5277
The CD-ROM version of this three-volume desk reference provides the same information as its printed companion. The database lists over 55,000 companies, including more than 12,000 public companies. In addition to contact information, which includes the names and titles of over 500,000 executives, you can find out about each company's primary and secondary sources of

business, annual revenues, number of employees, parent company, and subsidiaries. When available, the *Standard & Poor's Register* also lists the names of banks, accounting firms, and law firms used by each company. Also, the directory provides biographies of more than 70,000 top executives, which include information such as directorships held and schools attended. There are 55 different search modes available on the database. You can search geographically, by zip code, industry, SIC code, or stock symbol. You can also limit your search to only private or only public companies. This directory is updated quarterly.

# ACCOUNTING AND MANAGEMENT CONSULTING

*Accounting and management consulting firms are facing more competitive pressures than ever, coupled with declining profits. Competition is forcing accounting firms to redesign the services they offer, cut costs significantly, and upgrade their recruiting efforts to attract more highly-skilled accountants. Fortunately, innovations in tax software and other technologies have made accounting practices more efficient, though resulting in fewer overall job opportunities. However, the U.S. Department of Labor expects the number of opportunities in this industry to increase 10 to 20 percent by 2006, most notably in the areas of management consulting and other advisory positions.*

*The nation's largest and most dominant accounting firms are focusing more on management consulting. As a result, revenues in the consulting arena have grown significantly. The split of Arthur Andersen into a separate division, Andersen Consulting, reflects a trend that will continue to transform the larger accounting firms and push some business customers toward smaller divisions or private firms.*

*The largest firms are continuing to create partnerships worldwide, and some of the smaller firms are following suit. In July 1998, Price Waterhouse and Coopers & Lybrand merged to form PricewaterhouseCoopers, a global professional services firm. The majority of the mid-sized accounting firms, however, concentrate on maintaining strong regional client relationships. According to* Inc. *magazine, while some accounting firms will be forced out of business due to competition, many have responded by specializing in a particular area.*

## AON CONSULTING

125 Chubb Avenue, Lyndhurst NJ 07071. 201/460-6653. **Fax:** 201/460-6999. **Contact:** Human Resources. **Description:** An international human resources consulting and benefits brokerage firm providing integrated advisory and support services in retirement planning, health care management, organizational effectiveness, compensation, human resources-related communications, and information technologies. AON's organizational effectiveness services include advisory and support services in compensation, strategy development, organizational design, business process redesign, human resources development, management training and development, organizational communications, and information technology applications. Strategic health care services include advisory and support services in traditional group health and welfare programs, strategic health planning, strategic health care management, quality assurance, flexible benefits and compensation, financial management, data management, vendor oversight, and communications. Strategic retirement planning and educational services include consulting and support services in core actuarial applications, retirement health and welfare benefits, funding and investment strategy, recordkeeping and administration, employee sensing and communications, personalized retirement modeling, holistic lifestyle and family planning, database information, and proprietary studies. Information technologies services include human resources information systems development (information management strategies, systems, databases, software, and technology advisement) and human resource systems applications (human resources planning, recordkeeping, communication, and education). **Corporate headquarters location:** Chicago IL.

## BOWMAN & COMPANY LLP

601 White Horse Road, Voorhees NJ 08043. 609/435-6200. **Contact:** Human Resources Department. **World Wide Web address:** http://www.bowmanllp.com. **Description:** A certified public accounting firm. **Common positions include:** Accountant/Auditor. **Educational**

**backgrounds include:** Accounting. **Benefits:** 401(k); Daycare Assistance; Disability Coverage; Life Insurance; Medical Insurance. **Corporate headquarters location:** This Location. **Listed on:** Privately held. **Annual sales/revenues:** $5 - $10 million. **Number of employees at this location:** 90.

## DELOITTE & TOUCHE
2 Hilton Court, Parsippany NJ 07054. 973/683-7000. **Contact:** Personnel. **World Wide Web address:** http://www.dttus.com. **Description:** One of the nation's leading professional services firms. Deloitte & Touche provides accounting, auditing, tax, and management consulting services to over 16,000 people in more than 100 U.S. cities.

## ERNST & YOUNG
125 Chubb Avenue, Lyndhurst NJ 07071. 201/507-2200. **Contact:** Human Resources. **World Wide Web address:** http://www.ey.com. **Description:** A worldwide certified public accounting organization, with operations in three main areas: auditing and accounting; tax services; and management consulting. The company has approximately 5,000 professionals and 600 partners and directors in offices throughout the United States and abroad. **Corporate headquarters location:** New York NY.

## GEMINI CONSULTING
25 Airport Road, Morristown NJ 07960. 973/285-9000. **Fax:** 973/285-9020. **Contact:** Human Resources. **Description:** Provides management consulting services for *Fortune* 500 companies.

## KPMG PEAT MARWICK LLP
3 Chestnut Ridge Road, Montvale NJ 07645. **Contact:** Human Resources. **World Wide Web address:** http://www.kpmgcareers.com. **Description:** This location houses administrative offices. Overall, KPMG Peat Marwick LLP delivers a wide range of value-added assurance, tax, and consulting services. **NOTE:** For immediate consideration, job seekers need to mail, fax, or e-mail a resume to the following location: KPMG National Resume Processing Center, 8200 Brookriver Drive, Suite 400, Dallas TX 75247. Fax: 888/ONE-KPMG. E-mail address: resume@pa0015d5.us.kpmg.com. Please specify Department #NETCCY in all correspondence. **Corporate headquarters location:** This Location. **Other U.S. locations:** Nationwide. **Parent company:** KPMG International is a leader among professional services firms engaged in capturing, managing, assessing, and delivering information to create knowledge that will help its clients maximize shareholder value. The company has more than 85,000 employees worldwide, including 6,500 partners and 60,000 professional staff, serving clients in 844 cities in 155 countries.

## KEPNER-TREGOE, INC.
P.O. Box 704, Princeton NJ 08542. 609/252-2426. **Contact:** Human Resources. **World Wide Web address:** http://www.kepner-tregoe.com. **Description:** A worldwide management consulting firm. Product categories include strategy formulation, systems improvement, skill development, and specific issue resolution. Industry markets served are automotive, information technology, chemicals, financial services, and natural resources. Kepner-Tregoe operates in 44 countries and 14 languages. **Common positions include:** Accountant/Auditor; Administrator; Marketing Specialist; Operations/Production Manager; Planner. **Educational backgrounds include:** Business Administration; Education; Finance; Liberal Arts; Marketing. **Benefits:** Dental Insurance; Disability Coverage; Employee Discounts; Life Insurance; Medical Insurance; Pension Plan; Profit Sharing; Savings Plan; Tuition Assistance. **Corporate headquarters location:** This Location. **Operations at this facility include:** Administration; Sales; Service. **Listed on:** New York Stock Exchange.

## WILLIAM M. MERCER, INC.
212 Carnegie Center, CN-5323, Princeton NJ 08543-5323. 609/520-2500. **Contact:** Carol Bakely, Human Resources. **World Wide Web address:** http://www.mercer.com. **Description:** One of the world's largest actuarial and human resources management consulting firms, providing advice to organizations on all aspects of employee/management relationships. Services include retirement, health and welfare, performance and rewards, communication, investment, human resources administration, risk, finance and insurance, and health care provider consulting. **Corporate headquarters location:** New York NY.

## ROBBINS-GIOIA, INC.
28B Hill Road, Parsippany NJ 07054. 973/402-5824. **Contact:** Human Resources. **World Wide Web address:** http://www.rgalex.com. **Description:** Services include program and project management, configuration management, cost estimating, acquisition management, software development, systems design, technical support, life cycle management, and risk management. Robbins-Gioia functions as a prime contractor, team member, or subcontractor in various industries

including manufacturing, telecommunications, electronics, and state and local government. The company has experience managing large projects in logistics, mergers, personnel, finance, automated data processing, information resource management, systems integration, and new product development. Founded in 1980. **NOTE:** Interested jobseekers should address all inquiries to Robbins-Gioia, Inc., Human Resources, 11 Canal Center Plaza, Suite 200, Alexandria VA 22314-1595. **Corporate headquarters location:** Alexandria VA. **Other U.S. locations:** Montgomery AL; Englewood CO; Dayton OH. **International locations:** London, England.

## KURT SALMON ASSOCIATES, INC.
103 Carnegie Center, Suite 205, Princeton NJ 08540. 609/452-8700. **Contact:** Director of Recruiting. **World Wide Web address:** http://www.kurtsalmon.com. **Description:** Provides management consulting to logistics and consumer products companies.

## SIBSON AND COMPANY, LLC
504 Carnegie Center, Third Floor, Princeton NJ 08543-5211. 609/520-2700. **Contact:** Human Resources. **Description:** A management consulting firm.

*Note: Because addresses and telephone numbers of smaller companies can change rapidly, we recommend you call each company to verify the information below before inquiring about job opportunities. Mass mailings are not recommended.*

### Additional small employers:

**ACCOUNTING, AUDITING, AND BOOKKEEPING SERVICES**

**Arthur Andersen LLP**
101 Eisenhower Pkwy, Roseland NJ 07068-1028. 973/403-6100.

**Deloitte & Touche**
2 Tower Center Blvd, East Brunswick NJ 08816-1100. 732/296-6200.

**Ernst & Young**
99 Wood Ave S, Iselin NJ 08830-2715. 732/906-3200.

**JH Cohn LLP**
75 Eisenhower Pkwy, Roseland NJ 07068-1600. 973/228-3500.

**KPMG Peat Marwick LLP**
PO Box 7468, Princeton NJ 08543-7468. 609/896-2100.

**Lash Tamaron**
395 W Passaic St, Rochelle Park NJ 07662-3016. 201/368-5581.

**Moore Stephens PC**
340 North Ave E, Cranford NJ 07016-2461. 908/272-7000.

**PricewaterhouseCoopers**
101 Hudson St, Jersey City NJ 07302-3915. 201/521-3000.

**PricewaterhouseCoopers**
400 Campus Dr, Florham Park NJ 07932. 973/236-4000.

**Rothstein Kass & Co. PC**
85 Livingston Ave, Roseland NJ 07068-3702. 973/994-6666.

**BUSINESS CONSULTING SERVICES**

**Chauncey Group International Ltd.**
664 Rosedale Rd, Princeton NJ 08540-2218. 609/720-6689.

**Coastal Group Management Co.**
24 Bridge St, Bldg B, Metuchen NJ 08840-2276. 732/494-4300.

**Corning Donrolaar Inc.**
210 Carnegie Ctr, Princeton NJ 08540-6233. 609/452-8550.

**GGI**
500 International Dr, Budd Lake NJ 07828-1381. 973/347-1313.

**Hewitt Associates LLC**
PO Box 755, Bedminster NJ 07921-0755. 908/781-7100.

**Horizons Consulting**
119 Cherry Hll Rd, 2nd Fl, Parsippany NJ 07054-1112. 973/402-1616.

**Kwasha Lipton Group**
2100 N Central Rd, Fort Lee NJ 07024-7558. 201/592-1300.

**Peer Group Inc.**
379 Thornall St, Edison NJ 08837-2225. 732/321-3670.

**Roy F. Weston Inc.**
2890 Woodbridge Ave, Bldg 209, Edison NJ 08837. 732/321-4200.

**Sedgwick Noble Lowndes**
3 Becker Farm Rd, Ste 4, Roseland NJ 07068-1726. 973/533-4500.

**TMP/Worldwide Inc.**
600 International Dr, Budd Lake NJ 07828-4307. 973/347-9410.

**TMR Inc.**
2 0,Lynn Way, Morristown NJ 07960-4618. 973/829-1030.

**Walsh-Lowe and Associates**
47 Newark St, Hoboken NJ 07030-5604. 201/216-1100.

**MANAGEMENT SERVICES**

**Ron Lynn Management Consultants**
1037 Route 46, Clifton NJ 07013-2445. 973/916-0500.

### For more information on career opportunities in accounting and management consulting:

#### Associations

**AMERICAN ACCOUNTING ASSOCIATION**
5717 Bessie Drive, Sarasota FL 34233. 941/921-7747. World Wide Web address: http://www.aaa-edu.org. An academically-oriented accounting association that offers two quarterly journals, a semi-annual journal, a newsletter, and a wide variety of continuing education programs.

**AMERICAN INSTITUTE OF CERTIFIED PUBLIC ACCOUNTANTS**
1211 Avenue of the Americas, New York NY 10036. 212/596-6200. World Wide Web address:

http://www.aicpa.org. A national professional organization for all CPAs. AICPA offers a comprehensive career package to students.

**AMERICAN MANAGEMENT ASSOCIATION**
1601 Broadway, New York NY 10019. 212/586-8100. World Wide Web address: http://www.amanet.org. Provides a variety of publications, training videos, and courses, as well as an Information Resource Center, which provides management information, and a library service.

**ASSOCIATION OF GOVERNMENT ACCOUNTANTS**
2208 Mount Vernon Avenue, Alexandria VA 22301. 703/684-6931. World Wide Web address: http://www. rutgers.edu/accounting/raw/aga. Serves financial management professionals and offers continuing education workshops.

**ASSOCIATION OF MANAGEMENT CONSULTING FIRMS**
521 Fifth Avenue, 35th Floor, New York NY 10175. 212/697-9693. World Wide Web address: http://www. amcf.org.

**THE INSTITUTE OF INTERNAL AUDITORS**
249 Maitland Avenue, Altamonte Springs FL 32701. 407/830-7600. World Wide Web address: http://www. theiia.org. Publishes magazines and newsletters. Provides information on current issues, a network of more than 50,000 members in 100 countries, and professional development and research services. Also offers continuing education seminars.

**INSTITUTE OF MANAGEMENT ACCOUNTANTS**
10 Paragon Drive, Montvale NJ 07645. 201/573-9000. World Wide Web address: http://www.imanet.org. Offers a Certified Management Accountant Program, periodicals, seminars, educational programs, a research program, a financial management network, and networking services. The association has about 80,000 members and 300 local chapters.

**INSTITUTE OF MANAGEMENT CONSULTANTS**
521 Fifth Avenue, 35th Floor, New York NY 10175. 212/697-8262. World Wide Web address: http://www. imc.org. Offers certification programs, professional development, and a directory of members.

**NATIONAL ASSOCIATION OF TAX PRACTITIONERS**
720 Association Drive, Appleton WI 54914-1483. 414/749-1040. World Wide Web address: http://www. natptax.com. Offers seminars, research, newsletters, preparer worksheets, state chapters, insurance, and other tax-related services.

**NATIONAL SOCIETY OF ACCOUNTANTS**
1010 North Fairfax Street, Alexandria VA 22314. 703/549-6400. World Wide Web address:

http://www.nsacct.org. Offers professional development services, government representation, a variety of publications, practice aids, low-cost group insurance, annual seminars, and updates for members on new tax laws.

<u>Magazines</u>

**CPA JOURNAL**
The New York State Society, 530 Fifth Avenue, 5th Floor, New York NY 10036. 212/719-8300. World Wide Web address: http://www.nysscpa.org. Monthly.

**CPA LETTER**
American Institute of Certified Public Accountants, 1211 Avenue of the Americas, New York NY 10036. 212/596-6200. World Wide Web address: http://www. aicpa.org/pubs/cpaltr.

**THE FINANCE AND ACCOUNTING JOBS REPORT**
Career Advancement Publications, Jamestown NY. World Wide Web address: http://www.jobreports.net. This publication is dedicated to finance and accounting professionals who are looking for a job. Each issue includes several hundred job openings in the United States and abroad. This report also offers subscribers networking opportunities through its contact and referral program.

**JOURNAL OF ACCOUNTANCY**
American Institute of Certified Public Accountants, 1211 Avenue of the Americas, New York NY 10036. 212/596-6200. World Wide Web address: http://www. aicpa.org.

**MANAGEMENT ACCOUNTING**
Institute of Management Accountants, 10 Paragon Drive, Montvale NJ 07645. 201/573-9000. World Wide Web address: http://www.imanet.org.

<u>Online Services</u>

**ACCOUNTANTS FORUM**
Go: Aicpa. A CompuServe forum sponsored by the American Institute of Certified Public Accountants.

**FINANCIAL, ACCOUNTING, AND INSURANCE JOBS PAGE**
http://www.nationjob.com/financial. This Website provides a list of financial, accounting, and insurance job openings.

**JOBS IN ACCOUNTING**
http://www.cob.ohio-state.edu/dept/fin/jobs/account. htm#Link7. Provides information on the accounting profession, including salaries, trends, and resources.

**MANAGEMENT CONSULTING JOBS ONLINE**
http://www.cob.ohio-state.edu/~opler/cons. Provides information and resources for jobseekers looking to work in the field of management consulting.

# ADVERTISING, MARKETING, AND PUBLIC RELATIONS

*Professionals in advertising, marketing, and public relations face an industry that is constantly changing and extremely competitive due to the high salaries it commands. Growth is forecast for all areas of advertising, and the public relations sector is projected to be one of the fastest-growing through 2006.*

*Advertising executives are reporting that certain trends are dictating the industry's direction. Perhaps the most prominent are a renewed emphasis on corporate branding and the strategy of advertising products to individual consumers rather than larger groups or corporations.*

*Internet advertising is the fastest-growing area of the industry. Jobseekers with new media and interactive marketing skills will have an advantage over the competition. Companies are investing in "pop-up ads" that are linked to Websites related to the types of products and services they offer. This allows Internet advertisers to target specific audiences. New companies, such as AdKnowledge and Personify, contract with Internet advertisers to monitor the success of specific ads, detailing who bought products or services, how much they bought, and the overall profit from the sale. Online advertisers are also using well known search engines as springboards to their sites, but at great expense. It costs millions of dollars for companies to have their logos displayed on these high-traffic areas of the Web.*

*Direct mail is another advertising sector which has seen a great deal of recent success. The growth in this sector is fueled by newer, more precise data-collection databases, and the volume of "junk mail" is expected to triple in the next decade.*

**BRINKER DISPLAYS**
545 North Arlington Avenue, East Orange NJ 07017. 973/678-1200. Contact: Human Resources. **Description:** A display advertising company.

**CAPSTONE RESEARCH**
623 Ridge Road, Lyndhurst NJ 07071. 201/939-0600. **Contact:** Human Resources. **Description:** Conducts market research for client companies.

**THE HIBBERT GROUP**
400 Pennington Avenue, P.O. Box 8116, Trenton NJ 08650-0116. 609/394-7500. **Fax:** 609/392-5946. **Contact:** Jean Crawford, Human Resources Administrator. **Description:** Offers direct marketing services including literature fulfillment, data services, telemarketing, and direct mail. **Educational backgrounds include:** Computer Science; Marketing. **Benefits:** 401(k); Disability Coverage; Employee Discounts; Life Insurance; Medical Insurance; Tuition Assistance. **Corporate headquarters location:** This Location. **Other U.S. locations:** Denver CO. **Operations at this facility include:** Administration; Sales; Service. **Number of employees at this location:** 450. **Number of employees nationwide:** 600.

**IMS HEALTH**
100 Campus Road, Totowa NJ 07512. 973/790-0700. **Contact:** Human Resources. **World Wide Web address:** http://www.ims-health.com. **Description:** Conducts market research of the health care industry for pharmaceutical companies. **Common positions include:** Accountant/Auditor; Administrator; Attorney; Computer Programmer; Customer Service Representative; Department Manager; Financial Analyst; General Manager; Human Resources Manager; Instructor/Trainer; Operations/Production Manager; Public Relations Specialist; Statistician; Systems Analyst;

Teacher/Professor; Technical Writer/Editor. **Educational backgrounds include:** Business Administration; Computer Science; Marketing. **Benefits:** Dental Insurance; Disability Coverage; Employee Discounts; Life Insurance; Medical Insurance; Savings Plan; Tuition Assistance. **Special programs:** Internships. **Corporate headquarters location:** Plymouth Meeting PA. **Parent company:** Dun & Bradstreet. **Number of employees at this location:** 400.

## IMEDIA
233 South Street, Morristown NJ 07960. 973/267-8500. **Fax:** 973/267-8977. **Contact:** Human Resources. **Description:** Provides public relations and technological consulting services for large firms.

## IMPACT TELEMARKETING
15 East Centre Street, Woodbury NJ 08096. 609/384-1111. **Recorded jobline:** 609/770-1770. **Contact:** Human Resources. **Description:** Provides telemarketing services for *Fortune* 500 companies.

## LCS INDUSTRIES, INC.
120 Brighton Road, Clifton NJ 07012. 973/778-5588. **Fax:** 973/778-7485. **Contact:** Monica Ann Mahon, Human Resources Manager. **World Wide Web address:** http://www.lcsi.com. **Description:** A direct marketing firm. **Common positions include:** Accountant/Auditor; Clerical Supervisor; Computer Programmer; Customer Service Representative; Management Trainee; Systems Analyst. **Educational backgrounds include:** Business Administration; Computer Science; Marketing. **Benefits:** 401(k); Dental Insurance; Disability Coverage; Life Insurance; Medical Insurance; Stock Option. **Corporate headquarters location:** This Location. **Other U.S. locations:** Dover DE; Weehawken NJ. **Subsidiaries include:** Catalog Resources and Specialists. **Operations at this facility include:** Administration; District Headquarters; Sales; Service. **Listed on:** NASDAQ. **Number of employees at this location:** 500. **Number of employees nationwide:** 800.

## MOKRYNSKI & ASSOCIATES
401 Hackensack Avenue, Hackensack NJ 07601. 201/488-5656. **Contact:** Human Resources. **Description:** A direct mailing company which manages, acquires, and sells mailing lists for client companies.

## PRO DIRECT INTERVIEWING
One Cherry Hill Plaza, Suite 700, Cherry Hill NJ 08002. 609/482-8400. **Contact:** Personnel Manager. **Description:** Provides market research services.

## TOTAL RESEARCH CORPORATION
5 Independence Way, Princeton NJ 08543. 609/520-9100. **Fax:** 609/987-8839. **Contact:** Jane Giles, Human Resources Manager. **World Wide Web address:** http://www.totalres.com. **Description:** A full-service marketing research firm that provides information for use in strategic and tactical marketing decisions. **Common positions include:** Database Manager; Financial Analyst; Human Resources Manager; Market Research Analyst; Marketing Manager; Marketing Specialist; Project Manager; Purchasing Agent/Manager; Sales Executive; Statistician; Typist/Word Processor. **Educational backgrounds include:** Liberal Arts; Marketing. **Benefits:** 401(k); Dental Insurance; Disability Coverage; Life Insurance; Medical Insurance; Telecommuting; Tuition Assistance. **Corporate headquarters location:** This Location. **Other U.S. locations:** Tampa FL; Chicago IL; Minneapolis MN; Poughkeepsie NY. **Listed on:** NASDAQ. **Annual sales/revenues:** $21 - $50 million. **Number of employees at this location:** 130. **Number of employees nationwide:** 320. **Number of employees worldwide:** 350.

*Note: Because addresses and telephone numbers of smaller companies can change rapidly, we recommend you call each company to verify the information below before inquiring about job opportunities. Mass mailings are not recommended.*

**Additional small employers:**

**DIRECT MAIL ADVERTISING SERVICES**

**American List Counsel Inc.**
88 Orchard Rd, CN 5219, Princeton NJ 08543. 908/874-4300.

**Clark O'Neill Inc.**
1 Broad Ave, Fairview NJ 07022-1570. 201/945-3400.

**CSC Direct Mailers**
631 Grove St, Jersey City NJ 07310-1229. 201/659-8888.

**Database America**
100 Paragon Dr, Montvale NJ 07645-1718. 201/476-2300.

**Elite Mailing**
151 Heller Pl, Bellmawr NJ 08031-2503. 609/848-5506.

**Hann & DePalmer**
28 Englehard Dr, Cranbury NJ
08512-3721. 609/655-4646.

**J. Knipper & Co. Inc.**
1645 Oak St, Lakewood NJ
08701-5925. 732/905-7878.

**KMI Direct Mail Advertising**
355 New Albany Rd,
Moorestown NJ 08057-1117.
609/802-1900.

**Mailco Inc.**
150 S Main St, Wood Ridge NJ
07075-1002. 973/777-9500.

**MDM Technologies LLC**
333 1st St, Elizabeth NJ 07206-
2015. 908/353-7800.

**Pagex Systems**
100 Paragon Dr, Montvale NJ
07645-1718. 201/476-2000.

**Presort Partners**
1440 Lower Ferry Rd, Trenton NJ
08618-1415. 609/538-9200.

**Reliable Mail Service Inc.**
297 Kinderkamack Rd, Oradell
NJ 07649-2155. 201/262-7307.

**The Corporate
Communications Group**
26 Parsippany Rd, Whippany NJ
07981-1421. 973/386-1444.

**The Mail Box Inc.**
5 Independence Way, Princeton
NJ 08540-6627. 609/514-5156.

**Tri Tech Services**
4 Corporate Pl, Piscataway NJ
08854-4120. 732/878-6441.

**MISC. ADVERTISING
SERVICES**

**Common Health Advertising**
30 Lanidex Plaza W, Parsippany
NJ 07054-2717. 973/884-2200.

**CSC Advertising Inc.**
Campbell Pl, Camden NJ 08103.
609/342-3804.

**Integrated Communications**
989 Lenox Dr, Lawrenceville NJ
08648-2315. 609/406-9600.

**Integrated Communications**
5 Sylvan Way, Parsippany NJ
07054-3813. 973/984-2755.

**Irma Weiss Inc.**
125 73rd St, North Bergen NJ
07047-5810. 201/869-1693.

**Lewis Gace Bozell**
1 Bridge Plz S, Fort Lee NJ
07024-7325. 201/461-9600.

**National Telephone Directories**
PO Box 6765, Somerset NJ
08875-6765. 732/302-3000.

**National Telephone Directories**
115 Central Ave, Bogota NJ
07603-1405. 201/843-1100.

**Outdoor Systems Advertising**
185 Route 46, Fairfield NJ
07004-2321. 973/575-6900.

**RBT/Strum Inc.**
Rural Route 38, Cherry Hill NJ
08002. 609/488-5500.

**Redi Mail Direct Marketing**
5 Audrey Pl, Fairfield NJ 07004-
3401. 973/808-4500.

**Synergy Marketing Group**
17-17 Route 208 N, Fair Lawn NJ
07410. 201/791-7272.

**TAL International Marketing**
65 Madison Ave, Morristown NJ
07960-7307. 973/540-8333.

**Torre Lazur**
20 Waterview Blvd, Parsippany
NJ 07054-1229. 973/263-9100.

**PUBLIC RELATIONS
SERVICES**

**On-Campus Marketing
Concepts**
PO Box 558, Cherry Hill NJ
08003-0558. 609/795-1114.

**QLM Associates Inc.**
470 Wall St, Princeton NJ 08540-
1509. 609/683-1177.

## For more information on career opportunities in advertising, marketing, and public relations:

### Associations

**ADVERTISING RESEARCH FOUNDATION**
641 Lexington Avenue, 11th Floor, New York NY
10022. 212/751-5656. Fax: 212/319-5265. E-mail
address: email@arfsite.org. World Wide Web address:
http://www.arfsite.org. A nonprofit organization
comprised of advertising, marketing, and media
research companies. For institutions only.

**AMERICAN ASSOCIATION OF ADVERTISING
AGENCIES**
405 Lexington Avenue, 18th Floor, New York NY
10174. 212/682-2500. World Wide Web address:
http://www.commercepark.com/aaaa. Offers
educational and enrichment benefits such as
publications, videos, and conferences.

**AMERICAN MARKETING ASSOCIATION**
250 South Wacker Drive, Suite 200, Chicago IL
60606. 312/648-0536. World Wide Web address:
http://www.ama.org. An association with nearly
45,000 members worldwide. Offers a reference center,
25 annual conferences, and eight publications for
marketing professionals and students.

**THE DIRECT MARKETING ASSOCIATION**
1120 Avenue of the Americas, New York NY 10036-
6700. 212/768-7277. World Wide Web address:
http://www.the-dma.org. This association offers
monthly newsletters, seminars, and an annual
telephone marketing conference.

**INTERNATIONAL ADVERTISING ASSN.**
521 Fifth Avenue, Suite 1807, New York NY 10175.
212/557-1133. Fax: 212/983-0455. E-mail address:
iaa@ibnet.com. World Wide Web address:
http://www.iaaglobal.org. Over 3,600 members in 89
countries. Membership includes publications;
professional development; congresses, symposia, and
conferences; annual report and membership directory;
and worldwide involvement with governments and
other associations. Overall, the organization looks to
promote free speech and the self-regulation of
advertising.

**MARKETING RESEARCH ASSOCIATION**
1344 Silas Deane Highway, Suite 306, Rocky Hill CT
06067. 860/257-4008. World Wide Web address:
http://www.mra-net.org. Publishes several magazines
and newsletters.

**PUBLIC RELATIONS SOCIETY OF AMERICA**
33 Irving Place, New York NY 10003-2376. 212/995-
2230. World Wide Web address: http://www.prsa.org.
Publishes books and magazines for public relations
professionals.

### Directories

**AAAA ROSTER AND ORGANIZATION**
American Association of Advertising Agencies, 405
Lexington Avenue, 18th Floor, New York NY 10147.
212/682-2500.

**DIRECTORY OF MINORITY PUBLIC RELATIONS PROFESSIONALS**
Public Relations Society of America, 33 Irving Place, New York NY 10003-2376. 212/995-2230.

**O'DWYER'S DIRECTORY OF PUBLIC RELATIONS FIRMS**
J.R. O'Dwyer Company, 271 Madison Avenue, Room 600, New York NY 10016. 212/679-2471.

**PUBLIC RELATIONS CONSULTANTS DIRECTORY**
American Business Directories, Division of American Business Lists, 5711 South 86th Circle, Omaha NE 68137. 402/593-4500.

**STANDARD DIRECTORY OF ADVERTISING AGENCIES**
Reed Elsevier, 121 Chanlon Road, New Providence NJ 07974. Toll-free phone: 800/521-8110.

**Magazines**

**ADVERTISING AGE**
Crain Communications Inc., 220 East 42nd Street, New York NY 10017-5846. 212/210-0100. World Wide Web address: http://www.adage.com.

**ADWEEK**
BPI Communications, 1515 Broadway, 12th Floor, New York NY 10036-8986. 212/764-7300. World Wide Web address: http://www.adweek.com.

**BUSINESS MARKETING**
Crain Communications Inc., 220 East 42nd Street, New York NY 10017-5846. 212/210-0100. World Wide Web address: http://www.netb2b.com.

**JOURNAL OF MARKETING**
American Marketing Association, 250 South Wacker Drive, Suite 200, Chicago IL 60606. 312/648-0536.

**THE MARKETING NEWS**
American Marketing Association, 250 South Wacker Drive, Suite 200, Chicago IL 60606. 312/648-0536. A biweekly magazine offering new ideas and developments in marketing.

**PR REPORTER**
PR Publishing Company, P.O. Box 600, Exeter NH

03833. 603/778-0514. World Wide Web address: http://www.prpublishing.com.

**PUBLIC RELATIONS NEWS**
Phillips Business Information, Inc., 1201 Seven Locks Road, Suite 300, Potomac MD 20854. 301/424-3338. Fax: 301/309-3847. World Wide Web address: http://www.phillips.com.

**Newsletters**

**PUBLIC RELATIONS CAREER OPPORTUNITIES**
1575 I Street NW, Suite 1190, Washington DC 20005. 202/408-7900. Fax: 202/408-7907. World Wide Web address: http://www.careeropps.com/prcareer1. A newsletter listing public relations, public affairs, special events, and investor positions nationwide compensating above $35,000 annually. Available on a subscription basis, published 24 times a year. Produced by the Public Relations Society of America., which also publishes other newsletters, including *CEO Job Opportunities Update* and *ASAE Career Opportunities* (for the American Society of Association Executives).

**Online Services**

**ADVERTISING & MEDIA JOBS PAGE**
http://www.nationjob.com/media. This Website offers advertising and media job openings that can be searched by a variety of criteria including location, type of position, and salary. This site also offers a service that will perform the search for you.

**DIRECT MARKETING WORLD'S JOB CENTER**
http://www.dmworld.com. Posts professional job openings for the direct marketing industry. This site also provides a career reference library, a list of direct marketing professionals, and a list of events within the industry.

**MARKETING CLASSIFIEDS ON THE INTERNET**
http://www.marketingjobs.com. Offers job listings by state, resume posting, discussions with other marketing professionals, and links to other career sites and company home pages.

# AEROSPACE

*Slow growth is predicted for the aerospace industry through 2006. Recent U.S. Defense Department spending cuts have increased competition for aerospace jobs, yet that is being offset by the high demand for commercial aircraft. According to Standard & Poor, aerospace industry profits for the first two quarters of 1998 were down 24 percent from profits for the same period of 1997. This is causing major companies, such as Boeing, to make significant changes. At the end of 1998, Boeing announced it would cut 48,000 jobs by 2001. The layoffs demonstrate the company's new focus on efficiency, increasing worker productivity, and ultimately profit margins. Boeing planned on building and selling 550 aircraft during 1998; however, the Asian economic crisis forced Boeing to find new buyers for some aircraft ordered by Asian companies.*

**ALLIEDSIGNAL**
699 Route 46 East, Teterboro NJ 07608. 201/288-2000. **Contact:** Human Resources. **Description:** Develops and manufactures advanced aerospace products under government contract, including instrumentation for air and guidance systems.

**BFGOODRICH AEROSPACE**
197 Ridgedale Avenue, Cedar Knolls NJ 07927. 973/267-4500. **Contact:** Human Resources. **World Wide Web address:** http://www.bfgoodrich.com. **Description:** Manufactures aircraft systems and components and provides services for the aerospace industry worldwide. **Parent company:** BFGoodrich Company. **Listed on:** New York Stock Exchange.

**BREEZE-EASTERN**
700 Liberty Avenue, Union NJ 07083. 908/686-4000. **Fax:** 908/686-4279. **Contact:** Edward Chestnut, Human Resources. **Description:** Designs, develops, manufactures, and services sophisticated lifting and restraining products, principally helicopter rescue hoist and cargo hooks systems; winches and hoists for aircraft and weapon systems; and aircraft cargo tie-down systems. **Corporate headquarters location:** This Location. **Parent company:** TransTechnology designs, manufactures, sells, and distributes specialty fasteners through several subsidiaries. Breeze Industrial Products (Saltsburg PA) manufactures a complete line of standard and specialty gear-driven band fasteners in high-grade stainless steel for use in highly engineered applications. The Palnut Company (Mountainside NJ) manufactures light- and heavy-duty single- and multithread specialty fasteners. Industrial Retaining Ring (Irvington NJ) manufactures a variety of retaining rings made of carbon steel, stainless steel, and beryllium copper. The Seeger Group (Somerville NJ) manufactures retaining clips, circlips, spring pins, and similar components.

**CURTISS-WRIGHT FLIGHT SYSTEMS**
300 Fairfield Road, Fairfield NJ 07004. 973/575-2200. **Contact:** Human Resources. **Description:** An aerospace manufacturer specializing in flight control systems. **Corporate headquarters location:** Lyndhurst NJ. **Other U.S. locations:** Nationwide. **International locations:** Denmark. **Parent company:** Curtiss-Wright Corporation. **Listed on:** New York Stock Exchange. **Number of employees nationwide:** 1,600. **Number of employees worldwide:** 2,000.

**DASSAULT FALCON JET CORPORATION**
P.O. Box 2000, South Hackensack NJ 07606. 201/262-0800. **Contact:** Robert Basso, Human Resources. **Description:** Manufactures and sells a line of two- and three-engine business aircraft. Dassault Falcon Jet also operates an international group of jet aircraft service and maintenance centers (Falcon Jet Service Centers), engaged in a wide range of jet aircraft engine, airframe, avionics, instruments, and accessories service, repair, and maintenance. The company operates service centers in eight United States locations and throughout the world. **Corporate headquarters location:** This Location. **Parent company:** Dassault Breguet Aviation (France).

## DASSAULT FALCON JET CORPORATION

475 Wall Street, Princeton NJ 08540. 609/921-0450. **Contact:** Human Resources Department. **Description:** This location is a sales office. Overall, Dassault Falcon Jet Corporation manufactures and sells a line of two- and three-engine business aircraft. The company also operates an international group of jet aircraft service and maintenance centers (Falcon Jet Service Centers), engaged in a wide range of jet aircraft engine, airframe, avionics, instruments, and accessories service, repair, and maintenance. The company operates service centers in eight United States locations and throughout the world.

## GEC-MARCONI AEROSPACE INC.

110 Algonquin Parkway, Whippany NJ 07981. 973/428-9898. **Contact:** Russell J. Stehn, Vice President of Human Resources. **Description:** Engineers and manufactures electro-mechanical actuation control systems for the aerospace and commercial industries. **Common positions include:** Accountant/Auditor; Aerospace Engineer; Blue-Collar Worker Supervisor; Buyer; Computer Programmer; Credit Manager; Customer Service Representative; Department Engineer; Electrical/Electronics Engineer; Financial Analyst; Human Resources Manager; Industrial Engineer; Mechanical Engineer; Operations/Production Manager; Purchasing Agent/Manager; Quality Control Supervisor; Technical Writer/Editor. **Educational backgrounds include:** Accounting; Computer Science; Engineering. **Benefits:** 401(k); Dental Insurance; Disability Coverage; Life Insurance; Medical Insurance; Pension Plan; Tuition Assistance. **Parent company:** GEC Ltd. (Stanhope Gate, England). **Operations at this facility include:** Divisional Headquarters; Manufacturing; Research and Development; Sales. **Listed on:** New York Stock Exchange. **Number of employees at this location:** 250.

## ITT AEROSPACE/COMMUNICATIONS
## ITT AVIONICS

100 Kingsland Road, Clifton NJ 07014. 973/284-4238. **Contact:** Human Resources. **Description:** Designs and engineers software for satellite communications under government contracts.

## LYNTON GROUP, INC.

3 Airport Road, Morristown Municipal Airport, Morristown NJ 07960-4624. 973/292-9000. **Fax:** 973/292-1497. **Contact:** Human Resources. **Description:** Performs aviation services including the management, charter, maintenance, hangarage, and refueling of corporate helicopters and fixed-wing aircraft, and helicopter support services for industrial and utility applications. Lynton Group also provides aircraft sales and brokerage services to customers on an international level. **Corporate headquarters location:** This Location. **Subsidiaries include:** EHL (England) and Ramapo (Lincoln Park NJ) perform helicopter maintenance, component overhaul, avionics design, and aircraft parts sales.

## NAVAL AIR ENGINEERING STATION

Route 547, Lakehurst NJ 08733. 732/323-2011. **Contact:** Human Resources. **World Wide Web address:** http://www.lakehurst.navy.mil. **Description:** Researches, develops, and tests advanced technologies and equipment needed to support sophisticated aircraft.

## SMITHS INDUSTRIES AEROSPACE & DEFENSE SYSTEMS

7-9 Vreeland Road, Florham Park NJ 07932. 973/822-1300. **Toll-free phone:** 888/764-8470. **Fax:** 973/966-6138. **Contact:** Kathy Price, Manager of Employee Relations. **Description:** An aerospace engineering facility involved in avionics, weapons management, and navigation. **Common positions include:** Electrical/Electronics Engineer; Software Engineer; Systems Analyst. **Educational backgrounds include:** Computer Science; Engineering. **Benefits:** Dental Insurance; Disability Coverage; Life Insurance; Medical Insurance; Pension Plan; Savings Plan; Tuition Assistance. **Office hours:** Monday - Friday, 7:30 a.m. - 4:30 p.m. **Number of employees at this location:** 195.

**For more information on career opportunities in aerospace:**

**Associations**

**AHS INTERNATIONAL -- THE VERTICAL FLIGHT SOCIETY**
217 North Washington Street, Alexandria VA 22314. 703/684-6777. Fax: 703/739-9279. E-mail address: ahs703@aol.com. World Wide Web address: http://www.vtol.org. Promotes the advancement of vertical flight technology.

**AMERICAN ASTRONAUTICAL SOCIETY**
6352 Rolling Mill Place, Suite 102, Springfield VA 22152-2354. 703/866-0020. Fax: 703/866-3526. E-mail address: info@astronautical.org. World Wide Web address: http://www.astronautical.org. Offers conferences for members and scholarships for students.

**AMERICAN INSTITUTE OF AERONAUTICS AND ASTRONAUTICS, INC.**
1801 Alexander Bell Drive, Suite 500, Reston VA

20191-4344. 703/264-7500. Toll-free phone: 800/NEW-AIAA. Fax: 703/264-7551. World Wide Web address: http://www.aiaa.org. Membership required. Publishes 10 journals and books. The Website provides information on employment opportunities, resume services, aerospace news, career placement services, continuing education resources, and a mentor program.

**NATIONAL AERONAUTIC ASSOCIATION**
1815 North Fort Myer Drive, Suite 700, Arlington VA 22209. 703/527-0226. World Wide Web address: http://www.naa.ycg.org. Publishes a magazine. Membership required.

**PROFESSIONAL AVIATION MAINTENANCE ASSOCIATION**
636 Eye Street NW, Suite 300, Washington DC 20001-3736. 202/216-9220. World Wide Web address: http://www.pama.org. Conducts local and national seminars; publishes industry news journals; and addresses government issues. Members have access to the Worldwide Membership Directory.

## Newsletters

**AIR JOBS DIGEST**
World Air Data, Department 700, P.O. Box 42360, Washington DC 20015. World Wide Web address: http://www.tggh.net/wad. This monthly resource provides current job openings in aerospace, space, and aviation industries. Subscription rates: $96.00 annually, $69.00 for six months, and $49.00 for three months.

# APPAREL, FASHION, AND TEXTILES

*Employment in the apparel and textiles industry has been hurt by advances in labor-saving technology. Computer-controlled cutters, semi-automatic sewing machines, and automated material handling systems continue to reduce the need for apparel workers. However, positions are still available due to the industry's high turnover rate.*

*Increased overseas production of textiles has also decreased the need for domestic workers who perform sewing functions. In fact, the U.S. Department of Labor estimates that imports now comprise 50 percent of U.S. apparel consumption, a figure that will increase as the North American Free Trade Agreement (NAFTA) becomes fully implemented. The industry has responded by attempting to develop niche markets, strong brand names, and faster customer response systems, according to* Monthly Labor Review. *Despite these efforts, over 1 million U.S. textile and apparel jobs were eliminated between 1973 and 1997, and the U.S. Department of Labor expects employment to decline steadily through the year 2006.*

**ABERDEEN SPORTSWEAR, INC.**
P.O. Box 8413, Trenton NJ 08650. 609/587-2309. **Contact:** Human Resources. **Description:** A manufacturer of quality sportswear.

**BEACON LOOMS, INC.**
411 Alfred Avenue, Teaneck NJ 07666. 201/833-1600. **Contact:** Personnel. **Description:** Produces a wide range of textiles, primarily for sale to retailers throughout the country. **Corporate headquarters location:** This Location. **Other U.S. locations:** Englewood NJ.

**BISCAYNE APPAREL, INC.**
1373 Broad Street, Clifton NJ 07013. 973/473-3240. **Contact:** Human Resources. **Description:** Designs, manufactures, and markets apparel worldwide. Biscayne Apparel has several operations: Andy Johns Fashions imports and manufactures active outerwear and sportswear for women and children; Mackintosh of New England offers a line of premium wool coats for women; and Varon supplies girls' underwear, thermals, daywear, and intimate apparel, and boys' and women's thermal and cotton interlock underwear. **Corporate headquarters location:** This Location. **Parent company:** Biscayne Holdings, Inc. **Listed on:** American Stock Exchange.

**CONGOLEUM CORPORATION**
P.O. Box 3127, Mercerville NJ 08619. 609/584-3000. **Fax:** 609/584-3522. **Contact:** Human Resources. **World Wide Web address:** http://www.congoleum.com. **Description:** This location distributes vinyl floor products to wholesalers worldwide. Overall, Congoleum Corporation is a diversified manufacturer and distributor, operating in the areas of home furnishings, shipbuilding, and automotive and industrial distribution. The company developed one of the first no-wax floors, one of the first chemically embossed sheet vinyl floors, and one of the first types of domestically produced sheet vinyl that uses environmentally safe, water-based inks. **Common positions include:** Accountant; Claim Rep.; Customer Service Rep.; Secretary. **Benefits:** 401(k); Dental Insurance; Employee Discounts; Life Insurance; Medical Insurance; Pension Plan; Tuition Assistance. **Corporate headquarters location:** This Location. **Other area locations:** Cedarhurst NJ; Trenton NJ. **Listed on:** New York Stock Exchange.

**COOPER SPORTSWEAR MANUFACTURING COMPANY**
720 Frelinghuysen Avenue, Newark NJ 07114. 973/824-3400. **Contact:** Controller. **Description:** Imports and manufactures men's and boys' leather and cloth coats and jackets in the moderate-to-high price range. The company sells to department stores and private label distributors, and distributes products throughout the world.

**DREXEL SHIRT COMPANY**
402-412 Route 23, Franklin NJ 07416. 973/827-9135. **Contact:** Mrs. Pat Ward, Personnel Manager. **Description:** Manufactures men's shirts.

**S. GOLDBERG & COMPANY, INC.**
20 East Broadway, Hackensack NJ 07601. 201/342-1200. **Contact:** Personnel Manager. **Description:** Manufactures house slippers. **Common positions include:** Industrial Engineer. **Benefits:** Disability Coverage; Employee Discounts; Life Insurance; Medical Insurance; Pension Plan; Profit Sharing; Tuition Assistance. **Corporate headquarters location:** This Location. **Operations at this facility include:** Manufacturing.

**JACLYN, INC.**
5801 Jefferson Street, West New York NJ 07093. 201/868-9400. **Contact:** Personnel. **Description:** Designs, manufactures, and sells women's and children's handbag fashions, accessories, specialty items, and ready-to-wear apparel. **Common positions include:** Accountant/Auditor; Administrator; Blue-Collar Worker Supervisor; Buyer; Computer Programmer; Credit Manager; Department Manager; Financial Analyst; General Manager; Human Resources Manager; Operations/Production Manager; Purchasing Agent/Manager; Sales Executive; Transportation/Traffic Specialist. **Educational backgrounds include:** Accounting; Business Administration; Economics; Finance. **Benefits:** Disability Coverage; Employee Discounts; Life Insurance; Medical Insurance; Pension Plan; Profit Sharing. **Corporate headquarters location:** This Location. **Operations at this facility include:** Administration; Manufacturing; Research and Development; Sales; Service. **Listed on:** American Stock Exchange.

**MANNINGTON MILLS INC.**
P.O. Box 30, Salem NJ 08079. 609/935-3000. **Contact:** Kathleen Gaudet, Manager of Human Resources. **Description:** Manufactures and wholesales various floor coverings including vinyl, wood, and carpet.

**OLD DEERFIELD FABRICS INC.**
99 Commerce Road, Cedar Grove NJ 07009. 973/239-6600. **Contact:** Personnel Department. **Description:** Manufactures decorative fabrics and other household decorations. **Corporate headquarters location:** This Location.

**PHILLIPS-VAN HEUSEN CORPORATION**
1001 Frontier Road, Suite 100, Bridgewater NJ 08807-2955. 908/685-0050. **Contact:** Bette Chaves, Director of Human Resources. **Description:** Engaged in the manufacture, wholesale, and retail of men's and women's apparel. **Corporate headquarters location:** New York NY. **Other U.S. locations:** AL. **Listed on:** New York Stock Exchange. **Number of employees nationwide:** 14,000.

**SETON COMPANY**
849 Broadway, Newark NJ 07104. 973/485-4800. **Contact:** Lillian Bahamonde, Human Resources Manager. **Description:** Company operations are conducted primarily through two business segments. The Leather Division's operations include tanning, finishing, and distribution of whole-hide cattle leathers for the automotive and furniture upholstery industries; cattle hide side leathers for footwear, handbag, and other markets; and cattle products for collagen, rawhide pet items, and other applications. The Chemicals and Coated Products Division is engaged in the manufacture and distribution of epoxy and urethane chemicals, specialty leather finishes, industrial and medical tapes, foams, films, and laminates. Other manufacturing facilities are located in Wilmington DE (epoxy, urethane chemicals, leather finishes); Toledo OH (cattle hide processing); Malvern PA (industrial coated products); and Saxton PA (cutting of finished leathers). **Corporate headquarters location:** This Location. **Subsidiaries include:** Radel Leather Manufacturing Company; Seton Leather Company. **Listed on:** American Stock Exchange.

**DAVID STEVENS MANUFACTURING**
P.O. Box 1288, Blackwood NJ 08012. 609/227-0655. **Contact:** Human Resources. **Description:** Produces ladies' sportswear.

**SUNBRITE DYE COMPANY, INC.**
P.O. Box 1076, Passaic NJ 07055. 973/777-9830. **Contact:** Human Resources. **Description:** Dyes and finishes commercial textile goods.

**WELLMAN, INC.**
1040 Broad Street, Suite 302, Shrewsbury NJ 07702. 732/542-7300. **Contact:** Personnel. **World Wide Web address:** http://www.wellmanwlm.com. **Description:** Manufactures polyester fibers and recycles fibers, resins, and plastics. The company is organized into three groups: the Fibers Group, which is comprised of domestic and European fiber manufacturing operations, produces polyester and nylon staple fibers and polyester partially-oriented yarn; the Manufactured Products

Group, consisting of businesses which produce and process recycled raw materials and produce PET and nylon engineering resins, wool tops and anhydrous lanolin, polyester batting and needle-punched fabrics, and PET sheet and thermoformed packaging products; and New England CRInc., which designs, equips, and operates materials recovery facilities and 13 additional recycling plants. **Corporate headquarters location:** This Location. **Other U.S. locations:** Commerce CA; Rolling Meadows IL; Chelmsford MA; Bloomfield Hills MI; Charlotte NC; Bridgeport NJ; New York NY; Medina OH; Pawtucket RI; Florence SC; Johnsonville SC; Marion SC; Ripon WI. **Listed on:** New York Stock Exchange.

**WINER INDUSTRIES INC.**
404 Grand Street, Paterson NJ 07505. 973/684-8822. **Contact:** Human Resources. **Description:** Manufactures clothing, including women's jackets.

*Note: Because addresses and telephone numbers of smaller companies can change rapidly, we recommend you call each company to verify the information below before inquiring about job opportunities. Mass mailings are not recommended.*

**Additional small employers:**

**APPAREL WHOLESALE**

**Anne Klein & Company**
1170 Valley Brook Ave, Lyndhurst NJ 07071-3608. 201/531-2300.

**Berkshire Fashions Inc.**
930 New Durham Rd, Edison NJ 08817-2214. 732/287-9300.

**ES Sutton Inc.**
115 Kennedy Drive, Sayreville NJ 08872-1459. 732/721-0022.

**Escada**
10 Mulholland Dr, Hasbrouck Heights NJ 07604-3125. 201/462-6000.

**Haddad Organization Ltd. Incorporated**
90 E 5th St, Bayonne NJ 07002-4261. 201/339-8883.

**Mayfair Infantswear**
100 Wesley White Road, Carteret NJ 07008-1109. 732/382-4055.

**Polo Ralph Lauren LP**
9 Polito Ave, Lyndhurst NJ 07071-3406. 201/531-6000.

**Sasilo USA**
1 Gardner Rd, Fairfield NJ 07004-2205. 973/882-9494.

**TDS**
50 Rte 46 E, Totowa NJ 07512. 973/785-0210.

**Toppers Worldwide**
PO Box 561, Thorofare NJ 08086-0561. 609/845-0400.

**Van Mar Inc.**
PO Box 233, Milltown NJ 08850-0233. 732/254-5197.

**BROADWOVEN FABRIC MILLS**

**Absecon Mills Inc.**
PO Box 672, Cologne NJ 08213-0672. 609/965-5373.

**Allison Corporation**
15 Okner Pkwy, Livingston NJ 07039-1603. 973/992-3800.

**Kalkstein Silk Mills Inc.**
75 Wood St, Paterson NJ 07524-1017. 973/278-1600.

**CHILDREN'S AND INFANTS' CLOTHING**

**D. Glasgow & Sons Inc.**
382 Fayette St, Perth Amboy NJ 08861-3930. 732/826-3900.

**Little Champ**
100 Crows Mill Rd, Keasbey NJ 08832-1005. 732/738-6000.

**TLC for Girls Inc.**
1771 W Edgar Rd, Linden NJ 07036-6407. 908/523-1060.

**EMBROIDERY**

**Premiere Lace Inc.**
910 22nd St, Union City NJ 07087-2111. 201/863-8881.

**United Embroidery Inc.**
PO Box 520A, North Bergen NJ 07047-8098. 201/863-0070.

**FABRICATED TEXTILE PRODUCTS**

**Annin & Co.**
163 Bloomfield Ave, Verona NJ 07044-2702. 973/239-9000.

**Danco Manufacturing**
88 Llewellyn Ave, Bloomfield NJ 07003-2340. 973/748-4880.

**Danco Manufacturing**
1 Annin Dr, Roseland NJ 07068-1800. 973/228-9400.

**FOOTWEAR**

**Capezio**
PO Box 40, Totowa NJ 07511-0040. 973/595-9000.

**Kenneth Cole Productions**
2 Emerson Ln, Secaucus NJ 07094-2504. 201/864-8080.

**KNITTING MILLS**

**Fairfield Textiles**
55 Passaic Ave, Fairfield NJ 07004-3509. 973/227-1656.

**Nisha Knits Inc.**
100 3rd Ave, Kearny NJ 07032-4028. 201/955-2323.

**Oxford Textile Finishing**
1 Wall St, Oxford NJ 07863. 908/453-2121.

**Rebtex Inc.**
40 Industrial Pkwy, Somerville NJ 08876-3425. 908/722-3549.

**Westchester Lace Inc.**
3901 Liberty Ave, North Bergen NJ 07047-2538. 201/864-2150.

**LEATHER TANNING AND FINISHING**

**Elmo Leather of America Inc.**
PO Box 357, Edison NJ 08818-0357. 732/777-7800.

**MEN'S AND BOYS' CLOTHING**

**Bibong Apparel Corporation**
23 Greenwoods Rd, Old Tappan NJ 07675-7018. 201/784-1322.

**Crown Clothing Co.**
609 Paul St, Vineland NJ 08360-5626. 609/691-0343.

**DeRossi & Son Co. Inc.**
PO Box 190, Vineland NJ 08362-0190. 609/691-0061.

**Rennoc Corporation**
3501 South East Boulevard, Vineland NJ 08360-7780. 609/327-5400.

**MISC. APPAREL AND ACCESSORIES**

**Handcraft Manufacturing Corporation**
640 Frelinghuysen Avenue, Newark NJ 07114-1324. 973/565-0077.

**NARROW FABRIC AND OTHER SMALLWARES MILLS**

**FG Montabert Co.**
175 Paterson Avenue, Midland Park NJ 07432-1820. 201/444-1250.

**NONWOVEN FABRICS**

**PGI Nonwoven**
PO Box 360, Landisville NJ 08326-0360. 609/697-1600.

**STITCHING AND TUCKING**

**Avanti Linens Inc.**
PO Box 415, Wood Ridge NJ 07075-0415. 201/641-7766.

**Creative Embroidery Corporation**
PO Box 1485, Bloomfield NJ 07003-1485. 973/429-2740.

**Excel Embroidery LLC**
687 Lehigh Ave, Union NJ 07083-7625. 908/686-9006.

**Prime Time Merchandise Incorporated**
239 Lindbergh Place, Paterson NJ 07503-2821. 973/684-3667.

**TEXTILE FINISHING**

**Franco Manufacturing Co. Inc.**
555 Prospect St, Metuchen NJ 08840-2271. 732/494-0500.

**Marijon Dyeing & Finishing**
PO Box 408, East Rutherford NJ 07073-0408. 201/933-9770.

**Miss Brenner Inc.**
PO Box 1587, Clifton NJ 07015-1587. 973/777-6410.

**Spinnerin Inc.**
30 Wesley St, South Hackensack NJ 07606-1509. 201/343-5900.

**TEXTILE GOODS**

**Cardinal Fashion Co. Inc.**
1500 Hudson St, Hoboken NJ 07030-5511. 201/222-1998.

**WOMEN'S AND MISSES' CLOTHING**

**Akilis**
575 65th St, West New York NJ 07093-5301. 201/854-7779.

**Alexandra Fashion Inc.**
1453 75th St, North Bergen NJ 07047-4046. 201/854-2450.

**Alfred Dunner Inc.**
200 Walsh Dr, Parsippany NJ 07054-1044. 973/263-2727.

**Berlei USA**
75 Knickerbocker Rd, Moonachie NJ 07074-1613. 201/933-7766.

**Blue Fish Clothing Inc.**
3 6th St, Frenchtown NJ 08825-1148. 908/996-3844.

**Bonnell Manufacturing Co. Inc.**
9900 Church Rd, Mount Laurel NJ 08054-1108. 609/235-2883.

**Casablanca**
45 Enterprise Ave A, Secaucus NJ 07094. 201/392-1100.

**Couleurs Inc.**
641 59th St, West New York NJ 07093-1320. 201/295-2990.

**Cut Rite Inc.**
5 Columbia Ave, Passaic NJ 07055-6407. 973/779-1109.

**Harve Benard Ltd.**
225 Meadowlands Pkwy, Secaucus NJ 07094-2305. 201/319-0909.

**Hellas Fashions Inc.**
133 Kossuth St, Newark NJ 07105-3414. 973/589-2576.

**Inner Secrets Inc.**
1000 1st St, Harrison NJ 07029-2332. 973/485-0500.

**Jackie Evans Fashions**
18-26 3rd St, Passaic NJ 07055. 973/471-6991.

**Jean Michaels Inc.**
1 Ironside Ct, Willingboro NJ 08046-2533. 609/871-8888.

**Lido Fashions Inc.**
104 Gray St, Paterson NJ 07501-3504. 973/279-0030.

**Lilli Group Inc.**
34 Wesley St, South Hackensack NJ 07606-1509. 201/883-1800.

**Maidenform**
154 Avenue E, Bayonne NJ 07002-4435. 201/436-9200.

**Q&T Coat Corporation**
420 Grand St, Paterson NJ 07505-2005. 973/523-3445.

**Russ Togs**
1 Claibourne Ave, North Bergen NJ 07047-6448. 201/319-8500.

**Seoul Suits**
1072 W Side Ave, Jersey City NJ 07306-6307. 201/434-0110.

**Wacoal International Corp.**
40 Triangle Blvd, Carlstadt NJ 07072-2701. 201/933-8400.

**YARN AND THREAD MILLS**

**Robison-Anton Textile Co.**
PO Box 159, Fairview NJ 07022-0159. 201/941-0500.

## For more information on career opportunities in the apparel, fashion, and textiles industries:

### Associations

**AMERICAN APPAREL MANUFACTURERS ASSOCIATION**
2500 Wilson Boulevard, Suite 301, Arlington VA 22201. 703/524-1864. World Wide Web address: http://www.americanapparel.org. Publishes numerous magazines, newsletters, and bulletins for the benefit of employees in the apparel manufacturing industry.

**AMERICAN TEXTILE MANUFACTURERS INSTITUTE**
Office of the Chief Economist, 1130 Connecticut Avenue NW, Suite 1200, Washington DC 20036. 202/862-0500. Fax: 202/862-0570. World Wide Web address: http://www.atmi.org. The national trade association for the domestic textile industry. Members are corporations only.

**THE FASHION GROUP INTERNATIONAL**
597 Fifth Avenue, 8th Floor, New York NY 10017. 212/593-1715. World Wide Web address: http://www.fgi.org. A nonprofit organization for professionals in the fashion industries (apparel, accessories, beauty, and home). Offers career counseling workshops 18 times per year.

**INTERNATIONAL ASSOCIATION OF
CLOTHING DESIGNERS**
475 Park Avenue South, 9th Floor, New York NY
10016. 212/685-6602. Fax: 212/545-1709.

**Directories**

**AAMA DIRECTORY**
American Apparel Manufacturers Association, 2500
Wilson Boulevard, Suite 301, Arlington VA 22201.
703/524-1864. A directory of publications distributed
by the American Apparel Manufacturers Association.

**APPAREL TRADES BOOK**
Dun & Bradstreet Inc., One Diamond Hill Road,
Murray Hill NJ 07974. 908/665-5000.

**FAIRCHILD'S MARKET DIRECTORY OF
WOMEN'S AND CHILDREN'S APPAREL**
Fairchild Publications, 7 West 34th Street, New York
NY 10001. 212/630-4000.

**Magazines**

**ACCESSORIES**
Business Journals, 50 Day Street, Norwalk CT 06854.
203/853-6015.

**AMERICA'S TEXTILES INTERNATIONAL**
Billiam Publishing, 555 North Pleasantburg Drive,
Suite 132, Greenville SC 29607. 864/242-5300.

**APPAREL INDUSTRY MAGAZINE**
Shore Verone Inc., 6255 Barfield Road, Suite 200,

Atlanta GA 30328. 404/252-8831. Toll-free phone:
800/241-9034. World Wide Web address: http://www.
aimagazine.com.

**BOBBIN MAGAZINE**
Bobbin Publishing Group, P.O. Box 1986, 1110 Shop
Road, Columbia SC 29202. 803/771-7500.

**TEXTILE HILIGHTS**
American Textile Manufacturers Institute, Office of
the Chief Economist, 1130 Connecticut Avenue NW,
Washington DC 20036. A quarterly publication.
Subscriptions: $125.00 per year (domestic); $200.00
per year (international).

**WOMEN'S WEAR DAILY (WWD)**
Fairchild Publications, 7 West 34th Street, New York
NY 10001. 212/630-4000. World Wide Web address:
http://www.fairchildpub.com.

**Online Services**

**THE INTERNET FASHION EXCHANGE**
http://www.fashionexch.com. An excellent site for
those industry professionals interested in apparel and
retail. The extensive search engine allows you to
search by job title, location, salary, product line,
industry, and whether you want a permanent,
temporary, or freelance position. The Internet Fashion
Exchange also offers career services such as recruiting
and outplacement firms that place fashion and retail
professionals.

# ARCHITECTURE, CONSTRUCTION, AND ENGINEERING

*Building on its success of the mid-90's, the construction industry is flourishing. The Federal Reserve Board notes that new and existing home sales are strong in most areas of the U.S., and that construction may only be limited by a shortage of workers. Approximately 7.1 million workers were employed in the industry in 1997, a record year according to* U.S. Industry and Trade Outlook 1998.

*For jobseekers who choose construction, the best opportunities will be in projects at electric utilities, educational structures, and water supply facilities. In 1998, housing starts were expected to total 1.6 million, versus 1.5 million in 1997. Construction is likely to remain strongest in the Midwest and the South. Building trade workers such as architects, concrete masons, and sheet metal workers will see only average growth in their industries through 2005.*

*In engineering, the best opportunities through 2005 are in the civil, industrial, and electrical sectors. Aerospace engineers will continue to face fierce competition and chemical engineers will have more opportunities with companies focusing on the development of specialty chemicals.*

**ABB LUMMUS GLOBAL INC.**
1515 Broad Street, Suite 2, Bloomfield NJ 07003. 973/893-1515. **Contact:** Human Resources. **Description:** An engineering firm serving power plants, chemical plants, and petrochemical and oil refineries, as well as other industries such as aviation and storage. **Parent company:** Asea, Brown, Boveri, Inc. (Norwalk CT) is a supplier of industrial equipment and services for industries such as electric power generation, oil and gas exploration, and production and chemical refinement processing. Another subsidiary, ABB Simcon (Bloomfield NJ), specializes in chemical engineering.

**ARROW GROUP INDUSTRIES, INC.**
1600 Route 23 North, P.O. Box 928, Wayne NJ 07474-0928. 973/696-6900. **Fax:** 973/696-8539. **Contact:** Joanne Trezza, Human Resources Director. **Description:** Manufactures steel storage buildings. **Corporate headquarters location:** This Location. **Other U.S. locations:** Breese IL. **Listed on:** Privately held. **Number of employees at this location:** 115. **Number of employees nationwide:** 330.

**ASEA, BROWN, BOVERI, INC. (ABB, INC.)**
1460 Livingston Avenue, P.O. Box 6005, North Brunswick NJ 08902-6005. 732/932-6000. **Contact:** Human Resources Manager. **World Wide Web address:** http://www.abb.com/americas/usa. **Description:** Provides engineering, construction, and sales support services as part of the worldwide engineering firm. Internationally, the company operates through the following business segments: oil field equipment and services; power systems; engineering and construction; process equipment; and industrial products. **Corporate headquarters location:** Norwalk CT. **Other U.S. locations:** New York NY. **Subsidiaries include:** ABB Lumus Global Inc., Bloomfield NJ; ABB Susa (also at this location). **Parent company:** Asea Brown Boveri Ltd. (Zurich, Switzerland). **Number of employees worldwide:** 220,000.

**LOUIS BERGER INTERNATIONAL, INC.**
100 Halsted Street, East Orange NJ 07019. **Contact:** Richard Bergailo, Personnel Director. **E-mail address:** rbergailo@louisberger.com. **Description:** A diversified consulting firm. The company provides cultural, environmental, and transportation-related engineering and planning services in the United States. Louis Berger International also aids in urban and rural development projects in Africa, Asia, Latin America, and the Middle East. Founded in 1940. **NOTE:** Please do not contact by fax or phone. Send a scannable resume by regular mail or in ASCII format by e-mail. **Common positions include:** Biological Scientist; Civil Engineer; Draftsperson; Economist; Environmental

Engineer; Geologist/Geophysicist; Transportation/Traffic Specialist; Urban/Regional Planner. **Educational backgrounds include:** Biology; Economics; Engineering; Geology. **Benefits:** 401(k); Dental Insurance; Disability Coverage; Life Insurance; Medical Insurance; Public Transit Available. **Listed on:** Privately held. **Annual sales/revenues:** More than $100 million.

### BURNS AND ROE ENTERPRISES INC.
800 Kinderkamack Road, Oradell NJ 07649. 201/265-2000. **Contact:** Jennifer Morris, Human Resources. **Description:** An engineering and construction company. **NOTE:** Entry-level positions are offered. **Common positions include:** Electrical/Electronics Engineer; Environmental Engineer; Industrial Engineer; Manufacturing Engineer; Marketing Manager; Marketing Specialist; Mechanical Engineer; Metallurgical Engineer; MIS Specialist; Project Manager; Purchasing Agent/ Manager; Quality Control Supervisor; Secretary; Systems Analyst; Technical Writer/Editor; Transportation/Traffic Specialist. **Educational backgrounds include:** Computer Science; Engineering; Marketing. **Benefits:** 401(k); Dental Insurance; Disability Coverage; Life Insurance; Medical Insurance; Pension Plan; Tuition Assistance. **Special programs:** Internships. **Corporate headquarters location:** This Location. **Listed on:** Privately held. **Number of employees at this location:** 600. **Number of employees nationwide:** 1,200. **Number of employees worldwide:** 1,250.

### CALTON HOMES INC.
500 Craig Road, Manalapan NJ 07726. 732/780-1800. **Contact:** Human Resources. **World Wide Web address:** http://www.caltonhomes.com. **Description:** Calton and its subsidiaries design, construct, and sell single-family detached homes and townhouses primarily in central New Jersey, central Florida, eastern Pennsylvania, and the Chicago metropolitan area.

### CLAYTON BRICK
2 Porete Avenue, North Arlington NJ 07031. 201/998-7600. **Contact:** Human Resources Manager. **Description:** Engaged in precast concrete panel construction and installation.

### EDWARDS AND KELCEY INC.
299 Madison Avenue, P.O. Box 1936, Morristown NJ 07962-1936. 973/267-0555. **Fax:** 973/267-3555. **Contact:** Susan M. Timko, Corporate Human Resources Manager. **World Wide Web address:** http://www.ekwireless.com. **Description:** A consulting, engineering, planning, and wireless communications organization whose range of services includes location and economic feasibility studies; valuations and appraisals; cost analyses; computer technology; marketing studies; traffic and transportation studies; soils and foundation analyses; environmental impact studies; master planning; structural surveys; and preliminary and final designs. Services also include preparation of contract documents and observation of construction operations for public transit systems, terminals, railroads, stations, bus depots, parking garages, airports, ports, highways, streets, bridges, tunnels, traffic control systems, military facilities, communications systems, storm and sanitary sewers, water supply and distribution, flood control, and land development. Founded in 1946. **NOTE:** Entry-level positions are offered. **Common positions include:** Accountant; Civil Engineer; Environmental Engineer; Marketing Specialist; Systems Analyst. **Educational backgrounds include:** Accounting; Computer Science; Engineering; Marketing. **Benefits:** 401(k); Dental Insurance; Disability Coverage; Life Insurance; Medical Insurance; Tuition Assistance. **Special programs:** Internships. **Corporate headquarters location:** This Location. **Other U.S. locations:** Chicago IL; Boston MA; Minneapolis MN; Manchester NH; New York NY; West Chester PA; Providence RI; Milwaukee WI. **Operations at this facility include:** Administration; Divisional Headquarters. **Listed on:** Privately held. **Annual sales/revenues:** $51 - $100 million. **Number of employees at this location:** 170. **Number of employees nationwide:** 560.

### FACTORY MUTUAL ENGINEERING ASSOCIATION
30 Vreeland Road, Florham Park NJ 07932. 973/822-2010. **Contact:** District Office. **Description:** A loss control services organization owned by Allendale Insurance, Arkwright, and Protection Mutual Insurance, with 15 district offices located throughout the United States and Canada. Research facilities are located in Norwood MA and West Gloucester RI. The company helps owner company policyholders to protect their properties and occupancies from damage caused by fire, wind, flood, and explosion; boiler, pressure vessel, and machinery accidents; and many other insured hazards. **Common positions include:** Chemical Engineer; Civil Engineer; Electrical/Electronics Engineer; Fire Science/Protection Engineer; Mechanical Engineer. **Benefits:** Dental Insurance; Disability Coverage; Employee Discounts; Life Insurance; Medical Insurance; Pension Plan; Savings Plan; Tuition Assistance. **Corporate headquarters location:** Norwood MA.

### FLUOR DANIEL, INC.
301 Lippencott Center, Marlton NJ 08053. 609/985-6500. **Contact:** Human Resources. **World Wide Web address:** http://www.fluordaniel.com. **Description:** A full-service engineering and

construction company serving the power, industrial, hydrocarbon, and process industries as well as the federal government. **Common positions include:** Chemical Engineer; Civil Engineer; Designer; Draftsperson; Electrical/Electronics Engineer; Environmental Engineer; Mechanical Engineer; Structural Engineer. **Educational backgrounds include:** Engineering. **Other U.S. locations:** Nationwide. **Parent company:** Fluor Corporation (Irvine CA) engages in engineering and construction as well as the extraction of various natural resources. Fluor Corporation provides its services to energy, natural resource, industrial, commercial, utility, and government clients. Natural resources extracted are principally gold, silver, lead, zinc, iron ore, coal, oil, and gas. The corporation also provides contract drilling services. **Number of employees worldwide:** 20,000.

### GENTEK BUILDING PRODUCTS
11 Cragwood Road, Woodbridge NJ 07095. 732/381-0900. **Contact:** Human Resources. **Description:** Manufactures aluminum and steel residential siding.

### HILL INTERNATIONAL
One Levitt Parkway, Willingboro NJ 08046-1436. 609/871-5800. **Contact:** Michelle Jablonski, Manager of Human Resources. **World Wide Web address:** http://www.hillintl.com. **Description:** Provides construction management and consulting services to large corporations.

### HOBOKEN FLOORS
70 Demarest Drive, Wayne NJ 07470. 973/694-2888. **Contact:** Personnel. **Description:** Manufactures hardwood flooring used in construction. **Corporate headquarters location:** This Location.

### K. HOVNANIAN COMPANIES
10 Highway 35, P.O. Box 500, Red Bank NJ 07701. 732/747-7800. **Contact:** Human Resources. **World Wide Web address:** http://www.khov.com. **Description:** Designs, constructs, and sells condominium apartments, townhomes, and single-family residences in planned communities primarily in New Jersey, New York, eastern Pennsylvania, Florida, Virginia, North Carolina, and Southern California. The company is also engaged in mortgage banking. Founded in 1959. **NOTE:** Entry-level positions are offered. **Common positions include:** Accountant; Administrative Assistant; Architect; Attorney; Auditor; Civil Engineer; Computer Operator; Computer Programmer; Controller; Financial Analyst; Human Resources Manager; Market Research Analyst; Marketing Manager; Marketing Specialist; MIS Specialist; Online Content Specialist; Real Estate Agent; Sales Manager; Secretary; Systems Analyst; Systems Manager; Technical Writer/Editor; Webmaster. **Educational backgrounds include:** Accounting; Business Administration; Computer Science; Engineering; Marketing. **Benefits:** 401(k); Dental Insurance; Disability Coverage; Life Insurance; Medical Insurance; Profit Sharing; Tuition Assistance. **Corporate headquarters location:** This Location. **Subsidiaries include:** New Fortis Homes. **Listed on:** American Stock Exchange. **Stock exchange symbol:** HOV. **Annual sales/revenues:** More than $100 million. **Number of employees at this location:** 90. **Number of employees nationwide:** 1,150.

### INTERNATIONAL SPECIALTY PRODUCTS, INC.
1361 Alps Road, Wayne NJ 07470. 973/628-4000. **Contact:** Gary Schneid, Director/Employee Selection. **World Wide Web address:** http://www.ispcorp.com. **Description:** Manufactures specialty chemicals and building materials. Chemicals include high-pressure acetylene derivatives, industrial organic and inorganic chemicals, GAF filter systems, and GAF mineral products. Building materials include prepared roofing, roll roofing, built-up roofing systems, and single-ply roofing. The company maintains research and development facilities throughout the U.S. and abroad. **Common positions include:** Accountant/Auditor; Advertising Clerk; Attorney; Biological Scientist; Biomedical Engineer; Budget Analyst; Buyer; Chemical Engineer; Chemist; Computer Programmer; Financial Analyst; General Manager; Paralegal; Pharmacist; Systems Analyst. **Educational backgrounds include:** Chemistry; Engineering. **Benefits:** 401(k); Dental Insurance; Disability Coverage; Life Insurance; Medical Insurance; Savings Plan; Tuition Assistance. **Corporate headquarters location:** This Location. **Listed on:** New York Stock Exchange. **Number of employees at this location:** 700. **Number of employees nationwide:** 4,300.

### LIPINSKI LANDSCAPING
180 Elbow Lane, Mount Laurel NJ 08054. 609/231-7941. **Contact:** Human Resources. **World Wide Web address:** http://www.lipinskiland.com. **Description:** Provides landscaping services to commercial and residential clients.

### FRANK A. McBRIDE COMPANY
233 Central Avenue, Hawthorne NJ 07506. 973/423-1123. **Contact:** Ethel Vander Wers, Human Resources. **Description:** Mechanical contractors for the architecture and construction industries.

## MELARD MANUFACTURING CORPORATION
2 Paulison Avenue, Passaic NJ 07055. 973/472-8888. **Contact:** Human Resources. **Description:** Manufactures a broad range of hardware products including bath accessories and plumbing products. **Corporate headquarters location:** This Location.

## JOS. L. MUSCARELLE, INC.
99 West Essex Street & Route 17, Maywood NJ 07607. 201/845-8100. **Contact:** Joseph Muscarelle, Jr., President. **Description:** Engaged in construction and real estate development. **Common positions include:** Civil Engineer; Cost Estimator; Credit Manager; Draftsperson; Electrical/Electronics Engineer; General Manager; Human Resources Manager; Operations/ Production Manager; Project Manager; Purchasing Agent/Manager; Real Estate Agent; Sales Executive; Scheduler. **Educational backgrounds include:** Accounting; Business Administration; Engineering; Finance; Marketing. **Benefits:** Dental Insurance; Life Insurance; Medical Insurance; Tuition Assistance.

## PATENT CONSTRUCTION SYSTEMS
One Mack Centre Drive, Paramus NJ 07652. 201/261-5600. **Contact:** Bruce Bender, Manager of Human Resources and Labor Relations. **Description:** Manufactures and markets scaffolding as well as concrete forming and shoring products. Founded in 1909. **Parent company:** Harsco Corporation.

## PIONEER INDUSTRIES
401 Washington Avenue, Carlstadt NJ 07072. 201/933-1900. **Contact:** Nick Cartabona, Personnel Manager. **Description:** Produces industrial doors, fireproof and theft-proof doors, and other sheet metal specialties. **Corporate headquarters location:** Bloomfield Hills MI. **Parent company:** Core Industries. **Operations at this facility include:** Manufacturing.

## SCHIAVONE CONSTRUCTION COMPANY
1600 Paterson Plank Road, Secaucus NJ 07096. 201/867-5070. **Contact:** Recruiting. **Description:** A heavy construction firm engaged in large-scale projects such as highways, tunnels, and bridges. Clients include city, state, and federal governments.

## STONE & WEBSTER ENGINEERING CORPORATION
3 Executive Campus, P.O. Box 5200, Cherry Hill NJ 08034. 609/482-3000. **Contact:** Joseph Landolt, Manager of Human Resources. **World Wide Web address:** http://www.stoneweb.com. **Description:** Engineers, designs, and constructs oil and gas processing, petrochemical, chemical, electrical power, industrial, and civil-works facilities in the United States and internationally. **Benefits:** Dental Insurance; Disability Coverage; Employee Discounts; Life Insurance; Medical Insurance; Pension Plan; Tuition Assistance. **Corporate headquarters location:** Boston MA. **Other U.S. locations:** Denver CO; New York NY; Chattanooga TN; Houston TX. **Parent company:** Stone & Webster, Inc. **Listed on:** New York Stock Exchange. **Number of employees nationwide:** 6,000.

*Note: Because addresses and telephone numbers of smaller companies can change rapidly, we recommend you call each company to verify the information below before inquiring about job opportunities. Mass mailings are not recommended.*

**Additional small employers:**

**ARCHITECTURAL SERVICES**

**EI Associates**
115 Evergreen Place, East Orange NJ 07018-2005. 973/672-5100.

**Hillier Group Inc.**
500 Alexander Park, Princeton NJ 08540-6395. 609/452-8888.

**BRIDGE, TUNNEL, AND HIGHWAY CONSTRUCTION**

**Conti Enterprises Inc.**
3001 S Clinton Ave, South Plainfield NJ 07080-1440. 908/755-3185.

**ELECTRICAL WORK**

**Beach Electric Co. Inc.**
PO Box 878, New Providence NJ 07974-0878. 908/508-2660.

**Calvi Electric Co.**
PO Box 479, Atlantic City NJ 08404-0479. 609/345-0151.

**Daidone Electric Inc.**
200 Raymond Blvd, Newark NJ 07105-4608. 973/690-5216.

**EII Inc.**
PO Box 128, Cranford NJ 07016-0128. 908/276-1000.

**Forest Electric Corp.**
55 Carter Dr, Edison NJ 08817-2064. 732/819-0669,

**George E. Scholes Co.**
12 Gelb Ave, Union NJ 07083-6807. 908/688-3993.

**Goldsmith Associates Inc.**
8 Springdale Rd, Cherry Hill NJ 08003-4009. 609/751-4747.

**Hatzel & Buehler Inc.**
PO Box 477, Fords NJ 08863-0477. 732/442-3100.

**Kleinknecht Electric Company**
202 Rutgers St, Maplewood NJ
07040-3228. 973/761-1600.

**Lessner Electric Company**
PO Box 239, Elizabeth NJ 07207-
0239. 908/354-7880.

**Lightning Electric Company**
40 E Willow St, Millburn NJ
07041-1417. 973/379-6800.

**Modern Electric Co.**
PO Box 2697, Clifton NJ 07015-
2697. 973/478-1222.

**OTS of NJ Inc.**
640 Herman Road, Suite 3,
Jackson NJ 08527-3068. 732/833-
0600.

**Schoonover Electric Company**
PO Box 57, Westfield NJ 07091-
0057. 908/233-2400.

**SM Electric Co. Inc.**
PO Box 1144, Rahway NJ 07065-
1144. 732/388-3540.

**Star-Lo Electric Inc.**
PO Box 2385, Morristown NJ
07962-2385. 973/540-0111.

## ENGINEERING SERVICES

**Adams Rehmann Heggan &
Associates**
PO Box 579, Hammonton NJ
08037-0579. 609/561-0482.

**Atlantic Science & Technology**
1413 Cantillon Blvd, Mays
Landing NJ 08330-2023.
609/625-8633.

**Boswell Engineering Inc.**
330 Phillips Ave, South
Hackensack NJ 07606-1717.
201/641-0770.

**CDM**
1 Raritan Center Parkway, Edison
NJ 08837-3606. 732/225-7000.

**Dames & Moore Group**
12 Commerce Dr, Cranford NJ
07016-3506. 908/272-8300.

**Dimensions International Inc.**
PO Box 10, Mays Landing NJ
08330-0010. 609/625-5775.

**Egan-Davis Standard**
PO Box 671, Somerville NJ
08876-0671. 908/722-6000.

**Emcon**
1 International Blvd, Mahwah NJ
07495-0025. 201/512-5700.

**Galaxy Scientific Corp.**
2500 English Creek Ave, Egg
Harbor Township NJ 08234-
5562. 609/645-0900.

**Gasi Inc.**
379 Princeton Hightstown,
Cranbury NJ 08512-2961.
609/448-9111.

**Goodkind & Odea Inc.**
PO Box 1708, Rutherford NJ
07070-0708. 201/438-6166.

**HNTB Corporation**
330 Passaic Ave, Fairfield NJ
07004-2006. 973/227-6460.

**HRI Inc.**
100 Overlook Ctr, Ste 400,
Princeton NJ 08540-7814.
609/243-8700.

**JCA Associates Inc.**
1256 N Church St, Ste 3,
Moorestown NJ 08057-1129.
609/722-6700.

**Langan Engineering &
Environmental Services**
River Drive Center, Elmwood
Park NJ 07407. 201/794-6900.

**Lippincott Jacobs & Gouda**
PO Box 354, Riverside NJ 08075-
0354. 609/461-1239.

**Lockwood Greene Engineers**
270 Davidson Ave, Somerset NJ
08873-4140. 732/560-5700.

**Malcolm Pirnie Inc.**
1 International Blvd, Mahwah NJ
07495-0025. 201/529-4700.

**Michael Baker Corporation**
307 College Rd East, Princeton
NJ 08540-6608. 609/734-7900.

**MMSI**
2339 Route 70 West, Cherry Hill
NJ 08002-3315. 609/486-5000.

**Modern Technologies
Corporation**
494 Sycamore Ave, Ste 203,
Shrewsbury NJ 07702-4205.
732/542-5414.

**Nacco Materials Handling
Group**
15 Junction Rd, Flemington NJ
08822-5722. 908/788-3200.

**NDI Engineering Company**
PO Box 518, Thorofare NJ
08086-0518. 609/848-0033.

**On-Board Chemical
Corporation**
450 Raritan Center Parkway,
Edison NJ 08837-3944. 732/225-
4300.

**Paulus Sokolowski & Sartor**
PO Box 4039, Warren NJ 07059-
0039. 732/560-9700.

**RBA Group**
PO Box 1927, Morristown NJ
07962-1927. 973/898-0300.

**Remington & Vernick
Engineers**
232 Kings Highway, Haddonfield
NJ 08033. 609/795-9595.

**Remington & Vernick
Engineers**
845 North Main Street,
Pleasantville NJ 08232-1455.
609/645-7110.

**RG Vanderweil Engineers Inc.**
500 Alexander Park, Princeton NJ
08540-6307. 609/987-1144.

**Richard A. Alaimo Associates**
200 High St, Mount Holly NJ
08060-1404. 609/267-8310.

**Sadat Associates Inc.**
116 Village Blvd, Ste 230,
Princeton NJ 08540-5700.
609/987-2500.

**Sharp Design Inc.**
PO Box 250, Clarksboro NJ
08020. 609/853-6362.

**Site-Blauvelt Engineers Inc.**
200 E Park Dr, Suite 100, Mount
Laurel NJ 08054-1297. 609/273-
1224.

**The Austin Company**
1001 Durham Ave, South
Plainfield NJ 07080-2300.
908/756-9000.

**The M&T Company**
2494 Rte 547, Lakehurst NJ
08733. 732/657-5600.

**Townplan Associates**
PO Box 828, Red Bank NJ
07701-0828. 732/671-6400.

**URS Greiner Inc.**
Mack Centre, Paramus NJ 07652.
201/262-7000.

**Vitronics Inc.**
15 Meridian Rd, Eatontown NJ
07724-2242. 732/389-0244.

**Weidlinger Associates Inc.**
4 Research Way, Floor 1,
Princeton NJ 08540-6618.
609/514-7337.

**Woodward-Clyde International**
PO Box 290, Wayne NJ 07474-
0290. 973/785-0700.

## GENERAL CONTRACTORS

**Cherry Valley Construction Co.**
1544 The Great Rd, Skillman NJ
08558. 609/466-1888.

**Custom Living Homes Inc.**
415 State Route 24, Chester NJ
07930-2920. 908/879-7777.

**Lake Ridge Development
Company**
PO Box D, Lakehurst NJ 08759-
0904. 732/901-6011.

**Lake Ridge Development
Company**
55 Schoolhouse Rd, Whiting NJ
08759-3048. 732/350-1600.

**The Matzel Mumford
Organization**
100 Village Ct, Hazlet NJ 07730-
1546. 732/888-1055.

**Westminster Homes**
26 Columbia Turnpike, Florham
Park NJ 07932-2213. 973/822-
0050.

**GENERAL INDUSTRIAL
CONTRACTORS**

**Broadacres Realty Co.**
PO Box 2911, Edison NJ 08818-
2911. 732/548-2200.

**Damon G. Douglas Company**
PO Box 1030, Cranford NJ
07016-1030. 908/272-0100.

**Epic Incorporated**
136 11th St, Piscataway NJ
08854-1572. 732/752-6100.

**G&C Enterprises Inc.**
PO Box 370, Columbus NJ
08022-0370. 609/298-2234.

**Gilbane Building Company**
3705 Quakerbridge Road,
Trenton NJ 08619-1209. 609/588-
5667.

**Hall Construction Company
Inc.**
PO Box 1448, Belmar NJ 07719-
1448. 732/681-2500.

**Joseph A. Natoli Construction**
PO Box 619, Pine Brook NJ
07058-0619. 973/575-1500.

**Joule Maintenance of
Gibbstown**
429 Broad St, Gibbstown NJ
08027. 609/423-7500.

**Kajima Construction Service**
900 Sylvan Ave, Englewood
Cliffs NJ 07632-3301. 201/568-
1800.

**Murray Construction Co. Inc.**
51 Commerce St, Springfield NJ
07081-3014. 973/376-7650.

**NFF Construction Inc.**
619 Church St, Pleasantville NJ
08232-4208. 609/646-6353.

**Turner Construction Company**
265 Davidson Ave, Somerset NJ
08873-4120. 732/627-8300.

**HEAVY CONSTRUCTION**

**Henkels & McCoy Inc.**
PO Box 218, Burlington NJ
08016-0218. 609/387-9000.

**Henkels & McCoy Inc.**
1300 West Blancke Street,
Linden NJ 07036-6216. 908/474-
0500.

**JF Kiely Construction Co.**
PO Box 535, Long Branch NJ
07740-0535. 732/222-4400.

**Sambol Construction
Corporation**
PO Box 5110, Toms River NJ
08754-5110. 732/349-2900.

**MASONRY, STONEWORK,
AND PLASTERING**

**Frank Pantisano & Son**
PO Box 259, Blackwood NJ
08012-0259. 609/227-6696.

**Garden State Brickface
Windows & Siding**
217 Highland Pkwy, Roselle NJ
07203-2616. 908/241-5900.

**MISC. SPECIAL TRADE
CONTRACTORS**

**Avanti Demolition & Carting**
233 Wilson Ave, Newark NJ
07105-3824. 973/589-7662.

**Caruso Excavating Co.**
PO Box 2043, Asbury Park NJ
07712-2043. 732/919-7483.

**JA Jones Management Services**
PO Box 680, Pomona NJ 08240-
0680. 609/485-6081.

**Liberty Contracting**
2531 94th St, North Bergen NJ
07047-1411. 201/488-9300.

**Marshall Productions**
529 South Clinton Avenue,
Trenton NJ 08611-1809. 609/394-
7153.

**Unesco Inc.**
2531 94th St, North Bergen NJ
07047-1411. 201/939-4000.

**Vollers Excavating &
Construction**
PO Box 5297, Somerville NJ
08876-1303. 908/725-1026.

**W&H Systems Inc.**
120 Asia Pl, Carlstadt NJ 07072-
2412. 201/933-7840.

**Warren Inc.**
PO Box 413, Jersey City NJ
07303-0412. 201/433-9797.

**OPERATIVE BUILDERS**

**Hovnanian Pennsylvania Inc.**
110 Fieldcrest Ave, Edison NJ
08837-3620. 732/225-4001.

**PLUMBING, HEATING, AND
A/C**

**August Arace & Sons Inc.**
PO Box 24, Elizabeth NJ 07206-
0024. 908/354-1626.

**Bonland Industries Inc.**
PO Box 200, Wayne NJ 07474-
0200. 973/694-3211.

**Daniel Falasca Plumbing
Heating & Cooling**
3329 North Mill Road, Vineland
NJ 08360-1525. 609/794-2010.

**F&G Mechanical Corp.**
348 New County Road, Secaucus
NJ 07094-1622. 201/864-3580.

**Fritze Heating & Air
Conditioning**
10 School St, Whippany NJ
07981-1507. 973/887-0685.

**Monsen Engineering Company**
PO Box 10061, Fairfield NJ
07004-6061. 973/227-1880.

**PLUMBING, HEATING, AND
A/C EQUIPMENT
WHOLESALE**

**Honeywell**
574 Springfield Avenue,
Westfield NJ 07090-1001.
908/233-9200.

**Honeywell DMC Services Inc.**
150 Brick Blvd, Brick NJ 08723-
7125. 732/920-3000.

**L&H Plumbing & Heating
Supplies**
PO Box 3025, Lakewood NJ
08701-8125. 732/905-1000.

**ROAD CONSTRUCTION**

**Dannunzio & Sons Inc.**
136 Central Ave, Clark NJ
07066-1142. 732/574-1300.

**George Harms Construction**
PO Box 817, Farmingdale NJ
07727-0817. 732/938-4004.

**Monmouth Ocean Contracting**
1817 Old Mill Rd, Belmar NJ
07719-3613. 732/974-1300.

**Statewide Hi-Way Safety Inc.**
PO Box 616, Hammonton NJ
08037. 609/561-0713.

**For more information on career opportunities in architecture, construction, and engineering:**

<u>Associations</u>

**AACE INTERNATIONAL: THE ASSOCIATION FOR ADVANCEMENT OF COST ENGINEERING**
209 Prairie Avenue, Suite 100, Morgantown WV 26505. 304/296-8444. Toll-free phone: 800/858-2678. Fax: 304/291-5728. World Wide Web address: http://www.aacei.org. A membership organization which offers *Cost Engineering*, a monthly magazine; employment referral services; technical reference information and assistance; insurance; and a certification program accredited by the Council of Engineering Specialty Boards. Toll-free number provides information on scholarships for undergraduates.

**ASM INTERNATIONAL: THE MATERIALS INFORMATION SOCIETY**
9639 Kinsman Road, Materials Park OH 44073. 440/338-5151. World Wide Web address: http://www. asm-intl.org. Gathers, processes, and disseminates technical information to foster the understanding and application of engineered materials.

**AMERICAN ASSOCIATION OF ENGINEERING SOCIETIES**
1111 19th Street NW, Suite 403, Washington DC 20036-3690. 202/296-2237. World Wide Web address: http://www.aaes.org. A multidisciplinary organization of professional engineering societies. Publishes reference works, including *Who's Who in Engineering, International Directory of Engineering Societies*, and the *Thesaurus of Engineering and Scientific Terms*, as well as statistical reports from studies conducted by the Engineering Workforce Commission.

**AMERICAN CONSULTING ENGINEERS COUNCIL**
1015 15th Street NW, Suite 802, Washington DC 20005. 202/347-7474. Fax: 202/898-0068. World Wide Web address: http://www.acec.org. A national organization of more than 5,000 member firms. Offers *Last Word*, a weekly newsletter; *American Consulting Engineer* magazine; life and health insurance programs; books, manuals, video- and audiotapes, and contract documents; conferences and seminars; and voluntary peer reviews.

**AMERICAN INSTITUTE OF ARCHITECTS**
1735 New York Avenue NW, Washington DC 20006. 202/626-7300. Toll-free phone: 800/365-2724. World Wide Web address: http://www.aia.org. Contact toll-free number for brochures.

**AMERICAN INSTITUTE OF CONSTRUCTORS**
1300 North 17th Street, Suite 830, Arlington VA 22209. 703/812-2021. World Wide Web address: http://www.aicnet.org.

**AMERICAN SOCIETY FOR ENGINEERING EDUCATION**
1818 N Street NW, Suite 600, Washington DC 20036. 202/331-3500. World Wide Web address: http://www. asee.org. Publishes magazines and journals including the *Journal of Engineering Education*.

**AMERICAN SOCIETY OF CIVIL ENGINEERS**
1801 Alexander Bell Drive, Reston VA 20191-4400. 703/295-6300. World Wide Web address: http://www. asce.org. A membership organization which offers subscriptions to *Civil Engineering* magazine and *ASCE News*, discounts on various other publications, seminars, video- and audiotapes, specialty conferences, an annual convention, group insurance programs, and pension plans.

**AMERICAN SOCIETY OF HEATING, REFRIGERATING AND AIR CONDITIONING ENGINEERS**
1791 Tullie Circle NE, Atlanta GA 30329. 404/636-8400. Fax: 404/321-5478. World Wide Web address: http://www.ashrae.org. A society of 50,000 members which offers handbooks, a monthly journal, a monthly newspaper, discounts on other publications, group insurance, continuing education, and registration discounts for meetings, conferences, seminars, and expositions.

**AMERICAN SOCIETY OF LANDSCAPE ARCHITECTS**
636 Eye Street NW, Washington DC 20001. 202/898-2444. World Wide Web address: http://www.asla.org. Check out the Website's Joblink for listings of employment opportunities.

**AMERICAN SOCIETY OF MECHANICAL ENGINEERS**
3 Park Avenue, New York NY 10016. 212/591-7722. World Wide Web address: http://www.asme.org. Handles educational materials for certified engineers, as well as scholarships.

**AMERICAN SOCIETY OF NAVAL ENGINEERS**
1452 Duke Street, Alexandria VA 22314. 703/836-6727. World Wide Web address: http://www.jhuapl. edu/ASNE. Holds symposiums based on technical papers. Publishes a journal and newsletter bimonthly.

**AMERICAN SOCIETY OF PLUMBING ENGINEERS**
3617 Thousand Oaks Boulevard, Suite 210, Westlake CA 91362. 805/495-7120. Provides technical and educational information.

**AMERICAN SOCIETY OF SAFETY ENGINEERS**
1800 East Oakton Street, Des Plaines IL 60018-2187. 847/699-2929. Jobline service available at ext. 243. Fax: 847/768-3434. World Wide Web address: http://www.asse.org. A membership organization offering *Professional Safety*, a monthly journal; educational seminars; an annual professional development conference and exposition; technical publications; certification preparation programs; career placement services; and group and liability insurance programs.

**ASSOCIATED BUILDERS & CONTRACTORS**
1300 North 17th Street, 8th Floor, Arlington VA 22209. 703/812-2000. World Wide Web address: http://www.abc.org. Sponsors annual career fair.

**ASSOCIATED GENERAL CONTRACTORS OF AMERICA, INC.**
1957 E Street NW, Washington DC 20006. 202/393-2040. World Wide Web address: http://www.agc.org. A full-service construction association of subcontractors, specialty contractors, suppliers, equipment manufacturers, and professional firms. Services include government relations, education and

training, jobsite services, legal services, and information services.

**THE ENGINEERING CENTER (TEC)**
One Walnut Street, Boston MA 02108-3616. 617/227-5551. Contact: Abbie Goodman. World Wide Web address: http://www.engineers.org. An association that provides services for many engineering membership organizations.

**ILLUMINATING ENGINEERING SOCIETY OF NORTH AMERICA**
120 Wall Street, 17th Floor, New York NY 10005-4001. 212/248-5000. World Wide Web address: http://www.iesna.org. An organization for industry professionals involved in the manufacturing, design, specification, and maintenance of lighting systems. Conference held annually. Offers a Technical Knowledge Examination.

**JUNIOR ENGINEERING TECHNICAL SOCIETY**
1420 King Street, Suite 405, Alexandria VA 22314-2794. 703/548-JETS. Fax: 703/548-0769. E-mail address: jets@nae.edu. World Wide Web address: http://www.asee.org/jets. A nonprofit, educational society promoting interest in engineering, technology, mathematics, and science. Provides information to high school students and teachers regarding careers in engineering and technology.

**NATIONAL ACTION COUNCIL FOR MINORITIES IN ENGINEERING**
350 Fifth Avenue, Suite 2212, New York NY 10118. 212/279-2626. Offers scholarship programs for students. World Wide Web address: http://www.nacme.org.

**NATIONAL ASSOCIATION OF HOME BUILDERS**
1201 15th Street NW, Washington DC 20005. 202/822-0200. World Wide Web address: http://www.nahb.com. A trade association promoting safe and affordable housing. Provides management services and education for members.

**NATIONAL ASSOCIATION OF MINORITY ENGINEERING PROGRAM ADMINISTRATORS, INC.**
1133 West Morse Boulevard, Suite 201, Winter Park FL 32789. 407/647-8839. World Wide Web address: http://www.namepa.org.

**NATIONAL ELECTRICAL CONTRACTORS ASSOCIATION**
3 Bethesda Metro Center, Suite 1100, Bethesda MD 20814. 301/657-3110. World Wide Web address: http://www.necanet.org. Provides information on hiring and trade shows. The association also publishes a magazine called *Electrical Contractor*.

**NATIONAL SOCIETY OF BLACK ENGINEERS**
1454 Duke Street, Alexandria VA 22314. 703/549-2207. World Wide Web address: http://www.nsbe.org. A nonprofit organization run by college students. Offers scholarships, editorials, and magazines.

**NATIONAL SOCIETY OF PROFESSIONAL ENGINEERS**
1420 King Street, Alexandria VA 22314-2794. 703/684-2800. Call 703/684-2830 for scholarship information for students. Fax: 703/836-4875. World Wide Web address: http://www.nspe.org. A society of over 73,000 engineers. Membership includes the monthly magazine *Engineering Times*; continuing

education; scholarships and fellowships; discounts on publications; and health and life insurance programs.

**SOCIETY OF AMERICAN REGISTERED ARCHITECTS**
303 South Broadway, Suite 322, Tarrytown NY 10591. 914/631-3600. Fax: 914/631-1319. World Wide Web address: http://www.sara-national.org.

**SOCIETY OF FIRE PROTECTION ENGINEERS**
7315 Wisconsin Avenue, Suite 1225W, Bethesda MD 20814. 301/718-2910. Fax: 301/718-2242. World Wide Web address: http://www.sfpe.org. Offers members reports, newsletters, *Journal of Fire Protecting Engineering*, insurance programs, short courses, symposiums, tutorials, an annual meeting, and engineering seminars.

### Directories

**DIRECTORY OF ENGINEERING SOCIETIES**
American Association of Engineering Societies, 1111 19th Street NW, Suite 403, Washington DC 20036. 202/296-2237. $185.00. Lists other engineering association members, publications, and convention exhibits.

**DIRECTORY OF ENGINEERS IN PRIVATE PRACTICE**
National Society of Professional Engineers, 1420 King Street, Alexandria VA 22314-2794. 703/684-2800. $50.00. Lists members and companies.

### Magazines

**THE CAREER ENGINEER**
National Society of Black Engineers, 1454 Duke Street, Alexandria VA 22314. 703/549-2207.

**CHEMICAL & ENGINEERING NEWS**
American Chemical Society, 1155 16th Street NW, Washington DC 20036. 202/872-4600. World Wide Web address: http://www.acs.org.

**COMPUTER-AIDED ENGINEERING**
Penton Media, 1100 Superior Avenue, Cleveland OH 44114. 216/696-7000.

**EDN CAREER NEWS**
Cahners Business Information, 275 Washington Street, Newton MA 02158. 617/964-3030. World Wide Web address: http://www.cahners.com.

**ENGINEERING TIMES**
National Society of Professional Engineers, 1420 King Street, Alexandria VA 22314. 703/684-2800.

**NAVAL ENGINEERS JOURNAL**
American Society of Naval Engineers, 1452 Duke Street, Alexandria VA 22314. 703/836-6727. Subscription: $48.00.

### Online Services

**ARCHITECTURE & BUILDING FORUM**
Go: Arch. A CompuServe discussion group for architectural professionals.

**ARCHITECTURE AND LANDSCAPE ARCHITECTURE JOBS**
http://www.clr.toronto.edu/VIRTUALLIB/jobs.html. This Website provides job openings for architects and landscape architects, as well as links to other related sites.

**HOT JOBS! - CONSTRUCTION**
http://www.kbic.com/construction.htm. Provides
construction employment opportunities organized by
job title.

**P.L.A.C.E.S. FORUM**
Keyword: places. A discussion group available to
America Online subscribers who are professionals in
the fields of architecture, construction, and
engineering.

# ARTS AND ENTERTAINMENT/RECREATION

*Diversity is the trend in the entertainment industry. Recently, Business Week reported that media corporations and entertainment powerhouses are trying to gain revenue by creating new divisions. These companies have originated record labels, online services, movie studios, theme parks, and cable networks. As a result, the market is saturated and profits are falling.*

*A recent study predicted that the average television viewer will gain almost 1,000 channel choices by the time digital compression of television is complete and linking of TVs to the Internet becomes an option. With the creation of new channels comes more competition and as a result, programming costs have hit the roof. In an attempt to ease the sting of losing* Seinfeld, *NBC has agreed to pay $13 million for each new episode of* ER *(the network's highest ranking show), versus $2 million per episode in 1997. Advertising costs are rising as well, though not as dramatically. A 30 second spot on* ER *now goes for $565,000, versus $560,000 in 1997. Look for movie makers to create more distinct products that attract consumers in all areas. Fox and Paramount struck a golden iceberg with* Titanic, *which has spawned book tie-ins, a best-selling soundtrack, and a $30 million sale to NBC for the television rights.*

*Fans of professional sports continue to spend money on their teams and 1999 will likely be no exception. To retain its contract for* Monday Night Football, *ABC will be reportedly paying the National Football League a hard-hitting $550 million per season, as noted in* Fortune. *Major League Baseball has expanded by two more teams and is climbing back from its slump of the mid-'90s with the help of interleague play. The National Hockey League has also begun plans to expand, with four new teams possible by 2000. The National Basketball Association (NBA), however, is facing the possibility of a canceled 1998-99 season due to labor disputes. Prior to the labor disputes, the NBA reportedly inked a television deal with both TNT and NBC for $2.6 billion.*

*The U.S. Department of Labor expects employment opportunities for amusement and recreation services to increase by 41 percent between 1996 and 2006. Despite these projections, across much of the industry costs are being cut and joint ventures continue. Therefore, jobseekers with business savvy and a flair for marketing may find some solid opportunities.*

**AUDIO PLUS VIDEO INTERNATIONAL, INC.**
235 Pegasus Avenue, Northvale NJ 07647. 201/767-3800. **Contact:** Human Resources Department. **Description:** Audio Plus Video International provides services which include post-production work and audio and video restoration for a variety of networks including the Children's Television Network. **Corporate headquarters location:** New York NY. **Parent company:** International Post Limited is a provider of a wide range of post-production services primarily to the television advertising industry and a distributor of television programming to the international market through its operating subsidiaries: Manhattan Transfer/Edit, Inc.; Audio Plus Video International, Inc.; Big Picture/Even Time Limited; and The Post Edge, Inc. The company's services include creative editorial services, film-to-tape transfer, electronic video editing, computer-generated graphics, duplication, and audio services, all in multiple standards and formats, as well as network playback operations. The company's services are provided in the New York metropolitan area and South Florida.

**CME INFORMATION SERVICES**
2000 Crawford Place, Suite 100, Mount Laurel NJ 08054. 609/866-9100. **Contact:** Human Resources. **Description:** Produces educational videotapes, audiotapes, and CD-ROMS and holds live educational conferences.

**GARDEN STATE PARK**
P.O. Box 4274, Cherry Hill NJ 08034. 609/488-8400. **Contact:** Personnel. **World Wide Web address:** http://www.gspark.com. **Description:** A pari-mutuel horse racing track.

**INSTRUCTIVISION, INC.**
3 Regent Street, Suite 306, Livingston NJ 07039-1617. 973/992-9081. **Contact:** Human Resources. **World Wide Web address:** http://www.instructivision.com. **Description:** A multimedia publishing company. Instructivision develops educational video and computer programs and workbooks. The company operates a full-service video production facility encompassing a production stage, an interformat digital editing suite, offline editing, 3-D animation, and audio recording equipment.

**McCARTER THEATRE**
**CENTER FOR THE PERFORMING ARTS**
91 University Place, Princeton NJ 08540. 609/683-9100. **Fax:** 609/497-0369. **Contact:** General Manager. **Description:** A performing arts center which produces and presents artists in drama, music, dance, and special events. Established in 1963. **Common positions include:** Actor/Actress/Performer; Artist; Designer; Painter; Tailor. **Educational backgrounds include:** Art/Design; Business Administration; Communications; Liberal Arts; Marketing. **Benefits:** Dental Insurance; Life Insurance; Medical Insurance; Pension Plan. **Special programs:** Internships. **Corporate headquarters location:** This Location. **Number of employees at this location:** 200.

**MONMOUTH PARK**
175 Oceanport Avenue, Oceanport NJ 07757. 732/222-5100. **Contact:** Human Resources. **Description:** A horse-racing track.

**MOUNTAIN CREEK**
P.O. Box 391, Vernon NJ 07462. 973/827-2000. **Contact:** Human Resources. **Description:** A water amusement park in the summer and a ski resort in the winter.

**NEW JERSEY SHAKESPEARE FESTIVAL**
36 Madison Avenue, Madison NJ 07940. 973/408-3278. **Fax:** 973/408-3361. **Contact:** Joseph Discher, Artistic Associate. **E-mail address:** njsf@njshakespeare.org. **World Wide Web address:** http://www.njshakespeare.org. **Description:** A nonprofit professional theater devoted to producing the works of Shakespeare and other classic masterworks. Founded in 1962. **NOTE:** Entry-level positions are offered. **Common positions include:** Administrative Assistant; General Manager; Graphic Artist; Graphic Designer; Marketing Manager; Production Manager; Public Relations Specialist; Teacher/Professor. **Educational backgrounds include:** Business Administration; Liberal Arts; Marketing; Public Relations; Theater. **Benefits:** Dental Insurance; Employee Discounts; Flexible Schedule; Medical Insurance; On-Site Daycare; Pension Plan; Public Transit Available. **Special programs:** Internships; Apprenticeships; Training.

**NEW JERSEY SPORTS & EXPOSITION AUTHORITY**
50 Route 120, East Rutherford NJ 07073. 201/935-8500. **Contact:** Gina Klein, Assistant Director of Human Resources. **World Wide Web address:** http://www.njsea.com. **Description:** A state-appointed agency responsible for sports and entertainment activities at the Meadowlands Sports Complex, which includes Meadowlands Racetrack (harness and thoroughbred racing, as well as other events), Giants Stadium (New York Giants, New York Jets, concerts, and other events), and Meadowlands Arena (New Jersey Nets, New Jersey Devils, tennis, track, concerts, and other events). **Corporate headquarters location:** This Location.

**P.P.I. ENTERTAINMENT GROUP**
88 St. Francis Street, Newark NJ 07105. 973/344-4214. **Contact:** Personnel. **World Wide Web address:** http://www.peterpan.com. **Description:** Manufactures and distributes records, tapes, videos, and CD-ROMs. **Common positions include:** Accountant; Advertising Account Executive; Editorial Assistant; Graphic Artist; Graphic Designer; Marketing Manager; Production Manager; Public Relations Specialist; Purchasing Agent/Manager; Sales Manager; Sales Representative; Secretary; Video Production Coordinator. **Educational backgrounds include:** Accounting; Art/Design; Communications; Marketing. **Benefits:** 401(k); Employee Discounts; Life Insurance; Medical Insurance; Public Transit Available. **Corporate headquarters location:** This Location. **Listed on:** Privately held.

**SONY MUSIC**
400 North Woodbury Road, Pitman NJ 08071. 609/589-8000. **Contact:** Human Resources Department. **World Wide Web address:** http://www.sony.com. **Description:** Offices of the major record company.

*Note: Because addresses and telephone numbers of smaller companies can change rapidly, we recommend you call each company to verify the information below before inquiring about job opportunities. Mass mailings are not recommended.*

**Additional small employers:**

**AMUSEMENT AND RECREATION SERVICES**

**Livingston Recreation Dept.**
20 Robert H. Harp Dr, Livingston NJ 07039-3930. 973/535-7925.

**Parks and Recreation Administration**
Lincoln Park, Jersey City NJ 07304. 201/915-1391.

**Playday Distributors**
12 Grant Ave, Seaside Heights NJ 08751-2112. 732/793-1020.

**Powerhouse Company**
401 Hackensack Ave, Hackensack NJ 07601-6411. 201/488-3300.

**BOTANICAL AND ZOOLOGICAL GARDENS**

**Duke Gardens Foundation Inc.**
PO Box 2030, Somerville NJ 08876-1256. 908/722-3700.

**NJ State Aquarium at Camden**
One Riverside Dr, Camden NJ 08103-1037. 609/365-3300.

**ENTERTAINERS AND ENTERTAINMENT GROUPS**

**Magical Enterprises Inc.**
115 Route 37 E, Toms River NJ 08753-6624. 732/286-1950.

**New Jersey Symphony Orchestra**
2 Central Ave, Newark NJ 07102-3102. 973/624-3713.

**GOLF COURSES**

**Atrium Country Club Inc.**
609-615 Eagle Rock Ave, West Orange NJ 07052. 973/731-7900.

**Forsgate Country Club**
PO Box 269, Jamesburg NJ 08831-0269. 732/521-0070.

**Mac Wild Oaks Country Club**
Rural Route 30, Box 414, Sewell NJ 08080-9500. 609/468-0190.

**MOTION PICTURE AND VIDEO TAPE PRODUCTION AND DISTRIBUTION**

**Films For Humanities & Sciences**
PO Box 2053, Princeton NJ 08543-2053. 609/275-1400.

**NBA Entertainment Inc.**
PO Box 10602, Newark NJ 07193-0602. 201/865-1500.

**NFL Films Inc.**
330 Fellowship Road, Mount Laurel NJ 08054-1201. 609/778-1600.

**Phoenix Communications**
3 Empire Blvd, South Hackensack NJ 07606-1806. 201/807-0888.

**Video Services Corporation**
240 Pegasus Avenue, Northvale NJ 07647-1904. 201/767-1000.

**MUSEUMS AND ART GALLERIES**

**Liberty Science Center**
251 Phillip St, Jersey City NJ 07305-4600. 201/451-0006.

**Newark Museum Association**
PO Box 540, Newark NJ 07101-0540. 973/596-6550.

**PHYSICAL FITNESS FACILITIES**

**Eastern Athletic Club Inc.**
PO Box 331, Medford NJ 08055. 609/953-9090.

**Tilton Athletic Club**
3022 Hingston Ave, Egg Harbor NJ 08234-4412. 609/646-2590.

**RACING AND TRACK OPERATION**

**Freehold Raceway**
PO Box 4274, Cherry Hill NJ 08034-0649. 732/462-3800.

**SPORTING AND RECREATIONAL CAMPS**

**Brooklake Day Camp**
4 Foxcroft Dr, Livingston NJ 07039-2633. 973/533-1600.

**Camp Horizons**
4 Foxcroft Dr, Livingston NJ 07039-2633. 973/992-7767.

**Lake Bryn Mawr Camp**
PO Box 612, Short Hills NJ 07078-0612. 973/467-3518.

**Lake-Vu Day Camp**
505 Riva Ave, East Brunswick NJ 08816-2437. 732/821-8933.

**Tall Pines Day Camp Inc.**
1349 Sykesville Rd, Williamstown NJ 08094-3247. 609/262-3900.

**THEATRICAL PRODUCERS AND SERVICES**

**Hunterdon Hills Playhouse**
88 State Route 173, Hampton NJ 08827-4004. 908/730-8007.

**For more information on career opportunities in arts, entertainment, and recreation:**

Associations

**AMERICAN ASSOCIATION OF MUSEUMS**
1575 Eye Street NW, Suite 400, Washington DC 20005. 202/289-1818. Fax: 202/289-6578. World Wide Web address: http://www.aam-us.org. Publishes *Aviso,* a monthly newsletter containing employment listings for the entire country.

**AMERICAN CAMPING ASSOCIATION**
5000 State Road 67 North, Martinsville IN 46151. 765/342-8456.

**AMERICAN CRAFTS COUNCIL**
72 Spring Street, New York NY 10012-4019. 212/274-0630. Operates a research library. Publishes *American Crafts* magazine.

**AMERICAN DANCE GUILD**
31 West 21st Street, New York NY 10010. 212/627-3790. Holds an annual conference with panels, performances, and workshops. Operates a job listings service (available at a discount to members).

**AMERICAN FEDERATION OF MUSICIANS**
1501 Broadway, Suite 600, New York NY 10036. 212/869-1330. World Wide Web address: http://www.afm.org.

**AMERICAN FILM INSTITUTE**
2021 North Western Avenue, Los Angeles CA 90027. 323/856-7600. Toll-free phone: 800/774-4AFI. World Wide Web address: http://www.afionline.org. Membership is required, and includes a newsletter; and members-only discounts on events, seminars, workshops, and exhibits.

**AMERICAN MUSIC CENTER**
30 West 26th Street, Suite 1001, New York NY 10010-2011. 212/366-5260. Fax: 212/366-5265. World Wide Web address: http://www.amc.net. A nonprofit research and information center for contemporary music and jazz. Provides information services and grant programs.

**AMERICAN SOCIETY OF COMPOSERS, AUTHORS, AND PUBLISHERS (ASCAP)**
One Lincoln Plaza, New York NY 10023. 212/621-6000. World Wide Web address: http://www.ascap.com. A membership association which licenses members' work and pays members' royalties. Offers showcases and educational seminars and workshops. The society also has an events hotline: 212/621-6485.

**AMERICAN SYMPHONY ORCHESTRA LEAGUE**
1156 15th Street NW, Suite 800, Washington DC 20005. 202/776-0212. World Wide Web address: http://www.symphony.org.

**AMERICAN ZOO AND AQUARIUM ASSOCIATION**
8403 Colesville Road, Suite 710, Silver Spring MD 20910. 301/562-0777. E-mail address: azaoms@aol.com. World Wide Web address: http://www.aza.org. Publishes a monthly newspaper with employment opportunities for members.

**AMERICANS FOR THE ARTS**
One East 53rd Street, New York NY 10022. 212/223-2787. World Wide Web address: http://www.artsusa.org. A nonprofit organization for the literary, visual, and performing arts. Supports K-12 education and promotes public policy through meetings, forums, and seminars.

**ASSOCIATION OF INDEPENDENT VIDEO AND FILMMAKERS**
304 Hudson Street, 6th Floor, New York NY 10013. 212/807-1400. World Wide Web address: http://www.aivf.org.

**THE CENTER FOR THE STUDY OF SPORT IN SOCIETY**
360 Huntington Avenue, Suite 161 CP, Boston MA 02115. 617/373-4025. World Wide Web address: http://www.sportinsociety.org. Develops programs and provides publications on the interaction of sports and society.

**NATIONAL ARTISTS' EQUITY ASSOCIATION**
P.O. Box 28068, Central Station, Washington DC 20038-8068. 202/628-9633. A national, nonprofit organization dedicated to improving economic, health, and legal conditions for visual artists.

**NATIONAL ENDOWMENT FOR THE ARTS**
1100 Pennsylvania Avenue NW, Washington DC 20506. 202/682-5400. World Wide Web address: http://www.arts.endow.gov.

**NATIONAL RECREATION AND PARK ASSOCIATION**
22377 Belmont Ridge Road, Ashburn VA 20148. 703/858-0784. Fax: 703/858-0794. World Wide Web address: http://www.nrpa.org. A national, nonprofit service organization. Offers professional development and training opportunities in recreation, parks, and leisure services. Publishes a newsletter and magazine that offer employment opportunities for members only.

**PRODUCERS GUILD OF AMERICA**
400 South Beverly Drive, Suite 211, Beverly Hills CA 90212. 310/557-0807. Fax: 310/557-0436. World Wide Web address: http://www.producersguild.com. Membership is required, and includes credit union access; subscription to *P.O.V. Magazine* and the association newsletter; attendance at the organization's annual Golden Laurel Awards and other events; and special screenings of motion pictures at the time of the Academy Awards.

## Directories

**ARTIST'S AND GRAPHIC DESIGNER'S MARKET**
Writer's Digest Books, 1507 Dana Avenue, Cincinnati OH 45207. 513/531-2222.

**BLACK BOOK ILLUSTRATION**
The Black Book, 10 Astor Place, 6th Floor, New York NY 10003. 212/539-9800. World Wide Web address: http://www.blackbook.com.

**BLACK BOOK PHOTOGRAPHY**
The Black Book, 10 Astor Place, 6th Floor, New York NY 10003. 212/539-9800. World Wide Web address: http://www.blackbook.com.

**PLAYERS GUIDE**
165 West 46th Street, Suite 1305, New York NY 10036. 212/869-3570.

**ROSS REPORTS TELEVISION AND FILM**
BPI Communications, Inc., 1515 Broadway, 14th Floor, New York NY 10036-8986. 212/764-7300.

## Magazines

**AMERICAN CINEMATOGRAPHER**
American Society of Cinematographers, 1782 North Orange Drive, Hollywood CA 90028. Toll-free phone: 800/448-0154. World Wide Web address: http://www.cinematographer.com.

**ARTFORUM**
65 Bleecker Street, 13th Floor, New York NY 10012. 212/475-4000. World Wide Web address: http://www.artforum.com.

**AVISO**
American Association of Museums, 1575 Eye Street NW, Suite 400, Washington DC 20005. 202/289-1818.

**BACK STAGE**
BPI Communications, Inc., 1515 Broadway, New

York NY 10036-8986. 212/764-7300. World Wide
Web address: http://www.backstage.com.

**BILLBOARD**
BPI Communications, Inc., 1515 Broadway, New
York NY 10036-8986. 212/764-7300. World Wide
Web address: http://www.billboard.com.

**CRAFTS REPORT**
300 Water Street, Box 1992, Wilmington DE 19899.
302/656-2209. World Wide Web address: http://www.
craftsreport.com.

**DRAMA-LOGUE**
P.O. Box 38771, Los Angeles CA 90038. 213/464-
5079.

**HOLLYWOOD REPORTER**
BPI Communications, Inc., 5055 Wilshire Boulevard,
6th Floor, Los Angeles CA 90036. 213/525-2000.
World Wide Web address: http://www.
hollywoodreporter.com.

**VARIETY**
245 West 17th Street, 5th Floor, New York NY
10011. 212/337-7001. Toll-free phone: 800/323-4345.

**WOMEN ARTIST NEWS**
300 Riverside Drive, New York NY 10025. 212/666-
6990.

<u>**Online Services**</u>

**AMERICAN CAMPING ASSOCIATION**
http://www.aca-camps.org. Provides listings of jobs at
day and overnight camps for children and adults with
special needs.

**ARTJOB**
Gopher://gopher.tmn.com/11/Artswire/artjob.
Provides information on jobs, internships, and
conferences in theater, dance, opera, and museums.
This site is only accessible through America Online.

**COOLWORKS**
http://www.coolworks.com. Provides links to 22,000
job openings in national parks, summer camps, ski
areas, river areas, ranches, fishing areas, cruise ships,
and resorts. This site also includes information on
volunteer openings.

**VISUAL NATION ARTS JOBS LINKS**
http://fly.hiwaay.net/%7Edrewyor/art_job.html.
Provides links to other sites that post arts and
academic job openings and information.

# AUTOMOTIVE

*In the face of fierce worldwide competition, automotive manufacturers have been forced to lower car prices, grant low interest-rate financing, and offer better deals on leasing. With consumer* confidence relatively high, there is a strong buyer's market, but according to Business Week, *auto consumers are also more discriminating than ever.*

*Nineteen ninety-eight was a big year for the automotive industry. General Motors survived one of the worst strikes of its 91 year history, resulting in huge financial losses and the delayed introduction of new models. The industry as a whole continues to shift more production to Mexico, where auto production was at 1.5 million in 1998, and is estimated to reach 2.2 million by 2001 as the North American Free Trade Agreement (NAFTA) becomes fully implemented. Nineteen ninety-eight also saw the birth of DaimlerChrysler, the international partnership between Chrysler Corporation and Daimler Benz. It is expected that other automotive companies will follow suit in efforts to trim costs and share resources. Ford, for example, was recently outbid by Hyundai in the sale of Korea's troubled Kia Motors Corporation.*

*Despite the General Motors strike, industry profits were up 141 percent for the first two quarters of 1998 as compared to the same period of 1997.*

**BMW OF NORTH AMERICA, INC.**
P.O. Box 1227, Westwood NJ 07675-1227. 201/307-4000. **Physical address:** 300 Chestnut Ridge Road, Woodcliff Lake NJ 07675. **Contact:** Employment Manager. **Description:** As the U.S. headquarters, BMW of North America is responsible for United States marketing operations for BMW's extensive line of motorcycles and automobiles. **Parent company:** BMW - Bayerische Motoren Werke AG (Munich, Germany).

**FORD MOTOR COMPANY**
698 U.S. Highway 46, Teterboro NJ 07608. 201/288-9400. **Contact:** Robert Wildrick, Human Resources Manager. **Description:** This location is a parts distribution center. Overall, Ford is engaged in the manufacture, assembly, and sale of cars, trucks, and related parts and accessories. Ford is also one of the largest providers of financial services in the United States. The company has manufacturing, assembly, and sales affiliates in 29 countries outside the United States. The company's two core businesses are the Automotive Group and the Financial Services Group (Ford Credit, The Associates, USL Capital, and First Nationwide). Ford is also engaged in a number of other businesses, including electronics, glass, electrical and fuel-handling products, plastics, climate control systems, automotive service and replacement parts, vehicle leasing and rental, and land development. **Corporate headquarters location:** Dearborn MI. **Listed on:** New York Stock Exchange.

**FORD MOTOR COMPANY**
P.O. Box 3018, Edison NJ 08818. 732/632-5930. **Contact:** Human Resources. **Description:** This location is an assembly plant. Overall, Ford is engaged in the design, development, manufacture, and sale of cars, trucks, tractors, and related components and accessories. Ford is also one of the largest providers of financial services in the United States. The company has manufacturing, assembly, and sales affiliates in 29 countries outside the United States. The company's two core businesses are the Automotive Group and the Financial Services Group (Ford Credit, The Associates, USL Capital, and First Nationwide). Ford also is engaged in a number of other businesses, including electronics, glass, electrical and fuel-handling products, plastics, climate control systems, automotive service and replacement parts, vehicle leasing and rental, and land development. **Corporate headquarters location:** Dearborn MI. **Listed on:** New York Stock Exchange.

**GENERAL HOSE PRODUCTS INC.**
30 Sherwood Lane, Fairfield NJ 07004. 973/228-0500. **Contact:** Diana Taylor, Office Manager. **Description:** Manufactures heavy-duty hose products used primarily by auto manufacturers in air

conditioning systems. General Hose is also engaged in tube fabrication and assemblies. **Common positions include:** Accountant/Auditor; Blue-Collar Worker Supervisor; Manufacturer's/ Wholesaler's Sales Rep.; Mechanical Engineer; Operations/Production Manager. **Benefits:** Life Insurance; Medical Insurance. **Corporate headquarters location:** This Location. **Operations at this facility include:** Manufacturing. **Number of employees at this location:** 25.

### KEM MANUFACTURING COMPANY INC.
18-35 River Road, Fair Lawn NJ 07410. 201/796-8000. **Contact:** Personnel. **World Wide Web address:** http://www.kemparts.com. **Description:** Manufactures and markets a wide range of products for sale to the automotive aftermarket. **Common positions include:** Accountant/Auditor; Administrator; Advertising Clerk; Blue-Collar Worker Supervisor; Buyer; Computer Programmer; Credit Manager; Customer Service Representative; Department Manager; Draftsperson; General Manager; Human Resources Manager; Manufacturer's/Wholesaler's Sales Rep.; Mechanical Engineer; Operations/Production Manager; Purchasing Agent/Manager; Quality Control Supervisor. **Educational backgrounds include:** Accounting; Business Administration; Computer Science; Engineering; Liberal Arts; Marketing. **Benefits:** Disability Coverage; Employee Discounts; Life Insurance; Medical Insurance; Pension Plan; Tuition Assistance. **Corporate headquarters location:** This Location. **Operations at this facility include:** Manufacturing.

### MERCEDES-BENZ OF NORTH AMERICA
One Mercedes Drive, Montvale NJ 07645. 201/573-2530. **Contact:** Katherine Dronzek, Staffing/Employee Relations. **Description:** An importer of the complete line of Mercedes-Benz automobiles and related components. Mercedes-Benz of North America distributes Mercedes products to dealers throughout the United States. **Common positions include:** Accountant/Auditor; Automotive Engineer; Computer Programmer; Customer Service Rep.; Financial Analyst; Instructor/Trainer; Marketing Specialist; Systems Analyst; Technical Writer/Editor. **Educational backgrounds include:** Accounting; Computer Science; Engineering; Finance; Marketing. **Benefits:** Dental Insurance; Disability Coverage; Employee Discounts; Life Insurance; Medical Insurance; Pension Plan; Savings Plan; Tuition Assistance. **Corporate headquarters location:** This Location. **Parent company:** Daimler-Benz AG. **Number of employees nationwide:** 1,500.

### ROLLS-ROYCE MOTOR INC.
140 East Ridgewood Avenue, Paramus NJ 07652. 201/967-9100. **Contact:** Human Resources Manager. **Description:** This location is the North American sales headquarters. All Rolls-Royce cars and parts are manufactured in England. **Corporate headquarters location:** England.

### RYDER PUBLIC TRANSPORTATION
216 Haddon Avenue, Suite 300, Westmont NJ 08108. 609/858-1818. **Contact:** Anna Crouse, Human Resources. **Description:** Performs repair services on county and municipal vehicles such as police cars.

### SUBARU OF AMERICA
2235 Route 7 West, Cherry Hill NJ 08002. 609/488-8500. **Fax:** 609/488-3196. **Contact:** Scott Mogren, Director of Human Resources. **World Wide Web address:** http://www.subaru.com. **Description:** This location houses administrative offices. Overall, Subaru of America manufactures cars and trucks. **Benefits:** 401(k); Dental Insurance; Disability Coverage; Employee Discounts; Life Insurance; Matching Gift; Medical Insurance; Pension Plan; Tuition Assistance.

### VOLVO CARS OF NORTH AMERICA, INC.
6 Volvo Drive, Rockleigh NJ 07647. 201/767-4715. **Contact:** Ellen Andretta, Human Resources Services Representative. **Description:** Supports the sale and service of Volvo automobiles and related parts and accessories for approximately 400 dealers. **Common positions include:** Automotive Engineer. **Corporate headquarters location:** This Location.

*Note: Because addresses and telephone numbers of smaller companies can change rapidly, we recommend you call each company to verify the information below before inquiring about job opportunities. Mass mailings are not recommended.*

**Additional small employers:**

**AUTOMOTIVE REPAIR SHOPS**

**Faps Inc.**
303 Craneway St, Newark NJ 07114-3117. 973/589-0735.

**MOTOR VEHICLE EQUIPMENT WHOLESALE**

**Adesa Corporation**
200 N Main St, Manville NJ 08835-1357. 908/725-2200.

**American Honda Motor Co. Inc.**
PO Box 337, Moorestown NJ 08057-0337. 609/235-8700.

**Automotive Resources International**
9000 Midatlantic Dr, Mount Laurel NJ 08054. 609/439-7466.

**Jaguar Cars**
555 MacArthur Blvd, Mahwah NJ 07430-2326. 201/818-8500.

**Multech Inc.**
111 Corporate Blvd, South Plainfield NJ 07080-2409. 908/755-7227.

**NADE**
PO Box 188, Bordentown NJ 08505-0188. 609/298-3400.

**Nissan Motor Corp.**
PO Box 6750, Somerset NJ 08875-6750. 732/805-3100.

**Parts Plus Group Inc.**
20 River Rd, Bogota NJ 07603-1521. 201/487-7007.

**Toyota Motor Sales USA Inc.**
390 E Port St, Newark NJ 07114-3115. 973/589-2051.

**Volkswagen of America Inc.**
One Commerce Dr, Cranbury NJ 08512-3503. 609/860-8800.

**Volvo and GMC Truck Center**
PO Box 7052, North Brunswick NJ 08902-7052. 732/821-5440.

**MOTOR VEHICLES AND EQUIPMENT**

**FDP Brakes**
PO Box 5627, Trenton NJ 08638-0627. 609/396-6500.

**General Motors Corporation**
1016 West Edgar Road, Linden NJ 07036-6594. 908/474-4000.

**Hercules-Ajax Co.**
321 Valley Rd, Somerville NJ 08876-4056. 908/369-5544.

**Lo-Jack of New Jersey**
12 Rte 17, Ste 220, Paramus NJ 07652-2644. 201/368-8716.

**New Jersey American Inc.**
PO Box 158, Blackwood NJ 08012-0158. 609/228-7000.

**Precision Specialties Inc.**
PO Box 118, Pitman NJ 08071-0118. 609/589-0815.

**RMP Delaware Valley**
PO Box 615, Pennsauken NJ 08110-0615. 609/662-3811.

**Welles Manufacturing**
PO Box 155, Northvale NJ 07647-0155. 201/768-8200.

## For more information on career opportunities in the automotive industry:

### Associations

**AMERICAN AUTOMOBILE MANUFACTURERS ASSOCIATION**
1401 H Street NW, Suite 900, Washington DC 20005. 202/326-5500. Fax: 202/326-5567. World Wide Web address: http://www.aama.com. A trade association. Sponsors research projects, distributes publications, and reviews social and public policies pertaining to the motor vehicle industry and its customers.

**ASSOCIATION OF INTERNATIONAL AUTOMOBILE MANUFACTURERS, INC.**
1001 19th Street North, Suite 1200, Arlington VA 22209. 703/525-7788. World Wide Web address: http://www.aiam.org.

**AUTOMOTIVE SERVICE ASSOCIATION**
P O Box 929, Bedford TX 76095. 817/283-6205. World Wide Web address: http://www.asashop.org. Works with shops to find workers. Publishes a monthly magazine with classified advertisements.

**AUTOMOTIVE SERVICE INDUSTRY ASSOCIATION**
25 Northwest Point Boulevard, Suite 425, Elk Grove Village IL 60007-1035. 847/228-1310. World Wide Web address: http://www.aftmkt.com/asia. Members are manufacturers and distributors of automobile replacement parts. Sponsors a trade show. Publishes educational guidebooks and training manuals.

### Directories

**AUTOMOTIVE NEWS MARKET DATA BOOK**
Crain Communications, Automotive News, 1400 Woodbridge Avenue, Detroit MI 48207-3187. 313/446-6000.

**WARD'S AUTOMOTIVE YEARBOOK**
Ward's Communications, Inc., 3000 Town Center, Suite 2750, Southville MI 48075. 248/357-0800. World Wide Web address: http://www.wardsauto.com.

### Magazines

**AUTOMOTIVE INDUSTRIES**
Cahners Business Information, 201 King of Prussia Road, Radnor PA 19089. 610/964-4000.

**AUTOMOTIVE NEWS**
Crain Communications, 1400 Woodbridge Avenue, Detroit MI 48207-3187. 313/446-6000.

**WARD'S AUTO WORLD**
**WARD'S AUTOMOTIVE REPORTS**
Ward's Communications, Inc., 3000 Town Center, Suite 2750, Southville MI 48075. 248/357-0800. World Wide Web address: http://www.wardsauto.com.

# BANKING/SAVINGS AND LOANS

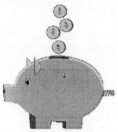

*Though the banking industry is expected to experience 10 to 20 percent job growth through 2006, it is still plagued by uncertainty heading into 2000. Mergers and acquisitions continue to be the norm, as in the case of the mega-merger between Citicorp and Travelers Group, with combined assets in excess of $700 billion. The Asian crisis continues to loom abroad, and the Year 2000 computer glitch is causing concerns for many banks. Although most banks remain unscathed and continue to prosper, some are still losing ground to security houses and financial divisions of large corporations. According to* Standard & Poor, *the industry saw a 15 percent increase in profits in the second quarter of 1998 from the second quarter of 1997, as well as an increase in profit margins.*

*An increasing number of smaller banks are finding the mega-mergers to be good for business. More and more consumers are choosing to take their money out of banking conglomerates and are giving their business to smaller, more personalized community banks. In fact,* Business Week *reports that even analysts in the field are beginning to lose faith in the promised efficiency of the mega-mergers of 1997.*

*One successful banking trend is automation. Automated teller machines (ATMs) will begin to offer more services including check cashing and printouts of account information. Jobseekers will find less opportunities as bank tellers and more opportunities as call center customer service representatives. The Bureau of Labor Statistics expects bank tellers to lose 152,000 jobs by 2005 and projects numerous layoffs for bank office workers and managers.*

**BANK OF GLOUCESTER COUNTY**
100 Park Avenue, Woodbury NJ 08096. 609/845-0700. **Contact:** Human Resources. **Description:** A bank.

**BANK OF NEW YORK**
385 Rifle Camp Road, West Paterson NJ 07424. 973/357-7405. **Contact:** Personnel. **World Wide Web address:** http://www.bankofny.com. **Description:** A bank serving individuals, corporations, foreign and domestic banks, governments, and other institutions through banking offices in New York City and foreign branches, representative offices, subsidiaries, and affiliates. **Corporate headquarters location:** New York NY. **Parent company:** Bank of New York Company, Inc. **Listed on:** New York Stock Exchange. **Number of employees nationwide:** 12,000.

**BRUNSWICK BANK & TRUST**
P.O. Box 29, New Brunswick NJ 08903. 732/247-5800. **Physical address:** 439 Livingston Avenue, New Brunswick NJ 08901. **Contact:** Human Resources. **Description:** A bank.

**COMMERCE BANK**
**OPERATIONS CENTER**
17000 Horizon Way, Mount Laurel NJ 08054. 609/751-9000. **Contact:** Human Resources. **World Wide Web address:** http://www.yesbank.com. **Description:** A full-service bank offering a variety of services, including Commerce Capital, an in-house stocks and bonds investment program. Commerce Bank, along with its affiliates Commerce Bank NJ, Commerce Bank Shore, Commerce Bank Harrisburg, and Independence Bank, constitute the Commerce Network.

**COMMUNITY NATIONAL BANK**
222 Haddon Avenue, Westmont NJ 08108. 609/869-7900. **Contact:** Human Resources. **World Wide Web address:** http://www.cnbnj.com. **Description:** A full-service bank. Community

National Bank is an active lender with a loan portfolio that includes commercial and residential mortgages, commercial loans, consumer installments, home equity loans, and credit card loans. **Parent company:** Community Financial.

**EQUITY NATIONAL BANK**
8000 Sagemore Drive, Suite 8101, Marlton NJ 08053. 609/983-4000. **Contact:** Barbara Niedosik, Assistant Vice President. **Description:** A bank whose operations include commercial and investment banking services.

**FMS FINANCIAL CORPORATION**
P.O. Box 397, Burlington NJ 08016. 609/386-2400. **Contact:** Nancy Parker, Human Resources. **Description:** A bank holding company. **Subsidiaries include:** Farmers & Mechanics Bank operates 13 branch offices in Burlington County NJ.

**FIRST UNION NATIONAL BANK**
190 River Road, Summit NJ 07901. 973/565-3200. **Contact:** Human Resources. **World Wide Web address:** http://www.firstunion.com. **Description:** A bank. In 1998, First Union Corporation acquired CoreStates Financial Corporation and The Money Store, Inc. **Parent company:** First Union Corporation (Charlotte NC).

**FIRST UNION NATIONAL BANK**
2 Broad Street, Woodbury NJ 08096. 609/384-3413. **Contact:** Human Resources. **World Wide Web address:** http://www.firstunion.com. **Description:** A bank. In 1998, First Union Corporation acquired both CoreStates Financial Corporation and The Money Store, Inc. **Common positions include:** Bank Officer/Manager; Bank Teller; Branch Manager; Customer Service Rep.; Loan Officer. **Educational backgrounds include:** Accounting; Business Administration; Communications; Economics; Finance; Liberal Arts; Marketing. **Benefits:** Dental Insurance; Disability Coverage; Employee Discounts; Life Insurance; Medical Insurance; Pension Plan; Savings Plan; Tuition Assistance. **Other U.S. locations:** CT; NY; PA. **Parent company:** First Union Corporation (Charlotte NC). **Number of employees at this location:** 800.

**FIRST UNION NATIONAL BANK**
120 Albany Street Plaza, New Brunswick NJ 08903. 732/843-4200. **Contact:** Human Resources. **Description:** A bank. In 1998, First Union Corporation acquired both CoreStates Financial Corporation and The Money Store, Inc. **Parent company:** First Union Corporation (Charlotte NC).

**FIRST UNION NATIONAL BANK**
370 Scotch Road, West Trenton NJ 08628. 609/771-5700. **Fax:** 609/530-7267. **Contact:** Human Resources. **World Wide Web address:** http://www.firstunion.com. **Description:** A bank. In 1998, First Union Corporation acquired both CoreStates Financial Corporation and The Money Store, Inc. **Parent company:** First Union Corporation (Charlotte NC).

**FLEET BANK**
1501 Tilton Road, Northfield NJ 08225. **Toll-free phone:** 800/620-0278. **Contact:** Branch Manager. **World Wide Web address:** http://www.fleet.com. **Description:** Provides banking services to commercial customers. **Parent company:** Fleet Financial Group was founded in 1971 and is a diversified financial services company with approximately 1,200 offices nationwide. Fleet Financial operates six banks, with branches throughout New England, New York, and London, England, and at more than 10 major financial services companies located throughout the United States including Atlanta GA, Long Beach CA, and New York NY. The company merged with Shawmut National Corporation in 1995. Affiliated banking companies include Fleet Bank, N.A.; Fleet Bank of Maine; Fleet Bank of Massachusetts, N.A.; Fleet Bank-NH; and Fleet Bank-RI. Affiliated financial services companies include AFSA Data Corp.; Fleet Brokerage Securities; Fleet Capital, Inc.; Fleet Credit Corp.; Fleet Private Equity; Fleet Investment Advisors; Fleet Investment Services; Fleet Securities, Inc.; Fleet Services Corp.; and RECOLL Management Corporation.

**FLEET BANK**
One Exchange Place, Jersey City NJ 07302. **Toll-free phone:** 800/841-4000. **Contact:** Human Resources. **World Wide Web address:** http://www.fleet.com. **Description:** A full-service bank engaged in a wide range of commercial and consumer banking services. **Corporate headquarters location:** Boston MA. **Parent company:** Fleet Financial Group was founded in 1971 and is a diversified financial services company with approximately 1,200 offices nationwide. Fleet Financial operates six banks, with branches throughout New England, New York, and London, England, and at more than 10 major financial services companies located throughout the United States including Atlanta GA, Long Beach CA, and New York NY. The company merged with Shawmut National Corporation in 1995. Affiliated banking companies include Fleet Bank, N.A.;

Fleet Bank of Maine; Fleet Bank of Massachusetts, N.A.; Fleet Bank-NH; and Fleet Bank-RI. Affiliated financial services companies include AFSA Data Corp.; Fleet Brokerage Securities; Fleet Capital, Inc.; Fleet Credit Corp.; Fleet Private Equity; Fleet Investment Advisors; Fleet Investment Services; Fleet Securities, Inc.; Fleet Services Corp.; and RECOLL Management Corporation.

## GREAT FALLS BANCORP
55 Union Boulevard, P.O. Box 269, Totowa NJ 07511. 973/942-1111. **Contact:** Human Resources. **Description:** A holding company. **Subsidiaries include:** Great Falls Bank conducts general commercial and retail banking encompassing a wide range of traditional deposits and lending functions along with other customary banking services.

## HUDSON CITY SAVINGS BANK
West 80 Century Road, Paramus NJ 07652. 201/967-1900. **Contact:** Douglas C. Yingling, Vice President/Personnel. **Description:** Operates a full-service mutual savings bank with 75 branches in Bergen, Burlington, Camden, Essex, Gloucester, Hudson, Middlesex, Monmouth, Morris, Ocean, Passaic, and Union Counties. Hudson City Savings Bank provides a wide range of traditional banking services, as well as other financial services, including IRAs.

## HUDSON UNITED BANK
P.O. Box 401, Basking Ridge NJ 07920-0401. **Contact:** Human Resources. **Description:** A bank. **NOTE:** Please send resumes to Marizel Fragoso, 1000 MacArthur Boulevard, Mahwah NJ 07430. 201/236-2600. **Corporate headquarters location:** This Location.

## INTERCHANGE STATE BANK
80 Park West, Plaza Two, Saddle Brook NJ 07663. 201/703-2265. **Contact:** Amanda Pascale, Human Resources. **Description:** A full-service bank with locations throughout Bergen County.

## PNC MORTGAGE
One Garret Mountain Plaza, 3rd Floor, West Paterson NJ 07424. 973/881-5400. **Contact:** Human Resources. **Description:** A full-service mortgage banking company that originates, acquires, and services residential mortgage loans. PNC's portfolio of serviced mortgages totals more than $38 billion. **Common positions include:** Accountant/Auditor; Attorney; Bank Officer/Manager; Branch Manager; Brokerage Clerk; Budget Analyst; Computer Programmer; Credit Manager; Economist; Financial Analyst; Human Resources Manager; Management Analyst/Consultant; Management Trainee; Paralegal; Securities Sales Rep.; Systems Analyst. **Educational backgrounds include:** Accounting; Business Administration; Communications; Computer Science; Economics; Finance; Liberal Arts; Marketing. **Benefits:** 401(k); Dental Insurance; Disability Coverage; Employee Discounts; Flexible Dependent Care; Life Insurance; Medical Insurance; Pension Plan; Tuition Assistance. **Parent company:** PNC Bank is one of the nation's largest financial service companies with assets of $60 billion. **Operations at this facility include:** Regional Headquarters. **Listed on:** New York Stock Exchange. **Number of employees nationwide:** 6,000.

## SOVEREIGN BANK
1120 Bloomfield Avenue, West Caldwell NJ 07006. 973/575-5800. **Toll-free phone:** 800/683-4663. **Contact:** Human Resources. **World Wide Web address:** http://www.sovereignbank.com. **Description:** A bank. **Parent company:** Sovereign Bancorp is one of the largest thrift holding companies, with community banking and loan offices serving eastern Pennsylvania, New Jersey, and northern Delaware.

## SUMMIT BANK
301 Carnegie Center, Princeton NJ 08543. 609/987-3200. **Contact:** James N. Ferrier, Staffing Manager. **Description:** A bank. **Corporate headquarters location:** This Location. **Listed on:** New York Stock Exchange.

## SUMMIT BANK
243 Route 130, Bordentown NJ 08505. 609/324-6802. **Contact:** Human Resources. **Description:** A bank. **Listed on:** New York Stock Exchange.

## SUMMIT CORPORATION
55 Challenger Road, Ridgefield Park NJ 07660. 201/296-3000. **Contact:** Human Resources. **Description:** A bank.

## SUN NATIONAL BANK
525 Route 72 East, Manahawkin NJ 08050. 609/597-1800. **Contact:** Director of Human Resources. **Description:** A bank. **NOTE:** Interested jobseekers should address all inquiries to

Marjorie Hart, Director of Human Resources, Sun National Bank, 226 Landis Avenue, Vineland NJ 08360.

## UNITED NATIONAL BANK
P.O. Box 6000, Bridgewater NJ 08807. 908/429-2200. **Physical address:** 1130 Route 22 East, Bridgewater NJ. **Contact:** Human Resources. **World Wide Web address:** http://www.united-national.com. **Description:** Operates a full-service commercial bank, offering a wide range of banking, trust, and other financial services. **Corporate headquarters location:** This Location.

## VALLEY NATIONAL BANK
1445 Valley Road, Wayne NJ 07470. 973/696-4020. **Contact:** Peter Verbout, Director of Human Resources. **Description:** Operates a commercial bank offering a wide range of traditional banking services. **Common positions include:** Bank Officer/Manager; Branch Manager; Computer Programmer; Credit Manager; Customer Service Representative; Department Manager; Financial Analyst; General Manager; Human Resources Manager; Management Trainee. **Educational backgrounds include:** Accounting; Business Administration; Computer Science; Economics; Finance; Mathematics. **Benefits:** Dental Insurance; Disability Coverage; Life Insurance; Medical Insurance; Pension Plan; Profit Sharing; Tuition Assistance. **Corporate headquarters location:** This Location. **Parent company:** Valley National Bancorp. **Operations at this facility include:** Administration. **Listed on:** New York Stock Exchange.

*Note: Because addresses and telephone numbers of smaller companies can change rapidly, we recommend you call each company to verify the information below before inquiring about job opportunities. Mass mailings are not recommended.*

**Additional small employers:**

### COMMERCIAL BANKS

**Amboy National Bank**
PO Box 1076, Old Bridge NJ 08857-1076. 732/591-8700.

**Broad National Bank**
905 Broad St, Newark NJ 07102-2622. 973/624-2300.

**Chase Manhattan Bank**
Broadway Markets St, Camden NJ 08102. 609/757-4094.

**Commerce Bank**
1101 Hooper Ave, Toms River NJ 08753-8324. 609/693-1111.

**First Union National Bank**
40 Main St, Toms River NJ 08753-7436. 732/914-3003.

**First Union National Bank**
765 Broad St, Newark NJ 07102-3717. 973/430-4000.

**Fleet Bank**
161 Harristown Rd, Glen Rock NJ 07452-3316. 201/670-2477.

**National Westminster Bank**
250 Corporate Ct, South Plainfield NJ 07080-2417. 908/769-2065.

**New Jersey National Bank**
PO Box CN1, Pennington NJ 08534. 609/989-5000.

**Shrewsbury State Bank**
465 Broad St, Red Bank NJ 07702-4001. 732/842-7700.

**The Yardville National Bank**
PO Box 8487, Trenton NJ 08650-0487. 609/585-5100.

**United Jersey Bank**
210 Main St, Hackensack NJ 07601-7372. 201/646-5000.

**United Jersey Bank**
335 Ridge Rd, Dayton NJ 08810-1534. 732/438-7467.

**United National Bank**
65 Readington Rd, Somerville NJ 08876-3557. 908/685-2340.

### CREDIT UNIONS

**Howmet Alloy Employees Credit Union**
Roy St, Dover NJ 07801. 973/361-2795.

### OFFICES OF BANK HOLDING COMPANIES

**Statewide Financial Corp.**
70 Sip Ave, Jersey City NJ 07306-3135. 201/795-7700.

**United National Bancorp**
630 Georges Rd, North Brunswick NJ 08902-3313. 732/247-8200.

### SAVINGS INSTITUTIONS

**First Savings Bank**
PO Box 16, Bayonne NJ 07002-0016. 201/437-1000.

**FSB Cenlar Inc,**
PO Box 77400, Trenton NJ 08628-6400. 609/883-3900.

**Pamrapo Savings Bank**
PO Box 98, Bayonne NJ 07002-0098. 201/339-4600.

**Provident Savings Bank**
PO Box 17, Jersey City NJ 07303. 201/333-1000.

**Summit Bank**
PO Box 316, Egg Harbor City NJ 08215-0316. 609/625-1110.

**For more information on career opportunities in the banking/savings and loans industry:**

### Associations

**AMERICA'S COMMUNITY BANKERS**
900 19th Street NW, Suite 400, Washington DC 20006. 202/857-3100. World Wide Web address: http://www.acbankers.org. A trade association representing the expanded thrift industry. Membership is limited to institutions.

**AMERICAN BANKERS ASSOCIATION**
1120 Connecticut Avenue NW, Washington DC
20036. 202/663-5221. World Wide Web address:
http://www.aba.com. Provides banking education and
training services, sponsors industry programs and
conventions, and publishes articles, newsletters, and
the *ABA Service Member Directory*.

**Directories**

**AMERICAN BANK DIRECTORY**
Thomson Financial Publications, 4709 West Golf
Road, Skokie IL 60076. Toll-free phone: 800/321-
3373.

**AMERICAN SAVINGS DIRECTORY**
Thomson Financial Publications, 4709 West Golf
Road, Skokie IL 60076. Toll-free phone: 800/321-
3373.

**MOODY'S BANK AND FINANCE MANUAL**
Moody's Investors Service, Inc., 99 Church Street, 1st
Floor, New York NY 10007-2701. 212/553-0300.
World Wide Web address: http://www.moodys.com.

**RANKING THE BANKS**
American Banker, Inc., One State Street Plaza, New
York NY 10004. 212/803-6700. World Wide Web
address: http://www.americanbanker.com.

**Magazines**

**ABA BANKING JOURNAL**
American Bankers Association, 1120 Connecticut
Avenue NW, Washington DC 20036. 202/663-5221.
World Wide Web address: http://www.aba.com.

**BANKERS MAGAZINE**
Faulkner & Gray, 11 Penn Plaza, New York NY
10001. Toll-free phone: 800/200-8963.

**BANKING STRATEGIES**
Bank Administrators Institute, One North Franklin,
Suite 1000, Chicago IL 60606. Toll-free phone:
800/224-9889. World Wide Web address: http://www.
bai.org.

**JOURNAL OF LENDING AND CREDIT RISK
MANAGEMENT**
Robert Morris Associates, 1650 Market Street, Suite
2300, Philadelphia PA 19103. 215/446-4000.

**Online Services**

**JOBS FOR BANKERS**
http://www.bankjobs.com. This site provides access to
a database of over 9,000 banking-related job
openings. Jobs for Bankers is run by Careers, Inc.
This Website also includes a resume database.

**JOBS IN COMMERCIAL BANKING**
http://www.cob.ohio-state.edu/dept/fin/jobs/
commbank.htm. Provides information and resources
for jobseekers looking to work in the field of
commercial banking.

**NATIONAL BANKING NETWORK:
RECRUITING FOR BANKING AND FINANCE**
http://www.banking-financejobs.com. Offers a
searchable database of job openings in banking and
financial services. The database is searchable by
region, keyword, and job specialty.

# BIOTECHNOLOGY, PHARMACEUTICALS, AND SCIENTIFIC R&D

*The forecast is bright for the biotechnology industry, with the advent of new technologies in drug research and a heightened demand for prescription drugs of all types.* As noted in The Wall Street Journal *and* The New York Times, *biotechnology and pharmaceutical companies, such as Amgen Inc. and Pharmacia & Upjohn, were experiencing strong earnings during the latter half of 1998. According to the Bureau of Labor Statistics, biological and medical scientists in particular can expect a 21 to 35 percent increase in the number of jobs through 2006. However, a large portion of research money comes from the federal government, funding which is expected to decline in coming years.*

*Large drug companies are preparing to release a plethora of new products and continue to face competition from generic drug makers. Advances in genetic research offer promising new developments, but capitalizing on them requires significant investment. Therefore, those companies with bigger research budgets currently dominate. However, a trend is developing whereby large drug companies form partnerships with smaller biotechnology firms that provide them with research services. Often, these partnerships allow a drug to move through the development process faster, thereby gaining FDA approval much sooner.*

*Among the industry leaders in breakthrough drug development is Merck & Company, Inc., which plans to introduce new painkillers; antidepressants; and drugs for arthritis, male pattern baldness, and asthma. Analysts project that Merck's new asthma drug, Singulair, could reap $1.5 billion in sales within the next three years. Other drug manufacturers anticipate new drugs for hepatitis-B as well as new AIDS drug combinations. In addition, drug-delivery companies are working to improve the ways in which drugs are absorbed by the body.*

**ALPHARMA**
One Executive Drive, Fort Lee NJ 07024. 201/947-7774. **Fax:** 201/947-6145. **Contact:** Lorraine Catarcio, Human Resources Director. **World Wide Web address:** http://www.alpharma.com. **Description:** A multinational pharmaceutical company which develops, manufactures, and markets specialty generic and proprietary human pharmaceuticals and animal health products. The U.S. Pharmaceuticals Division is a market leader in liquid pharmaceuticals and a prescription market leader in creams and ointments. Other divisions include the Animal Health Division, which manufactures and markets antibiotics and other feed additives to the poultry and swine industries; the Aquatic Animal Health Division, which serves the aquaculture industry and is a manufacturer and marketer of vaccines for farmed fish; and the Fine Chemicals Division, which is a basic producer of specialty bulk antibiotics. **Corporate headquarters location:** This Location. **Listed on:** NASDAQ. **Stock exchange symbol:** ALO.

**ALTEON INC.**
170 Williams Drive, Ramsey NJ 07446. 201/934-5000. **Fax:** 201/934-0090. **Contact:** Christine Blicharz, Human Resources. **World Wide Web address:** http://www.alteonpharma.com. **Description:** A pharmaceutical company engaged in the discovery and development of novel therapeutic and diagnostic products for treating complications associated with diabetes and aging.

**AMERICAN PHARMACEUTICAL COMPANY**
12 Dwight Place, Fairfield NJ 07004. 973/276-1310. **Contact:** Human Resources. **Description:** Repackages and distributes over-the-counter, nonprescription drugs and vitamin products

worldwide. The company markets its products under both store brand names and its own label to small- and medium-sized regional retail drug chains, drug wholesalers, and distributors. **Subsidiaries include:** American Rx Mail, Inc.; U.S. Labs, Inc.

## BASF CORPORATION
## KNOLL PHARMACEUTICALS
3000 Continental Drive North, Mount Olive NJ 07828-1234. 973/426-2600. **Contact:** Robert Stein, Director of Human Resources. **World Wide Web address:** http://www.basf.com. **Description:** This location serves as the United States headquarters and houses management offices as well as the pharmaceutical division, Knoll Pharmaceuticals. Overall, BASF Corporation is an international chemical products organization, doing business in five operating groups: agricultural chemicals; chemicals; colors and auxiliaries; pigments and organic specialties; and polymers. **Common positions include:** Accountant/Auditor; Chemical Engineer; Computer Programmer; Financial Analyst; Marketing Specialist. **Benefits:** Dental Insurance; Disability Coverage; Life Insurance; Medical Insurance; Pension Plan; Savings Plan; Tuition Assistance. **Corporate headquarters location:** This Location. **Other area locations:** South Brunswick NJ (produces ethoxylated textile auxiliary intermediates, specialty surfactants, and esters); and Washington NJ (produces polyether polyols). **Operations at this facility include:** Administration; Divisional Headquarters; Sales. **Number of employees worldwide:** 125,000.

## BERLEX LABORATORIES, INC.
300 Fairfield Road, Wayne NJ 07470. 973/694-4100. **Contact:** Human Resources. **World Wide Web address:** http://www.betaseron.com. **Description:** Researches, manufactures, and markets ethical pharmaceutical products in the fields of cardiovascular medicine, endocrinology and fertility control, diagnostic imaging, oncology, and central nervous system disorders. Berlex Laboratories has three strategic units: Pharmaceuticals and Imaging (New Jersey), Oncology/Central Nervous System (California), and Berlex Biosciences (California). The company also owns Berlex Drug Development and Technology and operates a national sales force. The sales force, which is divided into three geographic regions, markets the complete line of Berlex products including Betaseron, which is used to treat Multiple Sclerosis. **Corporate headquarters location:** This Location. **Parent company:** Schering Berlin, Inc. (Cedar Knolls NJ).

## BIO-IMAGING TECHNOLOGIES, INC.
830 Bear Tavern Road, West Trenton NJ 08628. 609/883-2000x223. **Contact:** Maria Kraus, Controller. **World Wide Web address:** http://www.bioimaging.com. **Description:** Mainly processes and analyzes data for clinics and labs. The company receives lab data from clinical tests including MRIs and ultrasounds and then digitizes the information.

## BIO-REFERENCE LABORATORIES, INC.
481 Edward H. Ross Drive, Elmwood Park NJ 07407. 201/791-2600. **Contact:** Personnel. **Description:** Operates a clinical laboratory serving the New York metropolitan area. Bio-Reference offers a list of chemical diagnostic tests including blood and urine analysis, blood chemistry, hematology services, serology, radioimmuno analysis, toxicology (including drug screening), Pap smears, tissue pathology (biopsies), and other tissue analyses. Bio-Reference markets its services directly to physicians, hospitals, clinics, and other health facilities. **Corporate headquarters location:** This Location.

## BIO-TECHNOLOGY GENERAL CORPORATION
70 Wood Avenue South, Iselin NJ 08830. 732/632-8800. **Contact:** Leah Berkovits, Human Resources. **Description:** Researches, develops, manufactures, and markets genetically engineered products for human health care. The company focuses primarily on the development of therapeutic products for serious conditions such as endocrine disorders, cardiopulmonary diseases, and ophthalmic and skin disorders. The company's key products include Oxandrin for the treatment of Turner syndrome; Androtest-SL for hypogonadism; BioLon for the protection of the corneal endothelium during intraocular surgery; Bio-Hep-B, a third-generation vaccine against the Hepatitis-B virus; a vitamin D derivative for the treatment of psoriasis; and Delatestryl for hypogonadism and delayed puberty. **Corporate headquarters location:** This Location. **International locations:** Rehovot, Israel. **Listed on:** NASDAQ. **Stock exchange symbol:** BTGC.

## BIOMATRIX INC.
65 Railroad Avenue, Ridgefield NJ 07657. 201/945-9550. **Contact:** Human Resources. **World Wide Web address:** http://www.biomatrix.com. **Description:** An international biomedical company that develops and commercializes products for matrix engineering in new medical therapeutic modalities. The company's products are used worldwide in a diverse range of medical applications including viscosurgery, viscosupplementation, and viscoprotection.

**BRADLEY PHARMACEUTICALS, INC.**
383 Route 46 West, Fairfield NJ 07004-2402. 973/882-1505. **Fax:** 973/575-5366. **Contact:** Human Resources. **World Wide Web address:** http://www.bradpharm.com. **Description:** Manufactures and markets over-the-counter and prescription pharmaceuticals, and health-related products including nutritional, personal hygiene, and internal medicine brands. Founded in 1985. **Corporate headquarters location:** This Location. **Subsidiaries include:** Bradley Pharmaceuticals (Canada) Inc.; Bradley Pharmaceuticals Overseas, Ltd., U.S. Virgin Islands; DOAK Dermatologics Co. Inc., Westbury NY. **Listed on:** NASDAQ. **Stock exchange symbol:** BPRX.

**BRISTOL-MYERS SQUIBB COMPANY**
P.O. Box 4000, Princeton NJ 08543-4000. 609/252-4000. **Contact:** Human Resources. **World Wide Web address:** http://www.bms.com. **Description:** This location houses research laboratories. Overall, Bristol-Myers Squibb manufactures pharmaceuticals, medical devices, nonprescription drugs, toiletries, and beauty aids. The company's pharmaceutical products include cardiovascular products, anti-infectives, anti-cancer agents, AIDS therapy treatments, central nervous system drugs, diagnostic agents, and other drugs. The company's line of nonprescription products includes formulas, vitamins, analgesics, remedies, and skin care products. Non-prescription drug brand names include Bufferin, Excedrin, Nuprin, and Comtrex. Beauty aids include Clairol and Ultress hair care, Nice n' Easy and Clairesse hair colorings, hair sprays, gels, and deodorants. **Corporate headquarters location:** New York NY.

**BRISTOL-MYERS SQUIBB COMPANY**
P.O. Box 191, New Brunswick NJ 08903-0191. 732/519-2000. **Contact:** Employment Department. **World Wide Web address:** http://www.bms.com. **Description:** This location is engaged in the research and manufacture of various pharmaceuticals and personal care products. Overall, Bristol-Myers Squibb manufactures pharmaceuticals, medical devices, nonprescription drugs, toiletries, and beauty aids. The company's pharmaceutical products include cardiovascular drugs, anti-infectives, anti-cancer agents, AIDS therapy treatments, central nervous system drugs, diagnostic agents, and other drugs. Nonprescription products include formulas, vitamins, analgesics, remedies, and skin care products. Non-prescription drug brand names include Bufferin, Excedrin, Nuprin, and Comtrex. Beauty aids include Clairol and Ultress hair care, Nice 'n Easy and Clairesse hair colorings, hair sprays, gels, and deodorants. **Corporate headquarters location:** New York NY. **Listed on:** New York Stock Exchange. **Stock exchange symbol:** BMY.

**CARTER-WALLACE INC.**
P.O. Box 1001, Cranbury NJ 08512. 609/655-6000. **Contact:** Human Resources. **Description:** A major manufacturer of ethical drugs and consumer products. Health care products include tranquilizers, laxatives, anti-bacterials, analgesics, decongestants, and cold and cough remedies. The company also manufactures tests for pregnancy, mononucleosis, rubella, and meningitis. Consumer products include Arrid antiperspirants and deodorants, Trojan condoms, hair lotions, and pet care items. **NOTE:** Entry-level positions and second and third shifts are offered. **Common positions include:** Account Manager; Account Representative; Administrative Assistant; Biochemist; Biological Scientist; Blue-Collar Worker Supervisor; Budget Analyst; Chemist; Clinical Lab Technician; Customer Service Representative; Finance Director; Financial Analyst; Human Resources Manager; Intellectual Property Lawyer; Marketing Manager; Operations/Production Manager; Paralegal; Production Manager; Quality Control Supervisor; Sales and Marketing Manager; Sales Representative; Secretary. **Educational backgrounds include:** Accounting; Biology; Chemistry; Finance; Liberal Arts; Marketing. **Benefits:** 401(k); Dental Insurance; Disability Coverage; Employee Discounts; Life Insurance; Medical Insurance; Pension Plan; Savings Plan; Tuition Assistance. **Corporate headquarters location:** New York NY. **Other U.S. locations:** Winsted CT; Decatur IL.; East Windsor NJ, Colonial Heights VA. **Listed on:** New York Stock Exchange. **Number of employees nationwide:** 2,200.

**CELFIS LABORATORY GROUP**
165 Fieldcrest Avenue, Edison NJ 08837. 732/346-5100. **Contact:** Human Resources. **Description:** An independent testing laboratory specializing in toxicology, microbiology, and analytical chemistry. **Common positions include:** Biological Scientist; Chemist; Computer Programmer; Credit Manager; General Manager; Quality Control Supervisor; Science Technologist; Toxicologist. **Educational backgrounds include:** Biology; Chemistry; Toxicology. **Benefits:** 401(k); Dental Insurance; Disability Coverage; Life Insurance; Medical Insurance; Pension Plan; Tuition Assistance. **Number of employees at this location:** 50.

**CELGENE CORPORATION**
7 Powder Horn Drive, Warren NJ 07059. 732/271-1001. **Contact:** Human Resources. **Description:** Engaged in the development and commercialization of a broad range of immunotherapeutic drugs

designed to control serious disease states. Celgene also manufactures and sells chiral intermediates, key building blocks in the production of advanced therapeutic compounds, and certain agrochemical and food-related products. The focus of Celgene's immunotherapeutics program is the development of small molecule compounds that modulate bodily production of tumor necrosis factor alpha, a hormone-like protein. Elevated levels of this cytokine are believed to cause significant symptoms associated with several debilitating diseases such as HIV and AIDS-related conditions, autoimmune disorders, sepsis, and inflammatory bowel disease. **Corporate headquarters location:** This Location.

## CHRYSALIS INTERNATIONAL CORPORATION
575 Route 28, Raritan NJ 08869. 908/722-7900. **Contact:** Human Resources. **World Wide Web address:** http://www.chrysalisintl.com. **Description:** Offers a continuum of preclinical and clinical services necessary to develop drugs emerging from research through to regulatory approval and market introduction. Chrysalis provides services to over 250 pharmaceutical and biotechnology industry clients in 26 countries. **NOTE:** All resumes should be sent to Helene Garibay, Associate Director of Human Resources, 100 Discovery Drive, Olyphant PA 18447. 717/586-2411. **Benefits:** 401(k); Dental Insurance; Disability Coverage; Life Insurance; Medical Insurance; Tuition Assistance. **Listed on:** NASDAQ. **Number of employees nationwide:** 40. **Number of employees worldwide:** 400.

## CISTRON BIOTECHNOLOGY INC.
10 Bloomfield Avenue, P.O. Box 2004, Pine Brook NJ 07058. 973/575-1700. **Contact:** Human Resources. **World Wide Web address:** http://www.cistronbio.com. **Description:** Uses recombinant DNA and immunological techniques to manufacture a line of cytokine pharmaceutical products which it sells to the research market worldwide.

## CYTOGEN CORPORATION
600 College Road East, Princeton NJ 08540. 609/987-8200. **Fax:** 609/452-2975. **Contact:** Jill Searing, Human Resources Director. **World Wide Web address:** http://www.cytogen.com. **Description:** Develops products using monoclonal antibodies for the targeted delivery of diagnostic and therapeutic substances directly to sites of disease. Proprietary antibody linking technology is used primarily to develop specific cancer diagnostic imaging and therapeutic products. Founded in 1981. **Common positions include:** Accountant/Auditor; Biological Scientist; Chemist; Human Resources Manager; Systems Analyst. **Educational backgrounds include:** Business Administration; Communications; Health Care; Liberal Arts; Medicine. **Benefits:** 401(k); Dental Insurance; Disability Coverage; Life Insurance; Medical Insurance; Pension Plan; Tuition Assistance. **Corporate headquarters location:** This Location. **Operations at this facility include:** Administration; Sales. **Listed on:** NASDAQ. **Number of employees at this location:** 120.

## DERMA SCIENCES, INC.
214 Carnegie Center, Suite 100, Princeton NJ 08540. 609/514-4744. **Contact:** Human Resources. **Description:** Engaged in the development, marketing, and sale of proprietary sprays, ointments, and dressings for the management of certain chronic, non-healing skin ulcerations such as pressure and venous ulcers, surgical incisions, and burns. **Benefits:** Stock Option.

## ENZON, INC.
20 Kingsbridge Road, Piscataway NJ 08854-3998. 732/980-4500. **Fax:** 732/980-5911. **Contact:** Sharon Thompson, Manager of Human Resources. **World Wide Web address:** http://www.enzon.com. **Description:** A biopharmaceutical company that develops advanced therapeutics for life threatening diseases primarily in the area of oncology. Enzon has two FDA-approved products. **Common positions include:** Administrative Assistant; Biochemist; Biological Scientist; Chemist; Secretary. **Educational backgrounds include:** Biology; Chemistry. **Benefits:** 401(k); Dental Insurance; Disability Coverage; Flexible Schedule; Life Insurance; Medical Insurance; On-Site Exercise Facility; Stock Option. **Office hours:** Monday - Friday, 8:30 a.m. - 5:00 p.m. **Other U.S. locations:** South Plainfield NJ. **Listed on:** NASDAQ. **Stock exchange symbol:** ENZN. **President/CEO:** Peter G. Tombros. **Annual sales/revenues:** $11 - $20 million. **Number of employees at this location:** 55. **Number of employees nationwide:** 90. **Number of projected hires for 1998 - 1999 at this location:** 25.

## FAULDING INC./PUREPAC
200 Elmora Avenue, Elizabeth NJ 07207. 908/527-9100. **Fax:** 908/659-2305. **Contact:** Ms. Sev Dimitropoulos, Human Resources Manager. **Description:** Manufactures generic pharmaceuticals.

## FISHER SCIENTIFIC
One Reagent Lane, Fair Lawn NJ 07410. 201/796-7100. **Contact:** Deb Myshkoff, Manager of Employee Relations. **World Wide Web address:** http://www.fisher1.com. **Description:**

Manufactures, distributes, and sells a wide range of products used in industrial and medical laboratories. Products include analytical and measuring instruments, apparatus, and appliances; reagent chemicals and diagnostics; glassware and plasticware; and laboratory furniture. Customers are primarily industrial laboratories, medical and hospital laboratories, and educational and research laboratories. Manufacturing operations are carried out by six operating divisions in 11 United States locations. **Common positions include:** Accountant/Auditor; Administrator; Biological Scientist; Biomedical Engineer; Blue-Collar Worker Supervisor; Buyer; Chemical Engineer; Chemist; Computer Programmer; Customer Service Representative; Department Manager; Draftsperson; Electrical/Electronics Engineer; Financial Analyst; General Manager; Human Resources Manager; Industrial Engineer; Materials Engineer; Mechanical Engineer; Operations/Production Manager; Purchasing Agent/Manager; Quality Control Supervisor; Systems Analyst. **Educational backgrounds include:** Accounting; Chemistry; Engineering; Finance; Liberal Arts; Marketing. **Benefits:** Dental Insurance; Disability Coverage; Life Insurance; Medical Insurance; Pension Plan; Profit Sharing; Savings Plan; Tuition Assistance. **Corporate headquarters location:** Pittsburgh PA. **Parent company:** Henley Group (La Jolla CA). **Operations at this facility include:** Administration; Manufacturing; Research and Development.

**HOECHST MARION ROUSSEL INC.**
P.O. Box 6800, Bridgewater NJ 08807. 908/231-5752. **Contact:** Human Resources. **Description:** An international pharmaceutical company working with respiratory, cardiac, and osteopathic medications. **Operations at this facility include:** Marketing; Research and Development.

**HOFFMANN-LA ROCHE**
340 Kingsland Street, Nutley NJ 07110-1199. 973/235-5000. **Contact:** Director of Staffing. **World Wide Web address:** http://www.roche.com. **Description:** An international health care company that produces a wide range of products based on intensive research in biology and chemistry. Hoffman-La Roche operates through the following divisions: Pharmaceuticals, Diagnostic Products, and Chemicals. **Common positions include:** Accountant/Auditor; Attorney; Biological Scientist; Biomedical Engineer; Blue-Collar Worker Supervisor; Buyer; Chemical Engineer; Chemist; Computer Programmer; Electrical/Electronics Engineer; Financial Analyst; Industrial Engineer; Mechanical Engineer; Purchasing Agent/Manager; Quality Control Supervisor; Sales Executive; Statistician; Systems Analyst; Technical Writer/Editor. **Educational backgrounds include:** Accounting; Biology; Chemistry; Engineering; Finance; Marketing. **Benefits:** Dental Insurance; Disability Coverage; Life Insurance; Medical Insurance; Pension Plan; Savings Plan; Tuition Assistance. **Corporate headquarters location:** This Location. **Other area locations:** Belleville NJ; Branchburg NJ; Clifton NJ; Fair Lawn NJ; Little Falls NJ; Paramus NJ; Raritan NJ; Totowa NJ. **Subsidiaries include:** Roche Biomedical Laboratories; Roche Diagnostics (ethical pharmaceuticals); Roche Vitamins Inc. **Parent company:** Roche SA is an international Swiss-based health products firm. Facilities are located throughout the United States. **Operations at this facility include:** Administration; Manufacturing; Research and Development.

**HUNTINGTON LIFE SCIENCES**
P.O. Box 2360, Mettlers Road, East Millstone NJ 08875. 732/873-2550. **Fax:** 732/873-3992. **Contact:** Human Resources. **Description:** Provides contract biological safety (toxicological) testing services on a worldwide basis through two laboratories in the United States and the United Kingdom. The toxicology divisions of Huntington Life Sciences conduct studies designed to test pharmaceutical products, biologicals, chemical compounds, and other substances in order to produce the data required to identify, quantify, and evaluate the risks to humans and the environment resulting from the manufacture or use of these substances. These divisions also perform analytical and metabolic chemistry services. Huntington Life Sciences also performs clinical trials of new and existing pharmaceutical and biotechnology products and medical devices in humans. The company is engaged in the clinical development process including analytical chemistry, evaluation of clinical data, data processing, biostatistical analysis, and the preparation of supporting documentation for compliance with regulatory requirements. **Corporate headquarters location:** Austin TX. **Other U.S. locations:** Columbia MD; Richmond VA. **Parent company:** Applied Bioscience International Inc. (Arlington VA).

**HYMEDIX**
2245 Route 130, Suite 101, Dayton NJ 08810. 732/274-2288. **Contact:** Michele Coda, Administrative Assistant. **World Wide Web address:** http://www.hymedix.com. **Description:** Develops medical and skin care body creams.

**IGI, INC.**
Wheat Road & Lincoln Avenue, P.O. Box 687, Buena NJ 08310. 609/697-1441. **Contact:** Beverly Baxter, Human Resources. **Description:** A diversified company engaged in three business segments: animal health products, cosmetic and consumer products, and biotechnology. The animal

health products business produces and markets poultry vaccines, veterinary products, nutritional supplements, and grooming aids. The cosmetic and consumer products business produces and markets dermatologic, cosmetic, and consumer products. The biotechnology business develops and markets various applications of IGI's lipid encapsulation technology primarily for human medicines and vaccines. **Corporate headquarters location:** This Location.

## IVC INDUSTRIES, INC.
500 Halls Mill Road, Freehold NJ 07728. 732/308-3000. **Fax:** 732/308-9793. **Contact:** Human Resources. **World Wide Web address:** http://www.ivco.com. **Description:** Manufactures and distributes vitamins and nutritional supplements including the brand names Fields of Nature, Pine Brothers throat drops, Rybutol, Nature's Wonder, Synergy Plus, and Liquafil vitamin supplements. **Corporate headquarters location:** This Location. **Listed on:** NASDAQ. **Stock exchange symbol:** IVCO.

## IMMUNOMEDICS, INC.
300 American Road, Morris Plains NJ 07950. 973/605-8200. **Fax:** 973/605-8282. **Contact:** Human Resources. **World Wide Web address:** http://www.immunomedics.com. **Description:** Manufactures products to treat and detect infectious diseases and cancer. Products include LeukoScan, a diagnostic imaging tool that can scan for cancers such as osteomyelitis. **Listed on:** NASDAQ. **Stock exchange symbol:** IMMU.

## JANSSEN PHARMACEUTICA INC.
1125 Trenton-Harbourton Road, Titusville NJ 08560. 609/730-2000. **Contact:** Human Resources. **Description:** A pharmaceutical research company that specializes in prescription drugs for use in a range of fields including dermatology and psychiatry. **Parent company:** Johnson & Johnson (New Brunswick NJ).

## LABORATORY CORPORATION OF AMERICA (LABCORP)
69 First Avenue, Raritan NJ 08869. 908/526-2400. **Contact:** Human Resources. **World Wide Web address:** http://www.lca.com. **Description:** A laboratory that conducts blood and urine testing for area medical centers and provides AIDS and allergy testing.

## LIFE MEDICAL SCIENCES, INC.
379 Thornall Street, Edison NJ 08837-2227. 732/494-0444. **Fax:** 732/494-6252. **Contact:** Human Resources. **E-mail address:** LMS@lifemed.com. **World Wide Web address:** http://www.lifemed. com. **Description:** Develops medical products for use in a variety of therapeutic applications. The company's products include REPEL, to prevent surgical scars; REPEL-CV, to prevent scars as a result of cardiovascular surgery; RESOLVE, for the reduction of surgical scars; and CLINICEL, a scar management product. **Corporate headquarters location:** This Location. **Listed on:** NASDAQ. **Stock exchange symbol:** CHAI. **President:** Robert P. Hickey.

## THE LIPOSOME COMPANY, INC.
One Research Way, Princeton Forrestal Center, Princeton NJ 08540. 609/452-7060. **Contact:** Human Resources. **World Wide Web address:** http://www.lipo.com. **Description:** Develops proprietary lipid- and liposome-based pharmaceuticals for the treatment, prevention, and diagnosis of cancer, systemic fungal infections, and inflammatory and vaso-occlusive diseases. **Corporate headquarters location:** This Location.

## MARSAM PHARMACEUTICALS INC.
P.O. Box 1022, Cherry Hill NJ 08034. 609/424-5600. **Fax:** 609/751-8784. **Contact:** Alice Z. Mahoney, Human Resources Manager. **Description:** Manufactures generic drugs. Founded in 1985. **NOTE:** Second and third shifts are offered. **Common positions include:** Administrative Assistant; Biological Scientist; Chemical Engineer; Chemist; Clinical Lab Technician; Electrical/Electronics Engineer; Industrial Engineer; Industrial Production Manager; Manufacturing Engineer; Marketing Manager; Marketing Specialist; Mechanical Engineer; Pharmacist; Production Manager; Secretary; Typist/Word Processor. **Educational backgrounds include:** Accounting; Biology; Business Administration; Chemistry; Engineering; Liberal Arts; Marketing. **Benefits:** 401(k); Disability Coverage; Employee Discounts; Life Insurance; Medical Insurance; Profit Sharing; Public Transit Available; Tuition Assistance. **Special programs:** Co-ops. **Office hours:** Monday - Friday, 8:30 a.m. - 5:00 p.m. **Corporate headquarters location:** Florham Park NJ. **Other U.S. locations:** Phoenix AZ; Danbury CT. **Parent company:** Schein Pharmaceuticals, Inc. **Operations at this facility include:** Administration; Manufacturing; Research and Development. **Listed on:** NASDAQ. **President:** Marvin Samson. **Annual sales/revenues:** $51 - $100 million. **Number of employees at this location:** 260. **Number of employees nationwide:** 2,000.

**MEDAREX, INC.**
P.O. Box 953, Annandale NJ 08801. 908/713-6000. **Fax:** 908/713-6002. **Contact:** Nancy Dawley, Human Resources Assistant. **Description:** Researches and develops antibody-based pharmaceutical products to be used for the treatment of AIDS and other infectious diseases; cancers (including breast, ovarian, prostate, colon, and pancreatic); autoimmune diseases; and cardiovascular disease. These products bind to cells in the immune system and to the diseased cells, then stimulate the immune system to destroy the diseased cells. Founded in 1987. **Corporate headquarters location:** Princeton NJ.

**MERCK & CO., INC.**
126 East Lincoln Avenue, P.O. Box 2000, Rahway NJ 07065. 732/594-4000. **Contact:** Human Resources. **World Wide Web address:** http://www.merck.com. **Description:** A worldwide organization engaged in discovering, developing, producing, and marketing products for the maintenance of health and the environment. Products include human and animal pharmaceuticals and chemicals sold to the health care, oil exploration, food processing, textile, paper, and other industries. Merck also runs an ethical drug mail-order marketing business. **NOTE:** Applicants should indicate position of interest. **Corporate headquarters location:** Whitehouse Station NJ. **Other U.S. locations:** Albany GA; Wilson NC; Montvale NJ; West Point PA; Elkton VA.

**MERCK & CO., INC.**
One Merck Drive, P.O. Box 100, Whitehouse Station NJ 08889-0100. 908/423-1000. **Contact:** Human Resources. **Description:** A worldwide organization engaged in discovering, developing, producing, and marketing products for the maintenance of health and the environment. Products include human and animal pharmaceuticals and chemicals sold to the health care, oil exploration, food processing, textile, paper, and other industries. Merck also runs an ethical drug mail-order marketing business. **Corporate headquarters location:** This Location. **Other U.S. locations:** Albany GA; Wilson NC; Montvale NJ; Rahway NJ; West Point PA; Elkton VA.

**NAPP TECHNOLOGIES**
299 Market Street, 4th Floor, Saddle Brook NJ 07663. 201/843-4664. **Contact:** Marie Galdo, Personnel Department. **World Wide Web address:** http://www.napptech.com. **Description:** Produces medicinal chemicals and bulk pharmaceuticals. **Corporate headquarters location:** This Location.

**NEUMAN DISTRIBUTORS**
250 Moonachie Road, Moonachie NJ 07074. 201/931-0022. **Toll-free phone:** 800/777-1780. **Fax:** 201/931-0046. **Contact:** Employment Manager. **Description:** One of the largest privately held distributors of pharmaceuticals and health and beauty aids in the United States. **NOTE:** Second and third shifts are offered. **Common positions include:** Accountant; Administrative Assistant; Computer Programmer; Customer Service Representative; Project Manager; Secretary; Systems Analyst; Systems Manager. **Educational backgrounds include:** Accounting; Business Administration; Computer Science; Marketing; Software Development; Software Tech. Support. **Benefits:** 401(k); Dental Insurance; Disability Coverage; Life Insurance; Medical Insurance; Pension Plan; Public Transit Available. **Number of employees nationwide.** 1,000.

**NOVARTIS PHARMACEUTICALS CORPORATION**
59 Route 10, East Hanover NJ 07936. 973/503-7500. **Contact:** Human Resources. **World Wide Web address:** http://www.novartis.com. **Description:** This location houses the administrative headquarters and Novartis's primary research facility in the country. Overall, Novartis has three major divisions: health care, agribusiness, and nutrition. The health care division specializes in pharmaceuticals, both proprietary and generic, and ophthalmic health care. The agribusiness division is involved in seed technology, animal health, and crop protection. The nutrition sector includes medical, health, and infant nutrition.

**NOVARTIS PHARMACEUTICALS CORPORATION**
556 Morris Avenue, Summit NJ 07901. **Contact:** Human Resources. **World Wide Web address:** http://www.novartis.com. **Description:** One of the largest life science companies in the world. The company has three major divisions: health care, agribusiness, and nutrition. The nutrition sector includes medical, health, and infant nutrition. The health care division specializes in pharmaceuticals, both proprietary and generic, and ophthalmic health care. The agribusiness division is involved in seed technology, animal health, and crop protection.

**NOVO NORDISK A/S**
100 Overlook Center, Suite 200, Princeton NJ 08540. 609/987-5800. **Fax:** 609/987-3915. **Contact:** Human Resources. **World Wide Web address:** http://www.novo.dk/index.html. **Description:** One of the world's largest producers of industrial enzymes and insulin for the treatment of diabetes.

## ORGANON INC.
375 Mount Pleasant Avenue, West Orange NJ 07052. 973/325-4500. **Contact:** Human Resources. **Description:** Manufactures ethical pharmaceuticals. **Common positions include:** Accountant/Auditor; Chemist; Computer Programmer; Industrial Engineer; Manufacturer's/Wholesaler's Sales Rep.; Mechanical Engineer. **Educational backgrounds include:** Chemistry; Marketing. **Benefits:** Dental Insurance; Disability Coverage; Employee Discounts; Life Insurance; Medical Insurance; Pension Plan; Profit Sharing; Savings Plan; Tuition Assistance. **Corporate headquarters location:** This Location.

## ORTHO BIOTECH INC.
700 Route 202 South, Raritan NJ 08869. 908/704-5000. **Contact:** Human Resources. **Description:** Markets pharmaceuticals. **NOTE:** All hiring is done out of the corporate offices. Resumes should be sent to Johnson & Johnson Recruiting Services, Employment Management Center, Room JH-215, 501 George Street, New Brunswick NJ 08906-6597. **Parent company:** Johnson & Johnson (New Brunswick NJ).

## ORTHO-McNEIL PHARMACEUTICAL
1000 Route 202, P.O. Box 300, Raritan NJ 08869. 908/218-6000. **Contact:** Human Resources. **Description:** Manufactures prescription pharmaceutical products. **NOTE:** All hiring is done out of the corporate offices. Resumes should be sent to Johnson & Johnson Recruiting Services, Employment Management Center, Room JH-215, 501 George Street, New Brunswick NJ 08906-6597. **Parent company:** Johnson & Johnson (New Brunswick NJ).

## OSTEOTECH INC.
51 James Way, Eatontown NJ 07724. 732/542-2800. **Fax:** 732/542-9312. **Contact:** Charles Jannetti, Human Resources Director. **Description:** Processes human bone and connective tissue for transplantation and develops and manufactures biomaterial and device systems for musculoskeletal surgery. Osteotech is a leader in volume and quality of tissue processing for the American Red Cross and the Musculoskeletal Tissue Foundation. Founded in 1986. **NOTE:** Entry-level positions and second and third shifts are offered. **Company slogan:** Innovators in Musculoskeletal Tissue Science. **Common positions include:** Accountant; Administrative Assistant; Biochemist; Biological Scientist; Biomedical Engineer; Buyer; Chemist; Database Manager; Environmental Engineer; Librarian; Marketing Specialist; Operations Manager; Pharmacist; Physician; Production Manager; Quality Control Supervisor; Sales Executive; Sales Rep.; Secretary; Surgical Technician; Systems Analyst; Technical Writer/Editor. **Educational backgrounds include:** Accounting; Biology; Chemistry; Computer Science; Finance; Health Care; Marketing; Physics. **Benefits:** 401(k); Dental Insurance; Disability Coverage; Employee Discounts; Life Insurance; Medical Insurance; Savings Plan; Tuition Assistance. **Special programs:** Training. **Office hours:** Monday - Friday, 8:00 a.m. - 5:00 p.m. **Corporate headquarters location:** This Location. **Other U.S. locations:** Nationwide. **International locations:** The Netherlands. **Listed on:** NASDAQ. **Stock exchange symbol:** OSTE. **President:** Richard Bauer. **Annual sales/revenues:** $21 - $50 million. **Number of employees at this location:** 180. **Number of employees nationwide:** 200. **Number of employees worldwide:** 225. **Number of projected hires for 1998 - 1999 at this location:** 30.

## PHARMACEUTICAL FORMULATIONS, INC.
460 Plainfield Avenue, Edison NJ 08818. 732/819-3308. **Fax:** 732/819-4264. **Contact:** Dolores Scotto, Human Resources. **Description:** Manufactures and distributes over-the-counter, solid dosage pharmaceutical products in tablet, caplet, or capsule form. **Common positions include:** Accountant/Auditor; Buyer; Chemical Engineer; Chemist; Customer Service Rep.; Electrician; General Manager; Human Resources Manager; Purchasing Agent/Manager; Science Technologist; Services Sales Rep.; Transportation/Traffic Specialist. **Educational backgrounds include:** Accounting; Business Administration; Chemistry; Computer Science; Engineering; Finance; Marketing. **Benefits:** 401(k); Dental Insurance; Disability Coverage; Employee Discounts; Life Insurance; Medical Insurance; Profit Sharing. **Corporate headquarters location:** This Location. **Operations at this facility include:** Administration; Manufacturing; Research and Development; Sales; Service. **Number of employees at this location:** 320.

## PHARMACIA & UPJOHN, INC.
95 Corporate Drive, Bridgewater NJ 08807. 908/306-4400. **Contact:** Human Resources. **World Wide Web address:** http://www.pnu.com. **Description:** This location houses administrative offices. Overall, Pharmacia and Upjohn is a pharmaceutical and biotechnology company offering products for the treatment of various forms of cancer including breast cancer, leukemia and lymphoma, and prostate cancer. Other products include soft surgical aids and intraocular lenses for cataract surgery; intravenous nutrient delivery systems; smoking cessation and asthma treatments; and pharmaceuticals manufactured by recombinant-DNA technology. **Corporate headquarters location:** This Location. **Other U.S. locations:** Kalamazoo MI; Piscataway NJ.

## PHARMACIA BIOTECH
800 Centennial Avenue, Piscataway NJ 08855. 732/457-8000. **Contact:** Human Resources. **Description:** This location markets ethical drugs and diagnostic equipment. **Parent company:** Pharmacia & Upjohn, Inc. (Bridgewater NJ) is a pharmaceutical and biotechnological company offering products for the treatment of various forms of cancer including breast cancer, leukemia and lymphoma, and prostate cancer. Other products include soft surgical aids and intraocular lenses for cataract surgery; intravenous nutrient delivery systems; smoking cessation and asthma treatments; and pharmaceuticals manufactured by recombinant-DNA technology.

## QMED, INC.
100 Metro Park South, 3rd Floor, Laurence Harbor NJ 08878. 732/566-2666. **Contact:** Human Resources. **Description:** Designs, manufactures, and markets testing devices which enable medical professionals to perform minimally-invasive diagnostic procedures for certain illnesses, such as silent myocardial ischemia, venous blood flow insufficiencies, and diabetic neuropathy. **Listed on:** NASDAQ. **Stock exchange symbol:** QEKG.

## QUEST DIAGNOSTICS INCORPORATED
One Malcolm Avenue, Teterboro NJ 07608. 201/393-5211. **Contact:** Human Resources. **World Wide Web address:** http://www.questdiagnostics.com. **Description:** A clinical and anatomic laboratory testing company. **Common positions include:** Biological Scientist; Chemist; Computer Programmer; Medical Technologist; Sales Executive; Systems Analyst. **Educational backgrounds include:** Chemistry; Finance. **Benefits:** 401(k); Dental Insurance; Disability Coverage; Employee Discounts; Life Insurance; Medical Insurance; Profit Sharing; Savings Plan; Tuition Assistance. **Corporate headquarters location:** This Location. **Operations at this facility include:** Administration; Regional Headquarters; Sales; Service. **Listed on:** New York Stock Exchange.

## ROBERTS PHARMACEUTICAL CORPORATION
Meridian Center II, 4 Industrial Way West, Eatontown NJ 07724. 732/389-1182. **Fax:** 732/389-1014. **Contact:** Susan Sedwin, Human Resources Director. **World Wide Web address:** http://www.robertspharm.com. **Description:** An international pharmaceutical company focused on acquiring, developing, and bringing to market new prescription products. Founded in 1983. **Corporate headquarters location:** This Location. **International locations:** Canada; United Kingdom. **Listed on:** American Stock Exchange. **Stock exchange symbol:** RPC. **President/CEO:** John T. Spitznagel. **Annual sales/revenues:** More than $100 million.

## ROCHE VITAMINS INC.
45 Waterview Boulevard, Parsippany NJ 07054-1298. 973/257-1063. **Contact:** Human Resources. **World Wide Web address:** http://www.roche.com. **Description:** A pharmaceutical company which manufactures pharmaceutical drugs, diagnostic kits, and vitamins for dietary, pharmaceutical, and cosmetic use. **Parent company:** Hoffmann-La Roche.

## SGS U.S. TESTING COMPANY INC.
291 Fairfield Avenue, Fairfield NJ 07004. 973/575-5252. **Toll-free phone:** 800/777-8378. **Fax:** 973/575-1071. **Contact:** Mr. Lee Fredericks, Human Resources Manager. **World Wide Web address:** http://www.ustesting.sgsna.com. **Description:** An independent laboratory specializing in the testing of a variety of industrial and consumer products. Services include biological, chemical, engineering/materials, environmental, electrical, paper/packaging, textiles, certification programs, and inspections. **Common positions include:** Account Representative; Administrative Assistant; Administrative Manager; Biological Scientist; Chemist; Civil Engineer; Clinical Lab Technician; Customer Service Representative; Electrical/Electronics Engineer; Industrial Engineer; Manufacturing Engineer; Marketing Manager; Marketing Specialist; Mechanical Engineer; Sales Engineer; Sales Representative; Secretary. **Educational backgrounds include:** Biology; Chemistry; Engineering. **Benefits:** 401(k); Dental Insurance; Disability Coverage; Flexible Schedule; Life Insurance; Medical Insurance; Pension Plan; Tuition Assistance. **Corporate headquarters location:** This Location. **Other U.S. locations:** Los Angeles CA; Tulsa OK. **Parent company:** SGS North America. **Operations at this facility include:** Administration; Sales; Service.

## SANI-TECH, INC.
40 White Lake Road, Sparta NJ 07871. 973/579-1313. **Fax:** 973/579-3908. **Contact:** Operations Manager. **Description:** Manufactures silicone tubing for the biotech industry.

## SCHERING-PLOUGH CORPORATION
2000 Galloping Hill Road, Kenilworth NJ 07033. 908/298-4000. **Contact:** Human Resources Department. **Description:** Engaged in the discovery, development, manufacture, and marketing of pharmaceutical and consumer products. Pharmaceutical products include prescription drugs, over-

the-counter medicines, eye care products, and animal health products promoted to the medical and allied health professions. The consumer products group consists of proprietary medicines, toiletries, cosmetics, and foot care products marketed directly to the public. Product brand names include Coricidin cough and cold medicines, Maybelline, Claritin, Coppertone, and Dr. Scholl's. **Corporate headquarters location:** Madison NJ. **Other U.S. locations:** Miami FL; Union NJ; Memphis TN.

## SCHERING-PLOUGH CORPORATION
One Giralda Farms, Madison NJ 07940. 973/822-7000. **Contact:** Human Resources. **Description:** Engaged in the discovery, development, manufacture, and marketing of pharmaceutical and consumer products. Pharmaceutical products include prescription drugs, over-the-counter medicines, eye care products, and animal health products promoted to the medical and allied health professions. The consumer products group consists of proprietary medicines, toiletries, cosmetics, and foot care products marketed directly to the public. Product brand names include Coricidin cough and cold medicines, Maybelline, Claritin, Coppertone, and Dr. Scholl's. **Corporate headquarters location:** This Location. **Other U.S. locations:** Miami FL; Kenilworth NJ; Union NJ; Memphis TN.

## SCHERING-PLOUGH CORPORATION
1011 Morris Avenue, Union NJ 07083. 908/820-6494. **Contact:** Human Resources. **Description:** This location houses administrative offices. Overall, Schering-Plough is engaged in the discovery, development, manufacture, and marketing of pharmaceutical and consumer products. Pharmaceutical products include prescription drugs, over-the-counter medicines, eye care products, and animal health products promoted to the medical and allied health professions. The consumer products group consists of proprietary medicines, toiletries, cosmetics, and foot care products marketed directly to the public. Product brand names include Coricidin cough and cold medicines, Maybelline, Claritin, Coppertone, and Dr. Scholl's. **Corporate headquarters location:** Madison NJ. **Other U.S. locations:** Miami FL; Kenilworth NJ; Memphis TN.

## SMITHKLINE BEECHAM PHARMACEUTICALS
101 Possumtown Road, Piscataway NJ 08854. 732/469-5200. **Contact:** Human Resource Manager. **Description:** Manufactures penicillin. **Corporate headquarters location:** Philadelphia PA. **Parent company:** SmithKline Beecham Corporation is health care company engaged in the research, development, manufacture, and marketing of ethical pharmaceuticals, animal health products, ethical and proprietary medicines, and eye care products. The company's principal divisions include SmithKline Beecham Pharmaceuticals, SmithKline Beecham Animal Health, SmithKline Beecham Consumer Healthcare, and SmithKline Beecham Clinical Laboratories. The company is also engaged in many other aspects of the health care field, including the production of medical and electronic instruments. SmithKline Beecham Corporation manufactures proprietary medicines through its subsidiary, Menley & James Laboratories, including such nationally known products as Contac Cold Capsules, Sine-Off sinus medicine, Love cosmetics, and Sea & Ski outdoor products.

## SYNAPTIC PHARMACEUTICAL CORPORATION
215 College Road, Paramus NJ 07652. 201/261-1331. **Contact:** Human Resources. **Description:** Researches and develops pharmaceuticals. **NOTE:** This is not a manufacturing facility. **Corporate headquarters location:** This Location.

## TEVA PHARMACEUTICALS
18-01 River Road, Fair Lawn NJ 07410. 201/703-0400. **Fax:** 201/703-9491. **Contact:** Tony Cerbone, Director of Human Resources. **World Wide Web address:** http://www.tevapharmusa. com. **Description:** Manufactures and markets generic drugs. A bulk semi-synthetic penicillin production plant and three finished dosage plants are located in northern New Jersey. **Corporate headquarters location:** This Location. **Other U.S. locations:** Mexico MO; Elmwood Park NJ; Fairfield NJ; Paterson NJ; Waldwick NJ. **Number of employees nationwide:** 790.

## TEVA PHARMACEUTICALS USA
209 McLean Boulevard, Paterson NJ 07504. 973/742-7494. **Contact:** Human Resources. **World Wide Web address:** http://www.tevapharmusa.com. **Description:** This location packages pharmaceuticals produced at the company's other plants. Overall, Teva Pharmaceuticals manufactures and markets generic drugs. **Corporate headquarters location:** Fair Lawn NJ. **Number of employees nationwide:** 790.

## UNIGENE LABORATORIES, INC.
110 Little Falls Road, Fairfield NJ 07004-2193. 973/882-0860. **Fax:** 973/227-6088. **Contact:** William Steinhauer, Controller. **World Wide Web address:** http://www.unigene.com.

**Description:** A biopharmaceutical research and manufacturing firm that has developed a patented method to produce calcitonin, a leading drug for treating osteoporosis. Founded in 1980. **Benefits:** 401(k). **Corporate headquarters location:** This Location. **Other U.S. locations:** Boonton NJ. **Listed on:** NASDAQ. **Stock exchange symbol:** UGNE. **President:** Warren P. Levy, Ph.D.

### UNILEVER HOME & PERSONAL CARE USA
45 River Road, Edgewater NJ 07020. 201/943-7100. **Contact:** Ms. Mikel Gittens, Manager of Human Resources. **Description:** Researches and develops household and personal care products.

### WARNER-LAMBERT COMPANY
201 Tabor Road, Morris Plains NJ 07950. 973/540-2000. **Contact:** Corporate Human Resources. **World Wide Web address:** http://www.warner-lambert.com. **Description:** Manufactures pharmaceuticals and consumer health products with significant international operations. The pharmaceuticals unit produces ethical drugs, biologicals, diagnostic agents, capsules, and hospital equipment. The consumer products unit includes oral antiseptics, mouthwashes, mints, antacids, razors and blades, cough tablets, and cold medications under brand names including Halls, Rolaids, Listerine, Benadryl, and Schick. **Corporate headquarters location:** This Location. **Listed on:** New York Stock Exchange.

### WEST PHARMACEUTICAL SERVICES
1200 Paco Way, Lakewood NJ 08701. 732/367-9000. **Contact:** Personnel. **Description:** Packages and ships pharmaceutical products manufactured by other companies.

### ZENITH GOLDLINE PHARMACEUTICALS
140 LeGrand Avenue, Northvale NJ 07647. 201/767-1700. **Contact:** Winifred Stavros, Personnel Director. **Description:** Produces ethical pharmaceuticals for the cardiovascular, nervous, digestive, and respiratory systems. **Corporate headquarters location:** This Location.

*Note: Because addresses and telephone numbers of smaller companies can change rapidly, we recommend you call each company to verify the information below before inquiring about job opportunities. Mass mailings are not recommended.*

**Additional small employers:**

**DIAGNOSTIC SUBSTANCES**

**Bracco Diagnostics Inc.**
PO Box 5225, Princeton NJ
08543-5225. 609/514-2200.

**Direct Access Diagnostics**
140 US Highway 22, Bridgewater
NJ 08807-2477. 908/218-7300.

**Nycomed Amersham Inc.**
101 Carnegie Center, Princeton
NJ 08540-6231. 609/514-6000.

**PBM**
PO Box 7139, Princeton NJ
08543-7139. 732/274-1000.

**MEDICINAL CHEMICALS**

**Akzo Nobel Chemicals Inc.**
340 Meadow Rd, Edison NJ
08837-4102. 732/985-6262.

**Ganes Chemicals Inc.**
PO Box 1114, Carlstadt NJ
07072. 201/507-4300.

**Ganes Chemicals Inc.**
33 Industrial Park Rd, Pennsville
NJ 08070-3244. 609/678-3601.

**Penick Corporation**
158 Mount Olivet Ave, Newark
NJ 07114-2114. 973/242-6655.

**PHARMACEUTICAL PREPARATIONS**

**Berlex Laboratories**
340 Change Bridge Rd, Montville
NJ 07045. 973/276-2000.

**Biocraft Laboratories**
209 McLean Blvd, Paterson NJ
07504. 973/742-7494.

**Bristol-Myers Squibb Company**
1350 Liberty Ave, Hillside NJ
07205-1891. 908/851-2400.

**Chem International Inc.**
201 US Highway 22, Hillside NJ
07205-1832. 973/926-0816.

**Ciba-Geigy Pharmaceuticals**
30 Vreeland Rd, Florham Park NJ
07932-1904. 973/822-4654.

**Elkins-Sinn**
2 Esterbrook Ln, Cherry Hill NJ
08003-4002. 609/424-3700.

**G&W Laboratories Inc.**
111 Coolidge St, South Plainfield
NJ 07080-3801. 908/753-2000.

**Invamed Inc.**
2400 Rte 130 N, Dayton NJ
08810. 732/274-2400.

**Knoll Pharmaceutical Company**
30 N Jefferson Rd, Whippany NJ
07981-1030. 973/428-4000.

**Master Pak Laboratories**
121 Moonachie Ave, Moonachie
NJ 07074-1802. 201/460-0500.

**Nutro Laboratories Inc.**
PO Box 707, South Plainfield NJ
07080-0707. 908/754-9308.

**PF Laboratories Inc.**
700 Union Blvd, Totowa NJ
07512-2210. 973/256-3103.

**Roche Vitamins Inc.**
206 Roche Dr, Belvidere NJ
07823-1110. 908/475-5300.

**Roche Vitamins Inc.**
45 Eisenhower Dr, Paramus NJ
07652-1416. 201/909-8200.

**Schein Pharmaceutical Inc.**
100 Campus Dr, Florham Park NJ
07932-1006. 973/593-5500.

**Schering Berlin Inc.**
340 Changebridge Rd, Montville
NJ 07045. 973/276-2200.

**Schering-Plough Corporation**
110 Allen Rd, Liberty Corner NJ
07938. 908/604-1640.

**Sidmak Laboratories Inc.**
PO Box 371, East Hanover NJ
07936-0371. 973/386-5566.

**Teva Pharmaceuticals USA Inc.**
92 Rte 46, Elmwood Park NJ
07407. 201/796-3436.

**Wyeth-Ayerst Research**
9 Deerpark Dr, Cranbury NJ
08512. 732/274-4397.

**Teva Pharmaceuticals USA Inc.**
8-10 Gloria Ln, Fairfield NJ
07004. 973/575-2775.

**Universal Labs**
3 Terminal Rd, New Brunswick
NJ 08901-3615. 732/545-3130.

**Wyeth-Ayerst Research**
PO Box CN 8000, Princeton NJ
08540. 732/329-2300.

**For more information on career opportunities in biotechnology, pharmaceuticals, and scientific R&D:**

<u>Associations</u>

**AMERICAN ASSOCIATION FOR CLINICAL CHEMISTRY**
2101 L Street NW, Suite 202, Washington DC 20037-1526. 202/857-0717. Toll-free phone: 800/892-1400. World Wide Web address: http://www.aacc.org. International scientific/medical society of individuals involved with clinical chemistry and other clinical lab science-related disciplines.

**AMERICAN ASSOCIATION OF COLLEGES OF PHARMACY**
1426 Prince Street, Alexandria VA 22314-2841. 703/739-2330. World Wide Web address: http://www. aacp.org. An organization composed of all U.S. pharmacy colleges and over 2,000 school administrators and faculty members. Career publications include *Shall I Study Pharmacy?*, *Pharmacy: A Caring Profession*, and *A Graduate Degree in the Pharmaceutical Sciences: An Option For You?*

**AMERICAN ASSOCIATION OF PHARMACEUTICAL SCIENTISTS**
1650 King Street, Suite 200, Alexandria VA 22314-2747. 703/548-3000. World Wide Web address: http://www.aaps.org.

**THE AMERICAN COLLEGE OF CLINICAL PHARMACY (ACCP)**
3101 Broadway, Suite 380, Kansas City MO 64111. 816/531-2177. World Wide Web address: http://www. accp.com. Operates ClinNet jobline at 412/648-7893 for members only.

**AMERICAN PHARMACEUTICAL ASSOCIATION**
2215 Constitution Avenue NW, Washington DC 20037-2985. 202/628-4410. World Wide Web address: http://www.aphanet.org.

**AMERICAN SOCIETY FOR BIOCHEMISTRY AND MOLECULAR BIOLOGY**
9650 Rockville Pike, Bethesda MD 20814-3996. 301/530-7145. Fax: 301/571-1824. World Wide Web address: http://www.faseb.org/asbmb. A nonprofit scientific and educational organization whose primary scientific activities are in the publication of the *Journal of Biological Chemistry* and holding an annual scientific meeting. Also publishes a career brochure entitled *Unlocking Life's Secrets: Biochemistry and Molecular Biology.*

**AMERICAN SOCIETY OF HEALTH-SYSTEM PHARMACISTS**
7272 Wisconsin Avenue, Bethesda MD 20814. 301/657-3000. World Wide Web address: http://www. ashp.org. Provides pharmaceutical education. Updates pharmacies on current medical developments. Offers a service for jobseekers for a fee.

**BIOTECHNOLOGY INDUSTRY ORGANIZATION (BIO)**
1625 K Street NW, Suite 1100, Washington DC 20006-1604. 202/857-0244. Fax: 202/857-0237. World Wide Web address: http://www.bio.org. Represents agriculture, biomedical, diagnostic, food, energy, and environmental companies. Publishes a profile of the U.S. biotechnology industry.

**INTERNATIONAL SOCIETY FOR PHARMACEUTICAL ENGINEERING**
3816 West Linebaugh Avenue, Suite 412, Tampa FL 33624. 813/960-2105. World Wide Web address: http://www.ispe.org.

**NATIONAL PHARMACEUTICAL COUNCIL**
1894 Preston White Drive, Reston VA 20191. 703/620-6390. Fax: 703/476-0904. An organization of research-based pharmaceutical companies.

<u>Directories</u>

**DRUG TOPICS RED BOOK**
Medical Economics Company, 5 Paragon Drive, Montvale NJ 07645. 201/358-7200.

<u>Magazines</u>

**DRUG TOPICS**
Medical Economics Company, 5 Paragon Drive, Montvale NJ 07645. 201/358-7200.

**PHARMACEUTICAL ENGINEERING**
International Society for Pharmaceutical Engineering, 3816 West Linebaugh Avenue, Suite 412, Tampa FL 33624. 813/960-2105. World Wide Web address: http://www.ispe.org.

<u>Online Services</u>

**MEDZILLA**
E-mail address: info@medzilla.com. World Wide Web address: http://www.medzilla.com. Lists job openings for professionals in the fields of biotechnology, health care, medicine, and science related industries.

Visit our exciting job and career site at http://www.careercity.com

# BUSINESS SERVICES AND NON-SCIENTIFIC RESEARCH

 Standard & Poor *forecasted 7.5 percent growth across the board for the business services industry in 1998. This sector covers a broad range of services, from adjustment and collection to data processing. While the outlook varies depending on the service, in general, the business services sector is among the fastest-growing in the nation. In fact, the Bureau of Labor Statistics expects computer and data processing services to be the fastest-growing industry through 2006.*

*Steady consolidation across many industries continued to result in a greater need for services in 1998, from temporary help to consulting and engineering services. Security firms expect a significant boost in employment through the year 2005, due to increased concern about crime and vandalism, and the surge in commercial use of sophisticated computer equipment and guards trained to operate such equipment.*

**ADP FINANCIAL INFORMATION**
2 Journal Square Plaza, Jersey City NJ 07306. 201/714-3000. **Contact:** Human Resources. **Description:** An information brokerage service. **Parent company:** Automatic Data Processing (Roseland NJ).

**ADT SECURITY SERVICES**
290 Veterans Boulevard, Rutherford NJ 07070. 201/804-8600. **Contact:** Human Resources. **World Wide Web address:** http://www.adtsecurityservices.com. **Description:** Services more than 15,000 burglar, fire, and other alarm systems in several area locations, including Newark NJ, Parsippany NJ, and Trenton NJ. ADT Security Services also manufactures a variety of alarms and monitoring equipment for use in alarm service operations and for sale to commercial and industrial users. **Corporate headquarters location:** Parsippany NJ. **Other U.S. locations:** Orlando FL; St. Petersburg FL; Tampa FL; Atlanta GA; Baltimore MD; Rockville MD.

**AGC SEDGWICK**
4390 Route 1, Princeton NJ 08540-9357. 609/452-1660. **Toll-free phone:** 800/433-1681. **Fax:** 609/734-0460. **Contact:** Human Resources. **Description:** Offers a full range of systems development and production services, including its Windows-based (Windows '95-compatible) Information Management System. AGC Sedgwick handles all aspects of a client's job, including input, database, scanning, design, printing, and distribution. In data collection, the company can convert data from all forms of electronic media and produce computer-generated questionnaires via fax broadcasting, telephone research, or high-speed laser printers. The company also offers a full range of editorial services including data entry and proofreading. In data preparation, the company can manipulate data to automatically create multiple sections, indexes, abstracts, management reports, questionnaires, CD-ROM and diskette products, and other output options, all from a client's single information source. The company also designs and develops customized search and retrieval systems for preparation of CD-ROMs, directories on diskette, and online services.

**AUTOMATIC DATA PROCESSING (ADP)**
99 Jefferson Road, Parsippany NJ 07054. 973/739-3000. **Contact:** Human Resources Department. **World Wide Web address:** http://www.adp.com. **Description:** One of the largest companies in the world that provides computerized transaction processing, data communications, and information services. ADP pays over 18 million U.S. employees. The company's Employer Services Division provides payroll processing, payroll tax filing, job costing, labor distribution, automated bill payment, management reports, unemployment compensation management, human resource information, and benefits administration support to over 300,000 businesses. **Common positions include:** Sales Executive. **Educational backgrounds include:** Accounting; Business Administration. **Benefits:** 401(k); Dental Insurance; Disability Coverage; Job Sharing; Life Insurance; Medical Insurance; Pension Plan; Savings Plan; Stock Option; Stock Purchase; Tuition Assistance. **Special programs:** Internships. **Corporate headquarters location:** Roseland NJ.

**Operations at this facility include:** Divisional Headquarters; Research and Development. **Listed on:** New York Stock Exchange. **Annual sales/revenues:** More than $100 million. **Number of employees nationwide:** 25,000.

## AUTOMATIC DATA PROCESSING (ADP)
One ADP Boulevard, Roseland NJ 07068. 973/994-5000. **Contact:** Human Resources. **Description:** This location houses administrative offices. Overall, ADP is one of the largest companies in the world that provides computerized transaction processing, data communications, and information services. ADP pays over 18 million U.S. employees. The company's Employer Services Division provides payroll processing, payroll tax filing, job costing, labor distribution, automated bill payment, management reports, unemployment compensation management, human resource information, and benefits administration support to over 300,000 businesses. **Corporate headquarters location:** This Location. **Listed on:** New York Stock Exchange. **Number of employees nationwide:** 25,000.

## BENEFICIAL DATA PROCESSING CORPORATION
500 Beneficial Center, Peapack NJ 07977. 908/781-3000. **Contact:** Deborah Melnick, Director of Personnel Services. **World Wide Web address:** http://www.beneficial.com. **Description:** Provides data processing services for the insurance and banking industries. **Common positions include:** Computer Programmer; Computer Scientist; Data Processor; Software Engineer. **Parent company:** Beneficial Corporation.

## BISYS GROUP, INC.
150 Clove Road, Little Falls NJ 07424. 973/812-8600. **Contact:** Vice President, Human Resources Department. **World Wide Web address:** http://www.bisys.com. **Description:** BISYS Group, Inc. is a national, third-party provider of computing, administrative, and marketing support services to financial organizations. Services are offered through three major business units: Information Services, Loan Services, and Investment Services. The company derives a majority of its revenues from services provided through a single integrated software product, TOTAL PLUS, which includes comprehensive loan and deposit administration; branch automation and electronic banking services; operations and new business systems support; and accounting, financial management, and regulatory reporting services. BISYS Group, Inc. was organized in 1989 to acquire certain banking and thrift data processing operations of Automatic Data Processing (ADP). **NOTE:** Interested jobseekers should send resumes to 11 Greenwood Plaza, Suite 300, Houston TX 77064-1102.

## BORG-WARNER PROTECTIVE SERVICES
2 Campus Drive, Parsippany NJ 07054. 973/267-5300. **Contact:** Human Resources. **Description:** A holding company whose subsidiaries offer protective services. **Corporate headquarters location:** This Location. **Subsidiaries include:** Wells Fargo Armored Service, Wells Fargo Alarm Services, Wells Fargo Guard Services, and Pony Express Courier offer armored transport, courier security guard, and alarm services and products in more than 35 states, the District of Columbia, Canada, Spain, and Puerto Rico. Another subsidiary, Pytronics, markets smoke, fire, and security protection products and systems. The Pyro Chem Division produces fire-extinguishing chemicals. **Parent company:** Borg-Warner, Inc.

## CENDANT CORPORATION
6 Sylvan Way, Parsippany NJ 07054. 973/428-9700. **Toll-free phone:** 800/932-4656. **Fax:** 973/428-9684. **Contact:** Staffing and Employment. **E-mail address:** jobs@hfsinc.com. **World Wide Web address:** http://www.cendant.com. **Description:** Provides a wide range of business services including dining services, hotel franchise management, mortgage programs, and timeshare exchanges. Cendant Corporation's Real Estate Division offers employee relocation and mortgage services through Century 21, Coldwell Banker, ERA, Cendant Mortgage, and Cendant Mobility. The Travel Division provides car rentals, vehicle management services, and vacation timeshares through brand names including Avia, Days Inn, Howard Johnson, Ramada, Travelodge, and Super 8. The Membership Division offers travel, shopping, auto, dining, and other financial services through Travelers Advantage, Shoppers Advantage, Auto Vantage, Welcom Wagon, netMarket, North American Outdoor Group, and PrivacyGuard. Founded in 1997. **Common positions include:** Accountant/Auditor; Computer Operator; Computer Programmer; Customer Service Representative; Marketing Manager; Marketing Specialist; Public Relations Specialist; Real Estate Agent; Sales Representative; Secretary. **Educational backgrounds include:** Accounting; Business Administration; Communications; Computer Science; Finance; Marketing; Public Relations; Software Development. **Benefits:** 401(k); Dental Insurance; Disability Coverage; Employee Discounts; Life Insurance; Medical Insurance; Profit Sharing; Savings Plan; Tuition Assistance. **Corporate headquarters location:** This Location. **Operations at this facility include:** Administration; Divisional Headquarters; Sales; Service. **Listed on:** New York Stock Exchange.

**Stock exchange symbol:** CD. **President/CEO:** Henry Silverman. **Number of employees at this location:** 1,100. **Number of employees worldwide:** 30,000.

## COMPUTER OUTSOURCING SERVICES, INC. (COSI)
2 Christie Heights Street, Leonia NJ 07605. 201/840-4700. **Fax:** 201/840-7100. **Contact:** Human Resources Department. **World Wide Web address:** http://www.cosi-us.com. **Description:** Computer Outsourcing Services, Inc. provides payroll, data processing, and tax filing services to companies in book publishing, apparel, direct response marketing, and other industries. **Corporate headquarters location:** This Location. **Listed on:** NASDAQ. **Stock exchange symbol:** COSI.

## CORRESPONDENCE MANAGEMENT
P.O. Box 2110, Cherry Hill NJ 08053. 609/596-2521. **Contact:** Human Resources Department. **Description:** Provides medical record copying services.

## DIGITAL SOLUTIONS, INC. (DSI)
300 Atrium Drive, Somerset NJ 08873. 732/748-7000. **Fax:** 732/748-3239. **Contact:** Human Resources Department. **World Wide Web address:** http://www.digitalsolutions.com. **Description:** Digital Solutions, Inc. is a full-line provider of human resource management services to employers in a wide variety of industries. The company's services include professional employer organization (employee leasing) services, placement of temporary and permanent staffing, and payroll and payroll tax service preparation. **Corporate headquarters location:** This Location.

## THE DUN & BRADSTREET CORPORATION
One Diamond Hill Road, Murray Hill NJ 07974. 908/665-5000. **Contact:** Human Resources. **Description:** Provides business information and services through three divisions: Dun & Bradstreet Credit Services (marketing and sales); Dun & Bradstreet Operations (data gathering); and Dun & Bradstreet Commercial Collections (debt management and collections). These units collect, store, and sell information on over 9 million businesses, which is used by the business community to make decisions on credit, insurance, marketing, financial, merger, and other issues. **Common positions include:** Accountant/Auditor; Computer Programmer; Customer Service Representative; Economist; Financial Analyst; Human Resources Manager; Manufacturer's/Wholesaler's Sales Rep.; Marketing Specialist. **Educational backgrounds include:** Accounting; Business Administration; Finance; Marketing. **Benefits:** Dental Insurance; Disability Coverage; Employee Discounts; Fitness Program; Life Insurance; Medical Insurance; Pension Plan; Profit Sharing; Savings Plan; Tuition Assistance. **Corporate headquarters location:** New York NY. **Other area locations:** Parsippany NJ. **Operations at this facility include:** Divisional Headquarters. **Listed on:** New York Stock Exchange.

## THE DUN & BRADSTREET CORPORATION
3 Sylvan Way, Parsippany NJ 07054. 973/455-0900. **Contact:** Human Resources Department. **Description:** Produces business information and services through three divisions: Dun & Bradstreet Credit Services (marketing and sales); Dun & Bradstreet Operations (data gathering); and Dun & Bradstreet Commercial Collections (debt management and collections). These units collect, store, and sell information on over 9 million businesses, which is used by the business community to make decisions on credit, insurance, marketing, financial, merger, and other issues. **Corporate headquarters location:** New York NY. **Other area locations:** Murray Hill NJ. **Listed on:** New York Stock Exchange.

## FAULKNER INFORMATION SERVICES
7905 Browning Road, 114 Cooper Center, Pennsauken NJ 08109-4319. 609/662-2070. **Toll-free phone:** 800/843-0460. **Fax:** 609/662-3380. **Contact:** Betsey Thomas, Operations/Personnel Administrator. **E-mail address:** faulkner@faulkner.com. **World Wide Web address:** http://www. faulkner.com. **Description:** An independent publishing and research company specializing in providing technical information to end users and communication and IT professionals. Faulkner Information Services publishes more than a dozen standard information services in both print and electronic formats. The company provides comprehensive intelligence on products, vendors, technological advancements, and management issues associated with a wide range of technologies from open systems and client/server to enterprise networking, workgroup computing, and telecommunications. Faulkner Information Services also offers custom research and publication capabilities in such areas as market studies, customer satisfaction surveys, competitive analysis reports, and custom databases. **Common positions include:** Accountant/Auditor; Customer Service Representative; Human Resources Manager; Systems Analyst; Technical Writer/Editor. **Educational backgrounds include:** Communications; Computer Science; English. **Benefits:** 401(k); Dental Insurance; Disability Coverage; Life Insurance; Medical Insurance; Tuition Assistance. **Corporate headquarters location:** This Location. **Operations at this facility include:**

Administration; Research and Development; Sales; Service. **Number of employees at this location:** 45.

## GREG MANNING AUCTIONS, INC.
775 Passaic Avenue, West Caldwell NJ 07006. 973/882-0004. **Fax:** 973/882-4933. **Contact:** Human Resources. **World Wide Web address:** http://www.gregmanning.com. **Description:** Conducts public auctions of rare stamps, stamp collections, and stocks. Items included in the auctions are rare stamps; sports trading cards and sports memorabilia; rare glassware and pottery; pre-Colombian art objects; Egyptian, Middle-Eastern, and Far Eastern antiquities; and rare coins. **Corporate headquarters location:** This Location.

## MATHEMATICA POLICY RESEARCH, INC.
P.O. Box 2393, Princeton NJ 08543-2393. 609/799-3535. **Contact:** Ester Siach-Bar, Human Resources Representative. **Description:** Mathematica Policy Research, Inc. is an employee-owned company which conducts social policy research (both data collection and data analysis) for government agencies, foundations, and private sector clients. The areas studied include health, labor, welfare, education, child care, and food and nutrition. **Common positions include:** Economist; Statistician. **Educational backgrounds include:** Economics; Statistics. **Benefits:** 401(k); Dental Insurance; Disability Coverage; Life Insurance; Medical Insurance; On-Site Exercise Facility; Paid Vacation; Pension Plan; Profit Sharing; Tuition Assistance. **Corporate headquarters location:** This Location. **Other U.S. locations:** Washington DC. **Number of employees at this location:** 200.

## SCIENCE MANAGEMENT COMPANY
721 Route 202 & Route 206, Bridgewater NJ 08807. 908/722-0300. **Contact:** Human Resources Department. **Description:** Science Management Company works with IBM to provide disaster recovery services to large corporations. SMC Consulting (also at this location) provides management consulting services. **Common positions include:** Accountant/Auditor; Computer Programmer; Financial Analyst; General Manager; Human Resources Manager; Industrial Engineer; Systems Analyst. **Educational backgrounds include:** Accounting; Business Administration; Computer Science; Engineering; Finance; Liberal Arts; Marketing. **Benefits:** Dental Insurance; Disability Coverage; Life Insurance; Medical Insurance; Pension Plan; Profit Sharing; Savings Plan; Tuition Assistance. **Corporate headquarters location:** This Location. **Listed on:** American Stock Exchange.

## SENTINEL SECURITY SERVICES
44 State Street, Hackensack NJ 07601. 201/487-9096. **Contact:** Human Services. **Description:** Provides uniformed security officers to other companies.

## STERIS-ISOMEDIX SERVICES
11 Apollo Drive, Whippany NJ 07981. 973/887-4700. **Fax:** 973/887-1476. **Contact:** Human Resources. **Description:** Provides contract sterilization services to manufacturers of pre-packaged products, such as health care and certain consumer products. The company uses gamma radiation and ethylene oxide in these operations. STERIS-Isomedix Services operates contract irradiation sterilization facilities in the United States and Canada. **Subsidiaries include:** Skyland Scientific Services, Inc. (Bozeman MT) provides validation services to the pharmaceutical, biotechnology, and medical device industries.

*Note: Because addresses and telephone numbers of smaller companies can change rapidly, we recommend you call each company to verify the information below before inquiring about job opportunities. Mass mailings are not recommended.*

Additional small employers·

**ADJUSTMENT AND COLLECTION SERVICES**

**JDR Holdings Inc.**
500 N Franklin Tpke, Ramsey NJ 07446-1160. 201/818-3800.

**Paychex**
PO Box 359, Mount Laurel NJ 08054-0359. 609/235-3400.

**CREDIT REPORTING SERVICES**

**Amalgamated Credit Bureau**
PO Box 1006, Old Bridge NJ 08857-1006. 732/679-9100.

**CBA Information Services**
111 Woodcrest Rd, Cherry Hill NJ 08003-3620. 609/795-2221.

**Credit Lenders**
PO Box 508, Cherry Hill NJ 08003-0508. 609/751-7400.

**DETECTIVE, GUARD, AND ARMORED CAR SERVICES**

**Aarguard International Detective Agency**
407 Allwood Rd, Clifton NJ 07012-1704. 973/614-8600.

**Absolute Security Network**
333 Meadowlands Pkwy,
Secaucus NJ 07094-1814.
201/864-4000.

**Allied Security Inc.**
501 Hoes Ln, Ste 105, Piscataway
NJ 08854-5070. 732/699-0341.

**APS**
200 Sheffield St, Ste 301,
Mountainside NJ 07092-2314.
908/789-5545.

**Burns International Security**
2 Campus Dr, Parsippany NJ
07054-4400. 973/397-2000.

**Burns International Security**
525 Fellowship Rd, Ste 310,
Mount Laurel NJ 08054-3415.
609/778-7222.

**Burns International Security**
250 Moonachie Rd, Moonachie
NJ 07074-1308. 201/229-1600.

**Colonial Security Service**
294 South Ave, Fanwood NJ
07023-1325. 908/889-1900.

**Command Security Corp.**
1185 Morris Ave, Ste 301, Union
NJ 07083-3320. 908/686-1400.

**Consec Security Group Inc.**
PO Box 730, Harrison NJ 07029-
0730. 201/998-3277.

**Danbee Investigations Corp.**
PO Box 159, Midland Park NJ
07432-0159. 201/652-5500.

**Effective Security Systems**
PO Box 2, Clifton NJ 07011-
0002. 973/471-1094.

**EIP**
PO Box 195, Kenilworth NJ
07033-0195. 908/272-3345.

**Gateway Security Inc.**
Gateway III, Gateway Center,
Newark NJ 07102. 973/643-2755.

**General Security Systems Inc.**
2070 Millburn Ave, Maplewood
NJ 07040-3704. 973/762-1002.

**Guardsmark Inc.**
60 Walnut Ave, Ste 150, Clark
NJ 07066-1606. 732/381-1818.

**Haynes Security Inc.**
PO Box 5005, Newark NJ 07105-
0005. 973/817-8300.

**HSC Security Corp.**
77 Wabash Ave, Clifton NJ
07011-1600. 973/622-5212.

**Initial Security Investigative
Service**
711 N Main St, Ste 6,

Pleasantville NJ 08232-1590.
609/383-8855.

**Internal Intelligence Services**
434 Union Blvd, Totowa NJ
07512-2562. 973/389-1312.

**Jowa Security Services Inc.**
PO Box 205, Bridgeton NJ
08302-0154. 609/455-8279.

**Labor Management Concepts**
200 Belleville Tpke, North
Arlington NJ 07031-6235.
201/955-2804.

**Lansdell Protective Agency**
Newark International Airport,
Bldg 51-2, Newark NJ 07114.
973/961-4880.

**Loomis Fargo Co.**
701 Kingsland Ave, Lyndhurst
NJ 07071-2821. 201/939-2700.

**Marion Security Agency**
PO Box 8624, Red Bank NJ
07701-8624. 732/530-7133.

**McRoberts Protective Agency**
73 Main St, Ste 1, Woodbridge
NJ 07095-2845. 732/381-8700.

**Motivated Guard Service Inc.**
27 Warren St, Somerville NJ
08876-2921. 908/526-1140.

**Nilsen Detective Agency Inc.**
1203 E Broad St, Elizabeth NJ
07201-1048. 908/355-8290.

**Pinkerton Investigative Security**
99 Morris Ave, Springfield NJ
07081-1421. 973/376-3500.

**Princeton Armored Service**
245 Whitehead Rd, Trenton NJ
00610-3750. 609/890-6700.

**Professional Security**
4270 US Highway 1, Monmouth
Junction NJ 08852-1905.
732/274-1414.

**Randolph Services**
PO Box 465, Dover NJ 07802-
0465. 973/927-3400.

**Safeguard International Inc.**
1 Woodbridge Ctr Dr,
Woodbridge NJ 07095-1143.
732/602-1130.

**Saya Security Services Inc.**
1255 Paterson Plank Rd,
Secaucus NJ 07094-3229.
201/330-9700.

**Selective Detective Service**
Newark International Airport,
Newark NJ 07114. 973/961-3470.

**SOS Security Incorporated**
PO Box 6373, Parsippany NJ
07054-7373. 973/402-6600.

**Stanley Smith Security Inc.**
55 Washington St, Ste 207, East
Orange NJ 07017. 973/672-5511.

**Unique Security Guard Service**
700 Park Ave, Ste 301, Plainfield
NJ 07060-1616. 908/756-5650.

**Wackenhut Corporation**
100 Davidson Ave, Ste 205,
Somerset NJ 08873-1312.
732/563-0200.

**Wells Fargo Guard Services**
200 Decadon Dr, Ste 230,
Atlantic City NJ 08401. 609/646-
7295.

**Wells Fargo Guard Services**
799 Bloomfield Ave, Verona NJ
07044-1301. 973/239-2828.

**Wells Fargo Guard Services**
255 Old New Brunswick Rd,
Piscataway NJ 08854-3734.
732/981-1995.

**Wells Fargo Guard Services**
29 Emmons Dr, Ste A-2,
Princeton NJ 08540-5919.
609/734-4900.

**Winfield Security Corporation**
554 Bloomfield Ave, Ste 38,
Bloomfield NJ 07003-3307.
973/680-0008.

**Yankee Security Systems Inc.**
2641 Kennedy Blvd, Jersey City
NJ 07306-5943. 201/333-4337.

## SECRETARIAL AND COURT
## REPORTING SERVICES

**AA Office Services Inc.**
201 East Spring Garden St,
Palmyra NJ 08065-2029.
609/829-9484.

## SECURITY SYSTEMS
## SERVICES

**ADT**
7895 Browning Road,
Pennsauken NJ 08109-4640.
609/964-3375.

**ADT**
2540 Route 130, Ste 100,
Cranbury NJ 08512-3519.
609/655-2200.

**Bell Security Inc.**
1896 Morris Ave, Union NJ
07083-3508. 908/851-7788.

**Cops Monitoring**
PO Box 836, Williamstown NJ
08094-0836. 609/629-1111.

**Response USA Inc.**
11 Princess Rd, Ste K,
Lawrenceville NJ 08648-2319.
609/896-4500.

**For more information on career opportunities in miscellaneous business services and non-scientific research:**

### Associations

**AMERICAN SOCIETY OF APPRAISERS**
P.O. Box 17265, Washington DC 20041. 703/478-2228. Toll-free phone: 800/ASA-VALU. Fax: 703/742-8471. World Wide Web address: http://www.appraisers.org. An international, nonprofit, independent appraisal organization. ASA teaches, tests, and awards designations.

**EQUIPMENT LEASING ASSOCIATION OF AMERICA**
4301 North Fairfax Drive, Suite 550, Arlington VA 22203. 703/527-8655. World Wide Web address: http://www.elaonline.com.

**NATIONAL ASSOCIATION OF PERSONNEL SERVICES**
3133 Mt. Vernon Avenue, Alexandria VA 22305.

703/684-0180. Fax: 703/684-0071. World Wide Web address: http://www.napsweb.org. Provides federal legislative protection, education, certification, and business products and services to its member employment service agencies.

### Online Services

**INTERNET BUSINESS OPPORTUNITY SHOWCASE**
http://www.clark.net./pub/ibos/busops.html. This Website offers links to franchise, small business, and related opportunities.

**PLANT MAINTENANCE RESOURCE CENTER**
http://www.plant-maintenance.com. A great resource for maintenance professionals offering links to maintenance consultants and vendors; information on conferences; and articles on maintenance.

# CHARITIES AND SOCIAL SERVICES

 *Charitable health organizations have come into the spotlight in recent years. The American Heart Association, the Arthritis Foundation, and the American Lung Association have all offered their names (for a fee) to promote the sale of brand name products. Many think that the charities are risking their reputations by choosing one product over another. Even with this controversy, there is still a growing need for professionals to work in charitable organizations. The industry faces a high turnover rate and opportunities are plentiful.*

*The need for qualified social workers continues to grow as the older population in need of such services increases. Other factors leading to increasing job opportunities include growth of the overall population; an increase in crime rates and juvenile delinquency; a growing number of mentally ill, AIDS patients, and families in crisis; and the need for more social workers to administer discharge plans at medical facilities.*

**AMERICAN RED CROSS**
203 West Jersey Street, Elizabeth NJ 07202. 908/353-2500. **Contact:** Human Resources. **Description:** A humanitarian organization that aids disaster victims, gathers blood for distribution in crisis situations, and provides a variety of other social services. These services include training individuals to respond to emergencies, educating them on various diseases, and raising funds for other charitable establishments.

**THE ARC OF BERGEN AND PASSAIC COUNTIES, INC.**
223 Moore Street, Hackensack NJ 07601. 201/343-0322. **Contact:** Human Resources. **Description:** A nonprofit organization that works with people who are mentally retarded.

**COMMUNITY OPTIONS - PASSAIC AND BERGEN COUNTIES**
56 Fanny Road, Suite C, Boonton NJ 07005. 973/427-8700. **Contact:** Human Resources. **Description:** A private, nonprofit organization that works with adults who have developmental disabilities to find them housing and employment opportunities.

**HOPE HOUSE**
19-21 Belmont Avenue, Dover NJ 07801. 973/361-5555. **Contact:** Human Resources. **World Wide Web address:** http://www.hopehouse.com. **Description.** A nonprofit organization that provides AIDS outpatient, substance abuse, and family counseling; house cleaning for the elderly, and performs household chores for those who are unable.

**HOPES**
124 Grand Street, Hoboken NJ 07030. 201/656-3711. **Contact:** Human Resources. **Description:** A nonprofit organization funded by the state of New Jersey that sponsors programs such as Head Start and a medical transportation program for senior citizens.

**SOUTH BERGEN ACTIVITIES CENTER**
2 East Passaic Avenue, Rutherford NJ 07070. 201/460-9488. **Contact:** Human Resources. **Description:** A nonprofit organization that works with individuals who have developmental disabilities to teach them vocational and basic life skills. **Parent company:** A.R.C.

**URBAN LEAGUE OF HUDSON COUNTY**
779 Bergen Avenue, Jersey City NJ 07306. 201/451-8888. **Contact:** Human Resources. **Description:** A nonprofit organization that sponsors a variety of social programs including employment services and parenting programs.

*Note: Because addresses and telephone numbers of smaller companies can change rapidly, we recommend you call each company to verify the information below before inquiring about job opportunities. Mass mailings are not recommended.*

## Additional small employers:

### MISC. SOCIAL SERVICES

**Abilities of Northwest Jersey**
PO Box 251, Washington NJ
07882-0251. 908/689-1118.

**Adult Protective Services of
Morris County**
PO Box 900, Morristown NJ
07963-0900. 973/326-7282.

**Association for Retarded
Citizens**
1158 Wayside Rd, Tinton Falls
NJ 07724. 732/493-1919.

**Cerebral Palsy Association**
Oak Dr, Edison NJ 08837.
732/549-5580.

**Council of Newark Tenants**
303 Washington St, Ste 300,
Newark NJ 07102-2718. 973/643-0307.

**Development Resources Corp.**
650 S White Horse Pike,
Hammonton NJ 08037-2014.
609/567-9055.

**Development Resources Corp.**
1130 US Highway 202, Raritan
NJ 08869-1490. 908/707-8844.

**Easter Seals**
171 Atlantic St, Hackensack NJ
07601-3322. 201/342-5739.

**New Community Corporation**
233 W Market St, Newark NJ
07103-2713. 973/623-2800.

**Shirley Eves Center**
313 N 10th St, Millville NJ
08332-3103. 609/825-5840.

**YMCA**
PO Box 130, Toms River NJ
08754. 732/341-9622.

**YMCA**
25 Park St, Montclair NJ 07042-3407. 973/744-3400.

**YMCA**
2 Green St, Somerville NJ 08876-1620. 908/722-4567.

## For more information on career opportunities in charities and social services:

### Associations

**ALLIANCE FOR CHILDREN AND FAMILIES**
11700 West Lake Park Drive, Park Place, Milwaukee
WI 53224. 414/359-1040. World Wide Web address:
http://www.fsanet.org. Membership required.

**AMERICAN COUNCIL OF THE BLIND**
1155 15th Street NW, Suite 720, Washington DC
20005. 202/467-5081. Toll-free phone: 800/424-8666.
World Wide Web address: http://www.acb.org.
Membership required. Offers an annual conference, a
monthly magazine, scholarships, and employment
listings.

**CAREER OPPORTUNITIES**
1575 I Street NW, Suite 1190, Washington DC
20005-1168. 202/408-7900. Fax: 202/408-7907.
World Wide Web address: http://www.careeropps.
com. Publishes *CEO Update*, a bimonthly newsletter
which lists job openings at associations and nonprofit
organizations, with salaries of at least $50,000 per
year.

**CATHOLIC CHARITIES USA**
1731 King Street, Suite 200, Alexandria VA 22314.
703/549-1390. World Wide Web address: http://www.
catholiccharitiesusa.org. Membership required.

**CLINICAL SOCIAL WORK FEDERATION**
P.O. Box 3740, Arlington VA 22203. 703/522-3866.
A lobbying organization. Offers newsletters and a
conference every two years to member organizations.

**NATIONAL ASSN. OF SOCIAL WORKERS**
750 First Street NE, Suite 700, Washington DC
20002-4241. 202/408-8600. World Wide Web
address: http://www.naswdc.org.

**NATIONAL COUNCIL ON FAMILY
RELATIONS**
3989 Central Avenue NE, Suite 550, Minneapolis MN

55421. 612/781-9331. Fax: 612/781-9348.
Membership required. Publishes two quarterly
journals. Offers an annual conference and newsletters.

**NATIONAL FEDERATION OF THE BLIND**
1800 Johnson Street, Baltimore MD 21230. 410/659-9314. World Wide Web address: http://www.nfb.org.
Membership of 50,000 in 600 local chapters.
Publishes a quarterly magazine.

**NATIONAL MULTIPLE SCLEROSIS SOCIETY**
733 Third Avenue, New York NY 10017. 212/986-3240. Toll-free phone: 800/344-4867. World Wide
Web address: http://www.nmss.org. Publishes
*InsideMS* magazine.

**NATIONAL ORGANIZATION FOR HUMAN
SERVICE EDUCATION**
Brookdale Community College, 765 Newman Springs
Road, Lyncroft NJ 07738. 732/842-1900x546.

### Online Services

**AMERICAN CAMPING ASSOCIATION**
World Wide Web address: http://www.aca-camps.org.
Provides listings of jobs at day and overnight camps
for children and adults with special needs.

**COOLWORKS**
World Wide Web address: http://www.coolworks.
com. This Website includes information on volunteer
openings. The site also provides links to 22,000 job
openings in national parks, summer camps, ski areas,
river areas, ranches, fishing areas, cruise ships, and
resorts.

**NONPROFIT JOBS**
World Wide Web address: http://www.philanthropy-journal.org. The *Philanthropy Journal's* site lists jobs
in nonprofit associations and philanthropic
occupations.

Visit our exciting job and career site at http://www.careercity.com

# CHEMICALS/RUBBER AND PLASTICS

 *Growth in the chemicals industry should be rather weak overall, but some sectors are expected to fare better than others. Since 1996, the industry has done poorly in terms of growth, trade, and earnings, according to the U.S. Department of Commerce.* Standard & Poor *reported a 7 percent drop in profits for the chemical industry through the first half of 1998 from the first half of 1997, and profit margins were down as well.*

*Partly responsible is the electrical sector, one of the major consumers of chemicals, which saw a sharp decline in profits through the first half of 1998. Conversely, two other major industrial consumers -- the housing and automotive industries -- are doing well. Jobseekers with chemical engineering backgrounds will likely find opportunities with specialty chemicals, pharmaceuticals, and plastics manufacturers.*

*The demand for and production of plastics continues to grow, most notably in the automotive industry. Additionally, industrial use of rubber will expand as the demand for synthetic rubber by the automotive industry increases.*

**AEP INDUSTRIES, INC.**
125 Phillips Avenue, South Hackensack NJ 07606. 201/807-2364. **Contact:** Judy Lipman, Manager of Corporate Human Resources. **World Wide Web address:** http://www.aepinc.com. **Description:** A leader in the polyethylene film industry. The company's products are used in the packaging, transportation, textile, food, automotive, pharmaceutical, chemical, electronics, construction, agricultural, and other industries. Founded in 1970. **Common positions include:** Accountant/Auditor; Blue-Collar Worker Supervisor; Credit Manager; Customer Service Representative; Manufacturer's/Wholesaler's Sales Rep. **Benefits:** Dental Insurance; Life Insurance; Medical Insurance; Tuition Assistance. **Corporate headquarters location:** This Location. **Other U.S. locations:** CA; IL; NC; TX. **Operations at this facility include:** Administration; Research and Development; Sales. **Number of employees nationwide:** 975.

**ALLIEDSIGNAL, INC.**
10 North Avenue East, Elizabeth NJ 07201. 908/558-5100. **Contact:** Human Resources. **World Wide Web address:** http://www.alliedsignal.com. **Description:** This location manufactures plastic inserts for pill bottles. Overall, AlliedSignal is an advanced technology and manufacturing company providing customers worldwide with aerospace and automotive products, chemicals, fibers, plastics, and advanced materials. The company manufactures products to be used by other manufacturers in the production or processing of industrial and consumer items. **Corporate headquarters location:** Morristown NJ. **Subsidiaries include:** Allied Chemical Company; Allied Fibers & Plastics Company; Allied Health & Scientific Products Company; Eltra Corporation; Union Texas Petroleum Corporation. **Parent company:** AlliedSignal Corporation serves a broad spectrum of industries through its more than 40 strategic businesses, which are grouped into three sectors: aerospace, automotive, and engineered materials. AlliedSignal is one of the nation's largest industrial organizations, and has locations in more than 30 countries.

**ARMIN CORPORATION**
301 West Side Avenue, Jersey City NJ 07305. 201/432-8032. **Contact:** Personnel Director. **Description:** Produces a wide range of plastic and molded plastic items.

**ASHLAND CHEMICAL COMPANY**
**DREW DIVISION**
One Drew Plaza, Boonton NJ 07005. 973/263-7600. **Fax:** 973/263-4487. **Contact:** Human Resources. **World Wide Web address:** http://www.ashchem.com. **Description:** This location supplies specialty chemicals and services to the international maritime industry and other industrial markets worldwide. Through its industrial chemical sector, the Drew Division also manufactures and markets products for water management and fuel treatment, as well as specialized chemicals for major industries. The Ameroid Marine Division provides chemical and sealing products and applications technology for these products to the maritime industry. Ashland provides shipboard technical service for more than 15,000 vessels in more than 140 ports around the world. **Common**

**positions include:** Chemical Engineer; Chemist; Computer Programmer; Manufacturer's/ Wholesaler's Sales Rep.; Marketing Specialist; Mechanical Engineer; Systems Analyst. **Educational backgrounds include:** Chemistry; Engineering. **Benefits:** Dental Insurance; Disability Coverage; Life Insurance; Medical Insurance; Pension Plan; Profit Sharing; Savings Plan; Tuition Assistance. **Corporate headquarters location:** Dublin OH. **Parent company:** Ashland Inc. **Operations at this facility include:** Administration; Divisional Headquarters; Manufacturing; Regional Claims Center; Research and Development; Sales; Service.

**BASF CORPORATION**
**KNOLL PHARMACEUTICALS**
3000 Continental Drive North, Mount Olive NJ 07828-1234. 973/426-2600. **Contact:** Robert Stein, Director of Human Resources. **World Wide Web address:** http://www.basf.com. **Description:** This location serves as the United States headquarters and houses management offices as well as the pharmaceutical division, Knoll Pharmaceuticals. Overall, BASF Corporation is an international chemical products organization, doing business in five operating groups: agricultural chemicals; chemicals; colors and auxiliaries; pigments and organic specialties; and polymers. **Common positions include:** Accountant/Auditor; Chemical Engineer; Computer Programmer; Financial Analyst; Marketing Specialist. **Benefits:** Dental Insurance; Disability Coverage; Life Insurance; Medical Insurance; Pension Plan; Savings Plan; Tuition Assistance. **Corporate headquarters location:** This Location. **Other area locations:** South Brunswick NJ (produces ethoxylated textile auxiliary intermediates, specialty surfactants, and esters); and Washington NJ (produces polyether polyols). **Operations at this facility include:** Administration; Divisional Headquarters; Sales. **Number of employees worldwide:** 125,000.

**BOC GASES**
575 Mountain Avenue, Murray Hill NJ 07974. 908/464-8100. **Contact:** Corporate Personnel. **World Wide Web address:** http://www.boc.com. **Description:** Manufactures and markets industrial gases and related products. BOC Gases also provides full engineering and technical services. **Corporate headquarters location:** This Location. **Other U.S. locations:** Nationwide.

**BENJAMIN MOORE & COMPANY**
51 Chestnut Ridge Road, Montvale NJ 07645. 201/573-9600. **Fax:** 201/573-6631. **Contact:** Anne Beliveau, Human Resources Services Representative. **World Wide Web address:** http://www. benjaminmoore.com. **Description:** Manufactures paints, varnishes, and other coatings. **Common positions include:** Accountant/Auditor; Administrative Manager; Advertising Clerk; Attorney; Budget Analyst; Buyer; Chemist; Computer Programmer; Credit Manager; Customer Service Representative; Economist; Financial Analyst; Human Resources Manager; Human Service Worker; Manufacturer's/Wholesaler's Sales Rep.; Paralegal; Public Relations Specialist; Purchasing Agent/Manager; Systems Analyst; Transportation/Traffic Specialist. **Benefits:** 401(k); Dental Insurance; Disability Coverage; Employee Discounts; ESOP; Life Insurance; Medical Insurance; Pension Plan; Tuition Assistance. **Corporate headquarters location:** This Location. **Other U.S. locations:** Nationwide. **Operations at this facility include:** Administration; Research and Development; Sales; Service. **Listed on:** Privately held. **Number of employees at this location:** 175. **Number of employees nationwide:** 1,800.

**BUSH BOAKE ALLEN INC.**
7 Mercedes Drive, Montvale NJ 07645-1855. 201/391-9870. **Contact:** Human Resources. **World Wide Web address:** http://www.bushboakeallen.com. **Description:** Manufactures and distributes flavors and fragrances for use in foods, beverages, detergents, cosmetics, and other personal care items. **Listed on:** New York Stock Exchange. **Stock exchange symbol:** BOA.

**CAMBREX CORPORATION**
One Meadowlands Plaza, East Rutherford NJ 07073. 201/804-3000. **Fax:** 201/804-9852. **Contact:** Melissa Lesko, Manager of Human Resources. **World Wide Web address:** http://www. cambrex.com. **Description:** Manufactures and markets a broad range of specialty chemicals and commodity chemical intermediates. Health and pharmaceutical chemicals include specialty compounds used in the formulation of cosmetics and toiletries and intermediates converted into active ingredients in a variety of food additives and over the counter medications. Agricultural intermediates are used in the manufacture of herbicides and insecticides. **Corporate headquarters location:** This Location.

**CHURCH & DWIGHT COMPANY, INC.**
469 North Harrison Street, Princeton NJ 08543. 609/683-5900. **Contact:** Human Resources. **World Wide Web address:** http://www.armhammer.com. **Description:** Manufactures Arm & Hammer brand products including soaps and detergents.

## COLORITE PLASTICS
## COLORITE POLYMERS
101 Railroad Avenue, Ridgefield NJ 07657. 201/941-2900. **Contact:** Manuel Aneiros, Personnel Manager. **Description:** Colorite Plastics manufactures plastic garden hoses. Colorite Polymers (also at this location) manufactures PVC compounds. **Parent company:** Plastic Specialties & Technology.

## CREANOVA INC.
220 Davidson Avenue, Somerset NJ 08873. 732/560-6800. **Fax:** 732/560-6306. **Contact:** Human Resources. **World Wide Web address:** http://www.creanovainc.com. **Description:** Manufactures specialty chemicals, polymers, colorants, additives, and raw materials for the coatings industry. **NOTE:** As of January 1999, Creanova was discussing merger plans with Degussa Corporation. Please contact this location for more information. **Corporate headquarters location:** This Location. **Other U.S. locations:** Theodore AL; Pleasanton CA; Piscataway NJ; Lockland OH. **Parent company:** Huls Group. **Annual sales/revenues:** More than $100 million. **Number of employees worldwide:** 1,000.

## CREST FOAM INDUSTRIES, INC.
100 Carol Place, Moonachie NJ 07074. 201/807-0809. **Contact:** Human Resources. **World Wide Web address:** http://www.crestfoam.com. **Description:** Manufactures reticulated and specialty foam.

## CROMPTON & KNOWLES COLORS INCORPORATED
10 Kingsland Street, Nutley NJ 07110. 973/235-1800. **Contact:** Human Resources. **Description:** This location manufactures dyes. Overall, Crompton & Knowles is a worldwide manufacturer and marketer of specialty chemicals and equipment. The company's business is grouped into two segments. The specialty chemicals operation produces dyes. Dyes are sold internationally to apparel, carpeting, home furnishing, industrial, and automotive manufacturers. The specialty process equipment and controls division is a world leader in extrusion systems, industrial blow molding equipment, and related electronic controls for the plastics industry. Crompton & Knowles is a member of the Chemical Manufacturers Association and a signatory of the association's Responsible Care Program. **Corporate headquarters location:** Stamford CT. **Stock exchange symbol:** CNK. **Number of employees nationwide:** 2,300.

## CYTEC INDUSTRIES INC.
5 Garret Mountain Plaza, West Paterson NJ 07424. **Contact:** Human Resources Department. **Description:** Cytec Industries Inc. is an integrated, industrial chemicals manufacturer. The majority of Cytec's products are specialty chemicals. These include products and technologies for water and wastewater treatment, paper manufacturing, mineral processing, and oil drilling and recovery. **NOTE:** This firm does not accept unsolicited resumes. Please only respond to advertised openings.

## DAICOLOR-POPE INC.
33 Sixth Avenue, Paterson NJ 07524. 973/278-5170. **Contact:** Human Resources. **Description:** Manufactures pigments which are used by printing companies to produce inks.

## DOCK RESINS CORPORATION
1512 West Elizabeth Avenue, Linden NJ 07036. 908/862-2351. **Contact:** Human Resources. **Description:** Manufactures acrylic resins.

## E.I. DuPONT DE NEMOURS & COMPANY
U.S. Highway 130 & Canal Road, Deepwater NJ 08023. 609/299-5000. **Contact:** Human Resources. **World Wide Web address:** http://www.dupont.com. **Description:** This location is a chemical manufacturing plant. Overall, E.I. DuPont de Nemours & Company's activities include the manufacturing of biomedical, industrial, and consumer products (such as photographic, data-recording, and video devices); the production of manmade fiber products (with applications in a variety of consumer and commercial industries), polymer products (such as plastic resins, elastomers, and films), agricultural and industrial chemicals (such as herbicides and insecticides, pigments, fluorochemicals, petroleum additives, and mineral acids); the exploration and production of crude oil and natural gas; the refining, marketing, and downstream transportation of petroleum; and the mining and distribution of steam and metallurgical coals. **Benefits:** Dental Insurance; Disability Coverage; Life Insurance; Medical Insurance; Pension Plan; Savings Plan; Tuition Assistance. **Corporate headquarters location:** Wilmington DE. **Listed on:** New York Stock Exchange.

**DYNASIL CORPORATION OF AMERICA**
385 Cooper Road, West Berlin NJ 08091. 609/767-4600. **Fax:** 609/767-6813. **Contact:** Charlene Trace, Administrative Manager. **World Wide Web address:** http://www.dynasil.com. **Description:** Manufactures synthetic fused silica. Founded in 1960. **Benefits:** 401(k); Disability Coverage; Financial Planning Assistance; Life Insurance; Medical Insurance; Profit Sharing. **Corporate headquarters location:** This Location. **Other U.S. locations:** San Luis Obispo CA. **Listed on:** NASDAQ. **Annual sales/revenues:** $5 - $10 million. **Number of employees at this location:** 35. **Number of employees nationwide:** 40.

**FAIRMOUNT CHEMICAL COMPANY, INC.**
117 Blanchard Street, Newark NJ 07105. 973/344-5790. **Toll-free phone:** 800/872-9999. **Fax:** 973/690-5298. **Contact:** Maria Hayducka, Human Resources. **Description:** Manufactures and distributes chemical intermediates for the imaging industry; hydrazine, its salts, and derivatives for use in products manufactured by the company; additives used in the manufacture of plastics; and specialty chemicals, primarily pharmaceutical intermediates.

**FISHER SCIENTIFIC**
One Reagent Lane, Fair Lawn NJ 07410. 201/796-7100. **Contact:** Deb Myshkoff, Manager of Employee Relations. **World Wide Web address:** http://www.fisher1.com. **Description:** This location produces reagents. Overall, Fisher Scientific manufactures, distributes, and sells a wide range of products used in industrial and medical laboratories. Products include analytical and measuring instruments, apparatus, and appliances; reagent chemicals and diagnostics; glassware and plasticware; and laboratory furniture. Customers are primarily industrial laboratories, medical and hospital laboratories, and educational and research laboratories. Manufacturing operations are carried out through six operating divisions in 11 United States locations. **Common positions include:** Accountant/Auditor; Administrator; Biological Scientist; Biomedical Engineer; Blue-Collar Worker Supervisor; Buyer; Chemical Engineer; Chemist; Computer Programmer; Customer Service Rep; Department Manager; Draftsperson; Electrical/Electronics Engineer; Financial Analyst; General Manager; Human Resources Manager; Industrial Engineer; Materials Engineer; Mechanical Engineer; Operations/Production Manager; Purchasing Agent/Manager; Quality Control Supervisor; Systems Analyst. **Educational backgrounds include:** Accounting; Chemistry; Engineering; Finance; Liberal Arts; Marketing. **Benefits:** Dental Insurance; Disability Coverage; Life Insurance; Medical Insurance; Pension Plan; Profit Sharing; Savings Plan; Tuition Assistance. **Corporate headquarters location:** Pittsburgh PA. **Parent company:** Henley Group (La Jolla CA). **Operations at this facility include:** Administration; Manufacturing; Research and Development.

**GENERAL CHEMICAL CORPORATION**
90 East Halsey Road, Parsippany NJ 07054. 973/515-0900. **Contact:** Human Resources. **World Wide Web address:** http://www.genchem.com. **Description:** Manufactures inorganic chemicals and soda ash. **Common positions include:** Accountant/Auditor; Chemical Engineer; Customer Service Representative; Financial Analyst; Financial Manager; Human Resources Manager; Manufacturer's/Wholesaler's Sales Rep.; Mining Engineer; Secretary. **Educational backgrounds include:** Accounting; Business Administration; Engineering; Finance; Liberal Arts; Marketing. **Benefits:** 401(k); Dental Insurance; Disability Coverage; Life Insurance; Medical Insurance; Pension Plan; Tuition Assistance. **Corporate headquarters location:** This Location. **Other U.S. locations:** CA; Claymont DE; Syracuse NY; Pittsburgh PA; Green River WY. **Operations at this facility include:** Administration; Manufacturing; Sales; Service. **Number of employees at this location:** 180. **Number of employees nationwide:** 2,000.

**THE GEON COMPANY**
P.O. Box 400, Pedricktown NJ 08067. 609/299-5400. **Contact:** Human Resources. **Description:** A leading North American producer of vinyl (PVC) resins and compounds marketed under the GEON trademark, with 13 manufacturing plants in the United States, Canada, and Australia. **Corporate headquarters location:** Avon Lakes OH.

**GOODALL RUBBER COMPANY**
100 Ludlow Drive, Ewing NJ 08638. 609/799-2000. **Contact:** Bonnie Gessner, Personnel. **Description:** Manufactures, distributes, and sells rubber through 45 U.S. and Canadian sales and service centers. Products include hose, belting products, lined pipe, and fittings. **Common positions include:** Accountant/Auditor; Blue-Collar Worker Supervisor; Computer Programmer; Customer Service Representative. **Educational backgrounds include:** Accounting; Business Administration; Chemistry; Engineering; Finance; Marketing. **Benefits:** Disability Coverage; Life Insurance; Medical Insurance; Pension Plan; Profit Sharing; Savings Plan; Tuition Assistance. **Corporate headquarters location:** This Location. **Operations at this facility include:** Administration; Sales; Service.

## HERCULES CHEMICAL COMPANY
111 South Street, Passaic NJ 07055. 973/778-5000. **Contact:** Human Resources. **Description:** Manufactures plumbing sealant chemicals and epoxies.

## HOECHST CORPORATION
30 Independence Boulevard, Warren NJ 07059. 908/231-2000. **Fax:** 908/231-3225. **Contact:** Human Resources. **World Wide Web address:** http://www.celanese.com. **Description:** This location houses the Specialty Chemicals and Life Sciences Groups. Overall, Hoechst Corporation is a science-based, market-driven, international company dedicated to producing and marketing chemicals, manufactured fibers for textile and industrial uses, plastics and high-performance advanced materials, polyester, film, printing plates, dyes and pigments, pharmaceuticals, and animal health and crop protection products. **Corporate headquarters location:** This Location. **Other U.S. locations:** Charlotte NC; Wilmington NC; Summit NJ; New York NY; Spartanburg SC; Bay City TX; Bishop TX. **Parent company:** Hoechst Group. **Listed on:** New York Stock Exchange. **Annual sales/revenues:** More than $100 million. **Number of employees worldwide:** 23,000.

## J.M. HUBER CORPORATION
333 Thornall Street, Edison NJ 08818. **Contact:** Human Resources Department. **Description:** A diversified company, producing oil and natural gas, carbon black, kaolin (china) clay, synthetic inorganic pigments, printing inks, and equipment for the petroleum and pipeline industries. Products are sold to oil refineries and pipelines and to rubber, paper, printing, paint, adhesives, plastics, insecticides, ceramics, animal feed, packaging, home construction, and wood-consuming industries. **NOTE:** This firm does not accept unsolicited resumes. Please only respond to advertised openings.

## INTERNATIONAL SPECIALTY PRODUCTS INC.
1361 Alps Road, Wayne NJ 07470. 973/628-4000. **Contact:** Gary Schneid, Director of Employee Selection. **World Wide Web address:** http://www.ispcorp.com. **Description:** Manufactures specialty chemicals and building materials. Chemicals include high-pressure acetylene derivatives, industrial organic and inorganic chemicals, GAF filter systems, and GAF mineral products. Building materials include prepared roofing, roll roofing, built-up roofing systems, and single-ply roofing. International Specialty Products maintains research and development facilities throughout the U.S. and abroad. **Common positions include:** AccountantAuditor; Advertising Clerk; Attorney; Biological Scientist; Biomedical Engineer; Budget Analyst; Buyer; Chemical Engineer; Chemist; Computer Programmer; Financial Analyst; General Manager; Paralegal; Pharmacist; Systems Analyst. **Educational backgrounds include:** Chemistry; Engineering. **Benefits:** 401(k); Dental Insurance; Disability Coverage; Life Insurance; Medical Insurance; Savings Plan; Tuition Assistance. **Corporate headquarters location:** This Location. **Listed on:** New York Stock Exchange. **Number of employees at this location:** 700. **Number of employees nationwide:** 4,300.

## KOHL & MADDEN PRINTING INK CORPORATION
222 Bridge Plaza South, Suite 701, Fort Lee NJ 07024. 201/886-1203. **Contact:** Human Resources Manager. **World Wide Web address:** http://www.kohlmadden.com. **Description:** Produces printing inks, compounds, and varnishes. The company's sales offices are located throughout the United States. **Common positions include:** Clinical Lab Technician; Services Sales Representative. **Educational backgrounds include:** Chemistry; Marketing. **Benefits:** 401(k); Dental Insurance; Disability Coverage; Life Insurance; Medical Insurance; Pension Plan; Tuition Assistance. **Corporate headquarters location:** This Location. **Parent company:** Sun Chemical Corporation is one of the world's largest producers of printing inks and organic pigments. The company also designs and manufactures graphic arts equipment. **Operations at this facility include:** Administration; Divisional Headquarters; Sales. **Listed on:** Privately held. **Number of employees at this location:** 25. **Number of employees nationwide:** 450.

## MILLENIUM CHEMICALS
230 Half Mile Road, Red Bank NJ 07701. 732/933-5000. **Contact:** Human Resources Department. **Description:** Millenium Chemicals produces a range of chemical products including detergents and fragrances. **Corporate headquarters location:** This Location. **Other U.S. locations:** Hunt Valley MD.

## NATIONAL STARCH AND CHEMICAL COMPANY
10 Finderne Avenue, Bridgewater NJ 08807. 908/685-5000. **Toll-free phone:** 800/366-4031. **Fax:** 908/685-6956. **Contact:** Colleen Twill, College Relations Manager. **World Wide Web address:** http://www.nationalstarch.com. **Description:** Manufactures industrial chemicals including adhesives, resins, starches, and specialty chemicals for the packaging, textile, paper, food,

furniture, electronic materials, and automotive markets. National Starch and Chemical operates 125 facilities worldwide. **NOTE:** Entry-level positions are offered. **Common positions include:** Accountant; Biochemist; Chemical Engineer; Chemist; Computer Programmer; Food Scientist/Technologist; MIS Specialist. **Educational backgrounds include:** Accounting; Chemistry; Engineering; Food Science. **Benefits:** 401(k); Dental Insurance; Disability Coverage; Life Insurance; Medical Insurance; Pension Plan; Profit Sharing; Savings Plan; Tuition Assistance. **Special programs:** Internships. **Corporate headquarters location:** This Location. **Parent company:** The ICI Group. **Listed on:** New York Stock Exchange. **Annual sales/revenues:** More than $100 million. **Number of employees nationwide:** 8,500.

## NATIONAL TOOL & MANUFACTURING COMPANY
100-124 North 12th Street, Kenilworth NJ 07033. 908/276-1600. **Contact:** Delores Winn, Human Resources Department. **Description:** A manufacturer of plastic moldings for a variety of industrial uses.

## NORTON PERFORMANCE PLASTICS CORPORATION
150 Dey Road, Wayne NJ 07470. 973/696-4700. **Contact:** William Mahoney, Human Resources Director. **World Wide Web address:** http://www.nortonplastics.com. **Description:** Manufactures a wide range of plastic products and shapes including pipes, rods, sheet, tape, rectangular stock, insulated wire, and coaxial cable core; finished plastic products such as laboratory wire; and nylon products such as rods, tubes, slabs, gear blands, and custom castings. **Common positions include:** Chemical Engineer; Customer Service Representative. **Benefits:** Employee Discounts; Life Insurance; Pension Plan; Savings Plan; Tuition Assistance. **Special programs:** Internships. **Corporate headquarters location:** This Location. **Other U.S. locations:** IL; NY; OH. **Parent company:** Norton Company (Worcester MA) produces abrasives, petroleum, mining products and services, engineering materials, and construction products. **Operations at this facility include:** Administration; Manufacturing; Research and Development; Service.

## OAKITE PRODUCTS, INC.
50 Valley Road, Berkeley Heights NJ 07922. 908/464-6900. **Contact:** Suzanne Watson, Recruiter. **World Wide Web address:** http://www.oakite.com. **Description:** Manufactures and markets specialty chemical products used primarily for industrial cleaning, metal conditioning, and surface preparation. Branch offices and manufacturing facilities are located throughout the United States and Canada. **Common positions include:** Accountant/Auditor; Chemist; Manufacturer's/Wholesaler's Sales Rep.; Marketing Specialist. **Educational backgrounds include:** Accounting; Business Administration; Chemistry; Marketing. **Benefits:** Dental Insurance; Disability Coverage; Life Insurance; Medical Insurance; Profit Sharing; Tuition Assistance. **Corporate headquarters location:** This Location. **Operations at this facility include:** Administration; Research and Development.

## PVC CONTAINER CORPORATION
401 Industrial Way West, Eatontown NJ 07724. 732/542-0060. **Contact:** Diane Murphy, Personnel Manager. **Description:** Designs and manufactures plastic bottles and polyvinyl chloride compounds.

## RED DEVIL, INC.
2400 Vauxhall Road, Union NJ 07083. 908/688-6900. **Contact:** Joseph Chiaro, Director of Human Resources. **Description:** Manufactures and distributes paint sundries; hand tools; and a full-line of caulks, sealants, and adhesives for home and professional use. **Corporate headquarters location:** This Location. **Number of employees at this location:** 150. **Number of employees nationwide:** 250.

## REEDY INTERNATIONAL
25 East Front Street, Suite 200, Key Port NJ 07735. 732/264-1777. **Contact:** Human Resources. **Description:** Produces chemical components for items such as styrofoam and car parts.

## RHEOX, INC.
P.O. Box 700, Highstown NJ 08520. 609/443-2467. **Contact:** Human Resources. **Description:** This location houses the executive offices. Overall, Rheox manufactures chemicals. **Corporate headquarters location:** This Location.

## RHODIA INC.
CN7500, Cranbury NJ 08542. 609/860-4000. **Contact:** Human Resources. **Description:** This location houses administrative offices. Overall, Rhodia supplies specialty and intermediate chemicals to consumers and industrial markets. **Other U.S. locations:** Nationwide.

**SETON COMPANY**
849 Broadway, Newark NJ 07104. 973/485-4800. **Contact:** Silva Homsi, Human Resources Representative. **Description:** Company operations are conducted primarily through two business segments. The Leather Division's operations include tanning, finishing, and distributing whole-hide cattle leathers for the automotive and furniture upholstery industries; cattle hide side leathers for footwear, handbag, and other markets; and cattle products for collagen, rawhide pet items, and other applications. The Chemicals and Coated Products Division is engaged in the manufacture and distribution of epoxy and urethane chemicals, specialty leather finishes, industrial and medical tapes, foams, films, and laminates. Other manufacturing facilities are located in Wilmington DE (epoxy, urethane chemicals, leather finishes); Toledo OH (cattle hide processing); Malvern PA (industrial coated products); and Saxton PA (cutting of finished leathers). **Corporate headquarters location:** This Location. **Other U.S. locations:** Norristown PA; Saxton PA. **Subsidiaries include:** Radel Leather Manufacturing Company; Seton Leather Company. **Listed on:** American Stock Exchange.

**SIKA CORPORATION**
201 Polito Avenue, Lyndhurst NJ 07071. 201/933-8800. **Fax:** 201/933-9379. **Contact:** Kimberly Beaudette, Human Resources Generalist. **Description:** Sika Corporation manufactures specialty chemicals including sealants and adhesives for the construction and transportation industries. Founded in 1937. **NOTE:** Second and third shifts are offered. **Common positions include:** Administrative Assistant; Chemist; Customer Service Rep.; Secretary; Services Sales Rep.; Systems Analyst. **Educational backgrounds include:** Accounting; Business Administration; Chemistry; Engineering; Finance; Marketing. **Benefits:** 401(k); Dental Insurance; Disability Coverage; Life Insurance; Medical Insurance; Tuition Assistance. **Corporate headquarters location:** This Location. **Parent company:** Sika Finanz AG. **Operations at this facility include:** Administration; Manufacturing; Research and Development; Sales; Service. **Annual sales/revenues:** More than $100 million. **Number of employees at this location:** 200. **Number of employees nationwide:** 700.

**STAR-GLO INDUSTRIES, INC.**
2 Carlton Avenue, East Rutherford NJ 07073. 201/939-6162. **Contact:** Beatriz Sanchez, Personnel Director. **Description:** Manufactures precision-molded rubber and plastic parts, often bonded to metal. Sales are made primarily to original equipment manufacturers in the business machine and computer, welding, food packaging equipment, chemical, and aerospace industries. **Corporate headquarters location:** This Location.

**STEPAN COMPANY**
100 West Hunter Avenue, Maywood NJ 07607. 201/845-3030. **Contact:** Tim O'Donnell, Office Manager. **Description:** Produces specialty chemicals and food ingredients. The company operates eight production plants, five of which are located in the United States. **Common positions include:** Accountant/Auditor; Chemical Engineer; Chemist; Clinical Lab Technician; Financial Manager; Food Scientist/Technologist. **Educational backgrounds include:** Accounting; Chemistry; Communications. **Benefits:** Dental Insurance; Disability Coverage; Life Insurance; Medical Insurance; Pension Plan; Profit Sharing; Savings Plan; Tuition Assistance. **Corporate headquarters location:** Northfield IL. **Operations at this facility include:** Administration; Manufacturing; Research and Development; Sales. **Listed on:** American Stock Exchange. **Number of employees at this location:** 100. **Number of employees nationwide:** 1,300.

**SYBRON CHEMICALS INC.**
Birmingham Road, Birmingham NJ 08011. 609/893-1100. **Contact:** Stephen Adler, Director of Human Resources. **Description:** An international supplier of chemical specialties and related technology to two markets: environmental products and services, primarily related to water and waste treatment; and textile processing. The company's chemical specialties are used to enhance the aesthetic and physical characteristics of textiles during textile preparation, printing, dyeing, and finishing. Sybron's environmental products soften and demineralize water, purify drinking water for safe consumption, and biologically break down waste matter into harmless components. **Corporate headquarters location:** This Location.

**TICONA**
90 Morris Avenue, Summit NJ 07901. 908/598-4000. **Contact:** Human Resources. **Description:** Produces and markets chemicals and manufactures fibers for industrial and textile uses.

**USA DETERGENTS**
1735 Jersey Avenue, North Brunswick NJ 08902. 732/828-1800. **Contact:** Human Resources. **Description:** Manufactures household and automotive cleaning products. Products are sold in retail stores under the company's name.

## UNION CARBIDE CORPORATION
One Riverview Drive, Somerset NJ 08875. 732/271-2000. **Contact:** Personnel. **Description:** This location is engaged in the research and development of plastics. Overall, Union Carbide Corporation is a worldwide chemicals and polymers company. The company possesses many of the industry's most advanced process and catalyst technologies at some of the most cost-efficient, large-scale production facilities in the world. Union Carbide operates two business segments: Specialties and Intermediates, and Basic Chemicals and Polymers. Union Carbide is a leading North American supplier of solvents and intermediates to the paint and coatings industry; a leading licenser of several technologies; and a leading manufacturer and supplier of specialty chemicals, polymers, and services used in the personal care products, pharmaceuticals, automotive, wire and cable, oil and gas, and industrial lubricant industries. Union Carbide is also among the largest manufacturers of polyethylene and polypropylene. The company is one of the world's largest producers of ethylene oxide, and its derivative, ethylene glycol, used for polyester fiber, resin and film, automotive anti-freeze, and other products. **Corporate headquarters location:** Danbury CT. **Other U.S. locations:** Taft LA; Houston TX; South Charlestown WV.

## UNIQEMA
76 East 24th Street, Paterson NJ 07544. 973/345-8220. **Contact:** Human Resources. **Description:** Manufactures surfactant chemicals.

## WALLACE & TIERNAN
1901 West Garden Road, Vineland NJ 08360. 973/759-8000. **Contact:** Personnel Administrator. **Description:** A manufacturer of chlorinates for water and wastewater treatment.

*Note: Because addresses and telephone numbers of smaller companies can change rapidly, we recommend you call each company to verify the information below before inquiring about job opportunities. Mass mailings are not recommended.*

### Additional small employers:

#### ADHESIVES AND SEALANTS

**Custom Building Products**
PO Box 346, Bridgeport NJ
08014-0346. 609/467-9226.

#### CHEMICALS AND CHEMICAL PREPARATIONS

**Fidelity Chemical Products**
470 Frelinghuysen Ave, Newark
NJ 07114. 973/242-4110.

**H&R Florasynth**
300 North St, Teterboro NJ
07608-1204. 201/288-3200.

**Lonza Inc.**
17-17 State Rte 208, Fair Lawn
NJ 07410-2819. 201/794-2400.

**Union Carbide Corporation**
PO Box 670, Bound Brook NJ
08805-0670. 732/563-5000.

#### CLEANING & SANITATION PREPARATIONS

**Ecolab Inc.**
255 Blair Rd, Avenel NJ 07001-
2140. 732/636-2100.

**Reckitt & Colman Inc.**
PO Box K, Belle Mead NJ 08502.
908/874-5181.

**Reckitt & Colman Inc.**
1655 Valley Rd, Wayne NJ
07470. 973/633-3600.

#### INDUSTRIAL GASES

**E. Davis International Inc.**
7 Turner Pl, Piscataway NJ
08854-3838. 732/777-5190.

**Matheson Gas Products Inc.**
PO Box 85, East Rutherford NJ
07073-0085. 201/933-2400.

#### INDUSTRIAL INORGANIC CHEMICALS

**FMC**
500 Roosevelt Ave, Carteret NJ
07008-3588. 732/541-3000.

**Kuehne Chemical Co. Inc.**
86 Hackensack Ave, Kearny NJ
07032-4620. 973/589-0700.

**MEI**
500 Point Breeze Rd, Flemington
NJ 08822-4719. 908/782-5800.

#### INDUSTRIAL ORGANIC CHEMICALS

**Caschem Inc.**
40 Avenue A, Bayonne NJ
07002-5265. 201/858-7900.

**Cookson Pigments Inc.**
256 Vanderpool St, Newark NJ
07114-2413. 973/242-1800.

**CPS Chemical Co. Inc.**
PO Box 162, Old Bridge NJ
08857-0162. 732/607-2700.

**Creanova Inc.**
PO Box 365, Piscataway NJ
08855-0365. 732/981-5000.

**Crompton & Knowles Corporation**
1595 MacArthur Blvd, Mahwah
NJ 07430-3601. 201/818-2100.

**Degussa Corporation**
65 Challenger Rd, Ridgefield
Park NJ 07660-2104. 201/641-
6100.

**Dragoco Inc.**
10 Gordon Drive, Totowa NJ
07512-2204. 973/256-3850.

**Givaudan-Roure Corporation**
100 Delawanna Ave, Clifton NJ
07014-1550. 973/365-8000.

**Haarmann & Reimer Corp.**
PO Box 175, Springfield NJ
07081-0175. 973/467-5600.

**IFF**
PO Box 439, Dayton NJ 08810-
0439. 732/329-4600.

**Indol Color Co.**
1029 Newark Ave, Elizabeth NJ
07208-3518. 973/242-1300.

**Mane USA**
60 Demarest Dr, Wayne NJ
07470-6702. 973/633-5533.

**Solutia**
PO Box 309, Bridgeport NJ
08014-0309. 609/467-3000.

**Witco Corporation**
1000 Convery Blvd, Perth Amboy
NJ 08861-1932. 732/826-6600.

**MISC. RUBBER AND
PLASTIC PRODUCTS**

**Plastiflex Company Inc.**
9 Whippany Rd, Whippany NJ
07981-1540. 973/560-0320.

**Tingley Rubber Corporation**
PO Box 100, South Plainfield NJ
07080-0100. 908/757-7474.

**PAINTS, VARNISHES, AND
RELATED PRODUCTS**

**Benjamin Moore & Company**
134 Lister Ave, Newark NJ
07105-4524. 973/344-1200.

**Daniel Products Company Inc.**
384-400 Claymont Ave, Jersey
City NJ 07304. 201/432-0800.

**Interlux**
PO Box 386, Union NJ 07083-
0386. 908/686-1300.

**Olympic Paint & Chemical**
148 E 5th St, Bayonne NJ 07002-
4252. 201/437-0770.

**Stonhard Inc.**
PO Box 308, Maple Shade NJ
08052-0308. 609/779-7500.

**William Zinsser & Co. Inc.**
173 Belmont Dr, Somerset NJ
08873-1218. 732/469-8100.

**PAINTS, VARNISHES, AND
SUPPLIES WHOLESALE**

**Five Star Group Inc.**
PO Box 1960, East Hanover NJ
07936-1960. 973/428-4600.

**Jay Squared Inc.**
35 Horizon Blvd, South
Hackensack NJ 07606-1804.
201/440-7000.

**PLASTIC MATERIALS
WHOLESALE**

**Rapid Industrial Plastics Co.**
PO Box 10629, Newark NJ
07193-0629. 201/433-5500.

**PLASTIC MATERIALS,
SYNTHETICS, AND
ELASTOMERS**

**Ausimont Industries Inc.**
10 Leonards Ln, Thorofare NJ
08086. 609/853-8119.

**Formosa Plastics Corp.**
9 Peach Tree Hill Rd, Livingston
NJ 07039-5702. 973/992-2090.

**Synergistics Industries**
10 Ruckle Ave, Farmingdale NJ
07727-3691. 732/938-5980.

**PLASTIC PRODUCTS**

**Action Technology**
18 Green Pond Rd, Rockaway NJ
07866-2002. 973/625-9400.

**AL Hyde Company**
1 Main St, Grenloch NJ 08032.
609/227-0500.

**Allardi**
510 Ryerson Rd, Lincoln Park NJ
07035-2032. 973/694-0202.

**Amaray International**
52 Green Pond Rd, Rockaway NJ
07866-2002. 973/586-2900.

**American Cellophane**
183 National Rd, Edison NJ
08817-2810. 732/287-3144.

**American Seal Cut Corp.**
80 Leuning St, South Hackensack
NJ 07606-1317. 201/488-7477.

**Basic Line Inc.**
PO Box 1337, Perth Amboy NJ
08862-1337. 732/826-2000.

**Bel-Art Products Inc.**
6 Industrial Rd, Pequannock NJ
07440-1920. 973/694-0500.

**Brunswick Container Corp.**
6 Joanna Ct, East Brunswick NJ
08816-2108. 732/254-9304.

**Cairns & Bros. Inc.**
PO Box 4076, Clifton NJ 07012-
0476. 973/473-5067

**Captive Plastics Inc.**
PO Box 277, Piscataway NJ
08855-0277. 732/469-7900.

**Champion Plastics**
220 Clifton Blvd, Clifton NJ
07011-3695. 973/777-1888.

**Detailed Designs**
PO Box 3012, Plainfield NJ
07063-0012. 908/753-1990.

**Eagle Affiliates Inc.**
505 Manor Ave, Harrison NJ
07029-2047. 973/482-1222.

**EJ Brooks Company**
164 N 13th St, Newark NJ 07107-
1225. 973/483-0335.

**FPI Thermoplastic Technology**
PO Box 1907, Morristown NJ
07962-1907. 973/539-4200.

**General Foam**
13 Manor Rd, East Rutherford NJ
07073-2119. 201/933-8540.

**Graber-Rogg Inc.**
22 Jackson Dr, Cranford NJ
07016-3609. 908/272-4422.

**ICI Polyurethanes**
286 Mantua Grove Rd, Paulsboro
NJ 08066-1731. 609/423-8300.

**J-M Manufacturing Company**
9 Peach Tree Hill Road,
Livingston NJ 07039-5702.
973/535-1633.

**Jersey Plastic Molders**
149 Shaw Ave 155, Irvington NJ
07111-4714. 973/926-1800.

**Lermer Packaging Corp.**
520 South Ave, Garwood NJ
07027-1297. 908/789-0900.

**Madan Plastics Inc.**
PO Box 487, Cranford NJ 07016-
0487. 908/276-8484.

**Modern Plastics**
160 Meister Ave, Somerville NJ
08876-3474. 908/218-7997.

**Modern Plastics**
222 Old Egg Harbor Rd, West
Berlin NJ 08091. 609/768-3232.

**Moldieco Plastic Products**
PO Box 48, Fords NJ 08863-
0048. 732/738-1400.

**Omega Plastics Corporation**
PO Box 808, Lyndhurst NJ
07071-0808. 201/933-5353.

**Oneida Pacquet Inc.**
PO Box 449, Clifton NJ 07015-
0449. 973/777-5600.

**Owens Brockway**
2900 Woodbridge Ave, Edison
NJ 08837-3406. 732/548-4100.

**Patriot Manufacturing Inc.**
PO Box 498, Hammonton NJ
08037-0498. 609/567-0090.

**Pierson Industries Inc.**
7 Astro Place, Rockaway NJ
07866. 973/627-7945.

**Primex Plastics Corporation**
65 River Dr, Garfield NJ 07026-
3145. 973/470-8000.

**Progard**
245 Livingston St, Northvale NJ
07647-1901. 201/750-1680.

**Ringwood Containers LP**
247 Margaret King Ave,
Ringwood NJ 07456-1417.
973/962-1979.

**Setco Inc.**
34 Englehard Dr, Cranbury NJ
08512-3721. 609/655-4600.

**Silvatrim Corporation**
140 South Ave, South Plainfield
NJ 07080-3816. 908/753-6066.

**Southeastern Plastics Corp.**
15 Home News Row, New
Brunswick NJ 08901-3601.
732/846-8500.

**Star Manufacturing Inc.**
101 Industrial Ave, Little Ferry
NJ 07643-1901. 201/641-3300.

**Stull Closure Technologies**
17 Veronica Ave, Somerset NJ
08873-3448. 732/873-2520.

**Stull Closure Technologies**
35 Righter Rd, Dover NJ 07869-
1703. 973/584-2140.

**Superseal Manufacturing Co.**
125 Helen St, South Plainfield NJ
07080-3806. 908/561-5910.

**Techniplast Incorporated**
231 Main St, Little Falls NJ
07424-1346. 973/785-1400.

**Tek-Pak America Inc.**
PO Box 2585, Clifton NJ 07015-
2585. 973/881-8880.

**Tekni-Plex Inc.**
201 Industrial Pkwy, Somerville
NJ 08876-3449. 908/722-4800.

**Therma Systems Corporation**
PO Box 307, South Plainfield NJ
07080-0307. 908/561-8111.

**Vinyline**
1 Raritan Rd, Oakland NJ 07436-
2709. 201/337-9151.

**Waddington Jaycare LLC**
202 Washington Ave, Carlstadt
NJ 07072-3001. 201/507-0900.

**Wheaton Injection Molding**
PO Box 5006, Millville NJ
08332-5006. 609/327-1540.

**Wincup Holdings LP**
190 Liberty St, Metuchen NJ
08840-1216. 732/494-1999.

**Zappa Plastics Inc.**
165 Howard St, Phillipsburg NJ
08865-3164. 908/454-4500.

**PRINTING INK**

**General Printing Ink**
PO Box 1302, Fort Lee NJ
07024-1302. 201/224-4600.

**Heritage Inks International**
100 Pershing Ave, Edison NJ
08837-3943. 732/225-1800.

**RUBBER PRODUCTS**

**Ames Rubber Corporation**
1440 County Rte 565, Sussex NJ
07461. 973/875-3162.

**Ames Rubber Corporation**
23-47 Ames Blvd, Hamburg NJ
07419-1514. 973/827-9101.

**Bumper Specialties Inc.**
PO Box 45, Mount Holly NJ
08060-0045. 609/261-8100.

**Rhein Chemie Corporation**
1014 Whitehead Road Extension,
Trenton NJ 08638-2406. 609/771-
9100.

**SOAP AND OTHER
DETERGENTS**

**Amerchol Corporation**
PO Box 4051, Edison NJ 08818-
4051. 732/248-6000.

**Ben Rickert Inc.**
PO Box 440, Wayne NJ 07474-
0440. 973/628-0200.

**UNSUPPORTED PLASTIC
PRODUCTS**

**American Fuji Seal Inc.**
17 Stewart Pl, Fairfield NJ
07004-1632. 973/882-5600.

**Armin Polyethylene Film NE**
PO Box 253, Elizabeth NJ 07206-
0253. 908/353-3850.

**Bemis Company Inc.**
PO Box 475, Flemington NJ
08822-0475. 908/782-5858.

**Custom Decorating Inc.**
505 N Michigan Ave, Kenilworth
NJ 07033-1076. 908/810-9292.

**GPC**
PO Box 334, Lodi NJ 07644-
0334. 973/473-0660.

**Inteplast Corp.**
9 Peach Tree Hill Rd, Livingston
NJ 07039-5702. 973/994-8000.

**ITW Thielex Plastics**
95 Commerce Dr, Somerset NJ
08873-3469. 732/968-5300.

**Mobil Chemicals**
PO Box 3140, Edison NJ 08818-
3140. 732/321-6100.

**Nexus Plastics Inc.**
1 Loretto Ave, Hawthorne NJ
07506-1303. 973/427-3311.

**Occidental Chemical Corp.**
PO Box 456, Burlington NJ
08016-0456. 609/499-6251.

**Rexam Medical Packaging Inc.**
PO Box 158, Mount Holly NJ
08060-0158. 609/267-5900.

**Zeus Industrial Products Inc.**
PO Box 298, Raritan NJ 08869-
0298. 908/526-0800.

**For more information on career opportunities in the chemicals/rubber and plastics industries:**

<u>Associations</u>

**AMERICAN ASSOCIATION FOR CLINICAL
CHEMISTRY**
2101 L Street NW, Suite 202, Washington DC 20037
1526. 202/857-0717. Toll-free phone: 800/892-1400.
World Wide Web address: http://www.aacc.org.
International scientific/medical society of individuals
involved with clinical chemistry and other clinical lab
science-related disciplines.

**AMERICAN CHEMICAL SOCIETY**
Career Services, 1155 16th Street NW, Washington
DC 20036. 202/872-4600. World Wide Web address:
http://www.acs.org.

**AMERICAN INSTITUTE OF CHEMICAL
ENGINEERS**
3 Park Avenue, New York NY 10016. 212/591-7338.

Toll-free phone: 800/242-4363. World Wide Web
address: http://www.aiche.org. Provides leadership in
advancing the chemical engineering profession as it
meets the needs of society.

**CHEMICAL MANAGEMENT & RESOURCES
ASSOCIATION**
1255 23rd Street NW, Washington DC 20037.
202/452-1620. Engaged in marketing, marketing
research, business development, and planning for the
chemical and allied process industries. Provides
technical meetings, educational programs, and
publications to members.

**CHEMICAL MANUFACTURERS
ASSOCIATION**
1300 Wilson Boulevard, Arlington VA 22209.
703/741-5000. World Wide Web address: http://www.
cmahq.com. A trade association that develops and

implements programs and services and advocates
public policy that benefits the industry and society.

**THE ELECTROCHEMICAL SOCIETY**
10 South Main Street, Pennington NJ 08534. 609/737-
1902. An international educational society dealing
with electrochemical issues. Also publishes monthly
journals.

**SOAP AND DETERGENT ASSOCIATION**
475 Park Avenue South, New York NY 10016.
212/725-1262. World Wide Web address: http://www.
sdahq.org. A trade association and research center.

**SOCIETY OF PLASTICS ENGINEERS**
P.O. Box 403, Brookfield CT 06804-0403. 203/775-
0471. World Wide Web address: http://www.4spe.org.
Dedicated to helping members attain higher
professional status through increased scientific,
engineering, and technical knowledge.

**THE SOCIETY OF THE PLASTICS INDUSTRY,
INC.**
1801 K Street NW, Suite 600K, Washington DC
20006. 202/974-5200. Promotes the development of
the plastics industry and enhances public
understanding of its contributions while meeting the
needs of society.

### Directories

**CHEMICAL INDUSTRY DIRECTORY**
State Mutual Book and Periodical Service, Order
Department, 521 Fifth Avenue, 17th Floor, New York
NY 10175. 718/261-1704.

**CHEMICALS DIRECTORY**
Cahners Business Information, 275 Washington
Street, Newton MA 02458. 617/964-3030. World
Wide Web address: http://www.cahners.com.

**DIRECTORY OF CHEMICAL ENGINEERING
CONSULTANTS**
American Institute of Chemical Engineers, 3 Park
Avenue, New York NY 10016. 212/591-7338. Toll-
free phone: 800/242-4363. World Wide Web address:
http://www.aiche.org.

**DIRECTORY OF CHEMICAL PRODUCERS**
SRI International, 333 Ravenswood Avenue, Menlo
Park CA 94025. 650/895-2000. World Wide Web
address: http://www.sri.com.

### Magazines

**CHEMICAL & ENGINEERING NEWS**
American Chemical Society, 1155 16th Street NW,
Washington DC 20036. 202/872-4600. World Wide
Web address: http://www.pubs.acs.org/cen.

**CHEMICAL MARKET REPORTER**
Schnell Publishing Company, 2 Rector Street, 26th
Floor, New York NY 10004. 212/791-4267.

**CHEMICAL WEEK**
888 Seventh Avenue, 26th Floor, New York NY
10106. 212/621-4900. World Wide Web address:
http://www.chemweek.com.

# COMMUNICATIONS: TELECOMMUNICATIONS AND BROADCASTING

*The telecommunications industry continued to evolve in 1998, with consolidation and intense competition between local and long-distance carriers. In reaction to price drops and increased competition across all segments of the industry, mergers and acquisitions have been an industry trend. The proposed mega-merger of AT&T and TCI is an attempt to pool the resources of one of the nation's telephone giants with a leading cable company.*

*The Telecommunications Act of 1996, coupled with promising new wireless technology, opened the door for major long-distance companies to break into the local phone market within their respective regions, which proved a very costly venture. However, a federal court decision to limit the FCC's regulation over long-distance carriers should give businesses more power over prices and the freedom to enter new territories.*

*Competition has increased in the wireless communications industry, which has resulted in lower prices for wireless minutes. According to* Business Week, *the number of wireless subscribers increased from 144.2 million in 1996 to 213.7 million in 1997. Despite the increase in subscribers, it is unlikely smaller wireless operators will fare well amidst the price wars of the larger operators.*

*Internet technologies continue to transform the telecommunications industry as companies begin to offer long-distance and fax services over the Internet. According to Action Information Services, these services will produce $1 billion in revenues by 2001, although companies must satisfy customers' demands for increasingly faster Internet access.*

**AT&T CORPORATION**
295 North Maple Avenue, Basking Ridge NJ 07920. 908/221-6035. **Contact:** Mr. H.W. Burlingame, Executive Vice President of Human Resources. **World Wide Web address:** http://www.att.com. **Description:** AT&T is a major long-distance telephone company which provides domestic and international voice and data communications and management services, telecommunications products, and leasing and financial services. The company manufactures data communications products, computer products, switching and transmission equipment, and components. **NOTE:** Please send resumes to the resume scanning center at 1200 Peachtree Street, Room 7075, Promenade 1, Atlanta GA 30309. **Common positions include:** Telecommunications Analyst. **Corporate headquarters location:** This Location. **Other U.S. locations:** Nationwide. **Subsidiaries include:** AT&T Capital Corporation offers financing and leases and provides consumer credit through its AT&T Universal credit card. **Listed on:** New York Stock Exchange.

**AT&T WIRELESS SERVICES**
15 East Midland Avenue, Paramus NJ 07652. 201/967-3000. **Contact:** Human Resources. **Description:** Provides wireless services including sales, service, and billing.

**BELL ATLANTIC COMMUNICATIONS**
540 Broad Street, Newark NJ 07101. 973/649-9900. **Contact:** Human Resources. **World Wide Web address:** http://www.bell-atl.com. **Description:** A major exchange telephone services provider. The company provides advanced voice and data services and wireless communications throughout the mid-Atlantic and Northeast, and parts of the Southeast and Southwest. Bell Atlantic also publishes telephone directories and is a major cellular telephone service provider. Bell Atlantic offers a paging service, computer services, CPE equity sales, training programs, and various financial and real estate services. The company has investments in Grupo Iusacell, S.A. de C.V. (Mexico); Telecom Corporation of New Zealand Limited; and Bell Communications Research, Inc. Bell Atlantic merged with NYNEX in 1997. **NOTE:** Send resumes to Bell Atlantic

Communications Human Resources, P.O. Box 17505, Arlington VA 22201. Please indicate the state in which you are interested in working.

**BELLCORE (BELL COMMUNICATIONS RESEARCH)**
6 Corporate Place, Piscataway NJ 08854. 732/699-2000. **Contact:** Human Resources. **World Wide Web address:** http://www.bellcore.com. **Description:** Develops, provides, and maintains telecommunications information-networking software and professional services for businesses, governments, and telecommunications carriers. **Common positions include:** Accountant/Auditor; Computer Engineer; Computer Scientist; Financial Analyst; Marketing Specialist; Sales Representative. **Parent company:** Science Applications International Corporation (SAIC).

**DIALOGIC CORPORATION**
1515 Route 10, Parsippany NJ 07050. 973/993-3000. **Contact:** Human Resources. **World Wide Web address:** http://www.dialogic.com. **Description:** Offers computer telephony services that provide telephone network access to computer terminals and information. **Corporate headquarters location:** This Location.

**THE FURST GROUP**
459 Oak Shade Road, Shamong NJ 08088. 609/268-8000. **Contact:** Human Resources. **World Wide Web address:** http://www.furst.com. **Description:** Provides long-distance phone service across the country. Founded in 1989.

**GARDEN STATE CABLE TV**
P.O. Box 5025, Cherry Hill NJ 08034. 609/354-1880. **Physical address:** 1250 Haddonfield Berlin Road, Cherry Hill NJ 08034. **Contact:** Human Resources. **Description:** A cable broadcaster.

**GEOTEK COMMUNICATIONS**
102 Chestnut Ridge Road, Montvale NJ 07645. 201/930-9305. **Fax:** 201/930-9660. **Contact:** Human Resources. **World Wide Web address:** http://www.geotek.com. **Description:** An international provider of wireless communications services and a manufacturer of telecommunications products. With the introduction of GeoNet, a national wireless telecommunications network, the company intends to become an international provider of integrated, multifunction, digital wireless communication services. The company's Wireless Communications Group owns interests in a joint venture that holds commercial rights to digital wireless telecommunication technology developed by an Israeli government agency. Communications Products Group develops, manufactures, and markets telephone and telecommunications peripherals, commercial audio, paging, data dispatch, and power supply products.

**KEPTEL, INC.**
56 Park Road, Tinton Falls NJ 07724. 732/389-8800. **Fax:** 732/460-5483. **Contact:** Peggy Morrissey, Human Resources Manager. **E-mail address:** peggy.morrissey@antec.com. **World Wide Web address:** http://www.antec.com. **Description:** Designs and manufactures telecommunications network interface systems and connection apparatus. These products are primarily needed as a result of the deregulation of customers' premise equipment and the divestiture by AT&T of the Bell Operating Companies. The majority of sales are made directly to the seven Regional Bell Operating Companies. Keptel also manufactures various interconnect and transmission devices used in fiberoptic networks, concentrating on products for standard telephone lines installed for voice transmission. **Common positions include:** Accountant/Auditor; Buyer; Designer; Draftsperson; Electrical/Electronics Engineer; Human Resources Manager; Mechanical Engineer; Purchasing Agent/Manager; Software Engineer. **Educational backgrounds include:** Accounting; Business Administration; Engineering; Finance; Marketing; Physics. **Benefits:** 401(k); Dental Insurance; Disability Coverage; Life Insurance; Medical Insurance; Tuition Assistance. **Corporate headquarters location:** This Location. **Other U.S. locations:** El Paso TX. **Parent company:** ANTEC Corporation. **Operations at this facility include:** Manufacturing; Research and Development; Sales; Testing. **Number of employees at this location:** 140.

**L3 COMMUNICATIONS CORPORATION**
One Federal Street, Camden NJ 08103. 609/338-3000. **Contact:** Human Resources. **Description:** Manufactures communication systems for satellites.

**LUCENT TECHNOLOGIES**
283 King George Road, Room B2C36, Warren NJ 07059. **Contact:** Human Resources. **Description:** This location is a research and development center. Overall, Lucent Technologies manufactures communications products including switching, transmission, fiberoptic cable,

wireless systems, and operations systems to fulfill the needs of telephone companies and other communications services providers.

**LUCENT TECHNOLOGIES**
600-700 Mountain Avenue, Murray Hill NJ 07974. **Contact:** Employment Manager. **World Wide Web address:** http://www.lucent.com. **Description:** Manufactures communications products including switching, transmission, fiberoptic cable, wireless systems, and operations systems to fulfill the needs of telephone companies and other communications services providers. **Corporate headquarters location:** This Location.

**MADGE NETWORKS**
625 Industrial Way West, Eatontown NJ 07724. 732/389-5700. **Fax:** 732/544-9890. **Contact:** Human Resources. **Description:** Manufactures a wide range of video telecommunications equipment including video routers and related equipment.

**MIKROS SYSTEMS CORPORATION**
P.O. Box 7189, Princeton NJ 08543. 609/987-1513. **Contact:** Human Resources. **Description:** Develops communications products for the transmission of digital data over AM and FM radio frequencies.

**MOBILECOMM**
25 Rockwood Place, Englewood NJ 07631. 201/894-8000. **Contact:** Christine Schopperth, Human Resources Manager. **World Wide Web address:** http://www.mobilecomm.com. **Description:** A telecommunications service company providing a wide variety of specialized data- and message-processing and communications services. MobileComm operates a nationwide computer-controlled network which electronically receives, processes, and transmits record and data communications. The company also operates a radio paging business. **Common positions include:** Customer Service Representative; Sales Representative. **Corporate headquarters location:** Fort Lee NJ.

**MOBILECOMM**
One Executive Drive, Suite 500, Fort Lee NJ 07024. 201/224-9200. **Contact:** Human Resources. **Description:** This location houses administrative offices. Overall, MobileComm is a telecommunications service company, providing a wide variety of specialized data- and message-processing and communications services. The company operates a nationwide computer-controlled network which electronically receives, processes, and transmits record and data communications. MobileComm also operates a radio paging business. **Corporate headquarters location:** This Location.

**NEXTEL COMMUNICATIONS**
201 Route 17 North, Rutherford NJ 07070. 201/438-1400. **Contact:** Human Resources. **Description:** This location provides customer service for cellular phones. Overall, Nextel Communications is engaged in the specialized mobile radio (SMR) wireless communications business. These services permit the company's customers to dispatch fleets of vehicles and place calls using their two-way mobile radios to or from any telephone in North America through interconnection with the public switched telephone network. Nextel Communications also sells and rents two-way mobile radio equipment and provides related installation, repair, and maintenance services. **Other U.S. locations:** Fort Lauderdale FL; McLean VA.

**RCN CORPORATION**
105 Carnegie Center, Princeton NJ 08540. 609/734-3700. **Fax:** 609/734-3789. **Contact:** Employment Administrator. **World Wide Web address:** http://www.rcn.com. **Description:** A full-service communications company that provides customers with cable, Internet, long-distance, and local telephone services. **NOTE:** Entry-level positions and second and third shifts are offered. **Common positions include:** Accountant; Administrative Assistant; Computer Programmer; Customer Service Rep.; Financial Analyst; General Manager; Graphic Artist; Human Resources Manager; Internet Services Manager; Market Research Analyst; MIS Specialist; Paralegal; Sales Executive; Sales Rep.; Typist/Word Processor; Webmaster. **Educational backgrounds include:** Accounting; Marketing; Software Tech. Support. **Benefits:** 401(k); Dental Insurance; Disability Coverage; Flexible Schedule; Life Insurance; Medical Insurance; Profit Sharing; Tuition Assistance. **Special programs:** Co-ops. **Corporate headquarters location:** This Location. **Other U.S. locations:** DC; MA; NY; PA; VA. **Subsidiaries include:** Starpower LLC. **Listed on:** NASDAQ. **Stock exchange symbol:** RCNC. **Annual sales/revenues:** $51 - $100 million. **Number of employees at this location:** 200. **Number of employees nationwide:** 1,400. **Number of projected hires for 1998 - 1999 at this location:** 100.

124/The New Jersey JobBank

## RFL ELECTRONICS INC.

353 Powerville Road, Boonton Township NJ 07005. 973/334-3100. **Contact:** Personnel Manager. **World Wide Web address:** http://www.rflelect.com. **Description:** Designs and manufactures a wide range of telecommunication and teleprotection products for the electric, water, gas, and telephone utilities; railroads; mines; pipelines; airlines; oil drilling and refining firms; private contractors; OEMs; and government agencies. **Common positions include:** Accountant/Auditor; Administrator; Applications Engineer; Assembly Worker; Buyer; Draftsperson; Electrical/ Electronics Engineer; Electronics Technician; Industrial Engineer; Sales Engineer. **Educational backgrounds include:** Accounting; Business Administration; Computer Science; Engineering; Finance.

## SIEMENS BUSINESS COMMUNICATION SYSTEMS, INC.

3 Computer Drive, Cherry Hill NJ 08003. 609/424-2400. **Contact:** Human Resources. **E-mail address:** careers@siemenscom.com. **World Wide Web address:** http://www.siemenscom.com. **Description:** This location is a manufacturing facility. Overall, Siemens Business Communication Systems is a leading provider of communications and communications integration technology, including OfficePoint ISDN systems, a high-speed integration product enabling transmission and reception of voice, data, image, and video over a single phone line. **Corporate headquarters location:** Santa Clara CA. **Parent company:** Siemens A.G. (Germany). **Annual sales/revenues:** More than $100 million. **Number of employees worldwide:** 24,000.

## TIMEPLEX GROUP

400 Chestnut Ridge Road, Woodcliff Lake NJ 07675. 201/391-1111. **Toll-free phone:** 800/776-2677. **Fax:** 201/391-0961. **Contact:** Beverly Petrone, Manager of Corporate Human Resources. **World Wide Web address:** http://www.timeplex.com. **Description:** A leader in enterprise networking solutions for voice, data, and video traffic in the telecommunications industry. Founded in 1969. **Common positions include:** Electrical/Electronics Engineer; Industrial Engineer; Software Engineer; Systems Analyst. **Educational backgrounds include:** Business Administration; Communications; Computer Science; Engineering; Finance; Marketing. **Benefits:** 401(k); Dental Insurance; Disability Coverage; Employee Discounts; Life Insurance; Medical Insurance; Profit Sharing; Tuition Assistance. **Special programs:** Internships. **Office hours:** Monday - Friday, 8:30 a.m. - 5:15 p.m. **Corporate headquarters location:** This Location. **International locations:** Worldwide. **Operations at this facility include:** Administration; Manufacturing; Research and Development; Sales; Service. **Number of employees at this location:** 180. **Number of employees nationwide:** 730. **Number of employees worldwide:** 1,000.

## WCTC/WMGQ

78 Veronica Avenue, Somerset NJ 08873. 732/249-2600. **Fax:** 732/249-9010. **Contact:** Maribell Lytle, Administrative Assistant. **Description:** A news, information, and entertainment radio station. **Parent company:** Greater Media, Inc.

## WESTERN UNION CORPORATION

One Mack Centre Drive, Paramus NJ 07652. 201/986-5100. **Contact:** Human Resources. **World Wide Web address:** http://www.westernunion.com. **Description:** Provides telecommunications systems and services to business, government, and the public. The company operates a nationwide communications network that includes Westar satellites in orbit.

*Note: Because addresses and telephone numbers of smaller companies can change rapidly, we recommend you call each company to verify the information below before inquiring about job opportunities. Mass mailings are not recommended.*

**Additional small employers:**

**CABLE/PAY TELEVISION SERVICES**

**Cablevision**
PO Box 58, Belmar NJ 07719-0058. 732/681-8222.

**Cablevision**
5 Legion Dr, Cresskill NJ 07626-2109. 201/569-3720.

**Cablevision**
360 Central Ave, Newark NJ 07103-2808. 973/622-0884.

**Clear TV Cable**
PO Box 847, Toms River NJ 08754-0847. 732/286-2971.

**Comcast Cablevision**
403 South St, Eatontown NJ 07724-1867. 732/739-3100.

**Comcast Cablevision**
800 Rahway Ave, Union NJ 07083-6652. 732/602-7400.

**Pinnacle Cable Services Inc.**
5 Greentree Ctr, Marlton NJ 08053-3422. 609/983-8330.

**Suburban Cable TV Co. Inc.**
901 W Leeds Ave, Pleasantville NJ 08232. 609/641-6700.

**TCI**
275 Centennial Ave, Piscataway NJ 08854-3909. 732/457-0131.

**TCI**
67B Mountain Blvd, Warren NJ
07059-5678. 732/356-1300.

**Time Warner Cable**
200 Roosevelt Pl, Palisades Park
NJ 07650-1177. 201/585-2737.

**COMMUNICATIONS
EQUIPMENT**

**Alcatel Data Networks Inc.**
PO Box 8900, Mount Laurel NJ
08054. 609/273-2300.

**Axiom Inc.**
351 New Albany Rd,
Moorestown NJ 08057-1117.
609/866-1000.

**Celwave**
2 Ryan Rd, Marlboro NJ 07746-
2438. 732/462-1880.

**Integrated Network Corp.**
PO Box 6875, Bridgewater NJ
08807-0875. 908/218-1600.

**Lucent Technologies**
475 South St, Morristown NJ
07960-6453. 973/606-2000.

**Phillips Consumer
Communications**
246 Industrial Way W, Eatontown
NJ 07724-2206. 732/544-3030.

**Pyrotronics**
8 Fernwood Rd, Florham Park NJ
07932-1906. 973/822-1010.

**Pyrotronics**
8 Ridgedale Ave, Cedar Knolls
NJ 07927-1104. 973/267-1300.

**RF Products Inc.**
Davis & Copewood Sts, Camden
NJ 08103. 609/365-5500.

**Wheelock Inc.**
273 Branchport Ave, Long
Branch NJ 07740-6830. 732/222-
6880.

**MISC. COMMUNICATIONS
SERVICES**

**GE Americom**
4 Research Way, Princeton NJ
08540-6618. 609/987-4000.

**ITT Federal Services Corp.**
500 Plainfield Ave, Edison NJ
08817-2515. 732/985-4800.

**RADIO BROADCASTING
STATIONS**

**Nassau Broadcasting Partners
LP**
619 Alexander Rd, Princeton NJ
08540-6003. 609/924-1515.

**New Wave Communications LP**
PO Box 2069, Asbury Park NJ
07712-2069. 732/922-8282.

**WDVR - FM 89.7**
PO Box 191, Sergeantsville NJ
08557. 609/397-1620.

**WMNB**
1 Bridge Plz N, Ste 145, Fort Lee
NJ 07024-7502. 201/461-6667.

**WPRB-FM 103.3**
PO Box 342, Princeton NJ 08542.
609/258-3655.

**TELEGRAPH AND OTHER
MESSAGE
COMMUNICATIONS**

**Q Net Inc.**
329 Alfred Ave, Teaneck NJ
07666-5755. 201/837-5100.

**Western Union**
201 Centennial Ave, Piscataway
NJ 08854-3909. 732/885-4000.

**Xpedite Systems Inc.**
1 Industrial Way, Bldg D,
Eatontown NJ 07724-2255.
732/389-3900.

**TELEPHONE
COMMUNICATIONS**

**AT&T**
400 Interpace Pkwy, Parsippany
NJ 07054-1117. 973/331-4002.

**Bell Atlantic-New Jersey Inc.**
1609 Pacific Ave, Atlantic City
NJ 08401-6910. 609/344-9959.

**Bell Atlantic-New Jersey Inc.**
315 N Florida Ave, Atlantic City
NJ 08401-3914. 609/641-9900.

**Bell Atlantic-New Jersey Inc.**
3500 Pacific Ave, Wildwood NJ
08260-4828. 609/696-9950.

**C-Tec Fiber Systems of NJ**
105 Carnegie Ctr, Princeton NJ
08540-6251. 609/734-3700.

**LDDS Worldcom**
Rural Route 38, Ste 201, Cherry
Hill NJ 08002. 609/661-4027.

**Locus Corp.**
2160 N Central Rd, Ste 302, Fort
Lee NJ 07024-7547. 201/585-
0400.

**Mitel Inc.**
15000 Commerce Pkwy, Mount
Laurel NJ 08054-2212. 609/273-
2910.

**MobileComm**
65 Challenger Rd, Ridgefield
Park NJ 07660-2104. 201/440-
8400.

**Omnipoint Communications
Inc.**
16 Wing Dr, Cedar Knolls NJ
07927-1007. 973/257-2400.

**Pagenet**
70 Wood Ave, 4th Fl, Iselin NJ
08830. 732/603-7200.

**SkyTel**
1680 State Route 23, Wayne NJ
07470-7501. 973/305-6000.

**Teleport Communications
Group**
437 Ridge Rd, Dayton NJ 08810-
1323. 732/392-2000.

**Total-Tel USA Communications**
PO Box 449, Little Falls NJ
07424-0449. 973/812-1100.

**TELEVISION
BROADCASTING STATIONS**

**CNBC Inc.**
2200 Fletcher Ave, Fort Lee NJ
07024-5005. 201/585-2622.

**New Jersey Public Broadcasting**
PO Box CN7777, Trenton NJ
08625. 609/777-5000.

**WNJU-TV Broadcasting Corp.**
47 Industrial Ave, Teterboro NJ
07608-1002. 201/288-5550.

**WWOR-TV**
9 Broadcast Plz, Secaucus NJ
07094-2913. 201/348-0009.

**WXTV Channel 41**
500 Frank W. Burr Blvd, Teaneck
NJ 07666-6701. 201/287-4200.

**For more information on career opportunities in the communications industries:**

Associations

**ACADEMY OF TELEVISION ARTS &
SCIENCES**
5220 Lankershim Boulevard, North Hollywood CA
91601. 818/754-2800. World Wide Web address:
http://www.emmys.org.

**AMERICAN DISC JOCKEY ASSOCIATION**
297 Route 72 West, Suite C-120, Manahawkin NJ
08050-2980. 609/978-2180. World Wide Web
address: http://www.adja.org. A membership
organization for professional disc jockeys that
publishes a newsletter of current events and new
products.

**AMERICAN WOMEN IN RADIO AND TELEVISION, INC.**
1650 Tysons Boulevard, Suite 200, McLean VA 22102. 703/506-3290. World Wide Web address: http://www.awrt.org. A national, nonprofit professional organization for the advancement of women who work in electronic media and related fields. Services include *News and Views,* a fax newsletter transmitted biweekly to members; *Careerline,* a national listing of job openings available to members only; and the AWRT Foundation, which supports charitable and educational programs and annual awards.

**THE COMPETITIVE TELECOMMUNICATIONS ASSOCIATION (COMPTEL)**
1900 M Street NW, Suite 800, Washington DC 20036. 202/296-6650. World Wide Web address: http://www.comptel.org. A national association providing a wide variety of resources including telecommunications trade shows.

**INTERNATIONAL TELEVISION ASSOCIATION**
6311 North O'Connor Road, Suite 230, Irving TX 75309. 972/869-1112. World Wide Web address: http://www.itva.org. Membership required.

**NATIONAL ASSOCIATION OF BROADCASTERS**
1771 N Street NW, Washington DC 20036. 202/429-5300, ext. 5490. Fax: 202/429-5343. World Wide Web address: http://www.nab.org. Provides employment information.

**NATIONAL CABLE TELEVISION ASSN.**
1724 Massachusetts Avenue NW, Washington DC 20036-1969. 202/775-3669. Fax: 202/775-3695. World Wide Web address: http://www.ncta.com. A trade association. Publications include *Cable Television Developments, Secure Signals,* and *Kids and Cable.*

**PROMAX INTERNATIONAL**
2029 Century Park East, Suite 555, Los Angeles CA 90067. 310/788-7600. Fax: 310/788-7616. A nonprofit organization for radio, film, television, video, and other broadcasting professionals. Ask for the jobline.

**U.S. TELEPHONE ASSOCIATION**
1401 H Street NW, Suite 600, Washington DC 20005. 202/326-7300. World Wide Web address: http://www.usta.org. A trade association for local telephone companies.

**Magazines**

**BROADCASTING AND CABLE**
Broadcasting Publications Inc., 1705 DeSales Street NW, Washington DC 20036. 202/659-2340.

**ELECTRONIC MEDIA**
Crain Communications, 740 North Rush Street, Chicago IL 60611-2590. 312/649-5200.

**Online Services**

**BROADCAST PROFESSIONALS FORUM**
Go: BPForum. A CompuServe discussion group for professionals in radio and television.

**CPB JOBLINE**
World Wide Web address: http://www.cpb.org/jobline/index.html. The Corporation for Public Broadcasting, a nonprofit company, operates this site which provides a list of job openings in the public radio and television industries.

**JOURNALISM FORUM**
Go: Jforum. A CompuServe discussion group for journalists in print, radio, or television.

**ON-LINE DISC JOCKEY ASSOCIATION**
World Wide Web address: http://www.odja.com. Provides members with insurance, Internet advertising, a magazine, and networking resources. This site also posts job opportunities.

# COMPUTER HARDWARE, SOFTWARE, AND SERVICES

*As the computer industry's expansion continues to gain strength in a diverse and competitive marketplace, a plethora of new products and services will open up even more opportunities for employment into the next decade. The Bureau of Labor Statistics projects that through 2006 four of the ten fastest-growing occupations will be in the computer field, from desktop publishers, with an anticipated growth rate of 74 percent, to various computer scientists, with an anticipated growth rate of 118 percent. The number of computer repair positions will increase with rising hardware sales, and computer programmers will be in high demand as companies strive to keep up with technology and upgrade systems. Projections also indicate an additional 520,000 systems analysts positions by 2006. Computer operators, however, will see a decline in opportunities due to automation and advances in user-friendly software.*

*The demand for software, particularly for education, entertainment, and communications, increased by 12 percent in 1997, and had increased by 3 percent through the first two quarters of 1998. Internet-related software sales are expected to double each year through 2000, according to the U.S. Department of Labor.*

*In 1998, Microsoft, though still a software powerhouse, was bumped out by SAP as the leading software company. Microsoft continues to fight off anti-trust accusations brought by the U.S. Department of Justice. Intel, having derived much success from its Pentium chips, has started to lose market share to chips such as the AMD K6, a leading alternative used in the booming sub-$1,000 computer market. Apple hit it big in 1998 with the introduction of the iMac, which drove the company's market share from 6.8 percent to 13.5 percent.*

*Telephone and cable companies are investing in new technologies, including ASDL (asynchronous digital subscriber line), that promise to link users to the Internet up to 200 times faster than traditional modems. According to Dataquest Inc., 80 percent of the nation's households will have these fast-access technologies available by 2001.*

*Mainframe programmers and consultants are being actively hired to correct the "Year 2000 problem" and will likely stay in demand after the January 2000 deadline. Personnel who can read old programming codes are needed, and many qualified workers from other segments of the computer industry are leaving their current jobs to work as Year 2000 consultants.*

**ACI AUTOMATED CONCEPTS, INC.**
90 Woodbridge Center Drive, Suite 400, Woodbridge NJ 07095. 732/602-0200. **Contact:** Human Resources. **World Wide Web address:** http://www.autocon.com. **Description:** Provides systems integration services.

**AM BEST COMPANY**
AM Best Road, Oldwick NJ 08858. 908/439-2200. **Fax:** 908/439-3296. **Contact:** Human Resources. **World Wide Web address:** http://www.ambest.com. **Description:** A database products

firm offering software, CD-ROMs, and diskette support products to the insurance industry. **Corporate headquarters location:** This Location.

### ACTEL CORPORATION
200 Valley Drive, Suite 300, Arlington NJ 07856. 973/770-4700. **Contact:** Human Resources. **World Wide Web address:** http://www.actel.com. **Description:** This location provides engineering services. Overall, Actel Corporation manufactures field programmable gate arrays and the software to program them. **Common positions include:** Administrative Assistant; Applications Engineer; Design Engineer; Electrical/Electronics Engineer; Human Resources Manager; Software Engineer; Systems Analyst. **Corporate headquarters location:** Sunnyvale CA. **Listed on:** NASDAQ. **Stock exchange symbol:** ACTL. **Number of employees worldwide:** 350.

### ADVANTAGE KBS
One Ethel Road, Suite 106B, Edison NJ 08817. 732/287-2236. **Contact:** Human Resources. **Description:** Develops problem resolution software.

### AFFINITI
16 Portland Road, Highlands NJ 07732. 732/872-2240. **Contact:** Human Resources Department. **Description:** Provides systems integration services and software development.

### ALPHANET SOLUTIONS, INC.
7 Ridgedale Avenue, Cedar Knolls NJ 07927. 973/267-0088. **Fax:** 973/267-5361. **Contact:** John Warren, Vice President of Human Resources. **World Wide Web address:** http://www. alphanetcorp.com. **Description:** A leading systems integrator. The company's services include computer network design, installation and administration, help desk support, technical education, cabling and telecommunications sales and service, computer product sales and services, and Internet services. Clients include many small and mid-range companies, national and global *Fortune* 1000 companies, and large government agencies. Founded in 1984. **Common positions include:** Computer Programmer; Internet Services Manager; MIS Specialist; Systems Analyst; Systems Manager; Webmaster. **Corporate headquarters location:** This Location. **Other U.S. locations:** NY; PA. **Listed on:** NASDAQ. **Annual sales/revenues:** More than $100 million.

### AMDAHL CORPORATION
85 Challenger Road, 3rd Floor, Ridgefield Park NJ 07660. 201/229-4400. **Contact:** Human Resources. **E-mail address:** jobs@amdahl.com. **World Wide Web address:** http://www.amdahl. com. **Description:** This location is engaged in sales, service, and support. Overall, Amdahl designs, develops, manufactures, markets, and services large-scale, high-performance, general purpose computer systems including both hardware and software. Customers are primarily large corporations, government agencies, and large universities with high-volume data processing requirements. Amdahl markets more than 470 different systems. **Corporate headquarters location:** Sunnyvale CA.

### ANALYSIS INTERNATIONAL CORPORATION (AiC)
111 Wood Avenue South, Iselin NJ 08830. 973/555-9844. **Contact:** Human Resources. **World Wide Web address:** http://www.analysts.com. **Description:** AiC is an international computer consulting firm. The company assists clients in analyzing, designing, and developing systems in a variety of industries using different programming languages and software. **Corporate headquarters location:** Minneapolis MN.

### ANDERSEN CONSULTING
10 Waterview Boulevard, Parsippany NJ 07054. 973/316-4000. **Contact:** Human Resources. **World Wide Web address:** http://www.andersenconsulting.com. **Description:** This location of Andersen Consulting is engaged in information systems services. Overall, Andersen Consulting's service line includes systems building and systems integration, change management services, technology services, strategic services, software products, and computer operations management and systems support. **Number of employees nationwide:** 5,600.

### ANSOFT CORPORATION
669 River Drive, Suite 200, Elmwood Park NJ 07407. 201/796-2003. **Contact:** Human Resources. **World Wide Web address:** http://www.ansoft.com. **Description:** Develops and distributes circuit design software.

### ASPECT COMPUTER CORPORATION
21 World's Fair Drive, Somerset NJ 08873. 732/563-1304. **Contact:** Human Resources. **World Wide Web address:** http://www.aspectcom.com. **Description:** Manufactures computers.

**BEECHWOOD**
100 Walnut Avenue, Clark NJ 07066. 732/382-5400. **Contact:** Human Resources. **Description:** Develops customized software for the telecommunications industry.

**BELLCORE (BELL COMMUNICATIONS RESEARCH)**
6 Corporate Place, Piscataway NJ 08854. 732/699-2000. **Contact:** Human Resources. **World Wide Web address:** http://www.bellcore.com. **Description:** Develops, provides, and maintains telecommunications information-networking software and professional services for businesses, governments, and telecommunications carriers. **Common positions include:** Accountant/Auditor; Computer Engineer; Computer Scientist; Financial Analyst; Marketing Specialist; Sales Representative. **Parent company:** Science Applications International Corporation (SAIC).

**BLUEBIRD AUTO RENTAL SYSTEMS INC.**
700 Lanidex Plaza, Parsippany NJ 07054. 973/984-1014. **Contact:** Human Resources. **World Wide Web address:** http://www.barsnet.com. **Description:** Designs computer applications for auto rental agencies.

**BLUESTONE INC.**
1000 Briggs Road, Mount Laurel NJ 08054. 609/727-4600. **Toll-free phone:** 800/555-0045. **Fax:** 609/727-0124. **Contact:** Liz Walsh, Human Resources Generalist. **World Wide Web address:** http://www.bluestone.com. **Description:** Develops computer technology programs and provides user training. Bluestone offers Web-based software including dynamic Web applications and GUIs. The company also offers training programs in many states. Founded in 1989. **NOTE:** Entry-level positions are offered. **Common positions include:** Administrative Assistant; Marketing Specialist; MIS Specialist; Sales Engineer; Sales Representative; Software Engineer. **Educational backgrounds include:** Computer Science; Engineering. **Benefits:** 401(k); Dental Insurance; Disability Coverage; Flexible Schedule; Life Insurance; Medical Insurance. **Special programs:** Training. **Corporate headquarters location:** This Location. **Other U.S. locations:** CA. **Listed on:** Privately held. **Annual sales/revenues:** $21 - $50 million. **Number of employees at this location:** 155. **Number of employees nationwide:** 275.

**CNS INC.**
100 Ford Road, Denville NJ 07834. 973/625-4056. **Fax:** 973/625-9489. **Contact:** Human Resources Department. **World Wide Web address:** http://www.cns-nj.com. **Description:** A full-service computer hardware repair center.

**CADAPULT GRAPHIC SYSTEMS**
110 Commerce Drive, Allendale NJ 07401. 201/236-1100. **Contact:** Human Resources. **Description:** Develops software. Cadapult Graphic Systems also sells, services, and provides support for its computer graphic systems.

**CANTERBURY INFORMATION TECHNOLOGY, INC.**
1600 Medford Plaza, Medford NJ 08055. 609/953-0044. **Fax:** 609/953-0062. **Contact:** Darcy Teibel, Administrative Assistant. **World Wide Web address:** http://www.canterburyciti.com. **Description:** A corporate training company providing information technology services. Training covers entry-level vocational, managerial, executive, and technical areas. **Corporate headquarters location:** This Location. **Subsidiaries include:** ATM/Canterbury Corp., a software development and consulting firm; CALC/Canterbury Corp., a computer software training company; MSI/Canterbury Corp., a management, sales, and communication training company; ProSoft/Canterbury Corp., a provider of technical staffing, applications development, and corporate training.

**CAP GEMINI AMERICA**
111 Wood Avenue South, Iselin NJ 08830. 732/906-0400. **Contact:** Human Resources, **World Wide Web address:** http://www.usa.capgemini.com. **Description:** A leading provider of information technology consulting services. CGA's principal focus is on three major activities: consultancy, implementation, and systems integration. **Other U.S. locations:** Nationwide. **Parent company:** The Cap Gemini Sogeti Group is a top-ranked provider of information technology services throughout Europe and its major markets. **Number of employees nationwide:** 3,000.

**CIBER, INC.**
Iselin Metro Park, 70 Wood Avenue, Iselin NJ 08830. 732/968-9310. **Toll-free phone:** 800/736-9310. **Fax:** 800/270-4946. **Contact:** Human Resources. **World Wide Web address:** http://www.ciber.com. **Description:** Provides consulting for client/server development, mainframe and legacy systems, industry-specific analysis, application-specific analysis, and network development. **Common positions include:** Account Representative; Applications Engineer; Computer Operator; Computer Programmer; Database Manager; Internet Services Manager; Project

Manager; Sales Executive; Sales Manager; Sales Representative; Secretary; Systems Analyst; Systems Manager. **Educational backgrounds include:** Computer Science. **Benefits:** 401(k); Dental Insurance; Disability Coverage; Life Insurance; Medical Insurance; Tuition Assistance.

## COMMVAULT SYSTEMS
2 Crescent Place, Oceanport NJ 07757. 732/870-4000. **Contact:** Human Resources. **World Wide Web address:** http://www.commvault.com. **Description:** Develops and sells software for businesses with computer backup systems.

## COMPUCOM INC.
100 Eagle Rock Avenue, East Hanover NJ 07936. 973/581-6000. **Contact:** Human Resources. **World Wide Web address:** http://www.compucom.com. **Description:** A leading PC integration services company providing product procurement, advanced configuration, network integration, and support services to large businesses. **NOTE:** Please send resumes to Human Resources, 7171 Forest Lane, Dallas TX 75230. **Corporate headquarters location:** Dallas TX. **Other U.S. locations:** Nationwide.

## COMPUTER ASSOCIATES INTERNATIONAL, INC.
2 Executive Drive, Fort Lee NJ 07024. 201/592-0009. **Contact:** Personnel. **World Wide Web address:** http://www.cai.com. **Description:** This location sells software, offers technical support, and is home to the marketing department. Overall, Computer Associates International develops, markets, and supports more than 300 integrated products including systems and database management, business applications, application development, and consumer solutions. Software products include systems management software, information management software, business application software, and desktop software. Computer Associates International, Inc. serves many of the world's businesses, governments, research organizations, and educational organizations. Founded in 1976. **Corporate headquarters location:** Islandia NY. **Other U.S. locations:** Nationwide. **Listed on:** New York Stock Exchange. **Annual sales/revenues:** More than $100 million. **Number of employees nationwide:** 4,000. **Number of employees worldwide:** 9,000.

## COMPUTER ASSOCIATES INTERNATIONAL, INC.
2000 Midlantic Drive, Mount Laurel NJ 08054. 609/273-9100. **Contact:** Human Resources. **World Wide Web address:** http://www.cai.com. **Description:** This location sells software and offers technical support. Overall, Computer Associates International develops, markets, and supports more than 300 integrated products including systems and database management, business applications, application development, and consumer solutions. Software products include systems management software, information management software, business application software, and desktop software. Computer Associates International, Inc. serves many of the world's businesses, governments, research organizations, and educational organizations. Founded in 1976. **Special programs:** Internships. **Corporate headquarters location:** Islandia NY. **Other U.S. locations:** Nationwide. **Listed on:** New York Stock Exchange. **Annual sales/revenues:** More than $100 million. **Number of employees nationwide:** 4,000. **Number of employees worldwide:** 9,000.

## COMPUTER HORIZONS CORPORATION
49 Old Bloomfield Avenue, Mountain Lakes NJ 07046. 973/402-7400. **Contact:** Human Resources. **World Wide Web address:** http://www.chccorp.com. **Description:** A full-service technology solutions company offering contract staffing, outsourcing, re-engineering, migration, downsizing, and network management. Founded in 1969. **Corporate headquarters location:** This Location. **Other U.S. locations:** Nationwide. **Subsidiaries include:** Birla Horizons International Ltd.; Horizons Consulting, Inc.; Strategic Outsourcing Services, Inc.; Unified Systems Solutions, Inc. **Listed on:** NASDAQ. **Number of employees nationwide:** 1,500. **Number of employees worldwide:** 3,000.

## COMPUTER SCIENCES CORPORATION
304 West Route 38, P.O. Box 1038, Moorestown NJ 08057-0902. 609/234-1166. **Contact:** Human Resources Department. **World Wide Web address:** http://www.csc.com. **Description:** This location configures software. Overall, Computer Sciences Corporation primarily serves the U.S. government. The four sectors of the company include the Systems Group division, the Consulting division, the Industry Services Group, and the CSC divisions. The Systems Group division designs, engineers, and integrates computer-based systems and communications systems, providing all the hardware, software, training, and related elements necessary to operate a system. The Consulting division includes consulting and technical services in the development of computer and communication systems to non-federal organizations. The Industry Services Group provides service to health care, insurance, and financial service industries, as well as providing large-scale claim processing and other insurance-related services. CSC Health Care markets business systems and services to the managed health care industry, clinics, and physicians. CSC Enterprises provides

consumer credit reports and account management services to credit grantors. **Corporate headquarters location:** El Segundo CA. **Other U.S. locations:** Nationwide.

## COMPUTER SYSTEMS REPAIR
190 Jony Drive, Carlstadt NJ 07072. 201/842-8300. **Contact:** Ms. Dana Hobbs, Human Resources. **World Wide Web address:** http://www.csr.com. **Description:** Offers computer repair services.

## COMPUTRON SOFTWARE INC.
301 Route 17 North, 12th Floor, Rutherford NJ 07070. 201/935-3400. **Contact:** Human Resources. **World Wide Web address:** http://www.ctronsoft.com. **Description:** Develops and markets various financial software products.

## COMTREX SYSTEMS CORPORATION
102 Executive Drive, Suite 1, Moorestown NJ 08057. 609/778-0090. **Fax:** 609/778-9322. **Contact:** Lisa Mudrick, Human Resources. **World Wide Web address:** http://www.comtrex.com. **Description:** Specializes in point-of-sale solutions for the food service and hospitality industries. The company designs, develops, assembles, and markets electronic terminals and computer software which provide retailers with transaction processing, in-store controls, and management information. Comtrex's products are sophisticated terminals which combine traditional cash register functions with the data gathering capabilities of a computerized system. The company develops and licenses the use of software programs which provide enhanced reporting capabilities for its terminals systems and facilitate local and remote polling of information transfer between computers and the company's terminal systems. Founded in 1981. **Corporate headquarters location:** This Location. **Listed on:** NASDAQ. **Stock exchange symbol:** COMX.

## CRADEN PERIPHERALS
7860 Airport Highway, Pennsauken NJ 08109. 609/488-0700. **Contact:** Human Resources. **World Wide Web address:** http://www.craden.com. **Description:** Manufactures and markets printers under the Craden brand name.

## DGM&S INC.
1025 Briggs Road, Suite 100, Mount Laurel NJ 08054. 609/866-1212. **Contact:** Human Resources. **World Wide Web address:** http://www.dgms.com. **Description:** Develops middleware applications.

## DMR CONSULTING GROUP INC.
333 Thornall Road, Edison NJ 08837-2246. 732/549-4100. **Fax:** 732/549-2375. **Contact:** Recruiting Administrator. **World Wide Web address:** http://www.dmr.com. **Description:** Provides computer consulting services including outsourcing solutions and systems integration. **Corporate headquarters location:** This Location.

## DATA DELAY DEVICES INC.
3 Mount Prospect Avenue, Clifton NJ 07013. 973/773-2299. **Contact:** Human Resources. **World Wide Web address:** http://www.datadelay.com. **Description:** Manufactures delay lines.

## DATA GENERAL CORPORATION
Park 80 West Plaza 1, Saddle Brook NJ 07663. 201/587-8700. **Contact:** Human Resources. **World Wide Web address:** http://www.dg.com. **Description:** This location is a sales office. Overall, Data General designs, manufactures, and markets general purpose computer systems and related products and services including peripheral equipment, software services, training, and maintenance. Data General markets directly to end users and OEMs and offers six product lines whose applications include industrial manufacturing for controlling discrete assembly line operations, monitoring continuous production processes, testing, production planning, inventory management, and environmental surveillance. The company's products are also used in business data systems. **Corporate headquarters location:** Westborough MA. **Other U.S. locations:** Nationwide.

## DATA SYSTEMS & SOFTWARE INC.
200 Route 17, Mahwah NJ 07430. 201/529-2026. **Contact:** Human Resources. **Description:** A leading provider of consulting and development services for computer software and systems to high-technology companies in Israel and the United States, principally in the area of embedded real-time systems.

## DATACOLOR INTERNATIONAL
5 Princess Road, Lawrenceville NJ 08648. 609/924-2189. **Contact:** Human Resources. **Description:** A manufacturer of color matching equipment and software.

## DATARAM CORPORATION

P.O. Box 7528, Princeton NJ 08543-7528. 609/799-0071. **Toll-free phone:** 800/DATARAM. **Fax:** 609/897-7021. **Contact:** Dawn Craft, Human Resources Administrator. **E-mail address:** dcraft@dataram.com. **World Wide Web address:** http://www.dataram.com. **Description:** Develops memory and storage products that improve the performance of computer systems. The company offers a broad range of memory and storage products for workstations, servers, and minicomputers. Dataram primarily serves HP, DEC, Sun, and IBM users in industries including manufacturing, finance, government, telecommunications, utilities, research, and education. **Common positions include:** Accountant; Design Engineer; Designer; Sales Representative; Test Engineer. **Benefits:** 401(k); Dental Insurance; Disability Coverage; Life Insurance; Medical Insurance; Tuition Assistance. **Corporate headquarters location:** This Location. **International locations:** Singapore; Twyford, Berkshire, England. **Listed on:** American Stock Exchange. **Stock exchange symbol:** DTM. **Number of employees at this location:** 55.

## DATATECH INDUSTRIES INC.

23 Madison Road, Fairfield NJ 07004. 973/808-4000. **Contact:** Human Resources. **World Wide Web address:** http://www.datatech.com. **Description:** Specializes in installing mainframes and networking hardware for businesses.

## DELTA COMPUTEC, INC. (DCI)

900 Huyler Street, Teterboro NJ 07608. 201/440-8585. **Contact:** Recruiting. **Description:** Provides businesses with integrated networking solutions.

## DESKTOP ENGINEERING INTERNATIONAL, INC.

1200 MacArthur Boulevard, Mahwah NJ 07430. 201/818-9700. **Contact:** Human Resources. **Description:** Designs and produces software for use in mechanical and structural engineering.

## ECCS, INC.

One Sheila Drive, Tinton Falls NJ 07724. 732/747-6995. **Contact:** Sharon Wallace, Director of Human Resources. **World Wide Web address:** http://www.eccs.com. **Description:** Designs and configures computer systems. ECCS's mass storage enhancement products include RAID (Redundant Array of Independent Disks) products and technology; external disk, optical, and tape systems; internal disk and tape storage devices; and RAM. The company also provides related technical services. **Corporate headquarters location:** This Location.

## EASTMAN KODAK COMPANY - HEALTH IMAGING

One Pearl Court, Allendale NJ 07401. 201/760-5627. **Fax:** 201/760-5707. **Contact:** Lisa Kessler, Staffing Specialist. **E-mail address:** lkessler@kodak.com. **World Wide Web address:** http://www.kodak.com. **Description:** Develops software for client/server image management systems for use with medical ultrasound instrumentation. **Common positions include:** Administrative Assistant; Applications Engineer; Computer Engineer; Computer Programmer; Computer Scientist; Computer Technician; Database Administrator; Quality Assurance Engineer; Secretary; Software Engineer. **Educational backgrounds include:** Computer Science; Engineering. **Corporate headquarters location:** Rochester NY. **Number of employees at this location:** 85. **Number of employees nationwide:** 125.

## EXECUTIVE IMAGING SYSTEMS INC.

P.O. Box 2380, Cherry Hill NJ 08034. 609/424-5898. **Contact:** Human Resources. **World Wide Web address:** http://www.1eis.com. **Description:** Resells computers, facsimiles, printers, and peripherals.

## FDS INTERNATIONAL

18 West Ridgewood Avenue, Paramus NJ 07652. 201/843-0800. **Contact:** Human Resources Department. **World Wide Web address:** http://www.fdsinternational.com. **Description:** Develops transportation and custom brokerage software.

## FORMATION, INC.

121 Whittendale Drive, Moorestown NJ 08057. 609/234-5020. **Fax:** 609/234-8543. **Contact:** Kathy Cava, Manager of Human Resources. **World Wide Web address:** http://www.formation.com. **Description:** Designs and manufactures communications products and real-time, high-performance storage and retrieval systems. The company's products are capable of integrating a number of inputs including video, audio, data/text, and radar, and can employ a variety of communications protocols. The company is supplying an open systems storage system using Redundant Array of Independent Disks (RAID) technology. Formation also supplies plug compatible data storage systems for IBM AS/400 computers, as well as data storage systems to open systems computer manufacturers and systems integrators. **Common positions include:**

Computer Engineer; Electrical/Electronics Engineer; Mechanical Engineer; Software Engineer. **Educational backgrounds include:** Engineering. **Benefits:** Dental Insurance; Disability Coverage; Flextime Plan; Investment Plan; Life Insurance; Medical Insurance; Profit Sharing; Savings Plan; Tuition Assistance. **Corporate headquarters location:** This Location. **Operations at this facility include:** Administration; Manufacturing; Regional Headquarters; Research and Development; Sales; Service. **Number of employees at this location:** 100.

### FOUNTAIN TECHNOLOGIES, INC.
50 Randolph Road, Somerset NJ 08873. 732/563-4800. **Fax:** 732/563-4999. **Contact:** Yvonne Walsh, Human Resources. **Description:** Manufactures IBM-compatible computers. Founded in 1984. **NOTE:** Entry-level positions are offered. **Common positions include:** Account Representative; Accountant/Auditor; Computer Operator; Computer Programmer; Customer Service Representative; Database Manager; Electrical/Electronics Engineer; Graphic Artist; Industrial Engineer; Internet Services Manager; Marketing Specialist; Mechanical Engineer; MIS Specialist; Multimedia Designer; Online Content Specialist; Operations/Production Manager; Production Manager; Public Relations Specialist; Purchasing Agent/Manager; Quality Control Supervisor; Sales Executive; Sales Representative; Software Engineer; Systems Analyst; Technical Writer/Editor; Webmaster. **Educational backgrounds include:** Accounting; Art/Design; Business Administration; Communications; Computer Science; Engineering; Finance; Liberal Arts; Marketing; Public Relations. **Benefits:** Dental Insurance; Disability Coverage; Employee Discounts; Life Insurance; Medical Insurance. **Corporate headquarters location:** This Location. **Listed on:** Privately held. **Annual sales/revenues:** More than $100 million. **Number of employees at this location:** 1,000.

### GE CAPITAL IT SOLUTIONS
109 Corporate Boulevard, Suite J, South Plainfield NJ 07080. 908/791-2200. **Contact:** Human Resources Department. **World Wide Web address:** http://www.solutions.gecits.ge.com. **Description:** A nationwide reseller of computer products and services to commercial, governmental, and educational users. The company's products and services include value-added systems, systems integration, networking services, support, maintenance, facilities management, outsourcing, software and business consulting services, and rental services. **Other U.S. locations:** Nationwide.

### GEAC SOFTWARE
61 South Paramus Road, 5th Floor, Paramus NJ 07652. 201/843-8700. **Contact:** Human Resources. **Description:** Develops and markets business applications software in the areas of finance, human resources, inventory, materials, management, manufacturing, health care, and higher education. Among the company's products is the SmartStream series of financial software.

### GLOBAL TURNKEY SYSTEMS, INC.
20 Waterview Boulevard, 3rd Floor, Parsippany NJ 07054. 973/331-1010. **Fax:** 973/331-0042. **Contact:** Vice President of Finance and Administration. **World Wide Web address:** http://www.gtsystems.com. **Description:** Offers midrange computer systems and software services for book and magazine publishers. **Common positions include:** Accountant/Auditor; Computer Programmer; Systems Analyst; Technical Writer/Editor. **Educational backgrounds include:** Accounting; Business Administration; Computer Science; Finance; Marketing. **Benefits:** 401(k); Dental Insurance; Disability Coverage; Life Insurance; Medical Insurance; Tuition Assistance. **Corporate headquarters location:** This Location. **Other U.S. locations:** Denver CO. **Operations at this facility include:** Sales; Service. **Listed on:** Privately held. **Number of employees at this location:** 60.

### GLOBE MANUFACTURING SALES, INC.
1159 U.S. Route 22 East, Mountainside NJ 07092. 908/232-7301. **Fax:** 908/232-0179. **Contact:** Human Resources. **World Wide Web address:** http://www.akstamping.com. **Description:** Manufactures computer brackets that hold computer chips and other plastic parts. **Parent company:** AK Stamping Company, Inc.

### HBO & COMPANY (HBOC)
700 East Gate Drive, Suite 500, Mount Laurel NJ 08054. 609/234-4041. **Contact:** Human Resources. **World Wide Web address:** http://www.hboc.com. **Description:** This location offers sales and technical support. Overall, HBO & Company provides networking solutions and software by supplying physicians, hospitals, and other health care facilities with network service and support. **NOTE:** To apply for a job at any regional HBO & Company office, first send a resume to the corporate headquarters at HBO & Company, Human Resources, 301 Perimeter Center North, Atlanta GA 30346.

**HRSOFT, INC.**
10 Madison Road, Morristown NJ 07962. 973/984-6334. **Fax:** 973/984-5427. **Contact:** Human Resources. **World Wide Web address:** http://www.hrsoft.com. **Description:** Develops and provides human resource-related business software and services.

**H.F. HENDERSON INDUSTRIES INC.**
45 Fairfield Place, West Caldwell NJ 07006. 973/227-9250. **Contact:** Human Resources. **Description:** Manufactures printed circuit boards, harnesses, battery packs, and other computer components.

**IBM CORPORATION**
1515 South Washington Avenue, Piscataway NJ 08854. 732/926-2000. **Recorded jobline:** 800/964-4473. **Contact:** Human Resources. **World Wide Web address:** http://www.ibm.com. **Description:** This location is a marketing office. Overall, IBM (International Business Machines) develops, manufactures, and markets advanced information processing products including computers and microelectronic technology, software, networking systems and information technology-related services. IBM operates in the United States, Canada, Europe, Middle East, Africa, Latin America and Asia Pacific. **NOTE:** Jobseekers should send a resume to IBM Staffing Services, Department 1DP, Building 051, P.O. Box 12195, Research Triangle Park NC 27709-2195. **Corporate headquarters location:** Armonk NY. **Subsidiaries include:** IBM Credit Corporation; IBM Instruments, Inc.; IBM World Trade Corporation. **Number of employees at this location:** 100.

**IMI SYSTEMS**
4 East Kings Highway, Haddonfield NJ 08033. 609/795-5000. **Fax:** 609/795-9850. **Contact:** Recruiting Manager. **World Wide Web address:** http://www.imisys.com. **Description:** An information technology consulting firm that provides computer consulting personnel to other corporations. **Corporate headquarters location:** Melville NY.

**ITT AEROSPACE/COMMUNICATIONS**
**ITT AVIONICS**
100 Kingsland Road, Clifton NJ 07014. 973/284-4238. **Contact:** Human Resources. **Description:** ITT Aerospace/Communications designs and engineers software for satellite communications under government contracts.

**IKEGAMI ELECTRONICS INC.**
37 Brook Avenue, Maywood NJ 07607. 201/368-9171. **Contact:** Human Resources. **Description:** Manufactures and sells computer and broadcast monitors.

**INACOM INFORMATION SYSTEMS**
1009 Lenox Drive, Building 4 East, Suite 105, Lawrenceville NJ 08648. 609/896-2927. **Contact:** Human Resources. **World Wide Web address:** http://www.inacom.com. **Description:** A microcomputer reseller also offering sales advice, technical and software support, customized training, and networking specialists. Primary customers are mid-sized to large corporate accounts.

**INFORMATION HORIZON**
20 Waterview Boulevard, 1st Floor, Parsippany NJ 07054. 973/402-9364. **Contact:** Human Resources Department. **Description:** Offers computer consulting services for financial applications.

**INSTRUCTIVISION, INC.**
3 Regent Street, Suite 306, Livingston NJ 07039-1617. 973/992-9081. **Contact:** Human Resources. **World Wide Web address:** http://www.instructivision.com. **Description:** A multimedia publishing company. Instructivision develops educational video and computer programs and workbooks. The company operates a full-service video production facility encompassing a production stage, an interformat digital editing suite, offline editing, 3-D animation, and audio recording equipment.

**INTERACTIVE SOLUTIONS, INC.**
377 Route 17 South, Hasbrouck Heights NJ 07604. 201/288-6699. **Contact:** Human Resources Department. **Description:** Interactive Solutions, Inc. develops custom applications to meet specific client needs. **Common positions include:** Account Representative; Applications Engineer; Computer Programmer; Database Manager; MIS Specialist; Multimedia Designer; Sales Representative; Software Engineer; Systems Analyst; Telecommunications Manager; Typist/Word Processor. **Educational backgrounds include:** Accounting; Art/Design; Computer Science; Mathematics; Physics. **Benefits:** Disability Coverage; Financial Planning Assistance; Life

Insurance; Medical Insurance; Tuition Assistance. **Corporate headquarters location:** This Location. **Annual sales/revenues:** $11 - $20 million. **Number of employees at this location:** 120.

## INTERIM TECHNOLOGY
9 Polito Avenue, 9th Floor, Lyndhurst NJ 07071. 201/392-0800. **Contact:** Human Resources. **World Wide Web address:** http://www.interimtechnology.com. **Description:** A nationwide computer outsourcing service company, providing short-run supplemental and long-term contractual support for computer operations, communications operations, PC help desks, local area networks, computer programming, and technology training. The company's computer services are provided from offices strategically located throughout the United States. The company also provides the expertise for meeting applications and systems development objectives within information systems organizations. Capabilities extend beyond evaluating computer software and hardware to providing technically qualified professionals for any task in the systems development life cycle -- from conception through feasibility analysis, system design, programming, testing, implementation, and full systems maintenance and support. **Corporate headquarters location:** Oak Brook IL. **International locations:** United Kingdom. **Listed on:** New York Stock Exchange. **Stock exchange symbol:** IS. **Number of employees nationwide:** 2,000. **Number of employees worldwide:** 2,500.

## INTERNATIONAL DISCOUNT TELECOMMUNICATIONS CORPORATION (IDT)
294 State Street, Hackensack NJ 07601. 201/928-1000. **Contact:** Human Resources Department. **World Wide Web address:** http://www.idt.net. **Description:** An Internet access provider that offers dial-up services, Web hosting, and e-mail by phone. **NOTE:** Interested jobseekers should address inquiries to the attention of Jonathan Rand, Manager of Human Resources, IDT Corporation, 190 Main Street, Hackensack NJ 07601.

## ION NETWORKS INC.
21 Meridian Road, Edison NJ 08820. 732/494-4440. **Contact:** Human Resources. **World Wide Web address:** http://www.ion-networks.com. **Description:** Develops and markets software and hardware for computer security.

## ITOX
8 Elkins Road, East Brunswick NJ 08816. 732/390-2815. **Contact:** Human Resources. **World Wide Web address:** http://www.itox.com. **Description:** Manufactures computer components including graphics accelerator boards, motherboards, and sound cards for commercial and industrial systems.

## JBA INTERNATIONAL INC.
161 Gaither Drive, Mount Laurel NJ 08054. 609/231-9400. **Contact:** Human Resources. **World Wide Web address:** http://www.jbaintl.com. **Description:** Wholesales computer systems and enterprise management software.

## JCC CORPORATION
One International Boulevard, Suite 400, Mahwah NJ 07495. 201/592-5023. **Contact:** Human Resources. **World Wide Web address:** http://www.jccusa.com. **Description:** Manufactures and sells Internet access devices.

## KEANE, INC.
100 Walnut Avenue, Suite 202, Clark NJ 07066. 732/396-4321. **Contact:** Human Resources. **World Wide Web address:** http://www.keane.com. **Description:** Keane is a software services company that designs, develops, and manages software for corporations and health care facilities. Keane's services enable clients to leverage existing information systems and more rapidly and proficiently develop and manage new software applications. The company serves clients through two operating divisions: the Information Services Division (ISD) and the Healthcare Services Division (HSD). ISD provides software design, development, and management services to corporations and government agencies with large and recurring software development needs. HSD develops, markets, and supports financial, patient care, and clinical application software for hospitals and long-term care facilities. Founded in 1965. **Corporate headquarters location:** Boston MA. **Other U.S. locations:** Nationwide. **Listed on:** American Stock Exchange. **Number of employees nationwide:** 1,000.

## LOGIC WORKS
111 Campus Drive, Princeton NJ 08540. 609/514-1177. **Fax:** 609/514-2906. **Contact:** Mike Sweeney, Human Resources Representative. **E-mail address:** mcsweeney@logicworks.com. **World Wide Web address:** http://www.logicworks.com. **Description:** Develops commercial software for data modeling and data warehouse applications. Founded in 1988. **Common positions**

**include:** Account Manager; Account Representative; Accountant; Administrative Assistant; Applications Engineer; Computer Programmer; Marketing Manager; Marketing Specialist; Software Engineer. **Educational backgrounds include:** Computer Science; Software Development; Software Tech. Support. **Benefits:** 401(k); Dental Insurance; Disability Coverage; Flexible Schedule; Life Insurance; Medical Insurance; Pension Plan; Profit Sharing; Savings Plan; Telecommuting; Tuition Assistance. **Corporate headquarters location:** This Location. **Other U.S. locations:** Nationwide. **Listed on:** NASDAQ. **Stock exchange symbol:** LGWX. **President/CEO:** Greg Peters. **Annual sales/revenues:** $21 - $50 million. **Number of employees at this location:** 150. **Number of employees nationwide:** 240. **Number of projected hires for 1998 - 1999 at this location:** 75.

**MDY ADVANCED TECHNOLOGIES**
21-00 Route 208 South, Fair Lawn NJ 07410. 201/797-6676. **Contact:** Human Resources Department. **Description:** MDY Advanced Technologies provides computer networking and record management services.

**MAINTECH**
39 Paterson Avenue, Wallington NJ 07057. 973/614-1700. **Contact:** Human Resources. **Description:** Provides on-site computer maintenance services.

**MARCAM SOLUTIONS**
Park 80 West, Plaza 2, 4th Floor, Saddle Brook NJ 07663. 201/291-8400. **Contact:** Human Resources Department. **World Wide Web address:** http://www.marcam.com. **Description:** Develops and sells manufacturing and business-related software. **Corporate headquarters location:** Newton MA. **Parent company:** Marcam Solutions is a supplier of enterprise application software and services for industrial and distribution companies. The company also provides product support, implementation consulting, education, and programming services. **Number of employees nationwide:** 965.

**MEGASOFT, L.L.C.**
819 Highway 33 East, Freehold NJ 07728. 732/431-5300. **Contact:** Jane Carlos-Stokroki, Controller. **World Wide Web address:** http://www.megasoft.com. **Description:** Megasoft provides a broad range of integrated software and information distribution options in multiple formats on disk, in print, and online to many industries including the technology, insurance, financial services, pharmaceutical, publishing, government, and transportation communities. Founded in 1983.

**MICROSTAR COMPUTERS INC.**
25 Kimberly Road, Building F, East Brunswick NJ 08816. 732/651-8686. **Contact:** Human Resources. **Description:** Manufactures laptop computers.

**MISCO**
One MISCO Plaza, Holmdel NJ 07733. 732/264-1000. **Contact:** Human Resources. **Description:** Resells computer supplies and peripherals including faxes and modems.

**MOTOROLA INFORMATION SYSTEMS GROUP**
777 Passaic Avenue, Clifton NJ 07012. 973/470-9001. **Fax:** 973/470-8537. **Contact:** Human Resources Department. **Description:** Motorola Information Systems Group develops and sells modems and other related equipment. **Parent company:** Motorola, Inc. (Schaumburg IL) manufactures communications equipment and electronic products including car radios, cellular phones, semiconductors, computer systems, cellular infrastructure equipment, pagers, cordless phones, and LAN systems. The company has production plants in the U.S. and 18 other countries.

**NCR CORPORATION**
2 Oak Way, Berkeley Heights NJ 07922. 908/790-2500. **Contact:** Human Resources. **World Wide Web address:** http://www.ncr.com. **Description:** This location is involved in the sale of computer products and scanning equipment, as well as software consulting and engineering. Overall, NCR Corporation is a worldwide provider of computer products and services. The company provides computer solutions to the retail, financial, and communications industries. NCR Computer Systems Group develops, manufactures, and markets computer systems. NCR Financial Systems Group is an industry leader in three target areas: financial delivery systems, relationship banking/data warehousing solutions, and payments systems/item processing. NCR Retail Systems Group is a world leader in end-to-end retail solutions serving the food, general merchandise, and hospitality industries. NCR Worldwide Services provides data warehousing services solutions; end-to-end networking services; and designs, implements, and supports complex open systems environments. NCR Systemedia Group develops, produces, and markets a complete line of information products

to satisfy customers' information technology needs including transaction processing media, auto identification media, business form communication products, managing documents and media, and a full line of integrated equipment solutions. NCR Corporation formerly operated as AT&T Global Information Solutions. **Educational backgrounds include:** Business Administration; Computer Science. **Benefits:** 401(k); Dental Insurance; Disability Coverage; Life Insurance; Medical Insurance; Pension Plan; Savings Plan; Tuition Assistance. **Corporate headquarters location:** Dayton OH. **Other U.S. locations:** Nationwide. **Listed on:** New York Stock Exchange. **Annual sales/revenues:** More than $100 million. **Number of employees at this location:** 450. **Number of employees nationwide:** 19,000.

### NATIONS, INC.
788 Shrewsbury Avenue, Tinton Falls NJ 07724. 732/530-1818. **Contact:** Human Resources. **Description:** Designs and engineers software for the federal government.

### NETWORK SPECIALISTS INC.
### dba NSI SOFTWARE
80 River Street, Suite 5B, Hoboken NJ 07030. 201/656-2121. **Fax:** 201/656-2727. **Contact:** Human Resources. **World Wide Web address:** http://www.nsisw.com. **Description:** Develops network performance and fault-tolerant software tools. Products are compatible with Novell NetWare, Microsoft Windows NT, and UNIX.

### NU DATA INC.
1950 Swarthmore Avenue, Lakewood NJ 08701. 732/842-5757. **Contact:** Human Resources. **Description:** Distributes workstation hardware and computer cables.

### OMR SYSTEMS CORPORATION
101 Business Park Drive, Suite 220, Skillman NJ 08558. 609/497-2000. **Contact:** Human Resources. **World Wide Web address:** http://www.omrsystems.com. **Description:** Develops backroom trading software.

### OKIDATA CORPORATION
532 Fellowship Road, Mount Laurel NJ 08054. 609/235-2600. **Contact:** Human Resources. **World Wide Web address:** http://www.okidata.com. **Description:** Manufactures computer printers and fax machines.

### OMNITECH CORPORATE SOLUTIONS
100 West Forest Avenue, Englewood NJ 07631. 201/569-0101. **Contact:** Human Resources Department. **Description:** Provides computer sales, training, and support services to large corporations.

### ORACLE CORPORATION
517 Route 1 South, Suite 4000, Iselin NJ 08830. 732/636-2000. **Contact:** Human Resources. **World Wide Web address:** http://www.oracle.com. **Description:** Designs and manufactures business software programs for small companies.

### PNY TECHNOLOGIES
299 Webro Road, Parsippany NJ 07054. 973/515-9700. **Fax:** 973/515-9700. **Contact:** Human Resources. **World Wide Web address:** http://www.pny.com. **Description:** Manufactures and designs computer memory products. Founded in 1985. **NOTE:** Entry-level positions are offered. **Common positions include:** Account Manager; Account Representative; Design Engineer; Quality Control Supervisor; Sales and Marketing Representative. **Educational backgrounds include:** Accounting; Computer Science; Engineering. **Benefits:** 401(k); Dental Insurance; Disability Coverage; Life Insurance; Medical Insurance; Tuition Assistance. **Corporate headquarters location:** This Location. **Listed on:** Privately held. **Annual sales/revenues:** More than $100 million. **Number of employees at this location:** 250. **Number of employees nationwide:** 320. **Number of employees worldwide:** 420.

### PARAGON COMPUTER PROS INC.
20 Commerce Drive, Suite 226, Cranford NJ 07016. 908/709-6767. **Contact:** Human Resources Administrative Assistant. **World Wide Web address:** http://www.paracomp.com. **Description:** Offers computer consulting services to a variety of businesses.

### PEGASUS CONSULTING GROUP
90 Woodbridge Center Drive, Woodbridge NJ 07095. 732/726-0800. **Contact:** Human Resources. **Description:** A computer software consulting firm.

## PHYSICIAN COMPUTER NETWORK
1200 The American Road, Morris Plains NJ 07950. 973/490-3100. **Contact:** Human Resources. **World Wide Web address:** http://www.pcn.com. **Description:** Develops software for medical practices.

## PRINCETON FINANCIAL SYSTEMS INC.
600 College Road East, Princeton NJ 08540. 609/987-2400. **Fax:** 609/987-9032. **Contact:** Cara Verba, Staffing Manager. **World Wide Web address:** http://www.pfs.com. **Description:** Develops and supports investment management software. Founded in 1969. **NOTE:** Entry-level positions are offered. **Common positions include:** Accountant/Auditor; Computer Programmer; Fund Manager; Sales Manager; Software Engineer; Systems Analyst; Technical Writer/Editor. **Educational backgrounds include:** Accounting; Computer Science; Finance. **Benefits:** 401(k); Dental Insurance; Disability Coverage; Life Insurance; Medical Insurance; Tuition Assistance. **Special programs:** Apprenticeships. **Corporate headquarters location:** This Location. **International locations:** London; Toronto. **Parent company:** State Street Boston Corporation. **Listed on:** New York Stock Exchange. **Number of employees at this location:** 150. **Number of employees nationwide:** 185. **Number of employees worldwide:** 200.

## PRINCETON INFORMATION
120 Wood Avenue South, Suite 404, Iselin NJ 08830. 732/906-5660. **Contact:** Human Resources. **World Wide Web address:** http://www.princetoninformation.com. **Description:** Offers computer consulting services.

## PRINCETON SOFTECH
1060 State Road, Princeton NJ 08540. 609/497-0205. **Contact:** Human Resources. **World Wide Web address:** http://www.princetonsoftech.com. **Description:** Provides IT professionals with software solutions. The company's products are focused on Y2K solutions, intelligent data migration, and database synchronization. **Parent company:** Computer Horizons.

## QAD INC.
10000 Midlantic Drive, Suite 200, Mount Laurel NJ 08054. 609/273-1717. **Contact:** Human Resources. **World Wide Web address:** http://www.qad.com. **Description:** This location serves as a technical support branch and regional sales office. Overall, QAD develops MFG/PRO, a software package designed to aid in supply and distribution management for large companies. **Corporate headquarters location:** Carpinteria CA.

## QUALITY SOFTWARE SYSTEMS INC.
200 Centennial Avenue, Suite 110, Piscataway NJ 08854. 732/885-1919. **Contact:** Human Resources. **World Wide Web address:** http://www.qssiwarehouse.com. **Description:** Develops software to aid in warehouse management and development.

## RARITAN COMPUTER, INC.
400 Cottontail Lane, Somerset NJ 08873. 732/764-8886. **Fax:** 732/764-8887. **Contact:** Esther A. Hsu, Human Resources Manager. **E-mail address:** esthcr@raritan.com. **World Wide Web address:** http://www.raritan.com. **Description:** Designs and manufactures a line of products for sharing PCs and peripherals. Products include MasterConsole, a keyboard/video/mouse switch; CompuSwitch, a KVM switch allowing central control for up to four PCs; and Guardian, a virtual keyboard and mouse device which emulates keyboard and mouse signals. Founded in 1985. **Common positions include:** Account Manager; Account Representative; Accountant/Auditor; Administrative Assistant; Advertising Clerk; Applications Engineer; Buyer; Clerical Supervisor; Computer Programmer; Customer Service Representative; General Manager; Human Resources Manager; Internet Services Manager; Marketing Manager; MIS Specialist; Operations/Production Manager; Project Manager; Purchasing Agent/Manager; Quality Control Supervisor; Sales Manager; Sales Representative; Secretary; Software Engineer; Systems Analyst; Technical Writer/Editor; Telecommunications Manager; Vice President of Marketing. **Educational backgrounds include:** Accounting; Art/Design; Computer Science; Engineering. **Benefits:** 401(k); Dental Insurance; Life Insurance; Medical Insurance; Profit Sharing; Savings Plan; Tuition Assistance. **Corporate headquarters location:** This Location. **International locations:** Taiwan; the Netherlands. **Annual sales/revenues:** $21 - $50 million. **Number of employees at this location:** 40. **Number of employees nationwide:** 100. **Number of employees worldwide:** 120.

## SQN PERIPHERALS INC.
### dba SQN SIGNATURE SYSTEMS
65 Indel Avenue, P.O. Box 423, Rancocas NJ 08073. 609/261-5500. **Contact:** Human Resources. **World Wide Web address:** http://www.sqnsigs.com. **Description:** Develops signature verification software for the banking industry.

## SILVERLINE INDUSTRIES INC.
53 Knights Bridge Road, Piscataway NJ 08854. 732/248-3363. **Contact:** Human Resources. **Description:** Offers computer consulting services.

## SOFTWARE PUBLISHING CORPORATION (SPC)
3A Oak Road, Fairfield NJ 07004. 973/808-1992. **Contact:** Human Resources. **World Wide Web address:** http://www.spco.com. **Description:** A developer of IBM- and World Wide Web-compatible visual communications software. Founded in 1980. **Common positions include:** Software Engineer. **Benefits:** 401(k); Stock Purchase. **Corporate headquarters location:** This Location. **Listed on:** NASDAQ. **Stock exchange symbol:** SPCO. **Number of employees nationwide:** 70.

## SUN MICROSYSTEMS INC.
400 Atrium Drive, 3rd Floor, Somerset NJ 08873. 732/469-1000. **Contact:** Human Resources Department. **World Wide Web address:** http://www.sun.com. **Description:** This location is a sales office. Overall, Sun Microsystems produces high-performance computer systems, workstations, servers, CPUs, peripherals, and operating system software. The company developed its own microprocessor called SPARC. **Corporate headquarters location:** Mountain View CA. **Listed on:** NASDAQ.

## SUPERCOM INDUSTRIES INC.
97 Sunfield Avenue, Edison NJ 08837. 732/417-1900. **Contact:** Human Resources. **Description:** Distributes computers.

## SYNCSORT
50 Tice Boulevard, Woodcliff Lake NJ 07675. 201/930-8200. **Contact:** Human Resources. **World Wide Web address:** http://www.syncsort.com. **Description:** Develops operating systems software for businesses.

## UNIGRAPHICS SOLUTIONS
25 Hanover Road, 3rd Floor, Florham Park NJ 07932. 973/301-7502. **Contact:** Human Resources. **World Wide Web address:** http://www.ugsolutions.com. **Description:** Provides integrated hardware, software, and network solutions to *Fortune* 500 companies. Unigraphics focuses primarily on international corporations in the service, wholesale, distribution, and transportation industries.

## UNISYS CORPORATION
45 Spring Street, New Providence NJ 07974. 908/771-5000. **Fax:** 908/771-5286. **Contact:** Human Resources. **E-mail address:** jobs@unn.unisys.com. **World Wide Web address:** http://www.unisys.com. **Description:** This location is an administrative facility. Overall, Unisys Corporation is a provider of information services, technology, and software. Unisys specializes in developing business critical solutions based on open information networks. The company's enabling software team creates a variety of software projects which facilitate the building of user applications and the management of distributed systems. The company's platforms group is responsible for UNIX Operating Systems running across a wide range of multiple processor server platforms including all peripheral and communication drivers. The Unisys commercial parallel processing team develops microkernel-based operating systems, I/O device drivers, ATM hardware, diagnostics, and system architectures. The system management group is chartered with the overall management of development programs for UNIX desktop and entry-server products. **Corporate headquarters location:** Blue Bell PA. **Number of employees worldwide:** 49,000.

## WANG GLOBAL
1095 Cranbury South River Road, Suite 1, Jamesburg NJ 08831. 609/409-2500. **Contact:** Human Resources. **World Wide Web address:** http://www.wang.com. **Description:** This location houses customer service and sales offices. Overall, Wang Laboratories, Inc. is a leader in workflow, integrated imaging, document management, and related office software for client/server open systems; and a worldwide provider of integration and support services for office software and networks. Wang's Software Business is a provider of integrated client/server software that enables customers to streamline office information processes, cut costs, and respond more quickly to changes in market dynamics or customer needs. Principal markets for the Software Business are banking, insurance, government, and other enterprises with large-scale business processes. Wang's Solutions Integration Business provides extensive systems integration and other services to the U.S. government. Principal markets are federal agencies, the U.S. Department of Defense, and commercial not-for-profit hospitals and medical enterprises. The Customer Services Business provides maintenance and support services, network integration, installation, training, and other services to customers worldwide. With service delivery operations in more than 130 countries,

Wang's Customer Service Business provides maintenance and support services for more than 3,500 products and 300 vendors. **NOTE:** Please send resumes to Wang Laboratories, Inc., Human Resources, Mail Stop 027-15E, 836 North Street, Tewksbury MA 01876. **Corporate headquarters location:** Billerica MA.

*Note: Because addresses and telephone numbers of smaller companies can change rapidly, we recommend you call each company to verify the information below before inquiring about job opportunities. Mass mailings are not recommended.*

**Additional small employers:**

**COMPUTER MAINTENANCE AND REPAIR**

**Telos**
55 North Gilbert Street, Red Bank NJ 07701-4929. 732/530-8444.

**COMPUTER MANUFACTURERS**

**American Computer Company**
6 Commerce Drive, Suite 2, Cranford NJ 07016-3515. 908/272-3330.

**Ariel Corporation**
2540 US Highway 130, Cranbury NJ 08512-3519. 609/860-2900.

**Compaq Computer Corporation**
701 East Gate Drive, Suite 300, Mount Laurel NJ 08054-3838. 609/273-2000.

**Dynamic Decisions Inc.**
104 Sunfield Avenue, Edison NJ 08837-3827. 732/225-8868.

**Micro Generation**
70 Newfield Ave, Edison NJ 08837-3817. 732/225-8899.

**Minta Technologies**
11 Cotters Ln, East Brunswick NJ 08816-2002. 732/651-0088.

**NCR Corporation**
2031 Old Trenton Rd, Cranbury NJ 08512-1417. 609/443-1800.

**NCR Corporation**
184 Liberty Corner Rd, Warren NJ 07059-6733. 908/604-3900.

**Quantex Micro Systems Inc.**
PO Box 5895, Somerset NJ 08875-5895. 732/563-4166.

**Quay Corp.**
10 Industrial Way E, Eatontown NJ 07724-3317. 732/542-7340.

**COMPUTER PERIPHERAL MANUFACTURERS**

**Cisco Systems Inc.**
379 Thornall Street, Suite 4, Edison NJ 08837-2226. 732/603-7400.

**Data Access/DataPatch Inc.**
40 Eisenhower Drive, Paramus NJ 07652-1404. 201/843-9363.

**Lexmark International Inc.**
50 Tice Blvd, Woodcliff Lake NJ 07675-7654. 201/307-4605.

**NER Data Products Inc.**
PO Box 524, Glassboro NJ 08028-0524. 609/881-5524.

**Silver Cloud Manufacturing**
525 Orange St, Millville NJ 08332-4030. 609/825-8900.

**Systech Solutions Inc.**
7 Cedar Brook Dr, Cranbury NJ 08512. 609/395-8400.

**COMPUTER PROCESSING AND DATA PREPARATION SERVICES**

**ADP**
1465 State Route 31, Ste 4, Annandale NJ 08801-3130. 908/730-7377.

**ADP**
205 Main Ave, Clifton NJ 07014-1723. 973/365-7300.

**Broad Data Systems Inc.**
2710 Yorktowne Blvd, Brick NJ 08723-7966. 732/255-6260.

**Cambria Corporation**
5090 Central Hwy, Ste 1, Pennsauken NJ 08109-4637. 609/665-3600.

**CDSI**
1919 Park Ave, Weehawken NJ 07087-6712. 201/601-7100.

**Commercial Data Processing**
4 Sperry Rd, Fairfield NJ 07004-2005. 973/882-1660.

**DCI**
PO Box 459, Manasquan NJ 08736-0459. 732/223-8984.

**DMC Data Management Inc.**
145 46th W Ave, Wayne NJ 07470. 973/890-9500.

**Dynatron**
1 Haynes Ave, Newark NJ 07114-1313. 973/648-6700.

**EDS (Electronic Data Systems Corporation)**
120 W Passaic St, Rochelle Park NJ 07662-3217. 201/291-1560.

**EDS (Electronic Data Systems Corporation)**
550 Route 202-206, Bedminster NJ 07921-1537. 908/781-4900.

**EDS (Electronic Data Systems Corporation)**
525 Fellowship Rd, Ste 330, Mount Laurel NJ 08054-3415. 609/722-9300.

**Envoy Corp.**
500 Plaza Dr, Secaucus NJ 07094-3619. 201/902-7000.

**G-Tech Corporation**
1333 Brunswick Ave, Trenton NJ 08648-4541. 609/392-6200.

**ISI**
53 Haddonfield Rd, Ste 330, Cherry Hill NJ 08002-4802. 609/667-1862.

**JCI Data Processing**
200 Route 130 N, Riverton NJ 08077-2892. 609/786-2600.

**Micro-Graphic Information Systems**
244 Saddle River Rd, Saddle Brook NJ 07663-4619. 201/909-0222.

**Salomon Brothers Inc.**
745 State Rte 3, Rutherford NJ 07070-2572. 201/896-7280.

**Silver Matlen Group Inc.**
140 Littleton Rd, Ste 305, Parsippany NJ 07054-1867. 973/335-3322.

**SMS**
555 College Rd E, Princeton NJ 08540-6616. 609/419-3561.

**Source Data Concepts Inc.**
401 Route 70 East, Cherry Hill NJ 08034-2410. 609/427-4300.

**Summit Service Corporation**
161 Gaither Dr, Mount Laurel NJ
08054-1740. 609/234-2804.

**Summit Service Corporation**
1313 Route 38, Mount Laurel NJ
08054. 609/784-8408.

**COMPUTER SOFTWARE,
PROGRAMMING, AND
SYSTEMS DESIGN**

**9 Net Avenue Inc.**
One Meadowlands Plaza, East
Rutherford NJ 07073-2100.
201/804-9944.

**ACC**
3535 Route 66, Neptune NJ
07753. 732/922-6611.

**Access Methods Inc.**
PO Box 171, Montclair NJ
07042-0171. 973/744-9126.

**Ace Technologies Inc.**
One Bethany Road, Hazlet NJ
07730-1663. 732/335-0640.

**American Management Systems
Inc.**
75 Livingston Ave, Suite 2,
Roseland NJ 07068-3701.
973/535-7000.

**Analytical Systems Engineering
Corporation**
180 Avenue at the Common,
Shrewsbury NJ 07702-4581.
732/389-7400.

**Atlantic Digital Inc.**
133 US Highway 9, Englishtown
NJ 07726-8268. 732/972-0088.

**Avenir Inc.**
6 Wyckoff Place, Franklin Park
NJ 08823-1816. 732/767-1050.

**BASF**
1100 American Road, Morris
Plains NJ 07950. 973/359-4604.

**BEA Systems Inc.**
140 Allen Road, Liberty Corner
NJ 07938. 908/580-3028.

**BEA Systems Inc.**
180 Park Avenue, Florham Park
NJ 07932-1004. 973/443-6000.

**Best Ware Inc.**
300 Round Hill Drive, Rockaway
NJ 07866-1227. 973/586-2200.

**Business Software Solutions**
401 Route 73 South, Marlton NJ
08053-2047. 609/810-0550.

**Cap Gemini America Inc.**
960 Holmdel Road, Holmdel NJ
07733-2138. 732/946-8900.

**Chesapeake Decision Sciences**
200 South Street, New
Providence NJ 07974-2151.
908/464-8300.

**Claremont Technology Group**
18 Cattano Avenue, Suite 1,
Morristown NJ 07960-6846.
973/538-9095.

**Claremont Technology Group**
180 Mount Airy Rd, Suite 205,
Bernardsville NJ 07924-2720.
908/204-0202.

**Commtech Operations Systems**
2555 Route 130, Cranbury NJ
08512-3509. 609/655-2277.

**Compaq Computer Services**
200 Route 9, Englishtown NJ
07726-3072. 732/577-6000.

**Computer Associates
International**
Orchard Road, Rural Route 206,
Princeton NJ 08543. 609/921-
3070.

**Computer Sciences Corporation**
100 Decadon Drive, Egg Harbor
Township NJ 08234-3831.
609/383-8142.

**Computer Sciences Corporation**
15 Christopher Way, Eatontown
NJ 07724. 732/460-2000.

**Computran Systems, Inc.**
100 1st Street, Hackensack NJ
07601-2124. 201/489-7500.

**Conversion Services
International**
100 Eagle Rock Avenue, East
Hanover NJ 07936-3149.
973/560-9400.

**Cover-All Technologies Inc.**
18-01 Pollitt Dr, Fair Lawn NJ
07410-2826. 201/794-4800.

**Cyberthink Inc.**
465 Union Avenue, Bridgewater
NJ 08807-3196. 908/429-8008.

**Datatec Systems Inc.**
20C Commerce Way, Totowa NJ
07512-1154. 973/890-4800.

**Delta Corporate Services Inc.**
129 Littleton Road, Parsippany
NJ 07054-1869. 973/334-6260.

**Dendrite International Inc.**
1200 Mount Kemble Avenue,
Morristown NJ 07960-6797.
973/425-1200.

**DSET Corporation**
1011 Route 22 West, Bridgewater
NJ 08807. 908/526-7500.

**DSQ Software Corporation**
339 Thornall Street, Edison NJ
08837-2221. 732/767-0007.

**Emtec**
PO Box 1329, Mount Laurel NJ
08054-7329. 609/235-2121.

**Essex Computers Inc.**
164 Brighton Road, Clifton NJ
07012-1413. 973/773-2300.

**Fourth Technologies Inc.**
1816 Springdale Road, Cherry
Hill NJ 08003. 609/751-4848.

**Global Consultants Inc.**
PO Box 5631, Parsippany NJ
07054-6631. 973/560-0558.

**Horizon Computers Inc.**
5 Lincoln Highway, Edison NJ
08820-3964. 732/603-0004.

**IBM**
140 E Ridgewood Ave, Paramus
NJ 07652-3915. 201/967-6500.

**IBM**
27 Commerce Dr, Cranford NJ
07016-3610. 908/931-4709.

**IBM**
34 Maple Avenue, Montville NJ
07045. 973/276-4000.

**Icon CMP Corporation**
1200 Harbor Boulevard, Suite 8,
Weehawken NJ 07087-6728.
201/601-2000.

**IDD Enterprises**
600 Plaza Two, 5th Floor, Jersey
City NJ 07311. 201/938-5900.

**IMI Services**
5 Greentree Center, Suite 201,
Marlton NJ 08053-3422.
609/988-3922.

**Info Technologies Inc.**
179 Avenue at the Common,
Shrewsbury NJ 07702-4804.
732/741-7510.

**Innodata Corporation**
3 University Plaza Drive,
Hackensack NJ 07601-6208.
201/488-1200.

**Janis Group Inc.**
201 W Passaic St, Ste 403,
Rochelle Park NJ 07662-3100.
201/712-0505.

**JD Edwards & Company**
300 Lighting Way, Secaucus NJ
07094-3622. 201/223-1800.

**Keep It Simple Software**
1 S Centre St, South Orange NJ
07079-2607. 973/763-3363.

**Lakewood Software Tech Center**
4567 Route 9, Howell NJ 07731.
732/905-9200.

**Livingston Group Inc.**
300 Executive Dr, Ste 250, West Orange NJ 07052-3325. 973/736-9100.

**Logical Design Solutions Inc.**
465 South St, Ste 103, Morristown NJ 07960-6439.
973/971-0100.

**Logistic Solutions Inc.**
PO Box 1422, Piscataway NJ 08855-1422. 732/457-0015.

**Marlboro Computer**
10 Parsonage Rd, Edison NJ 08837-2429. 732/321-4144.

**Metacreations Corporation**
40 Washington Rd, Princeton Junction NJ 08550-1012.
609/716-8080.

**MFS Transtech Inc.**
200 E Park Dr, Ste 600, Mount Laurel NJ 08054-1297. 609/235-5252.

**Microbank Software Inc.**
70 S Orange Ave, Livingston NJ 07039-4903. 973/994-2390.

**Microsoft Corporation**
379 Thornall St, Edison NJ 08837-2225. 732/632-3300.

**Minolta Information Systems**
1 International Blvd, Fl 9, Mahwah NJ 07495-0025.
201/512-5800.

**Mitre Corporation**
145 Wyckoff Rd, Ste 201, Eatontown NJ 07724-1070.
732/544-1414.

**MJM Software**
285 Davidson Ave, Ste 202, Somerset NJ 08873-4153.
732/563-8400.

**Modis**
242 Old New Brunswick Rd, Piscataway NJ 08854-3754.
732/562-0100.

**Molloy Group Inc.**
4 Century Dr, Parsippany NJ 07054-4606. 973/540-1212.

**MPL Systems Inc.**
409 Minnisink Rd, Totowa NJ 07512-1808. 973/256-8220.

**MS Millennium LLC**
270 Davidson Ave, Somerset NJ 08873-4140. 732/469-2866.

**Network Programs Inc.**
255 Old New Brunswick Rd,

Piscataway NJ 08854-3734.
732/562-1111.

**Noblestar Systems Corporation**
1055 Parsippany Blvd, Parsippany NJ 07054-1230.
973/984-1000.

**Novadigm Inc.**
1 International Blvd, Mahwah NJ 07495-0025. 201/512-1000.

**Novell Inc.**
190 River Rd, Summit NJ 07901-1444. 908/522-6000.

**Nuware Technology Corp.**
21 Ernston Rd, Parlin NJ 08859-1701. 732/727-4850.

**Opencon Systems Inc.**
377 Hoes Ln, Piscataway NJ 08854-4138. 732/463-3131.

**Optimark Technologies Inc.**
10 Exchange Pl, Jersey City NJ 07302. 201/946-9400.

**Oracle Corporation**
1 Harmon Meadow Blvd, Secaucus NJ 07094-3600.
201/617-4489.

**Philips Manufacturing Technologies**
1764 New Durham Rd, South Plainfield NJ 07080-2328.
732/819-3000.

**Pinnacle Systems Inc.**
7 Lincoln Hwy, Ste 222, Edison NJ 08820-3965. 732/767-0099.

**PLP**
4567 Highway 9, Howell NJ 07731-3382. 732/901-0856.

**RIS Information Services Inc.**
200 Broadacres Dr, Ste 4, Bloomfield NJ 07003-3154.
973/893-1119.

**Rumarson Technologies Inc.**
363 Market St, Kenilworth NJ 07033-2033. 908/298-9300.

**SAP America Inc.**
300 Interpace Pkwy, Parsippany NJ 07054-1100. 973/331-0316.

**Sapient Corporation**
10 Exchange Pl, Jersey City NJ 07302. 201/938-2600.

**SHL Systemhouse Corp.**
989 Lenox Dr, Princeton NJ 08544-0001. 609/259-9400.

**Siemens Corporate Research**
755 College Rd E, Princeton NJ 08540-6632. 609/734-6500.

**SPL Worldgroup Inc.**
67 W Park Pl, Fl 10, Morristown NJ 07960. 973/539-6268.

**Standard Data Corp.**
225 Phillips Blvd, Trenton NJ 08618-1426. 609/406-5027.

**Storis Management Systems**
7 Entin Rd, Parsippany NJ 07054-5020. 973/515-0300.

**Sumisho Computer Systems USA**
111 Pavonia Ave, Ste 615, Jersey City NJ 07310. 201/792-4497.

**Sybase Inc.**
2001 Route 46, 5th Floor, Parsippany NJ 07054-1315.
973/331-5200.

**Think Systems Corporation**
1055 Parsippany Blvd, Parsippany NJ 07054-1230.
973/299-7177.

**Tracor Inc.**
4002 Lincoln Dr W, Marlton NJ 08053-1524. 609/988-1700.

**Tribase Systems Inc.**
215 Ridgedale Avenue, Florham Park NJ 07932-1355. 973/593-8200.

**Unixpros Inc.**
10 Industrial Way East, Eatontown NJ 07724-3317.
732/389-3295.

**VIS**
21 Clyde Rd, Somerset NJ 08873-5002. 732/873-0550.

**Voxware Inc.**
305 College Rd E, Princeton NJ 08540-6608. 609/514-4100.

**Web-Sci Technologies Inc.**
4214 US Highway 1, Monmouth Junction NJ 08852-1905.
732/329-9000.

**Windsoft**
66 Ford Rd, Denville NJ 07834-1300. 973/586-4400.

## COMPUTERS AND RELATED EQUIPMENT

**DecisionOne**
14 Washington Rd, Bldg 2, Princeton Junction NJ 08550-1028. 609/936-2900.

**Techmedia Computer Systems Corp.**
9 Smith St, Englewood NJ 07631-4607. 201/567-1583.

## MISC. COMPUTER RELATED SERVICES

**Anthony & Associates Inc.**
270 Davidson Ave, Ste 107, Somerset NJ 08873-4140.
732/560-8275.

**ATC Insys Technology Inc.**
200 Cottontail Lane, Somerset NJ
08873-1231. 732/563-0002.

**Aztec Consulting Service Inc.**
530 Main St, Ste 101, Fort Lee
NJ 07024-4505. 201/461-7200.

**CMI**
140 Broad Street, Red Bank NJ
07701-1927. 732/450-1100.

**Computer Horizons Corp.**
100 Walnut Ave, Suite 307, Clark
NJ 07066-1247. 732/396-0011.

**Comsys Technical Services**
285 Davidson Avenue, Somerset
NJ 08873-4153. 732/469-6227.

**Concept To Implementation**
3 Hemlock Lane, Holmdel NJ
07733-2410. 732/946-0700.

**Cross Current Corporation**
201 South Main Street,
Lambertville NJ 08530-1837.
609/397-3980.

**Data Study Inc.**
119 Cherry Hill Road, Parsippany
NJ 07054-1112. 973/402-7802.

**Datasoft Technologies Inc.**
120 Woodbridge Ave S, Ste 300,
Iselin NJ 08830. 732/632-2690.

**Delphi Partners Inc.**
120 Wood Ave South, Suite 406,
Iselin NJ 08830-2709. 732/603-7782.

**EJR Computer Associates Inc.**
5 Marine View Plaza, Hoboken
NJ 07030-5722. 201/795-3601.

**FYI Systems Inc.**
160 Littleton Road, Parsippany
NJ 07054-1871. 973/331-9050.

**GE Capital Consulting**
100 Davidson Avenue, Suite 300,
Somerset NJ 08873-1312.
732/627-0840.

**Global Computer Associates**
3 Garret Mountain Plaza, West
Paterson NJ 07424-3352.
973/278-7100.

**Grace Technologies Inc.**
9 Campus Drive, Parsippany NJ
07054-4408. 973/292-6770.

**H&L Technique Inc.**
PO Box 729, Lincroft NJ 07738-0729. 732/946-7575.

**Hexaware Technologies Inc.**
13B Roszel Road, Suite 110,
Princeton NJ 08540-6205.
609/951-9195.

**Ilex Systems Inc.**
170 Patterson Avenue,
Shrewsbury NJ 07702-4167.
732/530-7766.

**International Business Software Solutions**
200 Middlesex Essex Tpke, Iselin
NJ 08830-2033. 732/283-9700.

**KMB & Associates Inc.**
34 Toad Ln, Ringoes NJ 08551-1021. 908/806-0007.

**Larsen & Toubro Ltd.**
400 Kelby Street, Fort Lee NJ
07024-2937. 201/461-2384.

**Matrix Information Consulting**
365 W Passaic St, Fl 2, Rochelle
Park NJ 07662-3017. 201/587-0777.

**Medix Incorporated**
PO Box 10079, Newark NJ
07101-3079. 973/808-0088.

**MJR Associates Inc.**
55 Madison Ave, Morristown NJ
07960-7397. 973/285-3244.

**Patel Consultants Corp.**
1525 Morris Ave, Union NJ
07083-6334. 908/964-7575.

**Pierce Technology Corporation**
33 Wood Ave S, Ste 8, Iselin NJ
08830-2719. 732/321-8600.

**Polaris Consulting Service**
30 Two Bridges Rd, Fairfield NJ
07004-1550. 973/882-5100.

**Prism Inc.**
163 Washington Valley Rd,
Warren NJ 07059-7121. 732/748-0800.

**RCG Information Technology**
379 Thornall St, Edison NJ
08837-2225. 732/744-3500

**Real Soft Inc.**
PO Box 1489, Woodbridge NJ
07095-0970. 732/744-2420.

**Ricomm Systems Inc.**
PO Box 1193, Marlton NJ 08053-6193. 609/596-9027.

**Sequel Concepts**
3001 Hadley Rd, Units 7&8,
South Plainfield NJ 07080-1109.
908/668-5300.

**Spectrum Technology Group**
3421 US Highway 22, Somerville
NJ 08876-6026. 908/725-4000.

**SPS**
1450 Highway 34, Neptune NJ
07753-6807. 732/938-9111.

**STI**
555 US Highway 1, Iselin NJ
08830-3179. 732/855-8800.

**Taratec Development Corp.**
1170 US Highway 22,
Bridgewater NJ 08807-2927.
908/725-8090.

**Tekmark Global Solutions LLC**
100 Metroplex Dr, Ste 102,
Edison NJ 08817. 732/572-5400.

**Total Business Solutions**
150 Clove Rd, Little Falls NJ
07424-2138. 973/812-9700.

**Transworld Information Systems**
33 Wood Ave S, Ste 7, Iselin NJ
08830-2719. 732/321-0500.

**Tropaion Inc.**
PO Box 995, Matawan NJ 07747-0995. 732/290-0080.

**Usertech**
4 Brighton Rd, Ste 410, Clifton
NJ 07012-1646. 973/473-4477.

**Visient Corporation**
4 Gatehall Dr, Parsippany NJ
07054-4518. 973/455-1800.

**Vital Computer Services International**
83 Hanover Rd, Ste 170, Florham
Park NJ 07932-1508. 973/377-3177.

**Winnertech Corp.**
75 W Front St, Red Bank NJ
07701-1621. 732/758-9500.

**For more information on career opportunities in the computer industry:**

<u>Associations</u>

**AMERICAN INTERNET ASSOCIATION**
World Wide Web address: http://www.amernet.org. A
nonprofit association providing assistance in the use
of the Internet. Membership required.

**ASSOCIATION FOR COMPUTING MACHINERY**
1515 Broadway, 17th Floor, New York NY 10036.
212/869-7440. World Wide Web address: http://www.
acm.org. Membership required.

**ASSOCIATION FOR MULTIMEDIA COMMUNICATIONS**
P.O. Box 10645, Chicago IL 60610. 312/409-1032. E-mail address: amc@amcomm.org. World Wide Web address: http://www.amcomm.org. A multimedia and Internet association.

**ASSOCIATION FOR WOMEN IN COMPUTING**
41 Sutter Street, Suite 1006, San Francisco CA 94104. 415/905-4663. E-mail address: awc@awe.org. World Wide Web address: http://www.awc-hq.org. A nonprofit organization promoting women in computing professions.

**ASSOCIATION OF INTERNET PROFESSIONALS**
1301 Fifth Avenue, Suite 3300, Seattle WA 98101. E-mail address: info@associp.org. World Wide Web address: http://www.associp.org. A nonprofit trade association providing a forum for Internet users and professionals.

**BLACK DATA PROCESSING ASSOCIATES**
1111 14th Street NW, Suite 700, Washington DC 20005-5603. Toll-free phone: 800/727-BDPA. E-mail address: nbdpa@bdpa.org. World Wide Web address: http://www.bdpa.org. An organization of information technology professionals serving the minority community.

**THE CENTER FOR SOFTWARE DEVELOPMENT**
111 West St. John, Suite 200, San Jose CA 95113. 408/494-8378. E-mail address: info@center.org. World Wide Web address: http://www.center.org. A nonprofit organization providing technical and business resources for software developers.

**COMMERCIAL INTERNET EXCHANGE ASSOCIATION (CIX)**
1041 Sterling Road, Suite 104A, Herndon VA 20170. 703/709-8200. E-mail address: helpdesk@cix.org. World Wide Web address: http://www.cix.org. A nonprofit trade association of data internetworking service providers.

**HTML WRITERS GUILD**
World Wide Web address: http://www.hwg.org. An international organization of Web page writers and Internet professionals.

**INFORMATION TECHNOLOGY ASSOCIATION OF AMERICA**
1616 North Fort Myer Drive, Suite 1300, Arlington VA 22209. 703/522-5055. World Wide Web address: http://www.itaa.org.

**INTERNET ALLIANCE**
1825 Eye Street, Suite 400, P.O. Box 65782, Washington DC 20035. 202/955-8091. World Wide Web address: http://www.isa.net.

**MIS NETWORK ASSOCIATES**
P.O. Box 336, Ridgewood NJ 07801. 201/804-5909. World Wide Web address: http://www.nylana.org/misna. A networking group for unemployed MIS and information technology professionals.

**MULTIMEDIA DEVELOPMENT GROUP**
520 Third Street, Suite 257, San Francisco CA 94107. 415/512-3556. Fax: 415/512-3569. E-mail address: geninfo@mdg.org. A nonprofit trade association dedicated to the business and market development of multimedia companies.

**THE OPEN GROUP**
29-B Montvale Avenue, Woburn MA 01801. 781/376-8200. World Wide Web address: http://www.opengroup.org. A consortium concerned with open systems technology in the information systems industry. Membership required.

**SOCIETY FOR INFORMATION MANAGEMENT**
401 North Michigan Avenue, Chicago IL 60611-4267. 312/644-6610. E-mail address: info@simnet.org. World Wide Web address: http://www.simnet.org. A forum for information technology professionals.

**SOFTWARE FORUM**
953 Industrial Avenue, Suite 117, Palo Alto CA 94303. 650/856-3706. E-mail address: info@softwareforum.org. World Wide Web address: http://www.softwareforum.org. An independent, nonprofit organization for software industry professionals.

**SOFTWARE PUBLISHERS ASSOCIATION**
1730 M Street NW, Suite 700, Washington DC 20036. 202/452-1600. World Wide Web address: http://www.spa.org.

**SOFTWARE SUPPORT PROFESSIONALS ASSOCIATION**
11858 Bernardo Plaza Court, Suite 101C, San Diego CA 92128. Toll-free phone: 877/ASK-SSPA. World Wide Web address: http://www.sspa-online.com. A forum for service and support professionals in the software industry.

**USENIX ASSOCIATION**
2560 Ninth Street, Berkeley CA 94710. 510/528-8649. World Wide Web address: http://www.usenix.org. An advanced computing systems professional association for engineers, systems administrators, scientists, and technicians.

**WORLD WIDE WEB TRADE ASSOCIATION**
World Wide Web address: http://www.web-star.com/wwwta.html. An association promoting responsible use of the World Wide Web.

**Career Fairs**

**HI-TECH CAREER FAIRS AND SALES & BUSINESS PROFESSIONAL CAREER FAIRS**
National Career Centers USA, Inc., P.O. Box 447, Fayetteville NC 28302. 910/487-1100. Toll-free phone: 800/326-9111. Held three times per year in the New Jersey area.

**Magazines**

**COMPUTER-AIDED ENGINEERING**
Penton Media, Inc., 1100 Superior Avenue, Cleveland OH 44114. 216/696-7000. World Wide Web address: http://www.penton.com/cae.

**DATA COMMUNICATIONS**
McGraw-Hill, 3 Park Avenue, 31st Floor, New York NY 10013. 212/512-2000.

**DATAMATION**
Earthweb Inc., 10 Post Office Square, Suite 600 South, Boston MA 02109. World Wide Web address: http://www.datamation.com.

**IDC REPORT**
International Data Corporation, 5 Speen Street, Framingham MA 01701. 508/872-8200.

## Online Services

### COMPUTER CONSULTANTS
Go: Consult. A CompuServe discussion group for computer professionals interested in networking and business development.

### COMPUTERWORLD
http://www.computerworld.com. A weekly online newspaper for information sciences professionals. Features the latest news and employment opportunities. *Computerworld* conducts a job search by skills, job level (entry-level or experienced), job title, company, and your choice of three cities and three states. One feature of this site is "Career Central," a service which e-mails you when a job matches the skills you have submitted online. This site also has corporate profiles, an events calendar, *Computerworld*'s publications, an index of graduate schools, and other informative and educational resources.

### IT JOBS
http://www.internet-solutions.com/itjobs/us/usselect. htm. This Website provides links to companies that have job openings in the information technology industry.

### JOBSERVE
http://www.jobserve.com. Provides information on job openings in the field of information technology for companies throughout Europe. The site also offers links to numerous company Web pages, resume posting services, and a directory of recruiters.

### SELECTJOBS
http://www.selectjobs.com. Post a resume and search the job database by region, discipline, special requirements, and skills on *SelectJOBS*. Once your search criteria has been entered, this site will automatically e-mail you when a job opportunity matches your requests.

### THE SOFTWARE JOBS HOMEPAGE
http://www.softwarejobs.com. This Website offers a searchable database of openings for jobseekers looking in the software and information technology industries. The site is run by Allen Davis & Associates.

# EDUCATIONAL SERVICES

Job prospects remain favorable in educational services, due to a healthy demand for qualified teachers at all levels. The U.S. Department of Labor projects that over the next 10 years, more than 2 million teachers will retire. Demand will be strong for elementary and secondary teachers, college and university faculty, education administrators, school counselors, kindergarten teachers, and teacher assistants. Special education teachers are still in strong demand, with a 56 percent projected increase in openings through 2005. According to the U.S. Department of Education, a need for additional educators in the areas of bilingual education, math, and science is likely.

It is estimated that national high school enrollment will increase 11 percent by 2008. As the enrollment swells in elementary and secondary schools, and at higher learning institutions, operating costs will rise significantly as well. Among the cost pressures schools face are the implementation of computer technology in the classroom and curriculum changes.

According to Business Week, colleges and universities under fiscal constraints are struggling to meet the challenges of sustaining a high level of teaching and curricula without increasing tuition to the point that they are not affordable for the majority of students. For their part, some states (such as Massachusetts) are currently implementing programs that require teachers to pass aptitude tests, in efforts of improving the quality of education.

**BERGEN COMMUNITY COLLEGE**
400 Paramus Road, Paramus NJ 07652-1508. 201/447-7442. **Contact:** Personnel Office. **Description:** A community college enrolling more than 12,000 students.

**BERLITZ INTERNATIONAL, INC.**
400 Alexander Park, Princeton NJ 08540. 609/514-9650. **Contact:** David Horn, Vice President of Personnel, North America. **World Wide Web address:** http://www.berlitz.com. **Description:** A language services firm providing instruction and translation services through 298 language centers in 28 countries around the world. The company also publishes travel guides, foreign language phrase books, and home study materials. **Common positions include:** Accountant/Auditor; Director; Instructor/Trainer; Services Sales Representative. **Educational backgrounds include:** Accounting; Business Administration; Finance; Foreign Languages; Liberal Arts. **Corporate headquarters location:** This Location. **Operations at this facility include:** Administration. **Listed on:** New York Stock Exchange. **Number of employees nationwide:** 3,500.

**BRICK TOWNSHIP BOARD OF EDUCATION**
101 Hendrickson Avenue, Brick NJ 08724. 732/785-3000. **Contact:** Personnel. **Description:** Provides administrative, transportation, maintenance, and personnel services for Brick Township, which encompasses two high schools, two middle schools, eight elementary schools, and a primary learning center kindergarten.

**CAMDEN COUNTY COLLEGE**
P.O. Box 200, College Drive, Blackwood NJ 08012. 609/227-7200. **Contact:** Personnel. **World Wide Web address:** http://www.camdencc.edu. **Description:** A community college with more than 11,500 students enrolled in over 80 academic areas.

**CANTERBURY INFORMATION TECHNOLOGY, INC.**
1600 Medford Plaza, Medford NJ 08055. 609/953-0044. **Fax:** 609/953-0062. **Contact:** Darcy Teibel, Administrative Assistant. **World Wide Web address:** http://www.canterburyxcel.com. **Description:** A corporate training company covering entry-level vocational, managerial, executive, and technical areas. **Corporate headquarters location:** This Location. **Subsidiaries include:**

ATM/Canterbury Corp., a software development and consulting firm; CALC/Canterbury Corp., a computer software training company; MSI/Canterbury Corp., a management, sales, and communication training company; ProSoft/Canterbury Corp., a provider of technical staffing, applications development, and corporate training.

**COLLEGE OF NEW JERSEY**
P.O. Box 7718, Ewing NJ 08628-0718. 609/771-1855. **Contact:** Michelle Kilcher-Reilly, Personnel Department. **Description:** College of New Jersey is a four-year, state college offering bachelor's and master's degrees to approximately 6,000 undergraduate and 1,000 graduate students.

**EDUCATIONAL TESTING SERVICE (ETS)**
Rosedale Road, Princeton NJ 08541. 609/921-9000. **Contact:** Human Resources. **Description:** An educational research and evaluation service that administers many aptitude and achievement tests including the SAT, CLEP, TOEFL, GRE, GMAT, and AP.

**HELENE FULD SCHOOL OF NURSING**
College Drive, P.O. Box 1669, Blackwood NJ 08012. 609/374-0100. **Contact:** Human Resources. **Description:** A nurse training center affiliated with Virtua Health.

**KEAN UNIVERSITY**
1000 Morris Avenue, Union NJ 07083. 908/527-2150. **Contact:** Human Resources Department. **World Wide Web address:** http://www.state.nj.us/personnel. **Description:** A four-year, state university.

**MONTCLAIR STATE UNIVERSITY**
**NEW JERSEY SCHOOL OF CONSERVATION**
One Normal Avenue, Upper Montclair NJ 07043. 973/655-4000. **Contact:** Personnel. **World Wide Web address:** http://www.montclair.edu. **Description:** A state college. **NOTE:** For more information about employment opportunities in the environmental school, please contact the New Jersey School of Conservation, Human Resources Department, One Wapalanne Road, Branchville NJ 07826. 973/948-4646.

**NEW JERSEY CITY UNIVERSITY**
2039 Kennedy Boulevard, Hepburn Hall 105, Jersey City NJ 07305. 201/200-2335. **Fax:** 201/200-2219. **Contact:** Carolyn Turner, Director of Human Resources. **World Wide Web address:** http://www.njcu.edu. **Description:** A state university with approximately 10,000 students enrolled in its undergraduate, graduate, and continuing education programs. Formerly Jersey City State College, New Jersey City University achieved university status in May 1998. **Common positions include:** Education Administrator; Teacher/Professor. **Benefits:** 403(b); Dental Insurance; Disability Coverage; Flexible Schedule; Life Insurance; Medical Insurance; Pension Plan; Tuition Assistance.

**NEW JERSEY INSTITUTE OF TECHNOLOGY**
323 Martin Luther King Jr. Boulevard, Cullimore Hall, Room 211, Newark NJ 07102. 973/596-3140. **Contact:** Human Resources. **World Wide Web address:** http://www.njit.edu. **Description:** A technical institute of higher learning.

**PRINCETON UNIVERSITY**
Clio Hall, Office of Human Resources, Princeton NJ 08544. 609/258-3000. **Contact:** Joan Doig, Director of Human Resources. **World Wide Web address:** http://www.princeton.edu. **Description:** A private, four-year university offering bachelor of arts and science degrees, as well as master's and doctoral degrees. Approximately 4,500 undergraduate and 1,800 graduate students attend Princeton.

**ROWAN COLLEGE OF NEW JERSEY**
201 Mullica Hill Road, Glassboro NJ 08028. 609/256-4134. **Contact:** Human Resources. **World Wide Web address:** http://www.rowan.edu. **Description:** A four-year, state college offering bachelor's and master's degrees (including MBAs). Approximately 9,000 students attend Rowan College.

**RUTGERS STATE UNIVERSITY OF NEW JERSEY**
56 Bevier Road, Piscataway NJ 08854-8010. 732/445-3020. **Contact:** Personnel Department. **World Wide Web address:** http://www.rutgers.edu. **Description:** A four-year, state university. **Other U.S. locations:** Newark NJ.

## RUTGERS STATE UNIVERSITY OF NEW JERSEY
## UNIVERSITY COLLEGE-NEWARK
249 University Avenue, Newark NJ 07102. 973/353-1766. **Contact:** Human Resources. **World Wide Web address:** http://www.rutgers.edu. **Description:** A division of the state university. **Other U.S. locations:** Brunswick NJ.

## SETON HALL UNIVERSITY
400 South Orange Avenue, Stafford Hall, South Orange NJ 07079. 973/761-9138. **Contact:** Deborah Raikes-Colbert, Assistant Vice President for Human Resources. **World Wide Web address:** http://www.shu.edu. **Description:** A university.

## THOMAS EDISON STATE COLLEGE
101 West State Street, Trenton NJ 08608-1176. 609/984-1114. **Contact:** Ms. Carron M. Albert, Director of Human Resources. **Description:** A state college. **Benefits:** Dental Insurance; Disability Coverage; Life Insurance; Medical Insurance; Pension Plan; Tuition Assistance. **Corporate headquarters location:** This Location.

## TOMS RIVER REGIONAL SCHOOLS
1144 Hooper Avenue, Toms River NJ 08753. 732/505-5500. **Contact:** Human Resources. **Description:** A regional school district.

## WILLIAM PATERSON UNIVERSITY OF NEW JERSEY
300 Pompton Road, Wayne NJ 07470. 973/720-2603. **Contact:** Director of Human Resources. **World Wide Web address:** http://www.willpaterson.edu. **Description:** A public university with approximately 9,000 students. Programs include liberal arts, nursing, sciences, English, history, and music. The student body consists primarily of students from New Jersey.

*Note: Because addresses and telephone numbers of smaller companies can change rapidly, we recommend you call each company to verify the information below before inquiring about job opportunities. Mass mailings are not recommended.*

**Additional small employers:**

**BUSINESS, SECRETARIAL, AND DATA PROCESSING SCHOOLS**

**Berkeley Educational Services of New Jersey**
PO Box 440, Little Falls NJ 07424-0440. 973/278-5400.

**CHILD DAYCARE SERVICES**

**Clinton Street Head Start**
90 Martin St, Paterson NJ 07501-3622. 973/345-9555.

**Holley Childcare and Development Center**
260 Union St, Hackensack NJ 07601-4203. 201/343-8803.

**COLLEGES, UNIVERSITIES, AND PROFESSIONAL SCHOOLS**

**Bloomfield College & Seminary**
467 Franklin St, Bloomfield NJ 07003-3425. 973/748-9000.

**Caldwell College**
9 Ryerson Ave, Caldwell NJ 07006-6109. 973/228-4424.

**Centenary College**
400 Jefferson St, Hackettstown NJ 07840-2184. 908/852-1400.

**College of St. Elizabeth**
2 Convent Rd, Morristown NJ 07960-6923. 973/290-4000.

**DeVry Institute of Technology**
630 US Highway 1, North Brunswick NJ 08902-3311. 732/545-3900.

**Drew University**
36 Madison Ave, Madison NJ 07940-1434. 973/408-3000.

**Edward Williams College**
1000 River Rd, Teaneck NJ 07666-1914. 201/692-2000.

**Essex County College**
303 University Ave, Newark NJ 07102-1719. 973/877-3000.

**Felician College**
262 S Main St, Lodi NJ 07644-2117. 973/778-1190.

**Georgian Court College**
900 Lakewood Ave, Lakewood NJ 08701-2600. 732/364-2200.

**Monmouth College**
Cedar Ave, West Long Branch NJ 07764. 732/571-3400.

**New Jersey Dental School**
110 Bergen St, Newark NJ 07103-2400. 973/982-4615.

**Ramapo College of New Jersey**
505 Ramapo Valley Rd, Mahwah NJ 07430-1623. 201/529-7500.

**Rutgers State University of New Jersey**
329 Cooper St, Camden NJ 08102-1519. 609/225-1766.

**Seton Hall University School of Law**
1 Newark Ctr, Newark NJ 07102-5211. 973/642-8500.

**St. Peter's College**
2641 Kennedy Blvd, Jersey City NJ 07306-5943. 201/915-9000.

**Stevens Institute of Technology**
Castle Point Station, Hoboken NJ 07030. 201/216-5000.

**Waksman Institute**
PO Box 759, Piscataway NJ 08855-0759. 732/445-4748.

**ELEMENTARY AND SECONDARY SCHOOLS**

**Abington Avenue School**
209 Abington Ave, Newark NJ 07107-2507. 973/268-5230.

**Abraham Clark High School**
122 E 6th Ave, Roselle NJ 07203-2026. 908/298-2002.

**Absegami High School**
201 S Wrangleboro Rd, Absecon
NJ 08201-9553. 609/652-1372.

**Alfred Reed School**
11 Buttonwood Dr, Trenton NJ
08638-2911. 609/771-4466.

**Allegro School**
125 Ridgedale Ave, Cedar Knolls
NJ 07927-1803. 973/267-8060.

**Allen Middle School**
801 N Stanwick Rd, Moorestown
NJ 08057-2034. 609/778-6620.

**Ann Street Elementary School**
30 Ann St, Newark NJ 07105-
3108. 973/465-4890.

**Anthiel School**
339 Ewingville Rd, Trenton NJ
08638-1721. 609/883-2212.

**Archbishop Damiano School**
1145 Delsea Dr, Westville NJ
08093-2252. 609/848-3838.

**Arthur J. Holland Middle
School**
1001 W State St, Trenton NJ
08618-5233. 609/989-2730.

**Arthur Johnson Regional High
School**
365 Westfield Ave, Clark NJ
07066-1706. 732/382-0910.

**Arthur Judd Elementary
School**
1601 Roosevelt Ave, North
Brunswick NJ 08902-2660.
732/297-3400.

**Asbury Park High School**
1001 Sunset Ave, Asbury Park NJ
07712-5033. 732/776-2638.

**Atlantic City High School**
3701 Atlantic Avenue, Atlantic
City NJ 08401-6004. 609/343-
7300.

**Barringer High School**
90 Parker St, Newark NJ 07104-
1028. 973/268-5125.

**Barringer Prep School**
63 Webster St, Newark NJ
07104-2529. 973/268-5100.

**Bayonne High School**
28th St & Ave A, Bayonne NJ
07002. 201/858-5900.

**Belvidere Board of Education**
Oxford St, Belvidere NJ 07823.
908/475-6605.

**Berkeley Heights Board of
Education**
PO Box 147, Berkeley Heights
NJ 07922-0147. 908/464-1718.

**Berkeley Township Board of
Education**
53 Central Pkwy, Bayville NJ
08721-2414. 732/269-2321.

**Berlin Township School District**
234 Mount Vernon Ave, West
Berlin NJ 08091-1231. 609/767-
9403.

**Bernice Young Elementary
School**
1203 Neck Rd, Burlington NJ
08016-3909. 609/386-3520.

**Blair Academy**
PO Box 600, Blairstown NJ
07825-0600. 908/362-6121.

**Bleshman Regional Day School**
333 E Ridgewood Ave, Paramus
NJ 07652-4819. 201/262-7444.

**Bloomfield High School**
160 Broad St, Bloomfield NJ
07003-2628. 973/680-8600.

**Board of Education**
Ave A & 29th St, Bayonne NJ
07002. 201/858-5560.

**Board of Education**
124 Willow Dr, Little Silver NJ
07739-1538. 732/741-2188.

**Board of Education**
510 Chestnut St, Roselle Park NJ
07204-1928. 908/245-2103.

**Bridgeton High School**
Cherry St, Bridgeton NJ 08302.
609/455-8030.

**Bridgeton Middle School**
251 Broad St W, Bridgeton NJ
08302-2315. 609/453-3278.

**Bridgewater Raritan High
School**
PO Box 6569, Bridgewater NJ
08807-0569. 908/231-8660.

**Bridgewater Raritan Middle
School**
PO Box 6933, Bridgewater NJ
08807-0933. 908/575-9262.

**Brigantine School District**
PO Box 947, Brigantine NJ
08203-6947. 609/266-7671.

**Burlington City High School**
100 Dewey St, Burlington NJ
08016-2746. 609/387-5800.

**Burlington Township Board of
Education**
PO Box 428, Burlington NJ
08016-0428. 609/387-3955.

**Butler School District**
38 Bartholdi Ave, Butler NJ
07405-1404. 973/492-2040.

**Byram Township Board of
Education**
12 Mansfield Dr, Stanhope NJ
07874-3123. 973/347-1047.

**Calabro Elementary School**
524 Park Ave, Hoboken NJ
07030-3906. 201/420-2343.

**Camden Board of Education**
3064 Stevens St, Camden NJ
08105-2367. 609/966-5111.

**Camden Catholic High School**
Cuthbert Blvd & Rural Route 38,
Cherry Hill NJ 08002. 609/663-
2247.

**Camden High School**
1700 Park Blvd, Camden NJ
08103-2806. 609/966-5100.

**Carl W. Goetz Middle School**
835 Patterson Rd, Jackson NJ
08527-4936. 732/928-5112.

**Carteret High School**
199 Washington Ave, Carteret NJ
07008-2706. 732/969-4000.

**Central High School**
100 Summit St, Newark NJ
07103-3520. 973/733-6897.

**Central High School**
259 Pennington Titusville,
Pennington NJ 08534-1617.
609/737-1411.

**Central Regional High School**
PO Box C, Bayville NJ 08721-
0288. 732/269-1100.

**Charles W. Lewis Middle
School**
875 Erial Rd, Blackwood NJ
08012. 609/227-8400.

**Chatham High School**
255 Lafayette Ave, Chatham NJ
07928-1830. 973/635-9075.

**Cherokee High School**
120 Tomlinson Mill Rd, Marlton
NJ 08053-2550. 609/983-5140.

**Cherry Hill East High School**
1750 Kresson Rd, Cherry Hill NJ
08003-2590. 609/424-2222.

**Cherry Hill School District**
PO Box 5015, Cherry Hill NJ
08034-0391. 609/429-5600.

**Cherry Hill West High School**
2101 Chapel Ave W, Cherry Hill
NJ 08002-2052. 609/663-8006.

**Christa McAuliffe Middle
School**
Hope Chapel Rd, Jackson NJ
08527. 732/901-0052.

**Churchill Junior High School**
18 Norton Rd, East Brunswick NJ
08816-1704. 732/613-6800.

**Clayton School District Board
of Education**
300 W Chestnut St, Clayton NJ
08312. 609/881-8868.

**Clearview Senior High School**
PO Box 2000, Mullica Hill NJ
08062-0120. 609/478-4400.

**Cleveland Elementary School**
388 Bergen St, Newark NJ
07103-2232. 973/733-6944.

**Clifford J. Scott High School**
129 Renshaw Ave, East Orange
NJ 07017-3308. 973/266-5900.

**Clifton Avenue Elementary
School**
625 Clifton Ave, Lakewood NJ
08701-2808. 732/905-3656.

**Clifton Board of Education**
PO Box 2209, Clifton NJ 07015-
2209. 973/470-2300.

**Clifton E. Lawrence Primary
School**
31 Ryan Rd, Sussex NJ 07461-
1705. 973/875-8820.

**Cold Springs School**
1 Cold Springs Ave, Gloucester
City NJ 08030-2100. 609/456-
0320.

**Collier School**
PO Box 300, Wickatunk NJ
07765-0300. 732/946-4771.

**Collingswood Senior High
School**
424 W Collings Ave,
Collingswood NJ 08108-3054.
609/962-5701.

**Colonia High School**
180 East St, Colonia NJ 07067-
2219. 732/499-6500.

**Columbia High School**
17 Parker Ave, Maplewood NJ
07040-1327. 973/762-5600.

**Columbus Middle School**
350 Piaget Ave, Clifton NJ
07011-2558. 973/470-2360.

**Cramer Elementary School**
29th & Mickle St, Camden NJ
08105. 609/966-8910.

**Cumberland Regional High
School**
PO Box 5115, Bridgeton NJ
08302-5115. 609/451-9400.

**Dag Hammarskjold Middle
School**
200 Rues Lane, East Brunswick
NJ 08816-3600. 732/613-6890.

**Davis Junior High School**
300 N 36th St, Camden NJ
08110-3102. 609/966-8920.

**Delaware Valley Regional
School District**
19 Senator Stout Road,
Frenchtown NJ 08825-3721.
908/996-2131.

**Delbarton School**
230 Mendham Rd, Morristown
NJ 07960-5089. 973/538-3231.

**Delran High School**
50 Hartford Rd, Beverly NJ
08010. 609/461-6100.

**Deptford Township High
School**
575 Fox Run Rd, Woodbury NJ
08096-4242. 609/232-2713.

**Dover High School**
100 Grace St, Dover NJ 07801-
2644. 973/989-2010.

**Dr. William Horton Elementary
School**
291 N 7th St, Newark NJ 07107-
1751. 973/268-5260.

**Dumont High School**
101 New Milford Ave, Dumont
NJ 07628-2913. 201/387-1600.

**Dwight-Englewood School**
PO Box 489, Englewood NJ
07631-0489. 201/569-9500.

**East Brunswick High School**
380 Cranbury Rd, East
Brunswick NJ 08816-3062.
732/613-6900.

**East Dover Elementary Schoool**
725 Vaughn Ave, Toms River NJ
08753-4567. 732/505-5840.

**East Orange High School**
34 N Walnut St, East Orange NJ
07017-3506. 973/266-5800.

**East Orange School District**
715 Park Ave, East Orange NJ
07017-1004. 973/266-5727.

**East Side High School**
238 Van Buren St, Newark NJ
07105-2512. 973/465-4900.

**Eastern Camden Board of
Education**
PO Box 2500, Voorhees NJ
08043-0995. 609/346-6730.

**Eastern High School**
1306 Laurel Oak Rd, Voorhees
NJ 08043-4310. 609/784-4441.

**Eastside High School**
150 Park Ave, Paterson NJ
07501-2327. 973/881-6300.

**Edgewood Regional Junior
High School**
200 Cooper Folly Rd, Atco NJ
08004-2649. 609/767-7222.

**Edison High School**
50 Boulevard of Eagles, Edison
NJ 08817-4002. 732/985-2900.

**Edison School**
507 West St, Union City NJ
07087-2811. 201/348-5965.

**Edison Township Board of
Education**
100 Municipal Blvd, Edison NJ
08817-3302. 732/287-4400.

**Elizabeth City Board of
Education**
500 N Broad St, Elizabeth NJ
07208-3302. 908/558-3000.

**Elizabeth High School**
600 Pearl St, Elizabeth NJ 07202-
3624. 908/558-3100.

**Emerson High School**
318 18th St, Union City NJ
07087-4424. 201/348-5901.

**Erial Elementary School**
20 Essex Ave, Sicklerville NJ
08081-1210. 609/627-5415.

**Ewing High School**
900 Parkway Ave, Trenton NJ
08618-2308. 609/771-1300.

**Fair Lawn High School**
14-00 Berdan Ave, Fair Lawn NJ
07410-2155. 201/794-5450.

**Fieldstone Middle School**
Spring Valley Rd, Montvale NJ
07645. 201/391-1662.

**Fisher Middle School**
1325 Lower Ferry Rd, Trenton NJ
08618-1409. 609/883-2882.

**Flemington-Raritan School
District**
50 Court St, Flemington NJ
08822-1325. 908/782-8074.

**Florence Board of Education**
201 Cedar St, Florence NJ 08518-
1502. 609/499-4603.

**Florence Memorial High School**
500 E Front St, Florence NJ
08518-1511. 609/499-4620.

**Fort Lee High School**
3000 Lemoine Ave, Fort Lee NJ
07024-6105. 201/585-4675.

**Forum School**
107 Wyckoff Ave, Waldwick NJ
07463-1734. 201/444-5882.

**Frank H. Morrell High School**
1253 Clinton Ave, Irvington NJ
07111-2437. 973/399-6897.

**Frankford Township School District**
PO Box 430, Branchville NJ
07826-0430. 973/948-3727.

**Franklin Borough School District**
49 Washington Ave, Franklin NJ
07416-1719. 973/827-9010.

**Franklin Elementary School**
42 Park Ave, Newark NJ 07104-
1004. 973/268-5250.

**Freehold High School**
65 Broadway, Freehold NJ
07728-1860. 732/431-8365.

**Freehold Township High School**
281 Elton Adelphia Rd, Freehold
NJ 07728-8021. 732/431-8464.

**Gateway Regional Board of Education**
775 Yanyard Rd, Woodbury NJ
08097. 609/848-8200.

**Gillette Public School**
759 Valley Rd, Gillette NJ
07933-1936. 908/647-2313.

**Glen Landing Middle School**
85 Little Gloucester Rd,
Blackwood NJ 08012-5253.
609/227-3534.

**Glen Rock High School**
400 Hamilton Ave, Glen Rock NJ
07452-3432. 201/445-7700.

**Glen Rock Middle School**
600 Harristown Rd, Glen Rock
NJ 07452-2328. 201/251-8930.

**Gloucester City Junior Senior High School**
131 Crescent Blvd, Gloucester
City NJ 08030. 609/456-7000.

**Gloucester City School District**
520 Cumberland St, Gloucester
City NJ 08030-1923. 609/456-
9394.

**Governor Livingston Regional High School**
175 Watchung Blvd, Berkeley
Heights NJ 07922-2726. 908/464-
3100.

**Green Brook Middle School**
132 Jefferson Ave, Dunellen NJ
08812-2608. 732/968-1051.

**HA Marsh Primary School**
Irelan Ave, Absecon NJ 08201.
609/641-5375.

**Hackensack High School**
1st & Beach, Hackensack NJ
07601. 201/646-7900.

**Hackettstown High School**
PO Box 465, Hackettstown NJ
07840-0465. 908/852-2800.

**Haddon Heights Board of Education**
300 2nd Ave, Haddon Heights NJ
08035-1408. 609/547-7164.

**Haddon Township High School**
406 Memorial Ave, Collingswood
NJ 08108. 609/869-7750.

**Hamilton North High School**
1055 Klockner Rd, Trenton NJ
08619-3046. 609/890-3758.

**Hamilton Township Board of Education**
90 Park Ave, Trenton NJ 08690-
2024. 609/890-3720.

**Hammonton Elementary School**
PO Box 308, Hammonton NJ
08037. 609/567-7006.

**Hanover Park High School**
63 Mount Pleasant Ave, East
Hanover NJ 07936-2601.
973/887-0300.

**Harry L. Bain Elementary School**
6200 Broadway, West New York
NJ 07093-3008. 201/902-1241.

**Hasbrouck Heights Junior Senior High School**
365 Boulevard, Hasbrouck
Heights NJ 07604-1402. 201/288-
3971.

**Helen A. Fort Middle School**
PO Box 98, Browns Mills NJ
08015-0098. 609/894-8223.

**Helen I. Smith Elementary School**
30 Cambridge Ave, Saddle Brook
NJ 07663-4538. 201/796-6650.

**Highland High School**
450 Erial Rd, Blackwood NJ
08012-4583. 609/227-4100.

**Highland Park High School**
102 N 5th Ave, Highland Park NJ
08904-2925. 732/572-2400.

**Highpoint Regional High School**
299 Pigeon Hill Rd, Sussex NJ
07461. 973/875-3101.

**Hillsborough High School**
466 Raider Blvd, Belle Mead NJ
08502-1443. 908/874-4200.

**Hillsborough Middle School**
260 Triangle Rd, Somerville NJ
08876-4878. 908/874-3420.

**Hillside High School**
1085 Liberty Ave, Hillside NJ
07205-2526. 908/352-7662.

**Hoboken High School**
9th & Clinton Sts, Hoboken NJ
07030. 201/420-2300.

**Hoboken School District**
1115 Clinton St, Hoboken NJ
07030-3201. 201/420-2162.

**Holland Township School District**
714 Milford Warren Glen Rd,
Milford NJ 08848-1647. 908/995-
2401.

**Holmdel High School**
36 Crawford Corner Rd, Holmdel
NJ 07733. 732/946-1832.

**Holy Cross High School**
5035 Route 130, Riverside NJ
08075-1702. 609/461-5400.

**Hooper Avenue School**
1517 Hooper Ave, Toms River
NJ 08753-2236. 732/505-5850.

**Hopatcong School District**
PO Box 1029, Hopatcong NJ
07843-0829. 973/398-8801.

**Horace Mann Elementary School**
1215 83rd St, North Bergen NJ
07047-4233. 201/295-2880.

**Howell High School**
405 Squankum Yellowbrook,
Farmingdale NJ 07727-3743.
732/431-8490.

**Howell Township Board of Education**
PO Box 579, Howell NJ 07731-
0579. 732/938-7161.

**Hudson County Vocational Technical School**
8511 Tonnelle Ave, North Bergen
NJ 07047-4738. 201/854-3900.

**Hunterdon Central High School**
RR 31, Flemington NJ 08822.
908/782-5727.

**Hunterdon County Vocational School**
256 County Road 513, Glen
Gardner NJ 08826-3217.
908/638-5226.

**Indian Hills High School**
97 Yawpo Ave, Oakland NJ
07436-2740. 201/337-0100.

**Jackson Board of Education**
151 Don Connor Blvd, Jackson
NJ 08527-3407. 732/928-1464.

**James Caldwell Senior High School**
265 Westville Ave, Caldwell NJ
07006-7434. 973/228-6981.

**Jefferson Elementary School**
100 Prospect Ave, North
Arlington NJ 07031-6124.
201/955-5245.

**Jefferson Township Board of Education**
1010 Weldon Rd, Oak Ridge NJ 07438-9515. 973/697-3535.

**Jersey City Board of Education**
346 Claremont Avenue, Jersey City NJ 07305-1634. 201/915-6000.

**John Adams Elementary School**
1450 Redmond St, New Brunswick NJ 08902-1520. 732/247-6166.

**John F. Kennedy High School**
200 Washington Ave, Iselin NJ 08830-2371. 732/602-8650.

**Jonathan Dyton Regional High School**
Mountain Ave, Springfield NJ 07081. 973/376-6300.

**Jordan Elementary School**
129 Jordan Rd, Somers Point NJ 08244-1408. 609/927-7161.

**Joseph F. Cappell School**
1072 Old Trenton Rd, Trenton NJ 08690-1230. 609/588-8485.

**Joseph H. Brensinger School**
600 Bergen Ave, Jersey City NJ 07304-2539. 201/915-6120.

**Joseph Kushner Hebrew Academy**
110 S Orange Ave, Livingston NJ 07039-4904. 973/597-1115.

**Kearny High School**
336 Devon St, Kearny NJ 07032-2612. 201/955-5050.

**Kent Place School**
42 Norwood Ave, Summit NJ 07901-1913. 908/273-0900.

**Keyport Central Elementary School**
335 Broad St, Keyport NJ 07735-1600. 732/264-0561.

**Keyport High School**
PO Box 80, Keyport NJ 07735-0080. 732/264-0902.

**Lacey Township High School**
PO Box 206, Lanoka Harbor NJ 08734-0206. 609/971-2020.

**Lake Riviera Middle School**
171 Beaverson Blvd, Brick NJ 08723-7804. 732/477-2800.

**Lakeland Regional High School**
205 Conklintown Road, Wanaque NJ 07465-2122. 973/835-1900.

**Lakewood High School**
855 Somerset Ave, Lakewood NJ 08701-2127. 732/905-3500.

**Lanning Square Elementary School**
5th Berkley, Camden NJ 08103. 609/966-8950.

**Lawrence Senior High School**
2525 Princeton Pike, Trenton NJ 08648-3631. 609/530-8371.

**Lenape High School**
235 Hartford Rd, Medford NJ 08055-4001. 609/654-5111.

**Lenape Regional High School District**
93 Willow Grove Rd, Vincentown NJ 08088-8961. 609/268-2000.

**Liberty School**
PO Box 334, Great Meadows NJ 07838. 908/637-8672.

**Lincoln Elementary School**
80 Prospect Ave, Dumont NJ 07628-2736. 201/387-3040.

**Lincoln Middle School**
291 Lafayette Ave, Passaic NJ 07055-3748. 973/470-5504.

**Lindenwold School District**
1017 E Linden Ave, Lindenwold NJ 08021-1126. 609/784-4071.

**Little Egg Harbor Intermediate School**
305 Frog Pond Rd, Tuckerton NJ 08087-9700. 609/296-1719.

**Little Egg Harbor Township Board of Education**
950 Route 539, Tuckerton NJ 08087-4206. 609/296-7911.

**Little Falls Township School District**
Stevens Ave, Little Falls NJ 07424. 973/256-1034.

**Livingston Park Elementary School**
1128 Livingston Ave, North Brunswick NJ 08902-1825. 732/247-5116.

**Livingston Senior High School**
30 Livingston High Rd, Livingston NJ 07039. 973/535-8100.

**Lloyd Road School**
401 Lloyd Rd, Matawan NJ 07747-1894. 732/290-2760.

**Logan Township Board of Education**
110 School Ln, Swedesboro NJ 08085-1545. 609/467-5133.

**Long Branch High School**
Westwood Ave, Long Branch NJ 07740. 732/229-7300.

**Long Branch Middle School**
364 Indiana Ave, Long Branch NJ 07740-6120. 732/229-5533.

**Lounsberry Hollow Middle School**
PO Box 219, Vernon NJ 07462-0219. 973/875-8813.

**Lower Cape May Regional High School**
Rural Route 9, Box 687, Cape May NJ 08204. 609/884-3475.

**Lyndhurst Board of Education**
281 Ridge Rd, Lyndhurst NJ 07071-1928. 201/438-5683.

**Macopin Middle School**
70 Highlander Dr, West Milford NJ 07480-1511. 973/697-5691.

**Mainland Regional High School**
1301 Oak Ave, Linwood NJ 08221-1653. 609/927-4151.

**Malcom X Shabazz High School**
80 Johnson Ave, Newark NJ 07108-2729. 973/733-6760.

**Manalapan Englishtown Middle School**
155 Millhurst Rd, Englishtown NJ 07726-4002. 732/446-8108.

**Manalapan High School**
Church Ln, Englishtown NJ 07726. 732/431-8320.

**Manchester Middle School**
2759 Ridgeway Rd, Lakehurst NJ 08733-4712. 732/657-1717.

**Manchester Township Elementary School**
101 N Colonial Dr, Lakehurst NJ 08733-3915. 732/323-9600.

**Manchester Township High School**
101 S Colonial Dr, Lakehurst NJ 08733-3701. 732/657-2121.

**Maple Shade High School**
Frederick Ave, Maple Shade NJ 08052. 609/779-2880.

**Marie Katzenbach School for the Deaf**
PO Box 535, Trenton NJ 08625-0535. 609/530-3112.

**Marlboro High School**
95 N Main St, Marlboro NJ 07746-1019. 732/431-8420.

**Marlboro Middle School**
355 County Road 520, Marlboro NJ 07746-1107. 732/972-2100.

**Marlboro Township Board of Education**
1980 Township Dr, Marlboro NJ 07746-2247. 732/972-2010.

**Marquis de Lafayette School**
1071 Julia St, Elizabeth NJ
07201-1554. 908/558-3281.

**Matawan Regional High School**
450 Atlantic Ave, Matawan NJ
07747-2326. 732/290-2800.

**McKinley Avenue Elementary School**
1000 McKinley Ave,
Manahawkin NJ 08050-2807.
609/978-5700.

**McKinley Elementary School**
1 Colonnade Pl, Newark NJ
07104-1810. 973/268-5270.

**Memorial High School**
5501 Park Ave, West New York
NJ 07093-3523. 201/902-1131.

**Memorial Middle School**
375 River Dr, Elmwood Park NJ
07407-1696. 201/794-2823.

**Memorial Middle School**
424 S Main Rd, Vineland NJ
08360-7843. 609/794-6918.

**Mercer Junior Senior High School**
1030 Old Trenton Rd, Trenton NJ
08690-1230. 609/588-8450.

**Meridian Academy**
150 Oberlin Ave N, Lakewood
NJ 08701-4523. 732/905-1228.

**Middle Township School**
1 Penkethman Way, Cape May
Courthouse NJ 08210. 609/465-
1852.

**Middlesex County Vocational & Technical School**
PO Box 1070, East Brunswick NJ
08816-1070. 732/257-3300.

**Middletown High School South**
501 Nutswamp Rd, Middletown
NJ 07748-3114. 732/706-6111.

**Midland Park Board of Education**
31 Highland Ave, Midland Park
NJ 07432-1803. 201/444-1400.

**Millburn Senior High School**
462 Millburn Ave, Millburn NJ
07041-1210. 973/376-3600.

**Millroad Middle School**
400 W Mill Rd, Northfield NJ
08225-1850. 609/641-1731.

**Millstone Township Board of Education**
Schoolhouse Ln, Clarksburg NJ
08510. 732/446-0890.

**Milltown School District**
Violet Ter, Milltown NJ 08850.
732/828-8620.

**Monmouth Regional High School**
1 Norman J. Field Way,
Eatontown NJ 07724-4005.
732/542-1170.

**Montclair High School**
100 Chestnut St, Montclair NJ
07042-2908. 973/509-4100.

**Moorestown Township School District**
803 N Stanwick Rd, Moorestown
NJ 08057-2034. 609/778-6600.

**Morris County Vocational School District**
400 E Main St, Denville NJ
07834-2500. 973/627-4600.

**Morris Hills High School**
520 W Main St, Rockaway NJ
07866-3729. 973/989-2800.

**Morris Hills Regional School**
48 Knoll Top Ct, Denville NJ
07834-3623. 973/627-3512.

**Morristown High School**
50 Early St, Morristown NJ
07960-3820. 973/292-2106.

**Mount Olive Middle School**
99 Sunset Dr, Budd Lake NJ
07828-3511. 973/691-4065.

**Mount Vernon Elementary School**
142 Mount Vernon Pl, Newark
NJ 07106-3143. 973/374-2090.

**Neptune Middle School**
2300 Heck Ave, Neptune NJ
07753-4432. 732/776-2100.

**Neptune Senior High School**
55 Neptune Blvd, Neptune NJ
07753-4838. 732/776-2200.

**Neptune Township Board of Education**
2106 W Bangs Ave, Neptune NJ
07753-4536. 732/776-2050.

**New Brunswick Board of Education**
PO Box 2683, New Brunswick
NJ 08903-2683. 732/745-5427.

**New Brunswick High School**
1125 Livingston Ave, New
Brunswick NJ 08901-3309.
732/745-5476.

**New Providence Board of Education**
356 Elkwood Ave, New
Providence NJ 07974-1838.
908/464-9050.

**Newark Board of Education**
131 13th Ave, Newark NJ 07103-
3440. 973/733-7068.

**Newark School District**
2 Cedar St, Newark NJ 07102-
3015. 973/733-6700.

**Newton Board of Education**
57 Trinity St, Newton NJ 07860-
1824. 973/383-1900.

**North Arlington High School**
222 Ridge Rd, North Arlington
NJ 07031-6036. 201/991-6800.

**North Brunswick High School**
Raider Rd, North Brunswick NJ
08902. 732/821-8200.

**North Hunterdon-Voorhees Regional High School**
1445 State Route 31, Annandale
NJ 08801-3117. 908/735-2846.

**North Plainfield High School**
34 Wilson Ave, Plainfield NJ
07060-4075. 908/769-6000.

**North Warren Regional High School**
PO Box 410, Blairstown NJ
07825-0410. 908/362-8384.

**Northern Burlington County School District**
160 Mansfield Rd E, Columbus
NJ 08022-2113. 609/298-3900.

**Northern Valley Demarest Regional High School**
150 Knickerbocker Rd, Demarest
NJ 07627-1026. 201/768-3200.

**Northfield Board of Education**
1000 Burton Ave, Northfield NJ
08225-1246. 609/641-5129.

**Notre Dame High School**
601 Lawrence Rd, Lawrenceville
NJ 08648-4297. 609/882-7900.

**Nutley High School**
300 Franklin Ave, Nutley NJ
07110-2734. 973/661-8846.

**Ocean Academy Middle School**
148 Crest Haven Rd, Cape May
Courthouse NJ 08210-1651.
609/465-2720.

**Ocean City High School**
6th St & Atlantic Ave, Ocean
City NJ 08226. 609/399-1290.

**Ocean City Intermediate School**
1801 Bay Ave, Ocean City NJ
08226-2850. 609/399-5611.

**Ocean Township High School**
550 W Park Ave, Oakhurst NJ
07755-1030. 732/531-5650.

**Ocean Township Intermediate School**
1200 W Park Ave, Asbury Park
NJ 07712-7222. 732/531-5630.

**Ocean Township School District**
163 Monmouth Rd, Oakhurst NJ
07755-1514. 732/531-5600.

**Oliver Street School**
104 Oliver St, Newark NJ 07105-
1120. 973/465-4870.

**Orange Board of Education**
369 Main St, Orange NJ 07050-
2704. 973/677-4000.

**Orange High School**
400 Lincoln Ave, Orange NJ
07050-2208. 973/677-4050.

**Overbrook Senior High School**
1200 Turnerville Rd, Clementon
NJ 08021-6626. 609/767-8000.

**Oxycocous Elementary School**
250 N Main St, Manahawkin NJ
08050-3011. 609/978-5730.

**Paramus High School**
99 E Century Rd, Paramus NJ
07652-4346. 201/445-6465.

**Parkview Elementary School**
80 Violet Ter, Milltown NJ
08850-1643. 732/249-9625.

**Parsippany High School**
PO Box 52, Parsippany NJ
07054-0052. 973/263-7001.

**Parsippany Hills High School**
PO Box 223, Parsippany NJ
07054-0223. 973/682-2815.

**Pascack Hills High School**
225 W Grand Ave, Montvale NJ
07645-2001. 201/358-7020.

**Pascack Valley Regional High
School**
46 Akers Ave, Montvale NJ
07645-2028. 201/358-7000.

**Passaic High School**
101 Passaic, Passaic NJ 07055.
973/470-5600.

**Passaic Valley High School**
100 E Main St, Little Falls NJ
07424-1600. 973/890-2500.

**Paterson Public School**
98 Oak St, Paterson NJ 07501-
3108. 973/881-6077.

**Paulsboro Junior/Senior High
School**
670 N Delaware St, Paulsboro NJ
08066-1020. 609/423-2222.

**Paulsboro Public School
District**
662 N Delaware St, Paulsboro NJ
08066-1020. 609/423-5515.

**Peddie School**
PO Box A, Hightstown NJ
08520-1010. 609/490-7555.

**Pemberton Township High
School**
PO Box 98, Browns Mills NJ
08015-0098. 609/894-4833.

**Pennsauken Township Board of
Education**
1695 Hylton Rd, Pennsauken NJ
08110-1313. 609/662-8505.

**Pennsville School District**
110 S Broadway, Pennsville NJ
08070-2060. 609/540-6220.

**Perth Amboy Board of
Education**
178 Barracks St, Perth Amboy NJ
08861-3402. 732/826-3360.

**Phillipsburg School District**
575 Elder Ave, Phillipsburg NJ
08865-1544. 908/454-3400.

**Pine Point Middle School**
7 Erie St, Camden NJ 08102-
2723. 609/966-5360.

**Pinelands Regional School
District**
PO Box 248, Tuckerton NJ
08087-0248. 609/296-3106.

**Pingry School**
PO Box 366, Martinsville NJ
08836-0366. 908/647-5555.

**Piscataway High School**
100 Behmer Rd, Piscataway NJ
08854-4161. 732/981-0700.

**Plumsted Township School
District**
44 N Main St, New Egypt NJ
08533-1316. 609/758-7155.

**Point Pleasant Boro High
School**
Laura Herbert Dr, Point Pleasant
NJ 08742. 732/892-7500.

**Point Pleasant School District**
2100 Panther Path, Point Pleasant
NJ 08742-3770. 732/892-0265.

**Princeton Day School**
PO Box 75, Princeton NJ 08542-
0075. 609/924-6700.

**Princeton High School**
151 Moore St, Princeton NJ
08540-3312. 609/683-4480.

**Quitman Street Elementary
School**
21 Quitman St, Newark NJ
07103-4105. 973/733-6947.

**Radix Elementary School**
Radix Rd, Williamstown NJ
08094. 609/728-8650.

**Rahway High School**
1012 Madison Ave, Rahway NJ
07065-1803. 732/396-1090.

**Rancocas Valley Regional High
School**
Jacksonville Rd, Mount Holly NJ
08060. 609/267-0830.

**Ranney School Inc.**
235 Hope Rd, Eatontown NJ
07724-3066. 732/542-4777.

**Raphael de Cordero
Elementary School**
158 Erie St, Jersey City NJ
07302-1718. 201/714-4390.

**Redshaw Elementary School**
216 Livingston Ave, New
Brunswick NJ 08901-2930.
732/745-5344.

**Reynolds School**
2145 Yardville Ham Sq Rd,
Trenton NJ 08690. 609/890-3761.

**Richard C. Crockett Middle
School**
2631 Kuser Rd, Robbinsville NJ
08691-1805. 609/890-3800.

**Ridgefield Park Junior Senior
High School**
1 Ozzie Nelson Dr, Ridgefield
Park NJ 07660. 201/440-1440.

**Riletta T. Cream Elementary
School**
Mulford Budd St, Camden NJ
08104. 609/966-4760.

**Ringwood School District**
121 Carletondale Rd, Ringwood
NJ 07456-1611. 973/962-7028.

**Robert Waters Elementary
School**
2800 Summit Ave, Union City NJ
07087-2323. 201/348-5925.

**Roxbury High School**
1 Bryant Dr, Succasunna NJ
07876-1632. 973/584-1200.

**Rutgers Preparatory School**
1345 Easton Ave, Somerset NJ
08873-1412. 732/545-5600.

**Rutherford High School**
56 Elliott Ter, Rutherford NJ
07070-1976. 201/438-7675.

**Rutherford School District**
176 Park Ave, Rutherford NJ
07070-2310. 201/939-1717.

**Saddle Brook Community
School**
Mayhill St, Rochelle Park NJ
07662. 201/845-6682.

**Sampson G. Smith Intermediate
School**
1649 Amwell Rd, Somerset NJ
08873-2829. 732/873-2800.

**Sayreville Middle School**
PO Box 997, Sayreville NJ
08871-0997. 732/525-5200.

**Schuyler Colfax Junior High School**
1500 Hamburg Tpke, Wayne NJ
07470-4079. 973/633-3130.

**Shawnee High School**
600 Tabernacle Rd, Medford NJ
08055-9732. 609/654-7544.

**Shore Regional High School**
Monmouth Park Hwy, West Long
Branch NJ 07764. 732/222-9300.

**Solomon Schechter Day School**
Bergen Ave, New Milford NJ
07646. 201/262-8975.

**Solomon Schechter Day School**
1418 Pleasant Valley Way, West
Orange NJ 07052-1313. 973/669-
8000.

**Somerset County Technical School**
PO Box 6350, Bridgewater NJ
08807-0350. 908/526-4016.

**Somerville Public School Inc.**
51 W Cliff St, Somerville NJ
08876-1903. 908/218-4102.

**South Amboy Board of Education**
240 John St, South Amboy NJ
08879-1742. 732/525-2100.

**South Brunswick High School**
PO Box 183, Monmouth Junction
NJ 08852-0183. 732/329-4044.

**South Orange Middle School**
70 N Ridgewood Rd, South
Orange NJ 07079-1518. 973/378-
2733.

**South Plainfield Board of Education**
Cromwell Pl, South Plainfield NJ
07080. 908/754-4620.

**Southern Regional High School**
600 N Main St, Manahawkin NJ
08050-3022. 609/597-9481.

**Sparta High School**
70 W Mountain Rd, Sparta NJ
07871-3551. 973/729-6191.

**Spruce Street School**
90 Spruce St, Lakewood NJ
08701-5329. 732/905-3660.

**St. Mary School**
PO Box 624, New Monmouth NJ
07748-0624. 732/671-0129.

**St. Peter's Preparatory School**
144 Grand St, Jersey City NJ
07302-4431. 201/434-4400.

**Sterling High School District**
501 S Warwick Rd, Somerdale
NJ 08083-2174. 609/784-1287.

**Stillwater Township Public School**
77 Halszly Rd, Newton NJ
07860. 973/383-1800.

**Stuart Country Day School**
1200 Stuart Rd, Princeton NJ
08540-1234. 609/921-2330.

**Tabernacle Board of Education**
132 New Rd, Vincentown NJ
08088-8574. 609/268-0349.

**Teaneck Board of Education**
1 Merrison St, Teaneck NJ
07666-4616. 201/833-5510.

**The Lawrenceville School**
PO Box 6008, Trenton NJ 08648-
0008. 609/896-0400.

**The Midland School**
PO Box 5026, Somerville NJ
08876-1301. 908/722-8222.

**The Moriah School of Englewood**
53 S Woodland St, Englewood NJ
07631-3726. 201/567-0208.

**The Pennington School**
112 W Delaware Ave,
Pennington NJ 08534-1601.
609/737-1838.

**Thomas E. Harrington Middle School**
514 Mount Laurel Rd, Mount
Laurel NJ 08054-9523. 609/234-
1610.

**Thomas Jefferson Elementary School**
95 Altair Dr, Blackwood NJ
08012-2437. 609/589-8248.

**Trenton High School**
400 Chambers St, Trenton NJ
08609-2606. 609/989-2496.

**Union High School**
2350 N 3rd St, Union NJ 07083-
5049. 908/851-6500.

**Union Hill High School**
3808 Hudson Ave, Union City NJ
07087-6020. 201/348-5936.

**Upper Deerfield School District**
Highway 77, Bridgeton NJ
08302. 609/455-2267.

**Upper Pottsgrove Township School District**
235 Pine Tavern Rd, Monroeville
NJ 08343-1749. 609/358-8163.

**Upper Saddle River Board of Education**
395 W Saddle River Rd, Saddle
River NJ 07458. 201/327-4401.

**US Wiggins Elementary School**
400 Mount Vernon St, Camden
NJ 08103-2030. 609/966-5120.

**Valley View Elementary School**
Rural Route 514, Califon NJ
07830. 908/638-4521.

**Vernon School District**
PO Box 99, Vernon NJ 07462-
0099. 973/764-4486.

**Vineland North High School**
3010 E Chestnut Ave, Vineland
NJ 08360. 609/794-6800.

**Voorhees Middle School**
1000 Holly Oak Dr, Voorhees NJ
08043-1525. 609/795-2025.

**Voorhees Township Board of Education**
329 Route 73, Voorhees NJ
08043-9525. 609/751-8446.

**Wallace Elementary School**
1100 Willow Ave, Hoboken NJ
07030-3203. 201/420-2178.

**Wantage Elementary School**
815 State Rte 23, Sussex NJ
07461-3313. 973/875-4589.

**Warren County Vocational Technical High School**
1500 Route 57 W, Washington
NJ 07882-3538. 908/689-0122.

**Washington Borough Board of Education**
300 W Stewart St, Washington
NJ 07882-1250. 908/689-0241.

**Washington Elementary School**
3905 New York Ave, Union City
NJ 07087-4821. 201/348-5954.

**Washington Township Board of Education**
53 W Mill Rd, Long Valley NJ
07853-3435. 908/876-3616.

**Waterford Township School District**
1106 Old White Horse Pike,
Waterford Works NJ 08089-1852.
609/768-1473.

**Wayne Board of Education**
45 Reinhardt Rd, Wayne NJ
07470-2210. 973/790-6000.

**Wayne Hills High School**
272 Berdan Ave, Wayne NJ
07470-3240. 973/633-3090.

**Wayne Valley High School**
551 Valley Rd, Wayne NJ 07470-
3525. 973/633-3067.

**Weehawken Public School District**
Liberty Pl, Weehawken NJ
07087. 201/867-2243.

**Weequahic High School**
279 Chancellor Ave, Newark NJ
07112-1201. 973/705-3900.

**West Brook Middle School**
550 Roosevelt Blvd, Paramus NJ
07652-2012. 201/652-3907.

**West Deptford High School**
1600 Old Crown Point Rd,
Westville NJ 08093. 609/848-
6110.

**West Deptford Middle School**
675 Grove Rd, Paulsboro NJ
08066-1925. 609/848-1200.

**West Essex Regional High
School**
W Greenbrook Rd, Caldwell NJ
07006. 973/228-1200.

**West Milford Township High
School**
Highlander Dr, West Milford NJ
07480. 973/697-1700.

**West Morris Central High
School**
700 Bartley Rd, Chester NJ
07930. 908/879-5212.

**West Morris Mendham High
School**
65 E Main St, Mendham NJ
07945-1502. 973/543-7788.

**West Morris Regional High
School**
4 Bridges Rd, Chester NJ 07930.
908/879-6404.

**West Orange High School**
51 Conforti Ave, West Orange NJ
07052-2829. 973/669-5325.

**West Windsor Plainsboro High
School**
PO Box 248, Princeton Junction
NJ 08550-0248. 609/799-3200.

**West Windsor-Plainsboro
Middle School**
PO Box 410, Plainsboro NJ
08536-0410. 609/799-9600.

**Westfield Board of Education**
302 Elm St, Westfield NJ 07090-
3104. 908/789-4400.

**Westwood Regional Board of
Education**
PO Box 737, Westwood NJ
07675-0737. 201/664-0880.

**Whippany Park High School**
75 Mount Pleasant Ave,
Whippany NJ 07981-1122.
201/807-3004.

**Wildwood Board of Education**
4300 Pacific Ave, Wildwood NJ
08260-4625. 609/522-0786.

**William Dickinson High School**
2 Palisade Ave, Jersey City NJ
07306-1202. 201/714-4400.

**Williamstown High School**
561 Clayton Rd, Williamstown
NJ 08094-8827. 609/629-7444.

**Willingboro High School**
20 S John F. Kennedy Way,
Willingboro NJ 08046-3879.
609/835-8800.

**Willingboro Memorial Junior
High School**
451 Van Sciver Parkway,
Willingboro NJ 08046-1945.
609/835-8700.

**WM Yung Elementary School**
135 Stegman St, Jersey City NJ
07305-3208. 201/915-6440.

**Wood-Ridge School District**
89 Hackensack St, East
Rutherford NJ 07073-1415.
201/939-2566.

**Woodbridge High School**
Kelly St & St. George,
Woodbridge NJ 07095. 732/602-
8600.

**Woodrow Wilson Elementary
School**
529 Edgar Rd, Elizabeth NJ
07202-3301. 908/558-3424.

**Yavneh Academy**
155 Farview Ave, Paramus NJ
07652. 201/262-8494.

## JUNIOR COLLEGES AND
TECHNICAL INSTITUTES

**Atlantic Community College**
5100 Black Horse Pike, Mays
Landing NJ 08330-2623.
609/625-1111.

**Burlington County College**
Pemberton Browns Mall Rd,
Pemberton NJ 08068. 609/894-
9311.

**County College of Morris**
214 Center Grove Road,
Randolph NJ 07869-2007.
973/328-5000.

**Cumberland County College**
PO Box 517, Vineland NJ 08362-
0517. 609/691-8600.

**Essex County College**
730 Bloomfield Avenue,
Caldwell NJ 07006-6710.
973/228-3968.

**Gloucester County College**
PO Box 203, Sewell NJ 08080-
0203. 609/468-5000.

**Middlesex County College**
PO Box 3050, Edison NJ 08818-
3050. 732/548-6000.

**Ocean County College**
College Dr, Toms River NJ
08754. 732/255-0400.

**Passaic County Community
College**
PO Box 2868, Paterson NJ
07509-2868. 973/684-6800.

**Raritan Valley Community
College**
PO Box 3300, Somerville NJ
08876-1265. 908/526-1200.

**Salem Community College**
460 Hollywood Avenue, Carneys
Point NJ 08069. 609/299-2100.

**Sussex County Community
College**
1 College Hill Rd, Newton NJ
07860-1149. 973/579-5400.

**Union County College**
1033 Springfield Avenue,
Cranford NJ 07016-1528.
908/709-7000.

**Warren County Community
College**
475 Route 57 W, Washington NJ
07882-4343. 908/835-9222.

## MISC. SCHOOLS AND
EDUCATIONAL SERVICES

**HLS Corp.**
PO Box 422, Little Falls NJ
07424-0422. 973/785-8500.

**Westminster Conservatory**
101 Walnut Ln, Princeton NJ
08540-3819. 609/921-7104.

## VOCATIONAL SCHOOLS

**Atlantic County Vocational
School**
5080 Atlantic Avenue, Mays
Landing NJ 08330-2022.
609/625-2249.

**Burlington County Institute of
Technology**
695 Woodlane Road, Mount
Holly NJ 08060-3813. 609/267-
4226.

**Camden County Vocational
School**
343 Berlin Cross Keys Rd,
Sicklerville NJ 08081-9706.
609/767-7000.

**Cittone Institute**
1697 Oak Tree Rd, Edison NJ
08820-2806. 732/548-8798.

**Gloucester County Vocational & Technical School**
PO Box 800, Sewell NJ 08080-0800. 609/468-1445.

**Mercer County Vocational & Technical School**
1085 Old Trenton Rd, Trenton NJ 08690-1229. 609/586-2123.

**Piscataway Vocational School**
21 Suttons Ln, Piscataway NJ 08854-5715. 732/985-0717.

# For more information on career opportunities in educational services:

## Associations

### AMERICAN ASSOCIATION FOR HIGHER EDUCATION
One DuPont Circle, Suite 360, Washington DC 20036. 202/293-6440. World Wide Web address: http://www.aahe.org.

### AMERICAN ASSOCIATION OF SCHOOL ADMINISTRATORS
1801 North Moore Street, Arlington VA 22209. 703/528-0700. Fax: 703/841-1543. World Wide Web address: http://www.aasa.org. An organization of school system leaders. Membership includes a national conference on education; programs and seminars; *The School Administrator*, a monthly magazine; *Leadership News*, a monthly newspaper; *Leaders' Edge*, *Back Fence*, and *Edge City*, quarterly publications; and a catalog of other publications and audiovisuals.

### AMERICAN FEDERATION OF TEACHERS
555 New Jersey Avenue NW, Washington DC 20001. 202/879-4400. World Wide Web address: http://www.aft.org.

### COLLEGE AND UNIVERSITY PERSONNEL ASSOCIATION
1233 20th Street NW, Suite 301, Washington DC 20036. 202/429-0311. World Wide Web address: http://www.cupa.org. Membership required.

### NATIONAL ASSOCIATION FOR COLLEGE ADMISSION COUNSELING
1631 Prince Street, Alexandria VA 22314. 703/836-2222. World Wide Web address: http://www.nacac.com. An education association of school counselors and admissions officers who assist students in making the transition from high school to post-secondary education.

### NATIONAL ASSOCIATION OF BIOLOGY TEACHERS
11250 Roger Bacon Drive, Suite 19, Reston VA 20190. 703/471-1134. Toll-free phone: 800/406-0775. Fax: 703/435-5582. E-mail address: nabter@aol.com. World Wide Web address: http://www.nabt.org. A professional organization for biology and life science educators.

### NATIONAL ASSOCIATION OF COLLEGE AND UNIVERSITY BUSINESS OFFICERS
2501 M Street NW, Suite 400, Washington DC 20037. 202/861-2500. World Wide Web address: http://www.nacubo.org. Association for those involved in the financial administration and management of higher education. Membership required.

### NATIONAL COMMISSION FOR COOPERATIVE EDUCATION (NCCE)
360 Huntington Avenue, Suite 384 CP, Boston MA 02115. 617/373-3770. E-mail address: ncce@lynx.neu.edu. Offers free information to students interested in learning more about cooperative education programs.

### NATIONAL SCIENCE TEACHERS ASSOCIATION
1840 Wilson Boulevard, Arlington VA 22201-3000. 703/243-7100. World Wide Web address: http://www.nsta.org. Organization committed to the improvement of science education at all levels, preschool through college. Publishes five journals, a newspaper, and a number of special publications. Also conducts national and regional conventions.

### NATIONAL SOCIETY FOR EXPERIENTIAL EDUCATION (NSEE)
3509 Haworth Drive, Suite 207, Raleigh NC 27609-7299. 919/787-3263. E-mail address: info@nsee.org. World Wide Web address: http://www.nsee.org. A membership organization offering publications, conferences, and a resource center. Among the society's publications is *The Experienced Hand: A Student Manual for Making the Most of an Internship.*

## Books

### HOW TO GET A JOB IN EDUCATION
Adams Media Corporation, 260 Center Street, Holbrook MA 02343. 781/767-8100. World Wide Web address: http://www.adamsmedia.com.

## Directories

### WASHINGTON EDUCATION ASSOCIATION DIRECTORY
Council for Advancement and Support of Education, 1307 New York Avenue, Suite 1000, Washington DC 20005-4701. 202/328-5900. World Wide Web address: http://www.case.org.

## Online Services

### ACADEMIC EMPLOYMENT NETWORK
http://www.academploy.com. This site offers information for the educational professional, and allows you to search for positions nationwide. It also has information on other sites of interest, educational products, certification requirements by state, and relocation services.

### THE CHRONICLE OF HIGHER EDUCATION
http://chronicle.com/jobs. This Website provides job listings from the weekly published newspaper *The Chronicle of Higher Education*. Besides featuring articles from the paper, this site also offers employment opportunities. You can search for information by geographic location, type of position, and teaching fields.

### EDUCATION & INSTRUCTION JOBS
http://csueb.sfsu.edu/jobs/educationjobs.html. Offers a long list of links to other sites around the country that provide job openings and information for jobseekers looking in education. This site is part of the California State University Employment Board.

### EDUCATION FORUM
Go: Edforum. This CompuServe discussion group is open to educators of all levels.

**JOBWEB SCHOOL DISTRICTS SEARCH**
http://www.jobweb.org/search/schools. Provides a
search engine for school districts across the country.
The site is run by the National Association of
Colleges and Employers and it also provides
information on colleges and career fairs.

**THE TEACHER'S LOUNGE**
Keyword: teacher's lounge. An America Online
discussion group for teachers of kindergarten through
the twelfth grade.

**VISUAL NATION ARTS JOBS LINKS**
http://fly.hiwaay.net/%7Edrewyor/art_job.html.
Provides links to other sites that post academic and
arts job openings and information.

# ELECTRONIC/INDUSTRIAL ELECTRICAL EQUIPMENT

*Intense international competition is prompting the U.S. electronics industry to become more globalized. Companies are being forced to seek less expensive materials and labor. Standard & Poor reported a 92 percent decrease in second quarter 1998 profits for the electrical and electronics industry, and second quarter industry profit margins dropped from 9.9 percent in 1997 to 0.7 percent in 1998. The Bureau of Labor Statistics expects growth in non-manufacturing jobs, and well as positions for electrical consultants. Electrical assemblers, on the other hand, will see a decline in the number of positions through 2006.*

*U.S. Industry and Trade Outlook 1998 projects the best opportunities for jobseekers to be in the production of analog and memory ICs, microcomponents, and discrete semiconductors. Industry analysts worldwide predict that semiconductor markets will grow at an approximate rate of 15 percent annually through 2005. The outlook for the switchgear sector is highly favorable. U.S. electric utilities are expected to spend more than $300 million to automate power substations by 2000, and shipments of switchgear are forecasted to grow at an average rate of 4 to 5 percent through 2000.*

**ABACUS CONTROLS**
80 Readington Road, Somerville NJ 08876. 908/526-6010. **Contact:** Human Resources. **World Wide Web address:** http://www.abacuscontrols.com. **Description:** Manufactures frequency converters and uninterruptible power supplies.

**ALPHA WIRE CORPORATION**
711 Lidgerwood Avenue, Elizabeth NJ 07207. 908/925-8000. **Toll-free phone:** 800/522-5742. **Fax:** 908/925-3346. **Contact:** Hayley Jochnau, Human Resources Generalist. **World Wide Web address:** http://www.alphawire.com. **Description:** An international manufacturer and distributor of high-technology and high-reliability wire, cable, tubing, and connector products including communication and control cables, shrinkable and non-shrinkable tubing and insulation, instrumentation cables, flat cable and connectors, coaxial and data cables, plenum cable, and hook-up wire used for electrical and electronic equipment. Products are sold to a network of distributors and OEMs. **NOTE:** Entry-level positions are offered. **Common positions include:** Accountant/Auditor; Buyer; Credit Manager; Customer Service Representative; Electrical/Electronics Engineer; Electrician; General Manager; Industrial Engineer; Manufacturer's/Wholesaler's Sales Rep.; Operations/Production Manager; Purchasing Agent/Manager; Quality Control Supervisor. **Educational backgrounds include:** Accounting; Business Administration; Computer Science; Engineering; Finance; Liberal Arts; Marketing. **Benefits:** 401(k); Dental Insurance; Disability Coverage; Employee Discounts; Life Insurance; Medical Insurance; Profit Sharing; Savings Plan. **Corporate headquarters location:** This Location. **Subsidiaries include:** Cowen Cable Corporation; Insultab, Inc. **Operations at this facility include:** Administration; Research and Development; Sales; Service. **Listed on:** Privately held. **Number of employees at this location:** 170. **Number of employees nationwide:** 240.

**AMERICAN GAS & CHEMICAL COMPANY**
220 Pegasus Avenue, Northvale NJ 07647. 201/767-7300. **Fax:** 201/767-1741. **Contact:** Melanie Kershaw, Vice President. **E-mail address:** hr@amgas.com. **World Wide Web address:** http://www.amgas.com. **Description:** Manufactures electronic chemical and gas leak detectors. **Common positions include:** Accountant/Auditor; Applications Engineer; Buyer; Chemist; Chief Financial Officer; Clerical Supervisor; Computer Programmer; Customer Service Representative; Design Engineer; Draftsperson; Electrical/Electronics Engineer; Industrial Production Manager; Marketing Manager; Purchasing Agent/Manager; Quality Control Supervisor; Sales Engineer; Sales Manager. **Educational backgrounds include:** Chemistry; Engineering. **Benefits:** 401(k);

Dental Insurance; Life Insurance; Medical Insurance. **Corporate headquarters location:** This Location. **Operations at this facility include:** Administration; Manufacturing; Research and Development; Sales. **Listed on:** Privately held. **Number of employees at this location:** 125.

## ANADIGICS, INC.
35 Technology Drive, Warren NJ 07059. 908/668-5000. **Contact:** Human Resources. **Description:** Manufactures integrated circuits.

## ARIES ELECTRONICS
P.O. Box 130, Frenchtown NJ 08825. 908/996-6841. **Contact:** Human Resources. **E-mail address:** info@arieselec.com. **World Wide Web address:** http://www.arieselec.com. **Description:** Manufactures a wide variety of electronics components including pin grid array footprints, ZIF and test sockets, cable assemblies, DIP/SIP sockets/headers, display sockets, programming devices, and switches.

## AUTOMATIC SWITCH COMPANY
50-60 Hanover Road, Florham Park NJ 07932. 973/966-2000. **Contact:** Manager of Personnel. **Description:** An international manufacturer of an extensive line of electrical equipment used for the automation of machinery, equipment, and industrial processes and the control of electric power. Automatic Switch operates manufacturing facilities at this location, and in Elk Grove IL, Aiken SC, and Stockton CA (Delta Controls), with warehousing facilities in Elk Grove and Los Angeles. **Common positions include:** Accountant/Auditor; Electrical/Electronics Engineer; Industrial Engineer; Management Trainee; Mechanical Engineer; Operations/Production Manager. **Educational backgrounds include:** Accounting; Engineering; Finance; Liberal Arts; Marketing. **Benefits:** Dental Insurance; Disability Coverage; Employee Discounts; Life Insurance; Medical Insurance; Pension Plan; Profit Sharing; Savings Plan; Tuition Assistance. **Corporate headquarters location:** This Location. **Parent company:** Emerson Electric. **Subsidiaries include:** A&M Ludwig Corporation (Parsippany NJ), which manufactures screw machine parts; ASCO Electrical Products Company (Parsippany NJ), which makes metal enclosures and electrical distribution equipment; Auger Scientific (Cedar Knolls NJ), which makes miniature and microminiature solenoid valves and controls for medical, analytical, and pharmaceutical uses; ASCO Sisc Inc. (Dover DE); ASCO Investment Corporation; ASCO Services Inc. (also at this location).

## BASE TEN SYSTEMS, INC.
One Electronics Drive, Hamilton NJ 08619. 609/586-7010. **Contact:** Human Resources. **Description:** Designs, manufactures, and markets electronic systems employing safety critical software for the defense industry. The company also manufactures defense products to meet specifications set by prime government contractors, and designs and builds proprietary electronic systems for use in secure communications applications by various U.S. agencies. Base Ten Systems is developing commercial product programs involving medical screening, image processing, and pharmaceutical manufacturing software. **Corporate headquarters location:** This Location.

## BEL FUSE INC.
198 Van Borst Street, Jersey City NJ 07302. 201/432-0463. **Contact:** Human Resources. **World Wide Web address:** http://www.belfuse.com. **Description:** Designs, manufactures, and sells products used in local area networking, telecommunications, business equipment, and consumer electronic applications. The magnetic components manufactured by the company fall into four major groups: pulse transformers; delay lines, filters, and AC/DC converters; power transformers, line chokes, and coils; and packaged modules. The company manufactures miniature and micro fuses for supplementary circuit protection. Bel Fuse sells its products to approximately 550 customers throughout North America, Western Europe, and the Far East. Presently, the company has 52 sales representative organizations, 27 non-exclusive distributors, and a sales staff of 18 people. **Other U.S. locations:** CA; IN; NJ. **International locations:** France; Hong Kong; Macau.

## BLONDER TONGUE LABORATORIES, INC.
One Jake Brown Road, Old Bridge NJ 08857. 732/679-4000. **Fax:** 732/679-4353. **Contact:** Daniel J. Altiere, Senior Vice President. **World Wide Web address:** http://www.blondertongue.com. **Description:** Designs and manufactures signal processing equipment for the television and security industries. Products are for satellite communications, master antennae systems (MATV), industrial security, and other systems using RF technology. **Common positions include:** Accountant/Auditor; Buyer; Customer Service Representative; Draftsperson; Electrical/Electronics Engineer; General Manager; Industrial Engineer; Mechanical Engineer. **Educational backgrounds include:** Engineering. **Benefits:** 401(k); Dental Insurance; Disability Coverage; Life Insurance; Medical Insurance; Pension Plan; Tuition Assistance. **Corporate headquarters location:** This Location. **Operations at this facility include:** Administration; Divisional Headquarters;

Manufacturing; Regional Headquarters; Research and Development; Sales; Service. **Listed on:** American Stock Exchange. **Stock exchange symbol:** BDR. **Annual sales/revenues:** $51 - $100 million. **Number of employees at this location:** 500.

### CHECKPOINT SYSTEMS, INC.
101 Wolf Drive, Thorofare NJ 08086. 609/848-1800. **Contact:** Theresa McHale, Manager of Human Resources. **World Wide Web address:** http://www.checkpointsystems.com. **Description:** Develops, manufactures, and markets Electronic Article Surveillance systems to control shoplifting in retail stores and protect books and materials in libraries and universities; electronic access control systems to secure buildings and areas within buildings; and closed circuit television systems and solutions to control shoplifting and internal theft and to ensure the safety of people and assets. **Corporate headquarters location:** This Location.

### COMTREX SYSTEMS CORPORATION
102 Executive Drive, Suite 1, Moorestown NJ 08057. 609/778-0090. **Fax:** 609/778-9322. **Contact:** Lisa Mudrick, Human Resources. **World Wide Web address:** http://www.comtrex.com. **Description:** Specializes in point-of-sale solutions for the food service and hospitality industries. The company designs, develops, assembles, and markets electronic terminals and computer software which provide retailers with transaction processing, in-store controls, and management information. Comtrex's products are sophisticated terminals which combine traditional cash register functions with the data gathering capabilities of a computerized system. The company develops and licenses the use of software programs which provide enhanced reporting capabilities for its terminals systems and facilitate local and remote polling of information transfer between computers and the company's terminal systems. Founded in 1981. **Corporate headquarters location:** This Location. **Listed on:** NASDAQ. **Stock exchange symbol:** COMX.

### CONTINENTAL CONNECTOR CORPORATION
53 La France Avenue, Bloomfield NJ 07003. 973/429-8500. **Contact:** Iniabelle Paz, Personnel Department. **Description:** This location manufactures circuit connectors. Overall, Continental Connector Corporation is engaged in the development, manufacturing, and sale of a broad line of multiprecision rack and panel circuit connectors. Manufacturing operations consist primarily of the processing and assembly of plated metals, receptacles, and plugs of various types designed and molded from thermosetting molding compounds and other precision connector parts. **Corporate headquarters location:** Las Vegas NV.

### THE DEWEY ELECTRONICS CORPORATION
27 Muller Road, Oakland NJ 07436. 201/337-4700. **Contact:** Carol Grofsik, Director of Administration. **Description:** A systems-oriented civilian and military electronics development, design, engineering, and manufacturing firm. **Common positions include:** Buyer; Draftsperson; Electrical/Electronics Engineer; Industrial Engineer; Mechanical Engineer; Quality Control Supervisor. **Educational backgrounds include:** Business Administration; Computer Science; Engineering. **Benefits:** Disability Coverage; Life Insurance; Medical Insurance; Pension Plan; Tuition Assistance. **Corporate headquarters location:** This Location. **Operations at this facility include:** Administration; Manufacturing; Research and Development; Sales.

### DIAGNOSTIC RETRIEVAL SYSTEMS, INC. (DRS)
138 Bauer Drive, Oakland NJ 07436. 201/337-3800. **Contact:** Human Resources Department. **Description:** Designs, manufactures, and markets high-technology electronic products used to process, display, and store information for the U.S. Department of Defense, international defense departments, other U.S. prime defense contractors, and selected industrial corporations. The company's advanced signal processing, display, data storage, trainer, emulation, and electro-optical systems are utilized in numerous applications for military use and for the disk drive and television broadcast industries. Founded in 1968.

### ELECTRONIC MEASUREMENTS INC.
405 Essex Road, Neptune NJ 07753. 732/922-9300. **Contact:** Michele Vail, Human Resources Manager. **World Wide Web address:** http://www.emipower.com. **Description:** Manufactures DC power supplies. **Common positions include:** Accountant/Auditor; Administrator; Buyer; Customer Service Representative; Designer; Draftsperson; Electrical/Electronics Engineer; Electronics Technician; Industrial Engineer; Mechanical Engineer; Purchasing Agent/Manager; Quality Control Supervisor. **Educational backgrounds include:** Business Administration; Engineering. **Benefits:** 401(k); Dental Insurance; Life Insurance; Medical Insurance; Tuition Assistance. **Corporate headquarters location:** This Location. **Parent company:** Berwind Industries. **Operations at this facility include:** Administration; Manufacturing; Research and Development; Sales; Service. **Listed on:** Privately held. **Number of employees at this location:** 250.

**EMCORE CORPORATION**
394 Elizabeth Avenue, Somerset NJ 08873. 732/271-9090. **Contact:** Human Resources. **Description:** Manufactures semiconductors.

**EVENTIDE, INC.**
One Alsan Way, Little Ferry NJ 07643. 201/641-1200. **Contact:** Human Resources. **World Wide Web address:** http://www.eventide.com. **Description:** A manufacturer of electronic harmonizers.

**GENLYTE CORPORATION**
P.O. Box 3148, Union NJ 07083. 908/964-7000. **Contact:** Manager of Employment. **World Wide Web address:** http://www.genlyte.com. **Description:** Manufactures a range of lights, controls, and lighting fixtures through seven divisions. The Lightolier division features interior lighting fixtures for residential and commercial markets, including downlighting, track lighting, decorative, fluorescent, and controls. The controls division features electronic dimming and energy-saving lighting controls for both residential and commercial applications. The supply division, through electrical distributors Stonco, Crescent, and ExceLine, supplies standard, high-volume, contractor-friendly indoor and outdoor lighting. The Wide-Lite/Bronzelite division features energy-efficient, high-intensity discharge indoor and outdoor lighting and controls for commercial, industrial, and recreational lighting applications. The Hadco division features specification grade exterior architectural lighting for municipal, institutional, commercial, and landscape applications. The Diamond F division features decorative residential lighting fixtures sold through do-it-yourself home centers. The Canlyte division sells Lightolier, CFI, Keene, Wild-Lite, Stonco, and Hadco product lines in Canada. **Corporate headquarters location:** This Location.

**GOVERNMENT ELECTRONIC SYSTEMS (GES)**
199 Borton Landing Road, Moorestown NJ 08057. 609/722-5000. **Contact:** Human Resources. **Description:** Manufactures electronic systems for naval contracts. **Parent company:** Lockheed Martin Corporation provides turnkey systems development, engineering services, and spaceflight mission support for civil and commercial space programs worldwide. The company supports both space and ground-based systems, with an emphasis on command and control, data storage, and processing systems.

**HEWLETT-PACKARD COMPANY**
150 Green Pond Road, Rockaway NJ 07866. 973/627-6400. **Contact:** Employment Office. **World Wide Web address:** http://www.hp.com. **Description:** This location of Hewlett-Packard designs, markets, and manufactures AC and DC system power supplies, power test systems, and electronic loads. Overall, Hewlett-Packard designs and manufactures measurement and computation products and systems used in business, industry, engineering, science, health care, and education. The company's principal products are integrated instrument and computer systems (including hardware and software), computer systems and peripheral products, and medical electronic equipment and systems. **NOTE:** Jobseekers can also send resumes to Employment Response Center, Event #2498, Hewlett-Packard Company, Mail Stop 20-APP, 3000 Hanover Street, Palo Alto CA 94304-1181. **Corporate headquarters location:** Palo Alto CA. **Listed on:** New York Stock Exchange. **Number of employees nationwide:** 93,000.

**KEARFOTT GUIDANCE AND NAVIGATION CORPORATION**
150 Totowa Road, Wayne NJ 07474. 973/785-5908. **Fax:** 973/785-6255. **Contact:** Gregory MacNeil, Human Resources. **World Wide Web address:** http://www.kearfott.com. **Description:** Manufactures precision electromechanical and electronic components used to generate, sense, control, and display motion such as synchros, resolvers, cant angle sensors, and servo motors. Founded in 1917. **Common positions include:** Buyer; Electrical/Electronics Engineer; Mechanical Engineer; Software Engineer. **Benefits:** 401(k); Dental Insurance; Disability Coverage; Life Insurance; Medical Insurance; Profit Sharing; Tuition Assistance. **Corporate headquarters location:** This Location. **Other U.S. locations:** Asheville NC. **Parent company:** Astronautics Corporation of America manufactures electrical instruments for airplanes. **Number of employees at this location:** 1,300. **Number of employees nationwide:** 1,725.

**KULITE SEMICONDUCTOR PRODUCTS**
One Willow Tree Road, Leonia NJ 07605. 201/461-0900. **Contact:** Personnel Department. **World Wide Web address:** http://www.kulite.com. **Description:** Produces computerized metering systems for medical applications and for use in aircraft. Sales offices are located throughout the United States.

**LASER DIODE**
4 Olsen Avenue, Edison NJ 08820. 732/549-9001. **Contact:** Human Resources. **Description:** Manufactures semiconductors.

**MELCOR CORPORATION**
1040 Spruce Street, Trenton NJ 08820. 609/393-4178. **Contact:** Human Resources. **Description:** Manufactures semiconductors.

**MERRIMAC INDUSTRIES INC.**
41 Fairfield Place, West Caldwell NJ 07006. 973/575-1300. **Contact:** Personnel Department. **World Wide Web address:** http://www.merrimacind.com. **Description:** An international manufacturer of high-reliability signal-processing components. Products include IF-baseband components (used by electronics and military electronics OEMs); RF-microwave components (for military electronics and fiber-optics users); high-reliability space and missile products (electronic components used in military satellite and missile programs); integrated microwave products (for the military and commercial communications markets); and satellite reception products (products for the CATV and satellite master antenna systems). **Common positions include:** Accountant/Auditor; Buyer; Computer Programmer; Customer Service Representative; Draftsperson; Electrical/Electronics Engineer; Industrial Designer; Mechanical Engineer; Operations/Production Manager; Purchasing Agent/Manager; Quality Control Supervisor; Sales Executive; Technical Writer/Editor. **Educational backgrounds include:** Business Administration; Engineering; Marketing. **Benefits:** 401(k); Dental Insurance; Disability Coverage; Life Insurance; Medical Insurance; Profit Sharing; Tuition Assistance. **Corporate headquarters location:** This Location.

**MICRO METRICS INC.**
204 21st Avenue, Paterson NJ 07501. 973/345-9700. **Contact:** Human Resources. **Description:** Manufactures circuit boards on a contract basis.

**NOISECOM**
East 64 Midland Avenue, Paramus NJ 07652. 201/261-8797. **Contact:** Human Resources Department. **Description:** Manufactures test equipment for the wireless telecommunications industry.

**OKONITE COMPANY**
102 Hilltop Road, P.O. Box 340, Ramsey NJ 07446. 201/825-0300. **Contact:** Kathy Cuomo, Administrator of Personnel. **World Wide Web address:** http://www.okonite.com. **Description:** Manufactures power cable for large-scale users. **Corporate headquarters location:** This Location. **Other area locations:** Passaic NJ; Paterson NJ.

**PANASONIC INDUSTRIAL COMPANY**
2 Panasonic Way, 7C5, Secaucus NJ 07094. 201/348-7000. **Fax:** 201/392-6977. **Contact:** Recruitment Department. **Description:** This location houses the U.S. headquarters. Overall, Panasonic is one of the world's largest manufacturers of consumer and industrial electronic equipment and components. Brand names include Panasonic, Technics, and Quasar. **Common positions include:** Accountant/Auditor; Chemical Engineer; Clerical Supervisor; Computer Operator; Credit Clerk and Authorizer; Credit Manager; Electrical/Electronics Engineer; Employment Interviewer; Financial Manager; Human Resources Manager; Industrial Engineer; Manufacturer's/Wholesaler's Sales Representative; Mechanical Engineer; Nuclear Engineer; Purchasing Agent/Manager; Receptionist; Secretary; Systems Analyst. **Educational backgrounds include:** Accounting; Business Administration; Computer Science; Economics; Engineering; Finance; Marketing. **Parent company:** Matsushita Electronics Corporation of America. **Other U.S. locations:** Knoxville TN. **Number of employees at this location:** 300. **Number of employees nationwide:** 10,000.

**PHELPS DODGE HIGH PERFORMANCE CONDUCTORS**
666 Passaic Avenue, West Caldwell NJ 07006. 973/575-0400. **Fax:** 973/882-1297. **Contact:** Maria Escobar, Human Resources Manager. **Description:** One of the world's leading suppliers of sophisticated conductors. **Common positions include:** Ceramics Engineer; Electrical/Electronics Engineer; Electrician; Materials Engineer; Metallurgical Engineer. **Educational backgrounds include:** Engineering. **Benefits:** 401(k); Disability Coverage; Life Insurance; Medical Insurance. **Corporate headquarters location:** Inman SC. **Operations at this facility include:** Administration; Manufacturing; Sales. **Number of employees at this location:** 175. **Number of employees nationwide:** 400.

**POWERTECH, INC.**
0-02 Fair Lawn Avenue, Fair Lawn NJ 07410. 201/791-5050. **Fax:** 201/791-6805. **Contact:** Alex M. Polner, President. **E-mail address:** info@power-tech.com. **World Wide Web address:** http://www.power-tech.com. **Description:** A manufacturer of silicon power transistors.

## SCHLUMBERGER EMR PHOTOELECTRIC
20 Wallace Road, Princeton Junction NJ 08550. 609/799-1000. **Contact:** Carol Parker, Personnel. **World Wide Web address:** http://www.schlumberger.com. **Description:** This location is engaged in the engineering and manufacturing of critical, high-reliability transducers and transducer systems; nuclear sources and detectors for oil field services; and sensors/transducers for high-value measurement and control. Overall, Schlumberger EMR Photoelectric is a research, development, and manufacturing facility for Schlumberger Ltd. **Common positions include:** Chemical Engineer; Electrical/Electronics Engineer; Mechanical Engineer; Physicist. **Educational backgrounds include:** Engineering; Physics. **Benefits:** Dental Insurance; Disability Coverage; Life Insurance; Medical Insurance; Pension Plan; Profit Sharing; Savings Plan; Stock Option; Tuition Assistance. **Corporate headquarters location:** This Location. **Parent company:** Schlumberger Ltd. **Operations at this facility include:** Administration; Manufacturing; Research and Development. **Listed on:** New York Stock Exchange. **Number of employees at this location:** 83.

## TANON MANUFACTURING, INC.
185 Monmouth Parkway, West Long Branch NJ 07764. 732/229-1100. **Fax:** 732/571-0583. **Contact:** Patricia Burke, Director of Human Resources. **Description:** Provides contract electronic manufacturing services ranging from the assembly of printed circuit boards to the complete procurement, production, assembly, test, and delivery of entire electronic products and systems. **Common positions include:** Blue-Collar Worker Supervisor; Buyer; Electrical/Electronics Engineer; Industrial Engineer; Mechanical Engineer; Operations/Production Manager; Quality Control Supervisor; Systems Analyst. **Educational backgrounds include:** Business Administration; Engineering; Marketing. **Benefits:** 401(k); Dental Insurance; Disability Coverage; Employee Discounts; Life Insurance; Medical Insurance; Tuition Assistance. **Corporate headquarters location:** This Location. **Parent company:** E.A.I. **Operations at this facility include:** Manufacturing. **Listed on:** New York Stock Exchange. **Number of employees at this location:** 200.

## THERMO ELECTRIC COMPANY, INC.
109 North Fifth Street, Saddle Brook NJ 07663. 201/843-5800. **Contact:** Director of Corporate Services. **Description:** An international leader in industrial temperature instrumentation. Thermo Electric Company, Inc. is a resource for solutions to temperature control needs worldwide. Its products include temperature sensors, instrumentation, and specialty wire and cable. **Common positions include:** Accountant/Auditor; Electrical/Electronics Engineer; Manufacturer's/Wholesaler's Sales Rep.; Mechanical Engineer. **Educational backgrounds include:** Accounting; Engineering; Marketing. **Benefits:** 401(k); Dental Insurance; Disability Coverage; Life Insurance; Medical Insurance; Profit Sharing; Tuition Assistance. **Corporate headquarters location:** This Location. **Operations at this facility include:** Manufacturing; Research and Development; Sales; Service. **Number of employees at this location:** 200. **Number of employees nationwide:** 225.

## THOMAS ELECTRONICS, INC.
100 Riverview Drive, Wayne NJ 07470. 973/696-5200. **Contact:** Personnel Department. **Description:** Manufactures cathode-ray tubes for use by military and industrial OEMs. **Corporate headquarters location:** This Location.

*Note: Because addresses and telephone numbers of smaller companies can change rapidly, we recommend you call each company to verify the information below before inquiring about job opportunities. Mass mailings are not recommended.*

**Additional small employers:**

**AEROSPACE AND/OR NAUTICAL SYSTEMS AND INSTRUMENTS**

**GEC-Marconi Hazeltine Corp.**
150 Parish Dr, Wayne NJ 07470-6009. 973/305-2000.

**Raytheon Systems**
1300 MacArthur Blvd, Mahwah NJ 07430-2052. 201/529-1700.

**Strategic Technology Systems**
PO Box 3198, Trenton NJ 08619-0198. 609/584-0202.

**ELECTRIC LIGHTING AND WIRING EQUIPMENT**

**CN Burman Manufacturing Co.**
781 River St, Paterson NJ 07524-1318. 973/684-2200.

**Crescent Lighting**
PO Box 99, Barrington NJ 08007-0099. 609/546-5500.

**Diamond Communication Products**
500 North Ave, Garwood NJ 07027-1017. 908/789-1400.

**EGL Company Inc.**
100 Industrial Rd, Berkeley Heights NJ 07922-1523. 908/508-1111.

**Glasseal Products Inc.**
485 Oberlin Avenue South, Lakewood NJ 08701-6904. 732/370-9100.

**Kurt Versen Company**
PO Box 677, Westwood NJ 07675-0677. 201/664-8200.

**Mac Power**
PO Box 469, Kearny NJ 07032-0469. 973/344-0700.

**Mercury Lighting Products**
20 Audrey Pl, Fairfield NJ 07004-3416. 973/244-9444.

**Woodriver Industries**
PO Box 329, Riverside NJ 08075-0329. 609/764-0500.

## ELECTRICAL ENGINE EQUIPMENT

**AlliedSignal Aerospace**
118 Highway 35 S, Eatontown NJ 07724-1814. 732/542-2000.

## ELECTRICAL EQUIPMENT WHOLESALE

**Crystal Clear Industries Inc.**
300 Industrial Ave, Ridgefield Park NJ 07660. 201/229-0200.

**General Electric Company**
7 Ridge Rd, Fl 1, Parsippany NJ 07054-1614. 973/292-7001.

**General Electric Company**
14000 Horizon Way, Mount Laurel NJ 08054. 609/802-4600.

## ELECTRICAL EQUIPMENT, MACHINERY, & SUPPLIES

**Besam Automated Entrance System**
84 Twin Rivers Dr, Hightstown NJ 08520-5213. 609/443-5800.

**Crest Ultrasonics Corporation**
PO Box 7266, Trenton NJ 08628-0266. 609/883-4000.

**L&R Manufacturing Company Inc.**
577 Elm St, Kearny NJ 07032-3604. 201/991-5330.

**PRC Corporation**
N Frontage Rd, Landing NJ 07850. 973/347-0100.

**Sumtak**
615 Pierce St, Somerset NJ 08873-1262. 732/805-0008.

## ELECTRICAL INDUSTRIAL APPARATUS

**Valcor Engineering**
2 Lawrence Rd, Springfield NJ 07081-3121. 973/467-8400.

## ELECTRONIC CAPACITORS

**Electronic Concepts Inc.**
PO Box 1278, Eatontown NJ 07724-1081. 732/542-7880.

## ELECTRONIC COMPONENTS AND ACCESSORIES

**Ridge Associates Inc.**
198 Green Pond Rd, Rockaway NJ 07866-1219. 973/586-2717.

## ELECTRONIC PARTS AND EQUIPMENT WHOLESALE

**Aromat Corporation**
629 Central Ave, New Providence NJ 07974-1507. 908/464-3550.

**ASM**
PO Box 10095, Fairfield NJ 07004-6095. 973/244-9200.

**Harris Semiconductor**
PO Box 591, Somerville NJ 08876-0591. 908/685-6000.

**Heimann Systems**
186 Wood Ave S, Iselin NJ 08830-2704. 732/603-5914.

**Rolm Systems**
61 S Paramus Rd, Saddle Brook NJ 07663. 201/845-4005.

**Telquest International Corporation**
26 Commerce Rd, Fairfield NJ 07004-1606. 973/808-4588.

**TTSI**
18 Worlds Fair Dr, Somerset NJ 08873-1346. 732/563-6600.

**United Video Security**
11 Princess Rd, Suite H, Lawrenceville NJ 08648-2319. 609/896-4499.

## ELECTRONIC RESISTORS

**Thermometrics Inc.**
808 US Highway 1, Edison NJ 08817-4624. 732/287-2870.

**Ward Leonard Resistors**
605 Perkins Ln, Riverside NJ 08075-5034. 609/461-1900.

## MISC. ELECTRONIC COMPONENTS

**Adronics/Elrob Manufacturing**
9 Sand Park Rd, Cedar Grove NJ 07009 1243. 973/239-3800.

**EMC Technology Inc.**
1971 Old Cuthbert Rd, Cherry Hill NJ 08034-1417. 609/429-7800.

**KDI Triangle Corporation**
PO Box 10671, Newark NJ 07193-0671. 973/887-5700.

**London Harness & Cable Corporation**
330 Pennington Ave, Trenton NJ 08618-3609. 609/815-2100.

**Ocean Microwave Corporation**
3301 Highway 66 B, Neptune NJ 07753-2795. 732/531-0056.

**Ram Electronic Industries**
7980 National Highway, Pennsauken NJ 08110-1412. 609/488-0601.

## SEMICONDUCTORS AND RELATED DEVICES

**Entran Devices Inc.**
10 Washington Ave, Fairfield NJ 07004-3840. 973/227-1002.

**Epitaxx Inc.**
7 Graphics Drive, Trenton NJ 08628-1547. 609/538-1800.

**EPV**
PO Box 7456, Princeton NJ 08543-7456. 609/587-3000.

**NTE Electronics Inc.**
44 Farrand St, Bloomfield NJ 07003-2516. 973/748-5089.

**OPT Industries Inc.**
300 Red School Lane, Phillipsburg NJ 08865-2233. 908/454-2600.

**Silicon Technology Corporation**
48 Spruce St, Oakland NJ 07436-1830. 201/337-3731.

## SWITCHGEAR AND SWITCHBOARD APPARATUS

**Gunther America Inc.**
263 Hillside Ave, Nutley NJ 07110-1114. 973/667-6200.

## TRANSFORMERS

**GlobTek**
186 Veterans Dr, Northvale NJ 07647-2303. 201/784-1000.

**Hitran Corporation**
362 State Route 31, Flemington NJ 08822-5741. 908/782-5525,

**MagneTek Inc.**
487 Edward H. Ross Dr, Elmwood Park NJ 07407. 201/703-3311.

**NWL Capacitors**
312 Rising Sun Square Rd, Bordentown NJ 08505. 609/298-7300.

**For more information on career opportunities in the electronic/industrial electrical equipment industry:**

Associations

**AMERICAN CERAMIC SOCIETY**
P.O. Box 6136, Westerville OH 43086-6136. 614/890-4700. World Wide Web address: http://www. acers.org. Provides ceramics industry information. Membership required.

**ELECTROCHEMICAL SOCIETY**
10 South Main Street, Pennington NJ 08534. 609/737-1902. World Wide Web address: http://www. electrochem.org. An international society which holds bi-annual meetings internationally and periodic meetings through local sections.

**ELECTRONIC INDUSTRIES ASSOCIATION**
2500 Wilson Boulevard, Arlington VA 22201. 703/907-7500. World Wide Web address: http://www. eia.org.

**ELECTRONICS TECHNICIANS ASSOCIATION**
602 North Jackson Street, Greencastle IN 46135. 765/653-4301. World Wide Web address: http://www. eta-sda.com. Offers published job-hunting advice from the organization's officers and members. Also offers educational material and certification programs.

**FABLESS SEMICONDUCTOR ASSOCIATION**
Three Lincoln Centre, 5430 LBJ Freeway, Suite 280, Dallas TX 75240-6636. 972/866-7579. Fax: 972/239-2292. World Wide Web address: http://www.fsa.org. A semiconductor industry association.

**INSTITUTE OF ELECTRICAL AND ELECTRONICS ENGINEERS, INC. (IEEE)**
345 East 47th Street, New York NY 10017. 212/705-7900. Toll-free customer service line: 800/678-4333. World Wide Web address: http://www.ieee.org.

**INTERNATIONAL SOCIETY OF CERTIFIED ELECTRONICS TECHNICIANS**
2708 West Berry Street, Fort Worth TX 76109. 817/921-9061. World Wide Web address: http://www. iscet.org.

**NATIONAL ELECTRONICS SERVICE DEALERS ASSOCIATION**
2708 West Berry Street, Fort Worth TX 76109. 817/921-9101. World Wide Web address: http://www. nesda.com. Provides newsletters and directories to members.

**SEMICONDUCTOR EQUIPMENT AND MATERIALS INTERNATIONAL**
805 East Middlefield Road, Mountain View CA 94043-4080. 650/964-5111. E-mail address: semihq@ semi.org. World Wide Web address: http://www. semi.org. An international trade association concerned with the semiconductor and flat-panel display industries. Membership required.

# ENVIRONMENTAL AND WASTE MANAGEMENT SERVICES

*The United States is the world's largest producer and consumer of environmental goods and services. The industry continues to expand as a result of increasing public concern for the environment and the passing of both the Clean Air and Clean Water Acts. Global environmental revenues are expected to increase 33 percent by 2000. Jobseekers may look to private businesses for environmental jobs, as more and more companies start to self-regulate. Environmental jobs with the government, such as environmental inspectors and compliance officers, are subject to slow growth. However, once obtained, government jobs usually hold a great deal of security.*

*Solid waste management remains the largest of the environmental business segments. USA Waste acquired the industry leader, Waste Management, and is now left with Browning-Ferris as a main competitor. Another significant environmental segment is hazardous/toxic waste. In 1998, the Texas Natural Resource Conservation Commission denied a request to store nuclear waste from outside the state's borders. This is an issue that will continue to gain attention, as more states are faced with storing hazardous waste. Job opportunities will continue to be found primarily in the areas of environmental protection, natural resources, and education.*

**CLEAN HARBORS, INC.**
3 Sutton Place, Edison NJ 08817. 732/248-1997. **Contact:** Human Resources. **World Wide Web address:** http://www.cleanharbors.com. **Description:** Clean Harbors, Inc., through its subsidiaries, provides comprehensive environmental services in 35 states in the Northeast, Midwest, Central, and Mid-Atlantic regions. Clean Harbors provides a range of hazardous waste management and environmental support services to a customer base from over 40 locations. The company's hazardous waste management services include treatment, storage, recycling, transportation, risk analysis, site assessment, laboratory analysis, site closure, and disposal of hazardous materials through environmentally sound methods, including incineration. Environmental remediation services include emergency response, surface remediation, groundwater restoration, industrial maintenance, and facility decontamination. **Corporate headquarters location:** Braintree MA. **Number of employees nationwide:** 1,400.

**CLEAN HARBORS, INC.**
2301 Pennsylvania Avenue, Deptford NJ 08096. 609/589-5000. **Contact:** George Johnson, Human Resources. **World Wide Web address:** http://www.cleanharbors.com. **Description:** Clean Harbors, Inc., through its subsidiaries, provides comprehensive environmental services in 35 states in the Northeast, Midwest, Central, and Mid-Atlantic regions. Clean Harbors provides a range of hazardous waste management and environmental support services to a customer base from over 40 locations. The company's hazardous waste management services include treatment, storage, recycling, transportation, risk analysis, site assessment, laboratory analysis, site closure, and disposal of hazardous materials through environmentally sound methods, including incineration. Environmental remediation services include emergency response, surface remediation, groundwater restoration, industrial maintenance, and facility decontamination. **Corporate headquarters location:** Braintree MA. **Number of employees nationwide:** 1,400.

**DOOLAN INDUSTRIES, INC.**
1223 North Church Street, Moorestown NJ 08057. 609/231-0200. **Fax:** 609/231-1234. **Contact:** Juergen H. Weberbauer, CEO. **Description:** A holding company. Founded in 1938. **Common positions include:** Environmental Engineer; Sales Rep. **Educational backgrounds include:** Accounting; Finance; Marketing. **Benefits:** 401(k); Dental Insurance; Life Insurance; Medical Insurance. **Subsidiaries include:** Doolan Steel is a steel service center. Doolan Environmental

performs remediation and water filtration. Doolan Recovery Technologies recycles fluorescent lamps. Doolan General Services provides contract facility management for maintenance and repair. Psycho Design provides truck lettering, signs, graphics, and striping. **Operations at this facility include:** Administration; Divisional Headquarters; Sales. **Annual sales/revenues:** $5 - $10 million. **Number of employees at this location:** 10. **Number of employees nationwide:** 45.

### ENVIROGEN, INC.
4100 Quakerbridge Road, Lawrenceville NJ 08648. 609/936-9300. **Contact:** Judy Reed, Human Resources Department. **World Wide Web address:** http://www.envirogen.com. **Description:** A leading, technology-based, environmental systems and services company that provides solutions to industrial and hazardous waste remediation problems. Envirogen, Inc. uses biological and bio-complementary technologies for the treatment and/or cleanup of contaminated liquids, vapors, soils, and sludges. The company also designs and implements vapor extraction systems and other integrated systems for the on-site treatment of organic contaminants from various soils and groundwater.

### ENVIRON CORPORATION
214 Carnegie Center, Princeton NJ 08540. 609/452-9000. **Fax:** 609/452-0284. **Contact:** Human Resources Department. **World Wide Web address:** http://www.environcorp.com. **Description:** A multidisciplinary environmental and health sciences consulting firm that provides a broad range of services relating to the presence of hazardous substances found in the environment, consumer products, and the workplace. ENVIRON Corporation provides assessment and management of chemical risk, and supports private sector clients with complex, potentially high-liability concerns. **Corporate headquarters location:** Arlington VA. **Parent company:** Applied Bioscience International Inc.

### ENVIRONMENTAL MATERIALS CORPORATION
550 James Street, Lakewood NJ 08701. 732/370-3400. **Contact:** Human Resources Department. **Description:** Engaged in the marketing and sale of refrigerants and refrigerant reclaiming services. The company has also developed and commercialized a line of equipment designed to recycle and recover refrigerants contained in air conditioning and refrigeration systems. **Corporate headquarters location:** This Location. **Parent company:** Environmental Technologies Corporation.

### GROUNDWATER AND ENVIRONMENTAL SERVICES, INC.
1340 Campus Parkway, P.O. Box 1750, Wall NJ 07719. 732/919-1646. **Fax:** 732/919-0916. **Contact:** Human Resources. **E-mail address:** info@gesonline.com. **World Wide Web address:** http://www.gesnj.com. **Description:** An environmental engineering firm specializing in groundwater remediation. Founded in 1985.

### HAMON RESEARCH COTTRELL
P.O. Box 1500, Somerville NJ 08876. 908/685-4531. **Contact:** Carol Ames, Human Resources. **Description:** An environmental treatment and services company that provides a comprehensive range of services and technologies directed at controlling air pollution; protecting the integrity of the nation's water resources; providing services in support of the management and remediation of hazardous waste; and providing services for the operations, maintenance, and management of treatment facilities.

### HANDEX
500 Campus Drive, Morganville NJ 07751. 732/536-8500. **Contact:** Human Resources. **World Wide Web address:** http://www.handex.com. **Description:** Provides environmental remediation and educational services including comprehensive solutions to contamination of groundwater and soil resulting from leaking underground storage tanks; petroleum distribution systems; refineries; heavy industrial plants; chemical, aerospace, and pharmaceutical facilities; airports; auto and truck fleet facilities; and related contamination sources. Handex also offers 24-hour emergency response services and has 19 offices in 14 states.

### IDM ENVIRONMENTAL CORPORATION
396 Whitehead Avenue, South River NJ 08882. 732/390-9550. **Contact:** George Pasalano, Human Resources Director. **Description:** A full-service contractor specializing in environmental remediation, plant decommissioning services, and the relocation/re-erection of processing plants.

### IT/OHM
200 Horizon Center Boulevard, Trenton NJ 08691. 609/584-8900. **Contact:** Jay Earl, Recruiter. **Description:** Provides hazardous waste disposal services.

**KTI, INC.**
7000 Boulevard East, Guttenberg NJ 07093. 201/854-7777. **Contact:** Office Manager. **Description:** Develops and owns waste-to-energy facilities which provide a means of disposal of nonhazardous municipal solid waste.

**KILLAM ASSOCIATES**
27 Bleeker Street, Millburn NJ 07041. 973/379-3400. **Toll-free phone:** 800/832-3272. **Fax:** 973/379-1072. **Contact:** Ida C. Taliercio, Senior Human Resources Assistant. **E-mail address:** killam@earthlink.net. **World Wide Web address:** http://www.killam.com. **Description:** Provides hazardous waste clean-up services, as well as infrastructure planning and design. Founded in 1937. **NOTE:** Entry-level positions are offered. **Common positions include:** Account Manager; Accountant; Administrative Assistant; Administrative Manager; Advertising Executive; Architect; Assistant Manager; Attorney; Budget Analyst; Chemical Engineer; Chief Financial Officer; Civil Engineer; Clerical Supervisor; Computer Programmer; Controller; Database Manager; Design Engineer; Draftsperson; Editorial Assistant; Electrical/Electronics Engineer; Environmental Engineer; Finance Director; Financial Analyst; General Manager; Geologist/Geophysicist; Graphic Artist; Graphic Designer; Human Resources Manager; Industrial Engineer; Internet Services Manager; Management Trainee; Marketing Manager; Marketing Specialist; Mechanical Engineer; MIS Specialist; Paralegal; Purchasing Agent/Manager; Quality Control Supervisor; Sales Engineer; Sales Executive; Sales Manager; Sales Rep.; Secretary; Software Engineer; Systems Analyst; Systems Manager; Technical Writer/Editor; Transportation/Traffic Specialist; Typist/Word Processor; Vice President; Webmaster. **Educational backgrounds include:** Accounting; Business Administration; Communications; Computer Science; Engineering; Environmental Science; Finance; Geology; Liberal Arts; Marketing; Mathematics; Physics. **Benefits:** 401(k); Dental Insurance; Disability Coverage; Employee Discounts; ESOP; Life Insurance; Medical Insurance; Tuition Assistance. **Special programs:** Internships. **Internship information:** Internships are offered May through September, as well as during December and January. **Corporate headquarters location:** This Location. **Other U.S. locations:** Rocky Hill CT; Miami FL; Tampa FL; Boston MA; Raleigh NC; Concord NH; Cape May Court House NJ; Freehold NJ; Hackensack NJ; Randolph NJ; Toms River NJ; Whitehouse NJ; Buffalo NY; New York NY; Beachwood OH; Dublin OH; Fort Washington PA; Quakertown PA; Denville WV. **Subsidiaries include:** BAC Killam, Inc.; Carlan Killam Consulting Group, Inc.; E3-Killam, Inc.; Killam Associates - New England; Killam Management & Operational Services, Inc. **Parent company:** Thermo Electron Corporation (Waltham MA) manufactures environmental and analytical instruments, biomedical equipment, cogeneration systems, and processing equipment for industrial cleanup, medical, paper, recycling, natural gas, and bioengineering concerns. **Listed on:** American Stock Exchange; New York Stock Exchange. **Number of employees at this location:** 165. **Number of employees nationwide:** 850.

**MORETRENCH AMERICAN CORPORATION**
P.O. Box 316, Rockaway NJ 07866. 973/627-2100. **Contact:** Personnel. **Description:** A nationwide engineering and contracting firm specializing in groundwater control and hazardous waste removal. **Common positions include:** Accountant/Auditor; Civil Engineer; Draftsperson; Geologist/Geophysicist; Human Resources Manager; Purchasing Agent/Manager; Sales Executive. **Educational backgrounds include:** Engineering. **Benefits:** Disability Coverage; Life Insurance; Medical Insurance; Pension Plan; Profit Sharing; Tuition Assistance. **Corporate headquarters location:** This Location. **Operations at this facility include:** Manufacturing; Sales; Service.

**OGDEN ENERGY GROUP**
40 Lane Road, Fairfield NJ 07007-2615. 973/882-9000. **Contact:** Human Resources. **Description:** Develops waste-to-energy facilities nationwide through its subsidiaries and provides hazardous waste disposal and recycling services. **Subsidiaries include:** Ogden Martin Systems, Inc.; Ogden Waste Treatment Services, Inc. **Number of employees at this location:** 314.

**STATEWIDE**
11 Harmich Road, South Plainfield NJ 07080. 908/561-8380. **Contact:** Human Resources. **Description:** Provides integrated solid waste management services to residential, commercial, and industrial customers concentrated in the midwestern and mid-south regions of the U.S. and in Costa Rica, Central America. Principal services include nonhazardous landfill disposal, solid waste collection, and transfer station operations. **Parent company:** Republic Industries.

**TELEDYNE BROWN ENGINEERING ENVIRONMENTAL SERVICES**
50 Van Buren Avenue, Westwood NJ 07675. 201/664-7070. **Contact:** Human Resources. **World Wide Web address:** http://www.tbe.com. **Description:** An environmental laboratory specializing in the fields of isotopic analysis and nuclear technology.

*Note: Because addresses and telephone numbers of smaller companies can change rapidly, we recommend you call each company to verify the information below before inquiring about job opportunities. Mass mailings are not recommended.*

## Additional small employers:

### SANITARY SERVICES

**Burlington County Recycling**
10 Hartford Rd, Riverside NJ
08075-1874. 609/461-4141.

**Core Recycling**
5 Linden Ave, Jersey City NJ
07305-4722. 201/434-1100.

**Dauman Industries**
PO Box 610, Carteret NJ 07008-
0610. 732/541-1500.

**Foster Wheeler Environmental**
PO Box 479, Livingston NJ
07039-0479. 973/597-7000.

**IT/OHM**
92 N Main St, Building 14,
Windsor NJ 08561. 609/443-
2870.

**J&J Recycling Inc.**
666 S Front St, 5th Fl, Elizabeth
NJ 07202-3010. 908/351-2406.

**Midco Waste System**
5 Industrial Dr, New Brunswick
NJ 08901-3633. 732/545-8369.

**Monmouth County
Reclamation**
6000 Asbury Ave, Tinton Falls
NJ 07724. 732/922-8686.

**Passaic Valley Sewerage
Commission**
600 Wilson Ave, Newark NJ
07105-4814. 973/344-1800.

**Prins Recycling**
150 Saint Charles St, Newark NJ
07105-3902. 973/344-2222.

**Site Remediation**
401 E State St, Floor 6, Trenton
NJ 08608-1501. 609/292-1250.

**Somerset County Recycling**
40 Polhemus Ln, Bridgewater NJ
08807-3391. 732/469-3363.

## For more information on career opportunities in environmental and waste management services:

### Associations

**AIR & WASTE MANAGEMENT ASSOCIATION**
One Gateway Center, 3rd Floor, Pittsburgh PA 15222.
412/232-3444. E-mail address: info@awma.org.
World Wide Web address: http://www.awma.org. A
nonprofit, technical and educational organization
providing a neutral forum where all points of view
regarding environmental management issues can be
addressed.

**AMERICAN ACADEMY OF
ENVIRONMENTAL ENGINEERS**
130 Holiday Court, Suite 100, Annapolis MD 21401.
410/266-3311. World Wide Web address: http://www.
enviro-engrs.org.

**ENVIRONMENTAL INDUSTRY ASSNS.**
4301 Connecticut Avenue NW, Suite 300,
Washington DC 20008. 202/244-4700. World Wide
Web address: http://www.envasns.org.

**INSTITUTE OF CLEAN AIR COMPANIES**
1660 L Street NW, Suite 1100, Washington DC
20036. 202/457-0911. World Wide Web address:
http://www.icac.com.

**WATER ENVIRONMENT FEDERATION**
601 Wythe Street, Alexandria VA 22314. 703/684-
2452. World Wide Web address: http://www.wef.org.

### Magazines

**JOURNAL OF AIR AND WASTE
MANAGEMENT ASSOCIATION**
One Gateway Center, 3rd Floor, Pittsburgh PA 15222.

412/232-3444. Toll-free phone: 800/275-5851. World
Wide Web address: http://www.awma.org.

### Online Services

**ECOLOGIC**
World Wide Web address: http://www.eng.rpi.edu/
dept/union/pugwash/ecojobs.htm. This Website
provides links to a variety of environmental job
resources.

**ENVIRONMENTAL JOBS SEARCH
PAGE/UBIQUITY**
World Wide Web address: http://ourworld.
compuserve.com/homepages/ubikk/env4.htm. This
Website includes internships, tips, and links to other
databases of environmental job openings.

**INTERNATIONAL & ENVIRONMENTAL JOB
BULLETINS**
World Wide Web address: http://www.sas.upenn.edu/
African_Studies/Publications/International_Environm
ental_16621.html. Provides a wealth of information
on bulletins, magazines, and resources for jobseekers
who are looking to get into the environmental field.
Most of these resources are on a subscription basis
and provide job openings and other information. This
information was compiled by Dennis F. Desmond.

**LINKS TO SOURCES OF INFORMATION ON
ENVIRONMENTAL JOBS**
World Wide Web address: http://www.utexas.edu/ftp/
student/scb/joblinks.html. Provides links to numerous
sites that offer job openings and information in the
environmental field. The site is run by the University
of Texas at Austin.

# FABRICATED/PRIMARY METALS AND PRODUCTS

*The fabricated metals industry is on the rebound after a rough time in the early '90s. However, according to the Federal Reserve, the industry still suffers occasional setbacks, among them the decrease in steel production during the latter half of 1998. Steel production fell approximately 9 percent between January and September of 1998, due in large part to an increase in imports. Standard & Poor data indicated a 3 percent gain in sales for the steel industry, coupled with a 9 percent loss in profits for the first two quarters of 1998. The aluminum segment saw a 2 percent gain in sales for the same period, with a 23 percent decrease in profits.*

*As of September 1998, U.S. industrial production was 128 percent higher than at the same point in 1992. The transportation sector is expected to increase demand for metal castings, and commercial aircraft deliveries will still have a heavy reliance on plate products.*

**ACCURATE FORMING CORPORATION**
24 Ames Boulevard, Hamburg NJ 07419. 973/827-7155. **Fax:** 973/827-3678. **Contact:** Vickie Rodda, Controller. **Description:** Produces drawn metal stampings.

**ALPHA METALS, INC.**
600 Route 440, Jersey City NJ 07304. 201/434-6778. **Contact:** Human Resources. **World Wide Web address:** http://www.alphametals.com. **Description:** Manufactures specialized alloys, chemicals, and instrumentation for soldering applications used by electronics OEMs throughout the world. The company's consumer division manufactures solders for plumbing and hobbyists.

**ALUMINUM SHAPES INC.**
9000 River Road, Delair NJ 08110. 609/662-5500. **Contact:** Richard Gaunt, Managing Director of Human Resources. **Description:** An aluminum rolling and drawing company.

**ARVEY METAL FABRICATING CORPORATION**
20 Sand Park Road, Cedar Grove NJ 07009. 973/239-8100. **Contact:** Human Resources. **Description:** Engaged in aluminum steel fabricating.

**ATLANTIC METAL PRODUCTS, INC.**
21 Fadem Road, Springfield NJ 07081. 973/379-6200. **Contact:** Frank Schuller, Personnel Director. **Description:** Manufactures custom precision sheet metal parts for the computer and office equipment industries. **Corporate headquarters location:** This Location. **Other U.S. locations:** Hillside NJ.

**DOOLAN INDUSTRIES, INC.**
1223 North Church Street, Moorestown NJ 08057. 609/231-0200. **Fax:** 609/231-1234. **Contact:** Juergen H. Weberbauer, CEO. **Description:** A holding company. Founded in 1938. **Common positions include:** Environmental Engineer; Sales Representative. **Educational backgrounds include:** Accounting; Finance; Marketing. **Benefits:** 401(k); Dental Insurance; Life Insurance; Medical Insurance. **Subsidiaries include:** Doolan Steel is a steel service center. Doolan Environmental performs remediation and water filtration. Doolan Recovery Technologies recycles fluorescent lamps. Doolan General Services provides contract facility management for maintenance and repair. Psycho Design provides truck lettering, signs, graphics, and striping. **Operations at this facility include:** Administration; Divisional Headquarters; Sales. **Annual sales/revenues:** $5 - $10 million. **Number of employees at this location:** 10. **Number of employees nationwide:** 45.

**INDUSTRIAL RETAINING RING**
57 Cordier Street, Irvington NJ 07111. 973/926-5002. **Fax:** 973/926-4292. **Contact:** Human Resources. **Description:** Industrial Retaining Ring manufactures a variety of retaining rings made

of carbon steel, stainless steel, and beryllium copper. **NOTE:** Resumes should be sent to Human Resources, Industrial Retaining Ring, 152 Glenn Road, Mountainside NJ 07092-0214. **Corporate headquarters location:** Union NJ. **Parent company:** TransTechnology Corporation designs, manufactures, sells, and distributes specialty fasteners through several subsidiaries. Breeze Industrial Products (Saltsburg PA) manufactures a complete line of standard and specialty gear-driven band fasteners in high-grade stainless steel for use in highly engineered applications. The Palnut Company (Mountainside NJ) manufactures light- and heavy-duty single- and multi-thread specialty fasteners. The Seeger Group (Somerville NJ) manufactures retaining clips, circlips, spring pins, and similar components. Breeze-Eastern (Union NJ) designs, develops, manufactures, and services sophisticated lifting and restraining products, principally helicopter rescue hoist and cargo hooks systems; winches and hoists for aircraft and weapon systems; and aircraft cargo tie down systems.

## METEX CORPORATION
970 New Durham Road, Edison NJ 08818. 732/287-0800. **Fax:** 732/248-8739. **Contact:** Kim Wisk, Human Resources. **World Wide Web address:** http://www.metexcorp.com. **Description:** Manufactures and sells knitted wire mesh and products made from these materials. The company designs and manufactures knitted wire products and components through its Technical Products Division. Products are used in applications that include adverse environment protective materials used primarily as high-temperature gaskets; seals; shock and vibration isolators; noise reduction elements and shrouds; and phase separation devices used as air, liquid, and solid filtering devices. Metex is also an OEM for the automobile industry, supplying automobile manufacturers with seals and components for use in exhaust emission control devices. **Common positions include:** Blue-Collar Worker Supervisor; Computer Programmer; Cost Estimator; Designer; Electrical/Electronics Engineer; Electrician; Mechanical Engineer; Metallurgical Engineer; Quality Control Supervisor. **Educational backgrounds include:** Accounting; Business Administration; Engineering; Finance; Marketing. **Benefits:** 401(k); Dental Insurance; Disability Coverage; Life Insurance; Medical Insurance; Pension Plan; Tuition Assistance. **Corporate headquarters location:** Great Neck NJ. **Parent company:** United Capital Corporation. **Operations at this facility include:** Administration; Manufacturing; Research and Development; Sales. **Listed on:** American Stock Exchange. **Number of employees at this location:** 380.

## THE PALNUT COMPANY
152 Glen Road, Mountainside NJ 07092. 908/233-3300. **Fax:** 908/233-6566. **Contact:** Human Resource Manager. **Description:** The Palnut Company manufactures light- and heavy-duty single- and multi-thread specialty fasteners. **Corporate headquarters location:** Union NJ. **Parent company:** TransTechnology Corporation designs, manufactures, sells, and distributes specialty fasteners through several subsidiaries. Breeze Industrial Products (Saltsburg PA) manufactures a complete line of standard and specialty gear-driven band fasteners in high-grade stainless steel for use in highly engineered applications. Industrial Retaining Ring (Irvington NJ) manufactures a variety of retaining rings made of carbon steel, stainless steel, and beryllium copper. The Seeger Group (Somerville NJ) manufactures retaining clips, circlips, spring pins, and similar components. Breeze-Eastern (Union NJ) designs, develops, manufactures, and services sophisticated lifting and restraining products, principally helicopter rescue hoist and cargo hooks systems; winches and hoists for aircraft and weapon systems; and aircraft cargo tie down systems.

## PEERLESS TUBE COMPANY
58-76 Locust Avenue, Bloomfield NJ 07003. 973/743-5100. **Contact:** Personnel Department. **Description:** Manufactures collapsible metal tubes and one-piece extruded aluminum aerosol containers for the pharmaceutical, cosmetic, toiletries, and household products industries. Peerless Tube also manufactures and sells extruded aluminum shells for marking pens. The company operates a wholly-owned subsidiary in Puerto Rico which manufactures collapsible metal tubes. **Common positions include:** Blue-Collar Worker Supervisor; Computer Programmer; Manufacturer's/Wholesaler's Sales Rep.; Mechanical Engineer; Quality Control Supervisor. **Benefits:** Disability Coverage; Life Insurance; Medical Insurance; Pension Plan. **Corporate headquarters location:** This Location. **Listed on:** American Stock Exchange. **Number of employees at this location:** 500.

## SCHIAVONE-BONOMO CORPORATION
One Jersey Avenue, Jersey City NJ 07302. 201/333-4300. **Contact:** John Sariol, Personnel Manager. **Description:** A metals recycling firm, engaged primarily in the purchase, sale, and export of scrap metal. **Corporate headquarters location:** This Location.

## U.S. CAN COMPANY
669 River Drive, Suite 340, Elmwood Park NJ 07407. 201/794-4441. **Contact:** Human Resources. **World Wide Web address:** http://www.uscanco.com. **Description:** Manufactures a wide range of

steel container products. Principal clients include paint and ink manufacturers. **Common positions include:** Accountant/Auditor; Blue-Collar Worker Supervisor; Electrical/Electronics Engineer; Manufacturer's/Wholesaler's Sales Rep.; Purchasing Agent/Manager. **Educational backgrounds include:** Accounting; Computer Science; Engineering. **Benefits:** 401(k); Disability Coverage; Life Insurance; Medical Insurance; Pension Plan; Savings Plan. **Corporate headquarters location:** Oak Brook IL. **Other U.S. locations:** Baltimore MD; Hubbard OH; Racine WI. **Operations at this facility include:** Manufacturing. **Listed on:** New York Stock Exchange.

*Note: Because addresses and telephone numbers of smaller companies can change rapidly, we recommend you call each company to verify the information below before inquiring about job opportunities. Mass mailings are not recommended.*

**Additional small employers:**

**DIECASTINGS**

**Howmet Corp.**
Roy St, Dover NJ 07801.
973/361-0300.

**Premier Die Casting Company**
1177 Rahway Ave, Avenel NJ
07001-2185. 732/634-3000.

**ELECTROMETALLURGI-CAL PRODUCTS**

**SMC**
PO Box 768, Newfield NJ 08344-0768. 609/692-4200.

**FABRICATED METAL PRODUCTS**

**Garlock Bearings Inc.**
700 Midatlantic Pkwy, Thorofare
NJ 08086. 609/848-3200.

**FABRICATED STRUCTURAL METAL PRODUCTS**

**Allentown Caging Equipment Co.**
PO Box 698, Allentown NJ
08501-0698. 609/259-7951.

**Construction Specialties Inc.**
3 Werner Way, Lebanon NJ
08833-2223. 908/236-0800.

**Metro Steel Construction**
PO Box 300, Whitehouse NJ
08888-0300. 908/534-6644.

**Pepco Manufacturing Co.**
PO Box 68, Somerdale NJ 08083-0068. 609/783-3700.

**Pilot Technologies Corp.**
10 Pomeroy Rd, Parsippany NJ
07054-3722. 973/515-1010.

**Titanium Fabrication Corp.**
110 Lehigh Dr, Fairfield NJ
07004-3013. 973/227-5300.

**Westfield Sheet Metal Works**
PO Box 128, Kenilworth NJ
07033-0128. 908/276-5500.

**IRON AND STEEL FOUNDRIES**

**Atlantic States Cast Iron Pipes**
183 Sitgreaves St, Phillipsburg NJ
08865-3052. 908/454-1161.

**Campbell Foundry Co.**
800 Bergen St, Harrison NJ
07029-2034. 973/483-5480.

**Engineered Precision Cast Co.**
952 Palmer Ave, Middletown NJ
07748-1255. 732/671-2424.

**Griffin Pipe Products Co.**
1100 W Front St, Florence NJ
08518-1015. 609/499-1400.

**METAL FASTENERS**

**Audel Cherry Textron**
50 Lackawanna Ave, Parsippany
NJ 07054-1008. 973/263-8100.

**Waldes Truarc**
500 Memorial Dr, Somerset NJ
08873-1278. 732/469-7999.

**METAL FORGINGS**

**McWilliams Forge Co. Inc.**
385 Franklin Ave, Rockaway NJ
07866-4037. 973/627-0200.

**METAL HEAT TREATING**

**Alfred Heller Heat Treating**
PO Box 330, Clifton NJ 07011-0330. 973/772-4200.

**METAL STAMPINGS**

**Durex Inc.**
5 Stahuber Ave, Union NJ 07083-5037. 908/688-0800.

**National Manufacturing Corporation**
PO Box 409, Chatham NJ 07928-0409. 973/635-8846.

**Steel Craft Fluorescent Co.**
191 Murray St, Newark NJ
07114-2751. 973/824-5871.

**NONFERROUS ROLLING AND DRAWING OF METALS**

**American Modern Metal Corporation**
25 Belgrove Dr, Kearny NJ
07032-1502. 201/991-2100.

**Harrison Alloys Inc.**
PO Box 31, Harrison NJ 07029-0031. 973/483-4800.

**Swepco Tube Corp.**
PO Box 1899, Clifton NJ 07015-1899. 973/778-3000.

**SCREW MACHINE PRODUCTS**

**American Products Company**
PO Box 3143, Union NJ 07083-1943. 908/687-4100.

**SMELTING AND REFINING OF NONFERROUS METALS**

**Johnson Matthey Inc.**
2001 Nolte Dr, Paulsboro NJ
08066-1727. 609/853-8000.

**STEEL PIPE AND TUBES**

**Gibson Tube Inc.**
PO Box 5399, Somerville NJ
08876-1304. 908/218-1400.

**STEEL SHEET, STRIP, AND BARS**

**Sandvik Steel**
PO Box 428, Fair Lawn NJ
07410-0428. 201/794-5000,

**STEEL WIRE, NAILS, AND SPIKES**

**B. Willing Wire Corporation**
PO Box 8068, Willingboro NJ
08046. 609/871-8200.

**United Wire Hanger Corporation**
PO Box 2367, South Hackensack
NJ 07606-0967. 201/288-4540.

**STEEL WORKS, BLAST FURNACES, AND ROLLING MILLS**

**BRS Products Inc.**
550 9th St, Hoboken NJ 07030-6425. 201/418-8500.

**Costeel-Sayreville Inc.**
PO Box 96, Sayreville NJ 08871-0096. 732/721-6600.

**WHOLESALE METALS SERVICE CENTERS AND OFFICES**

**American Strip Steel Inc.**
55 Passaic Ave, Kearny NJ 07032-1185. 201/991-1500.

**Facile Holdings Inc.**
422 Erie St, Paterson NJ 07524. 973/684-1000.

**TW Metals Inc.**
Prospect Plains Rd, Cranbury NJ 08512. 609/655-4120.

**For more information on career opportunities in the fabricated/primary metals and products industries:**

Associations

**ASM INTERNATIONAL: THE MATERIALS INFORMATION SOCIETY**
9639 Kinsman Road, Materials Park OH 44073. 440/338-5151. World Wide Web address: http://www.asm-intl.org. Gathers, processes, and disseminates technical information to foster the understanding and application of engineered materials.

**THE ALUMINUM ASSOCIATION, INC.**
900 19th Street NW, Washington DC 20006. 202/862-5100. Fax: 202/862-5164. World Wide Web address: http://www.aluminum.org. A trade association for U.S. producers and recyclers of primary aluminum. Member companies operate over 200 plants throughout the nation.

**AMERICAN FOUNDRYMEN'S SOCIETY**
505 State Street, Des Plaines IL 60016. 847/824-0181. World Wide Web address: http://www.afsinc.org.

**AMERICAN WELDING SOCIETY**
550 NW LeJeune Road, Miami FL 33126. 305/443-9353. World Wide Web address: http://www.aws.org.

**ASSOCIATION OF IRON AND STEEL ENGINEERS**
3 Gateway Center, Suite 1900, Pittsburgh PA 15222-1004. 412/281-6323. World Wide Web address: http://www.aise.org.

**STEEL FOUNDERS' SOCIETY OF AMERICA**
455 State Street, Des Plaines IL 60016. 847/299-9160. World Wide Web address: http://www.sfsa.org.

Directories

**DIRECTORY OF STEEL FOUNDRIES AND BUYER'S GUIDE**
Steel Founders' Society of America, 455 State Street, Des Plaines IL 60016. 847/299-9160. World Wide Web address: http://www.sfsa.org.

Magazines

**AMERICAN METAL MARKET**
350 Hudson Street, New York NY 10014. 212/519-7550.

**IRON & STEEL ENGINEER**
Association of Iron and Steel Engineers, 3 Gateway Center, Suite 1900, Pittsburgh PA 15222-1004. 412/281-6323. World Wide Web address: http://www.aise.org.

**MODERN METALS**
Trend Publishing, 625 North Michigan Avenue, Suite 1500, Chicago IL 60611. 312/654-2300.

# FINANCIAL SERVICES

*Despite the economic turbulence of 1998, the future appears solid for the financial services sector. According to* Business Week, *profits for the financial services industry were up 18 percent for the first two quarters of 1998 from the same period of 1997, though profit margins were down. Merrill Lynch & Company had a strong year in 1997, posting over $1 trillion in customer assets. Attempting to match Merrill Lynch's success, Morgan Stanley and Dean Witter merged and Travelers Group subsidiary Salomon Inc. joined with Smith Barney Holdings Inc. Travelers Group was in the news again in 1998, when it merged with Citicorp, combining resources of more than $700 billion.*

*The best opportunities through the end of the decade will be for investment managers, specifically those with experience in high-technology, natural resources, and emerging markets. Mortgage and security brokerages are also showing significant growth, having added 7,000 and 4,000 jobs, respectively, in October 1998.*

**AFCO CREDIT CORPORATION**
525 Washington Boulevard, Suite 2300, Jersey City NJ 07310. 201/876-6600. **Contact:** Human Resources. **Description:** Finances insurance premiums, primarily for commercial policies. **Common positions include:** Branch Manager; Clerical Supervisor; Computer Programmer; Credit Manager; Financial Analyst; Systems Analyst; Underwriter/Assistant Underwriter. **Educational backgrounds include:** Business Administration; Liberal Arts; Marketing. **Benefits:** 401(k); Disability Coverage; Life Insurance; Medical Insurance; Pension Plan; Public Transit Available; Tuition Assistance. **Corporate headquarters location:** This Location. **Other U.S. locations:** Nationwide. **Parent company:** Mellon Bank Corporation (Pittsburgh PA) is a holding company for national commercial banks. Through its subsidiaries, the company offers consumer investment services (private asset management services and retail mutual funds); consumer banking services (consumer lending, branch banking, credit cards, mortgage loan origination and servicing, and jumbo residential mortgage lending); corporate/institutional investment services (institutional trust and custody, institutional asset and institutional mutual fund management and administration, securities lending, foreign exchange, cash management, and stock transfer); corporate/institutional banking services (large corporate and middle market lending, asset-based lending, certain capital market and leasing activities, commercial real estate lending, and insurance premium financing); and real estate workout (commercial real estate and mortgage banking recovery operations). **Listed on:** New York Stock Exchange. **Number of employees nationwide:** 350.

**AUTOINFO INC.**
One Paragon Drive, Suite 255, Montvale NJ 07645. 201/930-1800. **Contact:** Human Resources. **Description:** Provides automobile financing.

**BEAR, STEARNS & COMPANY, INC.**
115 South Jefferson Road, Whippany NJ 07981. 973/515-0012. **Contact:** Steve Lacoff, Managing Director of Personnel. **World Wide Web address:** http://www.bearstearns.com. **Description:** An investment banking, securities trading, and brokerage firm engaged in corporate finance, mergers, and acquisitions; institutional equities and fixed income sales and trading; individual investor services; asset management; and correspondent clearing. **Common positions include:** Accountant/Auditor; Computer Programmer; Management Trainee. **Educational backgrounds include:** Accounting; Business Administration. **Benefits:** 401(k); Dental Insurance; Disability Coverage; Life Insurance; Medical Insurance; Pension Plan; Profit Sharing; Tuition Assistance. **Corporate headquarters location:** New York NY. **Parent company:** The Bear Stearns Companies Inc. is a leading worldwide investment banking, securities trading, and brokerage firm with over $5.7 billion in total capital. **Listed on:** New York Stock Exchange.

**C.I.T. GROUP, INC.**
650 C.I.T. Drive, Livingston NJ 07039. 973/740-5000. **Contact:** Personnel Officer. **Description:** A diversified financial services organization. C.I.T. Group provides flexible funding alternatives,

secured business lending, and financial advisory services for corporations, manufacturers, and dealers. Founded in 1908. **International locations:** Worldwide. **Number of employees nationwide:** 2,500.

### CHAMPION MORTGAGE
20 Waterview Boulevard, Parsippany NJ 07054. 973/402-7700. **Contact:** Human Resources. **Description:** Provides refinancing and equity loans.

### DLJ SECURITIES CORPORATION
### PERSHING DIVISION
One Pershing Plaza, 9th Floor, Jersey City NJ 07399. 201/413-2000. **Contact:** Personnel Department. **World Wide Web address:** http://www.dljdirect.com. **Description:** A securities brokerage.

### FIRST MONTAUK FINANCIAL CORPORATION
328 Newman Springs Road, Red Bank NJ 07701. 732/842-4700. **Contact:** Human Resources. **World Wide Web address:** http://www.firstmontauk.com. **Description:** A diversified holding company which provides financial services throughout the United States to individuals, corporations, and institutions. **Subsidiaries include:** First Montauk Securities Corporation is a securities broker/dealer with a nationwide network of more than 300 registered representatives in 90 branch offices serving approximately 25,000 retail and institutional clients. Montauk Insurance Services, Inc. is an insurance agency. **Stock exchange symbol:** FMFK.

### G.E. CAPITAL MORTGAGE SERVICES
3 Executive Campus, Cherry Hill NJ 08002. 609/661-6100. **Contact:** Human Resources. **Description:** Provides real estate loans. **Parent company:** General Electric Company.

### J.B. HANAUER & COMPANY
4 Gatehall Drive, Parsippany NJ 07054. **Toll-free phone:** 888/524-8181. **Fax:** 973/829-0565. **Contact:** Human Resources. **Description:** A full-service brokerage firm specializing in fixed-income investments. J.B. Hanauer & Company provides a broad range of financial products and services. Founded in 1931. **NOTE:** Entry-level positions are offered. **Educational backgrounds include:** Accounting; Business Administration; Communications; Finance; Marketing; Mathematics. **Benefits:** 401(k); Dental Insurance; Disability Coverage; Employee Discounts; Financial Planning Assistance; Life Insurance; Medical Insurance. **Special programs:** Internships; Training. **Corporate headquarters location:** This Location. **Other U.S. locations:** North Miami FL; Tampa FL; West Palm Beach FL; Princeton NJ; Rye Brook NY; Philadelphia PA. **Listed on:** Privately held. **Annual sales/revenues:** More than $100 million. **Number of employees at this location:** 250. **Number of employees worldwide:** 600.

### K. HOVNANIAN COMPANIES
10 Highway 35, P.O. Box 500, Red Bank NJ 07701. 732/747-7800. **Contact:** Human Resources. **World Wide Web address:** http://www.khov.com. **Description:** Designs, constructs, and sells condominium apartments, townhomes, and single-family residences in planned residential communities primarily in New Jersey, New York, eastern Pennsylvania, Florida, Virginia, North Carolina, and Southern California. The company is also engaged in mortgage banking. Founded in 1959. **NOTE:** Entry-level positions are offered. **Common positions include:** Accountant; Administrative Assistant; Architect; Attorney; Auditor; Civil Engineer; Computer Programmer; Controller; Financial Analyst; Human Resources Manager; Market Research Analyst; Marketing Manager; Marketing Specialist; MIS Specialist; Online Content Specialist; Real Estate Agent; Sales Manager; Secretary; Systems Analyst; Systems Manager; Technical Writer/Editor; Webmaster. **Educational backgrounds include:** Accounting; Business Administration; Computer Science; Engineering; Marketing. **Benefits:** 401(k); Dental Insurance; Disability Coverage; Life Insurance; Medical Insurance; Profit Sharing; Tuition Assistance. **Corporate headquarters location:** This Location. **Subsidiaries include:** New Fortis Homes. **Listed on:** American Stock Exchange. **Stock exchange symbol:** HOV. **Annual sales/revenues:** More than $100 million. **Number of employees at this location:** 90. **Number of employees nationwide:** 1,150.

### JEFFERIES & COMPANY, INC.
51 JFK Parkway, Short Hills NJ 07078. 973/912-2900. **Contact:** Human Resources. **World Wide Web address:** http://www.jefco.com. **Description:** Engaged in equity, convertible debt and taxable fixed income securities brokerage and trading, and corporate finance. Jefferies is one of the leading national firms engaged in the distribution and trading of blocks of equity securities and conducts such activities primarily in the third market. Founded in 1962. **NOTE:** Please send resumes to Human Resources, 11100 Santa Monica Boulevard, Los Angeles CA 90025. **Parent company:** Jefferies Group, Inc. is a holding company which, through Jefferies & Company and its

three other primary subsidiaries, Investment Technology Group, Inc., Jefferies International Limited, and Jefferies Pacific Limited, is engaged in securities brokerage and trading, corporate finance, and other financial services.

## MERRILL LYNCH ASSET MANAGEMENT
P.O. Box 9011, Princeton NJ 08543. 609/282-2000. **Contact:** Human Resources Department. **Description:** A brokerage firm specializing in mutual funds. **Office hours:** Monday - Friday, 9:00 a.m. - 5:00 p.m.

## M.H. MEYERSON & COMPANY, INC.
525 Washington Boulevard, Jersey City NJ 07303. 201/459-9515. **Toll-free phone:** 800/888-8118. **Contact:** Human Resources. **World Wide Web address:** http://www.mhmeyerson.com. **Description:** Markets and trades approximately 2,000 securities. The company is also an active underwriter of small and mid-sized capitalization debt and equity services. M.H. Meyerson is licensed in 38 states and the District of Columbia and services approximately 8,500 retail accounts through its retail clearing agent, Bear, Stearns Securities Corporation. The company is also engaged in a variety of investment banking, underwriting, and venture capital activities. M.H. Meyerson provides comprehensive planning services to its corporate clients including public offerings and private placements of securities. Founded in 1960. **Corporate headquarters location:** This Location. **Other U.S. locations:** North Miami Beach FL. **Listed on:** NASDAQ. **Stock exchange symbol:** MHMY. **CEO:** Martin H. Meyerson. **Number of employees at this location:** 169.

## THE MONEY STORE INC.
2840 Morris Avenue, Union NJ 07083. 908/686-2000. **Contact:** Human Resources. **World Wide Web address:** http://www.themoneystore.com. **Description:** Originates, sells, and services consumer, commercial, and small business loans. The lending divisions include home equity, commercial, and student loans. The company operates through 211 offices in 49 states, Washington DC, Puerto Rico, and the UK. **NOTE:** Interested jobseekers should address resumes to The Money Store Inc., Human Resources, P.O. Box 997124, Sacramento CA 95899. 916/617-2000. **Corporate headquarters location:** This Location. **Listed on:** New York Stock Exchange. **Stock exchange symbol:** MON. **CEO:** Marc Turtletaub. **Annual sales/revenues:** More than $100 million. **Number of employees at this location:** 4,500.

## NEWCOURT
44 Whippany Road, Morristown NJ 07962-1983. 973/397-3000. **Contact:** Human Resources. **Description:** Provides financing of capital equipment for commercial customers worldwide.

## PHH MORTGAGE
6000 Atrium Way, Mount Laurel NJ 08054. 609/439-6000. **Contact:** Human Resources Department. **Description:** This location is involved in the origination, sale, and servicing of residential first mortgage loans and related insurance products. Overall, the company offers diverse business services to private and public sector organizations across North America, the United Kingdom, and Europe. The corporation specializes in three key areas: vehicle management services, relocation and real estate services, and mortgage banking services. Vehicle management services consist primarily of the management, purchase, leasing, and resale of vehicles for corporate clients and governmental agencies, including fuel and expense management programs and other fee-based services for clients' vehicle fleets. Relocation and real estate services consist primarily of the purchase, management, and resale of homes for transferred employees of corporate clients, governmental agencies, and affinity groups. **Other U.S. locations:** Hunt Valley MD.

## PAINE WEBBER INC.
1000 Harbor Boulevard, 10th Floor, Weehawken NJ 07087. 201/902-3000. **Contact:** Human Resources Department. **World Wide Web address:** http://www.painewebber.com. **Description:** Paine Webber Inc. is an investment banking firm assisting corporations, governments, and individuals in meeting their long-term financial needs. The company also has operations in equity and fixed-income securities. **Common positions include:** Services Sales Representative. **Educational backgrounds include:** Business Administration; Economics; Finance. **Benefits:** Disability Coverage; Employee Discounts; Life Insurance; Medical Insurance; Pension Plan; Savings Plan; Tuition Assistance. **Corporate headquarters location:** New York NY. **Parent company:** Paine Webber Group.

## PRUDENTIAL INVESTMENTS
Raritan Plaza #1, Raritan Center, Edison NJ 08837. 732/417-7000. **Contact:** Human Resources Department. **Description:** A national mutual fund management firm serving corporate and individual investors.

*Note: Because addresses and telephone numbers of smaller companies can change rapidly, we recommend you call each company to verify the information below before inquiring about job opportunities. Mass mailings are not recommended.*

## Additional small employers:

### CREDIT AGENCIES AND INSTITUTIONS

**Aegis Consumer Funding**
525 Washington Boulevard, Jersey City NJ 07310. 201/418-7300.

**Mosler Inc.**
415 Hamburg Tpke, Wayne NJ 07470-2164. 973/595-4000.

**New Jersey Mortgage & Investment**
5 Becker Farm Rd, Roseland NJ 07068-1727. 973/740-9200.

### INVESTMENT ADVISORS

**Summit Financial Resources**
4 Campus Dr, Parsippany NJ 07054-4401. 973/285-3600.

### MANAGEMENT INVESTMENT OFFICES

**Alliance Capital**
500 Plaza Drive, Secaucus NJ 07094. 201/319-4000.

**American Express Financial Advisors**
1200 Laurel Oak Rd, Voorhees NJ 08043-4317. 609/784-7500.

**Lexington Management Corporation**
PO Box 1515, Saddle Brook NJ 07663-1515. 201/845-7300.

### MORTGAGE BANKERS

**Alliance Funding**
135 Chestnut Ridge Rd, Montvale NJ 07645-1115. 201/930-1500.

**Chase Manhattan Mortgage**
PO Box 871, Perth Amboy NJ 08862-0871. 732/602-0900.

**Chase Manhattan Mortgage**
343 Thornall St, Edison NJ 08837-2206. 732/205-0600.

**PNC Mortgage Corp. of America**
1001 Durham Ave, South Plainfield NJ 07080-2300. 908/754-4200.

### SECURITY BROKERS AND DEALERS

**AG Edwards**
901 Lincoln Dr W, Marlton NJ 08053-3124. 609/596-0888.

**First Institutional Securities**
470 Colfax Ave, Clifton NJ 07013-1624. 973/778-9700.

**First Investors Corp.**
581 Main St, Woodbridge NJ 07095-1104. 732/855-2500.

**Gibraltar Securities Co.**
25 Hanover Rd, Florham Park NJ 07932-1410. 973/822-2500.

**Halpert and Company**
PO Box 1025, Millburn NJ 07041-1025. 973/379-6000.

**Herzog Heine Geduld Inc.**
525 Washington Blvd, Jersey City NJ 07310. 201/418-4000.

**Janney Montgomery Scott Inc.**
PO Box 6600, Mount Laurel NJ 08054-0660. 609/231-8400.

**Knight Securities LP**
525 Washington Blvd, 36th Fl, Jersey City NJ 07310. 201/222-9400.

**Mayer & Schweitzer Inc.**
111 Pavonia Avenue, Unit 15, Jersey City NJ 07310. 201/963-9100.

**Merrill Lynch**
PO Box 3997, Jersey City NJ 07302. 201/557-1000.

**Merrill Lynch**
PO Box 6707, Trenton NJ 08648-0707. 609/896-3500.

**Merrill Lynch**
PO Box 904, Moorestown NJ 08057. 973/301-7600.

**Merrill Lynch**
77 Broad St, Red Bank NJ 07701-1921. 732/530-3000.

**Noonan Astley & Pearce Inc.**
10 Exchange Pl, Jersey City NJ 07302-3905. 201/200-4500.

**Paine Webber**
PO Box 5270, Princeton NJ 08542. 609/951-5600.

**Princeton Venture Research**
5 Vaughn Dr, Princeton NJ 08540-6313. 609/924-3000.

**Prudential Securities Inc.**
4 Greentree Ctr, Ste 400, Marlton NJ 08053-3408. 609/985-0900.

**Salomon Smith Barney Inc.**
3000 Atrium Way, Ste 500, Mount Laurel NJ 08054-3914. 609/866-9292.

**Salomon Smith Barney Inc.**
1040 Broad St, Fl 2, Red Bank NJ 07702-4331. 732/389-8659.

**Sherwood Securities Corporation**
10 Exchange Pl, Jersey City NJ 07302. 201/946-2200.

**Troster Singer**
10 Exchange Place, Fl 9, Jersey City NJ 07302-3910. 201/332-3577.

## For more information on career opportunities in financial services:

### Associations

**FINANCIAL EXECUTIVES INSTITUTE**
P.O. Box 1938, Morristown NJ 07962-1938. 973/898-4600. World Wide Web address: http://www.fei.org. Fee and membership required. Publishes biennial member directory. Provides member referral service.

**INSTITUTE OF FINANCIAL EDUCATION**
55 West Monroe Street, Suite 2800, Chicago IL 60603-5014. Toll-free phone: 800/946-0488. World Wide Web address: http://www.theinstitute.com. Offers career development programs.

**NATIONAL ASSOCIATION OF BUSINESS ECONOMISTS**
1233 20th Street NW, Suite 505, Washington DC 20036. 202/463-6223. World Wide Web address: http://www.nabe.com. Offers a newsletter and Website that provide a list of job openings.

**NATIONAL ASSOCIATION OF CREDIT MANAGEMENT**
8815 Centre Park Drive, Suite 200, Columbia MD 21045. 410/740-5560. World Wide Web address: http://www.nacm.org. Publishes a business credit magazine.

**NATIONAL ASSOCIATION OF TAX PRACTITIONERS**
720 Association Drive, Appleton WI 54914-1483. Toll-free phone: 800/558-3402. E-mail address: natp@natptax.com. World Wide Web address: http://www.natptax.com. National Association of Tax Practitioners is a membership organization that offers newsletters and nationwide workshops.

**PUBLIC SECURITIES ASSOCIATION**
40 Broad Street, 12th Floor, New York NY 10004. 212/809-7000. Contact: Caroline Binn, extension 427. Public Securities Association publishes an annual report and several newsletters.

**SECURITIES INDUSTRY ASSOCIATION**
120 Broadway, 35th Floor, New York NY 10271. 212/608-1500. E-mail address: info@sia.com. World Wide Web address: http://www.sia.com. Contact: Phil Williams, Membership. Publishes several security industry resources. Membership required.

**TREASURY MANAGEMENT ASSOCIATION**
7315 Wisconsin Avenue, Suite 600-W, Bethesda MD 20814. 301/907-2862. World Wide Web address: http://www.tma-net.org.

**Directories**

**DIRECTORY OF AMERICAN FINANCIAL INSTITUTIONS**
Thomson Business Publications, 4709 West Golf Road, 6th Floor, Skokie IL 66076-1253. Sales: 800/321-3373.

**MOODY'S BANK AND FINANCE MANUAL**
Financial Information Services, 60 Madison Avenue, 6th Floor, New York NY 10010. Toll-free phone: 800/342-5647. World Wide Web address: http://www.moodys.com.

**Magazines**

**BARRON'S: NATIONAL BUSINESS AND FINANCIAL WEEKLY**
Barron's, 200 Liberty Street, New York NY 10281. 212/416-2700.

**FINANCIAL PLANNING**
Securities Data Publishing, 1290 Avenue of the Americas, 36th Floor, New York NY 10004. 212/765-5311.

**FUTURES: THE MAGAZINE OF COMMODITIES AND OPTIONS**
250 South Wacker Drive, Suite 1150, Chicago IL 60606. Toll-free phone: 888/898-5514. World Wide Web address: http://www.futuresmag.com.

**INSTITUTIONAL INVESTOR**
488 Madison Avenue, 12th Floor, New York NY 10022. 212/303-3300.

**Online Services**

**FINANCIAL, ACCOUNTING, AND INSURANCE JOBS PAGE**
http://www.nationjob.com/financial. This Website provides a list of financial, accounting, and insurance job openings.

**JOBS IN CORPORATE FINANCE**
http://www.cob.ohio-state.edu/dept/fin/jobs/corpfin.htm. Provides information and resources for jobseekers looking to work in the field of corporate finance.

**NATIONAL BANKING NETWORK: RECRUITING FOR BANKING AND FINANCE**
http://www.banking-financejobs.com. Offers a searchable database of job openings in financial services and banking. The database is searchable by region, keyword, and job specialty.

# FOOD AND BEVERAGES/AGRICULTURE

*The food and beverages industry constitutes the nation's largest sector of manufacturing, and the demand for processed food and beverages should increase moderately as the market becomes more globalized. With the popularity of pre-cooked meals, supermarkets have increased spending on prepared foods.* Standard & Poor *reported a 39 percent increase in food profits for the first two quarters of 1998 versus profits for the same period of 1997, and a 4 percent increase in beverage profits.*

*According to* Business Week, *about 15 percent of packaged food industry jobs were eliminated between 1996 and 1998. The trend in the packaged food business is toward cutbacks in the number of brands offered as well as fewer coupons for consumers. By reducing the number of brands, food companies are able to spend less money on marketing and focus on top-selling products. General Mills, for example, has eliminated all but its most profitable cereals.*

*Overall, the U.S. Department of Labor projects a slow decline in food industry employment through 2005, particularly for those occupations hurt by rising operations costs, including food processors and butchers. Agricultural careers are also expected to decline through 2005. Due to a high turnover rate, food and beverage service worker jobs will be available over the next decade. The dairy sector should see about 3 percent annual growth over the next few years, due mainly to strong demand for reduced-fat milk, natural cheese, and frozen desserts.*

## ANHEUSER-BUSCH, INC.
P.O. Box 879, Newark NJ 07101. 973/645-7700. **Physical address:** 200 U.S. Highway One, Newark NJ 07101. **Contact:** Human Resources Department. **World Wide Web address:** http://www.budweiser.com. **Description:** A beer producer with a high-tech brewing process and high-speed packaging lines. Anheuser-Busch, Inc. began operations in 1852 as the Bavarian Brewery and now ranks as one of the world's largest brewers. **Corporate headquarters location:** St. Louis MO. **Other U.S. locations:** Nationwide. **Parent company:** Anheuser-Busch Companies is a diverse company involved in the entertainment, brewing, baking, and manufacturing industries. The company is one of the largest domestic brewers, operating 13 breweries throughout the U.S. and distributing through over 900 independent wholesalers. Beer brands include Budweiser, Michelob, Busch, King Cobra, and O'Doul's (non-alcoholic) beverages. Related businesses include can manufacturing, paper printing, and barley malting. Anheuser-Busch Companies is also one of the largest operators of theme parks in the U.S., with locations in Florida, Virginia, Texas, Ohio, and California. Through subsidiary Campbell Taggart Inc., Anheuser-Busch Companies is also one of the largest commercial baking companies in the United States, producing foods under the Colonial brand name, among others. **Listed on:** New York Stock Exchange.

## BESTFOODS BAKING COMPANY
International Plaza, 700 Sylvan Avenue, Englewood Cliffs NJ 07632. 201/894-4000. **Contact:** Corporate Personnel Services. **World Wide Web address:** http://www.bestfoods.com. **Description:** This location houses the administrative and marketing offices and is also the world headquarters. Overall, Bestfoods produces and distributes a variety of food products including soups, sauces, and bouillons; dressings (including Hellmann's mayonnaise); starches and syrups; bread spreads (including Skippy peanut butter); desserts and baking aids; and pasta. **Corporate headquarters location:** This Location.

## BORDEN, INC.
## PRINCE SAUCES
1550 John Tipton Boulevard, Pennsauken NJ 08110. 609/661-3206. **Contact:** Cathi DeMarco, Manager of Human Resources. **Description:** Manufactures spaghetti sauce. **Common positions include:** Accountant/Auditor; Blue-Collar Worker Supervisor; Department Manager; Financial

Analyst; Food Scientist/Technologist; General Manager; Human Resources Manager; Industrial Engineer; Mechanical Engineer; Operations/Production Manager; Purchasing Agent/Manager; Quality Control Supervisor. **Educational backgrounds include:** Accounting; Biology; Business Administration; Chemistry; Engineering; Finance; Liberal Arts. **Benefits:** Dental Insurance; Disability Coverage; Employee Discounts; Life Insurance; Medical Insurance; Pension Plan; Profit Sharing; Savings Plan; Tuition Assistance. **Corporate headquarters location:** Columbus OH. **Operations at this facility include:** Administration; Manufacturing. **Listed on:** New York Stock Exchange.

## CAMPBELL SOUP COMPANY
One Campbell Place, Camden NJ 08103-1799. 609/342-4800. **Contact:** Human Resources. **World Wide Web address:** http://www.campbellsoup.com. **Description:** This location houses administrative offices. Overall, Campbell Soup Company is a producer of commercial soups, juices, pickles, frozen foods, canned beans, canned pasta products, spaghetti sauces, and baked goods. The company's products are distributed worldwide. U.S. brand names include Campbell's, Vlasic, V8, Chunky, Home Cookin', Prego, Pepperidge Farm, Inc., LeMenu, Mrs. Paul's, and Swanson. European foods are sold under brand names such as Pleybin, Biscuits Delacre, Freshbake, Groko, Godiva, and Betis. Campbell Soup Company also owns Arnotts Biscuits of Australia. **Corporate headquarters location:** This Location. **Listed on:** New York Stock Exchange.

## CLOFINE DAIRY PRODUCTS
P.O. Box 335, Linwood NJ 08221. 609/653-1000. **Contact:** Marie Losco, Personnel. **Description:** Provides brokerage services for dairy and other food products. Clofine Dairy Products buys directly from manufacturers and then sells to distributors.

## DRAKE BAKERIES
100 Demarest Drive, Wayne NJ 07470. 973/696-5010. **Contact:** Human Resources. **Description:** This location is a small sales office. Overall, Drake Bakeries is a national distributor and processor of bakery goods. **Corporate headquarters location:** This Location.

## EL JAY POULTRY CORPORATION
P.O. Box 778, Voorhees NJ 08043. 609/435-0900. **Contact:** Julia O'Connor, Personnel. **Description:** A poultry processing company.

## THE FRESH JUICE COMPANY
35 Walnut Avenue, Suite 4, Clark NJ 07066. 732/396-1112. **Contact:** Vice President. **Description:** Markets and sells frozen and fresh-squeezed Florida orange juice, grapefruit juice, apple juice, and other non-carbonated beverages under the brand name Just Pik't.

## GREENWICH MILLS
520 Secaucus Road, Secaucus NJ 07096. 201/865-0200. **Contact:** Lorraine Sadowski, Office Manager. **Description:** Produces and distributes coffee used in institutions, restaurants, and food service companies. **Corporate headquarters location:** This Location.

## INTERBAKE FOODS, INC.
891 Newark Avenue, Elizabeth NJ 07208-3599. 908/527-7000. **Contact:** Rita Palacios, Human Resources. **Description:** This location is a bakery for cookies. Overall, Interbake Foods operates in four business segments: Food Service; Grocery Products; Dairy Products; and Girl Scout Products. The Food Service segment offers a line of more than 160 items, including crackers, cookies, tart shells, and other products to institutional customers, such as health care institutions, schools and colleges, and commercial establishments; the Dairy Products segment produces wafers for ice-cream manufacturers; the Grocery Products segment includes a wide range of cookies and crackers; and the Girl Scout Products segment manufactures Girl Scout Cookies. **Parent company:** General Biscuits of America, Inc. is the American subsidiary of General Biscuit, S.A. (France).

## J&J SNACK FOODS CORPORATION
6000 Central Highway, Pennsauken NJ 08109. 609/665-9533. **Contact:** Human Resources. **Description:** Manufactures an expanding line of nutritional snack foods. Its principal products include frozen soft pretzels under Superpretzel and other brand names; Icee and Arctic Blast frozen carbonated beverages; frozen juice bars and desserts under Shapeups and other brand names; Luigi's Real Italian Ice; Mama Tish's Premium Italian Ices; Tio Pepe's churros; The Funnel Cake Factory funnel cakes; and Pride O' The Farm healthy baked goods. The snack foods are sold in snack bars and food stands in leading chain, department, discount, and convenience stores; malls and shopping centers; fast food outlets; stadiums and sports arenas; leisure and theme parks; movie theaters; airports; and schools, colleges, and other institutions.

**ORVAL KENT FOOD COMPANY**
164 Madison Street, East Rutherford NJ 07073. 973/779-2090. **Fax:** 973/779-7338. **Contact:** Human Resources. **Description:** Manufactures and markets a line of food products, primarily salads. **Common positions include:** Accountant/Auditor; Electrician; General Manager; Human Resources Manager; Purchasing Agent/Manager. **Benefits:** 401(k); Dental Insurance; Disability Coverage; Life Insurance; Medical Insurance; Tuition Assistance. **Corporate headquarters location:** Wheeling IL. **Operations at this facility include:** Administration; Manufacturing; Research and Development; Sales; Service. **Number of employees at this location:** 200.

**LIPTON**
800 Sylvan Avenue, Englewood Cliffs NJ 07632. 201/567-8000. **Contact:** Personnel Administrator. **Description:** Manufactures food and beverage products. Divisions include beverages, which produces and distributes tea bags, herbal teas, flavored teas, iced tea mixes, and instant tea; and foods, whose products include soup mixes and Cup-a-Soup products. **Corporate headquarters location:** This Location. **Other U.S. locations:** Flemington NJ.

**M&M/MARS INC.**
800 High Street, Hackettstown NJ 07840. 908/852-1000. **Contact:** Human Resources. **Description:** This location houses administrative offices. Overall, M&M/Mars produces candy and snack foods. **Corporate headquarters location:** This Location. **Other area locations:** 700 High Street, Hackettstown NJ 07840. **Other U.S. locations:** Albany GA; Burr Ridge IL.

**MCT DAIRIES, INC.**
15 Bleeker Street, Millburn NJ 07041. 973/378-8600. **Contact:** Human Resources. **Description:** MCT Dairies, Inc. (also at this location), which buys and sells cheeses and other industrial dairy products, including bulk domestic and imported cheeses, whey powders, dairy flavorings, and buttermilk.

**MARATHON ENTERPRISES INC.**
66 East Union Avenue, East Rutherford NJ 07073. 201/935-3330. **Contact:** Personnel Manager. **Description:** Manufactures Sabrett brand hot dogs. **Corporate headquarters location:** This Location.

**MINUTE MAID COMPANY**
480 Mercer Street, Hightstown NJ 08520. 609/448-5100. **Contact:** Human Resources. **Description:** Manufactures and sells a broad range of juice products. **Parent company:** One of the world's largest soft drink makers, The Coca-Cola Company manufactures concentrates and syrups which are sold to bottlers and wholesalers. Brand names include Coca-Cola, diet Coke, Coca-Cola light (international), Sprite, diet Sprite, Mr. PiBB, Mello Yello, Fanta, TAB, Fresca, Fruitopia, Powerade, and Minute Maid. The Coca-Cola Company owns 100 supporting brands around the world including PowerAde, Aquarius, Hi-C, Georgia (canned coffee, sold in Japan), Thums Up & Limca (India), Sparletta Brands (South Africa), Nestea (distributed by Coca-Cola Enterprises Inc.), and Seiryusabo (Japan). Other subsidiaries of The Coca-Cola Company include Coca-Cola Enterprises Inc., as well as Coca-Cola Foods, the world's largest seller of juice and juice-related products under brands such as FiveAlive, Hi-C, Bright & Early, and Bacardi.

**NABISCO FAIR LAWN BAKERY**
22-11 State Route 208, Fair Lawn NJ 07410-2608. 201/794-4000. **Contact:** Personnel. **Description:** This location is a bakery. Overall, Nabisco is a manufacturer of crackers, packaged food products, and wholesale bakery products. As one of the largest food companies in the United States, the firm has a strong market position in such areas as cookies, margarine, hot cereals, and pet snacks. Production and distribution facilities are located throughout the United States, Canada, Europe, and the Asia/Pacific region. **Corporate headquarters location:** Parsippany NJ. **Number of employees at this location:** 1,200.

**NABISCO INC.**
100 DeForest Avenue, East Hanover NJ 07936. 973/503-2000. **Contact:** Staffing Center. **World Wide Web address:** http://www.nabisco.com. **Description:** This location is the headquarters of the Bisquick Division. Overall, Nabisco is one of the largest consumer foods operations in the country with annual sales of almost $7.7 billion. The company markets a broad line of cookie and cracker products including brand names such as Oreo, Ritz, Premium, Teddy Grahams, Chips Ahoy!, and Wheat Thins. The company operates 13 cake and cookie bakeries, a flour mill, and a cheese plant. The bakeries produce over 1 billion pounds of finished products each year. Over 150 biscuit brands reach the consumer via one of the industry's largest distribution networks. **Common positions include:** Logistics Manager; Marketing Manager; Systems Analyst. **Educational backgrounds include:** Accounting; Computer Science; Marketing. **Benefits:** 401(k); Dental

Insurance; Employee Discounts; Life Insurance; Medical Insurance; Pension Plan; Savings Plan; Tuition Assistance. **Special programs:** Internships. **Corporate headquarters location:** Parsippany NJ. **Other U.S. locations:** Nationwide. **Parent company:** RJR Nabisco.

## NABISCO INC.
7 Campus Drive, P.O. Box 311, Parsippany NJ 07054-0311. 973/682-5000. **Contact:** Human Resources. **Description:** This location houses administrative offices. Overall, Nabisco is a manufacturer of crackers, packaged food products, and wholesale bakery products. As one of the largest food companies in the United States, the firm has a strong market position in such areas as cookies, margarine, hot cereals, and pet snacks. Production and distribution facilities are located throughout the United States, Canada, Europe, and the Asia/Pacific region. **Corporate headquarters location:** This Location.

## OCEAN SPRAY CRANBERRIES, INC.
104 East Park Street, Bordentown NJ 08505. 609/298-0905. **Fax:** 609/298-8353. **Contact:** Human Resources. **World Wide Web address:** http://www.oceanspray.com. **Description:** Manufactures cranberry juices and sauces. **Common positions include:** Accountant/Auditor; Blue-Collar Worker Supervisor; Budget Analyst; Customer Service Representative; Electrician; Human Resources Manager; Mechanical Engineer; Operations/Production Manager. **Educational backgrounds include:** Accounting; Business Administration; Engineering; Finance; Liberal Arts. **Benefits:** 401(k); Dental Insurance; Disability Coverage; Employee Discounts; Life Insurance; Medical Insurance; Pension Plan; Profit Sharing; Savings Plan; Tuition Assistance. **Special programs:** Internships. **Corporate headquarters location:** Lakeville MA. **Other U.S. locations:** Vero Beach FL; Middleboro MA; Las Vegas NV; Sulphur Springs TX; Kenosha WI. **Parent company:** Ocean Spray is a food processor engaged in the packaging, processing, and marketing of fresh cranberries, cranberry sauces, and cranberry and grapefruit juices. **Operations at this facility include:** Manufacturing. **Listed on:** Privately held. **Number of employees at this location:** 300. **Number of employees nationwide:** 2,000.

## PEPSI-COLA, INC.
8275 Route 130, Pennsauken NJ 08110. 609/665-6200. **Contact:** Human Resources. **World Wide Web address:** http://www.pepsi.com. **Description:** This location bottles Canada Dry products. Overall, Pepsi-Cola operates on a worldwide basis within two industry segments: beverages and snack foods.

## PHILADELPHIA BROKERAGE COMPANY
2201 Route 38, Suite 616, Cherry Hill NJ 08002. 609/482-0230. **Contact:** Richard Taubman, Partner. **Description:** A food brokerage.

## POLAND SPRINGS OF AMERICA
170 West Commercial Avenue, Moonachie NJ 07074. 201/531-2044. **Contact:** Human Resources. **Description:** Distributes bottled spring and distilled drinking water for home and industrial use. The company also provides water coolers, microwave ovens, and similar equipment for installation in commercial and industrial locations. **Common positions include:** Accountant/Auditor; Blue-Collar Worker Supervisor; Branch Manager; Customer Service Representative; Department Engineer; General Manager; Management Trainee; Operations/Production Manager; Sales Executive. **Educational backgrounds include:** Accounting; Computer Science; Finance; Liberal Arts; Marketing; Operations; Sales. **Benefits:** 401(k); Dental Insurance; Disability Coverage; Life Insurance; Medical Insurance; Tuition Assistance. **Parent company:** Perrier Group of America (Greenwich CT).

## R&R MARKETING
10 Patton Drive, West Caldwell NJ 07006. 973/228-5100. **Contact:** Human Resources. **Description:** Engaged in the wholesale importation and distribution of liquors and wines. **Corporate headquarters location:** This Location.

## RECKITT & COLMAN, INC.
1655 Valley Road, Wayne NJ 07470. 973/633-3600. **Fax:** 973/633-3734. **Contact:** Staffing Supervisor. **Description:** This location houses the corporate offices. Overall, Reckitt & Colman manufactures cleaning and specialty food products under such brand names as Easy-Off oven cleaner, French's mustard, Lysol, and Woolite detergent. **Common positions include:** Accountant; Administrative Assistant; Auditor; Computer Programmer; Food Scientist/Technologist; Market Research Analyst; Marketing Manager; Marketing Specialist; MIS Specialist. **Educational backgrounds include:** Accounting; Chemistry; Computer Science; Finance; Marketing. **Benefits:** 401(k); Dental Insurance; Disability Coverage; Employee Discounts; Medical Insurance; Pension

Plan; Savings Plan; Tuition Assistance. **Special programs:** Internships. **Office hours:** Monday - Friday, 8:30 a.m. - 4:30 p.m. **Corporate headquarters location:** This Location. **Parent company:** Reckitt & Colman plc. **Number of employees nationwide:** 1,600.

## SNOWBALL FOODS, INC.
1051 Sykes Lane, Williamstown NJ 08094. 609/629-4081. **Contact:** Matt Frese, Human Resources. **Description:** Engaged in poultry processing. **Common positions include:** Accountant; Blue-Collar Worker Supervisor; Buyer; Customer Service Rep.; Food Scientist/Technologist; Human Resources Manager; Management Trainee; Manufacturer's/Wholesaler's Sales Rep.; Operations/Production Manager; Quality Control Supervisor; Transportation/Traffic Specialist. **Educational backgrounds include:** Accounting; Business Administration; Marketing. **Benefits:** 401(k); Dental Insurance; Life Insurance; Medical Insurance; Tuition Assistance. **Special programs:** Internships. **Corporate headquarters location:** This Location. **Operations at this facility include:** Manufacturing; Research and Development; Sales; Service. **Number of employees at this location:** 250.

## SUPREMA SPECIALTIES INC.
P.O. Box 280, Park Station, Paterson NJ 07543. 973/684-2900. **Contact:** Ann Cocchiola, Employment. **Description:** Manufactures and markets a variety of premium gourmet natural cheese products from the U.S., Europe, and South America. Suprema's product line encompasses grated and shredded parmesan and pecorino romano cheeses, mozzarella and ricotta cheese products, low-fat versions of these products, and a provolone cheese. The company's products are sold to supermarkets and other retail customers, food service industry distributors, and food manufacturers. **Corporate headquarters location:** This Location.

## TUSCAN DAIRY FARM
750 Union Avenue, Union NJ 07083. 908/686-1500. **Contact:** Human Resources. **Description:** Produces and distributes milk and related products throughout northern New Jersey and adjacent areas. **Corporate headquarters location:** This Location.

## U.S. FOODSERVICE
244 High Hill Road, Bridgeport NJ 08014. 609/467-4900. **Fax:** 609/241-0973. **Contact:** Human Resources. **World Wide Web address:** http://www.usfoodservice.com. **Description:** An institutional food production and distribution company with clients in the restaurant and health care industries. **Corporate headquarters location:** Columbia MD. **Number of employees worldwide:** 12,000.

## VENICE MAID FOODS, INC.
P.O. Box 1505, Vineland NJ 08362. 609/691-2100x315. **Fax:** 609/696-1295. **Contact:** Patricia Haas, Human Resources Manager. **Description:** One of the nation's largest food manufacturers for private brands. The company produces over 375 institutional and retail products. Founded in 1927. **NOTE:** Entry-level positions and second and third shifts are offered. **Common positions include:** Accountant/Auditor; Administrative Assistant; Controller; Credit Manager; Customer Service Representative; Electrician; Food Scientist/Technologist; Food Service Manager; Purchasing Agent/Manager; Quality Control Supervisor; Sales Manager; Sales Representative; Secretary. **Educational backgrounds include:** Accounting; Business Administration. **Benefits:** 401(k); Dental Insurance; Disability Coverage; Employee Discounts; Life Insurance; Medical Insurance; Pension Plan; Tuition Assistance. **Operations at this facility include:** Administration; Manufacturing; Research and Development; Sales. **Listed on:** Privately held. **Number of employees at this location:** 190.

## WAKEFERN FOOD CORPORATION
505 Division Street, Elizabeth NJ 07207. 908/527-3300. **Contact:** Bill Britton, Manager of Human Resources. **Description:** Operates a retailer-owned, nonprofit, food cooperative. The company provides purchasing, warehousing, and distribution services to various grocery retailers throughout the metropolitan area. Many products are distributed under the Shop-Rite name. The company also provides a wide range of support services to member firms. **Educational backgrounds include:** Accounting; Liberal Arts. **Special programs:** Internships.

## WHITE ROSE FOOD CORPORATION
380 Middlesex Avenue, Carteret NJ 07008. 732/541-5555. **Contact:** Jackie Simmons, Personnel Director. **Description:** A major area distributor of a wide range of food products. **Corporate headquarters location:** San Francisco CA. **Other U.S. locations:** Farmingdale NY. **Parent company:** DiGiorgio Corporation.

*Note: Because addresses and telephone numbers of smaller companies can change rapidly, we recommend you call each company to verify the information below before inquiring about job opportunities. Mass mailings are not recommended.*

## Additional small employers:

### ALCOHOL WHOLESALE

**Allied Beverage Group LLC**
7800 Browning Rd, Pennsauken NJ 08109-4604. 609/486-4000.

**Federal Wine & Liquor Company**
PO Box 9, Mount Laurel NJ 08054-0009. 609/234-3200.

**Gallo Wine Sales Inc.**
520 Division St, Elizabeth NJ 07201-2003. 908/289-8000.

**Hygrade Co.**
PO Box 7092, North Brunswick NJ 08902-7092. 732/821-7600.

**Jaydor Corporation**
PO Box 1000, Millburn NJ 07041-1000. 973/379-1234.

**Kohler Distributing Co.**
PO Box 5655, Englewood NJ 07631-5655. 201/871-0777.

**Nash Distributors Inc.**
PO Box 384, Wood Ridge NJ 07075-0384. 201/896-1330.

**R&R Marketing**
2900 E State Street Extension, Trenton NJ 08619-4504. 609/587-6103.

**Rosrich Inc.**
PO Box 519, Kearny NJ 07032-0519. 973/624-6444.

**William Grant & Son USA**
130 Fieldcrest Ave, Edison NJ 08837-3620. 732/225-9000.

### BAKERY PRODUCTS

**Anthony & Son Italian Bakery**
1275 Bloomfield Ave, Fairfield NJ 07004-2708. 973/575-5865.

**Entenmann's Inc.**
24 Newark Pompton Turnpike, Little Falls NJ 07424-1152. 973/256-2907.

**Heinz Bakery Products Inc.**
1221 Little Gloucester Rd, Blackwood NJ 08012-4582. 609/228-0652.

**Iberia Foods Corp.**
PO Box 4168, South Hackensack NJ 07606-4168. 201/440-0659.

**Keebler Company**
PO Box 7, Sayreville NJ 08871-0007. 732/254-2000.

**Maple Leaf Foods USA Inc.**
220 S Orange Ave 203, Livingston NJ 07039-5800. 973/597-1991.

**Teixeira Bakery**
PO Box 5550, Newark NJ 07105-0550. 973/589-8875.

**Wonder Bread**
720 Washington Ave, Carlstadt NJ 07072-3007. 201/933-2424.

### BEVERAGES

**Coca-Cola**
1500 Livingston Ave, North Brunswick NJ 08902-1832. 732/246-3300.

**Coca-Cola**
1182655 Moonachie Rd, Carlstadt NJ 07072. 201/438-0400.

**Coca-Cola**
701 Jefferson Rd, Parsippany NJ 07054-3718. 973/884-2600.

**Concord Beverage Company**
535 Dowd Ave, Elizabeth NJ 07201-2103. 908/289-4600.

**Pepsi-Cola of Asbury Park**
3411 Sunset Ave, Asbury Park NJ 07712-3911. 732/922-9000.

### COFFEE

**Nestle USA-Beverage Division**
61 Jerseyville Ave, Freehold NJ 07728-2328. 732/462-1300.

**Tetley USA Inc.**
21 Grand Ave, Palisades Park NJ 07650-1027. 201/943-0600.

**Wechsler Coffee Corporation**
10 Empire Blvd, Moonachie NJ 07074-1303. 201/440-1700.

### DAIRY PRODUCTS

**Farmland Dairies**
PO Box 3340, Wallington NJ 07057-0340. 973/777-2500.

**Haagen-Dazs Company**
1 Amboy Ave, Woodbridge NJ 07095-2639. 732/634-7900.

**Mendez Dairy Inc.**
PO Box 1357, Perth Amboy NJ 08862-1357. 732/442-6337.

**Readington Farms Inc.**
PO Box 164, Whitehouse NJ 08888-0164. 908/534-2121.

**White Rose Dairy**
215 Blair Rd, Woodbridge NJ 07095. 732/636-0900.

### DOG AND CAT FOOD

**Hartz Mountain Corporation**
192 Bloomfield Ave, Bloomfield NJ 07003-5620. 973/743-8500.

**Hartz Mountain Pets**
305 Broadway, Jersey City NJ 07306-6712. 201/432-7200.

**Menu Foods Inc.**
9130 Griffith Morgan Ln, Pennsauken NJ 08110-3211. 609/662-7412.

### FLORICULTURE AND NURSERY PRODUCTS

**Princeton Nurseries**
PO Box 185, Allentown NJ 08501-0185. 609/259-7671.

### FOOD PREPARATIONS

**Fresh To Go Foods**
9 Campus Dr, Burlington NJ 08016-2281. 609/387-1316.

**Gel Spice Company Inc.**
48-52 Hook Rd, Bayonne NJ 07002. 201/339-0700.

**Sunnyside Fresh Foods**
730 Lebanon Rd, Millville NJ 08332-9773. 609/451-5077.

### FOOD WHOLESALE

**AFI**
One Center Dr, Elizabeth NJ 07207. 908/629-1800.

**Alliant Foodservice**
2101 91st St, North Bergen NJ 07047-4731. 201/854-1100.

**Atalanta Products**
1 Atalanta Plz, Elizabeth NJ 07206-2132. 908/351-8000.

**Compass Foods**
PO Box 418, Montvale NJ 07645-0418. 201/930-4088.

**Connell Company Inc.**
45 Cardinal Dr, Westfield NJ 07090-1019. 908/233-0700.

**Conolly Calhoun & Conolly**
945 Sherman Ave, Pennsauken NJ 08110-2614. 609/662-6800.

**Ferolie Corp.**
PO Box 409, Montvale NJ 07645-
0409. 201/307-9100.

**Ferrero**
600 Cottontail Lane, Somerset NJ
08873-1233. 732/764-9300.

**Food Enterprises of New York**
75 Lane Rd, Fairfield NJ 07004-
1011. 973/227-7070.

**Frito-Lay**
520 Jefferson Ave, Secaucus NJ
07094-2014. 201/319-0842.

**Garden State Nutritionals**
100 Lehigh Dr, Fairfield NJ
07004-3013. 973/575-9200.

**Gist-Brocades**
70 Lake Dr, Cranbury NJ 08512.
609/371-9169.

**GMB Enterprises Inc.**
1 Manischewitz Plaza, Jersey
City NJ 07302-2929. 201/333-
3700.

**Goya Foods Inc.**
100 Seaview Dr, Secaucus NJ
07094-1800. 201/348-4900.

**Haddon House Food Products**
PO Box 907, Medford NJ 08055-
0907. 609/654-7901.

**Hershey Import Co. Inc.**
700 E Lincoln Ave, Rahway NJ
07065-5712. 732/388-9000.

**JH Haar & Sons Inc.**
PO Box 524, Kearny NJ 07032-
0524. 201/955-2100.

**Kraft Foods**
203 Kuller Rd, Clifton NJ 07011-
2857. 973/881-2900.

**MAI-Metro LLC**
3 University Plz, Ste 24,
Hackensack NJ 07601-6208.
201/488-5511.

**MW Houck Inc.**
60 Craig Rd, Montvale NJ 07645-
1724. 201/476-9260.

**Nabisco Inc.**
100 Central Ave, Teterboro NJ
07608-1116. 201/288-2225.

**Nestle Food Co. Inc.**
500 Valley Rd, Wayne NJ 07470-
3528. 973/633-4900.

**Perrett Steele**
50 Knickerbocker Rd, Moonachie
NJ 07074-1613. 201/935-1600.

**Pezrow Corp. of New Jersey**
535 E Crescent Ave, Ramsey NJ
07446-2922. 201/825-9400.

**Porky Products**
135 Amity St, Jersey City NJ
07304-3509. 201/333-2333.

**Ritter Sysco Food Services**
PO Box 216, Elizabeth NJ 07207-
0216. 201/433-2000.

**RLB Food Distributors LP**
2 Dedrick Pl, West Caldwell NJ
07007. 973/575-9526.

**Roma Food Enterprises Inc.**
45 Stanford Rd, Piscataway NJ
08854-3725. 732/463-7662.

**William Wrigley Jr. Company**
1 Park 80 Plz W, Saddle Brook
NJ 07663. 201/845-3315.

**FRUITS AND TREE NUTS**

**Marino Brothers**
Rural Route 2, Box 32,
Swedesboro NJ 08085. 609/769-
3468.

**GRAIN MILL PRODUCTS**

**Caravan Products Co. Inc.**
PO Box 1004, Totowa NJ 07511-
1004. 973/256-8886.

**Pennant Food**
280 Jessup Rd, Thorofare NJ
08086-2128. 609/848-5314.

**MEAT AND POULTRY
PROCESSING**

**B&B Poultry Co. Inc.**
PO Box 307, Norma NJ 08347-
0307. 609/692-8893.

**Beef International Inc.**
PO Box 1340, Merchantville NJ
08109-0340. 609/663-6763.

**Garden State Sausage Co. Inc.**
50 Utter Ave, Hawthorne NJ
07506-2117. 973/427-1106.

**Nitta Casings Inc.**
PO Box 858, Somerville NJ
08876-0858. 908/218-4400.

**Thumann Inc.**
670 Dell Rd, Carlstadt NJ 07072-
2201. 201/935-3636.

**Vineland Kosher Poultry Inc.**
1050 S Mill Rd, Suite 1182,
Vineland NJ 08360-6202.
609/692-1871.

**Watsons Quality Food Products**
PO Box 215, Blackwood NJ
08012-0215. 609/227-0594.

**Western Beef**
1A New Main St, East Orange NJ
07018-4233. 973/674-8040.

**PRESERVED FRUITS AND
VEGETABLES**

**Del Monte Foods**
10 Corn Rd, Dayton NJ 08810-
1527. 732/329-2391.

**Johanna Foods Inc.**
PO Box 272, Flemington NJ
08822-0272. 908/788-2200.

**Joyce Food Products Inc.**
Bomar Pl, Elmwood Park NJ
07407. 201/791-4300.

**Lea & Perrins America Inc.**
15-01 Pollitt Dr, Fair Lawn NJ
07410-2728. 201/791-1600.

**McCain Ellio's Foods**
11 Gregg St, Lodi NJ 07644-
2704. 201/368-0600.

**Minot Food Packers Inc.**
PO Box 219, Bridgeton NJ
08302-0165. 609/451-2035.

**Mother's Kitchen Inc.**
499 Veterans Dr, Burlington NJ
08016-1269. 609/387-7200.

**Redpack Foods**
PO Box 436, Cedarville NJ
08311-0436. 609/447-3601.

**Seabrook Brothers & Sons Inc.**
PO Box 5103, Bridgeton NJ
08302-5103. 609/455-8080.

**Thomas J. Lipton Co.**
PO Box 71, Flemington NJ
08822-0071. 908/782-3838.

**Whitlock Packaging Corp.**
92 N Main St, Wharton NJ
07885-1607. 973/361-9794.

**SEAFOOD**

**Lamonica Brand**
PO Box 158, Cape May NJ
08204-0158. 609/465-4551.

**Mother's Food Products Inc.**
80 Avenue K, Newark NJ 07105-
3803. 973/589-4900.

**New York Fish House**
PO Box 1188, Elizabeth NJ
07207-1188. 908/351-1400.

**Snows/Doxsee Inc.**
994 Ocean Dr, Cape May NJ
08204-5400. 609/884-0440.

**The Lobster House**
PO Box 497, Cape May NJ
08204-0497. 609/884-3405.

**SUGAR/CONFECTIONERY
PRODUCTS**

**Henry Heide Inc.**
14 Terminal Rd, New Brunswick
NJ 08901-3616. 732/846-2400.

**Ingredient Technology Corp.**
1595 Macarthur Blvd, Mahwah
NJ 07430-3601. 201/818-1200.

**LA Dreyfus Co.**
3775 Park Ave, Edison NJ 08820-2505. 732/549-1600.

**Van Leer Chocolate Corporation**
PO Box 2006, Jersey City NJ 07303-2006. 201/798-8080.

**TOBACCO AND TOBACCO PRODUCTS WHOLESALE**

**Joseph H. Stomel & Sons**
1 Stomel Plz, West Berlin NJ 08091-9287. 609/768-9770.

**For more information on career opportunities in the food, beverage, and agriculture industries:**

Associations

**AMERICAN ASSOCIATION OF CEREAL CHEMISTS (AACC)**
3340 Pilot Knob Road, St. Paul MN 55121. 612/454-7250. E-mail address: aacc@scisoc.org. World Wide Web address: http://www.scisoc.org/aacc. Dedicated to the dissemination of technical information and continuing education in cereal science.

**AMERICAN CROP PROTECTION ASSN.**
1156 15th Street NW, Suite 400, Washington DC 20005. 202/296-1585. World Wide Web address: http://www.acpa.org.

**AMERICAN FROZEN FOOD INSTITUTE**
2000 Corporate Ridge, Suite 1000, McLean VA 22102. 703/821-0770. Fax: 703/821-1350. World Wide Web address: http://www.affi.com.

**AMERICAN SOCIETY OF AGRICULTURAL ENGINEERS**
2950 Niles Road, St. Joseph MI 49085-9659. 616/429-0300. World Wide Web address: http://www.asae.org.

**AMERICAN SOCIETY OF BREWING CHEMISTS**
3340 Pilot Knob Road, St. Paul MN 55121-2097. 612/454-7250. World Wide Web address: http://www.scisoc.org/asbc. Founded in 1934 to improve and bring uniformity to the brewing industry on a technical level.

**CIES - THE FOOD BUSINESS FORUM**
5549 Lee Highway, Arlington VA 22207. 703/534-8880. World Wide Web address: http://www.ciesnet.com. A global food business network. Membership is on a company basis.

**DAIRY MANAGEMENT, INC.**
10255 West Higgins Road, Suite 900, Rosemont IL 60018. 847/803-2000. World Wide Web address: http://www.dairyinfo.com. A federation of state and regional dairy promotion organizations that develop and execute programs to increase consumer demand for U.S.-produced milk and dairy products.

**INTERNATIONAL ASSOCIATION OF FOOD INDUSTRY SUPPLIERS**
1451 Dolley Madison Boulevard, McLean VA 22101. 703/761-2600. Fax: 703/761-4334. Contact: Dorothy Brady. E-mail address: info@iafis.org. World Wide Web address: http://www.iafis.org.

**MASTER BREWERS ASSOCIATION OF THE AMERICAS (MBAA)**
2421 North Mayfair Road, Suite 310, Wauwatosa WI 53226. 414/774-8558. World Wide Web address: http://www.mbaa.com. Promotes, advances, improves, and protects the professional interests of brew and malt house production and technical personnel.

**NATIONAL BEER WHOLESALERS' ASSN.**
1100 South Washington Street, Alexandria VA 22314-4494. 703/683-4300. Fax: 703/683-8965. Contact: Karen Craig.

**NATIONAL FOOD PROCESSORS ASSN.**
1350 I Street NW, Suite 300, Washington DC 20005. 202/639-5900. World Wide Web address: http://www.nfpa-food.org.

**NATIONAL SOFT DRINK ASSOCIATION**
1101 16th Street NW, Washington DC 20036. 202/463-6732. World Wide Web address: http://www.nsda.org.

**USA POULTRY AND EGG EXPORT COUNCIL**
2300 West Park Place Boulevard, Suite 100, Stone Mountain GA 30087. 770/413-0006. Fax: 770/413-0007. E-mail address: info@usapeec.org. World Wide Web address: http://www.usapeec.org.

Directories

**THOMAS FOOD INDUSTRY REGISTER**
Thomas Publishing Company, Five Penn Plaza, New York NY 10001. 212/290-7341. World Wide Web address: http://www.thomaspublishing.com.

Magazines

**FROZEN FOOD AGE**
Progressive Grocer Associates, 23 Old Kings Highway South, Darien CT 06820. 203/655 1600.

# GOVERNMENT

*The government remains the nation's largest employer. Be advised, however, that the number of federal jobs continues to decline. The Defense Department is expected to reduce the size of its workforce through attrition over the next decade. The outlook for state and local government workers is somewhat better. While opportunities vary by state and department, the Bureau of Labor Statistics forecasts a 10 percent increase in state and local positions through 2006, in response to growing populations and community development.*

*The U.S. Postal Service expected an operating surplus of approximately $500 to $600 million for 1998, though it still has a debt of approximately $4 billion. Forecasters predict that 1999 will be a record year for volume, as the U.S. Postal Service expects to handle nearly 200 billion pieces of mail. In order to remain competitive, the U.S. Postal Service has been looking for ways to increase first-class mail business, which has been sharply reduced by the convenience and efficiency of electronic mail, faxes, and teleconferencing. The U.S. Postal Service Fiscal Year 1999 Plan calls for improved delivery times, an increase in net earnings, and improved worker proficiency.*

*There will be a growing need for correctional officers and prison guards as many leave due to low salaries and unattractive rural locations. Positions in fire and police departments will be hardest to obtain as the number of candidates exceed new openings.*

*The Armed Forces are reducing personnel as a result of relative international peace. However, there are still opportunities for persons wishing to enter the military in the late 1990s. These candidates will finish their first enlistments in 2000 when personnel reductions will be complete. It is estimated that there will then be a need for 190,000 enlisted personnel and 15,000 officers to replace retirees and those who have completed their enlistments.*

**BURLINGTON, COUNTY OF**
49 Rancocas Road, Mount Holly NJ 08060-1317. 609/265-5020. **Contact:** Human Resources. **Description:** Administrative offices for Burlington County.

**CAMDEN, COUNTY OF**
520 Market Street, Camden NJ 08102. 609/225-5000. **Contact:** Human Resources. **Description:** Administrative offices for Camden County.

**DEPARTMENT OF TRANSPORTATION**
100 Daniels Way, Freehold NJ 07728. 732/308-4073. **Contact:** Human Resources. **Description:** Designs, builds, and maintains roads and highways throughout the state of New Jersey.

**DEPARTMENT OF TRANSPORTATION**
1035 Parkway Avenue, Trenton NJ 08618. 609/530-2000. **Contact:** Human Resources. **Description:** State headquarters of the agency responsible for designing, building, and maintaining roads and highways throughout the state of New Jersey.

**FEDERAL AVIATION ADMINISTRATION (FAA)**
Atlantic City International Airport, Atlantic City NJ 08405. 609/485-4000. **Contact:** Human Resources. **World Wide Web address:** http://www.faa.gov. **Description:** This location is a testing facility. Overall, the FAA is responsible for the development and maintenance of air navigation and air traffic control systems for both civil and military aircraft; the security of airports and stability of aircraft structures; and the certification of airports that meet certain safety requirements.

**JERSEY CITY POLICE DEPARTMENT**
8 Erie Street, Jersey City NJ 07302-2810. 201/547-5301. **Contact:** Human Resources. **Description:** Headquarters of Jersey City's police department.

**NEW JERSEY DEPARTMENT OF LABOR**
P.O. Box 110, Trenton NJ 08625. 609/292-2313. **Contact:** Human Resources. **Description:** Responsible for enforcing wage and hour laws, child labor laws, occupational health and safety regulations, unemployment, and disability insurance. The New Jersey Department of Labor also administers employment training and workers' compensation programs.

**NEW JERSEY DIVISION OF MOTOR VEHICLES**
225 East State Street, Trenton NJ 08608. 609/292-0800. **Contact:** Human Resources. **Description:** Registers motor vehicles and provides licenses to drivers.

**NEW JERSEY INTERNATIONAL BULK MAIL**
80 County Road, Jersey City NJ 07097. 201/714-6390. **Contact:** Human Resources. **Description:** A United States Post Office which processes foreign, military, and general bulk mail for distribution throughout the world.

**NEW JERSEY STATE POLICE HEADQUARTERS**
P.O. Box 7068, West Trenton NJ 08628-0068. 609/882-2000. **Contact:** Personnel Services. **Description:** Provides recruitment and testing information for state troopers and civilian positions including clerical staff and laboratory scientists.

**NEW JERSEY TURNPIKE AUTHORITY**
P.O. Box 1121, New Brunswick NJ 08903. 732/247-0900. **Contact:** Human Resources. **Description:** A state mandated, unsubsidized organization responsible for construction, maintenance, repair, and operation on New Jersey Turnpike projects.

**NEWARK, CITY OF**
920 Broad Street, Room 205, Newark NJ 07102-2609. 973/733-3780. **Contact:** Human Resources. **Description:** Administrative offices for the city of Newark.

**NEWARK POST OFFICE**
2 Federal Square, Newark NJ 07102. 973/693-5200. **Contact:** Human Resources. **Description:** A post office.

**ORANGE, CITY OF**
29 North Day Street, Orange NJ 07050. 973/266-4245. **Contact:** Personnel. **Description:** Administrative offices for the city of Orange.

**PASSAIC, CITY OF**
330 Passaic Street, Passaic NJ 07055. 973/365-5500. **Contact:** Human Resources. **Description:** Administrative offices for the city of Passaic.

**PASSAIC FIRE DEPARTMENT**
11 Hope Avenue, Passaic NJ 07055. 973/365-5686. **Contact:** Human Resources. **Description:** A fire department.

**PATERSON, CITY OF**
Division of Personnel, 111 Broadway, Paterson NJ 07505-1408. 973/881-3344. **Contact:** Personnel. **Description:** Administrative offices for the city of Paterson.

**SOMERSET, COUNTY OF**
P.O. Box 3000, Somerville NJ 08876-1262. 908/231-7000. **Contact:** Human Resources. **Description:** Administrative offices for Somerset County.

**TRENTON, CITY OF**
319 East State Street, Trenton NJ 08608-1809. 609/989-3030. **Contact:** Human Resources. **Description:** Administrative offices for the city of Trenton.

**U.S. POSTAL SERVICE**
46 Grove Street, Passaic NJ 07055. 973/779-0277. **Contact:** Human Resources. **Description:** One location of the United States postal service for the city of Passaic.

## UNION, COUNTY OF
Elizabethtown Plaza, Elizabeth NJ 07207. 908/527-4030. **Contact:** Human Resources. **Description:** Administrative offices for Union County.

## WEST MILFORD, CITY OF
1480 Union Valley Road, West Milford NJ 07480. 973/728-7000. **Contact:** Human Resources. **Description:** Administrative offices for the city of West Milford.

*Note: Because addresses and telephone numbers of smaller companies can change rapidly, we recommend you call each company to verify the information below before inquiring about job opportunities. Mass mailings are not recommended.*

### Additional small employers:

**ADMINISTRATION OF ECONOMIC PROGRAMS**

**New Jersey Economic Development Authority**
PO Box 990, Trenton NJ 08625-0990. 609/292-1800.

**ADMINISTRATION OF PUBLIC HEALTH PROGRAMS**

**Department of Health**
Broadway & Memorial Dr, Paterson NJ 07505. 973/881-6920.

**East Orange Health Department**
143 New St, East Orange NJ 07017-4110. 973/266-5482.

**Family Health Services**
50 E State St, Trenton NJ 08608-1715. 609/292-4043.

**New Jersey Commission of Blind/Visually Impaired**
153 Halsey St, Newark NJ 07102-2825. 973/648-2324.

**New Jersey Department of AIDS Prevention**
PO Box 363, Trenton NJ 08608. 609/984-5888.

**New Jersey Department of Human Services**
222 S Warren St, Suite 700, Trenton NJ 08608-2306. 609/292-3717.

**Ocean County Health Department**
PO Box 2191, Toms River NJ 08754-2191. 732/341-9700.

**ADMINISTRATION OF SOCIAL AND MANPOWER PROGRAMS**

**Board of Social Services**
4005 Route 9 S, Rio Grande NJ 08242-1911. 609/886-6200.

**Community Affairs Department**
101 S Broad St, Trenton NJ 08608-2401. 609/292-6420.

**Department of Social Services**
PO Box 3000, Freehold NJ 07728-1250. 732/431-6000.

**New Jersey Division of Pensions & Benefits**
PO Box 295, Trenton NJ 08625-0295. 609/292-3676.

**Passaic County Board of Social Services**
80 Hamilton St, Paterson NJ 07505-2024. 973/881-0100.

**Social Service Welfare Office**
400 Holly Dell Dr, Sewell NJ 08080-9384. 609/582-9200.

**COURTS**

**Adminstrative Office of Courts**
PO Box 37, Trenton NJ 08625-0037. 609/984-0275.

**County Superior Court**
PO Box 910, Morristown NJ 07963-0910. 973/285-6999.

**Jersey City Municipal Court**
769 Montgomery St, Jersey City NJ 07306-4603. 201/547-4327.

**EXECUTIVE, LEGISLATIVE, AND GENERAL GOVERNMENT**

**Aberdeen, Township of**
1 Aberdeen Sq, Matawan NJ 07747-2300. 732/583-4200.

**Asbury Park, City of**
1 Municipal Plaza, Asbury Park NJ 07712-7026. 732/775-2100.

**Atlantic City, City of**
1301 Bacharach Blvd, Atlantic City NJ 08401-4603. 609/347-5400.

**Atlantic, County of**
1333 Atlantic Ave, Atlantic City NJ 08401-8201. 609/345-6700.

**Avalon, Borough of**
3100 Dune Dr, Avalon NJ 08202-1706. 609/967-8200.

**Bayonne, City of**
630 Avenue C, Bayonne NJ 07002-3878. 201/858-6046.

**Belleville, Town of**
152 Washington Ave, Belleville NJ 07109-2589. 973/450-3300.

**Bergen, County of**
21 Main St, Hackensack NJ 07601-7021. 201/646-2000.

**Bergenfield, Borough of**
198 N Washington Ave, Bergenfield NJ 07621-1352. 201/387-4055.

**Berkeley, Township of**
PO Box B, Bayville NJ 08721-0287. 732/244-7400.

**Bloomfield, Town of**
Municipal Plz, Bloomfield NJ 07003. 973/680-4006.

**Bloomingdale, Borough of**
101 Hamburg Tpk, Bloomingdale NJ 07403-1236. 973/838-0778.

**Brick, Township of**
401 Chambersbridge Rd, Brick NJ 08723-2807. 732/477-3000.

**Brigantine, City of**
1417 W Brigantine Ave, Brigantine NJ 08203-2147. 609/266-7422.

**Burlington, City of**
437 High St, Burlington NJ 08016-4514. 609/386-0316.

**Burlington, Township of**
PO Box 340, Burlington NJ 08016-0340. 609/386-4444.

**Butler, Borough of**
1 Ace Rd, Butler NJ 07405-1348. 973/838-7200.

**Camden, City of**
Market Federal St, Camden NJ 08101. 609/757-7200.

**Cape May, County of**
4 Moore Rd, Cape May Courthouse NJ 08210-1654. 609/465-1000.

**Carteret, Borough of**
61 Cooke Ave, Carteret NJ
07008-3046. 732/541-3800.

**Cherry Hill, Township of**
PO Box 5002, Cherry Hill NJ
08034-0358. 609/488-7800.

**Clifton, City of**
900 Clifton Ave, Clifton NJ
07013-2708. 973/470-5800.

**Cranford, Town of**
8 Springfield Ave, Cranford NJ
07016-2181. 908/709-7200.

**Denville, Town of**
1 Saint Mary's Place, Denville NJ
07834-2122. 973/625-8330.

**Deptford, Township of**
1011 Cooper St, Deptford NJ
08096-3076. 609/845-5300.

**Dover, Town of**
PO Box 798, Dover NJ 07802-
0798. 973/366-2200.

**Dover, Township of**
PO Box 728, Toms River NJ
08754-0728. 732/341-1000.

**East Brunswick, Town of**
PO Box 1081, East Brunswick NJ
08816-1081. 732/390-6810.

**East Hanover, Town of**
411 Ridgedale Ave, East Hanover
NJ 07936-1440. 973/428-3000.

**East Orange, City of**
44 City Hall Plaza, East Orange
NJ 07017-4104. 973/266-5100.

**East Rutherford, Borough of**
1 Everett Place, East Rutherford
NJ 07073-1701. 201/933-3444.

**Eatontown, Borough of**
47 Broad St, Eatontown NJ
07724-1519. 732/542-2341.

**Edgewater, Borough of**
PO Box 120, Edgewater NJ
07020-0120. 201/943-1700.

**Edison, City of**
100 Municipal Blvd, Edison NJ
08817-3302. 732/248-7200.

**Elizabeth, City of**
50 Winfield Scott Plaza,
Elizabeth NJ 07201-2408.
908/820-4000.

**Franklin, Township of**
PO Box 6704, Somerset NJ
08875-6704. 732/873-2500.

**Franklin, Township of**
PO Box 300, Franklinville NJ
08322-0300. 609/694-1234.

**Freehold, Borough of**
51 W Main St, Freehold NJ
07728-2114. 732/462-4200.

**Haddon, Township of**
135 Haddon Ave, Collingswood
NJ 08108-1033. 609/854-1176.

**Haddonfield, Borough of**
242 Kings Hwy E, Haddonfield
NJ 08033-1907. 609/429-4700.

**Hamilton, Township of**
PO Box 150, Trenton NJ 08650-
0150. 609/890-3503.

**Hanover, Township of**
PO Box 250, Whippany NJ
07981-0250. 973/428-2500.

**Hawthorne, Borough of**
445 Lafayette Ave, Hawthorne
NJ 07506-2551. 973/427-1168.

**Highland Park, Borough of**
221 S 5th Ave, Highland Park NJ
08904-2611. 732/572-3400.

**Hillsborough, Township of**
555 Amwell Rd, Neshanic Station
NJ 08853-3409. 908/369-4313.

**Hillside, Township of**
Liberty Ave, Hillside NJ 07205.
973/926-3000.

**Hoboken, City of**
94 Washington St, Hoboken NJ
07030-4556. 201/420-2022.

**Hopewell, Township of**
201 Washington Crossing,
Titusville NJ 08560-1410.
609/737-0605.

**Howell, Township of**
PO Box 580, Howell NJ 07731-
0580. 732/938-4500.

**Hudson, County of**
567 Pavonia Ave, Jersey City NJ
07306-1803. 201/795-6000.

**Irvington, Town of**
Municipal Building, Irvington NJ
07111. 973/399-8111.

**Jackson, Township of**
95 W Veterans Hwy, Jackson NJ
08527-3409. 732/928-1200.

**Jefferson, Township of**
1033 Weldon Rd, Jefferson NJ
07849. 973/697-1500.

**Lakewood, Township of**
231 3rd St, Lakewood NJ 08701-
3220. 732/364-2500.

**Lavallette, Borough of**
PO Box 67, Lavallette NJ 08735-
0067. 732/793-7477.

**Lawrence, Township of**
PO Box 6006, Trenton NJ 08648.
609/844-7000.

**Lincoln Park, Borough of**
34 Chapel Hill Rd, Lincoln Park
NJ 07035-1939. 973/694-6100.

**Linden, City of**
301 N Wood Ave, Linden NJ
07036. 908/474-8493.

**Little Falls, Township of**
35 Stevens Ave, Little Falls NJ
07424-2248. 973/256-0170.

**Livingston, Township of**
357 S Livingston Ave, Livingston
NJ 07039-3927. 973/992-5000.

**Lodi, Borough of**
1 Memorial Dr, Lodi NJ 07644-
1626. 973/365-4005.

**Long Branch, City of**
344 Broadway, Long Branch NJ
07740. 732/222-7000.

**Long Hill, Township of**
1802 Long Hill Rd, Millington NJ
07946-1340. 908/647-8000.

**Lower, Township of**
2600 Bayshore Rd, Villas NJ
08251-1300. 609/886-2005.

**Lyndhurst, Township of**
367 Valley Brook Ave, Lyndhurst
NJ 07071-1810. 201/438-5120.

**Madison, Borough of**
Kings Rd, Madison NJ 07940.
973/593-3043.

**Mahwah, Township of**
PO Box 733, Mahwah NJ 07430-
0733. 201/529-2850.

**Manalapan, Township of**
120 Rte 522, Englishtown NJ
07726. 732/446-3200.

**Manchester, Township of**
1 Colonial Dr, Lakehurst NJ
08733-3801. 732/657-8121.

**Marlboro, Township of**
1979 Township Dr, Marlboro NJ
07746-2247. 732/536-0200.

**Matawan, Borough of**
PO Box 424, Matawan NJ 07747-
0424. 732/290-2001.

**Maywood, Borough of**
459 Maywood Ave, Maywood NJ
07607-1909. 201/845-7755.

**Mercer, County of**
PO Box 8068, Trenton NJ 08650-
0068. 609/989-6518.

**Metuchen, Borough of**
PO Box 592, Metuchen NJ
08840-0592. 732/632-8512.

**Middle, Township of**
33 Mechanic St, Cape May
Courthouse NJ 08210-2221.
609/465-8738.

**Middlesex, County of**
PO Box 871, New Brunswick NJ
08903-0871. 732/745-3000.

**Middletown, Township of**
1 Kings Hwy, Middletown NJ
07748-2502. 732/615-2000.

**Milltown, Borough of**
39 Washington Ave, Milltown NJ
08850-1219. 732/828-2100.

**Millville, City of**
PO Box 609, Millville NJ 08332-
0609. 609/825-7000.

**Monmouth, County of**
1 E Main St, Freehold NJ 07728-
2273. 732/431-7000.

**Monroe, Township of**
Perrineville Rd, Jamesburg NJ
08831. 732/521-4400.

**Montclair, Township of**
205 Claremont Ave, Montclair NJ
07042-3401. 973/744-1400.

**Montgomery, Township of**
2261 Route 206, Belle Mead NJ
08502-4012. 908/359-8211.

**Moorestown, Township of**
111 W Second St, Moorestown
NJ 08057-2480. 609/235-0912.

**Morristown, Town of**
PO Box 914, Morristown NJ
07963-0914. 973/292-6667.

**Mount Laurel, Township of**
100 Mount Laurel Rd, Mount
Laurel NJ 08054-1607. 609/234-
0001.

**Mount Olive, Township of**
US Hwy 46, Budd Lake NJ
07828. 973/691-0900.

**Neptune, Township of**
PO Box 1125, Neptune NJ
07754-1125. 732/988-5200.

**North Bergen, Township of**
4233 Kennedy Blvd, North
Bergen NJ 07047-2769. 201/392-
2000.

**North Brunswick, Township of**
PO Box 6019, North Brunswick
NJ 08902-6019. 732/247-0922.

**North Plainfield, Borough of**
263 Somerset St, Plainfield NJ
07060-4846. 908/769-2900.

**Nutley, Township of**
1 Kennedy Dr, Nutley NJ 07110-
2786. 973/284-4951.

**Oakland, Borough of**
Municipal Building, Oakland NJ
07436. 201/337-8111.

**Ocean City, City of**
9th St & Asbury Ave, Ocean City
NJ 08226. 609/399-6111.

**Ocean, County of**
PO Box 2191, Toms River NJ
08754. 732/244-2121.

**Ocean, Township of**
399 Monmouth Rd, Oakhurst NJ
07755-1550. 732/531-5000.

**Office of the Secretary of State**
125 W State St, Ste 300, Trenton
NJ 08608-1101. 609/777-1200.

**Old Bridge, Township of**
1 Old Bridge Plz, Old Bridge NJ
08857-2474. 732/721-5600.

**Oradell, Borough of**
355 Kinderkamack Rd, Oradell
NJ 07649-2182. 201/261-8202.

**Paramus, Borough of**
80 State Hwy 17, Paramus NJ
07652. 201/265-2100.

**Parsippany-Troy Hills,
Township of**
1001 Parsippany Blvd, Parsippany
NJ 07054-1222. 973/263-4350.

**Passaic, County of**
401 Grand St, Paterson NJ 07505-
2023. 973/881-4405.

**Pemberton, Township of**
500 Pemberton Browns Mill,
Pemberton NJ 08068-1539.
609/894-8201.

**Pequannock, Township of**
530 Newark Pompton Tpke,
Pompton Plain NJ 07444-1711.
973/835-5700.

**Phillipsburg, Town of**
675 Corliss Ave, Phillipsburg NJ
08865-1698. 908/454-5500.

**Piscataway, Township of**
455 Hoes Ln, Piscataway NJ
08854-5041. 732/562-2300.

**Plainfield, City of**
PO Box 431, Plainfield NJ
07061-0431. 908/753-3206.

**Pompton Lakes, Borough of**
25 Lenox Ave, Pompton Lakes
NJ 07442-1729. 973/835-0143.

**Princeton, Borough of**
PO Box 390, Princeton NJ 08542-
0390. 609/924-3118.

**Princeton, Township of**
369 Witherspoon St, Princeton NJ
08542-3404. 609/924-5176.

**Rahway, City of**
City Hall Plaza, Rahway NJ
07065. 732/827-2000.

**Ramsey, Borough of**
33 N Central Ave, Ramsey NJ
07446-1807. 201/825-3400.

**Randolph, Township of**
502 Millbrook Ave, Randolph NJ
07869-3702. 973/989-7100.

**Readington, Township of**
509 County Road, Whitehouse
Station NJ 08889-4004. 908/534-
4051.

**Red Bank, Borough of**
PO Box 868, Red Bank NJ
07701-0868. 732/530-2750.

**Ridgefield Park, Village of**
234 Main St, Ridgefield Park NJ
07660-2515. 201/641-4950.

**Ridgefield, Borough of**
604 Broad Ave, Ridgefield NJ
07657-1626. 201/943-5215.

**Ringwood, Borough of**
60 Margaret King Ave,
Ringwood NJ 07456-1703.
973/962-7002.

**River Edge, Borough of**
705 Kinderkamack Rd, River
Edge NJ 07661-2439. 201/599-
6300.

**Rockaway, Township of**
65 Mount Hope Rd, Rockaway
NJ 07866-1634. 973/627-7200.

**Roselle Park, Borough of**
110 E Westfield Ave, Roselle
Park NJ 07204-2021. 908/245-
0819.

**Roselle, Borough of**
210 Chestnut St, Roselle NJ
07203-1218. 908/245-5600.

**Salem, County of**
92 Market St, Salem NJ 08079-
1913. 609/935-7510.

**Sayreville, Borough of**
167 Main St, Sayreville NJ
08872-1149. 732/390-7000.

**Secaucus, Town of**
1203 Paterson Plank Rd,
Secaucus NJ 07094-3226.
201/330-2000.

**Somerville, Borough of**
PO Box 399, Somerville NJ
08876-0399. 908/725-2300.

**South Amboy, City of**
140 N Broadway, South Amboy
NJ 08879-1642. 732/727-4600.

**South Brunswick, Township of**
PO Box 190, Monmouth Junction
NJ 08852-0190. 732/329-4000.

**South Orange, Township of**
101 S Orange Ave, South Orange
NJ 07079-1901. 973/762-6000.

**South Plainfield, Borough of**
2480 Plainfield Ave, South
Plainfield NJ 07080-3531.
908/754-9000.

**South River, Borough of**
64 Main St, South River NJ
08882-1227. 732/257-1999.

**Sparta, Township of**
65 Main St, Sparta NJ 07871-
1903. 973/729-5133.

**Springfield, Township of**
100 Mountain Ave, Springfield
NJ 07081-1702. 973/912-2200.

**State of New Jersey**
W State St, Trenton NJ 08608.
609/292-2121.

**Summit, City of**
512 Springfield Ave, Summit NJ
07901-2607. 908/273-6400.

**Tinton Falls, Borough of**
556 Tinton Ave, Eatontown NJ
07724-3263. 732/542-3400.

**Vineland, City of**
PO Box 1508, Vineland NJ
08362-1508. 609/794-4000.

**Washington, Borough of**
100 Belvidere Ave, Washington
NJ 07882-1417. 908/689-3600.

**Washington, Township of**
350 Hudson Ave, Washington
Township NJ 07675-4716.
201/664-4404.

**Wayne, Township of**
475 Valley Rd, Wayne NJ 07470-
3532. 973/694-1800.

**Weehawken, Township of**
400 Park Ave, Weehawken NJ
07087-6711. 201/319-6005.

**West Deptford, Township of**
PO Box 89, Thorofare NJ 08086-
0089. 609/845-4004.

**West New York, Town of**
428 60th St, West New York NJ
07093-2231. 201/295-5200.

**West Orange, Township of**
60 Main St, West Orange NJ
07052-5404. 973/325-4000.

**West Windsor, Township of**
271 Clarksville Rd, Princeton
Junction NJ 08550-1401.
609/799-2400.

**Wildwood Crest, Borough of**
PO Box 529, Wildwood NJ
08260-0529. 609/522-7788.

**Wildwood, City of**
4400 New Jersey Ave, Wildwood
NJ 08260-1729. 609/522-2444.

**Willingboro, Township of**
One Salem Rd, Willingboro NJ
08046-2853. 609/877-2200.

**Winslow, Township of**
125 S Route 73, Hammonton NJ
08037-9423. 609/567-0700.

**Wyckoff, Township of**
Scott Plz, Wyckoff NJ 07481.
201/891-7000.

**FINANCE, TAXATION, AND
MONETARY POLICY
BODIES**

**Casino Control Commission**
Tennesse Ave & Boardwalk,
Atlantic City NJ 08401. 609/441-
3030.

**Office of Management &
Budget**
PO Box 221, Trenton NJ 08625-
0221. 609/292-6746.

**HOUSING AND URBAN
DEVELOPMENT
PROGRAMS**

**Housing Authority**
PO Box H, Paterson NJ 07509-
0208. 973/345-5080.

**Housing Authority**
57 Sussex Ave, Newark NJ
07103-3941. 973/430-2541.

**New Jersey Urban Development**
PO Box 990, Trenton NJ 08625-
0990. 609/633-1100.

**US Department of Housing &
Urban Development**
1 Newark Ctr, Newark NJ 07102-
5211. 973/622-7900.

**LAND, MINERAL, AND
WILDLIFE CONSERVATION
PROGRAMS**

**Liberty State Park Public
Advisory**
PO Box 404, Trenton NJ 08625-
0404. 609/984-0611.

**Mercer County Parks**
640 S Broad St, Trenton NJ
08611-1822. 609/989-6559.

**Monmouth County Park
Department**
805 Newman Springs Rd,
Lincroft NJ 07738-1605.
732/842-4000.

**Sandy Hook National Park**
PO Box 530, Highlands NJ
07732-0530. 732/872-5970.

**PUBLIC ENVIRONMENTAL
QUALITY PROGRAMS**

**Department of Environmental
Protection**
PO Box 402, Trenton NJ 08625-
0402. 609/292-2885.

**Passaic Valley Water
Commission**
PO Box 198, Little Falls NJ
07424-0198. 973/890-2480.

**PUBLIC ORDER AND
SAFETY**

**Atlantic County Sheriff's Office**
5903 Main St, Mays Landing NJ
08330-1701. 609/641-0111.

**Attorney General's Office**
25 Market St, Fl 8, Trenton NJ
08611-2148. 609/292-4925.

**Bayside State Prison**
PO Box F-1, Leesburg NJ 08327.
609/785-0040.

**Bergen County Jail**
160 S River St, Hackensack NJ
07601-6925. 201/646-2222.

**Bergen County Sheriff's Office**
1 Court St, Hackensack NJ
07601-7036. 201/646-2210.

**Burlington County Jail**
54 Grant St, Mount Holly NJ
08060-1309. 609/265-5173.

**Butler Fire Department**
26 Carey Ave 28, Butler NJ
07405-1446. 973/838-0063.

**Camden County Prosecutor's
Office**
25 N 5th St, Camden NJ 08102-
1231. 609/225-8400.

**Camden County Safety
Communications**
Egg Harbor Rd, Bldg 16,
Lindenwold NJ 08021. 609/783-
4808.

**Camden Police Department**
1 Police Plz, 800 Federal St,
Camden NJ 08101. 609/757-
7199.

**County Jail**
200 Market St, Trenton NJ
08611-2151. 609/989-6585.

**County Prosecutor's Office**
PO Box 71, New Brunswick NJ
08903-0071. 732/745-4264.

**County Prosecutor's Office**
PO Box 2002, Mays Landing NJ
08330-6350. 609/645-5885.

**Department of Corrections**
120 Hooper Ave, Toms River NJ
08753-7606. 732/929-2043.

**Department of Corrections**
PO Box 867, Trenton NJ 08625-
0867. 609/292-4397.

**Department of Public Safety**
330 Hook Rd, Bayonne NJ
07002-5011. 201/858-6000.

**Department of Public Safety**
647 Bloomfield Ave, Montclair
NJ 07042-2800. 973/509-4915.

**Department of Public Safety**
244 Perry St, Trenton NJ 08618-
3926. 609/989-4038.

**East Jersey State Prison**
Woodbridge Ave, Avenel NJ
07001. 732/499-5176.

**Elizabeth Fire Department**
316 Irvington Ave, Elizabeth NJ
07208-2012. 908/820-2800.

**Elizabeth Police Department**
1167 E Grand St, Elizabeth NJ
07201-2307. 908/558-2000.

**FCI Fairton**
PO Box 280, Fairton NJ 08320-
0280. 609/453-1177.

**FCI Fort Dix**
PO Box 38, Fort Dix NJ 08640-
0038. 609/723-1100.

**Hackensack Police Department**
225 State St, Hackensack NJ
07601-5506. 201/646-7777.

**Hanover Community Fire
District**
PO Box 165, Whippany NJ
07981-0165. 973/887-0100.

**Hoboken City Fire Department**
201 Jefferson St, Hoboken NJ
07030-1901. 201/420-2259.

**Hudson County Jail**
30 Hackensack Ave 35, Kearny
NJ 07032-4620. 973/491-5566.

**Irvington Fire Department**
Public Safety Bldg, Civic Sq,
Irvington NJ 07111. 973/399-
6555.

**Jersey City Fire Department**
465 Marin Blvd, Jersey City NJ
07302-2111. 201/547-4248.

**Mercer County Correction
Center**
PO Box 8068, Trenton NJ 08650-
0068. 609/882-4018.

**Mercer County Sheriff**
175 S Broad St, Trenton NJ
08608-2401. 609/989-6125.

**Monmouth County Prosecutor**
71 Monument St, Freehold NJ
07728-1747. 732/431-7186.

**Monmouth County Sheriff**
1 Waterworks Rd, Freehold NJ
07728-1330. 732/431-7863.

**New Jersey State Police**
Interchange 9, New Brunswick
NJ 08903. 732/247-3333.

**New Jersey State Prison**
PO Box CN 861, Trenton NJ
08625. 609/292-9700.

**Northern State Prison**
PO Box 2300, Newark NJ 07114-
0300. 973/465-0068.

**Paterson Fire Department**
850 Madison Ave, Paterson NJ
07501-3120. 973/881-6713.

**Plainfield Police Department**
200 E 4th St, Plainfield NJ
07060-1851. 908/753-3133.

**Police Department**
3339 Route 46, Parsippany NJ
07054-1226. 973/263-4395.

**Police Department**
593 Lincoln Ave, Orange NJ
07050-2015. 973/266-4117.

**Police Department**
2400 Bethel Ave, Pennsauken NJ
08109-2767. 609/488-0080.

**Police Department**
1270 Whitehorse Merc Rd,
Trenton NJ 08619-3814. 609/581-
4000.

**Riverfront State Prison**
PO Box 9104, Camden NJ 08101.
609/365-5700.

**Sheriff's Department**
2 Broad St, Elizabeth NJ 07201-
2202. 908/527-4450.

**South Brunswick Police
Department**
1 Police Plz, Monmouth Junction
NJ 08852. 732/329-4646.

**Southern State Correctional
Facility**
PO Box 150, Delmont NJ 08314-
0150. 609/785-1300.

**Teaneck Police Department**
900 Teaneck Rd, Teaneck NJ
07666-4502. 201/837-2600.

**Union County Jail**
15 Elizabethtown Plz, Elizabeth
NJ 07202-3410. 908/558-2686.

**Union Police Department**
981 Caldwell Ave, Union NJ
07083-6756. 908/686-0700.

**US Attorney's Office**
970 Broad St, Ste 502, Newark
NJ 07102-2506. 973/645-2700.

**REGULATION OF MISC.
COMMERCIAL SECTORS**

**Office of Thrift Supervision**
10 Exchange Pl, 18th Fl, Jersey
City NJ 07302. 201/413-1000.

**REGULATORY
ADMINISTRATION OF
TRANSPORTATION**

**Burlington County Bridge
Commission**
PO Box 6, Palmyra NJ 08065-
0006. 609/829-1900.

**Department of Motor Vehicles**
251 Market St, Paterson NJ
07505-1609. 973/742-7083.

**Department of Public Works**
101 South Orange Ave, South
Orange NJ 07079-1901. 973/378-
7741.

**Department of Public Works**
575 Highway 440, Jersey City NJ
07305-4823. 201/547-4400.

**Department of Public Works**
Plotts Rd, Newton NJ 07860.
973/579-0430.

**Department of Public Works**
836 Ridge Rd, Brick NJ 08724-
1007. 732/262-1087.

**Department of Public Works**
800 Commerce Street East,
Bridgeton NJ 08302-2279.
609/453-2192.

**Department of Transportation**
Coney Ave, Vineland NJ 08360.
609/794-6947.

**South Jersey Transportation
Authority**
25 S New York Ave, Atlantic
City NJ 08401-8008. 609/344-
4149.

**REGULATORY
ADMINISTRATION OF
UTILITIES**

**Atlantic County Utilities
Authority**
1701 Absecon Blvd, Atlantic City
NJ 08401-1711. 609/348-5500.

**Brick Township Municipal
Utilities Authority**
1551 Highway 88, Brick NJ
08724-2366. 732/458-7000.

**Ocean County Utility Authority**
PO Box P, Bayville NJ 08721-
0377. 732/269-4500.

## UNITED STATES POSTAL SERVICE

**Brick Post Office**
160 Chambersbridge Rd, Brick NJ 08723-3408. 732/477-0100.

**Clifton Post Office**
811 Paulison Ave, Clifton NJ 07011-3659. 973/472-7900.

**Freehold Post Office**
200 Village Center Dr, Freehold NJ 07728-2545. 732/431-4525.

**Hackensack Post Office**
560 Huyler St, South Hackensack NJ 07606-1544. 201/440-7785.

**Little Falls Post Office**
19 Warren St, Little Falls NJ 07424-2262. 973/256-0969.

**Mount Laurel Post Office**
200 Walt Whitman Ave, Mount Laurel NJ 08054-9998. 609/866-1573.

**Paramus Post Office**
PO Box 9998, Paramus NJ 07652. 201/262-6886.

**Paterson Post Office**
PO Box 998, Paterson NJ 07544-0998. 973/977-4601.

**Perth Amboy Post Office**
205 Jefferson St, Perth Amboy NJ 08861-4105. 732/826-2090.

**Pleasantville Post Office**
752 Black Horse Pike, Pleasantville NJ 08232-2340. 609/641-1858.

**Princeton Post Office**
213 Carnegie Center, Princeton NJ 08540-6213. 609/452-9044.

**Rutherford Post Office**
156 Park Ave, Rutherford NJ 07070-2310. 201/933-1213.

**Somerset Post Office**
500 Demott Ln, Somerset NJ 08873-2782. 732/873-8600.

**Somerville Post Office**
39 Division St, Somerville NJ 08876-2935. 908/725-0570.

**Teaneck Post Office**
751 Palisade Ave, Teaneck NJ 07666-3157. 201/836-6912.

**Union City Post Office**
301 30th St, Union City NJ 07087-4605. 201/867-0081.

**United States Postal Service**
171 Broad St, Red Bank NJ 07701-2015. 732/741-9200.

**United States Postal Service**
64 Midland Ave, Kearny NJ 07032-2211. 201/991-3700.

**United States Postal Service**
384 Main St, Orange NJ 07050-2722. 973/673-2372.

**United States Postal Service**
614 Cranbury Rd, East Brunswick NJ 08816-4030. 732/257-6270.

**United States Postal Service**
2101 Hwy 27, Edison NJ 08817. 732/287-4311.

**United States Postal Service**
1265 Hurffville Rd, Deptford NJ 08096-5619. 609/232-3919.

**United States Postal Service**
1 Brown Ave, Lakehurst NJ 08733-3025. 732/657-8562.

**United States Postal Service**
7895 Airport Highway, Pennsauken NJ 08109-4322. 609/661-9212.

**United States Postal Service**
525 Main St, Belleville NJ 07109-3322. 973/759-0339.

**United States Postal Service**
123 E Main St, Marlton NJ 08053-9998. 609/983-0350.

**United States Postal Service**
310 N Broad St, Elizabeth NJ 07208-3705. 908/352-8400.

**Vineland Post Office**
736 E Landis Ave, Vineland NJ 08360-8008. 609/691-0585.

**West Caldwell Post Office**
155 Clinton Rd, Caldwell NJ 07006. 973/227-6306.

## For more information about career opportunities in the government:

### Online Services

**FEDERAL JOB OPPORTUNITIES BOARD**
World Wide Web address: ftp://fjob.opm.gov/jobs. A Telnet bulletin board that allows jobseekers to search for government jobs by department, agency, or state. The site includes information about the application process as well as opportunities overseas.

**FEDERAL JOBS CENTRAL**
http://www.fedjobs.com. This resourceful site has only one drawback: Its services require a fee. Federal Jobs Central offers a subscription to a 64-page biweekly publication containing over 3,500 job listings; online listings that are accessible by occupation, salary, and location; and a service that pairs you with the job you are seeking.

**FEDERAL JOBS DIGEST**
http://www.jobsfed.com. An excellent site for jobseekers hoping to work for the government, this site offers over 3,500 opportunities in fields such as engineering, medical, administration, management, secretarial, computer services, and law enforcement. The site also includes employment links to government agencies. For a fee, you can let *FJD*'s matching service perform the job hunt for you.

**FEDWORLD**
http://www.fedworld.gov. Provides a wealth of information on all aspects of the government. Besides an employment link to federal job opportunities, this site also offers access to all government agencies and many government documents.

**JOBS IN GOVERNMENT**
http://www.jobsingovernment.com. E-mail address: info@jobsingovernment.com. A helpful search engine for individuals seeking employment in government or the public sector. The site offers profile based searches for thousands of open positions, the ability to post and e-mail resumes, and information about current topics and resources in government.

---

Visit our exciting job and career site at http://www.careercity.com

# HEALTH CARE: SERVICES, EQUIPMENT, AND PRODUCTS

*The rising cost of health care in the United States is influencing the move from the traditional fee-for-service plans to more cost-conscious managed care plans. Cost control is also creating a more demanding nation of health care customers who want the most for their money. Cost-cutting improvements in the field are beginning to take shape with the advent of new technology such as the use of telemedicine. This process allows electronic images of X-rays and test results to be transmitted anywhere in the world for further consultation and diagnosis.*

*Consolidation is still a dominant factor in the industry. Small, independent hospitals are being purchased by large corporations to form multi-hospital enterprises. As these hospitals merge, it is likely that costs will be cut, resources shared, and ultimately jobs eliminated.*

*Health care services are still a major source of job creation in the economy. That distinction is not expected to change as the elderly population continues to grow faster than the nation's total population. As this segment of the population continues to increase, opportunities in long-term care facilities, home health agencies, and doctors' offices will also continue to expand.*

*Industry trends point to a stronger demand for primary care physicians, rather than specialists. Non-traditional forms of medicine, such as acupuncture and home-infusion therapy, are gaining acceptance by consumers, as well as insurers, which should create more job opportunities. According to the Bureau of Labor Statistics, five of the ten fastest-growing occupations through 2006 will be health care related, specifically home health aides and occupational therapy assistants. Registered nurses may see as many as 411,000 new positions by 2006, and nurses aides and orderlies may see more than 300,000 new positions. Overall, it is estimated that the health care services industry will grow a vigorous 68 percent by 2006.*

**ANCORA PSYCHIATRIC HOSPITAL**
202 Spring Garden Road, Ancora NJ 08037. 609/561-1700. **Contact:** Human Resources Department. **Description:** A 500-bed, psychiatric hospital that offers a variety of inpatient services for adults.

**ATLANTIC CITY MEDICAL CENTER**
1925 Pacific Avenue, Atlantic City NJ 08401. 609/344-4081. **Contact:** Human Resources Department. **Description:** A hospital. **Other area locations:** Jim Leeds Road, Pomona NJ 08240, 609/652-1000.

**C.R. BARD, INC.**
730 Central Avenue, Murray Hill NJ 07974. 908/277-8000. **Fax:** 908/277-8412. **Contact:** Human Resources. **World Wide Web address:** http://www.crbard.com. **Description:** Produces and distributes medical, surgical, diagnostic, and disposable patient care products. The company's leading product lines include coronary angioplasty catheters, and equipment used in the cardiovascular, electrophysiology, urological, surgical, cardiopulmonary support, and open heart surgery systems. **Corporate headquarters location:** This Location. **Listed on:** New York Stock Exchange. **Stock exchange symbol:** BCR.

## BARNERT HOSPITAL

680 Broadway, Paterson NJ 07514. 973/977-6655. **Fax:** 973/279-2924. **Recorded jobline:** 973/977-6725. **Contact:** Personnel. **Description:** A 280-bed hospital. **Common positions include:** Computer Programmer; Dietician/Nutritionist; EKG Technician; Medical Records Technician; Nuclear Medicine Technologist; Occupational Therapist; Pharmacist; Physical Therapist; Physician; Radiological Technologist; Registered Nurse; Respiratory Therapist; Social Worker; Stationary Engineer; Surgical Technician. **Benefits:** Dental Insurance; Disability Coverage; Employee Discounts; Life Insurance; Medical Insurance; Pension Plan; Tuition Assistance. **Special programs:** Internships. **Operations at this facility include:** Administration; Service. **Number of employees at this location:** 1,000.

## BECTON DICKINSON & COMPANY

One Becton Drive, Franklin Lakes NJ 07417. 201/847-6800. **Contact:** Human Resources. **World Wide Web address:** http://www.bd.com. **Description:** A medical technology company engaged in the manufacture of health care products, medical instrumentation, diagnostic products, and industrial safety equipment. Major product lines for medical equipment include hypodermics, intravenous equipment, operating room products, thermometers, gloves, and specialty needles. The company also offers contract packaging services. **Corporate headquarters location:** This Location. **Other U.S. locations:** San Jose CA; Sparks MD; Detroit MI; Holdrege NE; Sumter SC; Sandy UT. **Listed on:** New York Stock Exchange.

## BIOSEARCH MEDICAL PRODUCTS INC.

35 Industrial Parkway, Somerville NJ 08876. 908/722-5000. **Toll-free phone:** 800/326-5976. **Fax:** 908/722-5024. **Contact:** Human Resources. **World Wide Web address:** http://www.biosearch. com. **Description:** Manufactures specialty medical devices for the gastroenterology, endoscopy, urology, and enteral feeding markets. The company's products are sold directly to hospitals and alternative care centers through domestic and international specialty dealers. Founded in 1978. **NOTE:** Entry-level positions are offered. **Common positions include:** Account Manager; Attorney; Buyer; Chief Financial Officer; Customer Service Representative; Design Engineer; Draftsperson; Human Resources Manager; Manufacturing Engineer; Production Manager; Purchasing Agent/Manager; Quality Control Supervisor; Sales Manager. **Educational backgrounds include:** Accounting; Engineering; Health Care; Marketing. **Benefits:** 401(k); Dental Insurance; Disability Coverage; Life Insurance; Medical Insurance; Tuition Assistance. **Special programs:** Training. **Listed on:** NASDAQ. **Stock exchange symbol:** BMPI. **Annual sales/revenues:** $5 - $10 million. **Number of employees at this location:** 30.

## BLOCK DRUG COMPANY

257 Cornelison Avenue, Jersey City NJ 07302. 201/434-3000. **Contact:** Human Resources. **Description:** Develops, manufactures, and sells products in four general categories: denture, dental care, oral hygiene, and professional dental products; proprietary products; ethical pharmaceutical products; and household products. Dental-related products include Polident denture cleansers. **Corporate headquarters location:** This Location.

## BURDETTE TOMLIN MEMORIAL HOSPITAL

2 Stone Harbor Boulevard, Cape May Court House NJ 08210. 609/463-2170. **Fax:** 609/463-2379. **Contact:** Human Resources Department. **World Wide Web address:** http://www.btmh.com. **Description:** Burdette Tomlin Memorial Hospital is a 242-bed, acute care, community hospital. **Common positions include:** Chef/Cook/Kitchen Worker; Construction Trade Worker; Dietician/Nutritionist; EEG Technologist; EKG Technician; Electrician; Emergency Medical Technician; Medical Records Technician; Nuclear Medicine Technologist; Occupational Therapist; Physical Therapist; Radiological Technologist; Registered Nurse; Respiratory Therapist; Social Worker; Speech-Language Pathologist; Stationary Engineer; Systems Analyst. **Benefits:** Dental Insurance; Disability Coverage; Life Insurance; Medical Insurance; Pension Plan; Tuition Assistance.

## CANTEL INDUSTRIES, INC.

1135 Broad Street, Suite 203, Clifton NJ 07013. 973/470-8700. **Contact:** Joanna Albrecht, Human Resources Department. **Description:** A holding company for a manufacturer of medical instruments. **Subsidiaries include:** Carson Group Inc. (Canada) markets and distributes medical instruments including flexible and rigid endoscopes; precision instruments including microscopes and image analysis systems; and industrial equipment including remote visual inspection devices, laser distance measurement and thermal imaging products, and online optical inspection and quality assurance systems for specialized industrial applications. Carson Industries, Inc. also offers a full range of photographic equipment and supplies for use by amateur and professional photographers.

**CAPITAL HEALTH SYSTEM AT FULD**
750 Brunswick Avenue, Trenton NJ 08638. 609/394-6000. **Contact:** Human Resources. **Description:** A medical center.

**CAPITAL HEALTH SYSTEM AT MERCER**
446 Bellevue Avenue, Trenton NJ 08618. 609/394-4000. **Contact:** Human Resources. **Description:** A 318-bed, community-based, acute care facility.

**CERAMCO INC.**
6 Terry Lane, Suite 100, Burlington NJ 08016. 609/386-8900x6004. **Toll-free phone:** 800/487-0100. **Fax:** 609/386-5266. **Contact:** Susan E. Race, Director of Human Resources. **E-mail address:** directhr@aol.com. **World Wide Web address:** http://www.ceramco.com. **Description:** A leading manufacturer and distributor of dental porcelain, raw materials, and equipment to dental laboratories for use in preparing crowns, bridges, and restorations. Founded in 1959. **Common positions include:** Materials Engineer; Sales Rep. **Educational backgrounds include:** Business Administration; Engineering. **Benefits:** 401(k); Dental Insurance; Disability Coverage; Life Insurance; Medical Insurance; Pension Plan; Tuition Assistance. **Office hours:** Monday - Friday, 8:00 a.m. - 5:00 p.m. **Corporate headquarters location:** This Location. **International locations:** England; Puerto Rico. **Parent company:** Dentsply International, Inc. **Annual sales/revenues:** $21 - $50 million. **Number of employees at this location:** 65. **Number of employees nationwide:** 90. **Number of employees worldwide:** 130.

**CHARTER BEHAVIORAL HEALTH SYSTEMS OF NEW JERSEY**
19 Prospect Street, Summit NJ 07902. 908/277-9094. **Toll-free phone:** 800/CHARTER. **Fax:** 908/522-7098. **Contact:** Keith Andreotta, Human Resources Director. **Description:** A psychiatric hospital. **NOTE:** Entry-level positions and second and third shifts are offered. **Common positions include:** Registered Nurse; Social Worker. **Educational backgrounds include:** Psychiatry; Social Work. **Benefits:** 401(k); Daycare Assistance; Dental Insurance; Disability Coverage; Employee Discounts; Life Insurance; Medical Insurance; Public Transit Available; Tuition Assistance. **Special programs:** Internships. **Corporate headquarters location:** Macon GA. **Other U.S. locations:** Nationwide. **Listed on:** American Stock Exchange. **CEO:** James Gallagher. **Annual sales/revenues:** Less than $5 million. **Number of employees at this location:** 200.

**COMMUNITY MEDICAL CENTER**
99 Highway 37 West, Toms River NJ 08755. 732/240-8000. **Contact:** Human Resources. **Description:** An affiliate of Saint Barnabus Health Care System, Community Medical Center is a 596-bed, general/short-term care hospital.

**CONTINENTAL CHOICE CARE, INC.**
25-B Vreeland Road, Suite 201, Florham Park NJ 07932. 973/593-0500. **Contact:** Jay Thompson, Office Manager. **Description:** Provides alternate site and in-center dialysis-related equipment, services, and supplies, including nursing services. The company provides dialysis services to individuals in their homes and alternative residential treatment sites in New Jersey and New York, including prisons and nursing homes. Continental Choice Care owns and operates a dialysis treatment center and provides dialysis-related consulting services and supplies to dialysis facilities and corrections programs. The company also owns a pharmacy and home infusion therapy business that treats patients with cancer, various infectious diseases, AIDS, and Lyme disease. **Listed on:** NASDAQ. **Stock exchange symbol:** CCCI.

**COOPER HOSPITAL/UNIVERSITY MEDICAL CENTER**
One & 3 Cooper Plaza, Camden NJ 08103. 609/342-2000. **Contact:** Human Resources. **Description:** A 554-bed, nonprofit, academic medical center. Cooper Hospital/University Medical Center specializes in the care of seriously-ill and critically-injured patients.

**CORDIS, A JOHNSON & JOHNSON COMPANY**
40 Technology Drive, Warren NJ 07059. 908/755-8300. **Contact:** Human Resources. **World Wide Web address:** http://www.jnj.com. **Description:** This location handles administration, research and development, and quality assurance. Overall, Cordis manufactures medical devices such as stents and catheters to treat cardiovascular diseases. **NOTE:** All hiring is done through the parent company. Resumes should be sent to Johnson & Johnson Recruiting Services, Employment Management Center, Room JH-215, 501 George Street, New Brunswick NJ 08906-6597. **Parent company:** Johnson & Johnson (New Brunswick NJ).

**DATASCOPE CORPORATION**
14 Philips Parkway, Montvale NJ 07645-9998. 201/391-8100. **Contact:** Human Resources. **Description:** Manufactures cardiac assist systems for hospital use in interventional cardiology and

cardiac surgery; and patient monitors for use in the operating room, post-anesthesia care, and critical care. Datascope's VasoSeal product rapidly seals femoral arterial punctures after catheterization procedures, including coronary angioplasty and angiography. Datascope also manufactures a line of collagen hemostats, which are used to control bleeding during surgery. The company's cardiac assist product is an intra-aortic balloon pumping system used in the treatment of cardiac shock, heart failure, cardiac arrhythmia, and in cardiac surgery and coronary angioplasty. Datascope's patient monitoring products comprise a line of multifunction and stand-alone models that measure a broad range of physiological data including blood oxygen saturation, airway carbon dioxide, ECG, and temperature.

**DEBORAH HOSPITAL**
200 Trenton Road, Browns Mills NJ 08015-1705. 609/652-1000. **Contact:** Human Resources. **Description:** A hospital providing a variety of services including cardiac and pulmonary care through the Deborah Heart and Lung Center.

**EBI MEDICAL SYSTEMS, INC.**
100 Interpace Parkway, Parsippany NJ 07054. 973/299-9300. **Fax:** 973/402-1396. **Contact:** Human Resources. **World Wide Web address:** http://www.ebimedical.com. **Description:** Designs, develops, manufactures, and markets products used primarily by orthopedic medical specialists in both surgical and nonsurgical therapies, including electrical bone growth stimulators, orthopedic support devices, spinal fixation devices for spinal fusion, external fixation devices, and cold temperature therapy. Founded in 1977. **NOTE:** Entry-level positions are offered. **Common positions include:** Computer Programmer; Customer Service Rep.; Design Engineer; Electrical/Electronics Engineer; Marketing Manager; Mechanical Engineer; Sales Rep.; Secretary. **Educational backgrounds include:** Biology; Business Administration; Computer Science; Engineering; Marketing. **Benefits:** 401(k); Dental Insurance; Life Insurance; Medical Insurance; Tuition Assistance. **Special programs:** Summer Jobs; Training. **Corporate headquarters location:** This Location. **Other U.S. locations:** OK. **International locations:** Puerto Rico. **Parent company:** Biomet, Inc. **Number of employees at this location:** 330.

**EAST COAST TECHNOLOGIES**
223 Haddon Avenue, West Berlin NJ 08091. **Toll-free phone:** 800/527-3779. **Contact:** Human Resources. **World Wide Web address:** http://www.eastcoasttech.com. **Description:** Wholesales and repairs medical equipment, primarily laser and medical imaging systems.

**ELECTRO-CATHETER CORPORATION**
2100 Felver Court, Rahway NJ 07065. 732/382-5600. **Contact:** Personnel. **Description:** Manufactures and sells instruments and systems for the diagnosis and treatment of disorders of the human heart and vascular system.

**ELIZABETH GENERAL MEDICAL CENTER**
925 East Jersey Street, Elizabeth NJ 07201. 908/629-8153. **Fax:** 908/629-8973. **Contact:** Judi A. Meseck, Employment Manager. **Description:** A hospital. **Common positions include:** Budget Analyst; Clinical Lab Technician; Counselor; Dietician/Nutritionist; EEG Technologist; EKG Technician; Electrician; Emergency Medical Technician; Human Service Worker; Medical Records Technician; Nuclear Medicine Technologist; Occupational Therapist; Pharmacist; Physical Therapist; Physicist; Preschool Worker; Psychologist; Recreational Therapist; Registered Nurse; Respiratory Therapist; Social Worker; Speech-Language Pathologist; Teacher/Professor. **Educational backgrounds include:** Occupational Therapy; Physical Therapy. **Benefits:** 401(k); 403(b); Daycare Assistance; Dental Insurance; Disability Coverage; Employee Discounts; Flexible Benefits; Life Insurance; Medical Insurance; Savings Plan; Tuition Assistance. **Number of employees at this location:** 2,200.

**ETHICON, INC.**
U.S. Route 22, Somerville NJ 08876. 908/218-0707. **Contact:** Human Resources. **Description:** Manufactures products for precise wound closure including sutures, ligatures, mechanical wound closure instruments, and related products. The company also makes its own surgical needles and provides needle-suture combinations to surgeons. **Corporate headquarters location:** This Location. **Parent company:** Johnson & Johnson (New Brunswick NJ).

**FRANCISCAN HEALTH SYSTEMS OF NEW JERSEY**
25 McWilliams Place, Jersey City NJ 07302. 201/418-2065. **Fax:** 201/418-2063. **Contact:** Linda Halleran, Employment Manager. **Description:** Operates two community hospitals: St. Mary Hospital (Hoboken NJ) and St. Francis Hospital (Jersey City NJ). **NOTE:** Entry-level positions are offered. **Common positions include:** Accountant; Administrative Assistant; Certified Nurses Aide; Clinical Lab Technician; Credit Manager; Customer Service Rep.; Dietician/Nutritionist;

Emergency Medical Technician; Food Scientist/Technologist; Human Resources Manager; Licensed Practical Nurse; MIS Specialist; Nuclear Medicine Technologist; Occupational Therapist; Pharmacist; Physical Therapist; Physician; Psychologist; Registered Nurse; Respiratory Therapist; Social Worker; Speech-Language Pathologist. **Educational backgrounds include:** Health Care; Nutrition. **Benefits:** 403(b); Dental Insurance; Disability Coverage; Employee Discounts; Life Insurance; Medical Insurance; On-Site Daycare; Pension Plan; Tuition Assistance. **Special programs:** Internships. **Corporate headquarters location:** This Location. **Annual sales/revenues:** $11 - $20 million. **Number of employees at this location:** 1,500. **Number of projected hires for 1998 - 1999 at this location:** 100.

### GENESIS HEALTH VENTURES, INC.
433 Hackensack Avenue, Hackensack NJ 07601. 201/525-5925. **Fax:** 201/488-2990. **Contact:** Recruitment. **World Wide Web address:** http://www.ghv.com. **Description:** Manages nursing homes. Founded in 1985. **Corporate headquarters location:** Kennett Square PA. **Other U.S. locations:** Nationwide. **Listed on:** New York Stock Exchange. **Stock exchange symbol:** GHY. **Number of employees nationwide:** 30,000.

### HCR MANOR CARE
1412 Marlton Pike, Cherry Hill NJ 08034. 609/428-6100. **Contact:** Mary Camblin, Recruiter. **World Wide Web address:** http://www.manorcare.com. **Description:** An inpatient and outpatient rehabilitation center providing physical, occupational, and speech therapies. HCR Manor Care is a result of the September 1998 merger between Health Care and Retirement Corporation and ManorCare Health Services. **Benefits:** 401(k); Dental Insurance; Life Insurance; Medical Insurance; Profit Sharing; Tuition Assistance. **Corporate headquarters location:** Toledo OH. **Other U.S. locations:** Nationwide. **Subsidiaries include:** Milestone Healthcare provides a variety of services including inpatient acute physical rehabilitation, outpatient rehabilitation, sports and industrial medicine, and cardiac outpatient services. **Listed on:** New York Stock Exchange. **Stock exchange symbol:** HCR. **Number of employees nationwide:** 50,000.

### HAUSMANN INDUSTRIES
130 Union Street, Northvale NJ 07647. 201/767-0255. **Contact:** Human Resources. **Description:** Produces medical examination tables and physical therapy equipment. **Corporate headquarters location:** This Location.

### HEALTHCARE IMAGING SERVICES, INC.
200 Schultz Drive, 3rd Floor, Middletown NJ 07701. 732/224-9292. **Fax:** 732/224-9329. **Contact:** Human Resources. **Description:** Provides equipment and services to physicians, hospitals, and other health care providers. The company operates five fixed-site MRI centers and one fixed-site multimodality imaging center consisting of MRI, ultrasonography, and mammography facilities. **Corporate headquarters location:** This Location.

### HOOPER HOLMES, INC.
170 Mount Airy Road, Basking Ridge NJ 07920. 908/766-5000. **Contact:** Human Resources Manager. **World Wide Web address:** http://www.hooper.com. **Description:** Hooper Holmes, Inc. performs health exams for insurance companies. **Common positions include:** Accountant/Auditor; Administrative Manager; Attorney; Clerical Supervisor; Computer Programmer; Credit Manager; Customer Service Rep.; Financial Analyst; Human Resources Manager; Licensed Practical Nurse; Paralegal; Quality Control Supervisor; Registered Nurse; Systems Analyst. **Educational backgrounds include:** Accounting; Business Administration; Finance; Marketing. **Benefits:** 401(k); Dental Insurance; Disability Coverage; Life Insurance; Medical Insurance; Profit Sharing; Tuition Assistance. **Corporate headquarters location:** This Location. **Operations at this facility include:** Research and Development; Sales; Service. **Listed on:** American Stock Exchange. **Number of employees at this location:** 120. **Number of employees nationwide:** 2,500.

### HUNTERDON DEVELOPMENTAL CENTER
P.O. Box 4003, Clinton NJ 08809-4003. 908/735-4031. **Contact:** Human Resources. **Description:** A state-run residential facility for adults with developmental disabilities.

### i-STAT CORPORATION
104 Windsor Center Drive, East Windsor NJ 08520. 609/443-9300. **Fax:** 609/443-9310. **Contact:** Kim Lyon, Human Resources Department. **World Wide Web address:** http://www.i-stat.com. **Description:** Develops, manufactures, and markets medical diagnostic products that perform blood analysis. i-Stat Corporation's products provide health care professionals with immediate and accurate critical diagnostic information at the point of patient care. **Number of employees at this location:** 500.

**INFU-TECH, INC.**
910 Sylvan Avenue, Englewood Cliffs NJ 07632. 201/567-4600. **Fax:** 201/567-1072. **Contact:** Human Resources. **Description:** A national leader in providing products and services for at-home and subacute care. The company provides parenteral and enteral nutrition, hydration, chemotherapy, antibiotic and chronic pain management therapies, and related products and services to patients in nursing homes, as well as intravenous therapy to patients recovering at home. Under contract to managed care organizations, the company also provides subacute care for many additional nursing home patients. Infu-Tech is accredited by the Joint Commission for Accreditation of Health Care Organizations. The company's products and services are marketed in 23 states. **Corporate headquarters location:** This Location.

**INTEGRA LIFESCIENCES CORPORATION**
105 Morgan Lane, Plainsboro NJ 08536. 609/275-0500. **Contact:** Human Resources Department. **World Wide Web address:** http://www.integra-ls.com. **Description:** Researches and develops a wide range of medical devices including artificial skin for burn victims; collagen sponges for use in surgery; dental wound and dermal ulcer dressings; and packing agents for ear, nose, and throat surgery.

**ROBERT WOOD JOHNSON UNIVERSITY HOSPITAL**
One Hamilton Health Place, Hamilton NJ 08690. 609/586-7900. **Contact:** Human Resources. **Description:** A general and teaching hospital.

**THE LODGE**
3510 Route 66, Neptune NJ 07753. 732/922-1900. **Contact:** Human Resources. **Description:** A 159-bed nursing home.

**THE MATHENY SCHOOL AND HOSPITAL**
P.O. Box 339, Peapack NJ 07977. 908/234-0011x291. **Fax:** 908/234-9496. **Contact:** Ms. Nancy Bunte, Human Resources Manager. **Description:** A licensed hospital and school for people with severe physical disabilities including cerebral palsy and spina bifida. **NOTE:** Entry-level positions as well as second and third shifts are offered. **Common positions include:** Administrative Assistant; Certified Nurses Aide; Chief Financial Officer; Controller; Counselor; Dietician/Nutritionist; Human Resources Manager; Licensed Practical Nurse; Medical Records Technician; MIS Specialist; Occupational Therapist; Physical Therapist; Psychologist; Public Relations Specialist; Registered Nurse; Secretary; Social Worker; Speech-Language Pathologist; Teacher/Professor. **Benefits:** 403(b); Dental Insurance; Disability Coverage; Employee Discounts; Flexible Schedule; Job Sharing; Life Insurance; Medical Insurance; Pension Plan; Savings Plan; Tuition Assistance. **Special programs:** Internships; Apprenticeships; Training. **President:** Robert Schonhorn.

**MEDICAL RESOURCES, INC.**
155 State Street, Hackensack NJ 07601. 201/488-6230. **Fax:** 201/488-8455. **Contact:** Human Resources Department. **Description:** Provides diagnostic imaging equipment and management services to managed care providers. **Subsidiaries include:** StarMed Staffing L.P. supplies medical personnel to hospitals and other medical facilities. **Listed on:** NASDAQ. **Stock exchange symbol:** MRII.

**MEDIQ INC.**
One Mediq Plaza, Pennsauken NJ 08110. 609/665-9300. **Fax:** 609/665-2391. **Contact:** Human Resources Department. **Description:** Mediq Inc. rents life support equipment such as ventilators, monitors, and incubators to hospitals and nursing homes. **Corporate headquarters location:** This Location.

**MODERN MEDICAL MODALITIES CORPORATION**
95 Madison Avenue, Suite 301, Morristown NJ 07960. 973/538-9955. **Contact:** Human Resources Department. **Description:** Modern Medical Modalities Corporation provides high-technology, diagnostic imaging services to physicians, hospitals, and other health care facilities. The company's primary focus is on Magnetic Resonance Imaging (MRI) and Computer Axial Tomography (CT scan) technologies. Modern Medical Modalities also offers a range of services including full, partial, or joint venture financing; site selection, design, and construction; equipment supply, maintenance, and operation; personnel placement and training; and facility marketing, management, billing, and collections. **Corporate headquarters location:** This Location.

**NEW LISBON DEVELOPMENTAL CENTER**
Rural Route 72, New Lisbon NJ 08064. 609/894-4000. **Contact:** Human Resources. **Description:** A residential treatment facility for adolescents and adults with developmental disabilities.

**OCEAN COUNTY VETERINARY HOSPITAL**
838 River Avenue, Route 9, Lakewood NJ 08701. 732/363-7202. **Fax:** 732/370-4176. **Contact:** Human Resources. **World Wide Web address:** http://www.ocvh.com. **Description:** Provides health care services to dogs, cats, and exotic pets including surgery, hospitalization, and diagnostic testing.

**OSTEONICS**
59 Route 17 South, Allendale NJ 07401. 201/825-4900. **Contact:** Human Resources. **World Wide Web address:** http://www.osteonics.com. **Description:** Manufactures medical implants including artificial knees, hips, shoulders, and elbows.

**OVERLOOK HOSPITAL**
99 Beauvoir Avenue, P.O. Box 220, Summit NJ 07902-0220. 908/522-2241. **Contact:** Human Resources. **Description:** A part of Atlantic Health Systems, Overlook Hospital is a 490-bed, public hospital with extensive facilities for pediatrics, oncology, cardiology, and same-day surgery.

**PSA HOME HEALTHCARE**
4900 Route 33, Suite 100, Neptune NJ 07753. 732/286-0555. **Contact:** Human Resources. **Description:** Provides infusion therapy, nursing, and other home health care services to clients.

**PHILIPS HEARING INSTRUMENTS COMPANY**
91 McKee Drive, Mahwah NJ 07430. 201/529-5557. **Fax:** 201/529-0003. **Contact:** Lorraine DePol, Office Manager. **Description:** Markets and produces hearing aid devices, including the XP-Peritympanic hearing instrument. **Parent company:** Philips Electronics North America Corporation, one of the larger industrial companies in the United States, is a multimarket manufacturing organization with nationwide locations and various subsidiaries. Philips concentrates its efforts primarily in the fields of consumer electronics, consumer products, electrical and electronics components, and professional equipment.

**SJ NURSES**
850 Hamilton Avenue, Trenton NJ 08629. 609/396-7100. **Toll-free phone:** 800/727-2476. **Fax:** 609/396-7559. **Contact:** Sally Jane Poblete, Vice President. **E-mail address:** sjpoblete@aol.com. **Description:** A home health care agency. **Common positions include:** Certified Nurses Aide; Licensed Practical Nurse; Occupational Therapist; Physical Therapist; Registered Nurse; Respiratory Therapist. **Corporate headquarters location:** This Location.

**SAINT FRANCIS MEDICAL CENTER**
601 Hamilton Avenue, Trenton NJ 08629. 609/599-5000. **Contact:** Human Resources. **Description:** A medical center that provides health care services to Trenton and the surrounding areas, with a particular emphasis on the needs of the poor.

**SHORE MEMORIAL HOSPITAL**
One East New York Avenue, Somers Point NJ 08244-2387. 609/653-5000. **Contact:** Human Resources. **World Wide Web address:** http://www.shorememorial.org. **Description:** A 350-bed, nonprofit medical center providing medical, surgical, pediatric, and obstetrical services. Shore Memorial Hospital joined with Shore Care Home Health Services and Ocean Point Health Care Center to form Shore Memorial Health Care System. **Number of employees at this location:** 1,400.

**SIEMENS CORPORATION**
186 Wood Avenue South, Iselin NJ 08830. 732/321-3100. **Contact:** Personnel Office. **Description:** This location is the U.S. medical engineering headquarters for one of the world's leading companies in the electrical and electronics industry. Overall, Siemens operates internationally through the following groups: power engineering and automation; electrical installations; communications; medical engineering; data systems; and components. The company's manufacturing and sales organization is established in more than 100 countries. **Other U.S. locations:** Nationwide. **International locations:** Worldwide. **Parent company:** Siemens AG (Munich, Germany).

**SOUTH JERSEY HEALTH SYSTEM**
**SOUTH JERSEY HOSPITAL**
333 Irving Avenue, Bridgeton NJ 08302-2123. 609/451-6600. **Contact:** Personnel. **Description:** Provides extensive medical services throughout southern New Jersey. **NOTE:** The hiring for all four hospitals in the South Jersey Health System is done through this location. **Subsidiaries include:** Elmer Community Hospital has 91 beds. Millville Hospital has 109 beds. Newcomb Medical Center has 235 beds. South Jersey Hospital (also at this location) has 224 beds.

## STAFF BUILDERS
622 George's Road, North Brunswick NJ 08902. 609/452-0020. **Contact:** Manager. **World Wide Web address:** http://www.staffbuilders.com. **Description:** A home health care agency. **Corporate headquarters location:** Lake Success NY.

## UNDERWOOD MEMORIAL HOSPITAL
509 North Broad Street, Woodbury NJ 08096. 609/845-0100. **Contact:** Robert Cardillo, Manager of Human Resources. **Description:** A hospital.

## UNIVERSITY HOSPITAL
30 Bergen Street, Building 8, Newark NJ 07107. 973/972-0012. **Contact:** Human Resources. **Description:** A 466-bed teaching hospital of the University of Medicine and Dentistry of New Jersey.

## VINELAND DEVELOPMENTAL CENTER
1676 East Landis Avenue, Vineland NJ 08361. 609/696-6000. **Contact:** Human Resources. **Description:** A residential treatment facility for females who have mental retardation.

## VISITING NURSE SERVICE SYSTEM
P.O. Box 250, Runnemede NJ 08078. 609/939-9000. **Contact:** Human Resources. **World Wide Web address:** http://www.vnss.com. **Description:** Provides home-based health care services including nursing, physical therapy, occupational therapy, speech pathology, nutritional therapy, mental health and enterostomal therapy, medical social services, and hospice care. **Other U.S. locations:** Nationwide.

## VITAL SIGNS, INC.
20 Campus Road, Totowa NJ 07512. 973/790-1330. **Fax:** 973/790-4475. **Contact:** Liz Greenberg, Director of Human Resources. **World Wide Web address:** http://www.vital-signs.com. **Description:** Vital Signs manufactures disposable medical products such as face masks, manual resuscitators, anesthesia kits, and other respiratory-related critical care products. **Common positions include:** Computer Programmer; Customer Service Rep.; Electrical/Electronics Engineer; Materials Engineer; Operations/Production Manager; Systems Analyst. **Educational backgrounds include:** Business Administration; Computer Science; Engineering; Finance; Marketing. **Benefits:** 401(k); Dental Insurance; Disability Coverage; Life Insurance; Pension Plan; Savings Plan. **Corporate headquarters location:** This Location. **Other U.S. locations:** Englewood CO. **Listed on:** NASDAQ. **Number of employees at this location:** 350. **Number of employees nationwide:** 450.

## WOODBINE DEVELOPMENTAL CENTER
P.O. Box 601, DeHirsch Avenue, Woodbine NJ 08270. 609/861-2164. **Contact:** Human Resources Department. **Description:** A residential treatment facility for adult males with mental disabilities.

## WOODBRIDGE DEVELOPMENTAL CENTER
Rahway Avenue, P.O. Box 189, Woodbridge NJ 07095-0189. 732/499-5525. **Contact:** Human Resources. **Description:** A residential treatment facility for adolescents and adults with developmental disabilities.

## WYANT HEALTHCARE
P.O. Box 8609, Somerville NJ 08876. 908/707-1800. **Contact:** Maureen Buehler, Administrative Assistant. **Description:** Manufactures disposable underpads, cloths, and wipes for health care, industrial, food service, and janitorial businesses.

*Note: Because addresses and telephone numbers of smaller companies can change rapidly, we recommend you call each company to verify the information below before inquiring about job opportunities. Mass mailings are not recommended.*

**Additional small employers:**

**DOCTORS' OFFICES AND CLINICS**

**Camcare Health Corp.**
130 Mickle Blvd, Camden NJ 08103-1025. 609/541-3270.

**Pinnacle Medical Group**
165 Old Marlton Pike, Medford NJ 08055-9543. 609/654-9400.

**Princeton Back & Neck Inst.**
727 State Rd, Princeton NJ 08540-1413. 609/497-1700.

**Tris**
1000 Haddonfield Berlin Rd, Voorhees NJ 08043-3520. 609/346-1800.

## HOME HEALTH CARE SERVICES

**Alliance Nursing Services**
95 Madison Ave, Ste 4, Morristown NJ 07960-6092. 973/267-8800.

**Always There Inc.**
383 Lafayette Ave, Hawthorne NJ 07506-2544. 973/427-7459.

**Amserv Healthcare of NJ Inc.**
PO Box 387, Metuchen NJ 08840-0387. 732/494-3430.

**Bayada Nurses**
290 Chester Ave, Moorestown NJ 08057-3306. 609/231-1000.

**Bayada Nurses**
1501 Livingston Ave, North Brunswick NJ 08902-1876. 732/418-2273.

**Bayada Nurses**
PO Box 2221, Cherry Hill NJ 08034-0168. 609/354-1000.

**Bergen Community Health Care**
400 Old Hook Rd, Ste G6, Westwood NJ 07675-2720. 201/358-2666.

**Camden County VNA**
2201 Route 38, Ste 500, Cherry Hill NJ 08002-4309. 609/321-0200.

**Care at Home Inc.**
33 Evergreen Pl, East Orange NJ 07018-2166. 973/677-1189.

**Caremore In Home Services**
189 Lakeview Dr S, Gibbsboro NJ 08026-1019. 609/346-4484.

**Chrill Home Health Care**
60 S Fullerton Ave, Montclair NJ 07042-2632. 973/744-8103.

**Community Nursing Services**
PO Box 287, Mount Holly NJ 08060-0287. 609/267-1950.

**Concerned Nursing Care Inc.**
PO Box 703, Lafayette NJ 07848-0703. 973/579-5355.

**Coram Healthcare Corporation**
11H Commerce Way, Totowa NJ 07512-1154. 973/812-9100.

**Country Health Care Inc.**
15 N Gaston Ave, Somerville NJ 08876-2416. 908/526-6668.

**Custom Care**
14 Commerce Dr, Cranford NJ 07016-3505. 908/709-0530.

**Firstat Nursing Services**
1033 Clifton Ave, Clifton NJ 07013-3517. 973/458-0400.

**Homeaid Resources Inc.**
14-25 Plaza Rd, Ste 214, Fair Lawn NJ 07410-3549. 201/796-0202.

**Liberty Homecare Inc.**
574 Summit Ave, Jersey City NJ 07306-2799. 201/418-8000.

**Morris Home Care**
110 American Rd, Morris Plains NJ 07950-2443. 973/540-9000.

**National Home Care Inc.**
100 Executive Dr, Ste 130, West Orange NJ 07052-3309. 973/243-5900.

**Olsten Corporation**
1909 Route 70 East, Cherry Hill NJ 08003-4501. 609/424-6524.

**Passaic Valley Hospice**
PO Box 1007, Totowa NJ 07511-1007. 973/256-4636.

**Patient Care**
10 Rooney Cir, West Orange NJ 07052-3308. 973/325-3005.

**Preferred Healthmate Inc.**
192 Jack Martin Blvd, Brick NJ 08724-7728. 732/840-5566.

**Salemcare Inc.**
PO Box 126, Salem NJ 08079-0126. 609/935-1608.

**Samaritan Hospice**
5 Eves Dr, Suite 300, Marlton NJ 08053-3101. 609/596-1600.

**Valley Health Affiliates Inc.**
505 Goffle Rd, Ridgewood NJ 07450-4027. 201/444-0040.

**Visiting Health Services**
526 North Ave E, Westfield NJ 07090-1423. 908/272-7113.

**Visiting Homecare Service**
CN 2010, Toms River NJ 08754. 732/244-5565.

**Visiting Nurse Association**
907 Pleasant Valley Ave, Mount Laurel NJ 08054-1287. 609/235-0462.

**Visiting Nurse Association**
191 Woodport Rd, Ste 203-A, Sparta NJ 07871-2641. 973/729-7078.

**Visiting Nurse Association**
PO Box 478, Gladstone NJ 07934-0478. 908/234-2220.

**Visiting Nurse Association**
38 Elm St, Morristown NJ 07960-4110. 973/539-1216.

**Visiting Nurse Association**
325 Jersey St, Trenton NJ 08611-3113. 609/695-3461.

**Visiting Nurse Association**
PO Box 170, Elizabeth NJ 07207-0170. 908/352-5694.

**We Care Health Services Inc.**
941 White Horse Ave, Trenton NJ 08610-1407. 609/581-8400.

## HOSPITALS AND MEDICAL CENTERS

**Bacharach Institute for Rehabilitation**
PO Box 723, Pomona NJ 08240-0723. 609/652-7000.

**Brick Hospital**
425 Jack Martin Blvd, Brick NJ 08724-7732. 732/840-2200.

**Buttonwood Hospital-Burlington County**
600 Pemberton Browns Mall Rd, New Lisbon NJ 08064. 609/726-7000.

**Forensic Psychiatric Hospital**
PO Box 7717, Trenton NJ 08628-0717. 609/633-0900.

**Hackensack Hospital**
60 2nd St, Hackensack NJ 07601-2029. 201/996-2000.

**Hampton Health System**
PO Box 7000, Rancocas NJ 08073. 609/267-7000.

**HealthSouth Rehabilitation**
14 Hospital Dr, Toms River NJ 08755-6402. 732/244-3100.

**Holiday Medical Center**
685 River Ave, Lakewood NJ 08701-5228. 732/364-8300.

**Memorial Hospital Salem County**
310 Salem Woodstown Rd, Salem NJ 00070-2048. 609/935-1000.

**Newcomb Medical Center**
65 S State St, Vineland NJ 08360-4849. 609/691-9000.

**Pollak Hospital**
100 Clifton Pl, Jersey City NJ 07304-3104. 201/915-1001.

**Shoreline Behavorial Health**
1691 US Highway 9, CN 2025, Toms River NJ 08755. 732/914-1688.

**Southern Ocean County Hospital**
1140 Route 72 W, Manahawkin NJ 08050-2412. 609/978-8900.

**Trenton Psychiatric Hospital**
PO Box 7500, Trenton NJ 08628-0500. 609/633-1500.

**William B. Kessler Memorial Hospital**
600 S White Horse Pike, Hammonton NJ 08037-2014. 609/561-6700.

## MEDICAL EQUIPMENT

**Adam Spence Corp.**
PO Box 1467, Belmar NJ 07719-1467. 732/681-7070.

**Aircast Inc.**
PO Box 709, Summit NJ 07902-0709. 908/273-6349.

**Arrow International Inc.**
2 Berry Dr, Mount Holly NJ 08060-5017. 609/267-0001.

**B. Braun Medical Inc.**
18 Olney Ave, Bldg 44, Cherry Hill NJ 08003-1607. 609/751-2080.

**Coltene/Whaledent Inc.**
750 Corporate Dr, Mahwah NJ 07430-2009. 201/512-8000.

**Datascope Corp.**
15 Law Dr, Fairfield NJ 07004-3206. 973/244-6100.

**Datascope Corp.**
580 Winters Ave, Paramus NJ 07652-3902. 201/265-8800.

**Electric Mobility Corporation**
1 Mobility Plz, Sewell NJ 08080. 609/468-0270.

**Exogen Inc.**
PO Box 6860, Piscataway NJ 08855-6860. 732/981-0990.

**Fresenius Medical Products**
2 Volvo Dr, Northvale NJ 07647-2508. 201/767-7700.

**International Technidyne Co.**
23 Nevsky St, Edison NJ 08820-2425. 732/494-8441.

**Liberty Optical Manufacturing Company**
380 Verona Ave, Newark NJ 07104-1711. 973/484-4100.

**McNeil Specialty Products**
PO Box 2400, New Brunswick NJ 08903-2400. 732/524-6740.

**Meadox Medicals Inc.**
103 Bauer Dr, Oakland NJ 07436-3102. 201/337-6126.

**Nutramax Ophthalmics**
40 Main St, Fairton NJ 08320. 609/451-9350.

**Ohmeda Inc.**
110 Allen Rd, Liberty Corner NJ 07938. 908/647-9200.

**Oticon**
PO Box 6724, Somerset NJ 08875-6724. 732/560-1220.

**Roche Diagnostic Systems Inc.**
11 Franklin Ave, Belleville NJ 07109-3501. 973/235-8300.

**Siemens Hearing Instruments Inc.**
PO Box 1397, Piscataway NJ 08855-1397. 732/562-6600.

**SS White Burs Inc.**
1145 Towbin Ave, Lakewood NJ 08701-5932. 732/905-1122.

**Temco Health Care**
125 South St, Passaic NJ 07055-7316. 973/472-3173.

**Terumo Medical Corp.**
2101 Cottontail Ln, Somerset NJ 08873-5115. 732/302-4900.

## MEDICAL EQUIPMENT RENTAL AND LEASING

**RDS**
1080 US Highway 202 S, Somerville NJ 08876-3733. 908/253-7200.

## NURSING AND PERSONAL CARE FACILITIES

**Absecon Manor Nursing Home**
1020 Pitney Rd, Absecon NJ 08201-9717. 609/646-5400.

**Allendale Nursing Home**
85 Harreton Rd, Allendale NJ 07401-1317. 201/825-0660.

**Alps Manor Nursing Home**
1120 Alps Rd, Wayne NJ 07470-3704. 973/694-2100.

**Alternatives Inc.**
PO Box 338, Somerville NJ 08876-0338. 908/685-1444.

**Andover Intermediate Care Center**
PO Box 1279, Andover NJ 07821-1279. 973/383-6200.

**Applewood Manor Nursing Home**
689 W Main St, Freehold NJ 07728-2611. 732/431-3200.

**Arbor Glen Care Rehabilitation**
1263 Pompton Ave, Cedar Grove NJ 07009-1008. 973/256-7220.

**Arbors Care Center**
Rur Rte 37, Toms River NJ 08757. 732/914-0090.

**Arnold Walter Nursing Home**
622 Laurel Ave, Hazlet NJ 07730-2681. 732/787-6300.

**Atlantic Coast Rehabilitation**
485 River Ave, Lakewood NJ 08701-4720. 732/364-7100.

**Atlantic Highlands Nursing**
8 Middletown Ave, Atlantic Highlands NJ 07716-2103. 732/291-0600.

**Avante at Red Bank Inc.**
PO Box 2030, Red Bank NJ 07701-0901. 732/741-8811.

**Barn Hill Care Center**
249 High St, Newton NJ 07860-9600. 973/383-5600.

**Bartley Healthcare Nursing**
175 Bartley Rd, Jackson NJ 08527-1241. 732/370-4700.

**Bayview Convalescent Center**
395 Lakeside Blvd, Bayville NJ 08721-2807. 732/269-0500.

**Beachview Intermediate Care**
32 Laurel Ave, Keansburg NJ 07734-1125. 732/787-8100.

**Berkeley Heights Nursing Home**
35 Cottage St, Berkeley Heights NJ 07922-1508. 908/464-0048.

**Bridgeton Nursing Center**
99 Manheim Ave, Bridgeton NJ 08302-2114. 609/455-2100.

**Bristol Manor Health Care Center**
96 Parkway, Rochelle Park NJ 07662-4200. 201/845-0099.

**Burlington Woods Convalescent Center**
115 Sunset Rd, Burlington NJ 08016-4153. 609/387-3620.

**Burnt Tavern Convalescent Center**
1049 Burnt Tavern Rd, Brick NJ 08724-1967. 732/840-3700.

**Camden County Health Services**
Collier Dr & Lakeland Rd, Blackwood NJ 08012. 609/757-8000.

**Carriage House Manor**
901 Ernston Rd, South Amboy NJ 08879-2000. 732/721-8200.

**Castle Hill Health Care**
615 23rd St, Union City NJ 07087-3505. 201/348-0818.

**Cedar Grove Manor**
398 Pompton Ave, Cedar Grove NJ 07009-1813. 973/239-7600.

**Cedar Oaks Care Center**
1311 Durham Ave, South Plainfield NJ 07080-2309. 732/287-9555.

**Central New Jersey Jewish Home**
380 Demott Ln, Somerset NJ
08873-2762. 732/873-2000.

**Chestnut Hill Convalescent Home**
360 Chestnut St, Passaic NJ
07055-3124. 973/777-7800.

**Cinnaminson Manor Nursing Home**
1700 Wynwood Dr, Riverton NJ
08077-2440. 609/829-9000.

**Conva-Center at Neptune**
101 Walnut St, Neptune NJ
07753-4301. 732/774-3550.

**Cooper River West Convalescent Center**
5101 N Park Dr, Pennsauken NJ
08109-4643. 609/665-8844.

**Country Manor-Dover Inc.**
16 Whitesville Rd, Toms River
NJ 08753-4107. 732/341-1600.

**Cranbury Skilled Nursing Center**
292 Applegarth Rd, Cranbury NJ
08512-4907. 609/860-2500.

**Cranford Hall Nursing Home**
600 Lincoln Park E, Cranford NJ
07016-3125. 908/276-7100.

**Cranford Health Extended Care**
PO Box 97, Cranford NJ 07016-0097. 908/272-6660.

**Crestwood Manor**
50 Lacey Rd, Whiting NJ 08759-2951. 732/849-4900.

**Daughters of Miriam Center**
155 Hazel St, Clifton NJ 07011, 3423. 973/772-3700.

**Delaire Nursing Home**
400 W Stimpson Ave, Linden NJ
07036-4434. 908/862-3399.

**Dellridge Care Center Inc.**
532 N Farview Ave, Paramus NJ
07652-4130. 201/261-1589.

**Dover Christian Nursing Home**
65 N Sussex St, Dover NJ 07801-3949. 973/361-5200.

**Dunroven Health Care Center**
221 County Rd, Cresskill NJ
07626-1605. 201/567-9310.

**East Orange Nursing Home**
PO Box 517, East Orange NJ
07019-0517. 973/672-1700.

**Emerson Convalescent Center**
100 Kinderkamack Rd, Emerson
NJ 07630-1828. 201/265-3700.

**Emery Nursing Rehabilitation**
4 State Route 34, Matawan NJ
07747-3033. 732/566-6400.

**Ewing Nursing and Rehab Center**
1201 Parkway Ave, Trenton NJ
08628-3008. 609/882-6900.

**Foothill Acres Nursing Home**
PO Box 780, Neshanic Station NJ
08853-0780. 908/369-8711.

**Fountainview Care Center**
527 River Ave, Lakewood NJ
08701-4722. 732/905-0700.

**Franklin Care Center**
3371 Hwy 27, Franklin Park NJ
08823. 732/821-8000.

**Freehold Rehabilitation Nursing**
3419 US Highway 9, Freehold NJ
07728-3284. 732/780-0660.

**Friends Home at Woodstown**
PO Box 457, Woodstown NJ
08098-0457. 609/769-1500.

**Garden State Health Care Center**
PO Box 976, East Orange NJ
07019-0976. 973/677-1500.

**Genesis Eldercare Center**
2601 E Evesham Rd, Voorhees
NJ 08043-9509. 609/596-1113.

**Genesis Eldercare Center**
Church Rd, Mount Laurel NJ
08054. 609/235-7100.

**Genesis Eldercare Center**
1400 Woodland Ave, Plainfield
NJ 07060-3362. 908/753-1113.

**Genesis Eldercare Center**
390 Red School Lane,
Phillipsburg NJ 08865-2230.
908/859-0200.

**Genesis Eldercare Center**
916 Lacey Rd, Forked River NJ
08731-1107. 609/971-1400.

**Genesis Eldercare Center**
1515 Lamberts Mill Rd,
Westfield NJ 07090-4763.
908/233-9700.

**Genesis Eldercare Center**
1515 Hulse Rd, Point Pleasant NJ
08742-4527. 732/295-9300.

**Gloucester Manor Health Care**
Pension Rd, Englishtown NJ
07726. 732/446-1804.

**Gloucester Manor Health Care**
685 Salina Rd, Sewell NJ 08080-4602. 609/468-2500.

**Green Acres Manor Inc.**
1931 Lakewood Rd, Toms River
NJ 08755-1211. 732/286-2323.

**Green Hill Retirement Community**
103 Pleasant Valley Way, West
Orange NJ 07052-2905. 973/731-2300.

**Greenbriar Healthcare Center**
1511 Clements Bridge Rd,
Deptford NJ 08096-3007.
609/845-9400.

**Greenbriar Healthcare Center**
PO Box 751, Hammonton NJ
08037-0751. 609/567-3100.

**Greenbrook Manor Nursing Home**
303 Rock Ave, Dunellen NJ
08812-2616. 732/968-5500.

**Grove Health Care Center**
919 Green Grove Rd, Neptune NJ
07753-2907. 732/922-3400.

**Hamilton Continuing Care Center**
1059 Edinburgh Rd, Trenton NJ
08690-1229. 609/588-0091.

**Hamilton Plaza Nursing Center**
56 Hamilton Ave, Passaic NJ
07055-5131. 973/773-7070.

**Harbor View Health Care Center**
178 Ogden Ave 198, Jersey City
NJ 07307-1337. 201/963-1800.

**Hazlet Manor Nursing Center**
3325 Highway 35, Hazlet NJ
07730-1552. 732/264-5800.

**Heath Village Retirement Community**
Schooley's Mountain Rd,
Hackettstown NJ 07840. 908/852-4801.

**Heritage Hall Nursing Home**
524 Wardell Rd, Neptune NJ
07753-7305. 732/922-9330.

**Holiday Care Center**
4 Plaza Dr, Toms River NJ
08757-3756. 732/240-0900.

**Holly Manor Nursing Home**
84 Cold Hill Rd, Mendham NJ
07945-2021. 973/543-2500.

**Holmdel Convalescent Center**
188 State Route 34, Holmdel NJ
07733-2125. 732/946-4200.

**Hospitality Care Center**
300 Broadway, Newark NJ
07104-4003. 973/484-4222.

**Hudson View Care Rehab**
9020 Wall St, North Bergen NJ
07047-6011. 201/861-4040.

**Hunterdon Convalescent Center**
1 Leisure Ct, Flemington NJ 08822-5724. 908/788-9292.

**Inglemoor Care Center**
311 S Livingston Ave, Livingston NJ 07039-3927. 973/994-0221.

**Jackson Center**
11 History Ln, Jackson NJ 08527-2209. 732/367-6600.

**Jersey Shore Nursing & Rehab**
3 Industrial Way, Eatontown NJ 07724. 732/544-1557.

**Jewish Geriatric Home**
3025 Chapel Ave W, Cherry Hill NJ 08002-1503. 609/667-3100.

**Jewish Home & Rehabilitation Center**
198 Stevens Ave, Jersey City NJ 07305-2111. 201/451-9000.

**JFK Hartwyck**
465 Plainfield Ave, Edison NJ 08817-2514. 732/985-1500.

**JFK Hartwyck**
2048 Oak Tree Rd, Edison NJ 08820-2012. 732/906-2100.

**JFK Hartwyck**
1340 Park Ave, Plainfield NJ 07060-3227. 908/754-3100.

**Kenbrook Associates LP**
120 Park End Pl, East Orange NJ 07018-1116. 973/812-9777.

**King James Care Center**
1165 Easton Ave, Somerset NJ 08873-1613. 732/246-4100.

**King James Care Center**
1501 Route 33, Trenton NJ 08690-1705. 609/586-1114.

**King Manor Associates**
2303 W Bangs Ave, Neptune NJ 07753-4111. 732/774-3500.

**Lake View Manor Nursing & Rehab**
411 Hackensack Ave, 7th Fl, Hackensack NJ 07601-6328. 201/488-8818.

**Lakeland Health Care Center**
25 5th Ave, Haskell NJ 07420-1075. 973/839-6000.

**Lakewood Nursing Center**
285 River Ave, Lakewood NJ 08701-4808. 732/363-0400.

**Lakewood Voorhees Nursing Home**
1302 Laurel Oak Rd, Voorhees NJ 08043-4310. 609/346-1200.

**Laurelton Village Nursing Home**
475 Jack Martin Blvd, Brick NJ 08724-7732. 732/458-6600.

**Lawrenceville Nursing Home**
PO Box 6338, Trenton NJ 08648-0338. 609/896-1494.

**Leisure Chateau Care Center**
962 River Ave, Lakewood NJ 08701-5605. 732/370-8600.

**Liberty House Nursing Home**
620 Montgomery St, Jersey City NJ 07302-3130. 201/435-0033.

**Lincoln Park Intermediate Care**
499 Pine Brook Rd, Lincoln Park NJ 07035-1804. 973/696-3300.

**Linwood Convalescent Center**
New Road Central Ave, Linwood NJ 08221. 609/927-6131.

**Logan Manor Healthcare Ctr.**
23 Schoolhouse Rd, Whiting NJ 08759-3024. 732/849-4300.

**Lutheran Home at Moorestown**
255 E Main St, Moorestown NJ 08057-2982. 609/235-2189.

**Manahawkin Convalescent Center**
1211 Route 72 W, Manahawkin NJ 08050-2415. 609/597-8500.

**Manchester Manor Rehabilitation Center**
1770 Tobias Ave, Lakehurst NJ 08733-3103. 732/657-1800.

**Marcella Nursing & Rehabilitation Center**
2305 Rancocas Rd, Burlington NJ 08016-4113. 609/387-9300.

**Masonic Home of NJ**
902 Jacksonville Rd, Burlington NJ 08016-3814. 609/386-0300.

**Meadow View Nursing Home & Rehabilitation Center**
PO Box 808, Williamstown NJ 08094-0808. 609/875-0100.

**Medbridge Mountainside**
1180 Route 22, Mountainside NJ 07092-2810. 908/654-0020.

**Medford Convalescent Nursing Center**
185 Tuckerton Rd, Medford NJ 08055-8803. 609/983-8500.

**Mediplex**
300 Brick Rd, Marlton NJ 08053. 609/988-8778.

**Mediplex of Oradell**
600 Kinderkamack Rd, Oradell NJ 07649-1501. 201/967-0002.

**Mediplex Rehab-Camden Inc.**
2 Cooper Plz, Camden NJ 08103-1461. 609/342-7600.

**Mercerville Nursing & Convalescent Center**
2240 Whitehorse Mercer Rd, Trenton NJ 08619-2640. 609/586-7500.

**Millhouse Nursing Home**
325 Jersey St, Trenton NJ 08611-3113. 609/394-3400.

**Monroe Village**
David Brainerd Dr, Jamesburg NJ 08831. 732/521-5400.

**Morris Hills Nursing Home**
77 Madison Ave, Morristown NJ 07960-6089. 973/540-9800.

**Morris View Nursing Home**
PO Box 437, Morris Plains NJ 07950-0437. 973/285-2800.

**New Jersey Veterans Memorial Home**
524 N West Blvd, Vineland NJ 08360-2845. 609/696-6350.

**Newark Extended Care**
65 Jay St, Newark NJ 07103-3235. 973/483-6800.

**North Cape Nursing & Rehabilitation**
700 Town Bank Rd, Cape May NJ 08204-4411. 609/898-8899.

**North Jersey Developmental Home**
PO Box 169, Totowa NJ 07511-0169. 973/256-1700.

**Northfield Manor Nursing Home**
787 Northfield Ave, West Orange NJ 07052-1131. 973/731-4500.

**Nursing Center At Vineland**
1640 S Lincoln Ave, Vineland NJ 08361-6610. 609/692-8080.

**Oakland Care Center**
20 Breakneck Rd, Oakland NJ 07436-2402. 201/337-3300.

**Ocean Point Health Care Center**
555 Bay Ave, Somers Point NJ 08244-2533. 609/927-9151.

**Old Bridge Manor**
6989 Route 18, Old Bridge NJ 08857-3345. 732/360-2277.

**Parkway Manor Health Center**
480 Parkway Dr E, East Orange NJ 07017-4029. 973/674-2700.

**Pine Acres Nursing Home**
51 Madison Ave, Madison NJ 07940-1411. 973/377-2124.

**Pinebrook Nursing Home**
PO Box 338, Englishtown NJ
07726-0338. 732/446-3600.

**Plaza Nursing**
456 Rahway Ave, Elizabeth NJ
07202-2338. 908/354-1300.

**Princeton Nursing Home**
35 Quarry St, Princeton NJ
08542-3144. 609/924-9000.

**Rahway Geriatric Center Inc.**
1777 Lawrence St, Rahway NJ
07065-5111. 732/499-7927.

**Raritan Health Extended Care**
633 State Route 28, Raritan NJ
08869-1127. 908/526-8950.

**Regency Gardens**
PO Box 2039, Wayne NJ 07474-
2039. 973/790-5800.

**Regent Care Center Inc.**
50 Polifly Rd, Hackensack NJ
07601-3207. 201/646-1166.

**Ridgewood Manor**
330 Franklin Tpke, Ridgewood
NJ 07450-1932. 201/891-4266.

**Roosevelt Care Center**
1 Roosevelt Dr, Edison NJ
08837-2333. 732/321-6800.

**Rose Mountain Care Center**
US Highway 1, New Brunswick
NJ 08901. 732/828-2400.

**Rosewood Manor Inc.**
Mill Rd, Rural Route 38, Maple
Shade NJ 08052. 609/779-1500.

**Salem County Nursing Home**
438 Woodstown Rd, Salem NJ
08079-4220. 609/935-6677.

**Seacrest Village Care**
PO Box 1480, Tuckerton NJ
08087-5480. 609/296-9292.

**Seashore Gardens**
1000 Arctic Ave, Suite 3850,
Atlantic City NJ 08401-4755.
609/345-5941.

**Silver Care Center**
1417 Brace Rd, Cherry Hill NJ
08034-3524. 609/795-3131.

**South Mountain Health Care**
2385 Springfield Ave, Vauxhall
NJ 07088-1046. 908/688-3400.

**Southern Ocean Nursing**
1361 Route 72 West,
Manahawkin NJ 08050-2417.
609/978-0600.

**Southgate Healthcare Center**
307 S Pennsville Auburn Rd,
Carneys Point NJ 08069-2919.
609/299-8900.

**St. Joseph's Home for the Blind**
537 Pavonia Ave, Jersey City NJ
07306-1803. 201/653-8300.

**St. Mary's Nursing Home**
1730 Kresson Rd, Cherry Hill NJ
08003-2518. 609/424-9521.

**St. Vincent's Nursing Home**
45 Elm St, Montclair NJ 07042-
3231. 973/746-4000.

**Sterling Manor**
794 N Forklanding Rd, Maple
Shade NJ 08052-1049. 609/779-
9333.

**Stone Arch Health Center**
114 County Road, Pittstown NJ
08867-4224. 908/735-6600.

**Stratford Nursing &
Convalescent Center**
Laurel & Warwick Rds, Stratford
NJ 08084. 609/784-2400.

**Summer Hill Nursing Home**
PO Box 746, Old Bridge NJ
08857-0746. 732/254-8200.

**Summit Ridge Nursing
Rehabilitation Corp.**
20 Summit St, West Orange NJ
07052-1501. 973/736-2000.

**The Harborage**
7600 River Rd, North Bergen NJ
07047-6217. 201/854-5033.

**Troy Hills Nursing &
Rehabilitation**
200 Reynolds Ave, Parsippany
NJ 07054-3326. 973/887-8080.

**Valley Health Care Center**
300 Old Hook Rd, Westwood NJ
07675-3122. 201/664-8888.

**Van Dyk Manor**
304 S Van Dien Ave, Ridgewood
NJ 07450-5299. 201/445-8200.

**Victoria Manor**
3809 Bayshore Rd, Cape May NJ
08204-3259. 609/898-0677.

**Wanaque Center**
1433 Ringwood Ave, Haskell NJ
07420-1520. 973/839-2119.

**Warren Haven Nursing Home**
350 Oxford Rd, Oxford NJ
07863-3224. 908/453-2131.

**Waters Edge of New Jersey**
512 Union St, Trenton NJ 08611-
2800. 609/393-8622.

**Waterview Nursing Center**
536 Ridge Rd, Cedar Grove NJ
07009-1611. 973/239-9300.

**Wellington Hall Care Center**
301 Union St, Hackensack NJ
07601-4304. 201/487-4900.

**West Caldwell Care Center**
165 Fairfield Ave, Caldwell NJ
07006-6414. 973/226-1100.

**White House Nursing Home**
560 Berkeley Ave, Orange NJ
07050-2109. 973/672-6500.

**Whiting Health Care Center**
3000 Hilltop Rd, Whiting NJ
08759-1349. 732/849-4400.

**Woodcliff Lake Manor**
555 Chestnut Ridge Rd,
Woodcliff Lake NJ 07675-8417.
201/391-0900.

**Woodcrest Center**
800 River Rd, New Milford NJ
07646-3032. 201/967-1700.

**Woodland Care Center**
1105 Linden St, Camden NJ
08102-1062. 609/365-8500.

**Woods Edge Care Center**
875 US Highway 202/206,
Bridgewater NJ 08807-1861.
908/526-8600.

## OFFICES AND CLINICS OF HEALTH PRACTITIONERS

**Matson Chiropractic Center**
25 Route 31 S, Ste F, Pennington
NJ 08534-2511. 609/737-7600.

## RESIDENTIAL CARE

**Applewood Estates**
1 Applewood Dr, Freehold NJ
07728-3985. 732/780-7370.

**Bancroft Inc.**
PO Box 20, Haddonfield NJ
08033-0018. 609/429-0010.

**Bishop McCarthy Residence**
1045 E Chestnut Ave, Vineland
NJ 08360-5838. 609/692-1030.

**Buena Vista Group Home**
1900 Tuckahoe, Milmay NJ
08340. 609/691-0736.

**Cadbury Retirement
Community**
2150 Route 38, Cherry Hill NJ
08002-4302. 609/667-4550.

**Children's Home of Burlington
County**
243 Pine St, Mount Holly NJ
08060-2201. 609/267-1550.

**Cliffside Health Care Center**
200 Center St, Keyport NJ 07735-
5105. 732/566-8422.

**Essex County Youth House**
208 Sussex Ave, Newark NJ
07103-2846. 973/482-5510.

**Fellowship Village**
8000 Fellowship Rd, Basking
Ridge NJ 07920-2932. 908/580-
3800.

**Francis Asbury Manor**
70 Stockton Ave, Ocean Grove
NJ 07756-1150. 732/774-1316.

**Geraldine L. Thompson
Medical Home**
Hospital Rd, Allenwood NJ
08720. 732/938-5250.

**Hawthorne House**
700 Mountain Ave, Wyckoff NJ
07481-1047. 201/848-8005.

**Integrity Inc.**
PO Box 510, Newark NJ 07101-
0510. 973/623-0600.

**Lutheran Home of Ocean View**
2721 Route 9, Ocean View NJ
08230-1055. 609/624-3881.

**Meadowview Nursing Home**
235 Dolphin Ave, Northfield NJ
08225-2015. 609/645-5955.

**Morris Hall Home for the Aged**
2381 Lawrenceville Rd,
Lawrenceville NJ 08648-2024.
609/896-9500.

**Mountainview Youth
Correctional Facility**
PO Box 994, Annandale NJ
08801-0994. 908/638-6191.

**New Jersey Geriatric Center**
225 W Jersey St, Elizabeth NJ
07202-1301. 908/353-1220.

**Our Lady's Residence**
1100 Clematis Ave, Pleasantville
NJ 08232-3302. 609/646-2450.

**Pitman Manor**
535 N Oak Ave, Pitman NJ
08071-1025. 609/589-7800.

**Presbyterian Homes & Services**
PO Box 200, Hightstown NJ
08520. 609/448-4100.

**Ranch Hope For Boys Inc.**
PO Box 325, Alloway NJ 08001.
609/935-1555.

**Riverview Estates**
303 Bank Ave, Riverton NJ
08077-1113. 609/829-2274.

**Riverview Extended Care
Residence**
55 W Front St, Red Bank NJ
07701-1621. 732/842-3800.

**Shady Lane Nursing Home**
PO Box 275, Clarksboro NJ
08020-0275. 609/423-0020.

**St. Joe's Residential Center**
37 Sherman Ave, Trenton NJ
08638-3454. 609/633-2484.

**St. Joseph's Home for the
Elderly**
140 Shepherd Ln, Totowa NJ
07512-2170. 973/942-0300.

**The Evergreens**
309 Bridgeboro Rd, Moorestown
NJ 08057-1419. 609/273-0806.

**The House of The Good
Shepherd**
798 Willow Grove St,
Hackettstown NJ 07840-1718.
908/852-1430.

**Ward Home for Aged**
333 Elmwood Ave, Maplewood
NJ 07040-1819. 973/762-5050.

**SPECIALTY OUTPATIENT
FACILITIES**

**Jersey Cape Diagnostic
Training Center**
152 Crest Haven Rd, Cape May
Courthouse NJ 08210-1651.
609/465-4117.

**Summit Health Inc.**
PO Box 337, Voorhees NJ 08043-
0337. 609/325-5800.

## For more information on career opportunities in the health care industry:

### Associations

**ACCREDITING COMMISSION ON
EDUCATION FOR HEALTH SERVICES
ADMINISTRATION**
1911 North Fort Myer Drive, Suite 503, Arlington VA
22209. 202/822-8561.

**AMBULATORY INFORMATION
MANAGEMENT ASSOCIATION
BAY VALLEY MEDICAL GROUP**
27212 Calaroga Avenue, Hayward CA 94545.
510/293-5688. Contact: Martha Feinberg,
Membership Coordinator. E-mail address:
info@aim4.org. World Wide Web address:
http://www.aim4.org.

**AMERICAN ACADEMY OF ALLERGY,
ASTHMA, & IMMUNOLOGY**
611 East Wells Street, Milwaukee WI 53202.
414/272-6071. World Wide Web address:
http://www.aaaai.org.

**AMERICAN ACADEMY OF FAMILY
PHYSICIANS**
8880 Ward Parkway, Kansas City MO 64114.
816/333-9700. World Wide Web address: http://www.
aafp.org. Promotes continuing education for family
physicians.

**AMERICAN ACADEMY OF PEDIATRIC
DENTISTRY**
211 East Chicago Avenue, Suite 700, Chicago IL

60611-2616. 312/337-2169. World Wide Web
address: http://www.aapd.org.

**AMERICAN ACADEMY OF
PERIODONTOLOGY**
737 North Michigan Avenue, Suite 800, Chicago IL
60611-2690. 312/573-3218. World Wide Web
address: http://www.perio.org.

**AMERICAN ACADEMY OF PHYSICIAN
ASSISTANTS**
950 North Washington Street, Alexandria VA 22314-
1552. 703/836-2272. World Wide Web address:
http://www.aapa.org. Promotes the use of physician
assistants.

**AMERICAN ASSOCIATION FOR CLINICAL
CHEMISTRY**
2101 L Street NW, Suite 202, Washington DC 20037.
202/857-0717. World Wide Web address:
http://www.aacc.org. A nonprofit association for
clinical, chemical, medical, and technical doctors.

**AMERICAN ASSOCIATION FOR
RESPIRATORY CARE**
11030 Ables Lane, Dallas TX 75229. 972/243-2272.
World Wide Web address: http://www.aarc.org.
Promotes the art and science of respiratory care, while
focusing on the needs of the patients.

**AMERICAN ASSOCIATION OF COLLEGES OF
OSTEOPATHIC MEDICINE**
5550 Friendship Boulevard, Suite 310, Chevy Chase
MD 20815. 301/968-4100. World Wide Web address:

---

http://www.aacom.org. Provides application processing services for colleges of osteopathic medicine.

## AMERICAN ASSOCIATION OF COLLEGES OF PODIATRIC MEDICINE
1350 Piccard Drive, Suite 322, Rockville MD 20850-4307. 301/990-7400. Fax: 301/990-2807. World Wide Web address: http://www.aacpm.org. Provides applications processing services for colleges of podiatric medicine.

## AMERICAN ASSOCIATION OF DENTAL SCHOOLS
1625 Massachusetts Avenue NW, Suite 600, Washington DC 20036-2212. 202/667-9433. Fax: 202/667-0642. E-mail address: aads@aads.jhu.edu. World Wide Web address: http://www.aads.jhu.edu. Represents all 54 of the dental schools in the U.S. as well as individual members. This organization addresses research, education, and public health.

## AMERICAN ASSOCIATION OF HEALTHCARE CONSULTANTS
11208 Waples Mill Road, Suite 109, Fairfax VA 22030. 703/691-2242. World Wide Web address: http://www.aahc.net.

## AMERICAN ASSOCIATION OF HOMES AND SERVICES FOR THE AGING
901 E Street NW, Suite 500, Washington DC 20004. 202/783-2242. World Wide Web address: http://www.aahsa.org.

## AMERICAN ASSOCIATION OF MEDICAL ASSISTANTS
20 North Wacker Drive, Suite 1575, Chicago IL 60606. 312/899-1500. World Wide Web address: http://www.aama-ntl.org.

## AMERICAN ASSOCIATION OF NURSE ANESTHETISTS
222 South Prospect Avenue, Park Ridge IL 60068-4001. 847/692-7050. World Wide Web address: http://www.aana.com

## AMERICAN ASSOCIATION OF ORAL AND MAXILLOFACIAL SURGEONS
9700 West Bryn Mawr Avenue, Rosemont IL 60018-5701. 847/678-6200. World Wide Web address: http://www.aaoms.org.

## AMERICAN CHIROPRACTIC ASSOCIATION
1701 Clarendon Boulevard, Arlington VA 22209. 703/276-8800. World Wide Web address: http://www.amerchiro.org. A national, nonprofit professional membership organization offering educational services (through films, booklets, texts, and kits), regional seminars and workshops, and major health and education activities that provide information on public health, safety, physical fitness, and disease prevention.

## AMERICAN COLLEGE OF HEALTH CARE ADMINISTRATORS
325 South Patrick Street, Alexandria VA 22314. 703/739-7900. World Wide Web address: http://www.achca.org. A professional membership society for individual long-term care professionals. Sponsors educational programs, supports research, and produces a number of publications.

## AMERICAN COLLEGE OF HEALTHCARE EXECUTIVES
One North Franklin Street, Suite 1700, Chicago IL

60606-3491. 312/424-2800. World Wide Web address: http://www.ache.org. Offers credentialing and educational programs. Publishes *Hospital & Health Services Administration* (a journal), and *Healthcare Executive* (a magazine).

## AMERICAN COLLEGE OF MEDICAL PRACTICE EXECUTIVES
104 Inverness Terrace East, Englewood CO 80112-5306. 303/799-1111. World Wide Web address: http://www.mgma.com/acmpe.

## AMERICAN COLLEGE OF OBSTETRICIANS AND GYNECOLOGISTS
409 12th Street SW, P.O. Box 96920, Washington DC 20090-6920. World Wide Web address: http://www.acog.org.

## AMERICAN COLLEGE OF PHYSICIAN EXECUTIVES
4890 West Kennedy Boulevard, Suite 200, Tampa FL 33609-2575. 813/287-2000. Fax: 813/287-8993. World Wide Web address: http://www.acpe.org.

## AMERICAN DENTAL ASSOCIATION
211 East Chicago Avenue, Chicago IL 60611. 312/440-2500. World Wide Web address: http://www.ada.org.

## AMERICAN DENTAL HYGIENISTS' ASSN.
444 North Michigan Avenue, Suite 3400, Chicago IL 60611. 312/440-8900. World Wide Web address: http://www.adha.org.

## AMERICAN DIETETIC ASSOCIATION
216 West Jackson Boulevard, Suite 800, Chicago IL 60606. 312/899-0040. Toll-free phone: 800/877-1600. Promotes optimal nutrition to improve public health and well-being.

## AMERICAN HEALTH INFORMATION MANAGEMENT ASSOCIATION
919 North Michigan Avenue, Suite 1400, Chicago IL 60611. 312/787-2672. World Wide Web address: http://www.ahima.org.

## AMERICAN HOSPITAL ASSOCIATION
One North Franklin Street, Chicago IL 60606. 312/422-3000. World Wide Web address: http://www.aha.org.

## AMERICAN MEDICAL ASSOCIATION
515 North State Street, Chicago IL 60610. 312/464-5000. World Wide Web address: http://www.ama.org. An organization for medical doctors.

## AMERICAN MEDICAL INFORMATICS ASSOCIATION
4915 St. Elmo Avenue, Suite 401, Bethesda MD 20814. 301/657-1291. World Wide Web address: http://www.ama-assn.org.

## AMERICAN MEDICAL TECHNOLOGISTS
710 Higgins Road, Park Ridge IL 60068. 847/823-5169. World Wide Web address: http://www.amt1.com.

## AMERICAN MEDICAL WOMEN'S ASSN.
801 North Fairfax Street, Suite 400, Alexandria VA 22314. 703/838-0500. Fax: 703/549-3864. E-mail address: info@amwa-doc.org. World Wide Web address: http://www.amwa-doc.org. Supports the advancement of women in medicine.

**AMERICAN NURSES ASSOCIATION**
600 Maryland Avenue SW, Suite 100W, Washington
DC 20024. 202/554-4444. World Wide Web address:
http://www.nursingworld.org.

**AMERICAN OCCUPATIONAL THERAPY
ASSOCIATION, INC.**
4720 Montgomery Lane, P.O. Box 31220, Bethesda
MD 20824-1220. 301/652-2682. Toll-free phone:
800/377-8555. Fax: 301/652-7711. World Wide Web
address: http://www.aota.org.

**AMERICAN OPTOMETRIC ASSOCIATION**
243 North Lindbergh Boulevard, St. Louis MO 63141.
314/991-4100. Offers publications, discounts, and
insurance programs for members.

**AMERICAN ORGANIZATION OF NURSE
EXECUTIVES**
One North Franklin Street, 34th Floor, Chicago IL
60606. 312/422-2800. World Wide Web address:
http://www.aone.org.

**AMERICAN ORTHOPAEDIC ASSOCIATION**
6300 North River Road, Suite 300, Rosemont IL
60018. 847/318-7330. World Wide Web address:
http://www.aoassn.org.

**AMERICAN PHYSICAL THERAPY ASSN.**
111 North Fairfax Street, Alexandria VA 22314.
703/684-2782. World Wide Web address: http://www.
apta.org. Small fee required for information.

**AMERICAN PODIATRIC MEDICAL ASSN.**
9312 Old Georgetown Road, Bethesda MD 20814-
1698. 301/571-9200. World Wide Web address:
http://www.apma.org.

**AMERICAN PSYCHIATRIC ASSOCIATION**
World Wide Web address: http://www.psych.org.
Professional association for mental health
professionals.

**AMERICAN PUBLIC HEALTH ASSOCIATION**
1015 15th Street NW, Suite 300, Washington DC
20005. 202/789-5600. World Wide Web address:
http://www.apha.org.

**AMERICAN SOCIETY OF
ANESTHESIOLOGISTS**
520 North NW Highway, Park Ridge IL 60068.
847/825-5586. World Wide Web address: http://www.
asahq.org.

**AMERICAN SPEECH LANGUAGE HEARING
ASSOCIATION**
10801 Rockville Pike, Rockville MD 20852. Toll-free
phone: 800/498-2071. World Wide Web address:
http://www.asha.org. Professional, scientific, and
credentialing association for audiologists; speech-
language pathologists; and speech, language, and
hearing scientists.

**AMERICAN SUBACUTE CARE ASSOCIATION**
1720 Kennedy Causeway, Suite 109, North Bay
Village FL 33141. 305/864-0396. World Wide Web
address: http://members.aol.com/ascamail/index.htm.

**AMERICAN VETERINARY MEDICAL ASSN.**
1931 North Meacham Road, Suite 100, Schaumburg
IL 60173. 847/925-8070. World Wide Web address:
http://www.avma.org. Provides a forum for the
discussion of important issues in the veterinary
profession.

**ASSOCIATION OF AMERICAN MEDICAL
COLLEGES**
2450 N Street NW, Washington DC 20037-1126.
202/828-0400. World Wide Web address: http://www.
aamc.org.

**ASSOCIATION OF MENTAL HEALTH
ADMINISTRATORS**
60 Revere Drive, Suite 500, Northbrook IL 60062.
847/480-9626.

**ASSOCIATION OF UNIVERSITY PROGRAMS
IN HEALTH ADMINISTRATION**
1110 Vermont Avenue NW, Suite 220, Washington
DC 20005. 202/822-8550.

**BAYER QUALITY NETWORK**
4700 West Lake Avenue, Glenview IL 60025. Toll-
free phone: 888/BAYERNET. World Wide Web
address: http://www.bayerquality.org. An educational
site for health care professionals.

**HEALTHCARE FINANCIAL MANAGEMENT
ASSOCIATION**
2 Westbrook Corporate Center, Suite 700,
Westchester IL 60154-5700. 708/531-9600. World
Wide Web address: http://www.hfma.org.

**HEALTHCARE INFORMATION AND
MANAGEMENT SYSTEMS SOCIETY**
230 East Ohio Street, Suite 500, Chicago IL 60611.
312/664-4467. World Wide Web address: http://www.
himss.org.

**NATIONAL ASSOCIATION FOR
CHIROPRACTIC MEDICINE**
15427 Baybrook Drive, Houston TX 77062. 281/280-
8262. World Wide Web address: http://www.
chiromed.org.

**NATIONAL COALITION OF HISPANIC
HEALTH AND HUMAN SERVICES
ORGANIZATIONS**
1501 16th Street NW, Washington DC 20036.
202/387-5000. World Wide Web address: http://www.
cossmho.org. Strives to improve the health and well-
being of Hispanic communities throughout the United
States.

**NATIONAL HOSPICE ORGANIZATION**
1901 North Moore Street, Suite 901, Arlington VA
22209. 703/243-5900. World Wide Web address:
http://www.nho.org. Educates and advocates for the
principles of hospice care to meet the needs of the
terminally ill.

**NATIONAL MEDICAL ASSOCIATION**
1012 10th Street NW, Washington DC 20001.
202/347-1895. World Wide Web address: http://www,
nmanet.org.

**Magazines**

**AMERICAN MEDICAL NEWS**
American Medical Association, P.O. Box 10945,
Chicago IL 60610. 312/670-7827.

**HEALTHCARE EXECUTIVE**
American College of Health Care Executives, One
North Franklin Street, Suite 1700, Chicago IL 60606-
3491. 312/424-2800.

**MODERN HEALTHCARE**
Crain Communications, 740 North Rush Street,

Chicago IL 60611. 312/649-5350. World Wide Web address: http://www.modernhealthcare.com.

**NURSEFAX**
Springhouse Corporation, 1111 Bethlehem Pike, Springhouse PA 19477. 215/646-8700. World Wide Web address: http://www.springnet.com. This is a jobline service designed to be used in conjunction with *Nursing* magazine. Please call to obtain a copy of a magazine or the *Nursing* directory.

**Online Services**

**AMIA/MEDSIG**
Go: MedSIG. A CompuServe forum for health care professionals to discuss and exchange information about topics in medicine.

**ACADEMIC PHYSICIAN AND SCIENTIST**
Gopher://aps.acad-phy-sci.com. A great resource for jobseekers interested in administrative or clinical positions at teaching hospitals.

**HEALTH CARE JOBS ONLINE JOB BULLETIN BOARD**
http://www.hcjobsonline.com. This Website is for jobseekers who are looking for job opportunities in the health care industry. This site is maintained by Images, Ink.

**MEDSEARCH AMERICA**
http://www.medsearch.com. Site geared for medical professionals and a definite "must see" for those seeking positions in this area, Medsearch America offers national and international job searches, career forums, a resume builder, resume posting, recruiters' sites, listings of professional associations, and employer profiles. Over 4,000 job openings are posted on Medsearch America.

**MEDZILLA**
E-mail address: info@medzilla.com. World Wide Web address: http://www.medzilla.com. Lists job openings for professionals in the fields of biotechnology, health care, medicine, and science related industries.

**NURSING NETWORK FORUM**
Go: Custom 261. A CompuServe bulletin board for nurses that provides periodic "live" discussions with special guests.

**SALUDOS WEB CAREER GUIDE: HEALTH CARE**
http://www.saludos.com/cguide/hcguide.html. Provides information for jobseekers looking in the health care field. The site includes links to several health care associations and other sites that are sources of job openings in health care. This site is run by Saludos Hispanos.

# HOTELS AND RESTAURANTS

*Employment in the hotel and restaurant industry increased from 1.66 million workers in 1993 to 1.85 million workers in 1998. Hotels are doing considerable business with a shortage of lodging facilities and a relatively strong economy. However, some areas, such as Las Vegas, have actually seen occupancy rates decrease recently. Las Vegas is due to open $3 billion worth of new hotels, geared toward affluent travelers seeking a resort atmosphere. The city has seen the construction of more than 10,000 new rooms since 1997, resulting in supply outweighing demand.* U.S. Industry and Trade Outlook 1998 *reports that numerous U.S. cities are banking on the success of business meetings and conventions and are making significant investments in new and expanded convention facilities.*

*Jobs are plentiful for candidates with degrees in hotel and restaurant management. Both business and tourism travel are expected to increase, which may again increase the number of hotels. Hotel chains, like many other businesses, continue to consolidate, and there is an increase in the number of economy hotels offering clean, simple accommodations. These two factors combined may ultimately increase competition for hotel management positions, as fewer hotel managers will be needed.*

*According to a recent report by the National Restaurant Association, 44 percent of every dollar Americans spend on food goes toward dining out. Nine million people are employed in food services and that number is expected to climb to 11 million by 2005. According to* Business Week, *Americans are starting to spend more on casual dining and prepared meals, and less at fast food restaurants. Other restaurant chains are seeing strong sales growth, such as Dunkin' Donuts, which expected 1998 sales to reach $200 million for its bagels alone.*

**AMERICAN GAMING & ENTERTAINMENT LTD.**
P.O. Box 2341, Ventnor NJ 08406. 609/822-8505. **Contact:** Human Resources. **Description:** Develops and manages casino gaming ventures. The company owns and operates the Gold Shore Casino in Biloxi MS, and manages the video lottery and other gaming activities at Mountaineer Racetrack and Resort in Chester WV.

**ATLANTIC CITY HILTON CASINO RESORT**
Boston & Pacific Avenues, Atlantic City NJ 08401. 609/347-7111. **Contact:** Human Resources Department. **World Wide Web address:** http://www.hiltonac.com. **Description:** A 744-room hotel and casino.

**BALLY'S PARK PLACE**
Park Place & The Boardwalk, Atlantic City NJ 08401-6852. 609/340-2000. **Contact:** Human Resources. **Description:** A resort hotel and casino with 1254 rooms, nine restaurants, a bar, a theater, a ballroom, retail space, and convention facilities. **Subsidiaries include:** Bally's Wild Wild West casino is connected to Bally's Park Place, though it maintains separate gaming, dining, and retail facilities.

**CAESARS ATLANTIC CITY HOTEL CASINO**
2100 Pacific Avenue, Atlantic City NJ 08401. 609/348-4411. **Contact:** Personnel. **World Wide Web address:** http://www.caesars.com. **Description:** A hotel with 1,100 rooms.

## CANTEEN VENDING SERVICES
6 Pearl Court, Allendale NJ 07401. 201/760-9000. **Contact:** Janet Gleason, Office Manager. **Description:** One of the largest food service companies in the nation. Sales are primarily through food and vending operations, serving more than 800 manual food accounts nationwide, in both office and manufacturing facilities. The Concessions Division serves major accounts including Yankee Stadium and Yellowstone National Park. The Hospital Host Division services school districts, hospitals, nursing homes, universities, and various other major institutional customers. **Parent company:** Canteen Corporation. **Other U.S. locations:** Phoenix AZ; Tuxedo MD.

## CHEFS INTERNATIONAL, INC.
P.O. Box 1332, Point Pleasant Beach NJ 08742. 732/295-0350. **Contact:** Ann Liss, Office Manager. **World Wide Web address:** http://www.sunet.net/lobstershanty. **Description:** Operates eight Lobster Shanty restaurants in New Jersey and Florida. **Corporate headquarters location:** This Location.

## CROWNE PLAZA
650 Terrace Avenue, Hasbrouck Heights NJ 07604. 201/288-6100. **Contact:** Cynthia Schalabba, Human Resources Manager. **Description:** Provides a wide range of lodging, restaurant, lounge, meeting, and banquet facilities as part of an international chain. **Common positions include:** Customer Service Representative; Food and Beverage Service Worker; Hotel/Motel Clerk; Housekeeper. **Benefits:** Employee Discounts; Medical Insurance. **Operations at this facility include:** Administration. **Corporate headquarters location:** San Francisco CA. **Other U.S. locations:** Phoenix AZ; Atlanta GA; Detroit MI; Hilton Head Island SC; White Plains NY.

## DAYS INN OF AMERICA, INC.
3159 Route 46, Parsippany NJ 07054. 973/335-0200. **Contact:** Human Resources. **Description:** A hotel with 120 rooms. **Parent company:** Hospitality Franchise Systems, Inc.

## HARRAH'S ATLANTIC CITY
777 Brigantine Boulevard, Atlantic City NJ 08203. 609/441-5000. **Contact:** Human Resources. **Description:** A hotel and casino providing 1,174 rooms, theaters, retail space, and seven restaurants.

## OCEAN SHOWBOAT INC.
801 Boardwalk, Atlantic City NJ 08401. 609/343-4000. **Contact:** Personnel. **Description:** A hotel and casino.

## PRIME HOSPITALITY CORPORATION
700 Route 46 East, Fairfield NJ 07007-2700. 973/882-1010. **Contact:** Human Resources. **Description:** An independent hotel operating company with ownership or management of 86 full- and limited-service hotels in 19 states and one resort hotel in the U.S. Virgin Islands. The hotels typically contain 100 to 200 guest rooms or suites and operate under franchise agreements with national hotel chains or under the company's Wellesley Inns or AmeriSuites trade names. Founded in 1961. **Common positions include:** Accountant/Auditor; Administrative Manager; Advertising Account Executive; Architect; Attorney; Auditor; Budget Analyst; Buyer; Chief Financial Officer; Computer Operator; Construction Contractor; Controller; Credit Manager; Database Manager; General Manager; Human Resources Manager; Marketing Manager; Quality Control Supervisor; Secretary; Systems Analyst; Systems Manager; Telecommunications Manager; Typist/Word Processor. **Educational backgrounds include:** Accounting; Business Administration; Hotel Administration; Liberal Arts. **Benefits:** 401(k); Dental Insurance; Disability Coverage; Employee Discounts; Life Insurance; Medical Insurance. **Corporate headquarters location:** This Location. **Other U.S. locations:** Nationwide. **Operations at this facility include:** Administration. **Listed on:** New York Stock Exchange. **Annual sales/revenues:** More than $100 million. **Number of employees at this location:** 190. **Number of employees nationwide:** 6,050. **Number of projected hires for 1998 - 1999 at this location:** 15.

## RESORTS CASINO HOTEL
1133 Boardwalk, Atlantic City NJ 08401. 609/344-6000. **Fax:** 609/340-7751. **Contact:** Employment Office. **World Wide Web address:** http://www.resortsac.com. **Description:** Atlantic City's first casino hotel, with more than 800 deluxe rooms and suites. The hotel also houses a fine dining restaurant, a full-service beauty salon, and several shops and boutiques.

## SANDS HOTEL & CASINO
136 South Kentucky Avenue, Atlantic City NJ 08401. 609/441-4000. **Contact:** Human Resources. **Description:** A resort hotel with 532 rooms, extensive gaming facilities, five restaurants, and live entertainment.

## TROPICANA CASINO AND RESORT

Brighton Avenue & the Boardwalk, Atlantic City NJ 08401. 609/340-4000. **Toll-free phone:** 800/843-8767. **Fax:** 609/343-5256. **Contact:** Donald Hoover, Personnel Manager. **World Wide Web address:** http://www.tropicana.net. **Description:** Tropicana Casino and Resort is a large casino and hotel which offers casino gaming, gourmet dining, hotel facilities, and an indoor amusement park. **Common positions include:** Accountant/Auditor; Administrator; Budget Analyst; Buyer; Computer Programmer; Department Manager; Electrician; Financial Analyst; Hotel Manager; Human Resources Manager; Marketing Specialist; Public Relations Specialist; Purchasing Agent/Manager; Systems Analyst. **Educational backgrounds include:** Accounting; Business Administration; Communications; Computer Science; Finance; Liberal Arts; Marketing. **Benefits:** Dental Insurance; Employee Discounts; Life Insurance; Medical Insurance; Pension Plan; Profit Sharing; Savings Plan; Tuition Assistance. **Special programs:** Internships. **Corporate headquarters location:** Phoenix AZ. **Other U.S. locations:** Las Vegas NV; Laughlin NV. **Parent company:** Aztar operates in major domestic gaming markets with casino hotel facilities. In addition to Tropicana Casino and Resort, Aztar also owns and operates Tropicana Resort and Casino (Las Vegas NV) and Ramada Express Hotel and Casino (Laughlin NV). **Operations at this facility include:** Administration; Service. **Listed on:** New York Stock Exchange. **Number of employees at this location:** 5,000.

## TRUMP HOTEL AND CASINO RESORTS

The Boardwalk at Mississippi Avenue, Atlantic City NJ 08401. 609/441-6500. **Fax:** 609/441-6067. **Contact:** Employment Office. **World Wide Web address:** http://www.trumptaj.com. **Description:** Operates Trump Marina, Trump's Taj Mahal, and Trump Plaza. **NOTE:** All hiring for these subsidiaries is done through this location.

*Note: Because addresses and telephone numbers of smaller companies can change rapidly, we recommend you call each company to verify the information below before inquiring about job opportunities. Mass mailings are not recommended.*

### Additional small employers:

#### DRINKING PLACES

**Iguana Beach Club**
2310 Marlton Pike W, Cherry Hill NJ 08002. 609/486-4288.

**Irish Pub & Inn Inc.**
164 Saint James Pl, Atlantic City NJ 08401-7106. 609/344-9063.

#### EATING PLACES

**Afton Restaurant**
2 Hanover Rd, Florham Park NJ 07932-1819. 973/377-1871.

**Bennigan's**
412 S Van Brunt St, Englewood NJ 07631-4613. 201/569-9797.

**Bennigan's**
119 Columbia Turnpike, Florham Park NJ 07932-2900. 973/822-7930.

**Bennigan's**
1735 Route 46, Parsippany NJ 07054-2913. 973/335-6880.

**Bennigan's**
65 US Highway 1, Metuchen NJ 08840-2931. 732/548-5557.

**Bertucci's Brick Oven Pizzeria**
1220 Nixon Dr, Mount Laurel NJ 08054-1173. 609/273-0400.

**Binghamton Restaurant**
725 River Rd, Edgewater NJ 07020-1101. 201/941-2300.

**Boardwalk Cafe**
102 Boardwalk 6, Atlantic City NJ 08401. 609/398-3490.

**Bob's Big Boy**
PO Box 307, South Amboy NJ 08879-0307. 732/525-0306.

**Braddock's Tavern Inc.**
39 S Main St, Medford NJ 08055-2429. 609/654-1604.

**Buffet's Inc.**
1350 Hurffville Rd, Deptford NJ 08096-3818. 609/401-1200.

**Burger King**
PO Box 5, Belmar NJ 07719-0005. 732/681-4314.

**Burger King**
173 E 70 Sharp Runn Plz, Medford NJ 08055. 609/654-4070.

**Burger King**
4 Candlewood Dr, Madison NJ 07940-2728. 973/765-9011.

**Burger King**
100 Franklin Ave, Nutley NJ 07110-3266. 973/284-1111.

**Casa Lupita Mexican Restaurant**
PO Box 73, Marlton NJ 08053-0073. 609/596-7887.

**Casa Lupita Mexican Restaurant**
250 Mercer Mall, Trenton NJ 08648. 609/452-7070.

**Casa Maria Restaurant**
Rtes 4 & 17, Paramus NJ 07652. 201/843-8444.

**Checker Sub Shop**
PO Box 816, Mount Laurel NJ 08054-0816. 609/866-9700.

**Checker's Drive-In**
283 Market St, Paterson NJ 07501-1927. 973/357-0102.

**Chi-Chi's**
625 Rte 1 at Gill Lane, Iselin NJ 08830. 732/636-5200.

**Chi-Chi's**
335 State Route 18, East Brunswick NJ 08816-2107. 732/390-1122.

**Chi-Chi's**
1709 Deptford Center Rd, Deptford NJ 08096-5627. 609/848-9200.

**Chili's Grill & Bar**
1310 State Highway 73, Mount
Laurel NJ 08054. 609/273-0020.

**Chili's Grill & Bar**
1800 Clements Bridge Rd,
Deptford NJ 08096-2021.
609/384-1212.

**Chili's Grill & Bar**
1165 US Highway 46, Little Falls
NJ 07424-1855. 973/785-0005.

**Coastline Restaurant**
1240 Brace Rd, Cherry Hill NJ
08034-3211. 609/795-1773.

**Damon's Restaurant**
6055 Black Horse Pike, Egg
Harbor Township NJ 08234-
4801. 609/484-8692.

**Domino's Pizza**
147 Grove St, Bloomfield NJ
07003-5645. 973/680-9777.

**Domino's Pizza**
51 Niagara St, Newark NJ 07105-
3266. 201/339-3030.

**East Brunswick Chateau**
PO Box 908, East Brunswick NJ
08816-0908. 732/238-6600.

**Fiesta Banquet Rooms**
PO Box 212, Wood Ridge NJ
07075-0212. 201/939-5409.

**Fifth Avenue Ice Cream Inc.**
333 Route 46, Fairfield NJ
07004-2427. 973/882-0340.

**First Place Restaurant**
400 Commons Way, Ste 272,
Bridgewater NJ 08807-2821.
908/218-9333.

**Garcia's Restaurant**
308 Highway 35 S, Eatontown NJ
07724-2216. 732/389-0444.

**Ground Round Inc.**
395 North Almonesson Rd,
Deptford NJ 08096. 609/848-
0121.

**Hard Rock Cafe**
1000 Boardwalk, Atlantic City NJ
08401-7415. 609/441-0007.

**Highlawn Pavilion**
Eagle Rock Ave, West Orange NJ
07052. 973/731-3463.

**Houlihan's**
643 Route 46 W, Fairfield NJ
07004-1556. 973/808-1300.

**Houlihan's**
197 Riverside Sq, Hackensack NJ
07601-6307. 201/488-9321.

**Houlihan's**
372 W Mount Pleasant Ave,

Livingston NJ 07039-2748.
973/992-0455.

**Houlihan's**
2000 Route 38, Ste 300, Cherry
Hill NJ 08002. 609/662-9300.

**Houlihan's**
1200 Harbor Blvd, Weehawken
NJ 07087-6728. 201/863-4000.

**Houlihan's**
700 Plaza Dr, Secaucus NJ
07094-3604. 201/330-8856.

**Jose Teja's**
700 Route 1 N, Iselin NJ 08830.
732/283-3883.

**JP's**
820 Main St, Toms River NJ
08753-6544. 732/349-0800.

**Katmandu**
50 Riverview Executive Park,
Trenton NJ 08611. 609/393-7300.

**L'Affaire 22 Inc.**
1099 US Highway 22,
Mountainside NJ 07092-2809.
908/232-4454.

**Lambertville Station**
11 Bridge St, Lambertville NJ
08530-2134. 609/397-8300.

**Landmark 2 Banquet &
Meeting Room**
26 State St, Moonachie NJ
07074-1405. 201/438-3939.

**Lone Star Steakhouse**
2880 Highway 35, Hazlet NJ
07730-1504. 732/335-1711.

**Lone Star Steakhouse**
2452 Route 38, Cherry Hill NJ
08002-1238. 609/482-7727.

**Mac's Restaurant Inc.**
908 Shore Rd 10, Somers Point
NJ 08244-2336. 609/927-2759.

**Mastori's Restaurant and Diner**
144 Route 130, Bordentown NJ
08505-2226. 609/298-4650.

**McDonald's**
PO Box 1158, Bloomfield NJ
07003-1158. 973/338-4641.

**Napa Valley Grill**
Garden State Plaza 1146,
Rochelle Park NJ 07662.
201/845-5555.

**Ogden**
One Harbor Blvd, Camden NJ
08103-1056. 609/635-0011.

**Olga's Diner**
73 Rural Route 70, Marlton NJ
08053. 609/596-1700.

**Olive Garden Restaurant**
230 State Route 35 S, Eatontown
NJ 07724-2103. 732/389-4585.

**Olive Garden Restaurant**
2314 State Rd, Ste 38, Cherry
Hill NJ 08002. 609/482-2453.

**Olive Garden Restaurant**
227 Eisenhower Pkwy,
Livingston NJ 07039-1700.
973/992-0044.

**Olive Garden Restaurant**
275 Route 22, Springfield NJ
07081-3530. 973/376-2667.

**Ponzio's Restaurant Cherry
Hill**
7 Route 70 W, Cherry Hill NJ
08002-3098. 609/428-4808.

**Ram's Head Inn Restaurant**
111 Prospect Ave, West Orange
NJ 07052-4202. 973/731-2360.

**Ram's Head Inn Restaurant**
9 W White Horse Pike, Absecon
NJ 08201-9448. 609/652-1700.

**Red Lobster**
520 Hwy 46, Wayne NJ 07470.
973/785-3114.

**Red Lobster**
6000 Hwy 1, Iselin NJ 08830.
732/636-6230.

**Red Lobster**
1298 Hooper Ave, Toms River
NJ 08753-3341. 732/914-0183.

**Red Lobster**
500 Route 3, Secaucus NJ 07094-
3701. 201/865-6709.

**Rod's 1890s Restaurant**
PO Box 202, Convent Station NJ
07961-0202. 973/539-6666.

**Romano's Macaroni Grill**
1958 State Hwy 23, Wayne NJ
07470. 973/305-5858.

**Romano's Macaroni Grill**
138 State Route 10, Ste 2, East
Hanover NJ 07936-2107.
973/515-1121.

**Ruby Tuesday Restaurant**
Freehold Raceway Mill, Freehold
NJ 07728. 732/577-9644.

**Ruby Tuesday Restaurant**
4403 Black Horse Pike, Mays
Landing NJ 08330-3103.
609/272-1550.

**Rumbleseats Restaurant**
Routes 130 & 206, Bordentown
NJ 08505. 609/298-8807.

**Ruth's Chris Steak House**
1000 Harbor Blvd, Weehawken
NJ 07087-6727. 201/863-5100.

**Seasons Restaurant**
4160 Quakerbridge Rd,
Lawrenceville NJ 08648-4703.
609/275-0260.

**Short Hills West**
345 S Orange Ave, Livingston NJ
07039-5903. 973/992-6655.

**Sizzler**
804 Bloomfield Ave, Caldwell NJ
07006-6700. 973/575-1059.

**Sizzler**
Mount Pleasant Ave, Rockaway
NJ 07866. 973/366-7755.

**Sizzler**
Parsonage Ave, RR 1, Edison NJ
08817. 732/494-0777.

**Sizzler**
700 Plaza Dr, Secaucus NJ
07094-3604. 201/863-8110.

**Steak & Ale**
1287 Highway 35, Middletown
NJ 07748-2011. 732/957-9448.

**TGI Friday's**
1279 Hooper Ave, Toms River
NJ 08753-3323. 732/914-1113.

**TGI Friday's**
3535 US Route 1, Suite 275,
Princeton NJ 08540. 609/520-
0378.

**TGI Friday's**
411 Hackensack Ave,
Hackensack NJ 07601-6328.
201/342-7107.

**TGI Friday's**
970 N Route 73, Marlton NJ
08053-1230. 609/596-9117.

**TGI Friday's**
30 Vreeland Rd A, Florham Park
NJ 07932-1904. 973/822-0099.

**TGI Friday's**
Somerset Shopping Center,
Bridgewater NJ 08807. 908/707-
1991.

**TGI Friday's**
1701 Route 22, Ste 100,
Watchung NJ 07060-6500.
908/322-6412.

**TGI Friday's**
401 Gill Ln, Iselin NJ 08830-
3002. 732/636-1537.

**TGI Friday's**
379 Rte 17 S, Woodbridge NJ
07095. 201/438-2300.

**The Palisadium**
700 Palisadium Dr, Cliffside Park
NJ 07010-3239. 201/224-2211.

**The Westwood**
430-438 North Ave, Garwood NJ
07027. 908/789-0808.

**Wendy's**
30 Garfield Ave, Jersey City NJ
07305-2401. 201/332-5022.

**White Castle System Inc.**
600 Westfield Ave, Elizabeth NJ
07208-1326. 908/352-7170.

**HOTELS AND MOTELS**

**Best Western**
216-234 Route 46, Fairfield NJ
07004. 973/575-7700.

**Blackhorse Inn of Mendham**
1 W Main St, Mendham NJ
07945-1220. 973/543-7300.

**Brunswick Hilton**
3 Tower Center Blvd, East
Brunswick NJ 08816-1143.
732/828-2000.

**Clinton Inn**
PO Box 247, Tenafly NJ 07670-
0247. 201/871-3200.

**Coventry Inn**
50 Kenny Place, Saddle Brook NJ
07663-5916. 201/845-6200.

**Crowne Plaza Edison**
125 Raritan Center Pkwy, Edison
NJ 08837-3614. 732/225-8300.

**Days Inn**
Morris Ave & The Boardwalk,
Atlantic City NJ 08401. 609/344-
6101.

**Dutch Inn**
299 Swedesboro Ave, Gibbstown
NJ 08027-1647. 609/423-6600.

**East Hanover Ramada**
130 Route 10, East Hanover NJ
07936. 973/386-5622.

**Econo Lodge**
2016 Route 37 W, Jackson NJ
08527. 732/657-7100.

**Embassy Suites**
909 Parsippany Blvd, Parsippany
NJ 07054-1222. 973/334-1440.

**Embassy Suites**
455 Plaza Dr, Secaucus NJ
07094-3631. 201/864-7300.

**Fairfield Radisson**
44 Mandeville Dr, Wayne NJ
07470-6564. 973/694-8013.

**Forrestal at Princeton**
100 College Rd E, Princeton NJ
08540-6613. 609/452-7800.

**Four Points Hotel**
1450 Route 70 E, Cherry Hill NJ
08034-2230. 609/428-2300.

**Hamilton Park Conference
Center**
175 Park Ave, Florham Park NJ
07932-1095. 973/377-2424.

**Hanover Marriott Hotel**
1401 Rte 10 E, Whippany NJ
07981. 973/538-8811.

**Hilton Gateway**
Gateway Ctr Raymond, Newark
NJ 07102. 973/622-5000.

**Holiday Inn**
PO Box 304, Bridgeport NJ
08014-0304. 609/467-3322.

**Holiday Inn**
50 Kenny Pl, Saddle Brook NJ
07663-5916. 201/843-0600.

**Holiday Inn**
304 Route 22, Springfield NJ
07081-3510. 973/376-9400.

**Holiday Inn**
290 Highway 37, Toms River NJ
08755-8032. 732/244-4000.

**Holiday Inn**
160 Frontage Rd, Newark NJ
07114-3721. 973/589-1000.

**Holiday Inn**
4355 Route 1, Princeton NJ
08540-5705. 609/452-2400.

**Holiday Inn Jetport**
1000 Spring St, Elizabeth NJ
07201-2113. 908/355-1700.

**Holiday Inn Somerset**
195 Davidson Ave, Somerset NJ
08873-4117. 732/356-1700.

**Hyatt Cherry Hill**
2349 Marlton Pike W, Cherry
Hill NJ 08002-3315. 609/662-
1234.

**Hyatt Regency New Brunswick**
2 Albany St, New Brunswick NJ
08901-1236. 732/873-1234.

**Hyatt Regency Princeton**
102 Carnegie Ctr, Princeton NJ
08540-6200. 609/987-1234.

**Landmark Inn**
US Route 1/9 N, Woodbridge NJ
07095. 732/636-2700.

**Marriott Glenpointe**
100 Frank W. Burr Blvd, Teaneck
NJ 07666-6702. 201/836-0600.

**Marriott Hotel**
201 Village Blvd, Princeton NJ
08540-5737. 609/452-7900.

**Marriott Hotel**
110 Davidson Ave, Somerset NJ
08873-1303. 732/560-0500.

**Marriott Hotel**
300 Brae Blvd, Park Ridge NJ
07656-1829. 201/307-0800.

**Marriott Hotel**
180 Garden State Pkwy, Saddle
Brook NJ 07663. 201/843-9500.

**Marriott Hotel**
Newark International Airport,
Newark NJ 07114. 973/623-0006.

**Marriott Montvale**
Garden State Pkwy, Montvale NJ
07645. 201/391-8509.

**Meadowlands Hilton**
2 Harmon Plz, Secaucus NJ
07094-2802. 201/348-6900.

**Montvale Inn**
100 Chestnut Ridge Rd, Montvale
NJ 07645-1803. 201/391-7700.

**Nassau Inn LP**
10 Palmer Square East, Princeton
NJ 08542-3721. 609/921-7500.

**Quality Inn**
10 Polito Ave, Lyndhurst NJ
07071-3403. 201/933-9800.

**Radisson Hotel**
915 Routes 73 & 95, Moorestown
NJ 08057. 609/234-7300.

**Radisson Hotel**
128 Frontage Rd, Newark NJ
07114-3721. 973/690-5500.

**Ramada Inn**
38 Two Bridges Rd, Fairfield NJ
07004-1530. 973/575-1742.

**Ramada Inn**
265 Route 3, Clifton NJ 07014-
1911. 973/778-6500.

**Ramada Inn**
60 Cottontail Ln, Somerset NJ
08873-1133. 732/560-9880.

**Ramada Inn**
180 State Rte 17, Mahwah NJ
07430-1240. 201/529-5880.

**Ramada Plaza Hotel**
555 Fellowship Rd, Mount Laurel
NJ 08054-3404. 609/273-1900.

**Residence Inn**
PO Box 8388, Princeton NJ
08543-8388. 732/329-9600.

**Seasons Resort**
PO Box 637, McAfee NJ 07428-
0637. 973/827-6000.

**Sheraton Hotel**
6 Industrial Way E, Eatontown
NJ 07724-3317. 732/542-6500.

**Sheraton Hotel**
6821 Black Horse Pike, Egg
Harbor NJ 08234-4131. 609/272-
0200.

**Sheraton Hotel at Woodbridge Place**
515 US Highway 1, Iselin NJ
08830-3010. 732/634-3600.

**Sheraton Tara Hotel**
199 Smith Rd, Parsippany NJ
07054-2813. 973/515-2000.

**Somerset Hills Hotel**
200 Liberty Corner Rd, Warren
NJ 07059-6761. 908/647-6700.

**The Grand Summit Hotel**
570 Springfield Ave, Summit NJ
07901-4501. 908/273-3000.

**Wilmington Hilton**
120 Schor Ave, Leonia NJ 07605-
2208. 201/461-3750.

**Woodbridge Hilton**
120 Wood Ave S, Ste 603, Iselin
NJ 08830-2709. 732/494-6200.

**Woodcliff Lake Hilton**
200 Tice Blvd, Woodcliff Lake
NJ 07675-8410. 201/391-3600.

**For more information on career opportunities in hotels and restaurants:**

## Associations

**AMERICAN HOTEL & MOTEL ASSOCIATION**
1201 New York Avenue NW, Suite 600, Washington
DC 20005-3931. 202/289-3100. World Wide Web
address: http://www.ahma.com.

**THE EDUCATIONAL FOUNDATION OF THE
NATIONAL RESTAURANT ASSOCIATION**
250 South Wacker Drive, Suite 1400, Chicago IL
60606. 312/715-1010. World Wide Web address:
http://www.edfound.org.

**NATIONAL RESTAURANT ASSOCIATION**
1200 17th Street NW, Washington DC 20036.
202/331-5900. World Wide Web address: http://www.
restaurant.org.

## Directories

**DIRECTORY OF CHAIN RESTAURANT
OPERATORS**
Lebhar-Friedman, Inc., 425 Park Avenue, New York
NY 10022. 212/756-5000. World Wide Web address:
http://www.lf.com.

**DIRECTORY OF HIGH-VOLUME
INDEPENDENT RESTAURANTS**
Lebhar-Friedman, Inc., 425 Park Avenue, New York
NY 10022. 212/756-5000. World Wide Web address:
http://www.lf.com.

## Magazines

**CORNELL HOTEL AND RESTAURANT
ADMINISTRATION QUARTERLY**
Cornell University School of Hotel Administration,
Statler Hall, Ithaca NY 14853-6902. 607/255-9393.
World Wide Web address: http://www.cornell.edu.

**HOSPITALITY WORLD**
PO Box 84108, Seattle WA 98124. 206/362-7125.

**NATION'S RESTAURANT NEWS**
Lebhar-Friedman, Inc., 3922 Coconut Palm Drive,
Tampa FL 33619. 813/664-6700.

## Online Services

**COOLWORKS**
World Wide Web address: http://www.coolworks.
com. This Website provides links to 22,000 job
openings at resorts, summer camps, ski areas, river
areas, ranches, fishing areas, and cruise ships.

**HOSPITALITY NET VIRTUAL JOB
EXCHANGE**
World Wide Web address: http://www.hospitalitynet.
nl/job.

**JOBNET: HOSPITALITY INDUSTRY**
World Wide Web address: http://www.westga.edu:80/
~coop/joblinks/subject/hospitality.html.

# INSURANCE

*Shaped by a changing marketplace of consolidation and competitive pressures, the insurance industry will face a tough year. The industry is highly competitive, and the U.S. Department of Labor forecasts slower than average growth for the industry through 2006. The added use of computers and databases allows more work to be done by fewer agents. Many opportunities will come as a result of people either retiring or switching professions.*

*The industry did see a 14 percent rise in profits during the first six months of 1998 versus the same period of 1997, though profit margins were down. The continued drop in the unemployment rate will help this industry, as more people have more income and property which must be managed and insured. Health care and pension benefits, in relation to an aging population, will also require the services of insurance companies, as will the rise in the number of young drivers and their needs for automobile insurance.*

**ADMIRAL INSURANCE COMPANY**
1255 Caldwell Road, Cherry Hill NJ 08034. 609/429-9200. **Contact:** Human Resources. **World Wide Web address:** http://www.admiralins.com. **Description:** Underwrites casualty and property insurance.

**AMERICAN RE-INSURANCE COMPANY**
555 College Road East, Princeton NJ 08543. 609/243-4649. **Contact:** Virginia M. Zdanowicz, Employment Manager. **Description:** Underwrites property and casualty reinsurance in both the domestic and international markets. **Common positions include:** Accountant/Auditor; Actuary; Attorney; Claim Rep.; Environmental Engineer; Financial Analyst; Human Resources Manager; Paralegal; Software Engineer; Underwriter/Assistant Underwriter. **Educational backgrounds include:** Accounting; Business Administration; Communications; Computer Science; Finance; Marketing. **Benefits:** 401(k); Dental Insurance; Disability Coverage; Life Insurance; Medical Insurance; Pension Plan; Savings Plan; Tuition Assistance. **Corporate headquarters location:** This Location. **Other U.S. locations:** Nationwide. **International locations:** Worldwide. **Parent company:** American Re Corporation, through its wholly-owned subsidiaries, is one of the largest providers of property and casualty reinsurance in the U.S. **Listed on:** New York Stock Exchange. **Number of employees at this location:** 800. **Number of employees nationwide:** 1,200.

**ANTHEM HEALTH & LIFE INSURANCE COMPANY**
One Centennial Avenue, Piscataway NJ 08855. 732/980-4000. **Fax:** 732/980-4095. **Contact:** Paul Neill, Vice President of Human Resources. **World Wide Web address:** http://www.anthem.com. **Description:** A group health and life insurance carrier. **Common positions include:** Actuary; Administrator; Assistant Manager; Claim Representative; Computer Programmer; Customer Service Representative; Financial Analyst; Insurance Agent/Broker; Quality Control Supervisor; Systems Analyst; Technical Writer/Editor; Underwriter/Assistant Underwriter. **Educational backgrounds include:** Accounting; Business Administration; Communications; Geology; Liberal Arts; Marketing; Mathematics. **Benefits:** 401(k); Daycare Assistance; Dental Insurance; Disability Coverage; Employee Discounts; Life Insurance; Medical Insurance; Pension Plan; Tuition Assistance **Special programs:** Internships. **Corporate headquarters location:** This Location. **Other U.S. locations:** Nationwide. **Parent company:** Community Mutual Insurance Company. **Operations at this facility include:** Administration; Service. **Number of employees at this location:** 905. **Number of employees nationwide:** 1,200.

**BLUE CROSS BLUE SHIELD**
Three Penn Plaza East, Newark NJ 07105. 973/466-4000. **Contact:** Human Resources. **Description:** Primarily a health insurance provider.

**THE CHUBB GROUP OF INSURANCE COMPANIES**
15 Mountain View Road, Warren NJ 07059. 908/903-2000. **Contact:** Human Resources. **World Wide Web address:** http://www.chubb.com. **Description:** One of the largest insurers in the United

States. In addition to its traditional commercial, personal, property, and casualty insurance business, the company has operations in life and health insurance and retail development. Founded in 1882. **Corporate headquarters location:** This Location. **Listed on:** New York Stock Exchange. **Annual sales/revenues:** More than $100 million. **Number of employees worldwide:** 10,000.

## GAB ROBINS NORTH AMERICA INC.
9 Campus Drive, Suite 7, Parsippany NJ 07054. 973/993-3400. **Contact:** Human Resources. **World Wide Web address:** http://www.gab.com. **Description:** Provides adjustment, inspection, appraisal, and claims management services to 15,000 insurance industry customers. Specific services include the settlement of claims following major disasters; appraisal, investigation, and adjustment of auto insurance claims; casualty claims; and fire, marine, life, accident, health, and disability claims. **Common positions include:** Accountant/Auditor; Claim Representative; Computer Programmer; Customer Service Representative; Human Resources Manager. **Educational backgrounds include:** Accounting; Business Administration; Liberal Arts. **Benefits:** Dental Insurance; Disability Coverage; Life Insurance; Medical Insurance; Pension Plan; Savings Plan; Tuition Assistance. **Corporate headquarters location:** This Location. **Parent company:** SGS North America. **Number of employees nationwide:** 3,400.

## HOME STATE INSURANCE COMPANY
## HOME STATE HOLDINGS
3 South Revmont Drive, Shrewsbury NJ 07702. 732/935-2600. **Contact:** Human Resources. **Description:** Provides personal and commercial auto insurance throughout the state. **Corporate headquarters location:** This Location. **Parent company:** Home State Holdings (also at this location) is a property and casualty holding company engaged primarily in providing personal and commercial auto insurance through its operating subsidiaries. Home State writes standard and preferred personal auto lines. The company's commercial auto lines focus on public transportation, including school buses, charter buses, limousines, and similar transportation risks. Subsidiaries of Home State Holdings include: Quaker City Insurance Company (operating in Pennsylvania, Delaware, Maryland, Virginia, West Virginia, and Washington DC) provides personal and commercial auto insurance. Commercial automobile and commercial multiperil insurance is offered through New York Merchant Bankers Insurance Company (New York). Personal auto and homeowners insurance is provided through the company's Home Mutual Insurance Company (Binghamton NY). The Westbrook Insurance Company (Connecticut) focuses on both personal and commercial automobile insurance. The Pinnacle Insurance Company (Carrollton GA) serves as the company's southeastern operations center and offers personal and commercial auto insurance.

## JEFFERSON INSURANCE GROUP
Newport Tower, 525 Washington Boulevard, Jersey City NJ 07310. 201/222-8666. **Fax:** 201/222-9161. **Contact:** Stella O'Hara, Supervisor of Recruitment and Training. **World Wide Web address:** http://www.jeffgroup.com. **Description:** A property and casualty insurance company. Member companies include Jefferson Insurance Company of New York, Monticello Insurance Company, and Jeffco Management Company, Inc. **Common positions include:** Accountant/Auditor; Actuary; Administrative Manager; Attorney; Claim Representative; Clerical Supervisor; Computer Programmer; Human Resources Manager; Human Service Worker; Quality Control Supervisor; Systems Analyst; Underwriter/Assistant Underwriter. **Educational backgrounds include:** Accounting; Finance; Marketing. **Benefits:** 401(k); Dental Insurance; Disability Coverage; Employee Discounts; Life Insurance; Medical Insurance; Pension Plan; Profit Sharing; Tuition Assistance. **Corporate headquarters location:** This Location. **Parent company:** Allianz (Germany). **Operations at this facility include:** Administration. **Listed on:** Privately held.

## MDA SERVICES
P.O. Box 14000, New Brunswick NJ 08906. 201/703-8000. **Contact:** Human Resources. **Description:** This location houses an automobile claims office. Overall, MDA Services provides personal lines of insurance.

## MERCK-MEDCO MANAGED CARE, L.L.C.
100 Summit Avenue, Montvale NJ 07645. 201/358-5400. **Contact:** Human Resources/Staffing. **Description:** Manages pharmaceutical benefits through contracts with HMOs. **Common positions include:** Account Manager; Account Representative; Accountant; Administrative Assistant; Assistant Manager; Attorney; Computer Programmer; Customer Service Representative; Financial Analyst; Human Resources Manager; Market Research Analyst; Marketing Manager; Marketing Specialist; Paralegal; Pharmacist; Physician; Public Relations Specialist; Purchasing Agent/Manager; Sales Executive; Secretary; Systems Analyst; Technical Writer/Editor. **Educational backgrounds include:** Accounting; Finance; Health Care; Marketing. **Benefits:** 401(k); Dental Insurance; Disability Coverage; Employee Discounts; Flexible Schedule; Life Insurance; Medical Insurance; Pension Plan; Savings Plan; Tuition Assistance. **Special programs:** Training. **Parent**

company: Merck & Co., Inc. (Whitehouse Station NJ) is a worldwide organization engaged in discovering, developing, producing, and marketing products for the maintenance of health and the environment. Products include human and animal pharmaceuticals and chemicals sold to the health care, oil exploration, food processing, textile, paper, and other industries. Merck also runs an ethical drug mail-order marketing business. **Listed on:** New York Stock Exchange. **Number of employees at this location:** 2,000. **Number of employees nationwide:** 10,000.

## METLIFE
501 U.S. Highway 22, Bridgewater NJ 08807. 908/253-1000. **Contact:** Human Resources. **Description:** An insurance provider.

## MOTOR CLUB OF AMERICA
95 Route 17 South, Paramus NJ 07653-0931. 201/291-2000. **Contact:** Human Resources. **Description:** Provides automobile insurance and operates through its subsidiaries. Founded in 1926. **Common positions include:** Accountant/Auditor; Adjuster; Claim Representative; Clerical Supervisor; Computer Programmer; Human Resources Manager; Insurance Agent/Broker; Systems Analyst; Travel Agent; Underwriter/Assistant Underwriter. **Benefits:** 401(k); Dental Insurance; Disability Coverage; Life Insurance; Medical Insurance. **Corporate headquarters location:** This Location. **Subsidiaries include:** Motor Club of America Enterprises; Motor Club of America Insurance Company. **Listed on:** NASDAQ. **Number of employees at this location:** 130.

## NEW JERSEY MANUFACTURERS INSURANCE COMPANY
301 Sullivan Way, Trenton NJ 08628. 609/883-1300. **Contact:** Human Resources. **Description:** An insurance provider.

## PRUDENTIAL HEALTHCARE
200 Wood Avenue South, Iselin NJ 08830-2706. 732/632-7000. **Contact:** Human Resources. **Description:** This location manages health care policies. Overall, Prudential is one of the largest insurance companies in North America and one of the largest diversified financial services organizations in the world. The company's primary business is to offer a full range of products and services in three areas: insurance, investment, and home ownership for individuals and families; health care management and other benefit programs for employees of companies and members of groups; and asset management for institutional clients and their associates. With a sales force of approximately 19,000 agents, 3,400 insurance brokers, and 6,000 financial advisors, the company insures or provides other financial services to more than 50 million people worldwide.

## PRUDENTIAL INSURANCE COMPANY OF AMERICA
23 Main Street, Holmdel NJ 07733. 732/946-5000. **Contact:** Human Resources. **Description:** One of the largest insurance and diversified financial services organizations in the world. The company's primary business is to offer a full range of products and services in three areas: insurance, investment, and home ownership for individuals and families; health care management and other benefit programs for employees of companies and members of groups; and asset management for institutional clients and their associates. With a sales force of approximately 19,000 agents, 3,400 insurance brokers, and 6,000 financial advisors, the company insures or provides other financial services to more than 50 million people worldwide. **Corporate headquarters location:** Newark NJ. **Number of employees worldwide:** 100,000.

## PRUDENTIAL INSURANCE COMPANY OF AMERICA
751 Broad Street, Newark NJ 07102. 973/802-8348. **Fax:** 973/802-7763. **Contact:** Human Resources Department. **Description:** One of the largest insurance companies in North America and one of the largest diversified financial services organizations in the world. The company's primary business is to offer a full range of products and services in three areas: insurance, investment, and home ownership for individuals and families; health care management and other benefit programs for employees of companies and members of groups; and asset management for institutional clients and their associates. With a sales force of approximately 19,000 agents, 3,400 insurance brokers, and 6,000 financial advisors, Prudential Insurance Company of America insures or provides other financial services to more than 50 million people worldwide. **Common positions include:** Accountant/Auditor; Actuary; Administrator; Computer Programmer; Human Resources Manager; Purchasing Agent/Manager; Underwriter/Assistant Underwriter. **Educational backgrounds include:** Accounting; Business Administration; Communications; Computer Science; Economics; Finance; Liberal Arts; Mathematics. **Benefits:** Daycare Assistance; Dental Insurance; Disability Coverage; Life Insurance; Medical Insurance; Pension Plan; Savings Plan; Tuition Assistance. **Special programs:** Internships. **Corporate headquarters location:** This Location. **Other U.S. locations:** Woodland Hills CA; Jacksonville FL; Minneapolis MN; Holmdel NJ; Roseland NJ; Philadelphia PA; Houston TX. **Listed on:** American Stock Exchange; NASDAQ; New York Stock

Exchange. **Annual sales/revenues:** More than $100 million. **Number of employees worldwide:** 100,000.

## PRUDENTIAL INSURANCE COMPANY OF AMERICA
80 Livingston Avenue, Roseland NJ 07068. 973/716-6000. **Contact:** Human Resources. **Description:** One of the largest insurance companies in North America and one of the largest diversified financial services organizations in the world. The company's primary business is to offer a full range of products and services in three areas: insurance, investment, and home ownership for individuals and families; health care management and other benefit programs for employees of companies and members of groups; and asset management for institutional clients and their associates. With a sales force of approximately 19,000 agents, 3,400 insurance brokers, and 6,000 financial advisors, the company insures or provides other financial services to more than 50 million people worldwide.

## ROBERT PLAN OF NEW JERSEY
P.O. Box 14000, New Brunswick NJ 08906. 732/777-5223. **Fax:** 732/777-5870. **Contact:** Lynn Schleckser, Human Resources Manager. **Description:** Provides insurance and insurance services for private passenger and homeowner risks. **NOTE:** Entry-level positions are offered. **Common positions include:** Adjuster; Attorney; Claim Representative; Clerical Supervisor; Computer Programmer; Customer Service Representative; Human Resources Manager; Paralegal; Underwriter/Assistant Underwriter. **Educational backgrounds include:** Business Administration; Liberal Arts. **Benefits:** 401(k); Dental Insurance; Disability Coverage; Employee Discounts; Flexible Schedule; Life Insurance; Medical Insurance. **Special programs:** Training. **Corporate headquarters location:** Uniondale NY. **Other U.S. locations:** CA; CT; FL; NY; PA; TX. **Subsidiaries include:** American Loss Control; Eagle Insurance; National Consumers Insurance Company; Newark Insurance Company. **Parent company:** The Robert Plan Corporation. **Listed on:** Privately held. **Number of employees at this location:** 450. **Number of employees nationwide:** 2,700.

## SELECTIVE INSURANCE COMPANY OF AMERICA
40 Wantage Avenue, Branchville NJ 07890-1000. 973/948-3000. **Contact:** Kim Burnett, Manager of Human Resources. **World Wide Web address:** http://www.selectiveinsurance.com. **Description:** Engaged in fire, marine, and casualty insurance.

*Note: Because addresses and telephone numbers of smaller companies can change rapidly, we recommend you call each company to verify the information below before inquiring about job opportunities. Mass mailings are not recommended.*

**Additional small employers:**

**INSURANCE AGENTS, BROKERS, AND SERVICES**

**Aegis Insurance Services Incorporated**
10 Exchange Pl, Jersey City NJ 07302. 201/521-1200.

**Associated Aviation Underwriters**
51 John F. Kennedy Pkwy, Short Hills NJ 07078-2702. 973/379-0800.

**Bollinger Fowler Co.**
PO Box 5000, Short Hills NJ 07078-5000. 973/467-0444.

**Citron Agency Inc.**
6 Carter Dr, Marlboro NJ 07746-1110. 732/972-9500.

**Crum & Forster Holdings Incorporated**
305 Madison Avenue, Morristown NJ 07960. 973/490-6600.

**Fireman's Fund Insurance Company**
PO Box 230, Parsippany NJ 07054-0230. 973/299-2989.

**GRE Insurance Group**
600 College Rd E, Ste 3000, Princeton NJ 08540-6636. 609/275-2760.

**Greater New York Mutual Insurance**
PO Box 1064, East Brunswick NJ 08816-1064. 732/238-6300.

**Hartford Fire Insurance Co.**
PO Box 1000, Rockaway NJ 07866-0700. 973/361-3700.

**J&H Marsh & McLennan Inc.**
PO Box 1966, Morristown NJ 07962-1966. 973/285-4600.

**J&H Marsh & McLennan Inc.**
PO Box 499, Parsippany NJ 07054-0499. 973/326-9300.

**Meeker Sharkey & MacBean**
PO Box 550, Cranford NJ 07016-0550. 908/272-8100.

**MIC**
PO Box 6770, Somerset NJ 08875-6779. 732/805-0100.

**National Insurance Association**
PO Box 285, Paramus NJ 07653-0285. 201/845-6600.

**Prudential Insurance**
PO Box 5500, Rockaway NJ 07866-5500. 973/989-4718.

**Prudential Insurance**
71 Hanover Rd, Florham Park NJ 07932-1502. 973/966-3000.

**Prudential Insurance**
PO Box 471, Millville NJ 08332-0471. 609/293-2000.

**Tribus Companies**
PO Box 927, Wayne NJ 07474-0927. 973/890-1818.

## INSURANCE COMPANIES

**Aetna US Healthcare**
55 Lane Rd, Fairfield NJ 07004-1011. 973/575-5600.

**Allstate Insurance Company**
1000 Midlantic Dr, Mount Laurel NJ 08054-1511. 609/273-2600.

**Allstate Insurance Company**
721 Rte 202-206, Bridgewater NJ 08807. 908/722-8100.

**American Insurance Company**
PO Box 230, Parsippany NJ 07054-0230. 973/299-1598.

**Amerihealth HMO**
8000 Midlantic Dr, Ste 333, Mount Laurel NJ 08054-1518. 609/778-6500.

**Atlas Assurance Company of America**
600 College Rd E, Princeton NJ 08540-6636. 609/275-2600.

**CGU Insurance**
PO Box 5028, Cherry Hill NJ 08034-0409. 609/273-8000.

**CGU Insurance**
PO Box 750, Florham Park NJ 07932-0750. 973/966-6060.

**Cigna Corporation**
401 White Horse Rd, Voorhees NJ 08043-2605. 609/346-5000.

**Cigna Corporation**
PO Box 2000, Marlton NJ 08053. 609/782-4300.

**Everest Reinsurance Company**
100 Mulberry Street, Ste 3, Newark NJ 07102. 973/802-8000.

**First Trenton Indemnity Company**
402 Lippincott Dr, Marlton NJ 08053-4112. 609/983-2400.

**Great American Insurance Co.**
PO Box 318, Parsippany NJ 07054-0318. 973/887-4800.

**Hanover Insurance Company**
860 Centennial Ave, Piscataway NJ 08854-3936. 732/457-0577.

**Harleysville Mutual Insurance Co.**
PO Box 967, Marlton NJ 08053-0967. 609/983-7022.

**Kemper Insurance Co.**
25 De Forest Ave, Summit NJ 07901. 908/522-4000.

**Liberty Mutual Insurance Co.**
Park 80 Plz E, Rochelle Park NJ 07662. 201/845-4300.

**Liberty Mutual Insurance Co.**
100 Franklin Square Drive, Somerset NJ 08873-4109. 732/563-6800.

**Maryland Casualty Company**
20 Waterview Blvd, Parsippany NJ 07054-1229. 973/402-8300.

**MBI Life Assurance Corp.**
520 Broad St, Newark NJ 07102-3111. 973/481-8000.

**Medical Inter-Insurance Exchange**
2 Princess Rd, Trenton NJ 08648-2302. 609/896-2404.

**MetLife**
600 Parsippany Road, Parsippany NJ 07054-3715. 973/884-6500.

**MTF**
293 Eisenhower Pkwy, Livingston NJ 07039-1711. 973/533-1165.

**New Jersey Manufacturers Insurance Co.**
1599 Littleton Rd, Parsippany NJ 07054-3803. 973/455-7200.

**Nile Care Health Plans**
400 Kelby St, Fort Lee NJ 07024-2937. 201/363-5500.

**Oxford Health Plans Incorporated**
399 Thornall St, Edison NJ 08837-2236. 732/632-9494.

**Princeton Insurance Company**
PO Box 5322, Princeton NJ 08543-5322. 609/452-9404.

**Prudential Insurance**
1201 New Rd, Linwood NJ 08221-1129. 609/926-2400.

**Seaboard Surety Company**
Burnt Mills Rd, RR 206, Bedminster NJ 07921. 908/658-3500.

**Signet Star Reinsurance Company**
PO Box 853, Florham Park NJ 07932-0853. 973/301-8000.

**St. Paul Fire & Marine Insurance Co.**
PO Box 203, Iselin NJ 08830-0203. 732/494-3800.

**State Farm Fire & Casualty**
1750 Rte 23, Wayne NJ 07470. 973/305-7441.

**Sumitomo Marine & Fire Insurance Co.**
15 Independence Boulevard, Warren NJ 07059-2713. 908/604-2900.

**Wausau Insurance Companies**
10 Rooney Cir, West Orange NJ 07052-3308. 973/736-5000.

**Western World Insurance Company**
PO Box 607, Franklin Lakes NJ 07417-0607. 201/847-8600.

## For more information on career opportunities in insurance:

### Associations

**ALLIANCE OF AMERICAN INSURERS**
3025 Highland Parkway, Suite 800, Downers Grove IL 60515. 630/724-2100. World Wide Web address: http://www.allianceai.org.

**HEALTH INSURANCE ASSOCIATION OF AMERICA**
555 13th Street NW, Suite 600E, Washington DC 20004. 202/824-1600. World Wide Web address: http://www.hiaa.org.

**INSURANCE INFORMATION INSTITUTE**
110 William Street, New York NY 10038. 212/669-9200. World Wide Web address: http://www.iii.org. Provides information on property/casualty insurance issues.

**NATIONAL ASSOCIATION OF PROFESSIONAL INSURANCE AGENTS**
400 North Washington Street, Alexandria VA 22314. 703/836-9340 World Wide Web address: http://www.pianet.com.

**SOCIETY OF ACTUARIES**
475 North Martingale Road, Suite 800, Schaumburg IL 60173. 847/706-3500. World Wide Web address: http://www.soa.org.

### Directories

**NATIONAL DIRECTORY OF HEALTH PLANS**
American Association of Health Plans, 1129 20th Street NW, Suite 600, Washington DC 20036. 202/778-3200. World Wide Web address: http://www.aahp.org.

**INSURANCE ALMANAC**
Underwriter Printing and Publishing Company, 50 East Palisade Avenue, Englewood NJ 07631. 201/569-8808. Available at libraries.

**INSURANCE PHONE BOOK**
Reed Elsevier Inc., 121 Chanlon Road, New Providence NJ 07974. Toll-free phone: 800/521-8110. $89.95, new editions available every other year. Also available at libraries.

Magazines

**BEST'S REVIEW**
A.M. Best Company, Ambest Road, Oldwick NJ 08858. 908/439-2200. World Wide Web address: http://www.ambest.com. Monthly.

**INSURANCE JOURNAL**
Wells Publishing, 9191 Towne Centre Drive, Suite 550, San Diego, CA 92122-1231. 619/455-7717. World Wide Web address: http://www.insurancejrnl.

com. A biweekly magazine covering the insurance industry for the western United States.

Online Services

**FINANCIAL, ACCOUNTING, AND INSURANCE JOBS PAGE**
http://www.nationjob.com/financial. This Website provides a list of financial, accounting, and insurance job openings.

**THE INSURANCE CAREER CENTER**
http://connectyou.com/talent. Offers job openings, career resources, and a resume database for jobseekers looking to get into the insurance field.

**INSURANCE NATIONAL SEARCH**
http://www.insurancerecruiters.com/insjobs/jobs.htm. Provides a searchable database of job openings in the insurance industry. The site is run by Insurance National Search, Inc.

# LEGAL SERVICES

*Prospective lawyers will continue to face intense competition through the year 2006, due to the overabundance of law school graduates. Consequently, fewer lawyers are working for major law firms, and are working instead for smaller firms, corporations, and associations, according to the U.S. Department of Commerce. Large corporations are establishing in-house legal departments to avoid paying for the services of expensive, big-name law offices.*

*According to the U.S. Department of Labor, paralegals comprise the fastest-growing profession in legal services, and will be one of the fastest-growing professions overall through 2006. Paralegals are assuming more responsibilities in areas such as real estate and trademark law. Private law firms will hire the most paralegals, but a vast array of other organizations also employ them including insurance companies, real estate firms, and banks. Legal secretaries will see moderate growth through 2006.*

**GREENBAUM, ROWE, SMITH, RAVIN, DAVIS**
P.O. Box 5600, Woodbridge NJ 07095. 732/549-5600. **Contact:** Pauline Dawson, Recruiting. **Description:** A law firm specializing in leveraged buy-outs, employment, and environmental law.

**HANNOCH WEISMAN**
4 Becker Farm Road, Roseland NJ 07068. 973/535-5417. **Fax:** 973/994-7198. **Contact:** Ms. Gayle Englert, Human Resources Director. **E-mail address:** genglert@hannoch.com. **World Wide Web address:** http://www.hannoch.com. **Description:** A law firm with main practice areas in business and counseling litigation and environmental law. Founded in 1960. **Common positions include:** Accountant; Administrative Assistant; Administrative Manager; Attorney; Chief Financial Officer; Controller; Database Manager; Human Resources Manager; Internet Services Manager; Marketing Manager; MIS Specialist; Paralegal; Secretary; Software Engineer; Systems Analyst; Typist/Word Processor. **Educational backgrounds include:** Accounting; Business Administration; Finance; Health Care; Marketing; Software Development; Software Tech. Support. **Benefits:** 401(k); Dental Insurance; Flexible Schedule; Life Insurance; Medical Insurance; Profit Sharing; Tuition Assistance. **Corporate headquarters location:** This Location. **Managing Partner:** William Heller. **Facilities Manager:** Martin McCaffrey. **Number of employees at this location:** 200.

**LeBOEUF, LAMB, GREENE & MACRAE LLP**
One Riverfront Plaza, Newark NJ 07102. 973/643-8000. **Contact:** Theodore Aden, Hiring Attorney. **Description:** A law firm.

**SMITH STRATTON WISE HEHER & BRENNAN**
600 College Road East, Princeton NJ 08540. 609/924-6000. **Contact:** Personnel. **Description:** A law firm. Founded in 1948.

**WILENTZ, GOLDMAN & SPITZER**
90 Woodbridge Center Drive, Suite 900, P.O. Box 10, Woodbridge NJ 07095. 732/636-8000. **Contact:** Human Resources. **Description:** A law firm.

*Note: Because addresses and telephone numbers of smaller companies can change rapidly, we recommend you call each company to verify the information below before inquiring about job opportunities. Mass mailings are not recommended.*

**Additional small employers:**

**LEGAL SERVICES**

**Archer & Greiner PC**
PO Box 3000, Haddonfield NJ 08033-0968. 609/795-2121.

**Bathgate Wegener and Wolf PC**
PO Box 2043, Lakewood NJ 08701-8043. 732/363-0666.

**Bressler Amery & Ross**
PO Box 1980, Morristown NJ 07962-1980. 973/514-1200.

**Brown & Connery LLP**
PO Box 539, Collingswood NJ
08108-0539. 609/854-8900.

**Buchanan Ingersoll**
500 College Rd E, Princeton NJ
08540-6635. 609/987-6800.

**Budd Larner Gross Rosenbaum**
150 John F. Kennedy Pkwy,
Short Hills NJ 07078-2701.
973/379-4800.

**Capehart & Scatchard**
8000 Midlantic Dr, Mount Laurel
NJ 08054-1518. 609/234-6800.

**Cole Schotz Meisel Forman**
PO Box 800, Hackensack NJ
07602-0800. 201/489-3000.

**Connell Foley & Geiser**
85 Livingston Ave, Roseland NJ
07068-3702. 973/535-0500.

**Dan Riker Scherer Hyland**
PO Box 1981, Morristown NJ
07962-1981. 973/538-0800.

**Davis Reberkenny & Abramowitz**
PO Box 5459, Cherry Hill NJ
08034-0480. 609/667-6000.

**Drinker Biddle & Reath**
105 College Rd E, Princeton NJ
08540-6622. 609/921-6336.

**Giordano Halleran & Ciesla**
PO Box 190, Middletown NJ
07748-0190. 732/741-3900.

**Goldenberg Mackler & Sayegh**
1030 Atlantic Ave, Atlantic City
NJ 08401-7427. 609/344-7131.

**Goldfein & Joseph**
3 Vaughn Dr Ste 115, Princeton
NJ 08540-6313. 609/683-9030.

**Green Lundgren & Ryan**
PO Box 70, Haddonfield NJ
08033-0085. 609/428-5800.

**Grotta Glassman & Hoffman**
75 Livingston Ave, Roseland NJ
07068-3701. 973/992-4800.

**Hill Wallack**
CN 5226, Princeton NJ 08543.
609/924-0808.

**Hoagland Longo Moran Dunst & Doukas**
PO Box 480, New Brunswick NJ
08903-0480. 732/545-4717.

**Hoffman DiMuzio & Hoffman**
PO Box 7, Woodbury NJ 08096-
7007. 609/845-8243.

**Horn Goldberg Gorney Plackter Wyce & Perskie**
1300 Atlantic Ave, Ste 500,
Atlantic City NJ 08401-7228.
609/348-4515.

**Jamieson More Peskin Spicer**
300 Alexander Park, Princeton NJ
08540-6308. 609/452-0808.

**Katz Ettin Levine Kruzweil**
905 Kings Hwy N, Cherry Hill
NJ 08034-1536. 609/667-6440.

**Lowenstein Sandler Kohl**
65 Livingston Ave, Roseland NJ
07068-1725. 973/992-8700.

**McCarter & English**
PO Box 652, Newark NJ 07101-
0652. 973/622-4444.

**McCarter & English**
1820 Chapel Ave W, Ste 80,
Cherry Hill NJ 08002-4610.
609/662-8444.

**Morgan Melhuish Monaghan**
651 W Mount Pleasant Ave,
Livingston NJ 07039-1600.
973/994-2500.

**Norris McLaughlin Marcus**
PO Box 1018, Somerville NJ
08876-1018. 908/722-0700.

**Parker McCay & Criscuolo PC**
3 Greentree Center, Marlton NJ
08053-3215. 609/596-8900.

**Pellettier & Altman**
PO Box CN 5301, Princeton NJ
08540. 609/520-0900.

**Pitney Hardin Kipp & Szuch**
PO Box 1945, Morristown NJ
07962-1945. 973/966-6300.

**Porzio Bromberg & Newman**
163 Madison Ave, Morristown
NJ 07960-7324. 973/538-4006.

**Reed Smith Shaw & McClay**
136 Main St, Princeton NJ 08540-
5735. 609/951-2200.

**Shanley & Fisher PC**
131 Madison Ave, Morristown
NJ 07960-6086. 973/285-1000.

**Sherman Silverstein Kohl**
4300 Haddonfield Rd,
Merchantville NJ 08109-3376.
609/662-0700.

**Sills Cummis Zuckerman**
1 Riverfront Plz, Newark NJ
07102-5401. 973/643-3232.

**Slimm & Goldberg**
PO Box 2222, Camden NJ 08108-
0220. 609/858-7200.

**Stark & Stark**
PO Box 5315, Princeton NJ
08543-5315. 609/896-9060.

**Sterns & Weinroth PC**
PO Box 1298, Trenton NJ 08607-
1298. 609/392-2100.

**Tomar Sominoff Adurian O'Brien PC**
20 Brace Rd, Cherry Hill NJ
08034-2633. 609/429-1100.

**Wolff & Samson**
5 Becker Farm Rd, Roseland NJ
07068-1727. 973/740-0500.

## For more information on career opportunities in legal services:

### Associations

**AMERICAN BAR ASSOCIATION**
750 North Lake Shore Drive, Chicago IL 60611.
312/988-5000. World Wide Web address: http://www.
abanet.org.

**FEDERAL BAR ASSOCIATION**
1815 H Street NW, Suite 408, Washington DC 20006-
3697. 202/638-0252. World Wide Web address:
http://www.fedbar.org.

**NATIONAL ASSOCIATION OF LEGAL ASSISTANTS**
1516 South Boston Avenue, Suite 200, Tulsa OK
74119-4013. 918/587-6828. World Wide Web
address: http://www.nala.org. An educational
association. Memberships are available.

**NATIONAL FEDERATION OF PARALEGAL ASSOCIATIONS**
P.O. Box 33108, Kansas City MO 64114-0108.
816/941-4000. World Wide Web address: http://www.
paralegals.org. Offers magazines, seminars, and
Internet job listings.

**NATIONAL PARALEGAL ASSOCIATION**
Box 406, Solebury PA 18963. 215/297-8333. World
Wide Web address: http://www.nationalparalegal.org.

### Directories

**MARTINDALE-HUBBELL LAW DIRECTORY**
121 Chanlon Road, New Providence NJ 07974.
800/526-4902. World Wide Web address: http://www.
martindale.com. A directory consisting exclusively of
the names of legal employers. In all, listings for over

900,000 lawyers and law firms are available. In addition to information regarding firms and practices, the information includes biographies of many individual lawyers. Thus, you can search for firm names, law schools attended, and field of law.

## Newsletters

### LAWYERS WEEKLY USA
Lawyers Weekly, Inc., 41 West Street, Boston MA 02111. Toll-free phone: 800/444-5297. World Wide Web address: http://www.lawyersweekly.com. A newsletter that profiles law firms, provides general industry information, and provides information on jobs nationwide.

## Online Services

### COURT REPORTERS FORUM
Go: CrForum. A CompuServe networking forum that includes information from the *Journal of Court Reporting*.

### LEGAL EXCHANGE
Jump to: Legal Exchange. A debate forum for lawyers and other legal professionals, offered through Prodigy.

### LEGAL INFORMATION NETWORK
Keyword: LIN. An America Online networking resource for paralegals, family law specialists, social security specialists, and law students.

# MANUFACTURING: MISCELLANEOUS CONSUMER

*Greater globalization is the trend in consumer manufacturing as worldwide and regional trade agreements reduce barriers and provide more uniform trade standards. Demand for household goods is cyclical and depends on the state of the economy and the disposable income of consumers. The distribution of these goods is more dependent on large discount retailers, and despite the strong but turbulent economy of 1998, consumer confidence is still relatively high.*

*A new trend in manufacturing is toward supercontractors, businesses that contract with a major company to do its manufacturing, distributing, and product servicing. According to* Business Week, *one such company is the Solectron Corporation, which manufactures printers for Hewlett-Packard. Such arrangements allow the major company, such as Hewlett-Packard, to devote more of its resources to research and development. The relationship is helping the U.S. manufacturing process to become more efficient, and therefore, globally competitive.*

*In general, manufacturing jobs will continue to decrease as the economy shifts toward service industries. The Bureau of Labor Statistics estimates a loss of 350,000 manufacturing jobs by 2006. Companies such as Kodak and Gillette have recently laid off thousands of workers, and Kodak expects to cut more than 12,000 more jobs by 2000. Factory automation -- including wireless communications, distributed intelligence, and centralized computer control -- is one major cause for the loss of manufacturing jobs. Growing competition has forced some companies to streamline production by replacing workers with computers in the areas of inventory tracking, shipping, and ordering. Individuals who have a working knowledge of these software applications will have an edge over less technically experienced jobseekers.*

**AMERICAN HOME PRODUCTS CORPORATION**
5 Giralda Farms, Madison NJ 07940. 973/660-5000. **Contact:** Human Resources. **World Wide Web address:** http://www.ahp.com. **Description:** Manufactures and markets prescription drugs and medical supplies, packaged medicines, food products, household products, and housewares. Each division operates through one or more of American Home Products Corporation's subsidiaries. Prescription Drugs and Medical Supplies operates through: Wyeth-Ayerst Laboratories (produces ethical pharmaceuticals, biologicals, nutritional products, over-the-counter antacids, vitamins, and sunburn remedies); Ives Laboratories (ethical pharmaceuticals); Fort Dodge Laboratories (veterinary pharmaceuticals and biologicals); Sherwood Medical (medical devices, diagnostic instruments, test kits, and bacteria identification systems); and Corometrics Medical Systems (medical electronic instrumentation for obstetrics and neonatology). The Packaged Medicines segment operates through Whitehall Laboratories (produces analgesics, cold remedies, and other packaged medicines). The Food Products segment operates through American Home Foods (canned pasta, canned vegetables, specialty foods, mustard, and popcorn). The Household Products and Housewares segment operates through: Boyle-Midway (cleaners, insecticides, air fresheners, waxes, polishes, and other items for home, appliance, and apparel care); Dupli-Color Products (touch-up, refinishing, and other car care and shop-use products); Ekco Products (food containers, commercial baking pans, industrial coatings, food-handling systems, foilware, and plasticware); Ekco Housewares (cookware, cutlery, kitchen tools, tableware and accessories, and padlocks); and Prestige Group (cookware, cutlery, kitchen tools, carpet sweepers, and pressure cookers). **Corporate headquarters location:** This Location.

**AMERICAN HOME PRODUCTS CORPORATION**
One Campus Drive, Parsippany NJ 07054. 973/683-2000. **Contact:** Human Resources. **World Wide Web address:** http://www.ahp.com. **Description:** Manufactures and markets prescription drugs and medical supplies, packaged medicines, food products, household products, and housewares. Each division operates through one or more of American Home Products Corporation's subsidiaries. Prescription Drugs and Medical Supplies operates through: Wyeth-Ayerst Laboratories (produces ethical pharmaceuticals, biologicals, nutritional products, over-the-counter antacids, vitamins, and sunburn remedies); Ives Laboratories (ethical pharmaceuticals); Fort Dodge Laboratories (veterinary pharmaceuticals and biologicals); Sherwood Medical (medical devices, diagnostic instruments, test kits, and bacteria identification systems); and Corometrics Medical Systems (medical electronic instrumentation for obstetrics and neonatology). The Packaged Medicines segment operates through Whitehall Laboratories (produces analgesics, cold remedies, and other packaged medicines). The Food Products segment operates through American Home Foods (canned pasta, canned vegetables, specialty foods, mustard, and popcorn). The Household Products and Housewares segment operates through: Boyle-Midway (cleaners, insecticides, air fresheners, waxes, polishes, and other items for home, appliance, and apparel care); Dupli-Color Products (touch-up, refinishing, and other car care and shop-use products); Ekco Products (food containers, commercial baking pans, industrial coatings, food-handling systems, foilware, and plasticware); Ekco Housewares (cookware, cutlery, kitchen tools, tableware and accessories, and padlocks); and Prestige Group (cookware, cutlery, kitchen tools, carpet sweepers, and pressure cookers). **Corporate headquarters location:** Madison NJ.

**BAYER CORPORATION**
**AGFA CORPORATION**
100 Challenger Road, Ridgefield Park NJ 07660-2199. 201/440-2500. **Contact:** Human Resources. **World Wide Web address:** http://www.agfahome.com. **Description:** This location manufactures photographic imaging equipment and film. Overall, the company produces polyurethane raw materials, polymer thermoplastic resins and blends, coatings, industrial chemicals, and other related products.

**BROTHER INTERNATIONAL CORPORATION**
100 Somerset Corporate Boulevard, Bridgewater NJ 08807. 908/704-1700. **Contact:** Human Resources. **World Wide Web address:** http://www.brother.com. **Description:** One of America's largest manufacturers and distributors of personal word processors and portable electronic typewriters. Brother also markets many industrial products, home appliances, and business machines manufactured by its parent company. Founded in 1954. **Corporate headquarters location:** This Location. **Parent company:** Brother Industries, Ltd. (Nagoya, Japan). **Number of employees nationwide:** 1,300.

**C/S GROUP**
3 Werner Way, Lebanon NJ 08833. 908/236-0800. **Fax:** 908/236-0604. **Contact:** Lee DiRubbo, Director of Human Resources. **Description:** Manufactures decorative window products, including louvres and screens. Founded in 1948. **NOTE:** Entry-level positions are offered. **Common positions include:** Account Manager; Accountant/Auditor; Customer Service Rep.; Design Engineer; Draftsperson; Management Trainee; Sales Manager; Sales Rep.; Systems Analyst. **Educational backgrounds include:** Accounting; Computer Science; Engineering. **Benefits:** 401(k); Dental Insurance; Disability Coverage; Life Insurance; Medical Insurance; Profit Sharing; Savings Plan; Tuition Assistance. **Corporate headquarters location:** This Location. **Other U.S. locations:** Garden Grove CA; Muncy PA. **International locations:** France; Spain; United Kingdom. **Operations at this facility include:** Divisional Headquarters. **Listed on:** Privately held. **Annual sales/revenues:** More than $100 million. **Number of employees at this location:** 100. **Number of employees nationwide:** 420. **Number of employees worldwide:** 900.

**CCTV CORPORATION**
280 Huyler, South Hackensack NJ 07606. 201/489-9595. **Contact:** Gary Perlin, Sales Manager. **Description:** Produces a wide variety of video equipment, including cameras and monitors. **Corporate headquarters location:** This Location.

**CASIO INC.**
570 Mount Pleasant Avenue, Dover NJ 07801. 973/361-5400. **Contact:** Human Resources. **World Wide Web address:** http://www.casio.com. **Description:** A manufacturer of consumer electronics and computer-based products.

**COLGATE-PALMOLIVE COMPANY**
191 East Hanover Avenue, Morristown NJ 07962. 973/631-9000. **Contact:** Human Resources. **Description:** This location manufactures baby products and deodorant. Overall, Colgate-Palmolive

Company manufactures and markets a wide variety of products in the U.S. and around the world in two business segments: Oral, Personal, and Household Care; and Specialty Marketing. Oral, Personal, and Household Care products include toothpastes, oral rinses and toothbrushes, bar and liquid soaps, shampoos, conditioners, deodorants and antiperspirants, baby and shaving products, laundry and dishwashing detergents, fabric softeners, cleansers and cleaners, and bleach. Specialty Marketing products include pet dietary care products, crystal tableware, and portable fuel for warming food. Principal global trademarks and tradenames include Colgate, Palmolive, Mennen, Ajax, Fab, and Science Diet, in addition to various regional tradenames. **Corporate headquarters location:** New York NY. **Other U.S. locations:** Kansas City KS; Cambridge MA; Piscataway NJ.

**COLGATE-PALMOLIVE COMPANY**
**TECHNOLOGY CENTER**
909 River Road, Box 1343, Piscataway NJ 08855-1343. 732/878-7936. **Contact:** Human Resources Staffing Department. **Description:** This location houses a research and development facility. Overall, Colgate-Palmolive Company manufactures and markets a wide variety of products in the U.S. and around the world in two business segments: Oral, Personal, and Household Care; and Specialty Marketing. Oral, Personal, and Household Care products include toothpastes, oral rinses and toothbrushes, bar and liquid soaps, shampoos, conditioners, deodorants and antiperspirants, baby and shaving products, laundry and dishwashing detergents, fabric softeners, cleansers and cleaners, and bleach. Specialty Marketing products include pet dietary care products, crystal tableware, and portable fuel for warming food. Principal global trademarks and brand names include Colgate, Palmolive, Mennen, Ajax, Fab, and Science Diet, in addition to various regional brand names. **NOTE:** When submitting resumes, please include appropriate mail codes (for engineering or research positions, use Mail Code JHO and for secretarial or administrative positions, use Mail Code MG). **Common positions include:** Accountant/Auditor; Biological Scientist; Chemical Engineer; Chemist; Clinical Lab Technician; Computer Programmer; Dental Assistant/Dental Hygienist; Environmental Engineer; Financial Analyst; Human Resources Manager; Mechanical Engineer; Paralegal; Software Engineer; Systems Analyst; Technical Writer/Editor. **Educational backgrounds include:** Accounting; Biology; Business Administration; Chemistry; Computer Science; Engineering; Finance; Human Resources; Liberal Arts. **Benefits:** 401(k); Dental Insurance; Disability Coverage; Employee Discounts; Life Insurance; Medical Insurance; Pension Plan; Savings Plan; Tuition Assistance. **Special programs:** Internships. **Corporate headquarters location:** New York NY. **Other U.S. locations:** Kansas City KS; Cambridge MA; Morristown NJ. **Operations at this facility include:** Administration; Manufacturing; Research and Development. **Number of employees at this location:** 1,000.

**CONCORD CAMERA CORPORATION**
35 Mileed Way, Avenel NJ 07001. 732/499-8280. **Contact:** Human Resources. **Description:** Designs, engineers, manufactures, imports, markets, and distributes cameras and related accessories worldwide, including flashes and camera cases.

**COSMAIR, INC.**
222 Terminal Avenue, Clark NJ 07066. 732/499-2838. **Contact:** Human Resources Department. **Description:** Cosmair, Inc. is a manufacturer of personal care products including hair dyes and shampoo.

**DOUGLAS STEVEN PLASTICS**
P.O. Box 2775, Paterson NJ 07509. 973/523-3030. **Contact:** Human Resources. **Description:** Manufactures plastic food trays and serving platters.

**DURO-TEST CORPORATION**
9 Law Drive, Fairfield NJ 07004. 973/808-1800. **Contact:** Employment Manager. **Description:** Manufactures light bulbs.

**EDEN LLC**
812 Jersey Avenue, Jersey City NJ 07310. 201/656-3331. **Fax:** 201/656-3070. **Contact:** Human Resources. **Description:** A distributor and overseas manufacturer of children's toys and gifts. **Common positions include:** Accountant/Auditor; Administrative Assistant; Budget Analyst; Buyer; Claim Representative; Computer Programmer; Cost Estimator; Credit Manager; Customer Service Representative; Designer; Graphic Designer; Human Resources Manager; Marketing Manager; Mechanical Engineer; Purchasing Agent/Manager; Quality Control Supervisor; Systems Analyst. **Educational backgrounds include:** Accounting; Art/Design; Business Administration; Communications; Computer Science; Engineering; Finance; Liberal Arts; Marketing. **Benefits:** 401(k); Dental Insurance; Disability Coverage; Employee Discounts; Life Insurance; Medical Insurance; Pension Plan; Tuition Assistance. **Special programs:** Internships. **Corporate headquarters location:** This Location. **Other U.S. locations:** Los Angeles CA; San Francisco CA;

Atlanta GA; Chicago IL; Boston MA; Dallas TX. **Parent company:** Penguin Books. **Operations at this facility include:** Administration. **Number of employees at this location:** 170. **Number of employees nationwide:** 200.

## EFFANBEE DOLL COMPANY
19 Lexington Avenue, East Brunswick NJ 08816. 732/613-3852. **Contact:** Personnel Director. **Description:** Manufactures dolls. **Corporate headquarters location:** This Location.

## FEDDERS CORPORATION
505 Martinsville Road, P.O. Box 813, Liberty Corner NJ 07938. 908/604-8686. **Contact:** Human Resources. **World Wide Web address:** http://www.fedders.com. **Description:** One of the largest manufacturers and marketers of room air conditioners in North America. Brand names include Fedders, Emerson Quiet Kool, and Airtemp. The company also produces private-label brand air conditioners and dehumidifiers by Emerson Quiet Kool.

## GEMINI INDUSTRIES INC.
215 Entin Road, Clifton NJ 07014. 973/471-9050. **Contact:** Human Resources. **Description:** Manufactures PC and cellular telephone accessories, remote controls, and cable.

## GRAPHIC CONTROLS CORPORATION
One Carnegie Plaza, Cherry Hill NJ 08003-1020. 609/424-2200. **Contact:** Human Resources. **Description:** Manufactures and wholesales disposable writing instruments.

## GUEST SUPPLY INC.
4301 U.S. Highway One, P.O. Box 902, Monmouth Junction NJ 08852-0902. 609/514-9696. **Fax:** 609/514-7379. **Contact:** Joan Constanza, Human Resources Representative. **Description:** Manufactures, packages, and distributes personal care products, housekeeping supplies, room accessories, and textiles to the lodging industry. The company also manufactures and packages products for major retail and consumer products companies. Founded in 1979. **NOTE:** Entry-level positions and second and third shifts are offered. **Common positions include:** Account Manager; Account Rep.; Accountant; Blue-Collar Worker Supervisor; Buyer; Chemist; Chief Financial Officer; Controller; Credit Manager; Customer Service Rep.; Database Manager; Design Engineer; Finance Director; Financial Analyst; Graphic Artist; Graphic Designer; Human Resources Manager; Industrial Engineer; Industrial Production Manager; Manufacturing Engineer; Marketing Manager; Marketing Specialist; MIS Specialist; Operations/Production Manager; Purchasing Agent/Manager; Quality Control Supervisor; Sales Executive; Sales Manager; Sales Rep.; Secretary; Systems Analyst; Systems Manager; Telecommunications Manager; Transportation/ Traffic Specialist; Typist/Word Processor. **Benefits:** 401(k); Dental Insurance; Disability Coverage; Life Insurance; Medical Insurance; Savings Plan. **Corporate headquarters location:** This Location. **Other U.S. locations:** Nationwide. **Subsidiaries include:** Brecken-Ridge-Remy; Guest Distribution; Guest Packaging. **Operations at this facility include:** Divisional Headquarters; Regional Headquarters. **Listed on:** New York Stock Exchange. **Stock exchange symbol:** GSY. **Annual sales/revenues:** More than $100 million. **Number of employees at this location:** 1,000.

## HARTZ MOUNTAIN CORPORATION
400 Plaza Drive, Secaucus NJ 07094. 201/271-4800. **Contact:** Human Resources. **Description:** Engaged in the manufacture, packaging, and distribution of consumer products including pet foods, pet accessories, livestock feed and products; chemical products; home carpet-cleaning products; and equipment rentals. **Corporate headquarters location:** This Location. **Other U.S. locations:** Bloomfield NJ. **Subsidiaries include:** Cooper Pet Supply; Permaline Manufacturing Corporation; Sternco-Dominion Real Estate Corporation; The Pet Library Ltd. **Listed on:** American Stock Exchange.

## HOME CARE INDUSTRIES
One Lisbon Street, Clifton NJ 07013. 973/365-1600. **Contact:** Human Resources. **Description:** Manufactures vacuum cleaner bags.

## HUCK JACOBSON MANUFACTURING COMPANY INC.
One Mark Road, Kenilworth NJ 07033. 908/686-0200. **Contact:** Christine Sapienza, Personnel. **Description:** Manufactures and distributes a broad line of consumer home-maintenance equipment, including lawn mowers, and other lawn-care products, tractors, and snowblowers. **Parent company:** Textron Inc.

## JOHNSON & JOHNSON
One J&J Plaza, New Brunswick NJ 08933. **Contact:** Human Resources. **Description:** A health care products company. Products include pain relievers, contact lenses, pharmaceuticals, bandages,

toothbrushes, and surgical instruments under brand names including Reach, Band-Aid, and Acuvue. **NOTE:** This firm does not accept unsolicited resumes. Please only respond to advertised openings. **Corporate headquarters location:** This Location.

### JOHNSON & JOHNSON CONSUMER PRODUCTS, INC.
199 Grandview Road, Skillman NJ 08858. 908/874-1000. **Contact:** Employment Management Center. **World Wide Web address:** http://www.jnj.com. **Description:** A health care products company. Johnson & Johnson products include pain relievers, contact lenses, pharmaceuticals, bandages, toothbrushes, and surgical instruments under brand names, including Reach, Band-Aid, and Acuvue. The company has manufacturing subsidiaries in over 40 countries.

### KREMENTZ & COMPANY
375 McCarter Highway, Newark NJ 07114. 973/621-8300. **Contact:** Grace Reed, Personnel Director. **Description:** A manufacturer and distributor of fine jewelry and related items.

### LENOX INC.
100 Lenox Drive, Lawrenceville NJ 08648. 609/896-2800. **Contact:** Human Resources. **World Wide Web address:** http://www.lenox.com. **Description:** Manufactures china and crystal dinnerware and tableware.

### LETRASET/NIELSEN & BAINBRIDGE
40 Eisenhower Drive, Paramus NJ 07652. 201/845-6100. **Contact:** Dorothy Uhler, Personnel Director. **Description:** Produces and distributes graphic arts products, including transferable lettering and markers, color products, and software products. **Common positions include:** Accountant/Auditor; Administrator; Customer Service Representative; Sales Executive. **Educational backgrounds include:** Accounting; Finance; Marketing. **Benefits:** 401(k); Dental Insurance; Disability Coverage; Life Insurance; Medical Insurance. **Parent company:** Esselte. **Operations at this facility include:** Administration; Divisional Headquarters; Service.

### MAGLA PRODUCTS INC.
P.O. Box 1934, Morristown NJ 07962-1934. 973/377-0500. **Contact:** Human Resources. **Description:** Manufactures kitchen and domestic household textiles including ironing-board covers, dish towels, oven mitts, rubber gloves, disposable wipe cloths, and cling sheets. Principal customers are department store chains. **Corporate headquarters location:** This Location.

### MATTEL INC.
6000 Midlantic Drive, Mount Laurel NJ 08054. 609/234-7400. **Contact:** Barbara Rose, Personnel Manager. **World Wide Web address:** http://www.mattel.com. **Description:** This location performs marketing activities for the toy manufacturer. Overall, Mattel manufactures and distributes toys, electronic products, games, books, hobby products, and family entertainment products. **Corporate headquarters location:** El Segundo CA.

### MYRON MANUFACTURING CORPORATION
205 Maywood Avenue, Maywood NJ 07607. 201/845-6161. **Contact:** Human Resources. **Description:** Manufactures a line of custom-made vinyl products (including pocket calendars) for the office and business markets. **Common positions include:** Accountant; Computer Programmer; Customer Service Rep.; Department Manager; General Manager; Management Trainee; Marketing Specialist; Purchasing Agent/Manager; Quality Control Supervisor; Systems Analyst. **Educational backgrounds include:** Accounting; Business Administration; Finance; Marketing. **Benefits:** Dental Insurance; Disability Coverage; Employee Discounts; Life Insurance; Medical Insurance; Pension Plan; Savings Plan; Tuition Assistance. **Corporate headquarters location:** This Location.

### PENTECH INTERNATIONAL INC.
195 Carter Drive, Edison NJ 08817. 732/287-6640. **Contact:** Ms. Libby Melnick, Owner. **Description:** Designs, manufactures, and markets pencils, pens, markers, activity sets, and accessories. **Corporate headquarters location:** This Location.

### POWER BATTERY COMPANY
25 McLean Boulevard, Paterson NJ 07514. 973/523-8630. **Contact:** Human Resources. **Description:** Manufactures batteries for automobiles, computers, and small electronic appliances.

### PRINCE SPORTS GROUP
One Sportsystem Plaza, Bordentown NJ 08505-9630. 609/291-5800. **Toll-free phone:** 800/283-6647. **Fax:** 609/291-5791. **Contact:** Mike Soroker, Vice President of Human Resources. **World Wide Web address:** http://www.prince.com. **Description:** Manufactures sports equipment and related accessories. **Common positions include:** Accountant/Auditor; Adjuster; Administrative

Manager; Attorney; Blue-Collar Worker Supervisor; Collector; Computer Programmer; Credit Manager; Customer Service Representative; Draftsperson; Human Resources Manager; Human Service Worker; Investigator; Purchasing Agent/Manager; Systems Analyst; Transportation/Traffic Specialist; Travel Agent. **Educational backgrounds include:** Accounting; Art/Design; Business Administration; Communications; Computer Science; Finance; Marketing. **Benefits:** 401(k); Dental Insurance; Disability Coverage; Employee Discounts; Life Insurance; Medical Insurance; Pension Plan; Profit Sharing; Savings Plan; Tuition Assistance. **Corporate headquarters location:** This Location. **Parent company:** Other subsidiaries of Bennetton include: BSS Active; Nordica; and Eketelon. **Operations at this facility include:** Administration; Divisional Headquarters; Manufacturing; Regional Headquarters; Research and Development; Sales; Service. **Listed on:** NASDAQ. **Number of employees at this location:** 250.

**QUEST INTERNATIONAL FRAGRANCES COMPANY**
400 International Drive, P.O. Box 901, Mount Olive NJ 07828. 973/691-7100. **Contact:** Karen Molinaro, Human Resources. **Description:** A cosmetic fragrance company. **Corporate headquarters location:** This Location. **Operations at this facility include:** Administration; Manufacturing; Marketing; Sales.

**RECKITT & COLMAN, INC.**
1655 Valley Road, Wayne NJ 07470. 973/633-3600. **Fax:** 973/633-3734. **Contact:** Staffing Supervisor. **Description:** This location houses the corporate offices. Overall, Reckitt & Colman manufactures cleaning and specialty food products including the brand names Easy-Off oven cleaner, French's mustard, Lysol, and Woolite detergent. **Common positions include:** Accountant; Administrative Assistant; Auditor; Computer Operator; Computer Programmer; Food Scientist/Technologist; Market Research Analyst; Marketing Manager; Marketing Specialist; MIS Specialist. **Educational backgrounds include:** Accounting; Chemistry; Computer Science; Finance; Marketing. **Benefits:** 401(k); Dental Insurance; Disability Coverage; Employee Discounts; Medical Insurance; Pension Plan; Savings Plan; Tuition Assistance. **Special programs:** Internships. **Office hours:** Monday - Friday, 8:30 a.m. - 4:30 p.m. **Corporate headquarters location:** This Location. **Parent company:** Reckitt & Colman plc. **Operations at this facility include:** Regional Headquarters. **Number of employees nationwide:** 1,600.

**REVLON, INC.**
**IMPLEMENT DIVISION**
196 Coit Street, Irvington NJ 07111. 973/373-5803. **Contact:** Personnel Manager. **Description:** Manufactures nail files, scissors, tweezers, and other manicure and pedicure products. **Common positions include:** Accountant/Auditor; Blue-Collar Worker Supervisor; Department Manager; General Manager; Human Resources Manager; Industrial Engineer; Mechanical Engineer; Operations/Production Manager; Purchasing Agent/Manager; Quality Control Supervisor. **Educational backgrounds include:** Accounting; Business Administration; Engineering; Finance; Liberal Arts. **Benefits:** Disability Coverage; Employee Discounts; Life Insurance; Medical Insurance; Pension Plan; Profit Sharing; Savings Plan; Tuition Assistance. **Corporate headquarters location:** New York NY. **Listed on:** New York Stock Exchange.

**RUSS BERRIE & COMPANY, INC.**
111 Bauer Drive, Oakland NJ 07436. 201/337-9000. **Contact:** Gloria Fleischman, Personnel Manager. **World Wide Web address:** http://www.russberrie.com. **Description:** Designs and markets a line of more than 10,000 gift items in the U.S. and abroad. Products include toys, stuffed animals, novelties, and cards. A diverse customer base includes more than 100,000 retail stores including gift shops, florists, pharmacies, party shops, and stationery stores, as well as hotel, airport, and hospital gift shops. **Common positions include:** Accountant/Auditor; Commercial Artist; Customer Service Representative; Financial Analyst; Manufacturer's/Wholesaler's Sales Rep.; Marketing Specialist. **Educational backgrounds include:** Accounting; Art/Design; Business Administration; Finance; Liberal Arts; Marketing. **Benefits:** Dental Insurance; Employee Discounts; Life Insurance; Medical Insurance; Profit Sharing; Tuition Assistance. **Corporate headquarters location:** This Location. **Operations at this facility include:** Administration. **Listed on:** New York Stock Exchange. **Number of employees nationwide:** 2,000.

**SAFILO AMERICA INC.**
801 Jefferson Road, Parsippany NJ 07054. 973/952-2800. **Contact:** Human Resources. **Description:** Manufactures and distributes designer eyeglass frames.

**SANFORD KOH-I-NOOR**
P.O. Box 68, Bloomsbury NJ 08804. 908/479-4124. **Physical address:** 100 North Street, Bloomsbury NJ 08804. **Contact:** Director of Human Resources. **World Wide Web address:** http://www.kohinoor.com. **Description:** A manufacturer of artists' supplies.

234/The New Jersey JobBank

## SCHERING-PLOUGH CORPORATION
2000 Galloping Hill Road, Kenilworth NJ 07033. 908/298-4000. **Contact:** Human Resources Department. **Description:** Engaged in the research, development, manufacture, and marketing of pharmaceutical and consumer products. Pharmaceutical products include prescription drugs, over-the-counter medicines, eye care products, and animal health products promoted to the medical and allied health professions. The consumer products group consists of proprietary medicines, toiletries, cosmetics, and foot care products marketed directly to the public. Products include Coricidin cough and cold medicines and Maybelline products. **Subsidiaries include:** Schering Corporation, Madison NJ.

## SMITHKLINE BEECHAM CORPORATION
65 Industrial South, Clifton NJ 07012. 973/778-9000. **Contact:** Sinikka Laitamaki, Human Resource Manager. **Description:** This location manufactures toothpaste and Massengill products. Overall, SmithKline Beecham Corporation is a health care company engaged in the research, development, manufacture, and marketing of ethical pharmaceuticals, animal health products, ethical and proprietary medicines, and eye care products. The company's principal divisions include SmithKline Beecham Pharmaceuticals, SmithKline Beecham Animal Health, SmithKline Beecham Consumer Healthcare, and SmithKline Beecham Clinical Laboratories. The company is also engaged in many other aspects of the health care field, including the production of medical and electronic instruments. **Corporate headquarters location:** Philadelphia PA. **Subsidiaries include:** Menley & James Laboratories produces Contac Cold Capsules, Sine-Off sinus medicine, Love cosmetics, and Sea & Ski outdoor products.

## SONY ELECTRONICS, INC.
One Sony Drive, Park Ridge NJ 07656. 201/930-1000. **Contact:** Human Resources. **World Wide Web address:** http://www.sony.com. **Description:** This location houses the United States headquarters for the international electronics manufacturer. Overall, Sony's U.S. operations include manufacturing, engineering, design, sales, marketing, product distribution, and customer services. **Other U.S. locations:** Moonachie NJ; Paramus NJ; Teaneck NJ; New York NY. **Number of employees nationwide:** 24,000.

## SPRINGFIELD PRECISION INSTRUMENTS
76 Passaic Street, Wood-Ridge NJ 07075. 973/777-2900. **Contact:** Josie Giovinazzo, Personnel Manager. **Description:** Manufactures thermometers and barometers for consumer use. **Corporate headquarters location:** This Location.

## SQUARE TWO GOLF, INC.
18 Gloria Lane, Fairfield NJ 07004. 973/227-7783. **Contact:** Emily Force, Administrative Assistant. **World Wide Web address:** http://www.squaretwo.com. **Description:** Manufactures and markets a proprietary line of golf equipment including golf clubs, golf bags, golf balls, and accessories. The company markets these products under the trademarks Square Two, S2, PCX, XOR, ZCY, ONYX, Totally Matched, and Posiflow. Square Two Golf is also the exclusive golf club licensee of the Ladies Professional Golf Association. **Corporate headquarters location:** This Location.

## U.S. INDUSTRIES
101 Wood Avenue South, Iselin NJ 08830. 732/767-0700. **Contact:** Human Resources. **Description:** A holding company for four categories of manufacturing companies: bath and plumbing products, hardware and non-electric tools, commercial and residential lighting needs, and a variety of consumer products ranging from vacuum cleaners to toys. **Subsidiaries include:** Jacuzzi; Lighting Corporation of America; Selkirk; Spaulding.

## THE WELLA CORPORATION
12 Mercedes Drive, Montvale NJ 07645. 201/930-1020. **Fax:** 201/505-8156. **Contact:** Marybeth Bubert, Human Resources Director. **Description:** Manufactures a complete line of hair cosmetics including hair colors, permanent waves, hair conditioners, and shampoos. Founded in 1935. **Common positions include:** Accountant; Administrative Assistant; Clerical Supervisor; Customer Service Representative; Market Research Analyst; Marketing Manager; Public Relations Specialist; Purchasing Agent/Manager; Sales Manager; Sales Representative; Secretary. **Educational backgrounds include:** Accounting; Business Administration; Communications; Finance; Liberal Arts; Marketing. **Benefits:** 401(k); Dental Insurance; Disability Coverage; Employee Discounts; Life Insurance; Medical Insurance; Pension Plan; Savings Plan; Tuition Assistance. **Corporate headquarters location:** This Location. **Subsidiaries include:** Wella Manufacturing of Virginia, Inc., Richmond VA. **Parent company:** Wella AG. **Operations at this facility include:** Regional Headquarters. **Listed on:** Privately held. **Annual sales/revenues:** $51 - $100 million. **Number of employees at this location:** 90. **Number of employees nationwide:** 230.

*Note: Because addresses and telephone numbers of smaller companies can change rapidly, we recommend you call each company to verify the information below before inquiring about job opportunities. Mass mailings are not recommended.*

## Additional small employers:

### BATTERIES

**EAC**
PO Box 6058, Teterboro NJ
07608. 201/288-4477.

### COSMETICS AND RELATED PRODUCTS

**Beauty Sciences Inc.**
PO Box 767, Paterson NJ 07503.
973/278-1133.

**CCI**
20 Chestnut St, Garfield NJ
07026-2820. 973/546-1234.

**CCI**
171 Marsh St, Newark NJ 07114-
3236. 973/589-3900.

**CEI**
PO Box 6440, Edison NJ 08818-
6440. 732/225-2031.

**Chanel Inc.**
876 Centennial Ave, Piscataway
NJ 08854-3917. 732/885-5500.

**Consumer Health Care**
400 Webro Rd, Parsippany NJ
07054-2826. 973/952-7600.

**Cosmair Inc.**
81 New England Ave, Piscataway
NJ 08854-4195. 732/981-0365.

**Cosmair Inc.**
PO Box 5190, North Brunswick
NJ 08902. 732/297-7337.

**Davlyn Industries Inc.**
7 Fitzgerald Ave, Cranbury NJ
08512-3729. 609/655-5600.

**English Leather**
PO Box 909, Northvale NJ
07647-0909. 201/768-8080.

**Guest Packaging Inc.**
414 E Inman Ave, Rahway NJ
07065-4705. 732/382-7270.

**International Flavors & Fragrances**
800 Rose Ln, Union Beach NJ
07735-3550. 732/264-4500.

**ITS On The Dock**
PO Box 345, Totowa NJ 07511-
0345. 973/785-8121.

**Kasper Inc.**
200 Corporate Dr, Mahwah NJ
07430-2043. 201/529-1600.

**L'Oreal**
100 Commerce Dr, Franklin NJ
07416. 732/873-8200.

**Leeming-Pacquin**
100 Jefferson Rd, Parsippany NJ
07054-3708. 973/887-2100.

**PLC Specialties Inc.**
PO Box 335, Fair Lawn NJ
07410-0335. 973/423-1515.

**Procter & Gamble Co.**
100 Essex Ave E, Avenel NJ
07001-2020. 732/602-4500.

**Revlon Consumer Products Co.**
2147 Rte 27, Edison NJ 08818.
732/287-1400.

**Shisedio America Inc.**
178 Bauer Dr, Oakland NJ
07436-3105. 201/337-3750.

**Tsumura International**
300 Lighting Way, Secaucus NJ
07094-3622. 201/223-9000.

### HAND AND EDGE TOOLS

**Cobra Products Inc.**
1064 Industrial Dr, West Berlin
NJ 08091-9164. 609/768-2200.

**Hexacon Electric Company**
PO Box 36, Roselle Park NJ
07204-0036. 908/245-6200.

### HOUSEHOLD AUDIO AND VIDEO EQUIPMENT

**Bogen Communications Inc.**
PO Box 575, Ramsey NJ 07446-
0575. 201/934-8500.

**Maxell Corp. of America**
22-08 Route 208, Fair Lawn NJ
07410. 201/794-5900.

**Toshiba**
82 Totowa Rd, Wayne NJ 07470-
3114. 973/628-8000.

### HOUSEHOLD FURNITURE

**Huffman Koos Inc.**
1800 Lower Rd, Linden NJ
07036-6512. 732/574-1212.

**Room Plus Furniture**
91 Michigan Ave, Paterson NJ
07503-1807. 973/523-4600.

**Sharut Furniture Inc.**
220 Passaic St, Passaic NJ 07055-
6400. 973/473-1000.

### JEWELRY, SILVERWARE, AND PLATED WARE

**Gold & Diamond Merchants**
55 Metro Way, Secaucus NJ
07094-1905. 201/392-8181.

**Tessler & Weiss**
2389 Vauxhall Rd, Union NJ
07083-5036. 908/686-0513.

**Ultimate Trading Corp.**
563 Eagle Rock Ave, Roseland
NJ 07068-1501. 973/228-7700.

### MISC. FURNITURE AND FIXTURES

**Jewell Mercantile**
7 Jewell St, Garfield NJ 07026-
3710. 973/478-3900.

**Levolor**
25 Green Pond Rd, Rockaway NJ
07866-2001. 973/627-2200.

**Prestige Window Fashions**
PO Box 551, Edison NJ 08818-
0551. 732/225-2330.

### OFFICE AND ART SUPPLIES

**M&R Marking Systems Inc.**
PO Box 6969, Piscataway NJ
08855-6969. 732/562-9500.

**Type-Rite Ribbon Mfg. Inc.**
1413 Chestnut Ave, Hillside NJ
07205-1124. 908/810-9400.

### TOYS AND SPORTING GOODS

**Atlas Model Railroad Co. Inc.**
378 Florence Ave, Hillside NJ
07205-1102. 908/687-0880.

**Colorforms**
133 Williams Dr, Ramsey NJ
07446-1217. 201/327-2600.

**General Sportcraft Co. Ltd,**
140 Woodbine St, Bergenfield NJ
07621-3520. 201/384-4242.

**Marshall Clark Manufacturing**
20 Marshall St, Ste 40, Kearny
NJ 07032-1526. 201/991-2821.

**Mighty Star**
925 Amboy Ave, Perth Amboy
NJ 08861-1921. 732/826-5200.

**Playskool**
108 Fairway Ct, Northvale NJ
07647-2401. 201/767-0900.

**Reeves International Inc.**
34 Owens Dr, Wayne NJ 07470-
2341. 973/956-9555.

**Toy Pressman Corporation**
745 Joyce Kilmer Ave, New
Brunswick NJ 08901-3308.
732/545-4000.

**Tri-Chem Inc.**
1 Cape May St, Harrison NJ
07029-2404. 973/482-5500.

**Water World II Inc.**
700 Reading Ave, Hammonton
NJ 08037-3371. 609/561-5557.

**WATCHES & CLOCKS**

**Lucien Piccard/Arnex Watch**
120 Commerce Rd, Carlstadt NJ
07072-2502. 201/935-2200.

**Movado**
125 Chubb Ave, Lyndhurst NJ
07071-3504. 201/460-4800.

## For more information on career opportunities in consumer manufacturing:

### Associations

**ASSN. FOR MANUFACTURING EXCELLENCE**
380 West Palatine Road, Wheeling IL 60090.
847/520-3282. World Wide Web address: http://www.
ame.org.

**ASSN FOR MANUFACTURING TECHNOLOGY**
7901 Westpark Drive, McLean VA 22102. 703/893-
2900. World Wide Web address: http://www.mfgtech.
org. Offers research services.

**ASSOCIATION OF HOME APPLIANCE MANUFACTURERS**
20 North Wacker Drive, Suite 1231, Chicago IL
60606. 312/984-5800. World Wide Web address:
http://www.aham.org.

**NATIONAL ASSN. OF MANUFACTURERS**
1331 Pennsylvania Avenue NW, Suite 600,
Washington DC 20004. 202/637-3000. World Wide
Web address: http://www.nam.org.

**NATIONAL HOUSEWARES MANUFACTURERS ASSOCIATION**
6400 Schafer Court, Suite 650, Rosemont IL 60018.
847/292-4200. World Wide Web address: http://www.
housewares.org.

**SOCIETY OF MANUFACTURING ENGINEERS**
P.O. Box 930, One SME Drive, Dearborn MI 48121.
313/271-1500. World Wide Web address: http://www.
sme.org.

### Directories

**AMERICAN MANUFACTURER'S DIRECTORY**
5711 South 86th Circle, P.O. Box 37347, Omaha NE

68127. Toll-free phone: 800/555-5211. World Wide
Web address: http://www.infousa.com.

**APPLIANCE MANUFACTURER ANNUAL DIRECTORY**
Appliance Manufacturer, 5900 Harper Road, Suite
105, Solon OH 44139. 440/349-3060. $25.00.

**HOUSEHOLD & PERSONAL PRODUCTS INDUSTRY BUYERS GUIDE**
Rodman Publishing Group, 17 South Franklin
Turnpike, Ramsey NJ 07446. 201/825-2552. World
Wide Web address: http://www.happi.com.

### Magazines

**APPLIANCE**
Dana Chase Publications, 1110 Jorie Boulevard, Oak
Brook IL 60522-9019. 630/990-3484. World Wide
Web address: http://www.appliance.com.

**COSMETICS INSIDERS REPORT**
Advanstar Communications, 131 West First Street,
Duluth MN 55802-2065. Toll-free phone: 800/346-
0085. World Wide Web address: http://www.
advanstar.com.

### Online Services

**CAREER PARK - MANUFACTURING JOBS**
http://www.careerpark.com/jobs/manulist.html.

**MO'S GATEWAY TO MANUFACTURING-RELATED JOBS LISTINGS**
http://www.chesapk.com/mfgjobs.html.

# MANUFACTURING: MISCELLANEOUS INDUSTRIAL

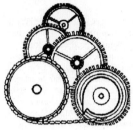

*The 1998 General Motors strike proved to be a hard blow for industrial manufacturing, but a strong economy is helping to sustain the industry. In fact, the automobile industry was expecting a record sales year for 1998, despite the GM strike. The Midwest, home to many of the nation's industrial manufacturing companies, continues to do well, recording an unemployment rate of 3.5 percent for August 1998. This was better than the national 4.5 percent rate.*

*However, the industry is still weak in areas. Deere & Company and Case Corporation both laid off workers in 1998, and due to falling steel prices and increased imports, midwestern steel mills are cutting payrolls and limiting production. Many companies are forging ahead with capital improvements, yet are not increasing their workforce. Companies which specialize in equipment for thriving industries, such as health care and construction, will show the most gains in the future.*

**AIRTRON**
200 East Hanover Avenue, Morris Plains NJ 07950. 973/539-5500. **Contact:** Bob Chapman, Personnel Director. **Description:** Operates a large crystal growing facility, producing single crystal rods for solid state lasers. Principal uses include target designators and range-finders for military applications; welding, cutting, and drilling in commercial markets; and precision optics and dielectric coatings used in laser systems. The company is also one of the nation's leading suppliers of microwave waveguide transmission lines and components.

**ALLIEDSIGNAL, INC.**
101 Columbia Road, Morristown NJ 07962. 973/455-2000. **Contact:** Human Resources Director. **World Wide Web address:** http://www.alliedsignal.com. **Description:** An advanced technology and manufacturing company serving customers worldwide with aerospace and automotive products, chemicals, fibers, plastics, and advanced materials. The company manufactures products to be used by other manufacturers in the production or processing of industrial and consumer items. **Corporate headquarters location:** This Location. **Other U.S. locations:** Elizabeth NJ. **Subsidiaries include:** Allied Chemical Company; Allied Fibers & Plastics Company; Allied Health & Scientific Products Company; Eltra Corporation; Union Texas Petroleum Corporation. **Parent company:** AlliedSignal Corporation serves a broad spectrum of industries through its more than 40 strategic businesses, which are grouped into three sectors: aerospace, automotive, and engineered materials. AlliedSignal is one of the nation's largest industrial organizations and has locations in more than 30 countries.

**AMERICAN STANDARD COMPANIES INC.**
One Centennial Avenue, P.O. Box 6820, Piscataway NJ 08855-6820. 732/980-6000. **Contact:** John Adams, Human Resources. **World Wide Web address:** http://www.americanstandard.com. **Description:** A global, diversified manufacturer. The company's operations are comprised of four segments: air conditioning products, plumbing products, automotive products, and medical systems. The air conditioning products segment (through subsidiary The Trane Company) develops and manufactures Trane and American Standard air conditioning equipment for use in central air conditioning systems for commercial, institutional, and residential buildings. The plumbing products segment develops and manufactures American Standard, Ideal Standard, and Standard bathroom and kitchen fixtures and fittings. The automotive products segment develops and manufactures truck, bus, and utility vehicle braking and control systems under the WABCO brand. The medical systems segment manufactures diagnostic products and systems. American Standard Companies Inc. and its 35 joint ventures operate 108 manufacturing facilities in 35 countries. **Corporate headquarters location:** This Location. **Listed on:** New York Stock Exchange. **Stock exchange symbol:** ASD. **Number of employees worldwide:** 51,000.

## ARROW FASTENER COMPANY
271 Mayhill Street, Saddle Brook NJ 07663. 201/843-6900. **Contact:** Mike Zeigler, Plant Manager. **World Wide Web address:** http://www.arrow-fastener.com. **Description:** Produces stapling machines, tackers, and similar products.

## BELCO TECHNOLOGIES, INC.
7 Entin Road, Parsippany NJ 07054. 973/884-4700. **Contact:** Joe Stehn, Personnel. **World Wide Web address:** http://www.belcotech.com. **Description:** A worldwide manufacturer of processes and equipment for the removal of air and water pollutants. Pollution control equipment includes electrostatic precipitators, baghouses, and related components used in pollution control. **Common positions include:** Accountant/Auditor; Administrator; Blue-Collar Worker Supervisor; Chemical Engineer; Department Manager; Draftsperson; Electrical/Electronics Engineer; General Manager; Human Resources Manager; Manufacturer's/Wholesaler's Sales Rep.; Mechanical Engineer; Operations/Production Manager; Purchasing Agent/Manager; Quality Control Supervisor. **Educational backgrounds include:** Accounting; Engineering. **Benefits:** Credit Union; Disability Coverage; Leave Time; Life Insurance; Tuition Assistance. **Corporate headquarters location:** This Location.

## BERES INDUSTRIES, INC.
1785 Swarthmore Avenue, Lakewood NJ 08701. 732/367-5700. **Contact:** Human Resources. **Description:** Designs, manufactures, and assembles precision engineered molds for use in the manufacture of molded plastic products and parts. **Subsidiaries include:** Athenia Plastic Mold Corporation; Supply Dynamics, Inc.

## BOBST GROUP, INC.
146 Harrison Avenue, Roseland NJ 07068. 973/226-8000. **Contact:** Ms. Jo Petruzzi, Personnel. **Description:** Produces a line of equipment for the converting, printing, and publishing industries. The company operates in the United States through three groups: Bobst, Bobst Champlain, and Bobst Registron. Products include die cutter/creasers, folder/gluers, flexo and gravure presses, electronic controls, and other sheet- and web-fed equipment. The company also manufactures converting equipment for the folding carton corrugated industries. **Common positions include:** Accountant/Auditor; Administrator; Advertising Clerk; Buyer; Credit Manager; Customer Service Representative; Department Manager; Draftsperson; Electrical/Electronics Engineer; General Manager; Human Resources Manager; Marketing Specialist; Mechanical Engineer; Operations/Production Manager; Systems Analyst; Transportation/Traffic Specialist. **Educational backgrounds include:** Accounting; Business Administration; Computer Science; Engineering; Finance; Marketing. **Parent company:** Bobst S.A. (Lausanne, Switzerland).

## CSM ENVIRONMENTAL SYSTEMS, INC.
200 Sheffield Street, Suite 305, Mountainside NJ 07092. 908/688-1177. **Contact:** Human Resources Department. **World Wide Web address:** http://www.csmsystems.net. **Description:** Markets, designs, manufactures, and installs air pollution control systems containing catalysts, blowers, burners, analyzers, heat exchangers, and other treatment and monitoring components. These air pollution control systems for hydrocarbon oxidation and nitrogen oxides reduction are used in a wide variety of industrial manufacturing and chemical processing applications. Environmental regulatory compliance, turnkey installation, and after-sale maintenance services are also available. The company is a leader in supplying controls for commercial bakeries, chemical plants, the pharmaceutical industry, and can and metal coating operations. The company sells to worldwide markets through the combination of a direct sales force and manufacturer representatives.

## CANTEL INDUSTRIES, INC.
1135 Broad Street, Suite 203, Clifton NJ 07013. 973/470-8700. **Contact:** Joanna Albrecht, Human Resources. **Description:** A holding company. **Subsidiaries include:** Carson Group Inc. (Canada) markets and distributes medical instruments including flexible and rigid endoscopes; precision instruments including microscopes and image analysis systems; and industrial equipment including remote visual inspection devices, laser distance measurement and thermal imaging products, and online optical inspection and quality assurance systems for specialized industrial applications. Carson also offers a full range of photographic equipment and supplies for amateur and professional photographers.

## CERTAINTEED CORPORATION
P.O. Box CN-E, Berlin NJ 08009. 609/767-7200. **Contact:** Human Resources. **World Wide Web address:** http://www.certainteed.com. **Description:** This location is a distribution center. Overall, Certainteed Corporation operates in three business segments: building materials including roofing products, vinyl siding, and door and sash products; fiberglass products including thermal and

acoustical insulation, and a wide range of other fiberglass products; and piping products, which produces pipes used in industrial, irrigation, sewer, mining, construction, and manufacturing applications. **NOTE:** Interested jobseekers should address inquiries to Kenneth Chiarello, Human Resources Manager, P.O. Box 860, Valley Forge PA 19482. **Corporate headquarters location:** Valley Forge PA. **Parent company:** Compagnie de Saint-Gobain (Paris, France) operates through four branches: Abrasives, Construction Materials, Industrial Ceramics, and Insulation and Reinforcements. The Saint-Gobain companies based in North America are organized under the umbrella of the Saint-Gobain Corporation, which includes the Certainteed Corporation, the Norton Company, and all of their subsidiaries. **Number of employees nationwide:** 8,000.

**CERTIFIED LABORATORIES INC.**
One Mack Center Drive, Paramus NJ 07652. 201/261-1215. **Contact:** Human Resources. **Description:** Manufactures and sells industrial and maintenance supplies.

**CHRONOS RICHARDSON INC.**
15 Gardner Road, Fairfield NJ 07004. 973/227-3522. **Contact:** Human Resources Department. **Description:** Chronos Richardson Inc. manufactures and distributes industrial weighing equipment, electronic bulk packagers, and vehicles for specialized industrial uses.

**COMPUTER POWER INC.**
124 West Main Street, High Bridge NJ 08829. 908/638-8000. **Contact:** Jessica Bacon, Personnel Manager. **Description:** Computer Power designs, manufactures, markets, sells, and services a broad range of power protection and conditioning systems and energy-efficient lighting products. Computer Power's power protection devices support and supplement electrical power furnished by utilities, manufacturing and industrial controllers, telecommunications systems, and medical equipment.

**CONSARC CORPORATION**
P.O. Box 156, Rancocas NJ 08073-0156. 609/267-8000. **Physical address:** 100 Indel Avenue, Rancocas NJ 08073. **Contact:** Ms. Pat Vogel, Executive Secretary. **Description:** Consarc Corporation sells, designs, and manufactures industrial melting furnaces. **Common positions include:** Buyer; Computer Programmer; Draftsperson; Electrical/Electronics Engineer; Mechanical Engineer; Operations/Production Manager. **Educational backgrounds include:** Computer Science; Engineering. **Benefits:** Disability Coverage; Life Insurance; Medical Insurance; Profit Sharing; Tuition Assistance. **Corporate headquarters location:** This Location. **Parent company:** Inducto Therm Industries. **Operations at this facility include:** Administration.

**COOPER ALLOY CORPORATION**
201 Sweetland Avenue, Hillside NJ 07205. 908/688-4120. **Contact:** Estelle Barone, Personnel Director. **Description:** Manufactures and distributes a line of plastic pumps to OEMs. The company also operates a stainless steel foundry at another location.

**CURTISS-WRIGHT CORPORATION**
1200 Wall Street West, Lyndhurst NJ 07071. 201/896-8400. **Contact:** Lorrainne Hielle, Corporate Benefits. **World Wide Web address:** http://www.curtisswright.com. **Description:** A diversified multinational manufacturing and service company that designs, manufactures, and overhauls precision components and systems and provides highly engineered services to the aerospace, automotive, shipbuilding, oil, petrochemical, agricultural equipment, power generation, metal working, and fire and rescue industries. Curtiss-Wright's principal operations include three domestic manufacturing facilities, 32 metal improvement service facilities located in North America and Europe, and two component overhaul facilities located in Florida and Denmark. **Common positions include:** Accountant/Auditor; Administrator; Aerospace Engineer; Attorney; Computer Programmer; Draftsperson; Electrical/Electronics Engineer; Financial Analyst; Human Resources Manager; Industrial Engineer; Mechanical Engineer; Metallurgical Engineer; Operations/Production Manager; Quality Control Supervisor; Systems Analyst. **Educational backgrounds include:** Accounting; Business Administration; Engineering; Finance. **Benefits:** 401(k); Dental Insurance; Disability Coverage; Life Insurance; Medical Insurance; Pension Plan; Tuition Assistance. **Corporate headquarters location:** This Location. **Subsidiaries include:** Curtiss-Wright Flight Systems, Inc.; Metal Improvement Company, Inc.; Target Rock Corporation. **Operations at this facility include:** Administration; Service. **Listed on:** New York Stock Exchange. **Number of employees nationwide:** 1,700.

**DEMAG DELAVAL TURBOMACHINERY CORPORATION**
P.O. Box 8788, Trenton NJ 08650. 609/890-5324. **Fax:** 609/890-5328. **Contact:** Cheryl Tatler-Pedersen, Human Resources Administrator. **Description:** Manufactures steam turbines and compressors. **Common positions include:** Accountant/Auditor; Blue-Collar Worker Supervisor;

Budget Analyst; Buyer; Computer Programmer; Credit Manager; Customer Service Representative; Designer; Draftsperson; Environmental Engineer; Financial Analyst; General Manager; Human Resources Manager; Industrial Engineer; Industrial Production Manager; Materials Engineer; Mechanical Engineer; Metallurgical Engineer; Petroleum Engineer; Public Relations Specialist; Quality Control Supervisor; Registered Nurse; Services Sales Representative; Systems Analyst. **Educational backgrounds include:** Accounting; Communications; Engineering; Finance; Liberal Arts; Marketing. **Benefits:** 401(k); Dental Insurance; Disability Coverage; Life Insurance; Medical Insurance; Pension Plan; Tuition Assistance. **Corporate headquarters location:** This Location. **Operations at this facility include:** Administration; Manufacturing; Regional Headquarters; Research and Development; Sales; Service. **Number of employees at this location:** 540.

### JOHN DUSENBERY COMPANY INC.
220 Franklin Road, Randolph NJ 07869. 973/366-7500. **Contact:** Alfred Guber, Controller. **Description:** Manufactures machinery for the paper, film, and foil industries. **Corporate headquarters location:** This Location.

### EDWARDS ENGINEERING CORPORATION
101 Alexander Avenue, Pompton Plains NJ 07444. 973/835-2800. **Fax:** 973/835-2822. **Contact:** Rich Lewin, Personnel and Material Manager. **World Wide Web address:** http://www.edwards-eng.com. **Description:** Manufactures coaxial condensers, coaxial evaporators, and vapor recovery systems using refrigeration and liquid nitrogen, baseboard heat, valance heating/cooling, liquid chillers, and hydronic control valves. **Common positions include:** Accountant/Auditor; Buyer; Chemical Engineer; Chemist; Computer Programmer; Credit Manager; Draftsperson; Electrical/Electronics Engineer; Electrician; Financial Analyst; Machinist; Manufacturer's/Wholesaler's Sales Rep.; Mechanical Engineer; Payroll Clerk; Purchasing Agent/Manager; Receptionist; Sheet-Metal Worker; Software Engineer; Stock Clerk; Systems Analyst; Tool and Die Maker; Typist/Word Processor; Welder. **Benefits:** 401(k); Dental Insurance; Disability Coverage; Employee Discounts; Life Insurance; Medical Insurance. **Corporate headquarters location:** This Location. **Operations at this facility include:** Administration; Manufacturing; Research and Development; Sales; Service. **Number of employees at this location:** 150.

### ELASTIMOLD
One Esna Park, Hackettstown NJ 07840. 908/852-1122. **Contact:** Kay Hedges, Manager of Human Resources. **Description:** A manufacturer of products and components for industrial and consumer markets. Products are classified in the following three segments: fluid power and metal components; electrical components and controls; and consumer and safety froducts. The fluid power and metal components segment includes hose and tubing, flexible hose assemblies, metal fastener products, and high-precision metal molds used by automotive, industrial equipment, aerospace, and plastics manufacturers. The electrical components and controls segment includes a variety of molded rubber connectors and distribution systems components marketed under the Elastimold trademark. These products are used predominantly by electrical power distribution companies, primarily for the underground installation of power lines serving residential, commercial, and industrial customers. Elastimold also manufactures electromechanical and solid state time delay relays and switches, controls, and motors; battery separators; aviation lighting transformers; splice caps; terminal blocks; electronic packaging components, and crimping tools used in electronic installation, switch gear, and other industrial electrical and electronic equipment. The consumer and safety products segment includes molded plastic key products for typewriters and telephones, and components for the automotive, appliance, computer, business machine, and hardware fields. **Corporate headquarters location:** This Location. **Listed on:** New York Stock Exchange.

### ENGELHARD CORPORATION
101 Wood Avenue, Iselin NJ 08830. **Contact:** Human Resources Department. **Description:** Engelhard Corporation is a diversified firm manufacturing catalysts, paper coatings, and fillers; precious metal components and mill products; products for the electronics industry; products for dental and medical requirements; sorbents; suspension agents; lime and industrial extenders; precious metals (supply, management, and refining); research and development process technology; catalyst products; and new metallurgical specialties. **NOTE:** This firm does not accept unsolicited resumes. Please only respond to advertised openings. **Corporate headquarters location:** This Location.

### FALSTROM COMPANY
P.O. Box 118, Passaic NJ 07055. 973/777-0013. **Contact:** Human Resources Department. **Description:** Manufactures steel cabinets for various clients including the defense industry.

## FEDDERS CORPORATION

P.O. Box 498, Whitehouse NJ 08888. 908/725-0500. **Physical address:** 3421 Route 22 East, Whitehouse NJ. **Contact:** Human Resources Department. **World Wide Web address:** http://www.fedders.com. **Description:** Fedders Corporation manufactures rotary compressors, principally for use in room air conditioners, and produces thermoelectric heating and cooling modules used in a variety of applications in which space and weight are considerations or precise temperature control is required. **Corporate headquarters location:** This Location.

## FLEXITALLIC LP

1300 Route 73, Suite 311, Mount Laurel NJ 08054. 609/234-5200. **Contact:** Office Manager. **Description:** Flexitallic manufactures spiral gaskets. **Common positions include:** Accountant/Auditor; Chemical Engineer; Customer Service Representative; General Manager; Industrial Engineer; Industrial Production Manager; Mechanical Engineer; Meteorologist; Operations/Production Manager; Petroleum Engineer; Purchasing Agent/Manager; Quality Control Supervisor. **Educational backgrounds include:** Business Administration; Engineering. **Benefits:** 401(k); Dental Insurance; Disability Coverage; Life Insurance; Medical Insurance; Pension Plan; Tuition Assistance. **Corporate headquarters location:** Houston TX. **Parent company:** TNN Industries, Inc. **Operations at this facility include:** Administration; Manufacturing; Regional Headquarters; Sales. **Number of employees at this location:** 28. **Number of employees nationwide:** 200.

## FOSTER WHEELER CORPORATION

Perryville Corporate Park, Clinton NJ 08809-4000. 908/730-4000. **Contact:** Bob Austin, Manager of Recruiting. **World Wide Web address:** http://www.fwc.com. **Description:** Foster Wheeler has three business segments: a process plants segment, engaged in the design, engineering, and construction of process plants and fired heaters for oil refiners and chemical producers; a utility and engine segment, engaged in the design and fabrication of steam generators, condensers, feedwater heaters, electrostatic precipitators, and other pollution abatement equipment; and an industrial segment that supplies pressure vessels and internals, electrical copper products, industrial insulation, welding wire, and electrodes. **Common positions include:** Accountant/Auditor; Chemical Engineer; Civil Engineer; Computer Programmer; Draftsperson; Electrical/Electronics Engineer; Financial Analyst; Industrial Designer; Mechanical Engineer. **Educational backgrounds include:** Accounting; Engineering; Finance. **Benefits:** Disability Coverage; Employee Discounts; Life Insurance; Medical Insurance; Pension Plan; Profit Sharing; Tuition Assistance. **Corporate headquarters location:** This Location. **International locations:** Worldwide. **Listed on:** New York Stock Exchange.

## FREQUENCY ENGINEERING LABORATORIES

Central Avenue, Farmingdale NJ 07727. 732/919-2420. **Fax:** 732/919-2455. **Contact:** David Fursman, Director of Human Resources Administration. **Description:** Engaged in prime and subcontract manufacturing of weapons, missile systems, test equipment, airborne systems, communication systems, and EW and ASW systems. **Common positions include:** Accountant; Administrative Assistant; Buyer; Clerical Supervisor; Computer Operator; Controller; Design Engineer; Draftsperson; Finance Director; Financial Analyst; Industrial Engineer; Manufacturing Engineer; Mechanical Engineer; Project Manager; Purchasing Agent/Manager; Secretary; Software Engineer; Typist/Word Processor. **Educational backgrounds include:** Accounting; Computer Science; Engineering; Finance. **Benefits:** 401(k); Dental Insurance; Disability Coverage; Life Insurance; Medical Insurance; Tuition Assistance. **Corporate headquarters location:** This Location. **Operations at this facility include:** Administration; Manufacturing; Research and Development; Sales. **Listed on:** Privately held. **Number of employees at this location:** 250.

## STEPHEN GOULD CORPORATION

35 South Jefferson Road, Whippany NJ 07981. 973/428-1500. **Contact:** Debbie Habbart, Executive Assistant. **Description:** Stephen Gould Corporation designs, produces, and supplies packaging including plastic, paper, and metal for a variety of industries. The corporation has several area locations and 26 national locations. **Corporate headquarters location:** This Location.

## HANOVIA/COLITE, INC.

825 Lehigh Avenue, Union NJ 07083. 908/688-0050. **Contact:** Patrick Cullen, Director of Human Resources. **Description:** Designs, develops, produces, and markets plasma arc lamps and related equipment including commercial and industrial ultraviolet products and accessories; produces various phosphorescent pigments, compounds, and films; and designs, develops, manufactures, assembles, and markets high-intensity lighting equipment. **Common positions include:** Ceramics Engineer; Chemist; Electrical/Electronics Engineer; Mechanical Engineer; Metallurgical Engineer.

**Educational backgrounds include:** Chemistry; Engineering; Physics. **Benefits:** Dental Insurance; Disability Coverage; Life Insurance; Medical Insurance; Pension Plan; Profit Sharing; Savings Plan; Tuition Assistance. **Corporate headquarters location:** This Location. **Operations at this facility include:** Manufacturing; Research and Development.

### HAYWARD INDUSTRIES

620 Division Street, Elizabeth NJ 07207. 908/351-5400. **Contact:** Wayne Wilson, Human Resources Representative. **Description:** Hayward Industries manufactures swimming pool equipment. The company is engaged in all aspects of production including design and sales. Principal clients use equipment in construction, repair, and maintenance of private and commercial swimming pools. The company also manufactures and distributes a standard line of industrial pipeline strainers and valves. The company operates an international subsidiary located in Belgium. **Educational backgrounds include:** Accounting; Business Administration; Communications; Economics; Engineering; Finance; Liberal Arts; Marketing. **Benefits:** 401(k); Dental Insurance; Disability Coverage; Employee Discounts; Life Insurance; Medical Insurance; Pension Plan; Savings Plan; Tuition Assistance. **Corporate headquarters location:** This Location. **Operations at this facility include:** Administration; Manufacturing; Research and Development; Sales; Service.

### HOLOPAK TECHNOLOGIES, INC.

9 Cotters Lane, East Brunswick NJ 08816. 732/238-2883. **Toll-free phone:** 800/225-FOIL. **Fax:** 732/613-1018. **Contact:** Bonnie Eichel, Personnel Manager. **Description:** HoloPak, through its subsidiaries Transfer Print Foils, Inc. and Alubec Industries Inc., is a producer and distributor of hot stamping foils, holographic foils, and metallized paper. Hot stamping foils are key elements of the graphics and packaging industries, and are used extensively to decorate a wide variety of products. Holographic foils are high-precision images embossed into specialized coatings, which are used to discourage counterfeiting and provide specialty decorative effects. HoloPak has manufacturing facilities in East Brunswick NJ and Montreal, Quebec, with sales offices located across the country. **Corporate headquarters location:** This Location. **Other U.S. locations:** Nationwide. **International locations:** Canada.

### HOSOKAWA MICRON POWDER SYSTEMS

10 Chatham Road, Summit NJ 07901. 908/273-6360. **Contact:** Human Resources Administrator. **Description:** Develops and manufactures air pollution control and process equipment. Products are used by the primary metals, non-metallic minerals, powder, protective coatings, paper, fertilizer, chemical, pharmaceutical, and food processing industries. **Common positions include:** Accountant/Auditor; Administrator; Buyer; Computer Programmer; Department Engineer; Draftsperson; Electrical/Electronics Engineer; Human Resources Manager; Mechanical Engineer; Operations/Production Manager; Purchasing Agent/Manager; Quality Control Supervisor; Sales Executive. **Educational backgrounds include:** Accounting; Business Administration; Chemistry; Computer Science; Engineering; Finance; Marketing. **Benefits:** Dental Insurance; Disability Coverage; Employee Discounts; Life Insurance; Medical Insurance; Pension Plan; Savings Plan; Tuition Assistance. **Corporate headquarters location:** New York NY. **Parent company:** Hosokawa Micron International Inc. **Operations at this facility include:** Administration; Manufacturing; Research and Development; Sales; Service.

### INGERSOLL-RAND COMPANY

200 Chestnut Ridge Road, Woodcliff Lake NJ 07675. 201/573-0123. **Contact:** Human Resources. **World Wide Web address:** http://www.ingersoll-rand.com. **Description:** Manufactures compressors, pumps, and other nonelectrical industrial equipment and machinery. Ingersoll-Rand Company's products include air compression systems, antifriction systems, construction equipment, air tools, bearings, locks, tools, and pumps. The company operates 93 production facilities throughout the world. **Corporate headquarters location:** This Location. **Other U.S. locations:** Nationwide. **Subsidiaries include:** The Torrington Company. **Listed on:** New York Stock Exchange.

### K-TRON INTERNATIONAL INC.

P.O. Box 888, Pitman NJ 08071-0888. 609/589-0500. **Contact:** Patricia Daniels, Human Resources. **World Wide Web address:** http://www.ktron.com. **Description:** Produces industrial feeders and blenders.

### LANGSTON CORPORATION

111 Woodcrest Road, Cherry Hill NJ 08034. 609/795-7100. **Contact:** Human Resources. **World Wide Web address:** http://www.langstoncorp.com. **Description:** Manufactures machines used in the production of boxes.

## LAWSON MARDON WHEATON INC.
1101 Wheaton Avenue, Millville NJ 08332-2003. 609/825-1400. **Contact:** Human Resources. **Description:** This location houses administrative offices. Overall, Lawson Mardon Wheaton is a manufacturer of glass and plastic tubes and containers used in the pharmaceutical and cosmetic industries. **Corporate headquarters location:** This Location.

## MAROTTA SCIENTIFIC CONTROLS INC.
P.O. Box 427, Montville NJ 07045-0427. 973/334-7800. **Contact:** Robert Cooper, Personnel Manager. **Description:** Manufactures high-pressure valves for pneumatic and hydraulic equipment. The company is also a custom manufacturer of fluid control products. Principal clients are companies in various industries and government agencies. **Common positions include:** Mechanical Engineer. **Educational backgrounds include:** Engineering. **Corporate headquarters location:** This Location.

## MIKRON INSTRUMENT COMPANY, INC.
16 Thornton Road, Oakland NJ 07436. 201/891-7330. **Contact:** Human Resources. **World Wide Web address:** http://www.mikroninst.com. **Description:** Mikron Instrument Company, Inc. develops, manufactures, markets, and services equipment and instruments for noncontact temperature measurement. The company's products are typically used to measure the temperature of moving objects; of stationary objects in environments or situations where contact temperature measurement would be difficult, hazardous, or impractical; and wherever rapid temperature changes must be accurately tracked instantaneously. The company also manufactures and/or markets calibration sources and a variety of accessories and optional equipment for its infrared thermometers.

## MINOLTA CORPORATION
101 Williams Drive, Ramsey NJ 07446. 201/825-4000. **Fax:** 201/825-7605. **Contact:** Linda Loveland, Employment and Compensation Manager. **World Wide Web address:** http://www. minoltausa.com. **Description:** Markets, sells, and distributes photographic and business equipment, as well as document imaging systems. **Common positions include:** Accountant/Auditor; Credit Manager; Customer Service Representative; Software Engineer. **Educational backgrounds include:** Accounting; Business Administration; Computer Science; Marketing. **Benefits:** 401(k); Dental Insurance; Disability Coverage; Employee Discounts; Life Insurance; Medical Insurance; Pension Plan; Tuition Assistance. **Corporate headquarters location:** This Location. **Parent company:** Minolta Co., Ltd. (Osaka, Japan). **Operations at this facility include:** Administration; Divisional Headquarters; Regional Headquarters; Sales; Service. **Listed on:** Privately held. **Number of employees at this location:** 500.

## OHAUS CORPORATION
29 Hanover Road, Florham Park NJ 07932. 973/377-9000. **Contact:** Human Resources Department. **World Wide Web address:** http://www.ohaus.com. **Description:** One of the world's largest manufacturers of precision weighing equipment for use in laboratory, education, and specialty markets.

## OLIVETTI OFFICE USA
## ROYAL SUPPLY CENTER
P.O. Box 6945, Bridgewater NJ 08807. 908/526-8200. **Physical address:** 765 U.S. Highway 202 North, Bridgewater NJ. **Contact:** Vince Boles, Personnel. **World Wide Web address:** http://www.royalnet.com. **Description:** Part of an international corporation which manufactures and distributes a broad line of electronic office products including typewriters, calculators, word processors, cash registers, copiers, personal and small computers, business computers, complete data processing systems, teleprinters, video terminals, telephone-switching systems, minicomputers, automatic tellers, and associated equipment. **Corporate headquarters location:** This Location.

## PERMACEL
## A NITTO DENKO COMPANY
P.O. Box 671, New Brunswick NJ 08903. 732/418-2455. **Fax:** 732/828-2474. **Contact:** Ms. C.M. Grobelny, Supervisor of Human Resources and Payroll. **Description:** Manufactures pressure-sensitive tape. **Common positions include:** Accountant/Auditor; Administrator; Blue-Collar Worker Supervisor; Chemical Engineer; Chemist; Computer Programmer; Credit Manager; Customer Service Representative; Department Manager; Economist; Electrical/Electronics Engineer; Financial Analyst; General Manager; Human Resources Manager; Industrial Engineer; Manufacturer's/Wholesaler's Sales Rep.; Marketing Specialist; Mechanical Engineer; Operations/Production Manager; Quality Control Supervisor; Systems Analyst; Transportation/Traffic Specialist. **Educational backgrounds include:** Accounting; Business

Administration; Chemistry; Computer Science; Engineering; Finance; Liberal Arts; Marketing. **Benefits:** 401(k); Dental Insurance; Disability Coverage; Life Insurance; Medical Insurance; Pension Plan; Savings Plan; Tuition Assistance. **Corporate headquarters location:** This Location. **Operations at this facility include:** Administration; Manufacturing; Regional Headquarters; Research and Development; Sales; Service. **Listed on:** Privately held. **Number of employees at this location:** 500.

## PHILIPS LIGHTING COMPANY
P.O. Box 6800, Somerset NJ 08875-6800. 732/563-3000. **Physical address:** 200 Franklin Square Drive, Somerset NJ. **Fax:** 732/563-3200. **Contact:** Human Resources Manager. **World Wide Web address:** http://www.philips.com/lighting. **Description:** Philips Lighting Company manufactures and markets lighting products and systems for industry and home including incandescent, fluorescent, automotive, high-intensity discharge, compact fluorescent, specialty, and projection lamps. **Parent company:** Philips Electronics North America Corporation, one of the larger industrial companies in the United States, is a multi-market manufacturing organization with nationwide locations and various subsidiaries. Philips concentrates its efforts primarily in the fields of consumer electronics, consumer products, electrical and electronics components, and professional equipment.

## SEALED AIR CORPORATION
Park 80 East, Saddle Brook NJ 07663. 201/791-7600. **Contact:** Manager of Employee Benefits. **Description:** Sealed Air Corporation produces specialized protective packaging materials and systems which reduce or eliminate the damage to products that may occur during shipment. The company operates over 25 manufacturing plants and administrative and sales offices in the United States, and six plants and nine sales offices in foreign countries. Sealed Air also has fully-staffed packaging and testing laboratories around the world and major technical facilities in Saddle Brook NJ (Technical Center) and Danbury CT. **Benefits:** 401(k); Dental Insurance; Disability Coverage; Life Insurance; Medical Insurance; Profit Sharing; Tuition Assistance. **Corporate headquarters location:** This Location. **Other U.S. locations:** Danbury CT; Holyoke MA; Scotia NY. **Listed on:** New York Stock Exchange. **Number of employees at this location:** 35. **Number of employees nationwide:** 2,000.

## TRANSTECHNOLOGY CORPORATION
150 Allen Road, Liberty Corner NJ 07938. 908/903-1600. **Contact:** Human Resources Department. **World Wide Web address:** http://www.ttcorp.com. **Description:** TransTechnology Corporation designs, manufactures, sells, and distributes specialty fasteners. **Corporate headquarters location:** This Location. **Subsidiaries include:** Breeze-Eastern designs, develops, manufactures, and services sophisticated lifting and restraining products, principally helicopter rescue hoist and cargo hooks systems, winches and hoists for aircraft and weapon systems, and aircraft cargo tie down systems; Breeze Industrial Products (Saltsburg PA) manufactures a complete line of standard and specialty gear-driven band fasteners in high-grade stainless steel for use in highly engineered applications; Industrial Retaining Ring (Irvington NJ) manufactures a variety of retaining rings made of carbon steel, stainless steel, and beryllium copper; The Palnut Company (Mountainside NJ) manufactures light- and heavy-duty single- and mutithread specialty fasteners; The Seeger Group (Somerville NJ) manufactures retaining clips, circlips, spring pins, and similar components.

## VICTORY ENGINEERING CORPORATION
Victory Road, Box 710, Springfield NJ 07081. 973/379-5900. **Contact:** Personnel. **World Wide Web address:** http://www.veco-net.com. **Description:** Manufactures and distributes thermistors, varistors, and specialty temperature sensing assemblies. **Common positions include:** Accountant/Auditor; Administrator; Blue-Collar Worker Supervisor; Buyer; Chemist; Department Manager; Electrical/Electronics Engineer; General Manager; Human Resources Manager; Manufacturer's/Wholesaler's Sales Representative; Operations/Production Manager; Purchasing Agent/Manager; Quality Control Supervisor. **Educational backgrounds include:** Accounting; Chemistry; Computer Science; Engineering; Finance; Marketing. **Benefits:** Disability Coverage; Life Insurance; Medical Insurance; Pension Plan; Tuition Assistance. **Corporate headquarters location:** This Location. **Operations at this facility include:** Manufacturing; Research and Development; Sales; Service.

## WEISS-AUG COMPANY INC.
P.O. Box 520, East Hanover NJ 07936. 973/887-7600. **Fax:** 973/887-6924. **Contact:** Mary Dante, Director of Human Resources. **World Wide Web address:** http://www.weiss-aug.com. **Description:** Manufactures stampings, moldings, insert moldings, and assemblies. Industries served include automotive, telecommunications, electronic and electrical connector, medical, and several specialty markets. Services include design, tooling, production, and quality control.

Founded in 1972. **NOTE:** Part-time jobs and second and third shifts are offered. **Common positions include:** Account Manager; Accountant; Administrative Assistant; Blue-Collar Worker Supervisor; Chief Financial Officer; Computer Programmer; Customer Service Representative; Department Manager; Design Engineer; Draftsperson; Environmental Engineer; Industrial Engineer; Human Resources Manager; Machinist; Manufacturing Engineer; Marketing Specialist; Mechanical Engineer; Network/Systems Administrator; Operations Manager; Production Manager; Purchasing Agent/Manager; Quality Assurance Engineer; Sales Engineer; Systems Manager; Tool and Die Maker; Vice President of Engineering; Vice President of Manufacturing. **Educational backgrounds include:** Accounting; Business Administration; Computer Science; Engineering; Microsoft Word; Microsoft Windows NT; Software Technical Support; Spreadsheets. **Benefits:** 401(k); Casual Dress - Fridays; Dental Insurance; Disability Coverage; Fitness Center; Life Insurance; Medical Insurance; Tuition Assistance. **Special programs:** Apprenticeships (for tool and die mold makers); Co-ops; Training. **Office hours:** Monday - Friday, 8:00 a.m. - 5:00 p.m. **Corporate headquarters location:** This Location. **Operations at this facility include:** Administration; Sales; Service. **Listed on:** Privately held. **President/CEO:** Dieter Weissenrieder. **Facilities Manager:** Phil DiParisi. **Information Systems Manager:** William Perlack. **Purchasing Manager:** Bob Traetta. **Annual sales/revenues:** $21 - $50 million. **Number of employees at this location:** 200. **Number of projected hires for 1999 - 2000 at this location:** 50.

## WYANT HEALTHCARE
P.O. Box 8609, Somerville NJ 08876. 908/707-1800. **Contact:** Maureen Buehler, Administrative Assistant. **Description:** Manufactures disposable underpads, cloths, and wipes for health care, industrial, food service, and janitorial businesses.

*Note: Because addresses and telephone numbers of smaller companies can change rapidly, we recommend you call each company to verify the information below before inquiring about job opportunities. Mass mailings are not recommended.*

**Additional small employers:**

### AMMUNITION

**Alliant Techsystems Incorporated**
PO Box H, Kenvil NJ 07847-1007. 973/584-1507.

**Ferrulmatic Inc.**
11 Jackson Rd, Totowa NJ 07512-1001. 973/256-5533.

### COMMERCIAL FURNITURE AND FIXTURES

**Bon-Art International Incorporated**
99 Evergreen Avenue, Newark NJ 07114-1124. 973/623-6615.

**Center Core Group Incorporated**
1355 West Front Street, Plainfield NJ 07063-1159. 908/561-7662.

**Frazier Industrial Company**
PO Box F, Long Valley NJ 07853. 908/876-3001.

**Global Industries Incorporated**
PO Box 562, Marlton NJ 08053-0562. 609/596-3390.

**Handy Manufacturing Company**
337 Sherman Avenue,

Newark NJ 07114-1507. 973/242-1600.

**Stylex Incorporated**
PO Box 5038, Riverside NJ 08075-0438. 609/461-5600.

**Vira Manufacturing Incorporated**
970 New Brunswick Ave, Rahway NJ 07065-3814. 732/382-8400.

### COMPRESSORS

**Fluid Enterprises Incorporated**
107 Bauer Dr, Oakland NJ 07436-3102. 201/337-1240.

**Gusmer**
PO Box 2055, Lakewood NJ 08701-8055. 732/370-9000.

### FANS, BLOWERS, AND AIR PURIFICATION EQUIPMENT

**Filtra Corp.**
1 North Corporate Drive, Riverdale NJ 07457-1715. 973/616-7300.

**McLean Engineering**
PO Box 127, Princeton Junction NJ 08550-0127. 609/799-0100.

### GASKETS, PACKING, AND SEALING DEVICES

**Seals Eastern Inc.**
PO Box 520, Red Bank NJ 07701-0520. 732/747-9200.

### HEATING EQUIPMENT

**Stamm International Corporation**
PO Box 602, Palisades Park NJ 07650-0602. 201/947-1700.

**The Trane Co.**
2231 East State Street Extension, Trenton NJ 08619. 609/587-3400.

### INDUSTRIAL AND COMMERCIAL MACHINERY AND EQUIPMENT

**Metem Corporation**
700 Parsippany Road, Parsippany NJ 07054-3712. 973/887-6635.

### MEASURING AND CONTROLLING EQUIPMENT

**Acrison Inc.**
20 Empire Blvd, Moonachie NJ 07074-1303. 201/440-8300.

**DPC Cirrus Inc.**
111 Canfield Ave, Bldg B, Randolph NJ 07869-1114. 973/927-2828.

**New Brunswick Scientific Company**
PO Box 4005, Edison NJ 08818-4005. 732/287-1200.

**Omega Engineering Incorporated**
PO Box 336, Bridgeport NJ 08014-0336. 609/467-4200.

**SP Industries**
PO Box 686, Buena NJ 08310-0686. 609/697-4700.

**Spex Industries**
3880 Park Ave, Edison NJ 08820-3012. 732/494-8660.

**Sterling Instrument**
38 Brunswick Avenue, Edison NJ 08817-2578. 732/287-6500.

**Westlock Controls Corporation**
280 Midland Avenue, Saddle Brook NJ 07663-6404. 201/794-7650.

**MISC. INDUSTRIAL MACHINE TOOLS**

**Mapal Inc.**
81 Suttons Lane, Piscataway NJ 08854-5723. 732/572-6700.

**MISC. INDUSTRIAL MACHINERY AND EQUIPMENT**

**Heller Industries Inc.**
4 Vreeland Rd, Florham Park NJ 07932-1501. 973/377-6800.

**Parmatic Filter Corporation**
88 Ford Rd, Denville NJ 07834-1357. 973/586-9200.

**MISC. PIPE FITTINGS AND/OR VALVES**

**Hahn Industries**
29 East Halsey Road, Parsippany NJ 07054-3704. 973/887-6400.

**Hoke Controls**
1 Tenakill Park, Cresskill NJ 07626-2028. 201/568-9100.

**Taylor Forge Stainless Incorporated**
PO Box 610, Somerville NJ 08876-0610. 908/722-1313.

**Versa Products Company Inc.**
PO Box 219, Paramus NJ 07653-0219. 201/843-2400.

**MOTORS AND GENERATORS**

**Howell Electric Motor**
PO Box 952, Plainfield NJ 07061-0952. 908/756-8800.

**PACKAGING MACHINERY**

**Cozzoli Machine Company**
401 E 3rd St, Plainfield NJ 07060-1825. 908/757-2040.

**PLUMBING FIXTURE FITTINGS AND TRIM**

**Hago Manufacturing Co. Inc.**
1120 Globe Ave, Mountainside NJ 07092-2904. 908/232-8687.

**POWER TRANSMISSION EQUIPMENT**

**SS White Technologies Inc.**
151 Old New Brunswick Rd, Piscataway NJ 08854-3708. 732/752-8300.

**SERVICE INDUSTRY MACHINERY**

**Graver Company**
750 Walnut Ave, Cranford NJ 07016-3348. 908/653-4200.

**For more information on career opportunities in industrial manufacturing:**

### Associations

**ASSOCIATION FOR MANUFACTURING EXCELLENCE**
380 West Palatine Road, Wheeling IL 60090. 847/520-3282. World Wide Web address: http://www.trainingforum.com/ASN/AME.

**ASSOCIATION FOR MANUFACTURING TECHNOLOGY**
7901 Westpark Drive, McLean VA 22102. 703/893-2900. A trade association. World Wide Web address: http://www.mfgtech.org.

**INSTITUTE OF INDUSTRIAL ENGINEERS**
25 Technology Park, Norcross GA 30092. 770/449-0460. World Wide Web address: http://www.iienet.org. Institute of Industrial Engineers is a nonprofit organization with 27,000 members. Conducts seminars and offers reduced rates on its books and publications.

**NATIONAL ASSOCIATION OF MANUFACTURERS**
1331 Pennsylvania Avenue NW, Suite 1500, Washington DC 20004. 202/637-3000. World Wide Web address: http://www.nam.org. A lobbying association.

**NATIONAL TOOLING & MACHINING ASSOCIATION**
9300 Livingston Road, Fort Washington MD 20744. Toll-free phone: 800/248-6862. World Wide Web address: http://www.ntma.org. Reports on wages and operating expenses, produces monthly newsletters, and offers legal advice.

**PRECISION MACHINED PRODUCTS ASSOCIATION**
6700 West Snowville Road, Brecksville OH 44141. 440/526-0300. Provides resource information.

**SOCIETY OF MANUFACTURING ENGINEERS**
P.O. Box 930, One SME Drive, Dearborn MI 48121. 313/271-1500. World Wide Web address: http://www.sme.org. Society of Manufacturing Engineers offers educational events and educational materials on manufacturing.

### Directories

**AMERICAN MANUFACTURER'S DIRECTORY**
5711 South 86th Circle, P.O. Box 37347, Omaha NE 68127. Toll-free phone: 800/555-5211. World Wide Web address: http://www.infousa.com. *American Manufacturer's Directory* lists over 531,000 manufacturing companies of all sizes and industries. The directory contains product and sales information, company size, and a key contact name for each company.

### Online Services

**CAREER PARK - MANUFACTURING JOBS**
http://www.careerpark.com/jobs/manulist.html. This Website provides a list of current job openings in the manufacturing industry. The site is run by Parker Advertising Service, Inc.

**MO'S GATEWAY TO MANUFACTURING-RELATED JOBS LISTINGS**
http://www.chesapk.com/mfgjobs.html. Provides links to sites that post job openings in manufacturing.

<u>**Special Programs**</u>

**BUREAU OF APPRENTICESHIP AND TRAINING**
U.S. Department of Labor, 200 Constitution Avenue NW, Room N4649, Washington DC 20210. 202/219-5921.

# MINING/GAS/PETROLEUM/ENERGY RELATED

*Crude oil prices fell more than 30 percent between November 1997 and November 1998, according to the U.S. Department of Energy. The decline is due to ailing economies in the Far East, mild winters in the U.S. and Europe, and an abundant supply. The trend is likely to continue with Asia in turmoil and a surplus of commodities from heating oil to gasoline. This is good news for consumers who benefited from lower prices.*

*Metal mining and oil and gas extraction all experienced decreased output during 1998, and the Bureau of Labor Statistics projects that employment opportunities in the mining industry will decrease by 2.5 percent by 2006. Other sectors are expected to remain steady, specifically service companies and drillers. Standard & Poor reported a 22 percent rise in profits for the petroleum services industry through the first half of 1998 versus the same period of 1997.*

*In other mining sectors, lime production has been reaching higher levels since 1993. The coal mining industry has undergone some changes in order to regain profits, and production is expected to rise 1 percent annually through 2002. Factors that may negatively affect this sector include higher transportation costs, labor disruptions, and government restrictions.*

**AMERADA HESS**
One Hess Plaza, Woodbridge NJ 07095-1229. 732/636-3000. **Contact:** Human Resources. **World Wide Web address:** http://www.hess.com. **Description:** Sells petroleum and provides refining services. **Corporate headquarters location:** New York NY.

**BEL-RAY COMPANY, INC.**
P.O. Box 526, Farmingdale NJ 07727. 732/938-2421. **Contact:** Human Resources. **Description:** Manufactures lubricants used in the aerospace, automotive, food, marine, mining, steel, and textiles industries.

**CASTROL NORTH AMERICA, INC.**
1500 Valley Road, Wayne NJ 07470. 973/633-2200. **Contact:** Janet Tuffy, Director of Human Resources. **Description:** Manufactures and markets lubricants and petroleum products. **Common positions include:** Petroleum Engineer. **Corporate headquarters location:** This Location. **Parent company:** Burmah Castrol USA, Inc. **Number of employees at this location:** 200. **Number of employees nationwide:** 2,500.

**HATCO CORPORATION**
1020 King George Post Road, Fords NJ 08863. 732/738-1000. **Contact:** Human Resources. **Description:** Manufactures jet lubricants and oils.

**MOBIL OIL CORPORATION**
600 Billingsport Road, Paulsboro NJ 08066. 609/224-0200. **Contact:** Human Resources. **Description:** This location houses sales and distribution offices for New Jersey and Pennsylvania. Overall, Mobil Oil Corporation is an integrated oil company engaged in petroleum and chemical products marketing, refining, manufacturing, exploration, production, transportation, and research and development in more than 100 countries. Exploration is conducted in 34 countries. The company has interests in 21 refineries in 12 countries, owns 28 oil tankers, and has interests in over 36,000 miles of pipeline worldwide. Mobil markets its products through more than 19,000 company-owned retail outlets in over 90 countries. Other products include fabricated plastics, films, food bags, housewares, garbage bags, and building materials. The company also has subsidiaries involved in real estate development and mining operations. **NOTE:** In December 1998, a merger was proposed whereby Exxon Corporation would purchase Mobil Oil Corporation for $80 billion in stock, creating the world's largest company with annual sales of $204 billion.

**TOSCO REFINING COMPANY**
1400 Park Avenue, Linden NJ 07036. 908/523-5000. **Contact:** Human Resources. **World Wide Web address:** http://www.tosco.com. **Description:** An oil refinery.

**WILSHIRE OIL COMPANY**
921 Bergen Avenue, Jersey City NJ 07306. 201/420-2796. **Contact:** Human Resources. **Description:** A diversified corporation engaged in oil and gas exploration and production, real estate operations, and investment activities. **Corporate headquarters location:** This Location.

**For more information on career opportunities in the mining, gas, petroleum, and energy industries:**

## Associations

**AMERICAN ASSOCIATION OF PETROLEUM GEOLOGISTS**
P.O. Box 979, Tulsa OK 74101. 918/584-2555. World Wide Web address: http://www.aapg.org. International headquarters for petroleum geologists.

**AMERICAN GEOLOGICAL INSTITUTE**
4220 King Street, Alexandria VA 22302-1502. 703/379-2480. World Wide Web address: http://www.agiweb.org. Scholarships available. Publishes monthly *Geotimes*. Offers job listings.

**AMERICAN NUCLEAR SOCIETY**
555 North Kensington Avenue, La Grange Park IL 60526. 708/352-6611. World Wide Web address: http://www.ans.org. Offers educational services.

**AMERICAN PETROLEUM INSTITUTE**
1220 L Street NW, Suite 900, Washington DC 20005. 202/682-8000. World Wide Web address: http://www.api.org. A trade association.

**GEOLOGICAL SOCIETY OF AMERICA**
3300 Penrose Place, P.O. Box 9140, Boulder CO 80301. 303/447-2020. World Wide Web address: http://www.geosociety.org. Membership of over 17,000. Offers sales items and publications. Also conducts society meetings.

**NUCLEAR ENERGY INSTITUTE**
1776 I Street NW, Suite 400, Washington DC 20006. 202/739-8000. World Wide Web address: http://www.nei.org. Provides a wide variety of information on nuclear energy issues.

**SOCIETY FOR MINING, METALLURGY, AND EXPLORATION, INC.**
8307 Shaffer Parkway, Littleton CO 80127. 303/973-9550. World Wide Web address: http://www.smenet.org.

**SOCIETY OF EXPLORATION GEOPHYSICISTS**
P.O. Box 702740, Tulsa OK 74170-2740. 918/497-5500. World Wide Web address: http://www.seg.org. A membership association. Offers publications.

**SOCIETY OF PETROLEUM ENGINEERS**
P.O. Box 833836, Richardson TX 75083. 972/952-9393. World Wide Web address: http://www.spe.org.

## Directories

**BROWN'S DIRECTORY OF NORTH AMERICAN & INTERNATIONAL GAS COMPANIES**
Advanstar Communications, 7500 Old Oak Boulevard, Cleveland OH 44130. Toll-free phone: 800/225-4569. World Wide Web address: http://www.advanstar.com.

**OIL AND GAS DIRECTORY**
Geophysical Directory, Inc., P.O. Box 130508, Houston TX 77219. 713/529-8789.

## Magazines

**AMERICAN GAS**
1515 Wilson Boulevard, Suite 100, Arlington VA 22209. 703/841-8686.

**GAS INDUSTRIES**
Gas Industries News, Inc., 6300 North River Road, Suite 505, Rosemont IL 60018. 847/696-2394.

**NATIONAL PETROLEUM NEWS**
Adams Business Media, 2101 South Arlington Heights Road, Suite 150, Arlington Heights IL 60005. 847/427-9512. Fax: 847/427-2006. World Wide Web address: http://www.petroretail.net.

**OIL AND GAS JOURNAL**
PennWell Publishing Company, P.O. Box 1260, Tulsa OK 74101. 918/835-3161. World Wide Web address: http://www.ogjonline.com.

## Online Services

**NATIONAL CENTRE FOR PETROLEUM GEOLOGY AND GEOPHYSICS**
http://www.ncpgg.adelaide.edu.au/ncpgg.html. This Website provides links to sites that post job openings in mining, petroleum, energy, and related fields.

**PETROLEUM & GEOSYSTEMS ENGINEERING**
http://www.pe.utexas.edu/Dept/Reading/pejb.html. Offers a vast list of links to sites that post current job openings in petroleum and geosystems engineering and related fields. The site is run by the University of Texas at Austin. Links to many relevant associations are also offered.

# PAPER AND WOOD PRODUCTS

*Despite an increased demand for U.S. market pulp, the Bureau of Labor Statistics expects a decline in the number of paper industry jobs through 2006. According to the U.S. Department of Commerce, while the pulp sector is expected to enjoy higher sales through 2002, overseas shipment growth should be slower, at 1.8 percent annually.*

*Profits for the industry as a whole increased 89 percent for the first two quarters of 1998 versus profits for the same period of 1997. Profits rose an amazing 211 percent in the second quarter alone, according to* Standard & Poor. *At the same time, industry profit margins more than tripled. Companies such as the Mead Corporation saw varying demand for paper products in 1998.*

*Automation is causing a decline in employment opportunities for precision woodworkers and woodworking machine operators, according to the U.S. Department of Labor. Woodworkers who specialize in furniture, cabinets, moldings, and fixtures should find more abundant opportunities. A significant upswing in the demand for wooden household furniture should result in improved employment prospects.*

**BALTEK CORPORATION**
10 Fairway Court, P.O. Box 195, Northvale NJ 07647. 201/767-1400. **Fax:** 201/387-6631. **Contact:** Human Resources. **Description:** Manufactures wood panels and other balsa wood products for marine and industrial use. **Corporate headquarters location:** This Location.

**BERLIN & JONES COMPANY, INC.**
2 East Union Avenue, East Rutherford NJ 07073. 201/933-5900. **Contact:** Walt Lypowy, Office Manager. **Description:** Manufactures envelopes. **Corporate headquarters location:** This Location.

**BOX USA**
100 Frontage Road, Newark NJ 07114. 973/589-7400. **Contact:** Gene Faulk, Human Resources. **Description:** Manufactures and sells corrugated cartons and displays. Design work is done on the premises.

**CUSTOM INDEX**
50 Furler Street, Totowa NJ 07512. 973/890-2414. **Contact:** Personnel. **Description:** Manufactures index tabs for paper products.

**DOCUSYSTEMS INC.**
151 Cortlandt Street, Belleville NJ 07109. 973/759-6500. **Fax:** 973/450-4703. **Contact:** Leonard Pondiscio, Human Resources Manager. **Description:** Manufactures plastic and paper airline baggage tags. **Benefits:** 401(k); Dental Insurance; Disability Coverage; Employee Discounts; Life Insurance; Medical Insurance; Pension Plan; Tuition Assistance. **Other U.S. locations:** Los Angeles CA; San Francisco CA; Nashville TN; Dallas TX. **Operations at this facility include:** Manufacturing. **Listed on:** Privately held. **Number of employees at this location:** 80. **Number of employees nationwide:** 4,000.

**GARDEN STATE PAPER COMPANY**
669 River Drive, Center 2, Elmwood Park NJ 07407. 201/796-0600. **Contact:** Human Resources. **Description:** A paper mill. **NOTE:** Send resumes to Human Resources, 950 River Drive, Garfield NJ 07026.

**INTERNATIONAL PAPER COMPANY**
75 Chestnut Ridge Road, Montvale NJ 07645. 201/391-1776. **Contact:** Personnel Department. **World Wide Web address:** http://www.ipaper.com. **Description:** This location houses sales offices for paperboard and paper products. Overall, International Paper Company is a manufacturer of pulp and paper, packaging, and wood products, as well as a range of specialty products. Millions

of acres of timberland are controlled by International Paper, making it one of the largest private landowners in the United States. The company is organized into five business segments, including Printing Papers, in which principal products include uncoated papers, coated papers, bristles, and pulp; Packaging, which includes industrial packaging, consumer packaging, and kraft and specialty papers; Distribution, which includes sales of printing papers, graphic arts equipment and supplies, packaging materials, industrial supplies, and office products; Specialty Products, which include imaging products, specialty panels, nonwovens, chemicals, and minerals; and Forest Products, including logs and wood products. **Corporate headquarters location:** Purchase NY. **Number of employees worldwide:** 72,500.

## MAIL-WELL ENVELOPE
25 Linden Avenue East, Jersey City NJ 07305. 201/434-2100x605. **Toll-free phone:** 800/526-3020. **Fax:** 201/434-4048. **Contact:** Nettie Hales, Human Resources Assistant. **World Wide Web address:** http://www.mail-well.com. **Description:** Manufactures and prints envelopes and tags. Primary customers are publishing houses, insurance agencies, banks, direct mail companies, pharmaceutical companies, brokers, and jobbers. **NOTE:** A college education is required of all applicants. Sales experience with industrial accounts is preferred. **Common positions include:** Customer Service Representative; Manufacturer's/Wholesaler's Sales Rep.; Marketing Specialist. **Benefits:** Dental Insurance; Disability Coverage; Savings Plan. **Corporate headquarters location:** Englewood CO. **Operations at this facility include:** Administration; Manufacturing; Research and Development; Sales.

## MANNINGTON MILLS INC.
P.O. Box 30, Salem NJ 08079. 609/935-3000. **Contact:** Kathleen Gaudet, Manager of Human Resources. **Description:** Manufactures and wholesales various floor coverings including vinyl, wood, and carpet.

## MARCAL PAPER MILLS, INC.
One Market Street, Elmwood Park NJ 07407. 201/796-4000. **Contact:** James H. Nelson, Director of Human Resources. **World Wide Web address:** http://www.marcalpaper.com. **Description:** Manufactures and distributes a broad range of nationally advertised paper products including paper towels, toilet tissue, and napkins. **Common positions include:** Accountant/Auditor; Chemical Engineer; Computer Programmer; Customer Service Representative; Manufacturer's/Wholesaler's Sales Rep.; Mechanical Engineer; Operations/Production Manager. **Educational backgrounds include:** Accounting; Business Administration; Engineering. **Benefits:** 401(k); Dental Insurance; Disability Coverage; Employee Discounts; Life Insurance; Medical Insurance; Savings Plan; Tuition Assistance. **Corporate headquarters location:** This Location.

## SCHIFFENHAUS INDUSTRIES
2013 McCarter Highway, Newark NJ 07104. 973/484-5000. **Contact:** Ms. Terri Bissel, Human Resources. **Description:** Manufactures corrugated boxes and flexographic, preprinted liner board. **Common positions include:** Accountant/Auditor; Blue-Collar Worker Supervisor; Computer Programmer; Customer Service Representative; Manufacturer's/Wholesaler's Sales Rep.; Marketing Specialist; Operations/Production Manager; Purchasing Agent/Manager; Quality Control Supervisor. **Educational backgrounds include:** Accounting; Business Administration; Finance; Marketing. **Benefits:** Disability Coverage; Life Insurance; Medical Insurance; Pension Plan; Profit Sharing; Savings Plan; Tuition Assistance. **Corporate headquarters location:** This Location. **Listed on:** New York Stock Exchange. **Number of employees at this location:** 168.

## SIMKINS INDUSTRIES
## LOWE PAPER COMPANY
P.O. Box 239, Ridgefield NJ 07657. 201/945-4900. **Contact:** Marie Flores, Personnel Manager. **Description:** Produces recycled, clay-coated, and specialty boxboard, including extrusion boxboards and specialties. Clients include food, cosmetic, pharmaceutical, and hardware manufacturers and distributors. **Common positions include:** Accountant/Auditor; Administrator; Customer Service Rep.; General Manager; Human Resources Manager; Management Trainee; Mechanical Engineer; Operations/Production Manager; Purchasing Agent/Manager; Quality Control Supervisor; Transportation/Traffic Specialist. **Educational backgrounds include:** Engineering; Science. **Benefits:** Dental Insurance; Disability Coverage; Life Insurance; Medical Insurance; Pension Plan. **Operations at this facility include:** Sales; Service.

## TENSION ENVELOPE CORPORATION
19 Wesley Street, South Hackensack NJ 07606. 201/487-1880. **Contact:** Personnel Manager. **Description:** A manufacturer of specialty envelopes. **Common positions include:** Blue-Collar Worker Supervisor; Commercial Artist; Department Manager; Manufacturer's/Wholesaler's Sales Rep.; Sales Manager. **Educational backgrounds include:** Business Administration; Marketing.

**Benefits:** Dental Insurance; Disability Coverage; Life Insurance; Medical Insurance; Pension Plan; Tuition Assistance. **Corporate headquarters location:** Kansas City MO. **Operations at this facility include:** Administration; Manufacturing; Sales.

## UNION CAMP CORPORATION
1600 Valley Road, Wayne NJ 07470. 973/628-2000. **Contact:** Bathsheba Sams, Personnel. **World Wide Web address:** http://www.unioncamp.com. **Description:** Manufactures forest-based products. Other fields of operation include minerals, land development, chemicals, school supplies, retail building supplies, printing machinery, packaging machinery and systems, plastic products, and cartons and containers. United States facilities include pulp and paper mills, lumber mills, plywood and particleboard plants, and chemical plants. Union Camp's research and development activities are centered in Princeton NJ. **Corporate headquarters location:** This Location.

*Note: Because addresses and telephone numbers of smaller companies can change rapidly, we recommend you call each company to verify the information below before inquiring about job opportunities. Mass mailings are not recommended.*

### Additional small employers:

**COATED AND LAMINATED PAPER**

**Frost King**
PO Box 2547, Paterson NJ 07509-2547. 973/684-5000.

**Holland Manufacturing Co.**
PO Box 404, Succasunna NJ 07876-0404. 973/584-8141.

**Polyken Technologies**
87 Lincoln Blvd, Middlesex NJ 08846-1020. 908/354-2870.

**CONVERTED PAPER AND PAPERBOARD PRODUCTS**

**BCI Book Covers**
84 Lockwood St, Newark NJ 07105-4719. 973/817-9000.

**BMI Holdings Inc.**
1200 Madison Ave, Paterson NJ 07503-2813. 973/345-8300.

**CCL Label Inc.**
120 Stockton St, Hightstown NJ 08520-3706. 609/443-3700.

**Rockline Industries Inc.**
227 Changebridge Rd, Montville NJ 07045-9514. 973/257-9346.

**Stephen Lawrence Co. Inc.**
35 State St, Moonachie NJ 07074-1402. 201/807-0500.

**DIE-CUT PAPER AND PAPER PRODUCTS**

**Recycled Paperboard Inc.**
1 Ackerman Ave, Clifton NJ 07011-1501. 973/546-0030.

**INDUSTRIAL PAPER AND RELATED PRODUCTS WHOLESALE**

**Bunzl New Jersey Inc.**
PO Box 668, Dayton NJ 08810-0668. 732/821-7000.

**VIP Packaging**
487 Hillside Ave, Hillside NJ 07205-1121. 908/964-0033.

**LUMBER AND WOOD WHOLESALE**

**Adam Wholesalers Inc.**
PO Box 529, Woodbury Heights NJ 08097-0529. 609/848-8000.

**Allied Building Products Co.**
PO Box 511, East Rutherford NJ 07073-0511. 201/507-8400.

**BWI**
210 Industrial Pkwy, Somerville NJ 08876-3450. 908/526-7555.

**Thermo Guard Inc.**
PO Box 682, Hammonton NJ 08037-0682. 609/567-3600.

**MILLWORK, PLYWOOD, AND STRUCTURAL MEMBERS**

**Joffe Lumber & Supply Co. Inc.**
PO Box K, Vineland NJ 08360. 609/825-9550.

**PAPER BAGS**

**Alpha Industries Inc.**
PO Box 808, Lyndhurst NJ 07071-0808. 201/933-6000.

**S&G Packaging Co.**
750 Dowd Ave, Elizabeth NJ 07201-2108. 908/351-2400.

**Zeta Consumer Products Corp.**
555 State Route 57, Port Murray NJ 07865-4335. 908/835-0215.

**PAPER MILLS**

**Amco Folding Cartons Inc.**
PO Box 98, Towaco NJ 07082-0098. 973/334-3030.

**Arko Paper Products Co. Inc.**
4100 New Brunswick Ave, Piscataway NJ 08854-3424. 732/424-2100.

**Crown Vantage**
404 Frenchtown Rd, Milford NJ 08848-1331. 908/995-2411.

**Fibermark Inc.**
PO Box 1140, Alpha NJ 08865-1140. 908/995-2424.

**Gift Box Corporation of America**
305 Veterans Blvd, Carlstadt NJ 07072-2708. 201/933-9777.

**Innovative Folding Carton**
901 Durham Ave, South Plainfield NJ 07080-2401. 908/757-6000.

**Lawrence Packaging Supply**
10 Caesar Pl, Moonachie NJ 07074-1701. 201/438-3515.

**Rock-Tenn Company**
164 Laidlaw Ave, Jersey City NJ 07306-2513. 201/653-0606.

**Sharp Ivers-Lee**
147 Clinton Rd, Caldwell NJ 07006-6601. 973/575-9000.

**PAPERBOARD CONTAINERS AND BOXES**

**Bell Container Corp.**
615 Ferry St, Newark NJ 07105-4404. 973/344-4400.

**Delta Corrugated Paper Products**
W Ruby Railroad Ave, Palisades Park NJ 07650. 201/941-1910.

**Express Container Corp.**
105 Avenue L, Newark NJ 07105-3807. 973/589-2155.

**Greater New York Box Co. Inc.**
PO Box 907, Clifton NJ 07014-0907. 973/472-3600.

**Inland Paperboard & Packaging**
140 Summerhill Rd, Spotswood NJ 08884-1235. 732/251-2000.

**Integrated Packaging**
122 Quentin Ave, New Brunswick NJ 08901-3263. 732/247-5200.

**MacMillan Bloedel Container**
PO Box 6697, Jersey City NJ 07306-0697. 201/656-5550.

**PCI Services Inc.**
1665 John Tipton Blvd, Pennsauken NJ 08110-2305. 609/486-0566.

**Phoenix Display and Packaging**
1300 Metropolitan Ave, Paulsboro NJ 08066-1823. 609/853-7000.

**President Container Inc.**
PO Box 247, Moonachie NJ 07074. 201/933-7500.

**Republic Container Corp.**
1561 John F. Kennedy Blvd, Jersey City NJ 07305-1721. 201/333-2564.

**Rock-Tenn Company**
PO Box H, Vineland NJ 08360. 609/691-9610.

**Smurfit Stone Container Corp.**
200 Hollister Rd, Teterboro NJ 07608-1134. 201/288-1541.

**Smurfit Stone Quality Partition**
PO Box 2200, Flemington NJ 08822-2200. 908/782-0505.

**Southern Container**
1 Corn Rd, Dayton NJ 08810-1527. 732/329-2664.

**Union Camp Corporation**
PO Box 555C, Clifton NJ 07012-0995. 973/779-1700.

**Union Camp Corporation**
480 Alfred Ave, Teaneck NJ 07666-5756. 201/568-6900.

**Union Camp Corporation**
PO Box 3301, Princeton NJ 08543-3301. 609/896-1200.

**Union Camp Corporation**
65 Oxford Dr, Moonachie NJ 07074-1020. 201/296-3900.

**Union Camp Corporation**
PO Box 2040, Trenton NJ 08607-2040. 609/587-2000.

**Universal Folding Box Co. Inc.**
Madison & 13th Streets, Hoboken NJ 07030. 201/659-7373.

**Victory Box Corp.**
645 W 1st Ave, Roselle NJ 07203-1027. 908/245-5100.

**Weyerhaeuser**
Railroad Ave, Closter NJ 07624. 201/768-6161.

## WOOD PRODUCTS

**Ginsey Industries Inc.**
281 Benigno Blvd, Bellmawr NJ 08031-2513. 609/933-1300.

**Homasote Company**
PO Box 7240, Trenton NJ 08628-0240. 609/883-3300.

## For more information on career opportunities in the paper and wood products industries:

### Associations

**FOREST PRODUCTS SOCIETY**
2801 Marshall Court, Madison WI 53705-2295. 608/231-1361. World Wide Web address: http://www.supranet.com/forestprod. An international, nonprofit, educational association that provides an information network for all segments of the forest products industry, as well as an employment referral service.

**NATIONAL PAPER TRADE ASSOCIATION**
111 Great Neck Road, Great Neck NY 11021. 516/829-3070. World Wide Web address: http://www.papertrade.com. Offers management services to paper wholesalers, as well as books, seminars, and research services.

**PAPERBOARD PACKAGING COUNCIL**
201 North Union Street, Suite 220, Alexandria VA 22314. 703/836-3300. Offers statistical and lobbying services.

**TECHNICAL ASSOCIATION OF THE PULP AND PAPER INDUSTRY**
P.O. Box 105113, Norcross GA 30092. 770/446-1400. World Wide Web address: http://www.tappi.org A nonprofit organization offering conferences and continuing education.

### Directories

**DIRECTORY OF THE WOOD PRODUCTS INDUSTRY**
Miller Freeman, Inc., 600 Harrison Street, San Francisco CA 94107. 415/905-2200. World Wide Web address: http://www.woodwideweb.com.

**INTERNATIONAL PULP AND PAPER DIRECTORY**
Miller Freeman, Inc., 600 Harrison Street, San Francisco CA 94107. 415/905-2200. World Wide Web address: http://www.pulp-paper.com.

**LOCKWOOD-POST'S DIRECTORY OF THE PULP, PAPER AND ALLIED TRADES**
Miller Freeman, Inc., 600 Harrison Street, San Francisco CA 94107. 415/905-2200. World Wide Web address: http://www.pulp-paper.com/lpdisk.htm.

### Magazines

**PAPERBOARD PACKAGING**
Advanstar Communications, 131 West First Street, Duluth MN 55802. 218/723-9200. World Wide Web address: http://www.advanstar.com.

**PULP & PAPER**
Miller Freeman, Inc., 600 Harrison Street, San Francisco CA 94107. 415/905-2200. World Wide Web address: http://www.mfi.com.

**WOOD TECHNOLOGY**
Miller Freeman, Inc., 600 Harrison Street, San Francisco CA 94107. 415/905-2200. World Wide Web address: http://www.woodtechmag.com.

# PRINTING AND PUBLISHING

The publishing industry saw profit gains of 20 percent during the first six months of 1998 as compared to the same period of 1997. New printing production and editorial systems, Web publishing software, and digital color proofs are just a few of the high-tech offerings which continue to revolutionize the book publishing industry. At this point, technology is outpacing the industry and analysts think it will take a few more years before these new technologies are fully integrated into book publishing.

A recent survey by Arthur Andersen reveals that industry mergers may be a continuing trend. Results showed that 79 percent of book publishing executives are considering a merger or acquisition transaction. Bertelsmann AG purchased Random House, Inc. from Advance Publications, Inc. in 1998. Other acquisitions included Pearson Plc.'s purchase of Viacom's educational, professional, and reference publishing divisions, and Barnes and Noble's purchase of the Ingram Book Group, a leading U.S. book distributor. The Arthur Andersen survey also indicates that publishers are motivated to agree to these deals in order to broaden product lines and increase market share in the industry. Overall, book sales have risen only about 5 percent since 1992, according to Veronis Suhler & Associates Inc.

According to the Association of American Publishers, the best book sales in 1997 were in education and professional book publishing. Another area that will be looking to expand is travel publishing. The World Tourism Organization predicts that by 2020 travel will be one of the leading industries in the United States. Look for publishers to expand their selections of travel books in an attempt to capture very specific audiences.

Newspapers lost 5.5 million customers between 1986 and 1996, due in part to higher prices and online news access. However, several newspapers are starting to see incremental sales growth. This growth is the result of new advertising campaigns, changes in production schedules to deliver papers earlier, and utilization of the Internet. Most regional and national newspapers now have their own Websites, allowing for topical research and access to current news and archives.

**ALEXANDER HAMILTON INSTITUTE INC.**
70 Hilltop Road, Ramsey NJ 07746-1119. **Toll-free phone:** 800/879-2441. **Fax:** 201/825-8696. **Contact:** Human Resources. **World Wide Web address:** http://ahipubs.com. **Description:** Publishes newsletters and manuals focused on employment law.

**APPLIED GRAPHICS TECHNOLOGIES (AGT)**
463 Barell Avenue, Carlstadt NJ 07072. 201/935-3200. **Fax:** 201/935-5108. **Contact:** Human Resources Director. **World Wide Web address:** http://www.agt.com. **Description:** This location offers publication and catalog services, satellite transmission services, a desktop service bureau, four-color facsimile or digital transmittal, and packaging services. Overall, Applied Graphics Technologies (AGT) is one of the largest providers of integrated graphic communications services to advertising agencies, magazine and catalog publishers, and corporate clients in various industries. The company's services include commercial printing, color separation and retouching,

facilities management, photo CD and digital image archiving, electronic imaging services, flexo/packaging services, publication and catalog services, satellite transmission services, creative design services, technical support and training services, and black and white ad production. **Corporate headquarters location:** New York NY. **Other U.S. locations:** Washington DC; Jericho NY.

## APPLIED PRINTING TECHNOLOGIES
77 Moonachie Avenue, Moonachie NJ 07074. 201/896-6600. **Fax:** 201/896-1893. **Contact:** Human Resources Department. **World Wide Web address:** http://www.aptlp.com. **Description:** Applied Printing Technologies offers commercial printing services, bindery services, a desktop service bureau, and advertising agency services. **Corporate headquarters location:** New York NY.

## THE ASBURY PARK PRESS
3601 Highway 66, P.O. Box 1550, Neptune NJ 07754. 732/922-6000x3111. **Fax:** 732/918-9144. **Contact:** Human Resources Department. **Description:** A publisher of a daily newspaper. **Common positions include:** Advertising Clerk; Blue-Collar Worker Supervisor; Branch Manager; Broadcast Technician; Computer Programmer; Credit Manager; Customer Service Representative; Electrician; General Manager; Human Resources Manager; Industrial Engineer; Management Analyst/Consultant; Management Trainee; Manufacturer's/Wholesaler's Sales Representative; Operations/Production Manager; Property and Real Estate Manager; Public Relations Specialist; Purchasing Agent/Manager; Radio/TV Announcer/Broadcaster; Services Sales Representative; Systems Analyst; Technical Writer/Editor; Transportation/Traffic Specialist; Travel Agent. **Educational backgrounds include:** Accounting; Art/Design; Business Administration; Communications; Computer Science; Economics; Finance; Liberal Arts; Marketing; Mathematics. **Benefits:** 401(k); Dental Insurance; Disability Coverage; Employee Discounts; Life Insurance; Medical Insurance; Pension Plan; Savings Plan; Tuition Assistance; Vision Insurance. **Special programs:** Internships. **Corporate headquarters location:** This Location. **Other U.S. locations:** Orlando FL. **Operations at this facility include:** Administration; Sales; Service. **Number of employees nationwide:** 1,900.

## BAKER & TAYLOR BOOKS
44 Kirby Avenue, Somerville NJ 08876. 908/722-8000. **Contact:** Human Resources Department. **Description:** Baker & Taylor Books produces, sells, and distributes books.

## BERLITZ INTERNATIONAL, INC.
400 Alexander Park, Princeton NJ 08540. 609/514-9650. **Contact:** David Horn, Vice President of Personnel, North America. **World Wide Web address:** http://www.berlitz.com. **Description:** Berlitz International, Inc. is a language services firm that provides instruction and translation services through 298 language centers in 28 countries around the world. The company also publishes travel guides, foreign language phrase books, and home study materials. **Common positions include:** Accountant/Auditor; Director; Instructor/Trainer; Services Sales Representative. **Educational backgrounds include:** Accounting; Business Administration; Finance; Foreign Languages; Liberal Arts. **Corporate headquarters location:** This Location. **Operations at this facility include:** Administration. **Listed on:** New York Stock Exchange. **Number of employees nationwide:** 3,500.

## BOOKAZINE COMPANY INC.
75 Hook Road, Bayonne NJ 07002. 201/339-7777. **Contact:** Richard Kallman, Vice President. **Description:** A general trade book wholesaler serving retail bookstores with a full line of titles. **Corporate headquarters location:** This Location.

## CAHNERS TRAVEL GROUP
500 Plaza Drive, Secaucus NJ 07094. 201/902-2000 **Contact:** Staffing Manager. **World Wide Web address:** http://www.travelcr.net. **Description:** Cahners Travel Group is a publisher of travel books and maps. **Common positions include:** Designer; Editor; Systems Analyst. **Educational backgrounds include:** Art/Design. **Special programs:** Internships. **Parent company:** Cahners Business Information (Newton MA) is one of the largest publishing companies in the U.S. The company produces over 50 magazines focusing on specialized business and consumer fields. Cahners Travel Group also provides many marketing and publishing services such as direct mail, economic forecasts, and advertising and marketing research. **Operations at this facility include:** Sales.

## CONSTRUCTION DATA CORPORATION
1911 Princeton Avenue, Lawrenceville NJ 08648. 609/394-4800. **Toll-free phone:** 800/395-1400. **Fax:** 800/395-1162. **Contact:** H.A. Sonier, Jr., Managing Editor. **World Wide Web address:**

http://www.cdcnews.com. **Description:** A construction trade publication which provides planning news and bidding opportunities in Connecticut, Delaware, New Jersey, New York, and Pennsylvania. **NOTE:** Entry-level positions are offered. **Common positions include:** Data Entry Clerk; Editor; Editorial Assistant; Reporter; Typist/Word Processor. **Educational backgrounds include:** Business Administration; Communications; Liberal Arts. **Benefits:** 401(k); Dental Insurance; Life Insurance; Medical Insurance; Public Transit Available; Tuition Assistance. **Special programs:** Internships. **Corporate headquarters location:** Vero Beach FL. **Other U.S. locations:** Rockland MA; Austin TX. **Listed on:** Privately held. **Annual sales/revenues:** $11 - $20 million. **Number of employees at this location:** 65. **Number of employees nationwide:** 175.

### COURIER-POST NEWSPAPER
P.O. Box 5300, Cherry Hill NJ 08034. 609/663-6000. **Contact:** Human Resources. **Description:** A newspaper with a circulation of approximately 100,000.

### THE DAILY RECORD INC.
800 Jefferson Road, Parsippany NJ 07054. 973/428-6200. **Contact:** Ellen Houlihan, Benefits Administrator. **World Wide Web address:** http://www.dailyrecord.com. **Description:** Publishes a morning newspaper, *The Daily Record.* Circulation is approximately 63,000 weekdays and 72,000 on Sunday. **Common positions include:** Accountant/Auditor; Administrative Manager; Advertising Clerk; Computer Programmer; Credit Manager; Customer Service Rep.; Editor; General Manager; Purchasing Agent/Manager; Reporter; Sales Representative; Services Sales Rep. **Educational backgrounds include:** Accounting; Business Administration; Communications. **Benefits:** 401(k); Dental Insurance; Disability Coverage; Employee Discounts; Life Insurance; Medical Insurance. **Operations at this facility include:** Administration; Sales; Service.

### DELUXE FINANCIAL SERVICES
105 Route 46 West, Mountain Lakes NJ 07046-1645. 973/334-8000. **Contact:** Russ Perry, Personnel Director. **Description:** Engaged in printing and selling a variety of checks, deposit tickets, and related forms to banks and other financial institutions. The company also manufactures documents printed with magnetic ink. Printing operations are carried out at more than 15 plants throughout the United States. **Corporate headquarters location:** Shoreview MN. **Parent company:** Deluxe Corporation provides check printing, electronic funds transfer processing services, and related services to the financial industry; check authorization and collection services to retailers; and electronic benefit transfer services to state governments. Deluxe also produces forms, specialty papers, and other products for small businesses, professional practices, and medical/dental offices; and provides tax forms and electronic tax filing services to tax preparers. Through the direct-mail channel, Deluxe sells greeting cards and gift wrap. Deluxe is a *Fortune* 500 company with facilities located in the United States, Canada, and the United Kingdom. Founded in 1915.

### DOW JONES & COMPANY, INC.
P.O. Box 300, Princeton NJ 08543-0300. 609/520-4000. **Contact:** Lisa Charles, Employee Relations. **World Wide Web address:** http://www.dowjones.com. **Description:** A financial news service and publishing company. Publications include *The Wall Street Journal* and *Barron's* educational book services.

### DOWDEN PUBLISHING COMPANY
110 Summit Avenue, Montvale NJ 07645. 201/391-9100. **Contact:** Human Resources. **Description:** Publishes newsletters for the health care industry.

### THE ECONOMICS PRESS, INC.
12 Daniel Road, Fairfield NJ 07004. 973/227-1224. **Toll-free phone:** 800/526-2554. **Fax:** 973/227-9742. **Contact:** Human Resources. **E-mail address:** info@epinc.com. **World Wide Web address:** http://www.epinc.com. **Description:** A publisher of books, audio and video programs, and computer programs focused on employee training, motivation, and business information.

### FAULKNER INFORMATION SERVICES
7905 Browning Road, 114 Cooper Center, Pennsauken NJ 08109-4319. 609/662-2070. **Toll-free phone:** 800/843-0460. **Fax:** 609/662-3380. **Contact:** Betsey Thomas, Operations/Personnel Administrator. **E-mail address:** faulkner@faulkner.com. **World Wide Web address:** http://www.faulkner.com. **Description:** An independent publishing and research company specializing in providing technical information and insight to end users and communication and IT professionals for nearly three decades. Faulkner Information Services publishes more than a dozen standard information services in both print and electronic formats. The company provides comprehensive intelligence on products, vendors, technological advancements, and management issues associated with a wide range of technologies from open systems and client/server to

enterprise networking, workgroup computing, and telecommunications. Faulkner also offers custom research and publication capabilities in such areas as market studies, customer satisfaction surveys, competitive analysis reports, and custom databases. **Common positions include:** Accountant/Auditor; Customer Service Representative; Human Resources Manager; Systems Analyst; Technical Writer/Editor. **Educational backgrounds include:** Communications; Computer Science; English. **Benefits:** 401(k); Dental Insurance; Disability Coverage; Life Insurance; Medical Insurance; Tuition Assistance. **Corporate headquarters location:** This Location. **Operations at this facility include:** Administration; Research and Development; Sales; Service. **Number of employees at this location:** 45.

### HOME NEWS TRIBUNE
35 Kennedy Boulevard, East Brunswick NJ 08816. 732/246-5500. **Contact:** Personnel Department. **World Wide Web address:** http://www.injersey.com/hnt. **Description:** Publishes an independently-owned daily newspaper with a weekday circulation of more than 51,000. **Corporate headquarters location:** This Location.

### IMTEK, INC.
P.O. Box 621, Bridgeport NJ 08014. 609/467-0047. **Physical address:** 110 High Hill Road, Bridgeport NJ 08014. **Contact:** Personnel Director. **Description:** Provides complete lithography and bookbinding services. **Corporate headquarters location:** This Location.

### THE JERSEY JOURNAL
30 Journal Square, Jersey City NJ 07306. 201/653-1000. **Contact:** Managing Editor. **Description:** Publishes a daily morning newspaper with a circulation of more than 55,000. **NOTE:** The Circulation Manager or the Advertising Manager can also be contacted. **Parent company:** Newhouse Newspapers Group.

### MACNAUGHTON EINSON GRAPHICS
20-10 Maple Avenue, Fair Lawn NJ 07410. 973/423-1900. **Contact:** Kathy Green, Personnel. **Description:** Provides a full range of commercial printing services.

### MACROMEDIA, INC.
150 River Street, Hackensack NJ 07601-7172. 201/646-4545. **Contact:** Human Resources. **Description:** A holding company for newspaper publishers. **Subsidiaries include:** Bergen Record Corporation publishes *The Record*, a daily newspaper with a circulation of 150 and 220 for the Sunday edition. Gremac publishes *Herald* and *News* as well as 17 other weekly publications.

### MARS GRAPHIC SERVICES INC.
One Deadline Drive, P.O. Box 167, Westville NJ 08093. 609/456-8666. **Contact:** Cynthia Yula, Human Resources. **Description:** A printer and lithographer.

### McBEE SYSTEMS
299 Cherry Hill Road, Parsippany NJ 07054. 973/263-3225. **Fax:** 973/263-8165. **Contact:** Cynthia Burke, National Recruiting, T&D Manager. **World Wide Web address:** http://www. mcbeesystems.com. **Description:** Manufactures business forms designed specifically for small businesses and professional offices. **Common positions include:** Customer Service Representative; Sales Representative. **Educational backgrounds include:** Accounting; Business Administration. **Benefits:** Dental Insurance; Disability Coverage; Life Insurance; Medical Insurance; Savings Plan; Tuition Assistance. **Corporate headquarters location:** This Location. **Parent company:** Romo Corporation. **Operations at this facility include:** Administration. **Number of employees nationwide:** 530.

### THE McGRAW-HILL COMPANIES
148 Princeton Hightstown Road, Hightstown NJ 08520. 609/426-5000. **Contact:** Recruitment Manager. **Description:** This location houses administrative offices. Overall, McGraw-Hill is a provider of information and services through books, magazines, newsletters, software, CD-ROMs, and online data, fax, and TV broadcasting services. The company operates four network-affiliated TV stations and also publishes *Business Week* magazine and books for the college, medical, international, legal, and professional markets. McGraw-Hill also offers financial services including Standard & Poor's, commodity items, and international and logistics management products and services.

### MEDICAL ECONOMICS COMPANY
5 Paragon Drive, Montvale NJ 07645. 201/358-7500. **Fax:** 201/722-2668. **Contact:** Human Resources. **World Wide Web address:** http://www.medec.com. **Description:** Publishes medical books and journals. **Common positions include:** Accountant/Auditor; Advertising Clerk; Artist;

Commercial Artist; Computer Programmer; Customer Service Representative; Designer; Editor; Financial Manager; Human Resources Manager; Librarian; Marketing Specialist; Receptionist; Services Sales Representative; Systems Analyst; Technical Writer/Editor; Typist/Word Processor. **Educational backgrounds include:** Accounting; Art/Design; Business Administration; Communications; Finance; Marketing. **Benefits:** Dental Insurance; Disability Coverage; Life Insurance; Medical Insurance; Pension Plan; Savings Plan; Tuition Assistance; Vision Insurance. **Special programs:** Internships. **Corporate headquarters location:** This Location. **Other U.S. locations:** DC; IL; KS. **Operations at this facility include:** Research and Development; Sales; Service. **Number of employees at this location:** 425. **Number of employees nationwide:** 510.

**NEWARK STAR-LEDGER**
One Star Ledger Plaza, Newark NJ 07102-1200. 973/877-4141. **Contact:** Human Resources. **World Wide Web address:** http://www.nj.com. **Description:** Publishes a large circulation daily newspaper.

**PANTONE**
590 Commerce Boulevard, Carlstadt NJ 07072. 201/935-5500. **Contact:** Manager of Human Resources. **Description:** Produces color charts and color specification materials used by the printing and publishing industries. **Common positions include:** Accountant; Assistant Manager; Blue-Collar Worker Supervisor; Chemist; Credit Manager; Customer Service Rep.; General Manager; Human Resources Manager; Manufacturer's/Wholesaler's Sales Rep.; Marketing Manager; Operations/Production Manager; Public Relations Specialist. **Educational backgrounds include:** Accounting; Chemistry; Computer Science; Finance; Marketing. **Benefits:** Dental Insurance; Life Insurance; Medical Insurance; Pension Plan; Savings Plan; Tuition Assistance. **Corporate headquarters location:** This Location. **Operations at this facility include:** Administration; Manufacturing; Research and Development; Sales.

**PARIS BUSINESS PRODUCTS, INC.**
122 Kissel Road, Burlington NJ 08016. 609/387-7300. **Fax:** 609/387-2114. **Contact:** Vince Thompson, Personnel Manager. **World Wide Web address:** http://www.pariscorp.com. **Description:** Produces business forms.

**PERMANENT LABEL**
801 Bloomfield Avenue, Clifton NJ 07012. 973/471-6617. **Contact:** Human Resources. **Description:** Engaged in decorating and printing labels for plastic products, primarily bottles. **Corporate headquarters location:** This Location.

**QUALEX, INC.**
16-31 Route 208, Fair Lawn NJ 07410. 201/797-0600. **Contact:** Karen Mergenthaler, Senior Human Resources Manager. **Description:** A photofinishing company providing processing services for print and reversal type films. **Common positions include:** Administrative Worker/Clerk; Customer Service Representative; Electronics Technician; Maintenance Technician; Photographic Process Worker; Print Coordinator. **Educational backgrounds include:** Electronics; Phototechnology. **Benefits:** Dental Insurance, Employee Discounts; Life Insurance; Medical Insurance; Pension Plan; Profit Sharing; Savings Plan; Tuition Assistance. **Corporate headquarters location:** Durham NC. **Parent company:** Eastman Kodak Company. **Operations at this facility include:** Administration; Customer Service; Sales; Service.

**REED ELSEVIER NEW PROVIDENCE**
121 Chanlon Road, New Providence NJ 07974. 908/665-6775. **Toll-free phone:** 800/521-8100. **Contact:** Human Resources. **World Wide Web address:** http://www.reedref.com. **Descript** A reference publisher of marketing, advertising, and corporate directories.

**RIDGEWOOD NEWSPAPERS/RIDGEWOOD NEWS**
988 Main Avenue, Passaic NJ 07055. 973/365-3000. **Contact:** Charles McDermott, Personnel. **Description:** Publishes several area newspapers including *Ridgewood News/Ridgewood Sunday News*, an area weekly with a circulation of more than 19,000. **Corporate headquarters location:** This Location.

**ROYAL/HOROWITZ/RAE**
282 Grove Avenue, Cedar Grove NJ 07009. 973/239-1601. **Contact:** Bob Kessler, Director of Human Resources. **Description:** A book bindery.

**SHOPPER'S GUIDE INC.**
8 Ranauldo Drive, Cherry Hill NJ 08034. 609/616-4900. **Contact:** Human Resource Manager. **World Wide Web address:** http://www.theshoppersguide.com. **Description:** One of the

Northeast's largest, free, weekly, shopper newspapers. **Common positions include:** Administrative Assistant; Collections Agent; Sales Executive; Sales Manager; Systems Analyst. **Parent company:** Newport Media, Inc.

**SIMON & SCHUSTER, INC.**
100 Front Street, Riverside NJ 08075. 609/461-6500. **Fax:** 609/461-4205. **Contact:** Dee Chassey, Human Resources Manager. **World Wide Web address:** http://www.simonandschuster.com. **Description:** This location is a distribution center. Overall, Simon & Schuster publishes consumer, educational, and professional books. **Other U.S. locations:** CA; MA; NY; OH. **Subsidiaries include:** Macmillan. **Parent company:** Viacom. **Number of employees nationwide:** 4,000.

**SIMON & SCHUSTER, INC.**
200 Old Tappan Road, Old Tappan NJ 07675. 201/767-5000. **Contact:** Staffing Manager. **World Wide Web address:** http://www.simonandschuster.com. **Description:** This location is a customer service center. Overall, Simon & Schuster publishes consumer, educational, and professional books. **Common positions include:** Accountant/Auditor; Budget Analyst; Computer Programmer; Credit Manager; Customer Service Representative; Data Entry Clerk; Financial Analyst; Human Resources Manager; Systems Analyst. **Educational backgrounds include:** Accounting; Communications; Finance. **Benefits:** 401(k); Dental Insurance; Disability Coverage; Employee Discounts; Life Insurance; Medical Insurance; Pension Plan; Savings Plan; Tuition Assistance. **Other U.S. locations:** CA; MA; NY; OH. **Subsidiaries include:** Macmillan; Prentice-Hall. **Parent company:** Viacom. **Operations at this facility include:** Administration; Service. **Number of employees nationwide:** 4,000.

**SIMON & SCHUSTER, INC.**
**PRENTICE HALL INC.**
One Lake Street, Upper Saddle River NJ 07458. 201/236-7000. **Contact:** Human Resources. **World Wide Web address:** http://www.simonandschuster.com. **Description:** This location houses corporate offices. Overall, Simon & Schuster publishes consumer, educational, and professional books. Prentice Hall (also at this location) specializes in business and professional books, as well as college-level resource materials. **Subsidiaries include:** Macmillan; Prentice Hall Inc. **Parent company:** Viacom. **Number of employees nationwide:** 4,000.

**SOUTH JERSEY PUBLISHING COMPANY**
1000 West Washington Avenue, Pleasantville NJ 08232. 609/272-7103. **Fax:** 609/272-7135. **Contact:** Kathleen Leonard, Personnel Director. **World Wide Web address:** http://www.pressplus.com. **Description:** Publishes the *Atlantic City Press*. **Common positions include:** Advertising Manager; Customer Service Representative; Reporter. **Educational backgrounds include:** Accounting; Business Administration; Marketing. **Benefits:** 401(k); Dental Insurance; Disability Coverage; Employee Discounts; Life Insurance; Medical Insurance; Pension Plan; Savings Plan; Tuition Assistance. **Special programs:** Internships. **Corporate headquarters location:** Pittsburgh PA. **Parent company:** Abarta Inc. **Operations at this facility include:** Administration; Manufacturing; Sales; Service. **Listed on:** Privately held. **Number of employees at this location:** 360. **Number of employees nationwide:** 430.

**L.P. THEBAULT COMPANY**
P.O. Box 169, 249 Pomeroy Road, Parsippany NJ 07054. 973/884-1300. **Fax:** 973/952-8232. **Contact:** Human Resources Manager. **Description:** One of the largest commercial printing establishments in the United States. The company specializes in the print-buying market, with projects ranging from annual reports to promotional pieces worldwide. **Common positions include:** Management Trainee. **Educational backgrounds include:** Accounting; Business Administration; Finance. **Benefits:** 401(k); Dental Insurance; Disability Coverage; Employee Discounts; Life Insurance; Medical Insurance; Tuition Assistance. **Special programs:** Internships. **Corporate headquarters location:** This Location. **Other U.S. locations:** Detroit MI; New York NY. **Subsidiaries include:** LPT Express Graphics. **Operations at this facility include:** Administration; Manufacturing; Sales. **Number of employees nationwide:** 400.

**JOHN WILEY & SONS, INC.**
One Wiley Drive, Somerset NJ 08875. 732/469-4400. **Toll-free phone:** 800/225-5945. **Contact:** Tracy Mazza, Human Resources. **World Wide Web address:** http://www.wiley.com. **Description:** This location houses the United States distribution center. Overall, John Wiley & Sons, Inc. is an international publishing house that publishes in four categories: Educational; Professional; Trade; and Scientific, Technical, and Medical (STM). In Educational, Wiley publishes textbooks and instructional packages for undergraduate and graduate students in the U.S. and internationally. Publishing programs focus on the physical and life sciences, mathematics, engineering, and accounting, with an increasing emphasis on economics, finance, business, MIS/CIS, and foreign

languages. In Professional, Wiley publishes books and subscription products for lawyers, architects, accountants, engineers, and other professionals. In Trade, Wiley publishes nonfiction books in areas such as business, computers, science, and general interest. In STM, Wiley publishes approximately 260 scholarly and professional journals, as well as encyclopedias, other major reference works, and books for the research and academic communities. Major subject areas include chemistry, the life sciences, and technology. **Corporate headquarters location:** New York NY. **Other U.S. locations:** Colorado Springs CO. **Listed on:** NASDAQ. **Number of employees nationwide:** 1,500.

**WORRALL COMMUNITY NEWSPAPERS INCORPORATED**
P.O. Box 3109, Union NJ 07083-1919. 908/686-7700. **Contact:** Human Resources. **Description:** A publisher of 18 weekly newspapers in Union and Essex Counties with a total circulation of over 40,000.

*Note: Because addresses and telephone numbers of smaller companies can change rapidly, we recommend you call each company to verify the information below before inquiring about job opportunities. Mass mailings are not recommended.*

**Additional small employers:**

**BLANK BOOKS AND BOOKBINDING**

**Bind Rite Service Inc.**
16 Horizon Blvd, South Hackensack NJ 07606-1804. 201/440-5585.

**GH Alliance Inc.**
7115 Airport Hwy, Pennsauken NJ 08109-4301. 609/665-8700.

**Remco Bindery**
265 Coles St, Jersey City NJ 07310-1027. 201/656-2520.

**BOOKS, PERIODICALS, AND NEWSPAPERS WHOLESALE**

**Blackwell's**
100 University Ct, Blackwood NJ 08012-3214. 609/629-0700.

**Curtis Circulation Company**
2500 McClellan Blvd, Fl 4, Pennsauken NJ 08109-4613. 609/488-5700.

**Harcourt Brace & Company**
151 Benigno Blvd, Bellmawr NJ 08031-2515. 609/931-5228.

**Hudson News**
1305 Paterson Plank Rd, North Bergen NJ 07047. 201/867-3600.

**Koen Book Distributors Inc.**
PO Box 600, Moorestown NJ 08057-0600. 609/235-4444.

**Sher Distributing Co.**
PO Box CN 0417, Totowa NJ 07511. 973/256-4050.

**BOOKS: PUBLISHING AND/OR PRINTING**

**Penguin Putnam Inc.**
390 Murray Hill Pkwy, East Rutherford NJ 07073-2109. 201/933-9292.

**Quinn-Woodbine Inc.**
1585 Dehirsch Ave, Woodbine NJ 08270-2405. 609/861-5352.

**Silver Burdett Ginn Inc.**
PO Box 480, Parsippany NJ 07054-0480. 973/739-8000.

**Troll Associates**
100 Corporate Dr, Mahwah NJ 07430. 201/529-4000.

**Visual Education Corporation**
PO Box 2321, Princeton NJ 08543-2321. 609/799-9200.

**Watson Duptill Publications**
1695 Oak St, Lakewood NJ 08701-5925. 732/363-4511.

**COMMERCIAL ART AND GRAPHIC DESIGN**

**Digital Color Image Inc.**
1055 Central Hwy, Pennsauken NJ 08109-4605. 609/662-5532.

**Graphic Design Technologies**
485 Bloy St, Hillside NJ 07205-1707. 908/687-0200.

**MC Decorating Co. Inc.**
PO Box 201, Rio Grande NJ 08242-0201. 609/886-6700.

**Scancelli**
PO Box 416, East Rutherford NJ 07073-0416. 201/933-0720.

**COMMERCIAL PRINTING**

**AQL Decorating Co. Inc.**
215 Bergen Blvd, Fairview NJ 07022-1301. 201/941-1610.

**Bowne Business Communications**
215 County Ave, Secaucus NJ 07094-2006. 201/271-2000.

**Butler Printing and Laminate**
PO Box 836, Butler NJ 07405-0836. 973/838-8550.

**Celebration**
PO Box 370, Mount Holly NJ 08060-0370. 609/261-5200.

**Chapel Company Inc.**
PO Box 830, Moorestown NJ 08057-0830. 609/727-1144.

**Comvestrix Corp.**
1100 Valley Brook Ave, Lyndhurst NJ 07071-3608. 201/935-8300.

**CR Wildman Graphic Communications**
9100 Pennsauken Hwy, Pennsauken NJ 08110-1206. 609/662-9119.

**Cunningham Graphics Inc.**
629 Grove St, Jersey City NJ 07310-1243. 201/217-1000.

**Decora**
86 Industrial Rd, Pennsville NJ 08070. 609/678-4330.

**Decora**
PO Box 448, Williamstown NJ 08094-0448. 609/728-9300.

**Evergreen Printing & Publishing Co.**
PO Box 786, Bellmawr NJ 08099-0786. 609/933-0222.

**Graphicdata LLC**
2 Manhatten Dr, Burlington NJ 08016-4120. 609/778-1560.

**Howard Press Inc.**
PO Box 379, Roselle NJ 07203-0379. 908/245-4400.

**Lehigh Press Lithographers**
7001 N Park Dr, Pennsauken NJ 08109-4399. 609/665-5200.

**Merrill Corporation**
649 Rahway Ave, Union NJ
07083-6631. 908/688-5757.

**Metro Litho Inc.**
101 Moonachie Ave, Moonachie
NJ 07074-1820. 201/935-1450.

**Monarch Art Plastics LLC**
3838 Church Rd, Mount Laurel
NJ 08054-1106. 609/235-5151.

**Pace Press Inc.**
1 Caesar Pl, Moonachie NJ
07074-1702. 201/935-7711.

**Phototype Color Graphics Inc.**
PO Box 2738, Camden NJ 08101-
2738. 609/663-4100.

**Pictorial Offset Corporation**
PO Box 157, Carlstadt NJ 07072-
0157. 201/935-7100.

**Plymouth Printing Co. Inc.**
PO Box 68, Cranford NJ 07016-
0068. 908/276-8100.

**Ronpak Inc.**
4301 New Brunswick Ave, South
Plainfield NJ 07080-1205.
732/968-8000.

**Sancoa International Company**
11000 Midlantic Dr, Mount
Laurel NJ 08054-1566. 609/273-
0700.

**Sandy Alexander Inc.**
200 Entin Rd, Clifton NJ 07014-
1423. 973/470-8100.

**Scott Printing Corporation**
700 Central Ave, New
Providence NJ 07974-1139.
908/665-4100.

**Screen Place Inc.**
90 Dayton Ave, Passaic NJ
07055-7035. 973/473-7767.

**Thompson Printing Company**
100 Page Rd, Clifton NJ 07012-
1421. 973/778-0200.

**Toppan Printing Company**
1100 Randolph Rd, Somerset NJ
08873-1291. 732/469-8400.

**Trenton Litho**
PO Box 5064, Trenton NJ 08638-
0064. 609/883-4300.

**Union Graphics Inc.**
1634 E Elizabeth Ave, Linden NJ
07036-1725. 908/486-0300.

**USS Corporation**
780 Frelinghuysen Ave, Newark
NJ 07114-2221. 973/242-1110.

**Wace New York Prepress**
1 Kero Rd, Carlstadt NJ 07072-
2604. 201/933-8585.

**Webcraft Games Inc.**
PO Box 6023, North Brunswick
NJ 08902-6023. 732/297-5100.

## GREETING CARDS

**Art Quadriga Inc.**
825 Hylton Rd, Pennsauken NJ
08110-1307. 609/663-2500.

## MISC. PUBLISHING

**Daily Racing Form**
PO Box 1015, Hightstown NJ
08520-1068. 609/448-9100.

**Franklin Electronic Publishers**
PO Box 1208, Burlington NJ
08016. 609/386-2500.

## NEWS SYNDICATES

**Forbes Newpapers**
44 Franklin St, Somerville NJ
08876-2909. 908/722-3000.

## NEWSPAPERS: PUBLISHING AND/OR PRINTING

**Bridgeton Evening News**
PO Box 596, Bridgeton NJ
08302-0490. 609/451-1000.

**Burlington County Times**
4284 Route 130, Willingboro NJ
08046-2027. 609/871-8000.

**Courier-News**
PO Box 6600, Bridgewater NJ
08807-0600. 973/772-8800.

**Crestwood Village Sun**
48 Schoolhouse Rd, Whiting NJ
08759-3025. 732/350-0800.

**Greater Media Newspapers Inc.**
Edgeboro Rd, East Brunswick NJ
08816. 732/254-7000.

**Meadowlands Castle**
149 Polito Ave, Lyndhurst NJ
07071-3601. 201/933-3352.

**New Jersey Herald**
PO Box 10, Newton NJ 07860-
0010. 973/383-1500.

**News Transcript**
25 Kilmer Dr #109, Morganville
NJ 07751-1564. 732/972-6740.

**Ocean County Reporter**
PO Box 908, Toms River NJ
08754-0908. 732/349-3000.

**Princeton Packet**
PO Box 350, Princeton NJ 08542-
0350. 609/924-3244.

**Rutgers Daily Targum**
126 College Ave, Ste 431, New
Brunswick NJ 08901-1166.
732/932-7051.

**South Jersey Newspaper Co.**
309 S Broad St, Woodbury NJ
08096-2406. 609/845-3300.

**Southwind**
139 Santiago Dr, Toms River NJ
08757-6163. 732/341-8878.

**Star Ledger**
20 Duke Rd, Piscataway NJ
08854-3714. 732/560-1560.

**The Beacon**
345 E Bay Ave, Manahawkin NJ
08050-3314. 609/597-3211.

**The Journal of Commerce**
445 Marshall St, Phillipsburg NJ
08865-2658. 908/859-1300.

**The Press**
1000 W Washington Ave,
Pleasantville NJ 08232-3861.
609/272-1100.

**Times Graphic**
PO Box 1504, Vineland NJ
08362-1504. 609/691-5000.

**Today's Sunbeam**
PO Box 20, Salem NJ 08079.
609/935-1500.

**Wayne Offset**
22 Park Pl, Butler NJ 07405-
1380. 973/492-0211.

## PERIODICALS: PUBLISHING AND/OR PRINTING

**Business Today**
305 Aaron Burr Hill, Rm 305,
Princeton NJ 08544. 609/258-
1111.

**First For Women Magazine**
270 Sylvan Ave, Englewood
Cliffs NJ 07632-2521. 201/569-
0006.

**Journal of Accountancy**
PO Box 2208, Jersey City NJ
07303-2208. 201/938-3292.

**K-LII Press**
10 Lake Dr, Hightstown NJ
08520-5321. 609/371-7700.

**Newsweek Inc.**
PO Box 420, Mountain Lake NJ
07046-0420. 973/316-2000.

**Princeton University Press**
41 William St, Princeton NJ
08540-5237. 609/258-4900.

**Urner-Barry Publications Inc.**
PO Box 389, Toms River NJ
08754-0389. 732/240-5330.

**Want Ad Press**
120 N Central Ave, Ramsey NJ
07446-1442. 201/825-4887.

**PHOTOGRAPHIC EQUIPMENT AND SUPPLIES**

**Buhl Industries Inc.**
14-01 Maple Ave, Fair Lawn NJ 07410-1530. 973/423-2800.

**Charles Besseler Company**
PO Box 4219, Linden NJ 07036-8219. 908/862-7999.

**Kodak Polychrome**
160 Terminal Ave, Clark NJ 07066-1319. 732/574-0400.

**Testrite Instrument Company Inc.**
135 Monroe St, Newark NJ 07105-1710. 973/589-6767.

**PRINTING TRADE SERVICES**

**TSI Graphics Inc.**
70 Jackson Dr, Cranford NJ 07016-3510. 908/272-2520.

**University Graphics Inc.**
21 W Lincoln Ave, Atlantic Highlands NJ 07716-1121. 732/872-0800.

**For more information on career opportunities in printing and publishing:**

Associations

**AMERICAN BOOKSELLERS ASSOCIATION**
828 South Broadway, Tarrytown NY 10591. 914/591-2665. World Wide Web address: http://www. bookweb.org. Publishes *American Bookseller, Bookselling This Week*, and *Bookstore Source Guide*.

**AMERICAN INSTITUTE OF GRAPHIC ARTS**
164 Fifth Avenue, New York NY 10010. 212/807-1990. World Wide Web address: http://www.aiga.org. A nationwide organization sponsoring programs and events for graphic designers and related professionals.

**AMERICAN SOCIETY OF COMPOSERS, AUTHORS AND PUBLISHERS (ASCAP)**
One Lincoln Plaza, New York NY 10023. 212/621-6000. World Wide Web address: http://www.ascap.com. A membership association which licenses members' work and pays members' royalties. Offers showcases and educational seminars and workshops. The society also has an events hotline: 212/621-6485. Many events listed are free.

**AMERICAN SOCIETY OF NEWSPAPER EDITORS**
11690-B Sunrise Valley Drive, Reston VA 20191. 703/453-1122. World Wide Web address: http://www. asne.org.

**ASSOCIATION OF AMERICAN PUBLISHERS**
71 Fifth Avenue, New York NY 10001. 212/255-0200. Fax: 212/255-7007. World Wide Web address: http://www.publishers.org. A national trade association for the book publishing industry.

**ASSOCIATION OF GRAPHIC COMMUNICATIONS**
330 Seventh Avenue, 9th Floor, New York NY 10001-5010. 212/279-2100. World Wide Web address: http://www.agcomm.org. Offers educational classes and seminars.

**BINDING INDUSTRIES OF AMERICA**
70 East Lake Street, Suite 300, Chicago IL 60601. 312/372-7606. Offers credit collection, government affairs, and educational services.

**THE DOW JONES NEWSPAPER FUND, INC.**
P.O. Box 300, Princeton NJ 08543-0300. 609/452-2820. World Wide Web address: http://www. dowjones.com.

**GRAPHIC ARTISTS GUILD**
90 John Street, Suite 403, New York NY 10038. 212/791-3400. World Wide Web address: http://www.gag.org. A union for artists.

**THE GRAPHIC ARTS TECHNICAL FOUNDATION**
200 Deer Run Road, Sewickley PA 15143-2600. 412/741-6860. World Wide Web address: http://www. gatf.org. Provides information, services, and training to those in graphic arts professions.

**MAGAZINE PUBLISHERS OF AMERICA**
919 Third Avenue, 22nd Floor, New York NY 10022. 212/752-0055. World Wide Web address: http://www. magazine.org. A membership association.

**NATIONAL ASSOCIATION OF PRINTERS AND LITHOGRAPHERS**
75 West Century Road, Paramus NJ 07652. 201/634-9600. World Wide Web address: http://www.napl.org. Membership required. Offers consulting services and a publication.

**THE NATIONAL NEWSPAPER ASSOCIATION**
1010 North Glebe Road, Suite 450, Arlington VA 22201. 703/907-7900. World Wide Web address: http://www.oweb.com/nna.

**NATIONAL PRESS CLUB**
529 14th Street NW, 13th Floor, Washington DC 20045. 202/662-7500. World Wide Web address: http://npc.press.org. Offers professional seminars, career services, and conference facilities, as well as members-only restaurants and a health club.

**NEWSPAPER ASSOCIATION OF AMERICA**
1921 Gallows Road, Suite 600, Vienna VA 22182. 703/902-1600. World Wide Web address: http://www. naa.org. Focuses on marketing, public policy, diversity, industry development, and newspaper operations.

**PRINTING INDUSTRIES OF AMERICA**
100 Dangerfield Road, Alexandria VA 22314. 703/519-8100. World Wide Web address: http://www. printing.org. Members are offered publications and insurance.

**TECHNICAL ASSOCIATION OF THE GRAPHIC ARTS**
68 Lomb Memorial Drive, Rochester NY 14623. 716/475-7470. World Wide Web address: http://www. taga.org. Conducts an annual conference and offers newsletters.

**WRITERS GUILD OF AMERICA WEST**
7000 West Third Street, Los Angeles CA 90048. 310/550-1000. World Wide Web address: http://www. wga.org. A membership association which registers scripts.

## Directories

### EDITOR & PUBLISHER INTERNATIONAL YEARBOOK
Editor & Publisher Company, 11 West 19th Street, New York NY 10011. 212/675-4380. World Wide Web address: http://www.mediainfo.com. Offers newspapers to editors in both the United States and foreign countries.

### GRAPHIC ARTS BLUE BOOK
A.F. Lewis & Company, 245 Fifth Avenue, Suite 2201, New York NY 10016. 212/679-0770. $85.00. Manufacturers and dealers.

### JOURNALISM CAREER AND SCHOLARSHIP GUIDE
The Dow Jones Newspaper Fund, P.O. Box 300, Princeton NJ 08543-0300. 609/452-2820.

## Magazines

### AIGA JOURNAL OF GRAPHIC DESIGN
American Institute of Graphic Arts, 164 Fifth Avenue, New York NY 10010. 212/807-1990. World Wide Web address: http://www.aiga.org. $22.00. A 56-page magazine, published three times per year, that deals with contemporary issues.

### THE EDITOR & PUBLISHER
Editor & Publisher Co., 11 West 19th Street, New York NY 10011. 212/675-4380. World Wide Web address: http://www.mediainfo.com. A periodical focusing on the newspaper publishing industry.

### GRAPHIS
141 Lexington Avenue, New York NY 10016. 212/532-9387. $90.00. Magazine covers portfolios, articles, designers, advertising, and photos.

### PRINT
104 Fifth Avenue, 19th Floor, New York NY 10011. 212/463-0600. Offers a graphic design magazine. $55.00 for subscription.

### PUBLISHERS WEEKLY
245 West 17th Street, New York NY 10011. 212/463-6758. Toll-free phone: 800/278-2991. World Wide Web address: http://www.publishersweekly.com. Weekly magazine for book publishers, book sellers, and jobseekers looking for work in publishing. Each issue includes a listing of job openings.

## Special Book and Magazine Programs

### CENTER FOR BOOK ARTS
626 Broadway, 5th Floor, New York NY 10012. 212/460-9768. Offers bookbinding, printing, and papermaking workshops.

### EMERSON COLLEGE WRITING AND PUBLISHING PROGRAM
100 Beacon Street, Boston MA 02116. 617/824-8500. World Wide Web address: http://www.emerson.edu.

### THE NEW YORK UNIVERSITY SUMMER PUBLISHING PROGRAM
11 West 42nd Street, Room 400, New York NY 10036. 212/790-3232.

### THE RADCLIFFE PUBLISHING COURSE
6 Ash Street, Cambridge MA 02138. 617/495-8678.

### THE STANFORD PROFESSIONAL PUBLISHING COURSE
Stanford Alumni Association, Bowman Alumni House, Stanford CA 97305-4005. 650/723-2027. Fax: 650/723-8597. E-mail address: publishing.courses@stanford.edu. World Wide Web address: http://www.stanfordproed.org.

### UNIVERSITY OF DENVER PUBLISHING INSTITUTE
2075 South University Boulevard, #D-114, Denver CO 80210. 303/871-2570.

## Online Services

### BOOKS AND WRITING
Jump to: Books and Writing BB. A bulletin board service, available through Prodigy, that allows writers to discuss issues in publishing and gain advice on writing style.

### JOURNALISM FORUM
Go: Jforum. A CompuServe discussion group for journalists in print, radio, or television.

### PHOTO PROFESSIONALS
Go: Photopro. A CompuServe forum for imaging professionals.

### PROPUBLISHING FORUM
Go: Propub. CompuServe charges a fee for this forum which caters to publishing and graphic design professionals.

Visit our exciting job and career site at http://www.careercity.com

# REAL ESTATE

 *After rising from 7.96 million in 1993 to 9.14 million in 1997, employment growth in the real estate industry continues to level off. Support for the real estate industry may come from both a strong economy and a strong construction industry. For the period of January through September 1998, housing starts were up approximately 9 percent, according to the U.S. Census Bureau.*

*The trend that is sweeping the industry is ownership of real estate investment trusts (REITs). REITs are companies that own, manage, and develop a number of diversified properties. These companies must follow strict guidelines and in the end remain exempt from corporate taxation. The REIT industry saw profits soar from $8 billion in 1990 to $120 billion in 1997.*

*The best opportunities for investment and sales are in office space. Industry analysts say that suburbs and downtowns, specifically in the Boston, Chicago, New York, San Francisco, and Seattle areas, will be the hot-spots for new construction. Due to the high turnover rate, real estate agents and brokers should continue to see opportunities, though the sector will see slow growth through 2006. With the increase in apartment and rental space, real estate managers are expected to see average growth into the next decade.*

*Business Week reported that the retail sector may have been the hardest hit in 1998. Overbuilding and changes in shopping habits have produced a glutted market of malls and shopping centers. Another negative is a potential overabundance in apartment space, most notably in the Sunbelt.*

**AVALON PROPERTIES, INC.**
100 Canal Pointe Boulevard, Suite 110, Princeton NJ 08540. 609/452-0025. **Contact:** Human Resources. **World Wide Web address:** http://www.avalonbay.com. **Description:** A self-administered and self-managed equity real estate investment trust that specializes in the development, construction, acquisition, and management of apartment communities in the mid-Atlantic and northeastern U.S. Avalon's real estate consists of 10,005 apartment homes in 33 communities located in six states and Washington DC. **Corporate headquarters location:** New Canaan CT. **Other U.S. locations:** Braintree MA; Alexandria VA; Richmond VA.

**CENDANT CORPORATION**
6 Sylvan Way, Parsippany NJ 07054. 973/428-9700. **Toll-free phone:** 800/932-4656. **Fax:** 973/428-9684. **Contact:** Staffing and Employment. **E-mail address:** jobs@hfsinc.com. **World Wide Web address:** http://www.cendant.com. **Description:** Provides a wide range of business services including dining services, hotel franchise management, mortgage programs, and timeshare exchanges. Cendant Corporation's Real Estate Division offers employee relocation and mortgage services through Century 21, Coldwell Banker, ERA, Cendant Mortgage, and Cendant Mobility. The Travel Division provides car rentals, vehicle management services, and vacation timeshares through brand names including Avia, Days Inn, Howard Johnson, Ramada, Travelodge, and Super 8. The Membership Division offers travel, shopping, auto, dining, and other financial services through Travelers Advantage, Shoppers Advantage, Auto Vantage, Welcom Wagon, netMarket, North American Outdoor Group, and PrivacyGuard. Founded in 1997. **Common positions include:** Accountant/Auditor; Computer Programmer; Customer Service Rep.; Marketing Manager; Marketing Specialist; Public Relations Specialist; Real Estate Agent; Sales Rep.; Secretary. **Educational backgrounds include:** Accounting; Business Administration; Communications; Finance; Marketing; Public Relations; Software Development. **Benefits:** 401(k); Dental Insurance; Disability Coverage; Employee Discounts; Life Insurance; Medical Insurance; Profit Sharing; Savings Plan; Tuition Assistance. **Corporate headquarters location:** This Location. **Operations at this facility include:** Administration; Sales; Service. **Listed on:** New York Stock Exchange. **Stock exchange symbol:** CD. **President/CEO:** Henry Silverman. **Number of employees at this location:** 1,100. **Number of employees worldwide:** 30,000.

## CHELSEA GCA REALTY, INC.
103 Eisenhower Parkway, Roseland NJ 07068. 973/228-6111. **Contact:** Human Resources Department. **World Wide Web address:** http://www.chelseagca.com. **Description:** Chelsea GCA Realty, Inc. is a self-administered and self-managed real estate investment trust engaged in the development, leasing, marketing, and management of upscale and fashion-oriented manufacturers' outlet centers. Chelsea operates outlets in Cabazon CA, Camarillo CA, Folsom CA, Pacific Grove CA, Petaluma CA, Lawrence KS, Flemington NJ, Central Valley NY, Aurora OH, and Troutdale OR.

## K. HOVNANIAN COMPANIES
10 Highway 35, P.O. Box 500, Red Bank NJ 07701. 732/747-7800. **Contact:** Human Resources. **World Wide Web address:** http://www.khov.com. **Description:** Designs, constructs, and sells condominium apartments, townhomes, and single-family residences in planned residential communities primarily in New Jersey, New York, eastern Pennsylvania, Florida, Virginia, North Carolina, and Southern California. The company is also engaged in mortgage banking. Founded in 1959. **NOTE:** Entry-level positions are offered. **Common positions include:** Accountant; Administrative Assistant; Architect; Attorney; Auditor; Civil Engineer; Computer Operator; Computer Programmer; Controller; Financial Analyst; Human Resources Manager; Market Research Analyst; Marketing Manager; Marketing Specialist; MIS Specialist; Online Content Specialist; Real Estate Agent; Sales Manager; Secretary; Systems Analyst; Systems Manager; Technical Writer/Editor; Webmaster. **Educational backgrounds include:** Accounting; Business Administration; Computer Science; Engineering; Marketing. **Benefits:** 401(k); Dental Insurance; Disability Coverage; Life Insurance; Medical Insurance; Profit Sharing; Tuition Assistance. **Corporate headquarters location:** This Location. **Subsidiaries include:** New Fortis Homes. **Listed on:** American Stock Exchange. **Stock exchange symbol:** HOV. **Annual sales/revenues:** More than $100 million. **Number of employees at this location:** 90. **Number of employees nationwide:** 1,150.

## VORNADO REALTY TRUST
Park 80 West, Plaza 2, Saddle Brook NJ 07663. 201/587-1000. **Contact:** Robin Hubschman, Human Resources. **Description:** A real estate investment trust. **CEO:** Steven Roth.

## WEICHERT REALTORS
1625 Route 10 East, Morris Plains NJ 07950. 973/267-7777. **Contact:** Human Resources. **World Wide Web address:** http://www.weichert.com. **Description:** A real estate agency. **NOTE:** Jobseekers should specify which department they are interested in applying to in their cover letter. **Corporate headquarters location:** This Location.

*Note: Because addresses and telephone numbers of smaller companies can change rapidly, we recommend you call each company to verify the information below before inquiring about job opportunities. Mass mailings are not recommended.*

**Additional small employers:**

**CEMETERY SUBDIVIDERS AND DEVELOPERS**

**Woodbridge Memorial Gardens**
PO Box 706, Woodbridge NJ 07095-0706. 732/634-2100.

**LAND SUBDIVIDERS AND DEVELOPERS**

**American Investments**
PO Box 1470, Bloomfield NJ 07003-1470. 973/673-8712.

**Clinton Commons Association**
1621 North Olden Avenue, Trenton NJ 08638-3205. 609/396-6800.

**Gale Wentworth & Dillon Incorporated**
PO Box 1091, Bedminster NJ 07921-1091. 908/658-4400.

**REAL ESTATE AGENTS AND MANAGERS**

**DI Donato Realty Company Inc.**
PO Box 3126, Trenton NJ 08619-0126. 609/586-2344.

**Prudential Property Company**
8 Campus Dr, Parsippany NJ 07054-4401. 973/734-1300.

**Roseland Property Company**
140 Eagle Rock Avenue, Roseland NJ 07068-1320. 973/228-8675.

**REAL ESTATE OPERATORS**

**Atlantic City Convention Center Authority**
2301 Boardwalk, Atlantic City NJ 08401-6621. 609/348-7000.

**Bellemead Development Corp.**
4 Becker Farm Rd, Roseland NJ 07068-1734. 973/740-1110.

**Carpenter Realty Corporation**
549 S Broadway, Gloucester City NJ 08030-2447. 609/456-0008.

**Century Properties Inc**
365 W Passaic St, Rochelle Park NJ 07662-3017. 201/712-1300.

**Chad Holding Co. Inc.**
575 N Midland Ave, Saddle Brook NJ 07663. 201/797-7200.

**DKM Properties Corp.**
136 Main St, Ste 200, Princeton NJ 08540-5735. 609/799-7400.

**Frank Investment Inc.**
PO Box 33, Pleasantville NJ 08232-0033. 609/641-3595.

**Harmon Cove**
400 Plaza Drive, Secaucus NJ
07094-3605. 201/348-1200.

**Harvest Village**
114 Hayes Mill Rd, Atco NJ
08004-2457. 609/753-2000.

**Leisure Park**
1400 Route 70, Lakewood NJ
08701-5949. 732/370-0444.

**Longport Ocean Plaza Condominiums**
2700 Atlantic Avenue,
Longport NJ 08403-1263.
609/823-3300.

**McBride Enterprises**
PO Box 549, Franklin Lakes NJ
07417-0549. 201/891-3900.

**Sagemore Apartments**
8000 Sagemore Dr, Ste 8301,
Marlton NJ 08053-3941.
609/985-1200.

**Schur Realty Company Incorporated**
143 2nd Street, Jersey City NJ
07302-3042. 201/653-6000.

## For more information on career opportunities in real estate:

### Associations

**INSTITUTE OF REAL ESTATE MANAGEMENT**
430 North Michigan Avenue, Chicago IL 60611. 312/661-1930. World Wide Web address: http://www.irem.org. Dedicated to educating and identifying real estate managers who are committed to meeting the needs of real estate owners and investors.

**INTERNATIONAL ASSOCIATION OF CORPORATE REAL ESTATE EXECUTIVES**
440 Columbia Drive, Suite 100, West Palm Beach FL 33409. 561/683-8111. World Wide Web address: http://www.nacore.com. An international association of real estate brokers.

**INTERNATIONAL REAL ESTATE INSTITUTE**
1224 North Nokomis, Alexandria MN 56308. Offers seminars on issues relating to the real estate industry.

**NATIONAL ASSOCIATION OF REAL ESTATE INVESTMENT TRUSTS**
1875 Eye Street NW, Suite 600, Washington DC 20006. 202/739-9400. Toll-free phone: 800/3-NAREIT. Contact: Matt Lentz, Membership. World Wide Web address: http://www.nareit.com. Membership required.

**NATIONAL ASSOCIATION OF REALTORS**
430 North Michigan Avenue, Chicago IL 60611.

312/329-8200. World Wide Web address: http://www.realtor.com. A membership organization compiling statistics, advising the government, and publishing several magazines including *Real Estate Today* and *Today's Realtor*.

### Magazines

**JOURNAL OF PROPERTY MANAGEMENT**
Institute of Real Estate Management, 430 North Michigan Avenue, Chicago IL 60610. 312/329-6000. World Wide Web address: http://www.irem.org.

**NATIONAL REAL ESTATE INVESTOR**
PRIMEDIA Intertec, 6151 Powers Ferry Road NW, Suite 200, Atlanta GA 30339. 770/955-2500. World Wide Web address: http://www.intertec.com.

### Online Services

**JOBS IN REAL ESTATE**
World Wide Web address: http://www.cob.ohio-state.edu/dept/fin/jobs/realest.htm. This Website provides resources for jobseekers who are looking to work in the real estate field.

**REAL JOBS**
World Wide Web address: http://www.real-jobs.com. This Website is designed to help real estate professionals who are looking for jobs.

# RETAIL

*Retail trade will likely see annual employment growth of only 1 percent through 2006, according to the Bureau of Labor Statistics. Cashiers will see the largest gains, with the projected creation of 530,000 new positions. Retail salespersons are expected to see more than 400,000 new positions by 2006. Competition will be greatest for supervisory and management positions, which provide higher pay, yet often don't require an advanced degree. Overall, job growth will depend on the segment of the retail industry, such as computers or home furnishings. The Federal Reserve Board anticipates a continued drop in retail prices due to an increase in lower-priced imports, such as apparel and electronics products.*

*Frequent fluctuations in the stock market in 1998 helped large discounters, such as Kmart and Wal-Mart, to see an increase in sales. Over the past several years, large discounters have seen their market share increase by 20 percent, whereas major department store chains have seen their market share fall 10 percent. Kmart continues to increase its number of refurbished Big Kmart stores, and planned on converting 528 of its existing stores into modern Big Kmart stores in 1998. Supermarkets are reaping the benefits of lower food prices but facing increased competition. Wal-Mart, the number one discount retailer, is branching into the grocery business, having already opened three test stores.*

*Online buying totaled more than $4 billion in sales in 1998. Amazon.com, a leading online bookseller, expected sales of approximately $400 million in 1998. Barnes & Noble, a leading retail bookseller which has seen its market share rise more than 100 percent, recently started its own online bookstore, with $14 million in sales for 1997, and expected $100 million in sales for 1998.*

*In order to see profits continue to rise, retailers will need to consistently offer lower, fair prices. Stores that also provide consumers with added incentives and reward benefits will draw more customers.*

**BJ'S WHOLESALE CLUB**
1910 Deptford Center Road, Deptford NJ 08096. 609/232-8880. **Contact:** Human Resources. **Description:** Sells food and general merchandise through more than 60 warehouses.

**BED BATH & BEYOND INC.**
650 Liberty Avenue, Annex Building, Union NJ 07083. 908/688-0888. **Contact:** Human Resources. **Description:** Sells domestic merchandise and home furnishings. The company's domestic merchandise line includes items such as bed linens, bath accessories, and kitchen textiles, and the company's home furnishings line includes items such as cookware, dinnerware, glassware, and basic housewares. Founded in 1971. **Corporate headquarters location:** This Location. **Listed on:** NASDAQ. **Stock exchange symbol:** BBBY.

**BROWNSTONE STUDIO**
414 Alfred Avenue, Teaneck NJ 07666. 201/837-1999. **Contact:** Human Resources. **Description:** A catalog house for women's apparel and accessories. **Common positions include:** Accountant/Auditor; Buyer; Computer Programmer; Customer Service Representative; General Manager; Quality Control Supervisor; Systems Analyst. **Educational backgrounds include:** Accounting; Art/Design; Computer Science; Finance; Marketing. **Benefits:** 401(k); Dental Insurance; Disability Coverage; Employee Discounts; Flexible Benefits; Life Insurance; Medical Insurance; Pension Plan; Profit Sharing; Tuition Assistance. **Corporate headquarters location:**

New York City NY. **Operations at this facility include:** Administration. **Listed on:** Privately held. **Number of employees at this location:** 200.

## BURLINGTON COAT FACTORY
1830 Route 130 North, Burlington NJ 08016. 609/387-7800. **Contact:** Sarah R. Orleck, Executive Director of Human Resources. **World Wide Web address:** http://www.bcf.coat.com. **Description:** An off-price apparel discounter. Product lines consist of all name-brand apparel, including coats, sportswear, childrenswear, menswear, juvenile furniture, linens, shoes, and accessories. **Corporate headquarters location:** This Location. **Listed on:** New York Stock Exchange.

## EDMUND SCIENTIFIC COMPANY
101 East Gloucester Pike, Barrington NJ 08007. 609/547-3488x6824. **Contact:** Lisa Verrechia, Human Resources Representative. **Description:** This location is a retail store. Overall, Edmund Scientific Company is a retail supplier of industrial optics, lasers, telescopes, and precision optical instruments through two mail order catalogs.

## EPSTEIN, INC.
32 Park Place, P.O. Box 902, Morristown NJ 07963-0902. 973/538-5000. **Contact:** Personnel. **Description:** A department store offering a wide range of fashions and other soft and hard goods. **Common positions include:** Accountant/Auditor; Administrator; Advertising Clerk; Credit Manager; Department Manager; General Manager. **Educational backgrounds include:** Business Administration; Marketing. **Benefits:** Disability Coverage; Employee Discounts; Life Insurance; Medical Insurance. **Corporate headquarters location:** Cedar Knolls NJ. **Other U.S. locations:** Bridgewater NJ; Princeton NJ; Shrewsbury NJ. **Operations at this facility include:** Sales.

## FOODARAMA SUPERMARKETS
922 Highway 33, Building 6, Suite 1, Freehold NJ 07728. 732/462-4700. **Contact:** Bob Spires, Vice President of Personnel. **Description:** Operates supermarkets in New Jersey, New York, and Pennsylvania. **Common positions include:** Accountant/Auditor; Management Trainee. **Educational backgrounds include:** Accounting. **Benefits:** Dental Insurance; Disability Coverage; Life Insurance; Medical Insurance; Pension Plan. **Corporate headquarters location:** This Location. **Listed on:** American Stock Exchange.

## THE GREAT ATLANTIC & PACIFIC TEA COMPANY (A&P)
2 Paragon Drive, Montvale NJ 07645. 201/930-4416. **Contact:** Corinne Blake, Director of Personnel. **Description:** This location houses administrative offices for one of the nation's largest supermarket chains. Overall, The Great Atlantic & Pacific Tea Company maintains approximately 1,000 retail supermarkets throughout the East Coast, Mid-Atlantic, and Canada. **Common positions include:** Accountant/Auditor; Computer Programmer; Draftsperson; Financial Analyst; Systems Analyst. **Educational backgrounds include:** Accounting; Business Administration; Computer Science. **Benefits:** 401(k); Dental Insurance; Disability Coverage; Life Insurance; Medical Insurance; Prescription Drugs; Retirement Plan; Vision Insurance. **Corporate headquarters location:** This Location. **Listed on:** New York Stock Exchange. **Number of employees at this location:** 650. **Number of employees nationwide:** 85,000.

## HANOVER DIRECT, INC.
1500 Harbor Boulevard, Weehawken NJ 07087. 201/863-7300. **Fax:** 201/272-3465. **Contact:** Vice President of Human Resources. **Description:** A direct marketing company that sells products manufactured by other companies through its 12 core catalogs structured into operating groups. **NOTE:** Entry-level positions are offered. **Common positions include:** Accountant/Auditor; Buyer; Fashion Designer; Financial Analyst; Industrial Engineer; Market Research Analyst; Telemarketer. **Educational backgrounds include:** Accounting; Business Administration; Economics; Fashion; Finance; Liberal Arts; Marketing; Mathematics. **Benefits:** 401(k); Dental Insurance; Disability Coverage; Employee Discounts; Free Parking; Life Insurance; Medical Insurance; Public Transit Available; Tuition Assistance. **Corporate headquarters location:** This Location. **Other U.S. locations:** San Diego CA; San Francisco CA; Hanover PA; De Soto TX; Roanoke VA; La Crosse WI. **Operations at this facility include:** Administration; Divisional Headquarters; Sales. **Listed on:** American Stock Exchange. **Annual sales/revenues:** More than $100 million. **Number of employees at this location:** 250. **Number of employees nationwide:** 3,000.

## HIT OR MISS, INC.
10 South Park Street, Montclair NJ 07042. 973/746-5187. **Toll-free phone:** 800/528-5001. **Contact:** Heidi Krietzberg, Regional Manager. **Description:** A women's fashion store. Hit or Miss operates over 300 stores in 35 states. **NOTE:** For more information about opportunities at Hit or Miss's corporate headquarters, resumes should be sent to Hit or Miss Home Office, Staffing &

Career Development, 100 Campanelli Parkway, Stoughton MA 02072. **Common positions include:** Accountant/Auditor; Assistant Manager; Buyer; Computer Programmer; Management Trainee; Store Manager; Systems Analyst. **Corporate headquarters location:** Stoughton MA. **Other U.S. locations:** Nationwide.

### KMART CORPORATION
7373 West Side Avenue, North Bergen NJ 07047. 201/854-5787. **Fax:** 201/295-5565. **Contact:** Human Resources. **World Wide Web address:** http://www.kmart.com. **Description:** One of the largest non-food retailers in the United States. The company operates over 2,000 stores nationwide under the Kmart name, with more than 50 Kmart stores located in the New York metropolitan area. All stores offer a broad range of discounted general merchandise, both soft and hard goods. **Common positions include:** Accountant/Auditor; Computer Operator; Computer Programmer; Distribution Manager; Human Resources Manager; Systems Analyst. **Benefits:** Dental Insurance; Disability Coverage; Employee Discounts; Life Insurance; Medical Insurance; Pension Plan; Profit Sharing; Savings Plan; Tuition Assistance. **Corporate headquarters location:** Troy MI. **Parent company:** Kmart Corporation. **Operations at this facility include:** Administration; Divisional Headquarters; Service. **Listed on:** New York Stock Exchange. **Number of employees at this location:** 1,700. **Number of employees nationwide:** 330,000.

### LECHTERS, INC.
One Cape May Street, Harrison NJ 07029. 973/481-1100. **Contact:** Employee Relations Manager. **Description:** A specialty retailer of primarily brand-name, non-electric basic housewares; tabletop items; and kitchen textiles. These products include cookware, bakeware, kitchen gadgets, kitchen utensils, microwave accessories, glassware, frames, household storage items, towels, placemats, napkins, and aprons. **Common positions include:** Accountant/Auditor; Buyer; Human Resources Manager; Management Trainee; Paralegal; Real Estate Agent. **Educational backgrounds include:** Accounting; Business Administration; Economics; Finance; Liberal Arts; Marketing. **Benefits:** 401(k); Dental Insurance; Disability Coverage; Employee Discounts; Life Insurance; Medical Insurance; Pension Plan. **Special programs:** Internships. **Corporate headquarters location:** This Location. **Other U.S. locations:** Nationwide. **Operations at this facility include:** Administration; Regional Headquarters. **Listed on:** NASDAQ. **Number of employees at this location:** 400. **Number of employees nationwide:** 6,910.

### LINENS 'N THINGS
6 Brighton Road, Clifton NJ 07015. 973/778-1300. **Contact:** Personnel. **Description:** A nationwide specialty retailer selling linens, home furnishings, and domestics. Linens 'n Things operates over 145 stores. **Common positions include:** Assistant Manager; Shipping and Receiving Clerk; Store Manager. **Educational backgrounds include:** Business Administration; Liberal Arts; Marketing; Retail Management. **Corporate headquarters location:** This Location.

### MACY'S
Garden State Plaza, Paramus NJ 07652. 201/843-9100. **Contact:** Human Resources. **Description:** A location of the national chain of department stores.

### MACY'S
275 Menlo Park, Edison NJ 08837. 732/549-4400. **Contact:** Human Resources. **Description:** A location of the national chain of department stores.

### MERCK MEDCO RX SERVICES
399 Jefferson Road, Parsippany NJ 07054. 973/560-6000. **Contact:** Human Resources. **Description:** A mail-order pharmacy. **Parent company:** Merck & Co., Inc. (Whitehouse Station NJ) is a worldwide organization engaged in discovering, developing, producing, and marketing products for the maintenance of health and the environment. Products include human and animal pharmaceuticals and chemicals sold to the health care, oil exploration, food processing, textile, paper, and other industries. Merck also runs an ethical drug mail-order marketing business.

### MICRO WAREHOUSE, INC.
1720 Oak Street, Lakewood NJ 08701. 732/370-3801. **Fax:** 732/370-7061. **Contact:** Human Resources Department. **World Wide Web address:** http://www.warehouse.com. **Description:** A catalog retailer of brand-name Macintosh and IBM-compatible personal computer software, accessories, and peripherals. **Common positions include:** Blue-Collar Worker Supervisor; Credit Manager; Customer Service Representative; Human Resources Manager; Systems Analyst. **Educational backgrounds include:** Business Administration; Computer Science; Liberal Arts. **Benefits:** 401(k); Dental Insurance; Disability Coverage; Employee Discounts; Life Insurance; Medical Insurance; Tuition Assistance. **Corporate headquarters location:** South Norwalk CT. **Other U.S. locations:** Gibbsboro NJ; Wilmington OH. **International locations:** Canada; England;

France; Germany; Mexico; Netherlands; Sweden. **Listed on:** NASDAQ. **Number of employees at this location:** 600. **Number of employees nationwide:** 1,500.

## PATHMARK STORES INC.

200 Milik Street, Carteret NJ 07008. 732/499-4019. **Contact:** Renee Perlman, Manager of Selection/Placement. **Description:** A diversified retailer engaged primarily in the operation of large supermarket/drug stores located in the Mid-Atlantic and New England. The company operates one of the largest supermarket chains in the country. Its Rickel Home Center division is among the largest do-it-yourself home center chains in the nation. **Corporate headquarters location:** This Location.

## PETRIE RETAIL CORPORATION

150 Meadowlands Parkway, Secaucus NJ 07094. 201/866-3600. **Contact:** Human Resources Department. **Description:** Operates a chain of approximately 1,400 women's specialty stores in 49 states.

## POPULAR CLUB PLAN

22 Lincoln Place, Garfield NJ 07026. 973/471-4300. **Contact:** Kevin Gilrain, Human Resources. **Description:** Operates a full-service, mail-order catalog operation. **Corporate headquarters location:** This Location.

## SPENCER GIFTS INC.

6826 Black Horse Pike, Egg Harbor Township NJ 08234. 609/645-3300. **Contact:** Tony Martire, Personnel Manager. **Description:** Spencer Gifts is a retailer of novelty and joke items. **Common positions include:** Accountant/Auditor; Assistant Manager; Buyer; Management Trainee. **Educational backgrounds include:** Accounting; Business Administration; Liberal Arts; Marketing. **Operations at this facility include:** Administration; Sales; Service. **Number of employees nationwide:** 4,000.

## STERN'S DEPARTMENT STORES

Bergen Mall, Route 4, Paramus NJ 07652. 201/845-2426. **Fax:** 201/845-2383. **Contact:** Director of Executive Placement. **World Wide Web address:** http://www.federated-fds.com. **Description:** Operates a chain of full-line department stores. Stern's Department Stores has 22 area locations. **Common positions include:** Management Trainee. **Educational backgrounds include:** Business Administration; Liberal Arts; Marketing. **Benefits:** 401(k); Dental Insurance; Employee Discounts; Medical Insurance; Pension Plan; Profit Sharing. **Corporate headquarters location:** This Location. **Other U.S. locations:** Woodbridge NJ; Flushing NY; Hicksville NY. **Parent company:** Federated Department Stores, Inc. (Cincinnati OH) operates a department store chain with 219 stores in 26 states. The retail segments include Bloomingdale's, The Bon Marche, Burdine's, Lazarus, Rich's/Goldsmith's, and Stern's. **Listed on:** New York Stock Exchange.

## STRAUSS DISCOUNT AUTO

9A Brick Plant Road, South River NJ 08882. 732/390-9000. **Fax:** 732/651-3114. **Contact:** Human Resources Administrator. **Description:** Strauss Discount Auto is engaged in the retail trade of automotive aftermarket products. **Common positions include:** Accountant/Auditor; Advertising Clerk; Automotive Mechanic; Budget Analyst; Buyer; Computer Programmer; Construction Contractor; Customer Service Representative; Draftsperson; Human Resources Manager; Management Trainee; Property and Real Estate Manager; Systems Analyst. **Educational backgrounds include:** Accounting; Business Administration; Liberal Arts. **Benefits:** 401(k); Dental Insurance; Disability Coverage; Employee Discounts; Life Insurance; Medical Insurance; Tuition Assistance. **Corporate headquarters location:** This Location. **Operations at this facility include:** Administration. **Number of employees at this location:** 200. **Number of employees nationwide:** 2,200.

## SYMS CORPORATION

Syms Way, Secaucus NJ 07094. 201/902-9600. **Contact:** John Tyzbir, Personnel Director. **World Wide Web address:** http://www.symsclothing.com. **Description:** This location houses a retail location and a distribution center. Overall, Syms Corporation operates a chain of 34 off-price apparel stores located throughout the Northeast, Midwest, Southeast, and Southwest. All stores offer men's tailored clothing; women's dresses, suits, and separates; and children's apparel. **Corporate headquarters location:** This Location. **Subsidiaries include:** Syms Advertising, which creates and places advertising for Syms Corporation.

## TODAY'S MAN, INC.

835 Lancer Drive, Moorestown NJ 08057. 609/235-0725. **Contact:** Human Resources. **World Wide Web address:** http://www.todaysman.com. **Description:** A leading operator of menswear

superstores specializing in tailored clothing, sportswear, and accessories. The company operates a chain of 28 superstores in the Chicago, New York, Philadelphia, and Washington DC markets. Today's Man carries a broad assortment of current-season brand name and private-label menswear at discount prices. Today's Man carries brand names from the U.S. and Europe, as well as private-label brands. **Common positions include:** Accountant/Auditor; Advertising Clerk; Buyer; Computer Programmer; Human Resources Manager; Management Trainee; Systems Analyst; Wholesale and Retail Buyer. **Educational backgrounds include:** Accounting; Art/Design; Business Administration; Computer Science; Liberal Arts; Marketing. **Benefits:** 401(k); Employee Discounts; Life Insurance; Medical Insurance; Profit Sharing. **Corporate headquarters location:** This Location. **Other U.S. locations:** CT; DC; FL; IL; MD; NY; PA; VA. **Operations at this facility include:** Administration. **Number of employees at this location:** 200. **Number of employees nationwide:** 2,000.

## TOYS 'R US

461 From Road, Paramus NJ 07652. 201/262-7800. **Contact:** Director of Employment. **World Wide Web address:** http://www.toysrus.com. **Description:** One of the largest children's specialty retailers in the world. The company operates over 1,450 stores worldwide. Founded in 1948. **NOTE:** Entry-level positions are offered. **Common positions include:** Accountant; Administrative Assistant; Assistant Manager; Computer Programmer; Financial Analyst; Management Trainee; MIS Specialist; Secretary; Systems Analyst. **Educational backgrounds include:** Accounting; Business Administration; Computer Science; Finance; Marketing. **Benefits:** 401(k); Daycare Assistance; Dental Insurance; Disability Coverage; Life Insurance; Medical Insurance; Profit Sharing; Savings Plan; Stock Option. **Special programs:** Training. **Corporate headquarters location:** This Location. **Other U.S. locations:** Nationwide. **Subsidiaries include:** Babies 'R Us; Kids 'R Us. **Listed on:** New York Stock Exchange. **Stock exchange symbol:** TOY. **Annual sales/revenues:** More than $100 million. **Number of employees at this location:** 1,400. **Number of employees worldwide:** 60,000.

## UNITED RETAIL GROUP, INC.

365 West Passaic Street, Rochelle Park NJ 07662. 201/845-0880. **Contact:** Human Resources Manager. **Description:** A leading nationwide specialty retailer of larger-size women's apparel and accessories. The company operates 569 stores in 36 states, principally under the names The Avenue and Sizes Unlimited. New/remodeled stores will bear the name Avenue Plus. The company targets fashion-conscious women between 18 and 50 years of age who wear size 14 or larger. Founded in 1987. **Benefits:** Pension Plan. **Subsidiaries include:** United Retail Incorporated. **CEO:** Raphael Benaroya. **Number of employees nationwide:** 4,100.

## VILLAGE SUPERMARKET, INC.

733 Mountain Avenue, Springfield NJ 07081. 973/467-2200. **Contact:** Vic D'Anna, Personnel Director. **Description:** Operates 20 supermarkets, 17 of which are located in north central New Jersey and three of which are in eastern Pennsylvania. Village Supermarket offers traditional grocery, meat, produce, dairy, frozen food, bakery, and delicatessen departments, as well as health and beauty aids, housewares, stationery, and automotive and paint supplies. Six stores contain prescription pharmacy departments, and the company also owns and operates two retail package liquor stores and one variety store. **Corporate headquarters location:** This Location. **Other area locations:** Bernardsville NJ; Chester NJ; Florham Park NJ; Livingston NJ; Morristown NJ; The Orchards NJ; Union NJ. **Parent company:** Wakefern Food Corporation.

## ZALLIE SUPERMARKETS

1230 Blackwood-Clementon Road, Clementon NJ 08021. 609/627-6501. **Contact:** Laura Tabakin, Vice President of Human Resources. **Description:** This location houses administrative offices. Overall, Zallie Supermarkets operates a chain of six Shop-Rite supermarkets. **Corporate headquarters location:** This Location.

*Note: Because addresses and telephone numbers of smaller companies can change rapidly, we recommend you call each company to verify the information below before inquiring about job opportunities. Mass mailings are not recommended.*

**Additional small employers:**

**AUTO DEALERS**

**Autoland**
170 Route 22, Springfield NJ 07081-3123. 973/467-2900.

**Bob Ciasulli Auto Mall Inc.**
RR 46, Little Falls NJ 07424. 973/785-4710.

**Classic Honda**
Black Horse Pike & RR 42,

Blackwood NJ 08012. 609/728-2700.

**Crystal Auto Mall**
220 US Highway 22, Dunellen NJ 08812-1911. 732/968-1000.

**FC Kerbeck & Sons**
100 Route 73 N, Palmyra NJ
08065-1041. 609/829-8200.

**Fette Ford**
PO Box 1237, Clifton NJ 07012-
0737. 973/779-7000.

**Flemington
Chrysler/Plymouth/Dodge**
PO Box 1007, Flemington NJ
08822-1007. 908/782-3673.

**Fullerton Ford**
PO Box B, Somerville NJ 08876.
908/722-2500.

**Global Auto Mall**
PO Box 1305, Watchung NJ
07060. 908/757-4000.

**Hillside Lincoln/Mercury**
100 US Highway 22, Hillside NJ
07205-1837. 973/923-3100.

**Holman Lincoln/Mercury**
Kings Hwy & Rural Route 38,
Maple Shade NJ 08052. 609/234-
4900.

**Lynnes Sussex County Nissan**
59 US Highway 206, Stanhope
NJ 07874-3262. 973/347-2200.

**Ocean Chevrolet Inc.**
Hwy 37 & Peter Ave, Toms River
NJ 08753. 732/244-8400.

**Paramus Hyundai**
E 315 Route 4 W, Paramus NJ
07652. 201/488-9000.

**Planet Honda**
2285 US Highway 22 W, Union
NJ 07083-8404. 908/964-1600.

**Prestige Motors Inc.**
405 N State Rte 17, Paramus NJ
07652-2900. 201/265-7800.

**Rice & Holman Ford**
PO Box 909, Mount Laurel NJ
08054-0909. 609/866-0111.

**Route 22 Toyota**
105 Route 22, Hillside NJ 07205-
1831. 973/705-9300.

**Stillman Automotive**
386 Grand Ave, Englewood NJ
07631-4101. 201/569-9000.

**Touch of Class Leasing**
910 US Highway 1, Edison NJ
08817-4848. 732/549-6600.

**Warnock Automotive Inc.**
175 State Route 10, East Hanover
NJ 07936-2104. 973/884-2100.

**Winner Ford**
PO Box 886, Cherry Hill NJ
08003-0886. 609/428-4000.

## CAMERA AND PHOTOGRAPHIC SUPPLY STORES

**Konica Quality Photo East**
823 E Gate Dr, Ste 1, Mount
Laurel NJ 08054-1202. 609/234-
9698.

## CATALOG AND MAIL-ORDER HOUSES

**CFI**
711 Ridgedale Ave, East Hanover
NJ 07936-3125. 973/503-1000.

**Columbia House**
400 N Woodbury Rd, Pitman NJ
08071-1166. 609/582-3209.

**Genesis Direct Inc.**
100 Plaza Dr, Secaucus NJ
07094-3613. 201/867-2800.

**Marboro Books Corp.**
1 Pond Rd, Northvale NJ 07647-
2505. 201/767-6600.

**Musical Heritage Society**
1710 Highway 35 S, Oakhurst NJ
07755. 732/531-7000.

**Popular Club Plan**
1 Truman Dr S, Edison NJ 08817-
2430. 732/985-4600.

**Technique**
100 Plaza Dr, Secaucus NJ
07094-3613. 201/271-9300.

**Vitamin Shoppe**
4700 W Side Ave, North Bergen
NJ 07047-6446. 201/866-7711.

## CONSUMER ELECTRONICS STORES

**Centennial Security Inc.**
332 Main St, Madison NJ 07940-
2226. 973/966-9766.

## CONSUMER SUPPLY STORES

**Home Depot**
130 Docks Corner Rd, Cranbury
NJ 08512. 732/329-3566.

## DEPARTMENT STORES

**Abraham & Straus**
100 Paramus Park, Paramus NJ
07652-3527. 201/967-1400.

**Ames Department Store**
Rte 23, N Wantage Plaza, Sussex
NJ 07461. 973/702-7155.

**Ames Department Store**
RR 206, Newton NJ 07860.
973/383-6500.

**Big Kmart**
Bridgeton Pike, Mantua NJ
08051. 609/468-7575.

**Big Kmart**
1468 Clementon Rd, Clementon
NJ 08021. 609/627-1800.

**Big Kmart**
3371 Brunswick Ave, Trenton NJ
08648-1303. 609/452-2777.

**Big Kmart**
Delsea Dr, Glassboro NJ 08028.
609/589-5150.

**Big Kmart**
Brooklawn Shopping Center,
Gloucester City NJ 08030-2797.
609/742-0333.

**Big Kmart**
1930 State Highway 88, Brick NJ
08724-3153. 732/840-0800.

**Big Kmart**
7500 S Crescent Blvd,
Pennsauken NJ 08109-4104.
609/665-8505.

**Big Kmart**
1061 White Horse Hamilton,
Trenton NJ 08610. 609/585-9700.

**Big Kmart**
213 Highway 37, Toms River NJ
08755-8022. 732/244-3001.

**Big Kmart**
Black Horse Pike, Pleasantville
NJ 08232. 609/484-0300.

**Big Kmart**
1817 Mount Holly Rd, Burlington
NJ 08016-4700. 609/386-3011.

**Big Kmart**
3850 S Delsea Dr, Vineland NJ
08360-7454. 609/825-9411.

**Big Kmart**
328 S White Horse Pike, Berlin
NJ 08009-1962. 609/768-0090.

**Bloomingdale's**
The Mall, Short Hills NJ 07078.
973/379-1000.

**Boscov's**
Lenola & Rural Route 38,
Moorestown NJ 08057. 609/231-
1101.

**Boscov's**
332 Rural Route 40, Pleasantville
NJ 08232. 609/383-1880.

**Boscov's**
3849 S Delsea Dr, Vineland NJ
08360-7408. 609/327-3800.

**Bradlee's**
Black Horse Pike & RR 42,
Blackwood NJ 08012. 609/228-
7060.

**Bradlee's**
Ramsey Sq, RR 17, Ramsey NJ
07446. 201/825-3100.

**Bradlee's**
Cuthbert Blvd & Rural Route 38,
Cherry Hill NJ 08034. 609/665-
1073.

**Bradlee's**
Ratzer Rd, RR 23, Wayne NJ
07470. 973/696-4141.

**Bradlee's**
River View Dr, RR 46, Totowa
NJ 07512. 973/812-7311.

**Bradlee's**
450 Hackensack Ave,
Hackensack NJ 07601-6305.
201/489-6009.

**Bradlee's**
189 Rte 46, Saddle Brook NJ
07663. 201/843-4213.

**Bradlee's**
RR 9, Englishtown NJ 07726-
9809. 732/780-7665.

**Bradlee's**
Poole Ave, RR 36, Hazlet NJ
07730. 732/264-6250.

**Bradlee's**
Twin Brooks Rd, RR 35,
Middletown NJ 07748. 732/957-
0810.

**Bradlee's**
772 Route 46, Parsippany NJ
07054-3401. 973/334-1042.

**Bradlee's**
Tices Lane, RR 18, East
Brunswick NJ 08816. 732/238-
4670.

**Bradlee's**
222 S White Horse Pike, Stratford
NJ 08084-1200. 609/346-9300.

**Bradlee's**
10 Clearview Rd, Edison NJ
08837-3716. 732/225-7272.

**Bradlee's**
45 Central Ave, Clark NJ 07066-
1421. 732/574-8902.

**Bradlee's**
1555 Saint Georges Ave, Colonia
NJ 07067-3414. 732/388-2633.

**Bradlee's**
Parkville Station Rd, RR 45,
Woodbury NJ 08096. 609/468-
8200.

**Bradlee's**
686 Oak Tree Ave, South
Plainfield NJ 07080-5122.
908/754-2728.

**Bradlee's**
Nicholson Rd & Rural Route 168,
Audubon NJ 08106. 609/547-
3437.

**Bradlee's**
14 Main Ave, Clifton NJ 07014-
1908. 973/667-3921.

**Bradlee's**
Morris Ave, RR 22, Union NJ
07083. 908/687-8081.

**Bradlee's**
2 Route 37 W, Toms River NJ
08753-6588. 732/244-7200.

**Bradlee's**
440 RR 9, Woodbridge NJ 07095.
732/826-6010.

**Bradlee's**
Burlington Manor, Burlington NJ
08016-1746. 609/387-3332.

**Bradlee's**
6719 Black Horse Pike, Egg
Harbor Township NJ 08234-
3901. 609/646-8500.

**Bradlee's**
RR 440, Jersey City NJ 07307.
201/432-6128.

**Bradlee's**
5038 Wellington Ave, Ventnor
City NJ 08406-1443. 609/823-
0500.

**Bradlee's**
PO Box 183, Bordentown NJ
08505-0183. 609/298-9380.

**Caldor**
4340 Route 130, Willingboro NJ
08046-1441. 609/877-5800.

**Caldor**
295 Route 72 W, Manahawkin NJ
08050-2813. 609/597-0450.

**Caldor**
Rte 4, Spring Valley Rd, Paramus
NJ 07652. 201/845-5553.

**Caldor**
Washington Plz Shopping Ctr,
Blackwood NJ 08012. 609/228-
9000.

**Caldor**
Union Ave, RR 35, Holmdel NJ
07733. 732/888-1400.

**Caldor**
Route 66, Neptune Blvd, Neptune
NJ 07753. 732/774-1106.

**Caldor**
1601 W Edgar Rd, Linden NJ
07036-6421. 908/862-1236.

**Caldor**
6801 W Side Ave, North Bergen
NJ 07047-6441. 201/854-2822.

**Caldor**
202 RR 10, Morris Plains NJ
07950. 973/539-5900.

**Caldor**
Prospect Eagle Rock Ave, West
Orange NJ 07052. 973/731-8606.

**Caldor**
RR 22, Watchung NJ 07060.
908/322-8880.

**Caldor**
Chamber Bridge Rd, RR 70,
Brick NJ 08723. 732/920-8400.

**Caldor**
Alliance Ave & Rural Route 45,
Woodbury NJ 08097. 609/845-
1132.

**Caldor**
536 Milltown Rd, North
Brunswick NJ 08902-3327.
732/846-6250.

**Caldor**
4971 Stelton Rd, South Plainfield
NJ 07080-1113. 908/769-0520.

**Caldor**
1 River Rd, Edgewater NJ 07020.
201/840-0766.

**Caldor**
33 State Hwy 37 W, Toms River
NJ 08753. 732/341-6333.

**Caldor**
RR 3 W, Secaucus NJ 07094.
201/864-6611.

**Caldor**
877 Saint George Ave,
Woodbridge NJ 07095-2514.
732/750-1500.

**Caldor**
Browertown Rd, RR 46, West
Paterson NJ 07424. 973/785-
1533.

**Flemington Department Store**
151 State Route 31, Flemington
NJ 08822-5748. 908/782-7662.

**Hecht's**
Lenola Rd & Rural Route 38,
Moorestown NJ 08057. 609/235-
7000.

**JCPenney**
6002 Echelon Mall, Cherry Hill
NJ 08034. 609/772-0200.

**JCPenney**
260 State Routes 23 & 46, Wayne
NJ 07470-6823. 973/785-3200.

**JCPenney**
Rts 4 & 17, Garden State Pkwy,
Paramus NJ 07652. 201/843-
2910.

**JCPenney**
Rural Route 1, Trenton NJ 08648-
9801. 609/799-8100.

**JCPenney**
3710 Route 9, Freehold NJ
07728. 732/780-4001.

**JCPenney**
Mount Hope & RR 80, Rockaway
NJ 07866. 973/361-4500.

**JCPenney**
2501 Mount Holly Rd, Burlington
NJ 08016-4802. 609/239-9400.

**JCPenney**
2000 Route 38, Cherry Hill NJ
08002-2100. 609/488-0330.

**JCPenney**
Black Horse Pike & Nicholson,
Audubon NJ 08106. 609/546-
8200.

**JCPenney**
Bay & Hooper Ave, Toms River
NJ 08753. 732/240-5400.

**JCPenney**
Woodbridge Center Dr,
Woodbridge NJ 07095. 732/636-
6000.

**JCPenney**
14 Laurel St N, Bridgeton NJ
08302-1908. 609/451-1650.

**JCPenney**
4405 Black Horse Pike, Mays
Landing NJ 08330-3102.
609/645-9399.

**JCPenney**
10 Mall Dr W, Jersey City NJ
07310-1601. 201/217-1111.

**Kmart**
1020 Hamburg Turnpike, Wayne
NJ 07470-3226. 973/696-8312.

**Kmart**
2 Memorial Dr, Lodi NJ 07644-
1623. 973/471-7900.

**Kmart**
859 Route 17, Paramus NJ
07652-3103. 201/444-8550.

**Kmart**
700 Broadway, Westwood NJ
07675-1674. 201/666-6501.

**Kmart**
1825 Highway 35, Belmar NJ
07719-3541. 732/280-8010.

**Kmart**
3010 Highway 35, Hazlet NJ
07730-1505. 732/739-2800.

**Kmart**
4594 Route 9 S, Howell NJ
07731. 732/363-9191.

**Kmart**
1701 W Edgar Rd, Linden NJ
07036-6407. 908/474-9799.

**Kmart**
108 Monmouth Rd, West Long
Branch NJ 07764-1006. 732/542-
5747.

**Kmart**
RR 57, Hackettstown NJ 07840.
908/852-7440.

**Kmart**
140 US Hwy RR 10, Dover NJ
07869. 973/361-5950.

**Kmart**
247 N Broadway, Pennsville NJ
08070-1201. 609/678-7600.

**Kmart**
1159 Route 46, Parsippany NJ
07054-2101. 973/299-1566.

**Kmart**
7401 Tonnelle Ave, Dunellen NJ
08812. 201/868-1960.

**Kmart**
645 Highway 18, East Brunswick
NJ 08816-3721. 732/238-6464.

**Kmart**
US Hwy 22, Plainfield NJ 07060.
908/561-7050.

**Kmart**
1089 US Highway 9, Old Bridge
NJ 08857-2876. 732/727-2760.

**Kmart**
RR 70, Box E, Marlton NJ 08053.
609/983-7440.

**Kmart**
256 US Highway 206 S,
Somerville NJ 08876-4681.
908/359-1000.

**Kmart**
6801 Hadley Rd, South Plainfield
NJ 07080-1121. 908/561-3088.

**Kmart**
371 Main St 411, Belleville NJ
07109-3234. 973/751-3331.

**Kmart**
1550 Saint Georges Ave, Avenel
NJ 07001-1044. 732/574-3500.

**Kmart**
180 Broadway, Elmwood Park NJ
07407-3052. 201/791-7007.

**Laneco**
1 Laneco Plz, Clinton NJ 08809-
1259. 908/735-4300.

**Laneco**
RR 22, Phillipsburg NJ 08865.
908/454-1175.

**Lord & Taylor**
Willowbrook Shopping Ctr,
Wayne NJ 07470. 973/785-0300.

**Lord & Taylor**
Ridgewood Ave, RR 17, Paramus
NJ 07652. 201/447-0400.

**Lord & Taylor**
600 Quaker Bridge Mall, Trenton
NJ 08648-1902. 609/799-9500.

**Lord & Taylor**
3710 Highway 9, Ste 1500,
Freehold NJ 07728-4806.
732/308-1400.

**Lord & Taylor**
111 Eisenhower Pkwy,
Livingston NJ 07039. 973/994-
0800.

**Lord & Taylor**
Mount Hope Rd, RR 80,
Rockaway NJ 07866. 973/328-
9000.

**Lord & Taylor**
440 Commons Way, Bridgewater
NJ 08807-2804. 908/707-9000.

**Lord & Taylor**
609 N Ave, Westfield NJ 07090.
908/233-6600.

**Macy's**
100 US Highway 46, Wayne NJ
07470-6834. 973/785-9525.

**Macy's**
Monmouth Mall, Eatontown NJ
07724. 732/542-1212.

**Macy's**
Rural Route 1, Lawrenceville NJ
08648-9801. 609/799-8000.

**Macy's**
112 Eisenhower Pkwy,
Livingston NJ 07039-4900.
973/994-2000.

**Macy's**
75 Rockaway Ave, Rockaway NJ
07866-3918. 973/328-1234.

**Macy's**
400 Commons Way, Bridgewater
NJ 08807-2800. 908/725-1400.

**Macy's**
1220 Morris Tpke, Short Hills NJ
07078-2718. 973/467-0800.

**Macy's**
1201 Hooper Ave, Toms River
NJ 08753-3330. 732/240-6500.

**Macy's**
Haddonfield Rd & RR 38, Cherry
Hill NJ 08002. 609/665-5000.

**Marshall's**
Shrewsbury Plz, Shrewsbury NJ
07702. 732/542-1190.

**Neiman Marcus**
1200 Morris Tpke, Short Hills NJ
07078-2717. 973/912-0080.

**Rowe-Manse Emporium Inc.**
1065 Bloomfield Ave, Clifton NJ
07012-2120. 973/472-8170.

**Saks Fifth Avenue**
380 Hackensack Ave,
Hackensack NJ 07601-6310.
201/646-1800.

**Saks Fifth Avenue**
1200 Morris Tpke, Short Hills NJ
07078. 973/376-7000.

**Sealfons Inc.**
615 Route 35, Red Bank NJ
07701-4700. 732/530-0033.

**Sears, Roebuck & Co.**
50 Rte 46, Wayne NJ 07470.
973/890-2000.

**Sears, Roebuck & Co.**
436 Main St, Hackensack NJ
07601-5911. 201/525-5200.

**Sears, Roebuck & Co.**
Paramus Park Mall, Paramus NJ
07652. 201/967-0300.

**Sears, Roebuck & Co.**
Routes 66 & 35, Asbury Park NJ
07712. 732/918-2700.

**Sears, Roebuck & Co.**
Lenola Rd, Rural Route 38,
Moorestown NJ 08057. 609/778-
5200.

**Sears, Roebuck & Co.**
S Orange Ave, Livingston NJ
07039. 973/535-4500.

**Sears, Roebuck & Co.**
Mt Hope Rd, RR 80, Rockaway
NJ 07866. 973/989-7200.

**Sears, Roebuck & Co.**
1640 Route 22, Watchung NJ
07060-6503. 908/755-6000.

**Sears, Roebuck & Co.**
1750 Deptford Center Rd,
Deptford NJ 08096-5222.
609/384-2000.

**Sears, Roebuck & Co.**
1200 US Highway 22,
Phillipsburg NJ 08865-4111.
908/859-9000.

**Sears, Roebuck & Co.**
51 US Highway 1, New
Brunswick NJ 08901-1530
732/937-7355.

**Sears, Roebuck & Co.**
1201 Hooper Ave, Toms River
NJ 08753-3330. 732/240-4500.

**Sears, Roebuck & Co.**
150 Woodbridge Ctr Dr,
Woodbridge NJ 07095-1124.
732/602-5000.

**Sears, Roebuck & Co.**
8 W Landis Ave, Vineland NJ
08360-8107. 609/692-2000.

**Sears, Roebuck & Co.**
50 Mall Dr W, Jersey City NJ
07310-1601. 201/626-6363.

**Shoppers World**
325 State Route 18, East
Brunswick NJ 08816-2107.
732/613-1000.

**Shoppers World**
100 Broad St, Elizabeth NJ
07201-2302. 908/351-3488.

**Steinbach**
80 Brick Plz, Brick NJ 08723-
4045. 732/477-4000.

**Stern's Department Stores**
46 RR 23, Wayne NJ 07470.
973/785-1100.

**Stern's Department Stores**
Ledgewood Mall, Ledgewood NJ
07852. 973/252-9700.

**Strawbridge's**
2501 Burlington Rd, Burlington
NJ 08016. 609/387-8100.

**Value City**
E Bergen Mall, Paramus NJ
07652. 201/845-3000.

**Value City**
468 Chancellor Ave, Irvington NJ
07111-4001. 973/371-5000.

**Value City**
3849 S Delsea Dr, Suite 300,
Vineland NJ 08360-7410.
609/327-8067.

**Wal-Mart**
55 S White Horse Pike,
Hammonton NJ 08037-1872.
609/567-2700.

**Wal-Mart**
150 E Route 70, Marlton NJ
08053-1856. 609/983-2100.

**Wal-Mart**
101 Nassau Park Blvd, Princeton
NJ 08540-5918. 609/987-0202.

**Wal-Mart**
4900 US Highway 9, Howell NJ
07731-3724. 732/886-9100.

**Wal-Mart**
709 S Broadway, Pennsville NJ
08070-2637. 609/935-8200.

**Wal-Mart**
1872 Route 88, Brick NJ 08724-
3535. 732/840-7772.

**Wal-Mart**
979 US Highway 1, North
Brunswick NJ 08902-2712.
732/545-4499.

**Wal-Mart**
950 Route 37 W, Toms River NJ
08755-5018. 732/349-6000.

**Wal-Mart**
4620 Black Horse Pike, Mays
Landing NJ 08330-3213.
609/625-8200.

**Wal-Mart**
195 Fries Mill Rd, Blackwood NJ
08012-2006. 609/875-7013.

**Wal-Mart**
2291 N 2nd St, Millville NJ
08332-1305. 609/825-4200.

**Wal-Mart**
525 Route 72 West, Manahawkin
NJ 08050-2800. 609/978-8300.

**Wal-Mart**
2106 Mount Holly Rd, Burlington
NJ 08016-4192. 609/386-8400.

**Wal-Mart**
273 Route 79 N, Berlin NJ
08009. 609/753-8787.

**FUEL DEALERS**

**Suburban Propane Partners**
240 Rte 10 W, Whippany NJ
07981. 973/887-5300.

**GROCERY AND
CONVENIENCE STORES**

**A&P**
RR 23, Sussex NJ 07461.
973/875-3256.

**A&P**
19 Belleville Ave, Bloomfield NJ
07003-5220. 973/429-8754.

**A&P**
Ratzer RR 23, Wayne NJ 07470.
973/694-7707.

**A&P**
430 Greenwood Ave, Wyckoff
NJ 07481-2027. 201/848-1106.

**A&P**
289 Bergen Blvd, Fairview NJ
07022-1323. 201/945-5255.

**A&P**
105 South Ave, Fanwood NJ
07023-1547. 908/756-2118.

**A&P**
2007 Highway 35, Belmar NJ
07719-3543. 732/974-9090.

**A&P**
116 Highway 36, Port Monmouth
NJ 07758-1329. 732/787-9686.

**A&P**
125 W Main St, Denville NJ
07834-1621. 973/586-0601.

**A&P**
Rte 46E, Hackettstown NJ 07840.
908/852-6182.

**A&P**
2220 91st St, North Bergen NJ
07047-4729. 201/662-4700.

**A&P**
1425 Kennedy Blvd, North
Bergen NJ 07047-6307. 201/864-
9300.

**A&P**
35 Brunswick Ave, Edison NJ
08817-2576. 732/985-3100.

**A&P**
375 Paterson Ave, Wallington NJ
07057-2101. 201/935-7822.

**A&P**
427 Atlantic City Blvd, Bayville
NJ 08721-1877. 732/269-0236.

**A&P**
1185 Amboy Ave, Edison NJ
08837-2592. 732/906-1446.

**A&P**
PO Box 418, Montvale NJ 07645-
0418. 201/573-9700.

**A&P**
3600 Oak Tree Rd, South
Plainfield NJ 07080. 908/668-
1050.

**A&P**
1350 Galloping Hill Rd, Union
NJ 07083-8902. 908/687-9700.

**A&P**
45 W Allendale Ave, Allendale
NJ 07401-1701. 201/825-9822.

**A&P**
45 Demercurio Dr, Allendale NJ
07401-1711. 201/934-9161.

**A&P**
125 Franklin Turnpike, Mahwah
NJ 07430-1341. 201/512-9100.

**Acme**
Rural Route 45 & Berkley Rd,
Mantua NJ 08051. 609/468-3939.

**Acme**
1080 Broad St, Shrewsbury NJ
07702-4332. 732/542-4130.

**Acme**
246 Norwood Ave, Long Branch
NJ 07740-4582. 732/531-6000.

**Acme**
Delsea Dr & Heston Rd,
Glassboro NJ 08028. 609/582-
0305.

**Acme**
Mt. Hope Ave, RR 80, Rockaway
NJ 07866. 973/989-8503.

**Acme**
Cinnamison Ave & RR 130,
Riverton NJ 08077. 609/786-
0390.

**Acme**
64 Princeton Heightstown Rd,
Princeton Junction NJ 08550-
1103. 609/452-2354.

**Acme**
631 Mantua Ave, Woodbury NJ
08096-3234. 609/848-0224.

**Acme**
Nicholson Rd & Rural Route 168,
Audubon NJ 08106. 609/547-
3938.

**Acme**
400 Cuthbert Rd, Collingswood
NJ 08108. 609/858-2226.

**Acme**
Rural Route 533, Trenton NJ
08610. 609/585-5150.

**Acme**
3845 Bayshore Rd, Cape May NJ
08204-3261. 609/884-1203.

**Acme**
11 Dennis Magnolia Dr, Cape
May Courthouse NJ 08210.
609/463-9106.

**Acme**
63 Landis Ave, Sea Isle City NJ
08243. 609/263-3495.

**Acme**
4454 Black Horse Pike, Mays
Landing NJ 08330-3100.
609/625-4710.

**Acme**
2 Garfield Ave, Jersey City NJ
07305-2401. 201/432-7011.

**Acme**
46 Florence Ave, Berlin NJ
08009. 609/768-5888.

**Brown's Thriftway**
5000 N Crescent Blvd,
Pennsauken NJ 08109-2151.
609/665-6311.

**Clark Shop-Rite**
1184 Raritan Rd, Clark NJ
07066-1311. 732/381-2025.

**Community Supermarket Corp.**
233 W Market St, Newark NJ
07103-2713. 973/242-2510.

**Corrado's Family Affair**
1578 Main Ave, Clifton NJ
07011-2110. 973/340-0628.

**Cumberland Farms**
N Cumberland Blvd & RR 13,
Burlington NJ 08016. 609/499-
2600.

**Delran Shop-Rite**
1000 Route 130, Riverside NJ
08075. 609/764-1161.

**Edward's**
1556 N Olden Avenue Ext,
Trenton NJ 08638-3204. 609/396-
2777.

**Edward's**
Concordia Shopping Mall,
Cranbury NJ 08512. 609/655-
8900.

**Edward's**
133 Main St, Madison NJ 07940-
2154. 973/593-8484.

**Edward's**
233 Route 18, East Brunswick NJ
08816-1903. 732/247-4141.

**Edward's**
1328 River Ave, Lakewood NJ
08701-5645. 732/905-7744.

**Edward's**
1083 Inman Ave, Edison NJ
08820-1132. 908/769-6173.

**Edward's**
Middlesex Ave, RR 27,
Metuchen NJ 08840. 732/549-
1620.

**Edward's**
Somerset Ave & RR 206, Raritan
NJ 08869. 908/685-1204.

**Edward's**
980 Easton Ave, Somerset NJ
08873-1745. 732/545-9050.

**Edward's**
424 Raritan Ave, Highland Park
NJ 08904-2740. 732/572-4155.

**Edward's**
4999 Stelton Rd, South Plainfield
NJ 07080-1113. 908/769-0120.

**Edward's**
1201 Stuyvesant Ave, Union NJ
07083-3821. 908/688-6650.

**Edward's**
635 S Clinton Ave, Trenton NJ
08611-1831. 609/278-0500.

**Edward's**
RR 3, Secaucus NJ 07094.
201/864-6062.

**Edward's**
11 Lacey Rd, Whiting NJ 08759-
2920. 732/350-7750.

**Edward's**
1710 Route 38, Mount Holly NJ
08060-2218. 609/265-8060.

**Edward's**
232 Central Ave, Jersey City NJ
07307-3006. 201/653-6508.

**Edward's**
649 Route 206, Belle Mead NJ
08502-1520. 908/359-7274.

**Foodarama Shop-Rite**
2909 Washington Rd, Parlin NJ
08859-1513. 732/525-8282.

**Foodmart International Corp.**
100 Boyle Plaza, Jersey City NJ
07310. 201/656-6950.

**Foodtown**
597 Park Ave, Freehold NJ
07728-2351. 732/462-6474.

**Foodtown**
232-274 Passaic Ave, Kearny NJ
07032. 201/997-6444.

**Foodtown**
PO Box 3038, Long Branch NJ
07740-3038. 732/229-9411.

**Foodtown**
116 3rd Ave, Neptune NJ 07753-
6400. 732/776-9564.

**Foodtown**
52 Westfield Ave, Clark NJ
07066-3226. 732/388-7334.

**Foodtown**
401 Abbington Dr, Hightstown
NJ 08520. 609/443-3413.

**Foodtown**
RR 35 & Sea Girt Ave, Sea Girt
NJ 08750. 732/223-1930.

**Foodtown**
2465 S Broad St, Trenton NJ
08610-4701. 609/888-4000.

**Francis Markets Ltd.**
RR 9, Englishtown NJ 07726-
9809. 732/536-1774.

**Francis Markets Ltd.**
116 3rd Ave, Neptune NJ 07753-
6400. 732/776-5656.

**Franklin Shop-Rite**
270 State Rte 23, Franklin NJ
07416-2160. 973/827-6135.

**Funaris Thriftway**
401 Harmony Rd, Gibbstown NJ
08027-1723. 609/423-3440.

**Giant Food**
400 E Evesham Rd, Cherry Hill
NJ 08003-3399. 609/216-1400.

**Grand Union**
175 Franklin Ave, Ridgewood NJ
07450-3205. 201/444-6222.

**Grand Union**
201 Willowbrook Blvd, Wayne
NJ 07470-7025. 973/890-6000.

**Grand Union**
327 Franklin Ave, Wyckoff NJ
07481-2051. 201/848-1046.

**Grand Union**
1189 Broad St, Clifton NJ 07013-
3327. 973/473-7766.

**Grand Union**
875 N State Rte 17, Paramus NJ
07652-3103. 201/652-9830.

**Grand Union**
34 W Railroad Ave, Tenafly NJ
07670-1735. 201/894-5111.

**Grand Union**
RR 9, Englishtown NJ 07726-
9809. 732/294-8510.

**Grand Union**
4075 Aldrich Ave, Howell NJ
07731. 732/901-9200.

**Grand Union**
Lloyd Rd RR 34, Matawan NJ
07747. 732/566-0450.

**Grand Union**
1071 Rte 37 W, Dover NJ 07802.
732/240-9806.

**Grand Union**
Route 10, Eisenhower Pkwy,
Livingston NJ 07039. 973/992-
2299.

**Grand Union**
Lakeside Blvd Ctr, Landing NJ
07850. 973/398-0808.

**Grand Union**
60 Sparta Ave, Sparta NJ 07871-
1821. 973/729-7844.

**Grand Union**
404 Springfield Ave, Berkeley
Heights NJ 07922. 908/464-8997.

**Grand Union**
380 W Pleasantview Ave,
Hackensack NJ 07601-1068.
201/342-4011.

**Grand Union**
55 Brick Blvd, Brick NJ 08723-
7922. 732/255-9879.

**Grand Union**
1225 State Rd, Rocky Hill NJ
08553. 609/924-0011.

**Grand Union**
4095 US Highway 1, Ste 41,
Monmouth Junction NJ 08852-
2161. 732/329-8288.

**Grand Union**
Milltown Rd, North Brunswick
NJ 08902. 732/246-2050.

**Inserra Supermarkets Inc.**
RR 440, Jersey City NJ 07304.
201/333-2345.

**Kennedy Shop 'N Bag**
Levitt Parkway Kennedy W,
Willingboro NJ 08046. 609/871-
3131.

**King's Supermarkets**
2 Dedrick Pl, Caldwell NJ 07006-
6399. 973/575-3320.

**King's Supermarkets**
86 E Main St, Mendham NJ
07945-1831. 973/543-4493.

**Landis Shop-Rite**
3600 E Landis Ave, Vineland NJ
08361-3046. 609/691-0116.

**Laurel Hill Shop-Rite**
Gordon Ave & RR 42,
Williamstown NJ 08094.
609/728-5600.

**LML Supermarket**
20 Ridge Rd, Mahwah NJ 07430-
2021. 201/529-5900.

**McCaffrey's**
301 N Harrison St, Princeton NJ
08540-3512. 609/683-1600.

**McCaffrey's**
335 Princeton Heightstown,
Cranbury NJ 08512-1834.
609/799-3555.

**Pathmark Supermarket**
1600 Saint Georges Ave, Avenel
NJ 07001-1044. 732/499-9361.

**Pathmark Supermarket**
10 Triangle Plz, Ramsey NJ
07446-1253. 201/934-7600.

**Pathmark Supermarket**
1070 Peterson Hamburg Tpke,
Wayne NJ 07470. 973/694-3663.

**Pathmark Supermarket**
498 E 30th St, Paterson NJ
07504-2111. 973/278-7702.

**Pathmark Supermarket**
450 Hackensack Ave,
Hackensack NJ 07601-6305.
201/487-0145.

**Pathmark Supermarket**
405 S State Rte 17, Hackensack
NJ 07601-1002. 201/487-3745.

**Pathmark Supermarket**
895 Paulison Ave, Clifton NJ
07011-3640. 973/546-6090.

**Pathmark Supermarket**
80 New Bridge Rd, Bergenfield
NJ 07621-4112. 201/385-2627.

**Pathmark Supermarket**
481 River Rd, Edgewater NJ
07020-1145. 201/840-7759.

**Pathmark Supermarket**
10 South Ave, Garwood NJ
07027-1338. 908/789-0490.

**Pathmark Supermarket**
50 Highway 36, Eatontown NJ
07724-2508. 732/542-6400.

**Pathmark Supermarket**
120 Route 9, Englishtown NJ
07726-4759. 732/536-7770.

**Pathmark Supermarket**
100 Schanck Rd, Freehold NJ
07728-5311. 732/780-1700.

**Pathmark Supermarket**
1 Clark St, Hazlet NJ 07730-
1241. 732/739-2300.

**Pathmark Supermarket**
145 Passaic Ave, Kearny NJ
07032-1105. 201/991-7661.

**Pathmark Supermarket**
2216 Highway 9, Howell NJ
07731-3333. 732/364-6300.

**Pathmark Supermarket**
1123 Highway 35, Middletown
NJ 07748-2605. 732/957-0270.

**Pathmark Supermarket**
757 State Route 15 S, Jefferson
NJ 07849-2284. 973/663-1500.

**Pathmark Supermarket**
140 State Route 10, Dover NJ
07869-1542. 973/361-7530.

**Pathmark Supermarket**
2115 69th St, North Bergen NJ
07047-4513. 201/453-0009.

**Pathmark Supermarket**
240 State Route 10, East Hanover
NJ 07936-2602. 973/887-2200.

**Pathmark Supermarket**
345 Prospect Ave, West Orange
NJ 07052. 973/731-4100.

**Pathmark Supermarket**
1157 Route 46, Parsippany NJ
07054-2101. 973/334-9290.

**Pathmark Supermarket**
50 Race Track Rd, East
Brunswick NJ 08816-3728.
732/257-5100.

**Pathmark Supermarket**
561 US Highway 1, Edison NJ
08817-4400. 732/572-7081.

**Pathmark Supermarket**
Rural Route 1, Cranbury NJ
08512-9801. 609/951-0609.

**Pathmark Supermarket**
1188 Route 22, Plainfield NJ
07060-3516. 908/561-1000.

**Pathmark Supermarket**
242 Lincoln Blvd, Middlesex NJ
08846-2305. 732/356-0440.

**Pathmark Supermarket**
1043 US Highway 9, Old Bridge
NJ 08857-2875. 732/721-8822.

**Pathmark Supermarket**
95 New Brunswick Ave, Perth

Amboy NJ 08861-2294. 732/826-
6044.

**Pathmark Supermarket**
1930 Highway 88, Brick NJ
08724-3153. 732/840-9690.

**Pathmark Supermarket**
1450 Clements Bridge Rd,
Deptford NJ 08096-3067.
609/853-5533.

**Pathmark Supermarket**
100 Veterans Memorial Dr,
Somerville NJ 08876. 908/526-
8868.

**Pathmark Supermarket**
407 Valley St, South Orange NJ
07079-2807. 973/762-6608.

**Pathmark Supermarket**
977 Valley Rd, Gillette NJ
07933-1813. 908/647-2450.

**Pathmark Supermarket**
1345 US Highway 1, North
Brunswick NJ 08902-2001.
732/828-3101.

**Pathmark Supermarket**
6301 Hadley Rd, South Plainfield
NJ 07080-1116. 908/561-4020.

**Pathmark Supermarket**
989 Church Rd, Cherry Hill NJ
08002-1301. 609/482-5433.

**Pathmark Supermarket**
651 N Stiles St, Linden NJ
07036-5759. 908/925-6626.

**Pathmark Supermarket**
2881 Mount Ephraim Ave,
Camden NJ 08104-3233.
609/962-7113.

**Pathmark Supermarket**
Rte 22 E, Union NJ 07083.
908/964-8610.

**Pathmark Supermarket**
4100 Park Ave, Weehawken NJ
07087-6182. 201/867-8778.

**Pathmark Supermarket**
1334 Lakewood Rd, Toms River
NJ 08755-4075. 732/505-6440.

**Pathmark Supermarket**
281 Ferry St, Newark NJ 07105-
3443. 973/589-7565.

**Pathmark Supermarket**
6718 Black Horse Pike, Egg
Harbor Township NJ 08234-
3903. 609/646-8414.

**Pathmark Supermarket**
115 Belmont Ave, Belleville NJ
07109-1017. 973/751-1041.

**Pathmark Supermarket**
1933 Highway 35, Belmar NJ
07719-3502. 732/449-6611.

**Pathmark Supermarket**
726 Washington Ave, Belleville
NJ 07109-2820. 973/751-1308.

**Pathmark Supermarket**
47179 Lyons Ave, Irvington NJ
07111. 973/923-8655.

**Pathmark Supermarket**
211 Elmora Ave, Elizabeth NJ
07202-1105. 908/289-5350.

**Pathmark Supermarket**
517 Route 72 East, Manahawkin
NJ 08050-3541. 609/978-8630.

**Pathmark Supermarket**
Rural Route 70, Cherry Hill NJ
08034. 609/428-7230.

**Pathmark Supermarket**
2225 N 2nd St, Millville NJ
08332-1305. 609/293-8188.

**Pathmark Supermarket**
420 Grand St, Jersey City NJ
07302-4240. 201/432-8401.

**Pathmark Supermarket**
130 White Horse Pike North,
Lawnside NJ 08045-1130.
609/546-5885.

**Pathmark Supermarket**
Kellogg St, RR 440, Jersey City
NJ 07305. 201/434-0417.

**Pathmark Supermarket**
25 Kinnelon Rd, Butler NJ
07405-2340. 973/838-6699.

**Pathmark Supermarket**
22-00 Maple Ave, Fair Lawn NJ
07410-1526. 201/796-3332.

**Pathmark Supermarket**
Rte 46 W, West Paterson NJ
07424. 973/890-1135.

**Pathmark Supermarket**
2110 Route 130, Beverly NJ
08010. 609/877-6161.

**Renco Supermarket LP**
New York & Atlantic Aves,
Atlantic City NJ 08401. 609/340-
0130.

**Shop-Rite**
PO Box 183, Bayonne NJ 07002-
0183. 201/437-6000.

**Shop-Rite**
625 Hamburg Tpke, Wayne NJ
07470-2098. 973/595-0079.

**Shop-Rite**
23 Marshall Hill Rd, West
Milford NJ 07480-2144. 973/728-
3458.

**Shop-Rite**
Route 17, Hasbrouck Heights NJ
07604. 201/288-4403.

**Shop-Rite**
814 River Rd, New Milford NJ
07646-3014. 201/262-8834.

**Shop-Rite**
246 Livingston St, Northvale NJ
07647-1902. 201/784-0173.

**Shop-Rite**
Bergen Mall, Paramus NJ 07652.
201/843-6616.

**Shop-Rite**
321 Broad Ave, Ridgefield NJ
07657-2327. 201/941-6240.

**Shop-Rite**
533 Martin Luther King Jr Blvd,
East Orange NJ 07018. 973/674-
1500.

**Shop-Rite**
1355 Inwood Ter, Fort Lee NJ
07024-1738. 201/886-0244.

**Shop-Rite**
Rural Route 9, Freehold NJ
07728-9809. 732/462-3120.

**Shop-Rite**
Hwy 36, Hazlet NJ 07730.
732/264-4110.

**Shop-Rite**
100 Passaic Ave, Kearny NJ
07032-1128. 201/998-1595.

**Shop-Rite**
Lloyd Rd, Matawan NJ 07747.
732/566-9111.

**Shop-Rite**
35 Harmony Rd, Middletown NJ
07748-1712. 732/671-9444.

**Shop-Rite**
280 Highway 9 N, Morganville
NJ 07751-1572. 732/617-0404.

**Shop-Rite**
Hwy 36, Monmouth Rd, West
Long Branch NJ 07764. 732/542-
5222.

**Shop-Rite**
437 US Highway 46, Dover NJ
07801-3709. 973/624-4777.

**Shop-Rite**
483 S Livingston Ave, Livingston
NJ 07039-4327. 973/740-2004.

**Shop-Rite**
Rural Route 57, Hackettstown NJ
07840. 908/852-1200.

**Shop-Rite**
Rural Route 46, Netcong NJ
07857. 973/347-0137.

**Shop-Rite**
RR 206, Box N, Newton NJ
07860. 973/383-6900.

**Shop-Rite**
1225 Highway 33, Trenton NJ
08690-2713. 609/890-8088.

**Shop-Rite**
Roxbury Mall, Rural Route 10,
Succasunna NJ 07876. 973/584-
1322.

**Shop-Rite**
384 Route 57 W, Washington NJ
07882-4335. 908/689-2400.

**Shop-Rite**
Rural Route 202, Bernardsville
NJ 07924. 908/766-3129.

**Shop-Rite**
641 Shunpike Rd, Chatham NJ
07928-1567. 973/377-4788.

**Shop-Rite**
195 US Highway 206 S, Chester
NJ 07930-2402. 908/879-5836.

**Shop-Rite**
3115 Kennedy Blvd, North
Bergen NJ 07047-2303. 201/865-
0219.

**Shop-Rite**
202 Rural Route 10, Morris
Plains NJ 07950. 973/539-0281.

**Shop-Rite**
495 Prospect Ave, West Orange
NJ 07052-4111. 973/736-9374.

**Shop-Rite**
1153 Valley Rd, Stirling NJ
07980-1500. 908/604-2129.

**Shop-Rite**
14 W Prospect St, East
Brunswick NJ 08816-2115.
732/257-7575.

**Shop-Rite**
503 Paulison Ave, Passaic NJ
07055-3152. 973/471-0868.

**Shop-Rite**
Old Post Rd, Rural Route 1,
Edison NJ 08817. 732/819-0140.

**Shop-Rite**
711 Evesham Ave, Somerdale NJ
08083-3000. 609/435-7880.

**Shop-Rite**
1665 Oak Tree Rd, Edison NJ
08820-2843. 732/494-2440.

**Shop-Rite**
1700 Madison Ave, Unit 21,
Lakewood NJ 08701-1253.
732/363-8270.

**Shop-Rite**
1701 US Highway 22, Ste 20,
Watchung NJ 07060-6500.
908/322-6410.

**Shop-Rite**
272 US Highway 202,

Flemington NJ 08822-1718.
908/782-2553.

**Shop-Rite**
668 Route 70, Brick NJ 08723-
4026. 732/477-7906.

**Shop-Rite**
220 Main St, Millburn NJ 07041-
1104. 973/467-5436.

**Shop-Rite**
1306 Centennial Ave, Piscataway
NJ 08854-4324. 732/981-9111.

**Shop-Rite**
US Hwy 9, Fairway Plz, Old
Bridge NJ 08857. 732/727-3533.

**Shop-Rite**
365 Convery Blvd, Perth Amboy
NJ 08861-3741. 732/442-1717.

**Shop-Rite**
S Evergreen Ave, Woodbury NJ
08096. 609/845-6843.

**Shop-Rite**
629 Higgins Ave, Brielle NJ
08730-1427. 732/528-6100.

**Shop-Rite**
US Highway 9, Forked River NJ
08731. 609/693-1152.

**Shop-Rite**
9 S Orange Ave, South Orange
NJ 07079-1716. 973/763-4161.

**Shop-Rite**
2200 Highway 66, Neptune NJ
07753-4062. 732/775-4250.

**Shop-Rite**
727 Morris Tpke, Springfield NJ
07081-1514. 973/376-3028.

**Shop-Rite**
2661 Morris Ave, Union NJ
07083-5656. 908/686-7595.

**Shop-Rite**
860 Fischer Blvd, Toms River NJ
08753-3824. 732/270-8833.

**Shop-Rite**
60 Beaverbrook Rd, Lincoln Park
NJ 07035-1702. 973/694-1080.

**Shop-Rite**
616 White Horse Pike, Absecon
NJ 08201-2302. 609/646-2448.

**Shop-Rite**
877 St. George Ave, Woodbridge
NJ 07095-2514. 732/636-3500.

**Shop-Rite**
3001 Blackhorse Pike,
Pleasantville NJ 08232. 609/645-
7553.

**Shop-Rite**
1801 Highway 35, Belmar NJ
07719-3503. 732/681-0900.

**Shop-Rite**
437 Franklin Ave, Nutley NJ
07110-2309. 973/235-1213.

**Shop-Rite**
1700 Route, Ste 47, Rio Grande
NJ 08242-1406. 609/399-3534.

**Shop-Rite**
Bethel Rd & Route 9, Somers
Point NJ 08244. 609/927-8133.

**Shop-Rite**
865 W Grand St, Elizabeth NJ
07202-1001. 908/558-9126.

**Shop-Rite**
2555 Pennington Rd, Pennington
NJ 08534-3216. 609/882-0711.

**Shop-Rite**
1622 Kings Highway N, Cherry
Hill NJ 08034-2302. 609/429-
2244.

**Shop-Rite**
5100 Wellington Ave, Ventnor
City NJ 08406-1445. 609/823-
7090.

**Shop-Rite**
540 Passaic Ave, Caldwell NJ
07006-7449. 973/575-1770.

**Shop-Rite**
Browertown Rd & Ros St, Little
Falls NJ 07424. 973/256-0909.

**Shop-Rite**
Minck Ave, Rural Route 73,
Berlin NJ 08009. 609/768-6450.

**Shop-Rite**
739 Route 601, Belle Mead NJ
08502. 908/359-7400.

**Shop-Rite**
14 Post Rd, Oakland NJ 07436-
1616. 201/337-3900.

**Shop-Rite**
622 Martin Ave, Route 206 S,
Bordentown NJ 08505. 609/298-
8700.

**Shopwell Inc.**
PO Box 359, North Bergen NJ
07047-0359. 201/869-9897.

**Super Foodtown**
Ridgedale Ave, Cedar Knolls NJ
07927. 973/539-0655.

**Super Foodtown**
PO Box 156, Whippany NJ
07981-0156. 973/884-2404.

**Super Foodtown**
1 Route 37 W, Toms River NJ
08753-6500. 732/244-8300.

**Super Fresh Food Markets Inc.**
Delsea Dr & Heston Rd,
Glassboro NJ 08028. 609/589-
4411.

**Thriftway Supermarket**
1091 Washington Blvd, Trenton
NJ 08691-3119. 609/426-4400.

**Thriftway Supermarket**
12 Renaissance Plaza, Atlantic
City NJ 08401-7020. 609/340-
8577.

**Ultra IGA**
Rural Route 38, Box Ark, Mount
Laurel NJ 08054. 609/235-4311.

**Ultra IGA**
8000 Gibbsboro & Marlton,
Camden NJ 08102. 609/751-
9388.

## HOBBY, TOY, AND GAME SHOPS

**AC Moore Arts & Crafts**
500 University Court, Blackwood
NJ 08012-3230. 609/228-6700.

## MISC. FOOD STORES

**Delicious Orchards**
36 Highway 34 S, Colt's Neck NJ
07722-1737. 732/462-1989.

**Market Basket**
813 Franklin Lakes Rd, Franklin
Lakes NJ 07417-2113. 201/891-
1329.

**Penn Valley Farms**
Cumberland Blvd, Rural Rte 130,
Burlington NJ 08016. 609/499-
1185.

## MISC. GENERAL MERCHANDISE STORES

**Odd Job Warehouse**
383 Nordhoff Pl, Englewood NJ
07631-4622. 201/871-0885.

**Price Club**
2835 State Route 35, Hazlet NJ
07730-1516. 732/264-0815.

**Sam's Club**
100 Trotters Way, Freehold NJ
07728-4819. 732/780-4477.

**Sam's Club**
5011 Route 130, Riverside NJ
08075-1806. 609/764-7380.

**Sam's Club**
290 State Route 18, East
Brunswick NJ 08816-1905.
732/613-6500.

**Sam's Club**
1500 Almonesson Rd, Suite 18,
Deptford NJ 08096-5261.
609/228-9469.

**Sam's Club**
1025 Black Horse Pike,
Pleasantville NJ 08232-4103.
609/485-2277.

**Sam's Club**
301 Nassau Park Blvd, Princeton
NJ 08540-5934. 609/452-5959.

## OPTICAL GOODS STORES

**Royal Optical**
PO Box 124, Glendora NJ 08029-
0124. 609/228-1000.

## RETAIL BAKERIES

**Bakery Cafe**
Hwy 71 & 99 Taylor Ave,
Manasquan NJ 08736. 732/528-
7724.

## SPORTING GOODS STORES

**Sports Authority Inc.**
50 S Drive A, Paramus NJ 07652.
201/265-2995.

**Sports Authority Inc.**
310 Highway 36, Ste 002, West
Long Branch NJ 07764-1027.
732/389-8334.

## STATIONERY AND OFFICE SUPPLY STORES

**Office Depot**
80 Stemmers Ln, Mount Holly NJ
08060-5652. 609/702-0100.

## For more information on career opportunities in retail:

<u>Associations</u>

**INTERNATIONAL COUNCIL OF SHOPPING CENTERS**
665 Fifth Avenue, New York NY 10022. 212/421-
8181. World Wide Web address: http://www.icsc.org.
Offers conventions, research, education, a variety of
publications, and awards programs.

**NATIONAL AUTOMOTIVE DEALERS ASSOCIATION**
8400 Westpark Drive, McLean VA 22102. 703/821-
7000. World Wide Web address: http://www.nadanet.
com.

**NATIONAL INDEPENDENT AUTOMOTIVE DEALERS ASSOCIATION**
2521 Brown Boulevard, Arlington TX 76006.

817/640-3838. World Wide Web address: http://www. niada.com.

## NATIONAL RETAIL FEDERATION
325 Seventh Street NW, Suite 1000, Washington DC 20004. 202/783-7971. World Wide Web address: http://www.nrf.com. Provides information services, industry outlooks, and a variety of educational opportunities and publications.

## Directories

## AUTOMOTIVE NEWS MARKET DATA BOOK
Crain Communications, 1400 Woodbridge Avenue, Detroit MI 48207-3187. 313/446-6000.

## Online Services

## THE INTERNET FASHION EXCHANGE
http://www.fashionexch.com. An excellent site for those industry professionals interested in apparel and retail. The extensive search engine allows you to search by job title, location, salary, product line, industry, and whether you want a permanent, temporary, or freelance position. The Internet Fashion Exchange also offers career services such as recruiting, and outplacement firms that place fashion and retail professionals.

## RETAIL JOBNET
http://www.retailjobnet.com. This site is geared toward recruiting professionals and jobseekers in the retail industry.

# STONE, CLAY, GLASS, AND CONCRETE PRODUCTS

*Largely dependent on the success of the construction market, the stone, clay, glass, and concrete industry experienced steady demand in 1998, as new construction projects began nationwide. Overall population and business growth will require new buildings and the renovation of existing structures. Coupled with a trend in brick and stone decorative structures and a decrease in the number of people entering the trade, bricklayers and stonemasons should see plentiful opportunities. Concrete masons will see less growth, yet will be heavily relied upon in new infrastructure projects. Glaziers will see slow growth, but the strong construction market could increase opportunities for jobseekers in this trade. Technological advances may also increase opportunities for glaziers, as homeowners and businesses upgrade to more efficient windows. Ceramic tile imports will likely increase due to Mexico's duty-free access to the U.S. market and a projected 10 percent cut in tariffs.*

**ANCHOR GLASS CONTAINER CORPORATION**
83 Griffith Street, Salem NJ 08079. 609/935-4000. **Contact:** Paul Macionus, Personnel Manager. **Description:** Engaged in the manufacture and sale of a diversified line of household, hardware, and packaging products including glassware, commercial and institutional china, decorative and convenience hardware, glass containers, and metal and plastic closures. Operations encompass over 20 divisions and subsidiaries with 40 plants and distribution centers located in the U.S. and abroad.

**BALL-FOSTER GLASS CONTAINER COMPANY**
Minue Street, Carteret NJ 07008. 732/969-1400. **Contact:** Ginny Swanson, Human Resources. **Description:** Manufactures glass jars.

**BARRETT PAVING MATERIALS INC.**
3 Becker Farm Road, Roseland NJ 07068-1748. 973/533-1001. **Fax:** 973/533-1020. **Contact:** Joann Gooding, Director of Human Resources. **Description:** This location houses administrative offices. Overall, Barrett Paving Materials is engaged in the manufacture of road construction materials and the construction and paving of roads, airports, parking lots, race tracks, driveways, and hike paths. Founded in 1903. **NOTE:** Entry-level positions are offered. **Common positions include:** Accountant; Civil Engineer; Controller; Cost Estimator; Management Trainee; Mechanical Engineer; Quality Control Supervisor; Sales Manager; Sales Rep.; Secretary; Typist/ Word Processor. **Educational backgrounds include:** Accounting; Business Administration; Engineering; Finance. **Benefits:** 401(k); Dental Insurance; Disability Coverage; Life Insurance; Medical Insurance; Pension Plan; Tuition Assistance. **Special programs:** Training; Co-ops; Summer Jobs. **Corporate headquarters location:** This Location. **Other U.S. locations:** Hebron CT; Richmond IN; Bangor ME; Ypsilanti MI; Hooksett NH; Bridgewater NJ; East Syracuse NY; Utica NY; Cincinnati OH. **International locations:** Worldwide. **Parent company:** Colas Inc. **Annual sales/revenues:** More than $100 million. **Number of employees at this location:** 1,000.

**RALPH CLAYTON & SONS**
P.O. Box 3015, Lakewood NJ 08701. 732/363-1995. **Contact:** Wayne Tart, Human Resources. **World Wide Web address:** http://www.claytonco.com. **Description:** Manufactures concrete.

**EFTEK CORPORATION**
324 New Brooklyn Road, Berlin NJ 08009. 609/767-2300. **Contact:** Rick Decker, Human Resources. **Description:** Recycles glass and manufactures cullet, broken glass that can be remelted.

**INRAD INC.**
181 Legrand Avenue, Northvale NJ 07647. 201/767-1910. **Contact:** Human Resources. **World Wide Web address:** http://www.inrad.com. **Description:** Manufactures and finishes synthetic crystals.

## KIMBLE GLASS, INC.
537 Crystal Avenue, Vineland NJ 08360. 609/692-3600. **Contact:** Marla Miller, Human Resources Secretary. **Description:** Manufactures glass products such as pharmaceutical vials and coffee pots.

## LEONE INDUSTRIES
P.O. Box 400, Bridgeton NJ 08302. 609/455-2000. **Physical address:** 443 Southeast Avenue, Bridgeton NJ 08302. **Contact:** Personnel. **Description:** Manufactures glass containers. **Common positions include:** Accountant/Auditor; Buyer; Customer Service Representative; Draftsperson; Electrical/Electronics Engineer; General Manager; Industrial Engineer; Management Trainee; Mechanical Engineer; Operations/Production Manager; Purchasing Agent/Manager; Quality Control Supervisor. **Educational backgrounds include:** Accounting; Business Administration; Engineering; Finance; Marketing. **Benefits:** Dental Insurance; Life Insurance; Medical Insurance; Pension Plan; Tuition Assistance. **Corporate headquarters location:** This Location.

*Note: Because addresses and telephone numbers of smaller companies can change rapidly, we recommend you call each company to verify the information below before inquiring about job opportunities. Mass mailings are not recommended.*

## Additional small employers:

### ASPHALT

**GAF Corporation**
1361 Alps Rd, Wayne NJ 07470-3700. 973/628-3000.

**Gardner Asphalt Corp.**
80 Jacobus Ave, Kearny NJ 07032-4526. 973/589-0047.

**Trunbull Asphalt**
1249 Newark Tpke, Kearny NJ 07032-4303. 201/998-5666.

### CRUSHED AND BROKEN STONE

**Millington Quarry Inc.**
PO Box 407, Millington NJ 07946-0407. 908/580-3910.

### GLASS & GLASS PRODUCTS

**AFG Industries**
2600 River Rd, Riverton NJ 08077-1600. 609/829-0400.

**Amp Lytel**
61 Chubb Way, Somerville NJ 08876-3903. 908/685-2000.

**Anchor Glass Container Corp.**
PO Box 688, Vineland NJ 08362-0688. 609/692-3333.

**Anchor Glass Container Corp.**
PO Box 557, Cliffwood NJ 07721-0557. 732/566-4000.

**Ball-Foster Glass Container Co.**
328 S 2nd St, Millville NJ 08332-4208. 609/825-5000.

**Chemglass Inc.**
3861 N Mill Rd, Vineland NJ 08360-1527. 609/696-0014.

**Comar**
1 Comar Pl, Buena NJ 08310-1523. 609/507-5400.

**Comar**
615 Alvine Rd, Elmer NJ 08318-4128. 609/691-2130.

**Comar**
91 W Forest Grove Rd, Vineland NJ 08360-2016. 609/692-4734.

**Durand Glass Manufacturing**
PO Box 5012, Millville NJ 08332-5012. 609/327-4800.

**Potters Industries Inc.**
600 Industrial Rd, Carlstadt NJ 07072-1632. 201/288-4700.

### MINERAL PRODUCTS

**General Ceramics**
16 1st Ave, Haskell NJ 07420-1502. 973/839-1600.

### MINERAL WOOL

**Johns Manville International Group**
PO Box 130, Berlin NJ 08009-0130. 609/768-7000.

### MISC. MINERALS

**United States Gypsum Co.**
1255 Raritan Rd, Clark NJ 07066-1140. 732/388-9100.

## For more information on career opportunities in stone, clay, glass, and concrete products:

### Associations

**THE AMERICAN CERAMIC SOCIETY**
P.O. Box 6136, Westerville OH 43086-6136. 614/890-4700. World Wide Web address: http://www. acers.org. Offers a variety of publications, meetings, information, and educational services. Also operates Ceramic Futures, an employment service with a resume database.

**NATIONAL GLASS ASSOCIATION**
8200 Greensboro Drive, Suite 302, McLean VA 22102. 703/442-4890. World Wide Web address: http://www.glass.org.

### Magazines

**GLASS MAGAZINE**
National Glass Association, 8200 Greensboro Drive, McLean VA 22102. 703/442-4890. World Wide Web address: http://www.glass.org.

**ROCK PRODUCTS**
PRIMEDIA Intertec, 29 North Wacker Drive, Chicago IL 60606. 312/726-2805.

# TRANSPORTATION/TRAVEL

 *All sectors of the transportation industry appear stable, particularly the domestic airline sector, which boasted record profits for the 12-month period ending in June 1998. Despite an increase in labor costs and high fuel prices, air carriers have maintained high profits due to strong consumer demand coupled with high ticket prices. Budget airlines, such as Southwest Airlines, continue to do well and are attracting competition from industry leaders who want to get into this growing market. An increasing number of public airports, in need of capital to increase their services, are undergoing privatization, which is resulting in improved services for customers, and profits for new owners.*

*Rising labor costs and deregulation have forced the trucking industry to lower operating costs, but the U.S. Department of Commerce forecasts that industrial and commercial shipments should increase by about 17 percent annually through 2005. The Bureau of Labor Statistics estimates an increase of 404,000 truck driving jobs through 2006.*

*The acquisition of Southern Pacific by Union Pacific has caused a great deal of havoc for the railroad industry. The merger is estimated to have cost business customers more than $2 billion. To correct the problem, Union Pacific has ordered hundreds of millions of dollars worth of new locomotives and plans on hiring 2,000 new train operators.*

*As imports increase, ship travel will increase. Transport ships, the main vehicle for U.S. imports, are increasing in size, some greater than four football fields in length. According to* Business Week, *these large ships require deep channels in which to travel, and eastern ports are dredging and redredging to meet the requirements. New York, currently the hub for ships on the East Coast, is dredging its shipping channels, in fear of losing business to deeper ports such as Norfolk and Halifax.*

**CR ENGLAND**
403 Dultys Lane, Burlington NJ 08019. 609/386-7220. **Contact:** Human Resources. **Description:** A trucking company providing freight services.

**CENDANT CORPORATION**
6 Sylvan Way, Parsippany NJ 07054. 973/428-9700. **Toll-free phone:** 800/932-4656. **Fax:** 973/428-9684. **Contact:** Staffing and Employment. **E-mail address:** jobs@hfsinc.com. **World Wide Web address:** http://www.cendant.com. **Description:** Provides a wide range of business services including dining services, hotel franchise management, mortgage programs, and timeshare exchanges. Cendant Corporation's Real Estate Division offers employee relocation and mortgage services through Century 21, Coldwell Banker, ERA, Cendant Mortgage, and Cendant Mobility. The Travel Division provides car rentals, vehicle management services, and vacation timeshares through brand names including Avia, Days Inn, Howard Johnson, Ramada, Travelodge, and Super 8. The Membership Division offers travel, shopping, auto, dining, and other financial services through Travelers Advantage, Shoppers Advantage, Auto Vantage, Welcom Wagon, netMarket, North American Outdoor Group, and PrivacyGuard. Founded in 1997. **Common positions include:** Accountant/Auditor; Computer Programmer; Customer Service Rep.; Marketing Manager; Marketing Specialist; Public Relations Specialist; Real Estate Agent; Sales Rep.; Secretary. **Educational backgrounds include:** Accounting; Business Administration; Communications; Computer Science; Finance; Marketing; Public Relations; Software Development. **Benefits:** 401(k); Dental Insurance; Disability Coverage; Employee Discounts; Life Insurance; Medical Insurance; Profit Sharing; Savings Plan; Tuition Assistance. **Corporate headquarters location:** This Location. **Listed on:** New York Stock Exchange. **Stock exchange**

**symbol:** CD. **President/CEO:** Henry Silverman. **Number of employees at this location:** 1,100. **Number of employees worldwide:** 30,000.

## EMERY WORLDWIDE
100 Port Street, Newark NJ 07114. 973/565-9488. **Contact:** Personnel. **Description:** Operates internationally through the following divisions: Purolator Courier Corporation (Basking Ridge NJ), which provides overnight delivery of time-sensitive materials by ground and air transportation throughout the United States; Purolator Courier Ltd., which provides identical services to Purolator Courier Corporation in Canada; Purolator Products Inc. (Rahway NJ), which manufactures and markets automotive, truck, and off-road vehicle filters and related products in the United States and Canada; and Stant, Inc. (Connersville IN), which manufactures and markets fuel caps, oil caps, radiator caps, and other related automotive products. **Listed on:** New York Stock Exchange.

## FEDERAL EXPRESS CORPORATION (FEDEX)
285 Davidson Avenue, 1st Floor, Somerset NJ 08873. **Toll-free phone:** 800/238-5355. **Recorded jobline:** 732/560-5964. **Contact:** Personnel Department. **World Wide Web address:** http://www.fedex.com. **Description:** One of the world's largest express transportation companies serving 212 countries worldwide. FedEx ships approximately 3 million packages daily through an operating fleet of over 600 aircraft, 39,500 vehicles, 2,000 ship sites, 33,800 drop boxes, and Internet shipping. **Common positions include:** Administrative Assistant; Clerk; Courier; Customer Service Rep.; Driver; Marketing Specialist; Operations Manager; Sales Rep. **Benefits:** Dental Insurance; Disability Coverage; Employee Discounts; Life Insurance; Medical Insurance; Pension Plan; Profit Sharing; Retirement Plan; Savings Plan; Stock Purchase; Tuition Assistance; Vision Insurance. **Corporate headquarters location:** Memphis TN. **International locations:** Worldwide. **Listed on:** New York Stock Exchange. **Stock exchange symbol:** FDX. **Annual sales/revenues:** More than $100 million. **Number of employees worldwide:** 140,000.

## HARBOUR INTERMODAL LTD.
1177 McCarter Highway, Newark NJ 07104. 973/481-6474. **Contact:** Human Resources. **Description:** Provides local intermodal transportation services in the greater New York Harbor area. The company also develops and sells equipment for intermodal services, including waterborne vessels and mobile and fixed heavy materials handling equipment for transporting and sorting containers, trailers, and general cargo.

## THE HERTZ CORPORATION
225 Brae Boulevard, Park Ridge NJ 07656. 201/307-2000. **Fax:** 201/307-2644. **Contact:** Director of Personnel. **World Wide Web address:** http://www.hertz.com. **Description:** A large rental company which leases new and used cars, and industrial and construction equipment in 130 countries worldwide. The company also sells used cars in the U.S., Australia, New Zealand, and Europe. The fleet of cars consists of 283,000 automobiles, primarily U.S.-made, which are leased through 5,300 offices. **Corporate headquarters location:** This Location.

## JEVIC TRANSPORTATION INC.
P.O. Box 5157, Delanco NJ 08075. 609/461-7111. **Contact:** Human Resources. **Description:** This location houses a dispatching center. Overall, Jevic Transportation is a trucking company providing freight services. **Corporate headquarters location:** This Location.

## LAIDLAW EDUCATIONAL SERVICE, INC.
2100 Highway 35, Sea Girt NJ 08750. 732/449-3530. **Contact:** Human Resources. **Description:** This location houses administrative offices. Overall, Laidlaw Educational Service, Inc. provides school bus transportation services.

## MAERSK INC.
Giralda Farms, Madison Avenue, P.O. Box 880, Madison NJ 07940. 973/514-5000. **Contact:** Human Resources. **Description:** Provides overseas shipping services.

## NORTON, LILLY & COMPANY, INC.
200 Plaza Drive, Secaucus NJ 07096. 201/392-3000. **Contact:** Human Resources. **Description:** This location handles collection, brokerage, and documentation. Overall, Norton, Lilly & Company, Inc. is a sea transportation firm, specializing in cargo hauling in the United States. **Corporate headquarters location:** This Location.

## SEA-LAND SERVICE INC.
5080 McLester Avenue, Elizabeth NJ 07207. 908/558-6000. **Contact:** Human Resources. **Description:** This location houses Northeast regional headquarters operations. Overall, Sea-Land Service ships large containers.

## TITAN GLOBAL TECHNOLOGIES
P.O. Box 617, Montvale NJ 07645. 201/930-0300. **Contact:** Human Resources. **World Wide Web address:** http://www.titan-global-tech.com. **Description:** Designs, manufactures, and installs monorail transportation systems. **Common positions include:** Accountant/Auditor; Administrative Manager; Advertising Clerk; Architect; Civil Engineer; Computer Operator; Computer Programmer; Cost Estimator; Electrical/Electronics Engineer; Mechanical Engineer; Quality Control Supervisor; Systems Analyst; Transportation/Traffic Specialist. **Benefits:** Dental Insurance; Disability Coverage; Life Insurance; Medical Insurance. **Corporate headquarters location:** This Location. **Operations at this facility include:** Administration; Research and Development.

## UNITED AIR LINES, INC.
Newark International Airport, Newark NJ 07114. **Toll-free phone:** 800/241-6522. **Contact:** Human Resources. **Description:** An air carrier that provides transportation of people and goods through more than 1,100 daily scheduled flights at 100 airports in the United States, Canada, and Mexico. **NOTE:** Send resumes to United Air Lines-WHQES, P.O. Box 66100, Chicago IL 60666. **Corporate headquarters location:** Elk Grove Township IL. **Parent company:** UAL, Inc. is a holding company whose subsidiaries include United Air Lines, Westin Hotels (48 locations), and GAB Business Services. **Listed on:** New York Stock Exchange.

## UNITED PARCEL SERVICE (UPS)
Mail Center, 22 Church Street, Ramsey NJ 07446. 201/818-0050. **Contact:** Human Resources. **Description:** This location is a package handling center. Overall, UPS provides package delivery services nationwide.

## UNITED PARCEL SERVICE (UPS)
340 MacArthur Boulevard, Mahwah NJ 07430. 201/828-9606. **Contact:** Human Resources. **Description:** This location is an information services center. Overall, UPS provides package delivery services nationwide.

## VIKING YACHT COMPANY
Route 9, New Gretna NJ 08224. 609/296-6000. **Contact:** Drew Davala, Human Resources. **Description:** Manufactures yachts.

*Note: Because addresses and telephone numbers of smaller companies can change rapidly, we recommend you call each company to verify the information below before inquiring about job opportunities. Mass mailings are not recommended.*

**Additional small employers:**

**AIR TRANSPORTATION AND SERVICES**

**American Airlines Inc.**
American Airlines Terminal NW, Newark NJ 07114. 973/961-4123.

**Anthem Express Inc.**
30 Montgomery St, Ste 240, Jersey City NJ 07302-3821. 201/324-1166.

**Continental Express**
Newark International Airport, Newark NJ 07114. 973/961-0032.

**DHL Airways Inc.**
675 Division St, Elizabeth NJ 07201-2039. 908/820-4300.

**Jet Aviation Business Jets**
114 Charles Lindbergh Dr, Teterboro NJ 07608. 201/288-8400.

**Northwest Airlines Inc.**
Terminal B, Newark International Airport, Newark NJ 07114. 973/961-4628.

**SAS Airlines**
9 Polito Ave, Lyndhurst NJ 07071-3406. 201/896-3600.

**Signature Flight Support Co.**
Newark International Airport, Newark NJ 07114. 973/624-1660.

**Sky Trek International Airlines**
67 Scotch Rd, Trenton NJ 08628-2504. 609/671-0200.

**Trans World Airlines Inc.**
Newark International Airport, Newark NJ 07114. 973/961-3050.

**USAirways Inc.**
Newark International Airport, Newark NJ 07114. 973/674-5500.

**COURIER SERVICES**

**APD Courier**
PO Box 992, Mount Laurel NJ 08054-0992. 609/983-9634.

**Federal Express Corporation**
161 Meister Ave, Somerville NJ 08876-3464. 973/923-6000.

**General Messenger Service**
PO Box 2166, Morristown NJ 07962-2166. 973/538-4420.

**United Parcel Service**
4 Gatehall Corporate Ctr, Parsippany NJ 07054-4518. 973/490-7300.

**United Parcel Service**
700 W Leeds Ave, Absecon NJ 08201-2846. 609/646-1448.

**LOCAL AND INTERURBAN PASSENGER TRANSIT**

**A&A Charter Service Inc.**
297 Communipaw Ave, Jersey City NJ 07304-4047. 201/432-0183.

**A-1 Limousine Inc.**
2 Emmons Dr, Princeton NJ 08540-5927. 609/924-0070.

**Academy Bus Company**
1515 Jefferson St, Hoboken NJ 07030-2307. 201/420-7000.

**Academy Lines Inc.**
50 State Hwy 36, Leonardo NJ
07737. 732/291-1300.

**Adventure Trails**
350 N Georgia Ave, Atlantic City
NJ 08401-4032. 609/347-8873.

**AEG Monorail Systems Inc.**
Brewster Rd, Bldg 60, Newark
NJ 07114. 973/624-9300.

**Airporter Inc.**
2531 E State Street Extension,
Trenton NJ 08619-3317. 609/734-
9200.

**Babe's Yellow Cab**
2086 Hudson St, Fort Lee NJ
07024-7208. 201/944-3581.

**Camptown Bus Lines Inc.**
126 Frelinghuysen Ave, Newark
NJ 07114-1633. 973/242-6100.

**Coast Cities Varsity Transit**
35 Troy Lane, Lincoln Park NJ
07035-1423. 973/696-1441.

**Coast Cities Varsity Transit**
431 Corkery Ln, Williamstown
NJ 08094-3239. 609/767-1441.

**Coast Cities Varsity Transit**
175 Klockner Rd, Trenton NJ
08619-2813. 609/586-6262.

**Dapper Bus**
1020 Green St, Iselin NJ 08830-
2146. 732/283-1982.

**Decamp Tours**
PO Box 581, Montclair NJ
07042-0581. 973/783-7500.

**Delaware River Coach Lines**
604 Elder Ave, Phillipsburg NJ
08865-1525. 908/859-1125.

**Domenco Bus Service Inc.**
PO Box 47, Bayonne NJ 07002-
0047. 201/339-6000.

**Drogin Bus Co.**
53 Kennedy Blvd, Bayonne NJ
07002-5211. 201/339-0023.

**Empire International**
PO Box 423, Norwood NJ 07648-
0423. 201/784-1200.

**Enterprise Transit Corp.**
15 Pleasant Ave E, Paramus NJ
07652-2528. 201/845-0200.

**Flyte Tyme Transportation**
PO Box 717, Westwood NJ
07675-0717. 201/236-1444.

**Gem Limousine Service**
45 Kilmer Rd, Edison NJ 08817-
2421. 732/393-9200.

**Gray Line**
1500 Clinton St, Hoboken NJ
07030-3402. 201/714-9400.

**Hudson Transit Lines Inc.**
17 Franklin Tpke, Mahwah NJ
07430-1336. 201/529-3666.

**Independent Bus Co.**
465 Mulberry St, Newark NJ
07114-2736. 973/242-1577.

**Kevah Konner Inc.**
PO Box 683, Pine Brook NJ
07058-0683. 973/227-3100.

**Laidlaw Transit**
450 Union Hill Rd, Englishtown
NJ 07726-1849. 732/536-3485.

**Lakeland Bus Lines Inc.**
PO Box 898, Dover NJ 07802-
0898. 973/366-0600.

**Leisure Line**
740 W Delilah Rd, Pleasantville
NJ 08232-1250. 609/272-8000.

**Leisure Line**
4 Leisure Ln, Mahwah NJ 07430-
1038. 201/529-4070.

**LER Transportation Company**
750 Somerset St, New Brunswick
NJ 08901-3225. 732/249-1100.

**Milu Bus Service Inc.**
PO Box 163, Matawan NJ 07747-
0163. 732/566-4068.

**Mr. Taxi**
PO Box 100, Tenafly NJ 07670-
0100. 201/837-3100.

**New Jersey Transit Bus
Operations**
420 Thomas Blvd, Orange NJ
07050-2955. 973/672-4800.

**New Jersey Transit Bus
Operations**
350 Newton Ave, Camden NJ
08103-1612. 609/968-3800.

**Olympia Trails Bus Co. Inc.**
PO Box 9261, Elizabeth NJ
07202. 908/354-3330.

**Olympic Limousine**
PO Box 708, Farmingdale NJ
07727-0708. 732/938-6665.

**Orange Newark Elizabeth Bus
Co.**
889 Frelinghuysen Ave, Newark
NJ 07114-2121. 973/824-6200.

**Phoenix Transportation**
6103 Westfield Ave, Pennsauken
NJ 08110-1754. 609/488-4645.

**Rapid River Airport Shuttle**
5090 Central Hwy, Pennsauken
NJ 08109-4637. 609/428-1500.

**Red and Tan Inc.**
437 Tonnele Ave, Jersey City NJ
07306-4910. 201/653-2220.

**Ridgewood Taxi**
PO Box 701, Ridgewood NJ
07451-0701. 201/444-2900.

**Rockland Coaches Inc.**
PO Box 447, Bergenfield NJ
07621-0447. 201/384-2400.

**Royal Coachman Limited**
540 Thomas Blvd, Orange NJ
07050-2920. 973/676-0200.

**Ryder Student Transportation
Services**
270 Gloucester Pike, Lawnside
NJ 08045-1150. 609/546-8131.

**Ryder Student Transportation
Services**
757 US Highway 206, Andover
NJ 07821-5038. 973/786-5333.

**Ryder Student Transportation
Services**
PO Box 183, Cologne NJ 08213-
0183. 609/965-1818.

**Safety Bus Service Inc.**
7200 Park Ave, Pennsauken NJ
08109-3010. 609/665-2662.

**Starr Tours**
2531 E State Street Extension,
Trenton NJ 08619. 609/587-0626.

**University Bus Co. Inc.**
PO Box 339, Hillsdale NJ 07642-
0339. 201/664-6500.

**Village Bus Co. Inc.**
PO Box 442, Sparta NJ 07871-
0442. 973/579-1197.

**Vogel Bus Company Inc.**
PO Box 301, Garwood NJ 07027-
0301. 908/298-0045.

**Winsale Inc.**
976 Newark Ave, Jersey City NJ
07306-6301. 201/798-1111.

## MAINTENANCE FACILITIES FOR MOTOR FREIGHT TRANSPORTATION

**ABF Freight System**
580 Delaney St, Newark NJ
07105. 201/451-8990.

**Dynamic Delivery Corp.**
125 Avenue E, Bayonne NJ
07002-4439. 973/344-6300.

**New Penn Motor Express Inc.**
36 Hackensack Ave, Kearny NJ
07032-4620. 973/589-1818.

**New Penn Motor Express Inc.**
2300 Garry Rd, Ste 2304,
Riverton NJ 08077-2539.
609/786-7646.

## MARINE CARGO HANDLING

**Navieras**
PO Box 3170, Edison NJ 08818-3170. 732/225-2121.

**South Jersey Port Corporation**
PO Box 129, Camden NJ 08101. 609/541-8500.

## MISC. TRANSPORTATION SERVICES

**Delaware River Port Authority**
PO Box 1949, Camden NJ 08101-1949. 609/968-3300.

**Garden State Parkway**
PO Box 5050, Woodbridge NJ 07095-5050. 732/442-8600.

**Hudson County Towing**
114 Amity St, Jersey City NJ 07304-3510. 201/332-0800.

**New Jersey Turnpike Authority**
Mt. Laurel Rd, Mount Laurel NJ 08054. 609/273-3208.

## MISC. WATER TRANSPORTATION SERVICES

**Hanjin Shipping Co. Ltd.**
80 Rte 4, Ste 490, Paramus NJ 07652-2654. 201/291-4600.

**Land N Sea Inc.**
425 Ferry St, Newark NJ 07105-3903. 973/589-7725.

## PACKING AND CRATING

**Carteret Packaging Inc.**
1200 Milik St, Carteret NJ 07008-1119. 732/969-1600.

**Mebane Packaging Group Inc.**
PO Box 521, Kearny NJ 07032-0521. 201/991-4800.

**Reed-Lane Inc.**
550 Huyler St, South Hackensack NJ 07606-1544. 201/342-7502.

## PASSENGER TRANSPORTATION ARRANGEMENT SERVICES

**American Express Travel Related Services**
PO Box 1385, Piscataway NJ 08855-1385. 732/980-0101.

**Liberty Travel Inc.**
69 Spring St, Ramsey NJ 07446-1117. 201/934-3500.

**Stratton Travel Inc.**
795 Franklin Ave, Franklin Lakes NJ 07417-1354. 201/891-3456.

**Travel One**
5000 Atrium Way, Mount Laurel NJ 08054-3915. 609/222-3900.

**TWA Getaway Vacations Inc.**
10 E Stow Rd, Ste 100, Marlton NJ 08053-3162. 609/985-4100.

## RAILROAD TRANSPORTATION

**Conrail**
1000 Howard Blvd, Mount Laurel NJ 08054-2355. 609/231-2000.

## SHIP/BOAT BUILDING AND REPAIRING

**Ocean Yachts Inc.**
PO Box 312, Egg Harbor City NJ 08215-0312. 609/965-4616.

**Silverton Yacht**
301 Riverside Dr, Millville NJ 08332-6717. 609/825-4117.

## TRUCKING

**A-P-A Transport Corp.**
PO Box 831, North Bergen NJ 07047-0831. 201/869-6600.

**ABA Trucking**
PO Box 646, South Plainfield NJ 07080-0646. 908/561-3484.

**American Freightways Express**
1000 Port Carteret Rd, Carteret NJ 07008-3522. 732/541-3372.

**Anytime Delivery Systems Inc.**
300 Middlesex Ave, Carteret NJ 07008-3479. 732/969-3401.

**Brennan Transportation**
50 Connecticut Dr, Fl 1, Burlington NJ 08016-4102. 609/239-7950.

**Brust Transporters Inc.**
433 Oak Glen Rd, Howell NJ 07731-8932. 732/364-8100.

**Budd Van Lines**
PO Box 5960, Somerset NJ 08875-5960. 732/627-0600.

**CBL Trucking Inc.**
PO Box 5008, Riverside NJ 08075-0408. 609/461-1812.

**Chopper Express Inc.**
219 Changebridge Rd, Montville NJ 07045-9514. 973/402-1268.

**Crofutt & Smith Moving & Storage**
PO Drawer D1, Landing NJ 07850. 973/347-7200.

**ECM Transportation Inc.**
115 Burns Rd, Mount Holly NJ 08060. 609/702-8255.

**Federated Distributors**
1090 Thomas Brush Hwy, Audubon NJ 08106. 609/488-1911.

**Freehold Cartage Inc.**
PO Box 5010, Freehold NJ 07728-5010. 732/462-1001.

**Guaranteed Overnight Delivery**
PO Box 100, Kearny NJ 07032-0100. 973/344-3013.

**H&M International Transportation**
700 Belleville Tpke, Kearny NJ 07032-4407. 201/997-4400.

**Hygrade Distribution & Delivery Systems**
100 Central Ave, Bldg 73, Kearny NJ 07032. 973/344-8800.

**JB Hunt Transport**
19 Edgeboro Rd, East Brunswick NJ 08816-1636. 732/390-7001.

**Langer Industries Inc.**
PO Box 305, Jersey City NJ 07303-2305. 201/434-1600.

**Leaseway Auto Carriers**
1001 W Linden Ave, Linden NJ 07036-6521. 908/862-9220.

**Linden Motor Freight Co. Inc.**
PO Box 169, Linden NJ 07036-0169. 908/862-1400.

**LTA Group Inc.**
PO Box 1079, East Brunswick NJ 08816-1079. 732/656-0900.

**MGM Transport Corp.**
PO Box 536, Totowa NJ 07511-0536. 973/256-6500.

**Mount Hope Trucking Co.**
625 Mount Hope Rd, Wharton NJ 07885-2807. 973/366-7741.

**MPG Transport**
714 Division St, Elizabeth NJ 07201-2005. 908/355-6100.

**National Retail Transportation**
2820 16th St, North Bergen NJ 07047-1541. 201/330-1900.

**National Retail Transportation**
PO Box 2697, Secaucus NJ 07096-2697. 201/935-3500.

**NEMF**
171 North Ave E, Elizabeth NJ 07201-2936. 908/965-0100.

**New Deal Logistics**
84 Harbor Dr, Jersey City NJ 07305-4504. 201/985-0300.

**New England Motor Freight**
310 Hollywood Ave, South Plainfield NJ 07080-4202. 908/753-6200.

**NFI Industries Inc.**
71 W Park Ave, Vineland NJ
08360-3508. 609/691-7000.

**Nu-Car Carriers Inc.**
317 Port St, Newark NJ 07114-
3012. 973/589-8615.

**Old Dominion Freight Line**
55 Van Keuren Ave, Jersey City
NJ 07306-6110. 201/216-0060.

**Overnite Transportation Co.**
1000 Blair Rd, Carteret NJ
07008-1227. 732/750-3500.

**Owens New World Trucking**
1 Gourmet Ln, Edison NJ 08837-
2902. 732/906-1900.

**Preston Trucking Company
Inc.**
50 Harrison Ave, Kearny NJ
07032. 201/991-1800.

**Preston Trucking Company
Inc.**
821 Saint George Ave,
Woodbridge NJ 07095-2514.
732/636-7210.

**Riteway Express Inc.**
PO Box 439, Elmwood Park NJ
07407-0439. 201/794-6040.

**Roadway Express Inc.**
72 Second St, Central Ave,
Kearny NJ 07032. 973/344-5100.

**Roadway Express Inc.**
700 Commercial Ave, Carlstadt
NJ 07072-2602. 201/507-0010.

**Shanahan's Express Inc.**
PO Box 2245, Riverton NJ
08077-5245. 609/786-1550.

**St. George Trucking**
123 Pennsylvania Ave, Kearny
NJ 07032-4524. 973/578-8400.

**Supreme Delivery Services**
100 Caven Point Rd, Jersey City
NJ 07305-4606. 201/332-3000.

**The Clark Group Inc.**
PO Box 438, Trenton NJ 08603-
0438. 609/396-1100.

**Triangle Transport Inc.**
418 Duncan Ave, Jersey City NJ
07306-6724. 201/332-3333.

**United Van Lines**
PO Box 9, Burlington NJ 08016-
0009. 609/386-0600.

**USF Red Star Inc.**
400 Delancey St, Newark NJ
07105-3812. 973/344-7700.

**Viking Freight Inc.**
580 Delancey St, Newark NJ
07105-3800. 973/344-2277.

**Yellow Freight System Inc.**
100 3rd Ave, Elizabeth NJ 07206-
1525. 908/352-1001.

## WAREHOUSING AND STORAGE

**GATX Terminals Corporation**
78 Lafayette St, Carteret NJ
07008-3521. 732/541-2000.

**Gordon Terminal Service
Company**
PO Box 143, Bayonne NJ 07002-
0143. 201/437-8300.

**Hillside Warehouse & Trucking**
PO Box 6493, Edison NJ 08818-
6493. 732/225-1271.

**Impac**
587 Industrial Rd, Carlstadt NJ
07072-1611. 201/460-0900.

**IMTT-Bayonne**
PO Box 67, Bayonne NJ 07002-
0067. 201/437-2200.

**Novo Holdings Inc.**
520 Main Street, Ste 204, Fort
Lee NJ 07024-4501. 201/592-
9044.

**OPS Warehouse**
297 Getty Ave, Paterson NJ
07503-2650. 973/684-5600.

**Port Jersey Distribution Service**
PO Box 5200, Jersey City NJ
07305-0200. 201/333-1300.

**Ridge Services Inc.**
112 Truman Dr, Edison NJ
08817-2425. 732/819-9669.

**Ryder Dedicated Logistics**
96 Executive Ave, Edison NJ
08817-6016. 732/248-0623.

**Seaman Warehouse**
433 Blair Rd, Avenel NJ 07001-
2215. 732/382-7770.

**Statco Inc.**
301 16th St, Jersey City NJ
07310-1024. 201/792-7000.

**Vital Records Inc.**
PO Box 688, Flagtown NJ 08821-
0688. 908/369-6900.

## WATER TRANSPORTATION OF FREIGHT

**ACL**
50 Cragwood Rd, South
Plainfield NJ 07080-2406.
908/668-5400.

**Crowley Maritime Corporation**
36& Delaware Ave, Camden NJ
08102-2404. 609/541-7726.

**Marine Transport Lines Inc.**
150 Marsh St, Newark NJ 07114-
3236. 973/578-2900.

**NYK Inc.**
300 Lighting Way, 5th Fl,
Secaucus NJ 07094-3622.
201/330-3000.

**P&O Containers Limited**
1 Meadowlands Plz, East
Rutherford NJ 07073-2100.
201/896-6200.

## WATER TRANSPORTATION OF PASSENGERS

**Cape May Lewes Ferry**
PO Box 827, Cape May NJ
08204. 609/886-2718.

**New York Waterway**
Pershing Rd, Weehawken NJ
07087. 201/902-8850.

**Spirit of New Jersey**
1500 Harbor Boulevard,
Weehawken NJ 07087-6732.
201/867-9172.

## For more information on career opportunities in transportation and travel industries:

<u>Associations</u>

**AIR TRANSPORT ASSOCIATION OF
AMERICA**
1301 Pennsylvania Avenue NW, Suite 1100,
Washington DC 20004. 202/626-4000. World Wide
Web address: http://www.air-transport.org. A trade
association for the major U.S. airlines.

**AMERICAN BUREAU OF SHIPPING**
2 World Trade Center, 106th Floor, New York NY

10048. 212/839-5000. World Wide Web address:
http://www.abs-group.com.

**AMERICAN SOCIETY OF TRAVEL AGENTS**
1101 King Street, Suite 200, Alexandria VA 22314.
703/739-2782. World Wide Web address: http://www.
astanet.com.

**AMERICAN TRUCKING ASSOCIATIONS, INC.**
2200 Mill Road, Alexandria VA 22314-4677.

290/The New Jersey JobBank

703/838-1700. World Wide Web address: http://www.trucking.org.

## ASSOCIATION OF AMERICAN RAILROADS
50 F Street NW, Washington DC 20001. 202/639-2100. World Wide Web address: http://www.aar.com.

## INSTITUTE OF TRANSPORTATION ENGINEERS
525 School Street SW, Suite 410, Washington DC 20024. 202/554-8050. World Wide Web address: http://www.ite.org.

## MARINE TECHNOLOGY SOCIETY
1828 L Street NW, Suite 906, Washington DC 20036. 202/775-5966. World Wide Web address: http://www.cms.udel.edu/mts.

## NATIONAL MOTOR FREIGHT TRAFFIC ASSOCIATION
2200 Mill Road, Alexandria VA 22314-4654. 703/838-1810. World Wide Web address: http://www.erols.com/nmfta/index.htm.

## NATIONAL TANK TRUCK CARRIERS
2200 Mill Road, Alexandria VA 22314. 703/838-1700.

### Books

## FLIGHT PLAN TO THE FLIGHT DECK: STRATEGIES FOR A PILOT CAREER
Cage Consulting, Inc., 13275 East Fremont Place, Suite 315, Englewood CO 80112-3917. Toll-free phone: 888/899-CAGE. Fax: 303/799-1998. World Wide Web address: http://www.cageconsulting.com.

## WELCOME ABOARD! YOUR CAREER AS A FLIGHT ATTENDANT
Cage Consulting, Inc., 13275 East Fremont Place, Suite 315, Englewood CO 80112-3917. Toll-free phone: 888/899-CAGE. Fax: 303/799-1998. World Wide Web address: http://www.cageconsulting.com.

### Directories

## MOODY'S TRANSPORTATION MANUAL
Financial Information Services, 60 Madison Avenue, 6th Floor, New York NY 10010. Toll-free phone: 800/342-5647.

## NATIONAL TANK TRUCK CARRIER DIRECTORY
National Tank Truck Carriers, 2200 Mill Road, Alexandria VA 22314. 703/838-1700.

## OFFICIAL MOTOR FREIGHT GUIDE
CNC Publishing, 1700 West Cortland Street, Chicago IL 60622. 773/278-2454.

### Magazines

## AMERICAN SHIPPER
Howard Publications, P.O. Box 4728, Jacksonville FL 32201. 904/355-2601. Monthly.

## FLEET OWNER
PRIMEDIA Intertec, 11 Riverbend Drive South, P.O. Box 4211, Stamford CT 06907-0211.

## HEAVY DUTY TRUCKING
Newport Communications, P.O. Box W, Newport Beach CA 92658. 714/261-1636.

## ITE JOURNAL
Institute of Transportation Engineers, 525 School Street SW, Suite 410, Washington DC 20024-2797. 202/554-8050. World Wide Web address: http://www.ite.org. One year subscription (12 issues): $60.00.

## MARINE DIGEST AND TRANSPORTATION NEWS
Marine Publishing, Inc., P.O. Box 3905, Seattle WA 98124. 206/682-3607.

## SHIPPING DIGEST
Geyer-McAllister Publications, 51 Madison Avenue, New York NY 10010. 212/689-4411.

## TRAFFIC WORLD MAGAZINE
1230 National Press Building, Washington DC 20045-2200. 202/783-1101.

## TRANSPORT TOPICS
American Trucking Associations, Inc., 2200 Mill Road, Alexandria VA 22314. 703/838-1778. World Wide Web address: http://www.ttnews.com.

### Newsletters

## AIR JOBS DIGEST
World Air Data, Department 700, P.O. Box 42360, Washington DC 20015. World Wide Web address: http://www.tggh.net/wad. This monthly resource provides current job openings in aerospace, space, and aviation. Subscription rates: $96.00 annually, $69.00 for six months, and $49.00 for three months.

### Online Services

## THE AIRLINE EMPLOYMENT ASSISTANCE CORPS.
World Wide Web address: http://www.avjobs.com. Site for aviation jobseekers providing worldwide classified ads, resume assistance, publications, and over 350 links to aviation-related Websites and news groups. Certain resources are members-only access.

## COOLWORKS
World Wide Web address: http://www.coolworks.com. This Website provides links to 22,000 job openings on cruise ships, at national parks, summer camps, ski areas, river areas, ranches, fishing areas, and resorts.

## JOBNET: HOSPITALITY INDUSTRY
World Wide Web address: http://www.westga.edu/~coop/joblinks/subject/hospitality.html. Provides links to job openings for airlines and cruise ships.

## 1-800-DRIVERS
World Wide Web address: http://207.238.83.41/jobspage.html. Designed to help job hunters find employment as a driver. This site offers an online job application, job listings, and links to various trucking companies.

## TRAVEL PROFESSIONALS FORUM
Go: Travpro. To join this CompuServe forum, you will need to send an e-mail to the sysop for permission.

Visit our exciting job and career site at http://www.careercity.com

# UTILITIES: ELECTRIC/GAS/WATER

 *Deregulation has greatly increased competition throughout all segments of the utilities industry. For example, many states now permit independent power producers to build electric power generating plants. In an effort to lower prices and compete with the new entrants, many existing electric utilities have resorted to layoffs and other cost-cutting measures. Other electric companies, such as Illinova Corporation, are spending millions to increase capacity. Water utilities continue to see growth, and the Bureau of Labor Statistics estimates 51 percent growth for this segment through 2006. Philadelphia Suburban Corporation, a water utility, reported a significant rise in profits due to an increase in customers in 1998. Overall, Standard & Poor reports a drop in both profits and profit margins for the utilities industry, and the U.S. Department of Labor forecasts that job growth will only be 12 percent through 2005, a rate much slower than the average for all industries.*

**AMERICAN WATER WORKS SERVICE CO.**
1025 Laurel Oak Road, Voorhees NJ 08043. 609/346-8200. **Contact:** Jack Markel, Director, Personnel Administration. **World Wide Web address:** http://www.amwater.com. **Description:** Acquires, manages, and services water companies across the country.

**ATLANTIC CITY ELECTRIC COMPANY (ACE)**
6801 Black Horse Pike, Egg Harbor Township NJ 08234-4130. 609/645-4100. **Fax:** 609/645-4711. **Recorded jobline:** 609/625-5848. **Contact:** Employee Relations Department. **Description:** A public utility primarily engaged in the generation, transmission, distribution, and sale of electric energy. **Common positions include:** Accountant/Auditor; Buyer; Chemical Engineer; Chemist; Civil Engineer; Claim Representative; Computer Programmer; Draftsperson; Economist; Electrical/Electronics Engineer; Financial Analyst; Human Resources Manager; Industrial Engineer; Mechanical Engineer; Software Engineer; Systems Analyst. **Educational backgrounds include:** Accounting; Business Administration; Chemistry; Communications; Computer Science; Engineering; Finance; Marketing. **Benefits:** 401(k); Dental Insurance; Disability Coverage; Life Insurance; Medical Insurance; Pension Plan; Prescription Drugs; Savings Plan; Tuition Assistance; Vision Plan. **Corporate headquarters location:** This Location. **Other area locations:** Atlantic City NJ. **Parent company:** Atlantic Energy, Inc. is the parent company of a consolidated group of subsidiaries consisting of Atlantic City Electric Company (ACE) and the non-utility companies Atlantic Energy Technology, Inc. (AET); Atlantic Generation, Inc. (AGI); Atlantic Southern Properties, Inc. (ASP); ATE Investments, Inc. (ATE); and Atlantic Thermal Systems, Inc. (ATS). AGI develops and operates cogeneration power projects currently located in New Jersey and New York. ASP owns and manages a commercial office and warehouse facility located in southern New Jersey. ATE provides fund management and financing to affiliates and manages a portfolio of investments in leveraged leases for equipment used in the airline and shipping industries. ATS develops thermal heating and cooling systems. **Operations at this facility include:** Administration; Divisional Headquarters; Research and Development. **Listed on:** New York Stock Exchange. **Number of employees at this location:** 1,600.

**ELIZABETHTOWN GAS COMPANY**
One Elizabethtown Plaza, P.O. Box 3175, Union NJ 07083-1975. 908/289-5000. **Contact:** Patricia Southwell, Manager of Employment and Training. **World Wide Web address:** http://www.nui.com. **Description:** Through several area locations, Elizabethtown Gas Company is engaged in the distribution of natural gas through its subsidiaries and investments in joint ventures. The company serves more than 240,000 customers. **Subsidiaries include:** Energy Marketing Exchange, which buys and sells spot-market gas; Utility Propane, a retail and wholesale distributor. **Parent company:** NUI Corporation (Bedminster NJ).

**GPU ENERGY CORPORATION**
300 Madison Avenue, Morristown NJ 07962. 973/263-6500. **Contact:** Human Resources. **World Wide Web address:** http://www.gpu.com. **Description:** An electric utility holding company with

several operating subsidiaries. **Common positions include:** Accountant/Auditor; Administrator; Electrical/Electronics Engineer; Human Resources Manager; Industrial Engineer; Systems Analyst. **Educational backgrounds include:** Accounting. **Corporate headquarters location:** This Location. **Subsidiaries include:** GPU Service Corporation, a service company; GPU Nuclear Service Corporation, which operates and maintains the nuclear units of the subsidiaries; Energy Initiatives, Inc. and El Power, Inc., which develop, own, and operate nonutility generating facilities. The company also provides administrative services to Jersey Central Power & Light, Metropolitan Edison, and Pennsylvania Electric, which serve 1.9 million customers. **Operations at this facility include:** Administration. **Listed on:** New York Stock Exchange.

### NEW JERSEY RESOURCES
1415 Wyckoff Road, Wall NJ 07719. 732/938-1480. **Contact:** Ms. Hollis Cooper, Human Resources. **World Wide Web address:** http://www.njng.com. **Description:** A holding company for natural gas and energy companies. **Subsidiaries include:** New Jersey Natural Gas Company distributes natural gas to over 330,000 customers in Monmouth and Ocean Counties, and parts of Morris and Middlesex Counties. Other subsidiaries are engaged in exploration for natural gas and oil, real estate development, and the development of cogeneration projects.

### PASSAIC VALLEY WATER COMMISSION
1525 Main Avenue, Clifton NJ 07011. 973/340-4300. **Contact:** Jim Gallagher, Personnel Director. **Description:** Provides water utility services. **Corporate headquarters location:** This Location.

### PUBLIC SERVICE ENTERPRISE GROUP
80 Park Plaza, Newark NJ 07101. 973/430-7000. **Contact:** Human Resources. **World Wide Web address:** http://www.pseg.com. **Description:** An electric and gas utility holding company. **Corporate headquarters location:** This Location. **Other area locations:** P.O. Box 236, Hancock's Bridge NJ 08038, 609/339-2912. **Subsidiaries include:** Public Service Electric & Gas Company serves most of New Jersey's industrial and commercial population with nuclear, coal, gas, oil, and purchased and interchanged power. **Listed on:** New York Stock Exchange.

### UNITED WATER RESOURCES, INC.
200 Old Hook Road, Harrington Park NJ 07640. 201/784-9434. **Fax:** 201/767-7142. **Contact:** James Vaeth, Director of Human Resources. **World Wide Web address:** http://www.unitedwater.com/uwnj. **Description:** A holding company for regulated water utilities. **Subsidiaries include:** Hackensack Water Company supplies water service to over 175,000 customers in 60 communities in northern Hudson and Bergen Counties. Spring Valley Water Company, which has 59,000 customers, provides water service in Rockland County NY, outside of the Palisade Interstate Park, and in areas served by the water systems of the towns of Nyack and Suffern.

*Note: Because addresses and telephone numbers of smaller companies can change rapidly, we recommend you call each company to verify the information below before inquiring about job opportunities. Mass mailings are not recommended.*

### Additional small employers:

**COMBINATION UTILITY SERVICES**

**CEA USA Inc.**
1200 E Ridgewood Ave, Ridgewood NJ 07450-3937. 201/652-2772.

**Public Service Electric & Gas Co.**
181 Prospect St, Bergenfield NJ 07621. 201/967-3274.

**Public Service Electric & Gas Co.**
PO Box 1023, Cranford NJ 07016-1023. 908/709-3502.

**Public Service Electric & Gas Co.**
140 E Ridgewood Ave, Ste 1, Paramus NJ 07652-3915. 201/967-3240.

**Public Service Electric & Gas Co.**
665 Whitehead Rd, Trenton NJ 08648-4449. 609/365-0006.

**Public Service Electric & Gas Co.**
309 Fellowship Rd, Floor 2, Mount Laurel NJ 08054-1234. 609/273-3010.

**Public Service Electric & Gas Co.**
48 Middle Ave, Summit NJ 07901-4028. 908/522-7401.

**Public Service Electric & Gas Co.**
40 Rock Avenue, Plainfield NJ 07063-1045. 908/756-0700.

**Public Service Electric & Gas Co.**
350 Raritan Center Pkwy, Edison NJ 08837-3913. 908/668-3900.

**Public Service Electric & Gas Co.**
472 Weston Canal Rd, Somerset NJ 08873-7245. 732/764-3001.

**Public Service Electric & Gas Co.**
4000 Hadley Rd, South Plainfield NJ 07080-1124. 908/756-7000.

**Public Service Electric & Gas Co.**
900 W Grand St, Elizabeth NJ 07202-1098. 908/558-7501.

## ELECTRIC SERVICES

**GPU Nuclear Service Corp.**
PO Box 388, Forked River NJ
08731-0388. 609/971-4000.

**Vineland Municipal Electric
Utility**
415 N West Ave, Vineland NJ
08360-3680. 609/794-4276.

## GAS AND/OR WATER
## SUPPLY

**Elizabethtown Water Company**
PO Box 111, Plainfield NJ
07061-0111. 908/654-1234.

**Middlesex Water Company**
PO Box 1500, Iselin NJ 08830-
0452. 732/634-1500.

**New Jersey American Water
Commission**
PO Box 6002, Bellmawr NJ
08099-6002. 609/547-1700.

**New Jersey American Water
Commission**
661 Shrewsbury Ave, Shrewsbury
NJ 07702-4134. 732/842-6900.

**New Jersey Water Supply
Authority**
PO Box 5196, Clinton NJ 08809-
0196. 908/638-6121.

**North Jersey District Water
Commission**
1 FA Orechio Dr, Wanaque NJ
07465-1517. 973/835-3600.

**United Water Resources, Inc.**
135 Hackensack Ave,
Hackensack NJ 07601-6107.
201/646-6663.

## GAS UTILITY SERVICES

**Energis Resources Inc.**
499 Thornall St, Ste 5, Edison NJ
08837-2235. 732/744-2000.

**New Brunswick Gas**
150 How Ln, New Brunswick NJ
08901-3640. 732/220-6200.

**New Jersey Natural Gas Co.**
PO Box 1464, Belmar NJ 07719-
1464. 732/938-1000.

**New Jersey Natural Gas Co.**
775 Vassar Ave, Lakewood NJ
08701-6908. 732/905-4382.

**NUI Corporation**
PO Box 760, Bedminster NJ
07921-0760. 908/781-0500.

**South Jersey Gas Company**
S Jersey One, Hammonton NJ
08037. 609/561-9000.

**South Jersey Gas Company**
111 N Franklin Blvd,
Pleasantville NJ 08232-2507.
609/645-2690.

## For more information on career opportunities in the utilities industry:

### Associations

**AMERICAN PUBLIC GAS ASSOCIATION**
11094-D Lee Highway, Suite 102, Fairfax VA 22030.
703/352-3890. World Wide Web address: http://www.
apga.org. Publishes a bi-weekly newsletter.

**AMERICAN PUBLIC POWER ASSOCIATION
(APPA)**
2301 M Street NW, Washington DC 20037. 202/467-
2903. World Wide Web address: http://www.appanet.
org. Represents publicly-owned utilities. Provides
many services including government relations,
educational programs, and industry-related
information publications.

**AMERICAN WATER WORKS ASSOCIATION**
6666 West Quincy Avenue, Denver CO 80235.
303/794-7711. World Wide Web address: http://www.
awwa.org.

**NATIONAL RURAL ELECTRIC
COOPERATIVE ASSOCIATION**
4301 Wilson Boulevard, Arlington VA 22203.
703/907-5500. World Wide Web address: http://www.
nreca.org.

### Directories

**MOODY'S PUBLIC UTILITY MANUAL**
Financial Information Services, 60 Madison Avenue,
6th Floor, New York NY 10010. Toll-free phone:
800/342-5647. World Wide Web address: http://www.
fisonline.com. Annually available at libraries.

### Magazines

**PUBLIC POWER**
American Public Power Association, 2301 M Street
NW, Suite 300, Washington DC 20037-1484.
202/467-2900.

Visit our exciting job and career site at http://www.careercity.com

# MISCELLANEOUS WHOLESALING

 *According to the U.S. Department of Commerce, the need to cut costs is increasing as wholesaling and distributing businesses become more global and competitive, leading to changes in manufacturer-distributor working relationships. The most significant of these is an improved efficiency in inventory management, whereby the distributor manages inventory at the customer's site.*

*Wholesaling has evolved into an industry driven by customer needs, and while companies now prefer to do business with fewer suppliers, they still expect quality services. Overall, the wholesale industry may see employment growth of 1.1 percent by 2006, according to the Bureau of Labor Statistics.*

**CCA INDUSTRIES INC.**
200 Murray Hill Parkway, East Rutherford NJ 07073. 201/330-1400. **Contact:** Human Resources Department. **Description:** Markets a wide variety of health and beauty products manufactured by others under CCA's formulations. The large majority of its sales are made to retail drug and food chains and mass merchandisers. Nail treatment products are sold under the name Nutra Nail; hair treatment products are sold under the names Pro Perm, Wash 'n Curl, Wash 'n Tint, and Wash 'n Straight; depilatory products are sold under the Hair Off label; skin care products are sold under the Sudden Change name; oral hygiene products are sold under the Plus+White mark; meal replacement products are sold under the trademarks Eat 'n Lose; and diet products under the marks Hungrex and Permathene.

**CLARION OFFICE SUPPLIES INC.**
101 East Main Street, Little Falls NJ 07424. 973/785-8383. **Contact:** Human Resources. **Description:** Distributes a wide variety of office supplies including computer hardware. Clarion Office Supplies provides individuals and businesses with most major brands of CPUs and monitors.

**CREATIVE HOBBIES, INC.**
900 Creek Road, Bellmawr NJ 08031. 609/933-2540. **Contact:** Human Resources. **Description:** A wholesale distributor of hobby ceramics supplies including clay, kilns, pottery wheels, tools, glazes, and decorating supplies.

**ENGINE DISTRIBUTORS, INC.**
332 South 17th Street, Camden NJ 08105-1769. 609/365-8631. **Contact:** Glen Cummins, Jr., President. **Description:** Distributes industrial engines. **Common positions include:** Branch Manager; General Manager; Manufacturer's/Wholesaler's Sales Rep.; Operations/Production Manager.

**HOLMDEL JEWELRY EXCHANGE**
2145 Route 35, Holmdel NJ 07733. 732/888-1884. **Contact:** Human Resources. **Description:** A wholesaler of gold and diamond jewelry.

**McMASTER-CARR SUPPLY COMPANY**
P.O. Box 440, New Brunswick NJ 08903. 732/329-6666. **Contact:** Jim O'Neill, Personnel Manager. **World Wide Web address:** http://www.mcmaster.com. **Description:** Distributes industrial products and supplies primarily through catalog sales. Products are sold worldwide. **Common positions include:** Management Trainee. **Educational backgrounds include:** Business Administration; Communications; Computer Science; Economics; Engineering; Finance; Liberal Arts; Marketing. **Benefits:** Dental Insurance; Disability Coverage; Employee Discounts; Life Insurance; Medical Insurance; Pension Plan; Profit Sharing; Tuition Assistance. **Corporate headquarters location:** Elmhurst IL. **Operations at this facility include:** Service.

**MITA COPYSTAR AMERICA**
225 Sand Road, Fairfield NJ 07004. 973/808-8444. **Contact:** Human Resources. **World Wide Web address:** http://www.mita.com. **Description:** This location houses executive offices only. Overall, Mita Copystar America imports and distributes a large line of copier machines and related office equipment. **Corporate headquarters location:** This Location. **Other U.S. locations:** Clifton NJ.

**NEW YORK GOLD BROKERS**
2021 Pacific Avenue, Atlantic City NJ 08401. 609/348-9329. **Contact:** Human Resources.
**Description:** A wholesaler of gold and other jewelry.

**PHILIPS ANALYTICAL**
85 McKee Drive, Mahwah NJ 07430. 201/529-3800. **Fax:** 201/529-0896. **Contact:** Human
Resources. **Description:** Sells and services analytical X-ray systems. **Common positions include:**
Accountant/Auditor; Buyer; Computer Programmer; Customer Service Rep.; Designer;
Electrical/Electronics Engineer; Field Engineer; Mechanical Engineer; Sales Rep.; Software
Engineer; Systems Analyst. **Educational backgrounds include:** Accounting; Business
Administration; Computer Science; Engineering; Marketing; Material Sciences; Physics; Science.
**Benefits:** 401(k); Dental Insurance; Disability Coverage; Employee Discounts; Life Insurance;
Medical Insurance; Pension Plan; Savings Plan; Spending Account; Tuition Assistance. **Corporate
headquarters location:** New York NY. **Other U.S. locations:** Tempe AZ; Fremont CA;
Alpharetta GA; Roselle IL; Columbia MD; Bellaire TX. **Parent company:** Philips Electronics
North America. **Number of employees at this location:** 180.

**PITMAN COMPANY**
721 Union Boulevard, Totowa NJ 07512. 973/812-0400. **Contact:** David Gornstein, Operations
Manager. **Description:** A distributor of Kodak, 3M, and BisMarch products.

**PRIMESOURCE**
15 Twin Bridge Drive, Pennsauken NJ 08110. 609/488-7200. **Contact:** Human Resources. **World
Wide Web address:** http://www.primesource.com. **Description:** Distributes graphic arts
equipment and systems.

**RIVIERA TRADING CORPORATION**
P.O. Box 1555, Secaucus NJ 07096. 201/864-8686. **Contact:** Director of Industrial Relations.
**Description:** Imports and distributes hair accessories and sunglasses. **Common positions include:**
Accountant; Administrator; Customer Service Rep.; Department Manager; Human Resources
Manager; Management Trainee; Marketing Specialist; Operations/Production Manager; Purchasing
Agent/Manager. **Educational backgrounds include:** Accounting; Business Administration.
**Benefits:** Dental Insurance; Disability Coverage; Life Insurance; Medical Insurance; Pension Plan;
Profit Sharing. **Corporate headquarters location:** New York NY.

**VAN LEEUWEN**
20 Harmich Road, South Plainfield NJ 07080. 908/226-0700. **Contact:** Human Resources.
**Description:** Distributes pipes, valves, and fittings, serving both domestic and overseas customers.
**NOTE:** If applying for a warehouse position, please contact Martin Curley; for an office position,
contact Jim Gallagher, Regional Manager. **Corporate headquarters location:** This Location.

**VIVA INTERNATIONAL GROUP**
3140 Route 22 West, Somerville NJ 08876. 908/595-6200. **Contact:** Human Resources.
**Description:** Distributes eyewear.

**WHOLESALE FURNITURE FOR LESS**
286 Green Street, Old Bridge NJ 08857. 732/360-0042. **Fax:** 732/360-4880. **Contact:** Human
Resources. **Description:** A wholesaler of furniture.

**ZABAL INTERNATIONAL GROUP**
63 Woodland Avenue, West Orange NJ 07052-2930. 973/324-1780. **Contact:** Human Resources.
**Description:** A diverse import and export company dealing primarily with the Middle East.
Products exported include food and animals.

For more information on career opportunities in the wholesaling industry:

Associations

NATIONAL ASSOCIATION OF
WHOLESALERS (NAW)
1725 K Street NW, Suite 300, Washington DC 20006.
202/872-0885.

*Many people turn to temporary agencies, permanent employment agencies, or executive recruiters to assist them in their respective job searches. At their best, these resources can be a valuable friend -- it's comforting to know that someone is putting his or her wealth of experience and contacts to work for you. At their worst, however, they are more of a friend to the employer, or to more experienced recruits, than to you personally, and it is best not to rely on them exclusively.*

*That said, there are several types of employment services for jobseekers to check out as part of their job search efforts:*

## TEMPORARY EMPLOYMENT AGENCIES

Temporary or "temp" agencies can be a viable option. Often these agencies specialize in clerical and support work, but it's becoming increasingly common to find temporary assignments in other areas like accounting or computer programming. Working on temporary assignments will provide you with additional income during your job search and will add experience to your resume. It may also provide valuable business contacts or lead to permanent job opportunities.

Temporary agencies are listed in your local telephone directory and in *The JobBank Guide to Employment Services* (Adams Media Corporation), found in your local public library. Send a resume and cover letter to the agency, and call to schedule an interview. Be prepared to take a number of tests at the interview.

## PERMANENT EMPLOYMENT AGENCIES

Permanent employment agencies are commissioned by employers to find qualified candidates for job openings. The catch is that their main responsibility is to meet the employer's needs -- not necessarily to find a suitable job for the candidate.

This is not to say that permanent employment agencies should be ruled out altogether. There are permanent employment agencies specializing in specific industries that can be useful for experienced professionals. However, permanent employment agencies are not always a good choice for entry-level jobseekers. Some will try to steer inexperienced candidates in an unwanted direction or offer little more than clerical placements to experienced applicants. Others charge a fee for their services a condition that jobseekers should always ask about up front.

Some permanent employment agencies dispute the criticisms mentioned above. As one recruiter puts it, "Our responsibilities are to the applicant and the employer equally, because without one, we'll lose the other." She also maintains that entry-level people are desirable, saying that "as they grow, we grow, too, so we aim to move them up the ranks."

In short, as that recruiter states, "All services are not the same." If you decide to register with an agency, your best bet is to find one that is recommended by a friend or associate. Barring that, names of agencies across the country can be found in *The Adams Executive Recruiters Almanac* (Adams Media Corporation) or *The JobBank Guide to Employment Services* (Adams Media Corporation). Or you can contact:

**National Association of Personnel Services (NAPS)**
3133 Mount Vernon Avenue
Alexandria VA 22305
703/684-0180

Be aware that there are an increasing number of bogus employment service firms, often advertising in newspapers and magazines. These "services" promise even inexperienced jobseekers top salaries in exciting careers -- all for a sizable fee. Others use expensive 900 numbers that jobseekers are encouraged to call. Unfortunately, most people find out too late that the jobs they have been promised do not exist.

As a general rule, most legitimate permanent employment agencies will never guarantee a job and will not seek payment until after the candidate has been placed. Even so, every agency you are interested in should be checked out with the local chapter of the Better Business Bureau (BBB). Find out if the agency is licensed and has been in business for a reasonable amount of time.

If everything checks out, call the firm to find out if it specializes in your area of expertise and how it will go about marketing your qualifications. After you have selected a few agencies (three to five is best), send each one a resume with a cover letter. Make a follow-up phone call a week or two later, and try to schedule an interview. Once again, be prepared to take a battery of tests at the interview.

Above all, do not expect too much. Only a small portion of all professional, managerial, and executive jobs are listed with these agencies. Use them as an addition to your job search campaign, not a centerpiece.

## EXECUTIVE SEARCH FIRMS

Also known as "headhunters," these firms consist of recruiters who are paid by client companies that hire them to fill a specific position. Executive search firms seek out and carefully screen (and weed out) candidates for high-salaried technical, executive, and managerial positions and are paid by the employer. The prospective employee is generally not charged a fee. Unlike permanent employment agencies, they often approach viable candidates directly, rather than waiting for candidates to approach them. Some prefer to deal with already employed candidates. Whether you are employed or not, do not contact an executive search firm if you aren't ready to look for a job. If a recruiter tries to place you right away and finds out you are not really looking yet, it is unlikely they will spend much time with you in the future.

Many search firms specialize in particular industries, while generalist firms typically provide placements in a wide range of industries. Look for firms that specialize in your field of interest or expertise, as well as generalist firms that conduct searches in a variety of fields. While you should concentrate on firms in your geographic area, you do not have to limit yourself to these as many firms operate nationally or internationally.

There are two basic types of executive search firms -- retainer-based and contingency-based. Note, however, that some firms conduct searches of both types. Essentially, retainer firms are hired by a client company for a search and paid a fee by the client company regardless of whether or not a placement is made. Conversely, contingency firms receive payment from the client company only when their candidate is hired. Fees are typically based on the position's first-year salary. The range is usually between 20 and 35 percent, and retainer firm fees tend to be at the higher end of that scale, according to Ivan Samuels, President of Abbott's of Boston, an executive search firm that conducts both types of searches.

Generally, companies use retainer firms to fill senior-level positions, with salaries over $60,000. In most cases, a company will hire only one retainer firm to fill a given position, and part of the process is a thorough, on-site visit by the search firm to the client company so that the recruiter may check out the operation. These search firms are recommended for a highly experienced professional seeking a job in his or her current field. Confidentiality is more secure with these firms, since a recruiter may only use your file in consideration for one job at a time, and most retainer firms will not freely circulate your resume without permission. This is particularly important to a jobseeker who is currently employed and insists on absolute discretion. If that's the case, however, make sure you do not contact a retainer firm used by your current employer.

Contingency firms make placements that cover a broader salary range, so these firms are more ideal for someone seeking a junior or mid-level position. Unlike retainer firms, contingency firms may be competing with other firms to fill a particular opening. As a result, these firms can be quicker and more responsive to your job search. In addition, a contingency firm will distribute your resume more widely. Some firms require your permission before sending your resume to any given company, while others ask that you trust their discretion. You should inquire about this with your recruiter at the outset, and choose according to your needs.

That said, once you've chosen the specific recruiter or recruiters that you will contact, keep in mind that recruiters are working for the companies that hire them, not for you, the jobseeker. Attempting to fill a position -- especially amongst fierce competition with other firms -- means your best interests may not be the recruiter's only priority. For this reason, you should contact as many search firms as possible in order to increase your chances of finding your ideal position.

A phone call is your first step, during which you should speak with a recruiter and exchange all relevant information. Ask lots of questions to determine the firm's credibility, whether they operate on a retainer or contingency basis (or both), and any and all questions you have regarding the firm's procedures. Offer the recruiter information about your employment history, as well as what type of work you are seeking. Make sure you sound enthusiastic, but not pushy. The recruiter will ask that you send a resume and cover letter as soon as possible.

Occasionally, the recruiter will arrange to meet with you, but most often this will not occur until he or she has received your resume and has found a potential match. James E. Slate, President of F-O-R-T-U-N-E Personnel Consultants in Topsfield, Massachusetts, advises that you generally not expect an abundance of personal attention at the beginning of the relationship with your recruiter, particularly with a large firm that works nationally and does most of its work over the phone. You should, however, use your recruiter's inside knowledge to your best advantage. Some recruiters will help coach you before an interview and many are open about giving you all the facts they know about a client company.

Not all executive search firms are licensed, so make sure those you plan to deal with have solid reputations and don't hesitate to check with the Better Business Bureau. Also keep in mind that it is common for recruiters to search for positions in other states. For example, recruiters in Boston sometimes look for candidates to fill positions in New York City, and the reverse is true as well. Names of search firms nationwide can be found in *The Adams Executive Recruiters Almanac* or *The JobBank Guide to Employment Services*, or by contacting:

**Association of Executive Search Consultants (AESC)**
500 Fifth Avenue, Suite 930, New York NY 10110. 212/398-9556.

**Top Echelon, Inc.**
World Wide Web address: http://www.topechelon.com.

A cooperative placement networking service of recruiting firms.

## CONTRACT SERVICES FIRMS

Firms that place individuals on a contract basis commonly receive job orders from client companies that can last anywhere from a month to over a year. The function of these firms differs from that of a temporary agency in that the candidate has specific, marketable skills they wish to put to work, and the contract recruiter interviews the candidate extensively. Most often, contract services firms specialize in placing technical professionals, though some do specialize in other fields, including clerical and office support. The use of these firms is increasing in popularity, as jobseekers with technical skills recognize the benefit of utilizing and demonstrating their talents at a sampling of different companies, and establishing contacts along the way that could lead to a permanent position, if desired. Most contract services firms do not charge a fee to the candidate.

For more information on contract services, contact:

**C.E. Publications, Inc.**
Contract Employment Weekly Magazine
P.O. Box 3006, Bothell WA 98041-3006. 425/806-5200.
World Wide Web address: http://www.ceweekly.com.

## RESUME/CAREER COUNSELING/OUTPLACEMENT SERVICES

These firms are very diverse in the services they provide. Many nonprofit organizations -- colleges, universities, private associations -- offer free or very inexpensive counseling services. For-profit career/outplacement counseling services, on the other hand, can charge a broad range of fees, depending on what services they provide. Services offered include career counseling, outplacement, resume development/writing, interview preparation, assessment testing, and various workshops. Upon contacting one of these firms, you should ask about the specific services that firm provides. Some firms provide career counseling only, teaching you how to conduct your own job search, while others also provide outplacement services. The difference here is that those which provide outplacement will conduct a job search for you, in addition to the counseling services. Firms like these are sometimes referred to as "marketing firms."

According to a representative at Career Ventures Counseling Services in Salem, Massachusetts, fees for career counseling average about $85 per hour. Counseling firms located in major cities tend to be more expensive. Furthermore, outplacement fees can range from $170 to over $7,000! As results are not guaranteed, you may want to check on a firm's reputation through the local Better Business Bureau.

For more information on resume services, contact:

**Professional Association of Resume Writers**
3637 Fourth Street, Suite 330, St. Petersburg FL 33704.
Attention: Mr. Frank Fox, Executive Director.

*Note: On the following pages, you will find employment services for this* JobBank *book's coverage area. Because contact names and addresses can change regularly, we recommend that you call each company to verify the information before inquiring about opportunities.*

# TEMPORARY EMPLOYMENT AGENCIES

**ANGELORD INC.**
930 Stuyvesant Avenue, Union NJ 07083-6940. 908/687-5442. **Fax:** 908/688-5482. **Contact:** Bella Guariella, President. **Description:** A temporary agency. **Specializes in the areas of:** Sales; Secretarial. **Positions commonly filled include:** Accountant/Auditor; Services Sales Representative; Typist/Word Processor. **Average salary range of placements:** $20,000 - $29,999. **Number of placements per year:** 50 - 99.

**ARC MEDICAL AND PROFESSIONAL PERSONNEL, INC.**
36 State Route 10, Suite D, East Hanover NJ 07936. 973/428-0101. **Fax:** 973/428-8257. **Contact:** Roslyn Durkin, Assistant Director. **Description:** Arc Medical and Professional Personnel, Inc. is a temporary agency that also provides some permanent placements. **Specializes in the areas of:** Health/Medical; Pharmaceuticals. **Positions commonly filled include:** Biochemist; Biological Scientist; Chemist; Clinical Lab Technician; Medical Records Technician; Pharmacist; Physician; Registered Nurse; Scientist; Typist/Word Processor. **Number of placements per year:** 1 - 49.

**ENRICHED LIVING**
18 Davenport Street, Somerville NJ 08876. 908/707-9779. **Fax:** 908/707-4668. **Contact:** Monica Larsen, Nursing Coordinator. **Description:** A temporary agency. **Specializes in the areas of:** Health/Medical. **Positions commonly filled include:** Dietician/Nutritionist; Licensed Practical Nurse; Physical Therapist; Registered Nurse; Social Worker. **Number of placements per year:** 1 - 49.

**ITC TEMPS INC.**
232 Boulevard, Suite 8, Hasbrouck Heights NJ 07505. 201/462-0264. **Fax:** 973/345-1229. **Contact:** Manager. **Description:** ITC Temps Inc. is a temporary agency that also offers contract services. **Specializes in the areas of:** Personnel/Labor Relations; Secretarial. **Positions commonly filled include:** Customer Service Representative; Human Resources Specialist; Typist/Word Processor. **Benefits available to temporary workers:** Bonus Award/Plan; Medical Insurance; Paid Vacation. **Average salary range of placements:** $30,000 - $50,000. **Number of placements per year:** 1 - 49.

**INTEGRO STAFFING SERVICES**
One Gatehall Drive, Parsippany NJ 07054. 973/267-6363. **Fax:** 973/267-2158. **Contact:** Lauren Hodgin, Manager. **Description:** Integro Staffing Services is a temporary agency. **Specializes in the areas of:** Accounting/Auditing; Banking; Biology; Computer Science/Software; Finance; Legal; Secretarial; Technical. **Positions commonly filled include:** Accountant/Auditor; Administrative Manager; Biochemist; Biological Scientist; Brokerage Clerk; Chemical Engineer; Chemist; Clinical Lab Technician; Computer Programmer; Paralegal; Typist/Word Processor. **Benefits available to temporary workers:** Bonus Award/Plan; Paid Holidays; Paid Vacation. **Other U.S. locations:** Bridgewater NJ; Cherry Hill NJ; Iselin NJ; Lawrenceville NJ; Mount Olive NJ; Paramus NJ. **Number of placements per year:** 1000+.

**JOULE TECHNICAL STAFFING**
1235 Route 1 South, Edison NJ 08837. 732/494-8880. **Contact:** Manager. **Description:** A temporary agency. **Specializes in the areas of:** Administration; Chemicals; Engineering. **Positions commonly filled include:** Branch Manager; Chemical Engineer; Chemist; Civil Engineer; Designer; Draftsperson; Electrical/Electronics Engineer; Electrician; Industrial Engineer; Mechanical Engineer; Services Sales Representative; Stationary Engineer. **Number of placements per year:** 200 - 499.

**KAYE PERSONNEL INC.**
1868 Route 70 East, Cherry Hill NJ 08003. 609/489-1200. **Fax:** 609/489-1010. **Contact:** Carolyn Kaye, Staffing Coordinator. **Description:** Kaye Personnel Inc. is a temporary agency. **Specializes in the areas of:** Industrial; Manufacturing; Personnel/Labor Relations; Publishing; Secretarial; Technical. **Positions commonly filled include:** Customer Service Representative; Secretary;

Typist/Word Processor. **Other U.S. locations:** Nationwide. **Number of placements per year:** 1000+.

**KELLY SCIENTIFIC RESOURCES**
140 Route 17 North, Suite 271, Paramus NJ 07652. 201/599-5959. **Fax:** 201/599-8470. **Contact:** Diane R. Long, NY Metro District Manager. **World Wide Web address:** http://www.kellyscientific.com. **Description:** A temporary agency for scientific professionals. **Specializes in the areas of:** Biomedical; Biotechnology; Chemicals; Environmental; Food; Petrochemical; Pharmaceuticals. **Corporate headquarters location:** Troy MI.

**KELLY SCIENTIFIC RESOURCES**
242 Old New Brunswick Road, Suite 140, Piscataway NJ 08854. 732/981-1399. **Contact:** Branch Manager. **World Wide Web address:** http://www.kellyscientific.com. **Description:** A temporary agency for scientific professionals. **Specializes in the areas of:** Biomedical; Biotechnology; Chemicals; Environmental; Food; Petrochemical; Pharmaceuticals. **Corporate headquarters location:** Troy MI.

**KELLY SERVICES, INC.**
70 South Orange Avenue, Suite 107, Livingston NJ 07039. 973/540-1800. **Fax:** 973/992-6511. **Contact:** Branch Manager. **Description:** Kelly Services, Inc. is a temporary agency. **Specializes in the areas of:** Accounting/Auditing; Advertising; Engineering; Finance; Secretarial. **Positions commonly filled include:** Biochemist; Biological Scientist; Biomedical Engineer; Blue-Collar Worker Supervisor; Chemical Engineer; Chemist; Civil Engineer; Claim Representative; Clerical Supervisor; Clinical Lab Technician; Computer Programmer; Customer Service Representative; Human Resources Specialist; Industrial Engineer; MIS Specialist; Multimedia Designer; Paralegal; Pharmacist; Purchasing Agent/Manager; Quality Assurance Engineer; Software Engineer; Typist/Word Processor. **Benefits available to temporary workers:** Paid Holidays; Paid Vacation. **Corporate headquarters location:** Troy MI. **Number of placements per year:** 1000+.

**KELLY SERVICES, INC.**
313 Courtyard, Somerville NJ 08876. 908/526-6225. **Fax:** 908/526-1625. **Contact:** Regina Boyle, Office Manager. **Description:** A temporary agency. **Specializes in the areas of:** Accounting/Auditing; Administration; Engineering; Finance; Secretarial. **Positions commonly filled include:** Biochemist; Biological Scientist; Biomedical Engineer; Chemical Engineer; Chemist; Civil Engineer; Claim Representative; Clerical Supervisor; Clinical Lab Technician; Computer Programmer; Human Resources Specialist; Industrial Production Manager; Mechanical Engineer; MIS Specialist; Multimedia Designer; Paralegal; Purchasing Agent/Manager; Quality Assurance Engineer; Software Engineer; Typist/Word Processor. **Benefits available to temporary workers:** Paid Holidays; Paid Vacation. **Corporate headquarters location:** Troy MI. **Number of placements per year:** 1000+.

**LAB SUPPORT INC.**
475 Market Street, 1st Floor, Elmwood Park NJ 07407. 201/794-8077. **Contact:** Account Manager. **World Wide Web address:** http://www.labsupport.com. **Description:** Lab Support Inc. is a temporary agency. **Specializes in the areas of:** Biology; Food; Manufacturing; Technical. **Positions commonly filled include:** Biochemist; Biological Scientist; Chemist; Food Scientist/Technologist; Science Technologist. **Benefits available to temporary workers:** 401(k); Medical Insurance; Paid Holidays; Paid Vacation. **Other U.S. locations:** Nationwide. **Average salary range of placements:** $30,000 - $50,000. **Number of placements per year:** 200 - 499.

**MANPOWER TECHNICAL SERVICES**
51 Haddonfield Road, Suite 325, Cherry Hill NJ 08002. 609/665-8177. **Fax:** 609/665-8249. **Contact:** Lisa Christensen, Area Manager. **Description:** Manpower Technical Services is a temporary agency that also provides contract services. Founded in 1948. **Specializes in the areas of:** Accounting/Auditing; Administration; Biology; Computer Hardware/Software; Engineering; Finance; Manufacturing; Technical. **Positions commonly filled include:** Accountant/Auditor; Actuary; Aerospace Engineer; Biochemist; Biological Scientist; Buyer; Chemical Engineer; Chemist; Civil Engineer; Clinical Lab Technician; Computer Programmer; Credit Manager; Design Engineer; Designer; Dietician/Nutritionist; Draftsperson; Economist; Electrical/Electronics Engineer; Environmental Engineer; Geologist/Geophysicist; Industrial Engineer; Internet Services Manager; Mechanical Engineer; Metallurgical Engineer; Multimedia Designer; Nuclear Engineer; Petroleum Engineer; Purchasing Agent/Manager; Quality Control Supervisor; Science Technologist; Software Engineer; Stationary Engineer; Structural Engineer; Technical Writer/Editor. **Benefits available to temporary workers:** 401(k); Dental Insurance; Life Insurance; Medical Insurance; Paid Holidays; Paid Vacation. **Corporate headquarters location:** Milwaukee WI. **Average salary range of placements:** $40,000 - $70,000. **Number of placements per year:** 100 - 150.

**NORMANN TEMPORARIES**
P.O. Box 407, Paramus NJ 07652-0407. 201/261-1576. **Fax:** 201/261-0685. **Contact:** Robert Allison, President. **Description:** A temporary agency. **Specializes in the areas of:** Light Industrial; Secretarial. **Positions commonly filled include:** Administrative Assistant; Administrative Manager; Clerical Supervisor; Customer Service Representative; Management Trainee; Secretary; Services Sales Representative; Typist/Word Processor. **Benefits available to temporary workers:** Medical Insurance; Paid Holidays; Paid Vacation. **Corporate headquarters location:** This Location. **Other U.S. locations:** Mahwah NJ. **Average salary range of placements:** $20,000 - $29,999. **Number of placements per year:** 1 - 49.

**NORRELL SERVICES**
197 Route 18 South, Suite 110, East Brunswick NJ 08816. 732/828-9111. **Toll-free phone:** 800/848-JOBS. **Fax:** 732/828-7766. **Contact:** Corrie Kirklen, Office Manager. **Description:** A temporary agency. **Specializes in the areas of:** Accounting; Administration; Finance; General Management; Insurance; Light Industrial; Secretarial. **Positions commonly filled include:** Administrative Assistant; Customer Service Representative; Secretary. **Corporate headquarters location:** Atlanta GA. **Average salary range of placements:** $20,000 - $49,999. **Number of placements per year:** 200 - 499.

**OLSTEN STAFFING SERVICES**
10 Lanidex Plaza West, Parsippany NJ 07054. 973/560-1670. **Fax:** 973/560-1208. **Contact:** Branch Manager. **Description:** Olsten Staffing Services is a temporary agency that also provides some permanent placements. **Positions commonly filled include:** Administrative Assistant; Chemist; Clinical Lab Technician; Customer Service Representative; Secretary; Typist/Word Processor. **Benefits available to temporary workers:** Medical Insurance; Paid Vacation. **Corporate headquarters location:** Melville NY. **Other U.S. locations:** Nationwide. **Average salary range of placements:** $20,000 - $29,999. **Number of placements per year:** 200 - 499.

**OLSTEN STAFFING SERVICES**
200 Cottontail Lane, Building A, Somerset NJ 08873. 732/563-1660. **Fax:** 732/563-1665. **Contact:** Customer Service Manager. **Description:** A temporary agency. **Specializes in the areas of:** Accounting/Auditing; Sales. **Positions commonly filled include:** Accountant/Auditor; Advertising Clerk; Biochemist; Biological Scientist; Blue-Collar Worker Supervisor; Brokerage Clerk; Budget Analyst; Chemist; Clinical Lab Technician; Computer Programmer; Customer Service Representative; Industrial Production Manager; Operations/Production Manager; Paralegal; Systems Analyst; Technical Writer/Editor; Typist/Word Processor. **Benefits available to temporary workers:** Medical Insurance; Paid Vacation. **Corporate headquarters location:** Melville NY. **Other U.S. locations:** Nationwide. **Average salary range of placements:** $20,000 - $29,999. **Number of placements per year:** 1000+.

**OMNE STAFFING SERVICES, INC.**
15 Bleeker Street, Milburn NJ 07041. 973/379-4900. **Fax:** 973/379-9119. **Contact:** Manager. **Description:** Omne Staffing Services, Inc. is a temporary agency. **Specializes in the areas of:** Administration; Computer Science/Software; Engineering; Industrial; Manufacturing; Office Support; Technical. **Positions commonly filled include:** Blue-Collar Worker Supervisor; Chemical Engineer; Civil Engineer; Clerical Supervisor; Computer Programmer; Customer Service Representative; Design Engineer; Designer; Draftsperson; Electrical/Electronics Engineer; Electrician; Industrial Engineer; Mechanical Engineer; MIS Specialist; Software Engineer; Structural Engineer; Technical Writer/Editor. **Benefits available to temporary workers:** 401(k); Medical Insurance; Paid Holidays; Paid Vacation. **Other U.S. locations:** CA; DC; FL; PA; TX. **Average salary range of placements:** $20,000 - $29,999. **Number of placements per year:** 1000+.

**PAT'S SECRETARIAL SERVICE**
50 South 21st Street, Kenilworth NJ 07033. 908/276-6366. **Contact:** Recruiter. **Description:** A temporary agency. **Specializes in the areas of:** Engineering; Legal; Secretarial. **Positions commonly filled include:** Clerical Supervisor; Clinical Lab Technician; Typist/Word Processor.

**THE PROFESSIONAL JOB ROSTER**
842 State Road, Princeton NJ 08540-7702. 609/921-9561. **Fax:** 609/921-9572. **Contact:** Director. **Description:** A temporary agency. **Specializes in the areas of:** Administration; Communications; Computer Hardware/Software; Finance; Sales; Technical.

**PROTOCALL BUSINESS STAFFING SERVICES**
426 High Street, Burlington NJ 08016-4502. 609/387-0300. **Fax:** 609/779-7471. **Contact:** Vince Moore, Regional Recruitment Coordinator. **Description:** Protocall Business Staffing Services is a

temporary agency. **Specializes in the areas of:** Accounting/Auditing; Computer Science/Software; Health/Medical; Industrial; Manufacturing; Secretarial. **Positions commonly filled include:** Accountant/Auditor; Claim Representative; Clinical Lab Technician; Computer Programmer; Customer Service Representative; Electrical/Electronics Engineer; Human Service Worker; Licensed Practical Nurse; Management Trainee; Medical Records Technician; MIS Specialist; Physical Therapist; Purchasing Agent/Manager; Quality Control Supervisor; Registered Nurse; Respiratory Therapist; Systems Analyst; Typist/Word Processor; Underwriter/Assistant Underwriter. **Corporate headquarters location:** Voorhees NJ. **Average salary range of placements:** $20,000 - $29,000. **Number of placements per year:** 1000+.

### REMEDY INTELLIGENT STAFFING
1930 Route 70 East, Executive Mews, Suite W111, Cherry Hill NJ 08003. 609/751-1900. **Toll-free phone:** 888/751-1900. **Fax:** 609/751-1361. **Contact:** Tom Jenkins, President. **World Wide Web address:** http://www.remedystaff.com. **Description:** A temporary agency. **Specializes in the areas of:** Administration; Banking; Finance; Secretarial. **Positions commonly filled include:** Clerical Supervisor; Customer Service Representative; Human Resources Specialist; Management Trainee; Services Sales Representative; Typist/Word Processor. **Benefits available to temporary workers:** Medical Insurance. **Other U.S. locations:** Nationwide. **Average salary range of placements:** $20,000 - $29,999. **Number of placements per year:** 500 - 999.

### SNELLING PERSONNEL SERVICES
47 River Road, Summit NJ 07901. 908/273-6500. **Fax:** 908/273-4379. **Contact:** Marilyn Richards, Vice President. **Description:** A temporary agency that also provides some permanent placements. **Specializes in the areas of:** Administration; Clerical; Finance; Legal; Personnel/Labor Relations; Sales; Secretarial. **Positions commonly filled include:** Administrative Manager; Brokerage Clerk; Claim Representative; Clerical Supervisor; Customer Service Representative; Dental Assistant/Dental Hygienist; Human Resources Specialist; Management Trainee; Medical Records Technician; MIS Specialist; Paralegal; Receptionist; Securities Sales Representative; Services Sales Representative; Transportation/Traffic Specialist; Typist/Word Processor. **Benefits available to temporary workers:** 401(k); Paid Holidays. **Average salary range of placements:** $20,000 - $29,999. **Number of placements per year:** 500 - 999.

### STRATUS SERVICES GROUP
500 Craig Road, Suite 201, Manalapan NJ 07726. 732/866-0100. **Contact:** Manager. **Description:** A temporary agency.

### SUPPORTIVE CARE, INC.
383 North Kings Highway, Suite 213, Cherry Hill NJ 08034. 609/482-6630. **Fax:** 609/482-6632. **Contact:** Debbie Kramer, Manager. **Description:** A temporary agency. **Specializes in the areas of:** Health/Medical. **Positions commonly filled include:** Certified Nurses Aide; Home Health Aide; Licensed Practical Nurse; Registered Nurse. **Average salary range of placements:** Less than $20,000. **Number of placements per year:** 1 - 49.

### TRS STAFFING SOLUTIONS, INC.
P.O. Box 566, Marlton NJ 08053. 609/985-9721. **Toll-free phone:** 800/535-8374. **Fax:** 609/985-6772. **Contact:** Joanne Becmer, Staffing Consultant. **Description:** A temporary agency. **Specializes in the areas of:** Administration; Computer Science/Software; Engineering; Manufacturing; Personnel/Labor Relations; Secretarial; Technical. **Positions commonly filled include:** Architect; Chemical Engineer; Chemist; Civil Engineer; Clerical Supervisor; Computer Programmer; Construction and Building Inspector; Cost Estimator; Draftsperson; Electrical/Electronics Engineer; Environmental Engineer; Internet Services Manager; Mechanical Engineer; Metallurgical Engineer; Mining Engineer; MIS Specialist; Multimedia Designer; Petroleum Engineer; Software Engineer; Structural Engineer; Surveyor; Systems Analyst; Telecommunications Manager. **Benefits available to temporary workers:** 401(k); Medical Insurance.

### TEMPORARY CLAIM PROFESSIONAL (TCP)
The Pavillions, 12000 Lincoln Drive West, Suite 401, Marlton NJ 08053-3213. 609/988-0099. **Contact:** Patricia Winstein, Manager. **Description:** Temporary Claim Professional is a temporary agency. **Specializes in the areas of:** Insurance. **Positions commonly filled include:** Adjuster; Claim Representative; Underwriter/Assistant Underwriter. **Benefits available to temporary workers:** Bonus Award/Plan; Medical Insurance. **Other U.S. locations:** Bel Air MD. **Average salary range of placements:** $30,000 - $50,000. **Number of placements per year:** 50 - 99.

### TEMPORARY EXCELLENCE INC.
205 Robin Road, Suite 200, Paramus NJ 07652. 201/599-1010. **Fax:** 201/599-1122. **Contact:** Lupita Cunningham, President. **Description:** Temporary Excellence Inc. is a temporary agency.

Specializes in the areas of: Accounting/Auditing; Fashion; Finance; Health/Medical; Personnel/Labor Relations; Retail; Sales; Secretarial. **Positions commonly filled include:** Accountant/Auditor; Clerical Supervisor; Credit Manager; Customer Service Representative; Human Resources Specialist; Typist/Word Processor. **Benefits available to temporary workers:** Medical Insurance; Paid Vacation. **Average salary range of placements:** $30,000 - $50,000. **Number of placements per year:** 1000+.

**UNITEMP TEMPORARY PERSONNEL**
38 Meadowlands Parkway, Secaucus NJ 07094. 201/867-5600. **Fax:** 201/867-2581. **Contact:** Office Manager. **Description:** Unitemp Temporary Personnel is a temporary agency. Founded in 1969. **Specializes in the areas of:** Secretarial. **Positions commonly filled include:** Administrative Assistant; Bookkeeper; Clerk; Customer Service Manager; Data Entry Clerk; Factory Worker; Legal Secretary; Medical Secretary; MIS Specialist; Quality Control Supervisor; Receptionist; Secretary; Typist/Word Processor. **Corporate headquarters location:** Paramus NJ. **Other area locations:** Woodcliff Lake NJ. **Number of placements per year:** 1000+.

**UNITEMP TEMPORARY PERSONNEL**
95 Route 17 South, Paramus NJ 07652. 201/845-7444. **Toll-free phone:** 800/UNI-TEMP. **Fax:** 201/845-7451. **Contact:** Molly Kissel, PHR, Vice President. **Description:** A temporary agency. Founded in 1969. **Specializes in the areas of:** Administration; Computer Science/Software; Legal; Secretarial. **Positions commonly filled include:** Administrative Assistant; Computer Operator; Computer Programmer; Paralegal; Secretary; Systems Analyst; Typist/Word Processor. **Benefits available to temporary workers:** Bonus Award/Plan; Paid Vacation. **Corporate headquarters location:** This Location. **Other area locations:** Secaucus NJ; Woodcliff Lake NJ. **Number of placements per year:** 1000+.

**UNITEMP TEMPORARY PERSONNEL**
50 Tice Boulevard, Woodcliff Lake NJ 07675. 201/391-3800. **Contact:** Molly Kissel, PHR, Vice President. **Description:** A temporary agency. **Corporate headquarters location:** Paramus NJ. **Other area locations:** Secaucus NJ.

**WINSTON STAFFING SERVICES**
301 Route 17 North, Rutherford NJ 07070. 201/460-9200. **Contact:** Michael A. Gallo, Vice President. **E-mail address:** info@winston-data.com. **World Wide Web address:** http://www.winston-data.com. **Description:** Winston Staffing Services is a temporary agency. **Specializes in the areas of:** Accounting/Auditing; Advertising; Banking; Computer Science/Software; Fashion; Finance; General Management; Health/Medical; Legal; Personnel/Labor Relations; Sales; Secretarial. **Positions commonly filled include:** Accountant/Auditor; Administrator; Advertising Clerk; Attorney; Blue-Collar Worker Supervisor; Brokerage Clerk; Budget Analyst; Buyer; Claim Representative; Clerical Supervisor; Clinical Lab Technician; Computer Programmer; Counselor; Credit Manager; Customer Service Representative; Dental Assistant/Dental Hygienist; Dietician/Nutritionist; EEG Technologist; EKG Technician; Emergency Medical Technician; Health Services Manager; Human Resources Specialist; Licensed Practical Nurse; Management Trainee; Manufacturer's/Wholesaler's Sales Representative; Market Research Analyst; Medical Records Technician; MIS Specialist; Multimedia Designer; Occupational Therapist; Paralegal; Pharmacist; Physical Therapist; Physician; Public Relations Specialist; Purchasing Agent/Manager; Quality Control Supervisor; Radiological Technologist; Recreational Therapist; Registered Nurse; Respiratory Therapist; Securities Sales Representative; Software Engineer; Statistician; Systems Analyst; Telecommunications Manager; Typist/Word Processor. **Benefits available to temporary workers:** Paid Vacation. **Number of placements per year:** 1000+.

# PERMANENT EMPLOYMENT AGENCIES

**A CHOICE NANNY**
637 Wyckoff Avenue, Wyckoff NJ 07481-1442. 201/891-2273. **Fax:** 201/891-1722. **Contact:** Sue Vigil, General Manager. **Description:** A Choice Nanny is a permanent employment agency. **Specializes in the areas of:** Child Care, In-Home; Nannies. **Positions commonly filled include:** Nanny. **Average salary range of placements:** Less than $25,000. **Number of placements per year:** 100 - 199.

**A CHOICE NANNY**
248 Columbia Turnpike, Building One, Florham Park NJ 07932. 973/593-9090. **Contact:** Owner.
**Description:** A permanent employment agency. **Specializes in the areas of:** Child Care, In-Home;
Nannies. **Positions commonly filled include:** Nanny. **Average salary range of placements:** Less
than $25,000. **Number of placements per year:** 100 - 199.

**A CHOICE NANNY**
27 Mountain Boulevard, Suite 9-B, Warren NJ 07059. 908/754-9090. **Contact:** General Manager.
**Description:** A permanent employment agency. **Specializes in the areas of:** Child Care, In-Home;
Nannies. **Positions commonly filled include:** Nanny. **Average salary range of placements:** Less
than $25,000. **Number of placements per year:** 100 - 199.

**A+ PERSONNEL**
1017 Broadway, Bayonne NJ 07002. 201/437-5594. **Fax:** 201/437-2914. **Contact:** Jill G. Rowland,
Vice President. **Description:** A permanent employment agency. **Specializes in the areas of:**
Accounting/Auditing; Administration; Computer Science/Software; Finance; Legal; Manufacturing;
Personnel/Labor Relations; Secretarial. **Positions commonly filled include:** Accountant/Auditor;
Advertising Clerk; Bank Officer/Manager; Blue-Collar Worker Supervisor; Brokerage Clerk;
Budget Analyst; Buyer; Chemical Engineer; Civil Engineer; Claim Representative; Clerical
Supervisor; Computer Programmer; Credit Manager; Customer Service Representative; Financial
Analyst; General Manager; Human Resources Manager; Industrial Engineer; Industrial Production
Manager; Insurance Agent/Broker; Management Analyst/Consultant; Management Trainee;
Mechanical Engineer; Operations/Production Manager; Paralegal; Public Relations Specialist;
Purchasing Agent/Manager; Quality Control Supervisor; Restaurant/Food Service Manager;
Securities Sales Representative; Software Engineer; Systems Analyst; Travel Agent;
Underwriter/Assistant Underwriter; Wholesale and Retail Buyer. **Number of placements per year:**
50 - 99.

**ABC NATIONWIDE EMPLOYMENT**
241 Main Street, Hackensack NJ 07601. 201/487-5515. **Fax:** 201/487-5591. **Contact:** Recruiter.
**Description:** A permanent employment agency. **Specializes in the areas of:** Engineering; Finance;
Legal; Manufacturing; Personnel/Labor Relations; Secretarial. **Positions commonly filled include:**
Accountant/Auditor; Civil Engineer; Clerical Supervisor; Credit Manager; Customer Service
Representative; Electrical/Electronics Engineer; Human Resources Manager; Industrial Engineer;
Mechanical Engineer; Purchasing Agent/Manager.

**ADVANCED PERSONNEL SERVICE**
1341 Hamburg Turnpike, Suite 1, Wayne NJ 07470-4042. 973/694-0303. **Fax:** 973/696-3291.
**Contact:** Daniel C. Kees, Vice President. **Description:** A permanent employment agency that also
provides some temporary placements. **Specializes in the areas of:** Accounting/Auditing;
Administration; Advertising; Banking; Economics; Finance; Food; General Management; Industrial;
Insurance; Legal; Manufacturing; Personnel/Labor Relations; Sales; Secretarial. **Positions
commonly filled include:** Accountant/Auditor; Administrative Manager; Advertising Clerk; Bank
Officer/Manager; Branch Manager; Budget Analyst; Claim Rep.; Clerical Supervisor; Credit
Manager; Customer Service Rep.; Economist; Editor; Financial Analyst; General Manager; Human
Resources Specialist; Insurance Agent/Broker; Management Trainee; Manufacturer's/Wholesaler's
Sales Rep.; Operations/Production Manager; Public Relations Specialist; Purchasing Agent/
Manager; Securities Sales Representative; Services Sales Representative; Technical Writer/Editor;
Telecommunications Manager; Transportation/Traffic Specialist; Travel Agent; Typist/Word
Processor; Underwriter/Assistant Underwriter. **Benefits available to temporary workers:** Bonus
Award/Plan; Paid Holidays; Paid Vacation. **Number of placements per year:** 200 - 499.

**RAYMOND ALEXANDER ASSOCIATES**
420 Minnisink Road, Totowa NJ 07512. **Contact:** Ray Jezierski, Recruiting Manager. **Description:**
A permanent employment agency. **Specializes in the areas of:** Accounting; Finance. **Positions
commonly filled include** Accountant/Auditor; Financial Analyst. **Average salary range of
placements:** $30,000 - $50,000. **Number of placements per year:** 100 - 199.

**ALLEN ASSOCIATES, INC.**
33 Wood Avenue South, Suite 600, Iselin NJ 08830. 732/549-7555. **Fax:** 732/549-7550. **Contact:**
Amy Regan, President. **Description:** A permanent employment agency. **Specializes in the areas of:**
Finance; Office Support; Personnel/Labor Relations; Secretarial. **Positions commonly filled
include:** Accountant/Auditor; Administrative Manager; Clerical Supervisor; Credit Manager;
Customer Service Representative; Human Resources Specialist; Management Trainee; Secretary;
Transportation/Traffic Specialist; Typist/Word Processor. **Average salary range of placements:**
$20,000 - $40,000. **Number of placements per year:** 50 - 99.

**ALLIANCE CONSULTANTS**
4 Holiday Drive, Hopatcong NJ 07843-1449. 973/398-1776. **Contact:** Rose-Ellen Horan, President. **Description:** A permanent employment agency. **Specializes in the areas of:** Administration; General Management; Personnel/Labor Relations; Sales; Secretarial. **Positions commonly filled include:** Accountant/Auditor; Administrative Manager; Claim Representative; Clerical Supervisor; Computer Programmer; General Manager; Human Resources Specialist; Insurance Agent/Broker; Manufacturer's/Wholesaler's Sales Rep.; Paralegal; Typist/Word Processor. **Average salary range of placements:** $30,000 - $50,000. **Number of placements per year:** 1 - 49.

**AMERICAN STAFFING RESOURCES**
Lawrenceville Office Park, Suite 2, 168 Franklin County Road, Lawrenceville NJ 08648. 609/219-1011. **Toll-free phone:** 800/AMS-TAF9. **Fax:** 609/219-1411. **Contact:** Dee-Dee Ward, Branch Supervisor. **Description:** A permanent employment agency that also provides some temporary placements. **Specializes in the areas of:** Accounting; Administration; Industrial; Information Technology; Light Industrial; MIS/EDP; Office Support; Scientific; Secretarial; Technical. **Positions commonly filled include:** Accountant; Administrative Assistant; Blue-Collar Worker Supervisor; Chief Financial Officer; Computer Operator; Computer Programmer; Controller; Cost Estimator; Customer Service Representative; Editorial Assistant; Human Resources Manager; Secretary; Typist/Word Processor. **Benefits available to temporary workers:** Bonus Award/Plan; Legal Services; Medical Insurance; Paid Holidays; Tuition Assistance; Vacation Pay. **Corporate headquarters location:** Feasterville PA. **Other U.S. locations:** Fairless Hills PA; Philadelphia PA; Willow Grove PA. **Average salary range of placements:** $20,000 - $29,999. **Number of placements per year:** 500 - 999.

**ARDEN ASSOCIATES**
1605 John Street, Fort Lee NJ 07024. 201/346-0414. **Contact:** Manager. **Description:** A permanent employment agency. **Specializes in the areas of:** Office Support.

**BAI PERSONNEL SOLUTIONS, INC.**
One Independence Way, Princeton NJ 08540. 609/734-9631. **Fax:** 609/734-9637. **Contact:** Leigh Clayton, President. **Description:** A permanent employment agency that also conducts executive searches and provides some temporary placements. **Specializes in the areas of:** Accounting; Administration; Advertising; Banking; Broadcasting; Computer Science/Software; Economics; Finance; Health/Medical; Insurance; Legal; MIS/EDP; Nonprofit; Personnel/Labor Relations; Printing; Publishing; Sales; Scientific; Secretarial; Technical. **Positions commonly filled include:** Account Manager; Account Rep.; Administrative Assistant; Administrative Manager; Assistant Manager; Auditor; Bank Officer/Manager; Branch Manager; Broadcast Technician; Budget Analyst; Chief Financial Officer; Claim Rep.; Clerical Supervisor; Computer Operator; Computer Programmer; Controller; Cost Estimator; Credit Manager; Customer Service Rep.; Database Manager; Editor; Editorial Assistant; Finance Director; Financial Analyst; General Manager; Graphic Artist; Graphic Designer; Human Resources Manager; Internet Services Manager; Librarian; Management Analyst/Consultant; Managing Editor; Marketing Manager; Marketing Specialist; MIS Specialist; Multimedia Designer; Operations Manager; Paralegal; Public Relations Specialist; Purchasing Agent/Manager; Radio/TV Announcer/Broadcaster; Reporter; Sales Executive; Sales Manager; Sales Rep.; Secretary; Software Engineer; Statistician; Systems Analyst; Systems Manager; Technical Writer/Editor; Telecommunications Manager; Typist/Word Processor; Underwriter/Assistant Underwriter; Video Production Coordinator; Webmaster. **Number of placements per year:** 100 - 199.

**BERMAN & LARSON**
12 Route 17 North, Suite 209, Paramus NJ 07652. 201/262-9200. **Toll-free phone:** 800/640-0126. **Fax:** 201/262-7060. **Contact:** Bob Larson, CPC, President. **E-mail address:** jobsbl@cybernex.com. **World Wide Web address:** http://www.jobsbl.com. **Description:** A permanent employment agency. **Specializes in the areas of:** Computer Science/Software; Industrial; Information Systems. **Positions commonly filled include:** Computer Programmer; Internet Services Manager; MIS Specialist; Software Engineer; Systems Analyst; Technical Writer/Editor. **Benefits available to temporary workers:** 401(k); Medical Insurance. **Number of placements per year:** 200 - 499.

**CPS TECHNICAL PLACEMENTS**
10 North Gaston Avenue, Somerville NJ 08876. 908/704-1770. **Fax:** 908/704-1554. **Contact:** Robert Fisher, Technical Employment Specialist. **Description:** A permanent employment agency that also provides some temporary placements. **Specializes in the areas of:** Biology; Engineering; Food; Pharmaceuticals. **Positions commonly filled include:** Biochemist; Biological Scientist; Biomedical Engineer; Chemical Engineer; Chemist; Clinical Lab Technician; Computer Operator;

Computer Programmer; Electrician; Food Scientist/Technologist; MIS Specialist; Pharmacist; Quality Control Supervisor; Technical Writer/Editor. **Number of placements per year:** 50 - 99.

**CAPITOL SEARCH**
215 East Ridgewood Avenue, Ridgewood NJ 07450. 201/444-6666. **Fax:** 201/444-4121. **Contact:** Bob Sanders, Owner. **Description:** A permanent employment agency. **Specializes in the areas of:** Child Care, In-Home; Domestic Help; Eldercare, In-Home; Nannies. **Positions commonly filled include:** Computer Graphics Specialist; Domestic Help. **Number of placements per year:** 100 - 199.

**CAREER CENTER, INC.**
P.O. Box 1036, Hackensack NJ 07601. 201/342-1777. **Toll-free phone:** 800/227-3379. **Fax:** 201/342-1776. **Contact:** Sandra Franzino, CIS, Vice President. **Description:** A permanent employment agency that also provides some temporary placements. **Specializes in the areas of:** Accounting/Auditing; Administration; Advertising; Banking; Clerical; Communications; Computer Science/Software; Engineering; Fashion; Finance; Insurance; Manufacturing; Personnel/Labor Relations; Sales; Technical. **Positions commonly filled include:** Accountant/Auditor; Administrative Manager; Bank Officer/Manager; Customer Service Representative; Data Entry Clerk; Draftsperson; EDP Specialist; Electrical/Electronics Engineer; Financial Analyst; Human Resources Manager; Industrial Designer; Industrial Engineer; Legal Secretary; Marketing Specialist; Mechanical Engineer; Medical Secretary; Metallurgical Engineer; Mining Engineer; MIS Specialist; Operations/Production Manager; Petroleum Engineer; Purchasing Agent/Manager; Quality Control Supervisor; Receptionist; Sales Representative; Secretary; Stenographer; Systems Analyst; Technician; Typist/Word Processor; Underwriter/Assistant Underwriter. **Benefits available to temporary workers:** 401(k); Medical Insurance; Paid Holidays; Paid Vacation. **Number of placements per year:** 1000+.

**CAREERNET PERSONNEL CONSULTANTS**
515 Highway 70, Brick NJ 08723. 732/920-5555. **Contact:** Manager. **Description:** A permanent employment agency. **Specializes in the areas of:** Office Support; Technical.

**CAREERS FIRST, INC.**
305 U.S. Route 130, Cinnaminson NJ 08077-3398. 609/786-0004. **Contact:** Gail Duncan, President. **Description:** A permanent employment agency. **Specializes in the areas of:** Administration; Computer Hardware/Software; Technical.

**CAREERS USA**
533 North Evergreen Avenue, Woodbury NJ 08096. 609/384-1600. **Fax:** 609/384-1310. **Contact:** Carla Janoff, President/Owner. **Description:** A permanent employment agency. **Specializes in the areas of:** Accounting/Auditing; Administration; Computer Science/Software; General Management; Industrial; Manufacturing; Personnel/Labor Relations; Secretarial; Technical. **Positions commonly filled include:** Administrative Manager; Blue-Collar Worker Supervisor; Claim Representative; Clerical Supervisor; Customer Service Representative; Draftsperson; Editor; Financial Analyst; Human Resources Specialist; Industrial Production Manager; MIS Specialist; Operations/Production Manager; Paralegal; Purchasing Agent/Manager; Quality Control Supervisor; Typist/Word Processor. **Benefits available to temporary workers:** Paid Holidays; Paid Vacation. **Average salary range of placements:** $20,000 - $29,999.

**CASTLE CAREERS INC.**
141 South Avenue, Fanwood NJ 07023. 908/322-9140. **Contact:** Manager. **Description:** A permanent employment agency. **Specializes in the areas of:** Office Support.

**CENTRAL TECHNICAL SERVICE INC.**
389 Main Street, Hackensack NJ 07601. 201/342-0055. **Contact:** Manager. **Description:** A permanent employment agency. **Specializes in the areas of:** Engineering; Technical.

**CITIZENS EMPLOYMENT SERVICES, INC.**
One Magnolia Avenue, Montvale NJ 07645. 201/391-5144. **Fax:** 201/391-4477. **Contact:** Elaine Larfier, Manager. **Description:** A permanent employment agency. **Specializes in the areas of:** Banking; Clerical; Computer Science/Software; Industrial; Insurance; Manufacturing; Retail; Sales. **Positions commonly filled include:** Accountant/Auditor; Actuary; Bank Officer/Manager; Bookkeeper; Chemical Engineer; Claim Representative; Computer Operator; Computer Programmer; Credit Manager; Customer Service Representative; Data Entry Clerk; Draftsperson; EDP Specialist; Electrical/Electronics Engineer; Industrial Production Manager; Insurance Agent/Broker; Legal Secretary; Mechanical Engineer; Operations/Production Manager; Purchasing Agent/Manager; Quality Control Supervisor; Sales Representative; Secretary; Stenographer;

Systems Analyst; Technician; Travel Agent; Typist/Word Processor; Underwriter/Assistant Underwriter. **Other area locations:** Parsippany NJ. **Average salary range of placements:** $30,000 - $50,000. **Number of placements per year:** 1000+.

### GLENN DAVIS ASSOCIATES
P.O. Box 1, Ironian NJ 07845. 973/895-4242. **Contact:** Manager. **Description:** A permanent employment agency. **Specializes in the areas of:** Computer Science/Software. **Positions commonly filled include:** MIS Specialist. **Number of placements per year:** 50 - 99.

### EXECUTIVE SOFTWARE PLUS
24 Lyons Place, Westwood NJ 07675. 201/666-5484. **Fax:** 201/664-0693. **Contact:** Claire Monte, Vice President. **E-mail address:** exsoft@aol.com. **Description:** A permanent employment agency. **Specializes in the areas of:** Computer Science/Software. **Positions commonly filled include:** Computer Programmer; Systems Analyst.

### EXPRESS PERSONNEL SERVICES
2569 State Route 10, Morris Plains NJ 07950. 973/898-1001. **Fax:** 973/898-1005. **Contact:** Marianne Kemp, Operations Manager. **Description:** A permanent employment agency that also conducts executive searches and provides some temporary placements. **Specializes in the areas of:** Accounting/Auditing; Administration; Advertising; Computer Hardware/Software; Engineering; General Management; Industrial; Legal; Manufacturing; Publishing; Sales; Secretarial; Technical. **Positions commonly filled include:** Accountant/Auditor; Administrative Manager; Advertising Clerk; Blue-Collar Worker Supervisor; Claim Representative; Clerical Supervisor; Computer Programmer; Customer Service Representative; Design Engineer; Designer; Draftsperson; Editor; Electrical/Electronics Engineer; Electrician; General Manager; Human Resources Specialist; Management Trainee; Manufacturer's/Wholesaler's Sales Rep.; MIS Specialist; Paralegal; Quality Control Supervisor; Software Engineer; Typist/Word Processor. **Benefits available to temporary workers:** Medical Insurance; Paid Vacation. **Corporate headquarters location:** Oklahoma City OK. **Average salary range of placements:** $20,000 - $29,999. **Number of placements per year:** 500 - 999.

### GRAHAM FOSTER ASSOCIATES
One GreenTree Center, Suite 201, Marlton NJ 08053. 609/795-8282. **Fax:** 609/772-6296. **Contact:** Manager. **Description:** A permanent employment agency. **Specializes in the areas of:** Computer Science/Software. **Positions commonly filled include:** Computer Operator; Computer Programmer; Database Manager; Internet Services Manager; MIS Specialist; Project Manager; Software Engineer; Systems Analyst; Systems Manager; Telecommunications Manager; Webmaster. **Average salary range of placements:** More than $50,000.

### G.A. AGENCY
524 South Avenue East, Cranford NJ 07016. 908/272-2080. **Fax:** 908/272-2962. **Contact:** Mrs. Randy Ring, Manager. **Description:** A permanent employment agency. **Specializes in the areas of:** Education. **Positions commonly filled include:** Education Administrator; Teacher/Professor. **Other U.S. locations:** Nationwide. **Average salary range of placements:** $30,000 - $50,000. **Number of placements per year:** 200 - 499.

### HALLMARK PERSONNEL INC.
140 Route 17 North, Suite 302, Paramus NJ 07652. 201/261-9010. **Contact:** Manager. **Description:** A permanent employment agency.

### HORIZON GRAPHICS PERSONNEL
110 Cornelia Street, Boonton NJ 07005. 973/263-2126. **Fax:** 973/263-4601. **Contact:** John DeSalvo, Vice President. **Description:** A permanent employment agency that also provides some temporary placements. **Specializes in the areas of:** Advertising; Art/Design; Fashion; Health/Medical; Publishing; Retail. **Positions commonly filled include:** Advertising Account Executive; Computer Animator; Desktop Publishing Specialist; Draftsperson; Editor; Editorial Assistant; Graphic Artist; Graphic Designer; Librarian; Multimedia Designer; Proofreader; Technical Writer/Editor; Video Production Coordinator; Webmaster; Writer. **Benefits available to temporary workers:** Paid Holidays; Paid Vacation. **Corporate headquarters location:** This Location. **Average salary range of placements:** $30,000 - $50,000. **Number of placements per year:** 100 - 199.

### HUGHES & PODESLA PERSONNEL INC.
281 East Main Street, Somerville NJ 08876. 908/231-0880. **Contact:** Paul Podesla, President. **Description:** A permanent employment agency. **Specializes in the areas of:** Accounting/Auditing; Engineering; Finance; General Management; Industrial; Manufacturing; Personnel/Labor Relations;

Sales; Technical. **Positions commonly filled include:** Accountant/Auditor; Biomedical Engineer; Budget Analyst; Buyer; Credit Manager; Customer Service Representative; Design Engineer; Draftsperson; Electrical/Electronics Engineer; Financial Analyst; General Manager; Human Resources Manager; Industrial Engineer; Industrial Production Manager; Mechanical Engineer; Operations/Production Manager; Purchasing Agent/Manager; Quality Control Supervisor; Transportation/Traffic Specialist. **Number of placements per year:** 1 - 49.

**HUNT, LTD.**
1050 Wall Street West, Suite 330, Lyndhurst NJ 07071. 201/438-8200. **Fax:** 201/438-8372. **Contact:** Alex Metz, President. **E-mail address:** huntltd@bellatlantic.net. **World Wide Web address:** http://www.huntltd.com. **Description:** A permanent employment agency that also provides some temporary placements. Founded in 1965. **Specializes in the areas of:** Distribution; Logistics. **Positions commonly filled include:** Industrial Engineer; Logistics Manager; Logistics Support Worker; Management Analyst/Consultant; Transportation/Traffic Specialist; Warehouse Manager. **Corporate headquarters location:** This Location. **Other U.S. locations:** Nationwide. **Average salary range of placements:** More than $50,000. **Number of placements per year:** 100 - 199.

**IMPACT PERSONNEL, INC.**
1901 North Olden Avenue, Suite 26A, Ewing NJ 08618. 609/406-1200. **Contact:** Manager. **Description:** A permanent employment agency. **Specializes in the areas of:** Accounting/Auditing; Administration; Advertising; Banking; Computer Hardware/Software; Engineering; Fashion; Finance; Food; General Management; Health/Medical; Industrial; Insurance; Legal; Manufacturing; Publishing; Retail; Sales; Secretarial; Technical. **Positions commonly filled include:** Accountant/Auditor; Administrative Assistant; Bookkeeper; Chemical Engineer; Claim Representative; Clerk; Commercial Artist; Computer Operator; Computer Programmer; Customer Service Representative; Data Entry Clerk; Driver; Electrical/Electronics Engineer; Factory Worker; Hotel Manager; Industrial Designer; Industrial Engineer; Legal Secretary; Light Industrial Worker; Mechanical Engineer; Medical Secretary; Quality Control Supervisor; Receptionist; Recruiter; Sales Representative; Secretary; Software Engineer; Technician; Typist/Word Processor. **Number of placements per year:** 500 - 999.

**INFOSYSTEMS PLACEMENT SERVICES**
17 Holmes Lane, Marlton NJ 08053-1911. 609/596-7770. **Fax:** 609/596-7772. **Contact:** Joe Dougherty, Owner. **E-mail address:** jadips@aol.com. **World Wide Web address:** http://www.infoplacement.com. **Description:** A permanent employment agency. **Specializes in the areas of:** Administration; Computer Science/Software. **Positions commonly filled include:** Computer Operator; Computer Programmer; Database Manager; Internet Services Manager; MIS Specialist; Project Manager; Software Engineer; Systems Analyst; Systems Manager; Telecommunications Manager. **Average salary range of placements:** More than $50,000. **Number of placements per year:** 1 - 49.

**JOULE STAFFING SERVICES**
2333 Whitehorse-Mercerville Road, Trenton NJ 08619. 609/588-5900. **Fax:** 609/588-9642. **Contact:** Jeanine Smith, Manager. **Description:** A permanent employment agency. **Specializes in the areas of:** Accounting/Auditing; Education; Engineering; Industrial; Legal; Manufacturing; Personnel/Labor Relations; Secretarial; Technical. **Positions commonly filled include:** Accountant/Auditor; Administrative Manager; Blue-Collar Worker Supervisor; Claim Representative; Clerical Supervisor; Computer Programmer; Counselor; Customer Service Representative; Human Resources Specialist; Management Trainee; Typist/Word Processor. **Benefits available to temporary workers:** Incentive Plan; Medical Insurance; Paid Holidays; Paid Vacation. **Corporate headquarters location:** Edison NJ. **Other U.S. locations:** Nationwide. **Average salary range of placements:** $20,000 - $29,999. **Number of placements per year:** 1000+.

**JOSEPH KEYES ASSOCIATES**
275 Forest Avenue, Paramus NJ 07652. 201/261-7400. **Fax:** 201/261-4836. **Contact:** Ed Michaels, Vice President. **Description:** A permanent employment agency that also provides some temporary placements and career/outplacement counseling. **Specializes in the areas of:** Accounting/Auditing; Engineering; Finance; Industrial; Manufacturing; Publishing. **Positions commonly filled include:** Accountant/Auditor; Administrative Manager; Blue-Collar Worker Supervisor; Broadcast Technician; Budget Analyst; Buyer; Ceramics Engineer; Claim Representative; Clerical Supervisor; Credit Manager; Customer Service Rep.; Design Engineer; Designer; Draftsperson; Electrical/Electronics Engineer; Environmental Engineer; Financial Analyst; Human Resources Specialist; Industrial Engineer; Industrial Production Manager; Materials Engineer; Mechanical Engineer; Metallurgical Engineer; Purchasing Agent/Manager; Quality Control Supervisor; Services Sales Rep.; Software Engineer; Technical Writer/Editor; Transportation/Traffic Specialist. **Average salary range of placements:** $30,000 - $50,000. **Number of placements per year:** 50 - 99.

## MAYFAIR SERVICES

372 Buffalo Avenue, Paterson NJ 07503. 973/742-0990. **Fax:** 973/742-0991. **Contact:** Merry Costello, Owner. **Description:** A permanent employment agency that also provides some temporary placements. **Specializes in the areas of:** Administration; Art/Design; Biology; Computer Hardware/Software; Engineering; General Management; Health/Medical; Industrial; Manufacturing; Personnel/Labor Relations; Publishing; Technical; Transportation. **Positions commonly filled include:** Aerospace Engineer; Agricultural Engineer; Aircraft Mechanic/Engine Specialist; Architect; Biochemist; Biological Scientist; Biomedical Engineer; Blue-Collar Worker Supervisor; Buyer; Chemical Engineer; Chemist; Civil Engineer; Clinical Lab Technician; Construction and Building Inspector; Customer Service Representative; Design Engineer; Designer; Draftsperson; Electrical/Electronics Engineer; Electrician; Environmental Engineer; General Manager; Health Services Manager; Human Resources Specialist; Industrial Engineer; Industrial Production Manager; Library Technician; Management Trainee; Mathematician; Mechanical Engineer; Medical Records Technician; Metallurgical Engineer; MIS Specialist; Multimedia Designer; Nuclear Engineer; Nuclear Medicine Technologist; Occupational Therapist; Operations/Production Manager; Pharmacist; Quality Control Supervisor; Science Technologist; Software Engineer; Stationary Engineer; Structural Engineer; Typist/Word Processor; Veterinarian. **Average salary range of placements:** $20,000 - $29,999. **Number of placements per year:** 200 - 499.

## MINI CONGLOMERATE SERVICE

P.O. Box 7811, Atlantic City NJ 08404-7811. 609/348-2299. **Contact:** Tom Murphy, President. **Description:** A permanent employment agency. **Specializes in the areas of:** Advertising; Broadcasting; Entertainment; General Management; Sales. **Positions commonly filled include:** Management Trainee; Travel Agent. **Average salary range of placements:** Less than $20,000. **Number of placements per year:** 1 - 49.

## NANNIES PLUS

520 Speedwell Avenue, Suite 114, Morris Plains NJ 07950-2132. **Toll-free phone:** 800/752-0078. **Fax:** 973/285-5055. **Contact:** Consultant. **Description:** A permanent employment agency that provides placements for live-in child care professionals. **Specializes in the areas of:** Child Care, In-Home. **Positions commonly filled include:** Nanny. **Average salary range of placements:** Less than $20,000. **Number of placements per year:** 200 - 499.

## NEIGHBORHOOD NANNIES

5 Haddon Avenue, Haddonfield NJ 08033. 609/795-5833. **Contact:** Celia Sarajian, Executive Director. **Description:** A permanent employment agency that also provides career/outplacement counseling. **Specializes in the areas of:** Child Care, In-Home; Eldercare, In-Home; Nannies. **Positions commonly filled include:** Nanny. **Number of placements per year:** 50 - 99.

## OFFICEMATES5 OF ENGLEWOOD CLIFFS, INC.
## DAYSTAR TEMPORARY SERVICES

560 Sylvan Avenue, Englewood Cliffs NJ 07632. 201/871-2203. **Fax:** 201/871-1116. **Contact:** Alice Eckstein, President. **Description:** A permanent employment agency. DayStar Temporary Services (also at this location) provides temporary placements. **Specializes in the areas of:** Accounting/Auditing; Administration; Advertising; Banking; Computer Science/Software; Economics; Finance; General Management; Insurance; Legal; Personnel/Labor Relations; Publishing; Sales; Secretarial; Transportation. **Positions commonly filled include:** Accountant/Auditor; Administrative Manager; Advertising Clerk; Bank Officer/Manager; Branch Manager; Brokerage Clerk; Budget Analyst; Buyer; Claim Representative; Clerical Supervisor; Computer Programmer; Cost Estimator; Credit Manager; Customer Service Representative; Financial Analyst; General Manager; Hotel Manager; Human Resources Specialist; Human Service Worker; Management Analyst/Consultant; Market Research Analyst; MIS Specialist; Paralegal; Public Relations Specialist; Purchasing Agent/Manager; Quality Control Supervisor; Securities Sales Representative; Services Sales Representative; Systems Analyst; Typist/Word Processor; Underwriter/Assistant Underwriter; Video Production Coordinator. **Number of placements per year:** 50 - 99.

## OMNI STAFFING SERVICES GROUP

15 Bleeker Street, Millburn NJ 07041. 973/379-4900. **Toll-free phone:** 800/321-6663. **Contact:** Manager. **Description:** A permanent employment agency. **Corporate headquarters location:** This Location.

## PARK AVENUE PERSONNEL

41 Park Avenue, Rutherford NJ 07070-1713. 201/939-1911. **Fax:** 201/939-3555. **Contact:** Mary Falzarano, President/Owner. **Description:** A permanent employment agency. **Specializes in the areas of:** Accounting/Auditing; Banking; Finance; Personnel/Labor Relations; Sales; Secretarial.

**Positions commonly filled include:** Accountant/Auditor; Administrative Manager; Clerical Supervisor; Financial Analyst; Human Resources Manager. **Average salary range of placements:** $30,000 - $50,000. **Number of placements per year:** 1 - 49.

**THE PERSONNEL GROUP**
**ARTHUR JAMES & ASSOCIATES INC.**
P.O. Box 4582, Warren NJ 07059. 908/754-6000. **Contact:** Manager. **Description:** A permanent employment agency. Arthur James & Associates (also at this location) specializes in placing personnel in the field of solid waste management.

**PERSONNEL PLUS**
**TEMPS PLUS**
500 State Route 17 South, Hasbrouck Heights NJ 07604-3121. 201/288-7800. **Fax:** 201/288-7995. **Contact:** Judi Stewart, Placement Consultant. **Description:** A permanent employment agency. Temps Plus (also at this location) provides temporary placements. **Specializes in the areas of:** Accounting/Auditing; Clerical; Marketing; Personnel/Labor Relations; Sales. **Positions commonly filled include:** Account Representative; Accountant/Auditor; Administrative Assistant; Administrative Manager; Advertising Clerk; Clerical Supervisor; Controller; Credit Manager; Customer Service Representative; Financial Analyst; Human Resources Manager; Human Resources Specialist; Paralegal; Purchasing Agent/Manager; Sales Executive; Sales Manager; Sales Representative; Secretary; Services Sales Representative; Transportation/Traffic Specialist; Typist/Word Processor. **Average salary range of placements:** $30,000 - $50,000. **Number of placements per year:** 200 - 499.

**POMERANTZ PERSONNEL**
1375 Plainfield Avenue, Watchung NJ 07060. 908/757-5300. **Toll-free phone:** 800/754-7000. **Fax:** 908/757-0144. **Contact:** Keith Grade, Corporate Director. **World Wide Web address:** http://www.pomerantzstaffing.com. **Description:** A permanent employment agency. **Specializes in the areas of:** Accounting/Auditing; Administration; Banking; Computer Hardware/Software; Food; General Management; Industrial; Light Industrial; Personnel/Labor Relations; Retail; Sales; Secretarial. **Positions commonly filled include:** Account Manager; Account Representative; Administrative Assistant; Advertising Clerk; Assistant Manager; Blue-Collar Worker Supervisor; Branch Manager; Buyer; Chemical Engineer; Chemist; Chief Financial Officer; Claim Representative; Clerical Supervisor; Credit Manager; Customer Service Representative; Database Manager; Design Engineer; Draftsperson; Editorial Assistant; Electrical/Electronics Engineer; Electrician; Finance Director; Financial Analyst; Food Scientist/Technologist; General Manager; Graphic Artist; Human Resources Manager; Industrial Engineer; Internet Services Manager; Management Analyst/Consultant; Management Trainee; Manufacturing Engineer; Marketing Manager; Mechanical Engineer; MIS Specialist; Operations Manager; Paralegal; Production Manager; Project Manager; Public Relations Manager; Purchasing Agent/Manager; Quality Control Supervisor; Sales Executive; Sales Manager; Sales Representative; Secretary; Software Engineer; Systems Analyst; Systems Manager; Technical Writer/Editor; Typist/Word Processor. **Corporate headquarters location:** This Location. **Other U.S. locations:** Nationwide. **Average salary range of placements:** $20,000 - $50,000. **Number of placements per year:** 200 - 499.

**PREMIER PERSONNEL GROUP, INC.**
10 Woodbridge Center Drive, Woodbridge NJ 07095. 732/750-5600. **Fax:** 732/750-9787. **Contact:** Robert C. Walsh, Senior Recruiter. **Description:** A permanent employment agency. **Specializes in the areas of:** Accounting/Auditing; Advertising; Banking; Finance; Legal; Marketing; Personnel/Labor Relations; Sales; Secretarial. **Positions commonly filled include:** Account Representative; Accountant; Administrative Assistant; Claim Representative; Computer Operator; Database Manager; Human Resources Manager; Sales Engineer; Sales Representative; Secretary. **Corporate headquarters location:** This Location. **Average salary range of placements:** $20,000 - $29,999. **Number of placements per year:** 200 - 499.

**QUALITY DOMESTICS, INC.**
484 Bloomfield Avenue, 2nd Floor, Suite 7, Montclair NJ 07042-3417. 973/509-7376. **Contact:** Lewis Ross, President. **Description:** A permanent employment agency focusing on the placement of home health care professionals. **Average salary range of placements:** Less than $20,000. **Number of placements per year:** 100 - 199.

**RSVP SERVICES**
P.O. Box 8369, Cherry Hill NJ 08002-0369. 609/667-4488. **Toll-free phone:** 800/222-0153. **Contact:** Howard Levin, Director. **E-mail address:** hl@rsvpjobs.com. **World Wide Web address:** http://www.rsvpjobs.com. **Description:** A permanent employment agency. **Specializes in the areas of:** Administration; Computer Hardware/Software; Electrical; Electronics.

**READY PERSONNEL/READY TEMPS**
Harborside Financial Center, 145 Plaza 2, Jersey City NJ 07311. 201/434-1800. **Fax:** 201/434-0900. **Contact:** Denise Arthur, Owner. **Description:** A permanent employment agency. **Specializes in the areas of:** Accounting/Auditing; Finance.

**RECRUITMENT ALTERNATIVES, INC.**
York House East, P.O. Box 554, Moorestown NJ 08057. 609/273-1066. **Contact:** Thomas J. Jaskel, Senior Vice President. **Description:** A permanent employment agency. **Specializes in the areas of:** Personnel/Labor Relations. **Positions commonly filled include:** Human Resources Manager; Recruiter. **Number of placements per year:** 1 - 49.

**S-H-S OF CHERRY HILL**
929 North Kings Highway, Cherry Hill NJ 08034. 609/779-9030. **Fax:** 609/779-0898. **Contact:** Account Manager. **Description:** A permanent employment agency. **Specializes in the areas of:** Accounting/Auditing; Administration; Engineering; Human Resources; Insurance; Manufacturing; Office Support. **Positions commonly filled include:** Accountant/Auditor; Biomedical Engineer; Chemical Engineer; Chemist; Credit Manager; Electrical/Electronics Engineer; Financial Analyst; Human Resources Manager; Mechanical Engineer; Petroleum Engineer; Physical Therapist; Underwriter/Assistant Underwriter.

**SCIENTIFIC SEARCH, INC.**
560 Fellowship Road, Suite 309, Mount Laurel NJ 08054. 609/866-0200. **Fax:** 609/722-5307. **Contact:** Robert I. Greenberg, President. **E-mail address:** ssi0200@scisearch.com. **Description:** A permanent employment agency. **Specializes in the areas of:** Computer Science/Software; Health/Medical. **Positions commonly filled include:** AS400 Programmer Analyst; Computer Programmer; Computer Technical Support; Database Administrator; Database Manager; Health Services Manager; Internet Services Manager; MIS Specialist; Network/Systems Administrator; Software Engineer; SQL Programmer; Systems Analyst. **Average salary range of placements:** $50,000 - $100,000. **Number of placements per year:** 100 - 199.

**SELECTIVE PERSONNEL**
288 Summerhill Road, East Brunswick NJ 08816. 732/432-9500. **Contact:** Manager. **Description:** A permanent employment agency. **Specializes in the areas of:** Accounting/Auditing; Administration; Banking; Clerical; Computer Hardware/Software; Engineering; Finance; Health/Medical; Insurance; Legal; Manufacturing; Personnel/Labor Relations; Sales; Technical.

**ARLINE SIMPSON ASSOCIATES, INC.**
114 Essex Street, Rochelle Park NJ 07662. 201/843-1414. **Toll-free phone:** 800/843-1691. **Fax:** 201/843-6483. **Contact:** Arline Simpson, President. **Description:** Arline Simpson Associates, Inc. is a permanent employment agency that also provides some temporary placements. **Specializes in the areas of:** Accounting/Auditing; Administration; Advertising; Banking; Computer Science/Software; Engineering; Finance; Insurance; Legal; Publishing; Retail; Sales; Secretarial; Technical. **Positions commonly filled include:** Accountant/Auditor; Administrative Assistant; Bookkeeper; Buyer; Chemist, Computer Programmer; Credit Manager; Customer Service Representative; Designer; Draftsperson; Food Scientist/Technologist, Industrial Engineer; Legal Secretary; Manufacturer's/Wholesaler's Sales Rep.; Manufacturing Engineer; Mechanical Engineer; MIS Specialist; Paralegal; Receptionist; Sales Representative; Securities Sales Representative; Systems Analyst; Typist/Word Processor. **Average salary range of placements:** $20,000 - $29,999. **Number of placements per year:** 200 - 499.

**SNELLING PERSONNEL SERVICES**
5425 Route 70, Pennsauken NJ 08109. 609/662-5424. **Contact:** Chris Deegler, Owner/Manager. **Description:** Snelling Personnel Services is a permanent employment agency. **Specializes in the areas of:** Accounting/Auditing; Banking; Clerical; Finance; Food; Health/Medical; Personnel/Labor Relations; Sales.

**SOURCE ONE PERSONNEL**
133 Franklin Corner Road, Lawrenceville NJ 08648. 609/895-0895. **Fax:** 609/895-0574. **Contact:** Manager. **Description:** Source One Personnel is a permanent employment agency. **Specializes in the areas of:** Accounting/Auditing; Retail; Sales. **Positions commonly filled include:** Accountant/Auditor; Budget Analyst; Computer Programmer; Customer Service Representative; Internet Services Manager; MIS Specialist; Paralegal; Services Sales Representative; Software Engineer; Typist/Word Processor. **Benefits available to temporary workers:** Paid Holidays; Paid Vacation. **Average salary range of placements:** $20,000 - $29,999. **Number of placements per year:** 200 - 499.

## SOURCE ONE PERSONNEL
2490 Brunswick Pike, Suite 202, Lawrenceville NJ 08648. 609/883-3000. **Fax:** 609/883-8344. **Contact:** Linda Vallyo, Branch Manager. **Description:** A permanent employment agency. **Specializes in the areas of:** Accounting/Auditing; Retail; Sales. **Positions commonly filled include:** Accountant/Auditor; Budget Analyst; Computer Programmer; Customer Service Representative; Internet Services Manager; MIS Specialist; Paralegal; Services Sales Representative; Software Engineer; Typist/Word Processor. **Benefits available to temporary workers:** Paid Holidays; Paid Vacation. **Average salary range of placements:** $20,000 - $29,999. **Number of placements per year:** 200 - 499.

## SOURCE SERVICES CORPORATION
## A BUSINESS OF ROMAC INTERNATIONAL
15 Essex Road, Suite 201, Paramus NJ 07652. 201/843-2020. **Fax:** 201/843-7705. **Contact:** Branch Manager. **Description:** A permanent employment agency. **Specializes in the areas of:** Accounting/Auditing; Administration; Banking; Computer Science/Software; Engineering; Finance; Health/Medical; Legal; Manufacturing. **Positions commonly filled include:** Accountant/Auditor; Attorney; Budget Analyst; Computer Programmer; Credit Manager; Financial Analyst; Licensed Practical Nurse; MIS Specialist; Registered Nurse; Software Engineer. **Benefits available to temporary workers:** Profit Sharing. **Corporate headquarters location:** Dallas TX. **Other U.S. locations:** Nationwide. **Number of placements per year:** 1000+.

## ULTIMATE SOLUTIONS, INC.
154 West Passaic Street, Rochelle Park NJ 07662. 201/909-3717. **Fax:** 201/587-0772. **Contact:** Owner. **E-mail address:** jobs@ultimatesolutions.com. **World Wide Web address:** http://www.ultimatesolutions.com. **Description:** A permanent employment agency. **Specializes in the areas of:** Computer Science/Software; Scientific; Technical. **Positions commonly filled include:** Computer Programmer; Database Manager; MIS Specialist; Systems Analyst; Systems Manager; Telecommunications Manager. **Corporate headquarters location:** This Location. **Average salary range of placements:** More than $50,000. **Number of placements per year:** 200 - 499.

## DON WALDRON & ASSOCIATES
220 North Centre Street, Merchantville NJ 08109. 609/663-5151. **Contact:** Manager. **Description:** A permanent employment agency. **Specializes in the areas of:** Sales.

## WINTERS & ROSS
442 Main Street, Fort Lee NJ 07024. 201/947-8400. **Fax:** 201/947-1035. **Contact:** Marilyn Winters, Vice President. **Description:** Winters & Ross is a permanent employment agency focusing on the placement of office support personnel. **Specializes in the areas of:** Accounting/Auditing; Bilingual; Clerical; Finance; Legal; Personnel/Labor Relations; Secretarial. **Positions commonly filled include:** Accountant/Auditor; Administrative Assistant; Bookkeeper; Clerical Supervisor; Computer Programmer; Credit Manager; Customer Service Representative; Data Entry Clerk; EDP Specialist; Financial Analyst; Human Resources Specialist; Legal Secretary; Management Trainee; Receptionist; Secretary; Stenographer; Typist/Word Processor. **Average salary range of placements:** $20,000 - $29,999. **Number of placements per year:** 100 - 199.

## CLAIRE WRIGHT ASSOCIATES
1280 U.S. Highway 46, Parsippany NJ 07054-4911. 973/402-8400. **Fax:** 973/402-8519. **Contact:** K. Kelley, Counselor. **Description:** A permanent employment agency. **Specializes in the areas of:** Accounting/Auditing; Administration; Advertising; Computer Hardware/Software; Engineering; Finance; Insurance; Legal; Manufacturing; Sales; Technical. **Positions commonly filled include:** Accountant/Auditor; Advertising Clerk; Chemical Engineer; Claim Representative; Computer Programmer; Draftsperson; Electrical/Electronics Engineer; Environmental Engineer; Financial Analyst; Human Resources Specialist; Industrial Engineer; Insurance Agent/Broker; Internet Services Manager; Market Research Analyst; Mechanical Engineer; Metallurgical Engineer; MIS Specialist; Nuclear Engineer; Paralegal; Property and Real Estate Manager; Purchasing Agent/Manager; Securities Sales Representative; Software Engineer; Technical Writer/Editor; Telecommunications Manager; Typist/Word Processor; Underwriter/Assistant Underwriter. **Average salary range of placements:** $30,000 - $50,000. **Number of placements per year:** 1 - 49.

## YOURS IN TRAVEL PERSONNEL AGENCY, INC.
301 Route 17 North, Suite 800, Rutherford NJ 07070. 201/438-3500. **Contact:** Robyn Hering, Vice President. **Description:** Yours in Travel Personnel Agency, Inc. is a permanent employment agency. **Specializes in the areas of:** Travel. **Positions commonly filled include:** Travel Agent.

# EXECUTIVE SEARCH FIRMS

**AV SEARCH CONSULTANTS**
674 Route 202/206, Bridgewater NJ 08807. 908/429-7800. **Contact:** Carl Risino, Manager. **Description:** An executive search firm. **Specializes in the areas of:** Legal.

**ABBOTT ASSOCIATES INC.**
1099 Wall Street West, Lyndhurst NJ 07071. 201/804-8100. **Contact:** Manager. **Description:** An executive search firm. **Specializes in the areas of:** Accounting/Auditing; Finance.

**ABLE CAREERS**
240 West Passaic Street, Maywood NJ 07607. 201/845-7771. **Contact:** Manager. **Description:** An executive search firm.

**ACCESS SYSTEMS**
101 Gibraltar Drive, Suite 2F, Morris Plains NJ 07950-1287. 973/984-7960. **Fax:** 973/984-7963. **Contact:** Joanne Palzer, President. **Description:** An executive search firm operating on a contingency basis. The firm places high-level sales and technical sales support professionals. **Specializes in the areas of:** Computer Science/Software; Data Communications; Sales. **Positions commonly filled include:** Manufacturer's/Wholesaler's Sales Rep.; Services Sales Rep.. **Average salary range of placements:** More than $50,000. **Number of placements per year:** 1 - 49.

**ACCOUNTANTS EXECUTIVE SEARCH**
**ACCOUNTANTS ON CALL**
80 Route 4 East, Suite 230, Paramus NJ 07652. 201/368-9200. **Contact:** Manager. **Description:** An executive search firm. Accountants On Call (also at this location) offers temporary placements. **Specializes in the areas of:** Accounting/Auditing; Banking; Finance.

**ACCOUNTANTS EXECUTIVE SEARCH**
**ACCOUNTANTS ON CALL**
379 Thornall Street, Edison NJ 08837. 732/906-1100. **Contact:** Manager. **Description:** An executive search firm. Accountants On Call (also at this location) offers temporary placements, primarily for entry-level positions. **Specializes in the areas of:** Accounting/Auditing.

**ACCOUNTANTS EXECUTIVE SEARCH**
**ACCOUNTANTS ON CALL**
354 Eisenhower Parkway, Plaza One, 2nd Floor, Livingston NJ 07039. 973/533-0600. **Contact:** Manager. **Description:** An executive search firm. Accountants On Call (also at this location) offers temporary placements. **Specializes in the areas of:** Accounting/Auditing; Finance.

**ACCOUNTANTS PROFESSIONAL SEARCH**
114 Essex Street, Rochelle Park NJ 07662. 201/288-2888. **Contact:** Manager. **Description:** An executive search firm. **Specializes in the areas of:** Accounting/Auditing.

**ADEL-LAWRENCE ASSOCIATES**
1208 Highway 34, Suite 18, Aberdeen NJ 07747. 732/566-4914. **Fax:** 732/566-9326. **Contact:** Larry Radzely, President. **Description:** An executive search firm. **Specializes in the areas of:** Computer Science/Software; Engineering; Health/Medical; Technical. **Positions commonly filled include:** Biomedical Engineer; Clinical Lab Technician; Design Engineer; Electrical/Electronics Engineer; Mechanical Engineer; MIS Specialist; Software Engineer; Systems Analyst; Telecommunications Manager. **Average salary range of placements:** More than $50,000. **Number of placements per year:** 200 - 499.

**ADVANCE POSITIONS INC.**
9 South Main Street, Marlboro NJ 07746. 732/577-1122. **Contact:** President. **Description:** An executive search firm. **Specializes in the areas of:** Food; General Management; Logistics; Retail; Transportation. **Positions commonly filled include:** Buyer; Distribution Manager; Industrial Engineer; Logistics Manager; Operations/Production Manager; Purchasing Agent/Manager; Transportation/Traffic Specialist. **Number of placements per year:** 1 - 49.

**ADVANCED TECHNICAL SEARCH**
414 Eagle Rock Avenue, Suites 302-306, West Orange NJ 07052. 973/669-0400. **Contact:** Manager. **Description:** An executive search firm. **Specializes in the areas of:** Wireless Communications.

**ALLEN ASSOCIATES**
128 Elliot Place, South Plainfield NJ 07080. 908/753-3751. **Contact:** Manager. **Description:** An executive search firm.

**DAVID ALLEN ASSOCIATES**
P.O. Box 56, Haddonfield NJ 08033-0048. 609/795-6470. **Fax:** 609/795-0175. **Contact:** David Ritchings, Partner. **E-mail address:** david.allen.search@worldnet.att.net. **World Wide Web address:** http://www.allendavid.qpg.com. **Description:** An executive search firm operating on both retainer and contingency bases. Founded in 1980. **Specializes in the areas of:** Banking; Food; General Management. **Positions commonly filled include:** Account Manager; Account Rep.; Bank Officer/Manager; Budget Analyst; Chemical Engineer; Chief Financial Officer; Controller; Credit Manager; Economist; Finance Director; Financial Analyst; Fund Manager; General Manager; Human Resources Manager; Management Analyst/Consultant; Market Research Analyst; Marketing Manager; Marketing Specialist; Sales Representative; Securities Sales Representative. **Corporate headquarters location:** This Location. **Other U.S. locations:** Nationwide. **Average salary range of placements:** More than $50,000. **Number of placements per year:** 50 - 99.

**FRANK ALLEN & ASSOCIATES**
15 James Street, Florham Park NJ 07932. 973/966-1606. **Contact:** Manager. **Description:** An executive search firm. **Specializes in the areas of:** Human Resources.

**ALTA ASSOCIATES, INC.**
8 Bartles Corner Road, Suite 21, Flemington NJ 08822. 908/806-8442. **Fax:** 908/806-8443. **Contact:** Joyce Brocaglia, Vice President. **Description:** An executive search firm. **Specializes in the areas of:** Computer Hardware/Software. **Positions commonly filled include:** Computer Programmer; Database Manager; EDP Specialist; MIS Specialist. **Number of placements per year:** 50 - 99.

**ANDERSON WRIGHT ASSOCIATES**
375 Johnson Avenue Annex, Englewood NJ 07631. 201/567-8080. **Contact:** Manager. **Description:** An executive search firm. **Specializes in the areas of:** Finance; Pharmaceuticals.

**ANDOS ASSOCIATES INC.**
2 Stone House Road, Mendham NJ 07945. 201/934-7766. **Contact:** Manager. **Description:** An executive search firm. **Specializes in the areas of:** Pharmaceuticals.

**R.W. APPLE & ASSOCIATES**
P.O. Box 200, Manasquan NJ 08736. 732/223-4305. **Fax:** 732/223-4325. **Contact:** Richard Apple, Owner. **Description:** An executive search firm operating on a retainer basis. R.W. Apple & Associates focuses on the environmental science and engineering consulting industries. **Specializes in the areas of:** Environmental. **Positions commonly filled include:** Chemical Engineer; Civil Engineer; Environmental Engineer; Geologist/Geophysicist. **Average salary range of placements:** More than $50,000. **Number of placements per year:** 1 - 49.

**THE ASCHER GROUP**
7 Becker Farm Road, Roseland NJ 07068. 973/597-1900. **Contact:** Personnel. **Description:** An executive search firm that also provides some temporary placements. **Specializes in the areas of:** Accounting/Auditing; Finance; Personnel/Labor Relations; Secretarial. **Positions commonly filled include:** Accountant/Auditor; Bank Officer/Manager; Budget Analyst; Credit Manager; EKG Technician; Financial Analyst; Human Resources Specialist; Purchasing Agent/Manager; Typist/Word Processor. **Number of placements per year:** 1000+.

**ASSURANCE GROUP**
P.O. Box 465, Morris Plains NJ 07950. 973/538-7594. **Contact:** Manager. **Description:** An executive search firm. **Specializes in the areas of:** Health/Medical.

**ASSURANCE GROUP**
**ASSURANCE HEALTH CARE SERVICES**
25 East Spring Valley Avenue, Maywood NJ 07607. 201/845-4461. **Contact:** Manager. **Description:** An executive search firm. Assurance Health Care Services (also at this location) provides home health care placements. **Specializes in the areas of:** Health/Medical.

**BALCOR ASSOCIATES**
P.O. Box 873, Union City NJ 07087. 201/854-2525. **Contact:** Manager. **Description:** An executive search firm. **Specializes in the areas of:** Accounting/Auditing; Consumer Package Goods; Finance; Human Resources; Manufacturing.

**BARCLAY CONSULTANTS**
201 Union Lane, Brielle NJ 08730. 732/223-1131. **Contact:** Manager. **Description:** An executive search firm that specializes in placing computer sales professionals. **Specializes in the areas of:** Sales.

**R.P. BARONE ASSOCIATES**
P.O. Box 706, Allenwood NJ 08720-0706. 732/292-0900. **Contact:** L. Donald Rizzo, President. **Description:** An executive search firm operating on both retainer and contingency bases. **Specializes in the areas of:** Engineering; Manufacturing; Marketing. **Positions commonly filled include:** Architect; Biochemist; Biomedical Engineer; Chemical Engineer; Chemist; Civil Engineer; Construction and Building Inspector; Cost Estimator; Design Engineer; Draftsperson; Electrical/Electronics Engineer; Environmental Engineer; Food Scientist/Technologist; General Manager; Industrial Engineer; Industrial Production Manager; Market Research Analyst; Mechanical Engineer; Metallurgical Engineer; Operations/Production Manager; Purchasing Agent/Manager; Science Technologist; Structural Engineer. **Average salary range of placements:** More than $50,000. **Number of placements per year:** 1 - 49.

**GARY S. BELL ASSOCIATES, INC.**
55 Harristown Road, Glen Rock NJ 07452. 201/670-4900. **Fax:** 201/670-4940. **Contact:** Gary S. Bell, President. **E-mail address:** gsbassoc@aol.com. **Description:** An executive search firm. **Specializes in the areas of:** Biology; Biotechnology; Chemicals; Clinical Research; Engineering; Environmental; General Management; Health/Medical; Manufacturing; Pharmaceuticals. **Positions commonly filled include:** Biochemist; Biological Scientist; Biomedical Engineer; Chemical Engineer; Chemist; Computer Programmer; Design Engineer; Electrical/Electronics Engineer; Licensed Practical Nurse; Market Research Analyst; Mechanical Engineer; MIS Specialist; Pharmacist; Physician; Purchasing Agent/Manager; Quality Control Supervisor; Registered Nurse; Respiratory Therapist; Software Engineer; Statistician; Systems Analyst. **Average salary range of placements:** More than $50,000. **Number of placements per year:** 50 - 99.

**BESEN ASSOCIATES**
115 Route 46 West, Suite 25, Mountain Lakes NJ 07046. 973/334-5533. **Contact:** Manager. **Description:** An executive search firm. **Specializes in the areas of:** Pharmaceuticals.

**BLAIR ASSOCIATES**
210 Summit Avenue, Montvale NJ 07645. 201/573-0900. **Contact:** Manager. **Description:** An executive search firm.

**BLAKE & ASSOCIATES EXECUTIVE SEARCH**
P.O. Box 1425, Pleasantville NJ 08232-6425. 609/645-3330. **Fax:** 609/383-0320. **Contact:** Ed Blake, President. **Description:** An executive search firm. **Specializes in the areas of:** Accounting/Auditing; Administration; Advertising; Architecture/Construction; Art/Design; Banking; Biology; Computer Science/Software; Economics; Engineering; Finance; Food; General Management; Health/Medical; Industrial; Insurance; Legal; Manufacturing; Personnel/Labor Relations; Publishing; Retail; Sales; Secretarial. **Positions commonly filled include:** Accountant/Auditor; Actuary; Adjuster; Administrative Manager; Agricultural Engineer; Agricultural Scientist; Architect; Attorney; Bank Officer/Manager; Biological Scientist; Biomedical Engineer; Branch Manager; Brokerage Clerk; Budget Analyst; Buyer; Chemical Engineer; Chemist; Civil Engineer; Claim Representative; Clerical Supervisor; Collector; Computer Programmer; Construction and Building Inspector; Construction Contractor; Cost Estimator; Credit Manager; Customer Service Representative; Dental Lab Technician; Dentist; Dietician/Nutritionist; Draftsperson; EEG Technologist; EKG Technician; Electrical/Electronics Engineer; Electrician; Financial Analyst; Food Scientist/Technologist; General Manager; Geologist/Geophysicist; Health Services Manager; Human Resources Manager; Human Service Worker; Industrial Engineer; Industrial Production Manager; Insurance Agent/Broker; Investigator; Landscape Architect; Management Trainee; Manufacturer's/Wholesaler's Sales Rep.; Materials Engineer; Mechanical Engineer; Medical Records Technician; Metallurgical Engineer; Mining Engineer; Nuclear Engineer; Nuclear Medicine Technologist; Occupational Therapist; Paralegal; Petroleum Engineer; Physical Therapist; Property and Real Estate Manager; Public Relations Specialist; Purchasing Agent/Manager; Quality Control Supervisor; Radiological Technologist; Real Estate Agent; Recreational Therapist; Respiratory Therapist; Restaurant/Food Service Manager; Science Technologist; Securities Sales Representative; Services Sales Representative; Software Engineer; Speech-Language Pathologist; Stationary Engineer; Statistician; Structural Engineer; Surgical Technician; Surveyor; Systems Analyst; Technical Writer/Editor; Transportation/Traffic Specialist; Travel Agent; Underwriter/Assistant Underwriter; Urban/Regional Planner; Wholesale and Retail Buyer. **Number of placements per year:** 50 - 99.

## BONIFIELD ASSOCIATES
One Eves Drive, Suite 115, Marlton NJ 08053. 609/596-3300. **Fax:** 609/596-8866. **Contact:** Richard Tyson, President. **E-mail address:** info@bonifield.com. **World Wide Web address:** http://www.bonifield.com. **Description:** An executive search firm operating on a contingency basis. **Specializes in the areas of:** Banking; Insurance. **Positions commonly filled include:** Accountant/Auditor; Actuary; Attorney; Bank Officer/Manager; Claim Representative; Insurance Agent/Broker; Underwriter/Assistant Underwriter. **Average salary range of placements:** More than $50,000. **Number of placements per year:** 50 - 99.

## BOWMAN & COMPANY LLP
601 White Horse Road, Voorhees NJ 08043. 609/782-2891. **Fax:** 609/435-0440. **Contact:** Steven M. Packer, CPA, Manager. **E-mail address:** bhrc@bowmanllp.com. **World Wide Web address:** http://www.bowmanllp.com. **Description:** An executive search firm that also provides contract services. Founded in 1997. **Specializes in the areas of:** Accounting/Auditing; Finance. **Positions commonly filled include:** Accountant; Auditor; Budget Analyst; Chief Financial Officer; Computer Operator; Computer Programmer; Consultant; Controller; Finance Director; Financial Analyst; Fund Manager; MIS Specialist; Systems Analyst; Systems Manager; Vice President of Finance. **Benefits available to temporary workers:** 401(k); Disability Coverage; Flexible Schedule; Life Insurance; Medical Insurance. **Corporate headquarters location:** This Location.

## BRETT ASSOCIATES
2184 Morris Avenue, Union NJ 07083. 908/687-7772. **Contact:** Manager. **Description:** An executive search firm. **Specializes in the areas of:** Manufacturing.

## BROAD WAVERLY & ASSOCIATES
P.O. Box 741, 200 Broad Street, Red Bank NJ 07701. 732/747-4400. **Contact:** Manager. **Description:** An executive search firm. **Specializes in the areas of:** Accounting/Auditing; Insurance; Light Industrial; Technical.

## BROOKDALE SEARCH ASSOCIATES
P.O. Box 1293, Bloomfield NJ 07003. 973/338-0515. **Fax:** 973/338-1242. **Contact:** Manager. **Description:** An executive search firm. **Specializes in the areas of:** Electrical; Electronics; Heating, Air Conditioning, and Refrigeration; Technical.

## BUTTERFASS PEPE & McCALLAN
P.O. Box 721, Mahwah NJ 07430. 201/512-3330. **Contact:** Manager. **Description:** An executive search firm. **Specializes in the areas of:** Investment.

## CFB ASSOCIATES
94 Washington Street, Paterson NJ 07505. 973/881-8284. **Contact:** Manager. **Description:** An executive search firm. **Positions commonly filled include:** Biochemist.

## CAPITAL FINANCE RECRUITING
321 Commercial Avenue, Suite 220, Palisades Park NJ 07650. 201/585-8444. **Contact:** Manager. **Description:** An executive search firm. **Specializes in the areas of:** Administration; Data Processing.

## CAPSTONE ASSOCIATES
33 Wood Avenue South, 5th Floor, Iselin NJ 08830. 732/906-1300. **Contact:** Manager. **Description:** An executive search firm. **Specializes in the areas of:** Computer Hardware/Software.

## CAREER MANAGEMENT GROUP, LLC
434 Ridgedale Avenue, Suite 11-165, East Hanover NJ 07936. 973/428-5239. **Fax:** 973/428-5084. **Contact:** Toni Donofrio, Managing Member. **E-mail address:** careermanage@msn.com. **Description:** An executive search firm. **Specializes in the areas of:** Accounting; Administration; Computer Science/Software; Engineering; Finance; General Management; Marketing; Personnel/ Labor Relations; Sales; Secretarial. **Positions commonly filled include:** Account Manager; Accountant; Administrative Assistant; Administrative Manager; Applications Engineer; Auditor; Budget Analyst; Chemical Engineer; Computer Operator; Computer Programmer; Customer Service Rep.; Database Manager; Design Engineer; Electrical/Electronics Engineer; Environmental Engineer; Financial Analyst; General Manager; Human Resources Manager; Industrial Engineer; Management Trainee; Manufacturing Engineer; Marketing Manager; Mechanical Engineer; MIS Specialist; Operations Manager; Purchasing Agent/Manager; Sales Engineer; Sales Executive; Sales Manager; Sales Rep.; Secretary; Software Engineer; Systems Analyst; Technical Writer/Editor; Telecommunications Manager; Transportation/Traffic Specialist. **Average salary range of placements:** More than $50,000. **Number of placements per year:** 50 - 99.

**CAREER MANAGEMENT INTERNATIONAL**
197 Route 18, Suite 102, East Brunswick NJ 08816. 732/937-4800. **Fax:** 732/937-4770. **Contact:** Karen Geipel, Assistant to the President. **Description:** An executive search firm operating on a retainer basis. **Specializes in the areas of:** Fashion; Finance; General Management; Personnel/ Labor Relations; Retail; Sales. **Positions commonly filled include:** Administrative Manager; Buyer; Credit Manager; Designer; Human Resources Manager; Management Analyst/Consultant; MIS Specialist; Operations/Production Manager. **Average salary range of placements:** More than $50,000. **Number of placements per year:** 50 - 99.

**CAREERS ON TRACK**
P.O. Box 222, Tenafly NJ 07670. 201/894-0600. **Fax:** 201/894-0563. **Contact:** Gary Tabor, Owner. **E-mail address:** tabortrak@aol.com. **Description:** An executive search firm. **Specializes in the areas of:** Sales. **Positions commonly filled include:** General Manager; Management Analyst/Consultant; Marketing Manager. **Average salary range of placements:** More than $50,000. **Number of placements per year:** 1 - 49.

**CAREERWORKS**
520 Main Street, Suite 302, Fort Lee NJ 07024-4501. 201/592-1460. **Contact:** Mark Raskin, President. **E-mail address:** careerw@aol.com. **Description:** An executive search firm operating on a contingency basis. **Specializes in the areas of:** Accounting/Auditing; Administration; Engineering; Finance; General Management; Manufacturing; Personnel/Labor Relations; Sales. **Positions commonly filled include:** Accountant/Auditor; Financial Analyst; General Manager; Hotel Manager; Operations/Production Manager; Restaurant/Food Service Manager; Transportation/Traffic Specialist. **Number of placements per year:** 50 - 99.

**CARTER McKENZIE INC.**
300 Executive Drive, Suite 250, West Orange NJ 07052-3303. 973/736-7100. **Fax:** 973/736-9416. **Contact:** John Capo, Vice President. **E-mail address:** jcapo@carter-mckenzie.com. **World Wide Web address:** http://www.carter-mckenzie.com. **Description:** An executive search firm operating on both retainer and contingency bases. **Specializes in the areas of:** Administration; Computer Science/Software. **Positions commonly filled include:** Computer Programmer; MIS Specialist; Software Engineer; Systems Analyst; Telecommunications Manager. **Average salary range of placements:** More than $50,000. **Number of placements per year:** 100 - 199.

**CARTER/MACKAY PERSONNEL INC.**
777 Terrace Avenue, Hasbrouck Heights NJ 07604. 201/288-5100. **Fax:** 201/288-2660. **Contact:** Bruce Green, Vice President. **E-mail address:** cartmackay@aol.com. **World Wide Web address:** http://www.cartermackay.com. **Description:** An executive search firm. **Specializes in the areas of:** Computer Hardware/Software; Computer Science/Software; Data Communications; Health/ Medical; Pharmaceuticals; Sales; Technical. **Positions commonly filled include:** General Manager; Manufacturer's/Wholesaler's Sales Rep.; Marketing Manager; Sales Manager; Systems Analyst. **Other U.S. locations:** Framingham MA; Cary NC; Great Neck NY. **Average salary range of placements:** More than $50,000.

**L. CAVALIERE & ASSOCIATES**
2300 State Route 27, North Brunswick NJ 08902. 732/940-3100. **Fax:** 732/940-2266. **Contact:** Louis Cavaliere, Managing Director. **Description:** An executive search firm operating on both retainer and contingency bases. **Specializes in the areas of:** MIS/EDP. **Positions commonly filled include:** Computer Programmer; Management Analyst/Consultant; Software Engineer; Systems Analyst. **Average salary range of placements:** More than $50,000. **Number of placements per year:** 1 - 49.

**CERTIFIED PERSONNEL CORPORATION**
P.O. Box 36, Berkeley Heights NJ 07922. 908/322-0404. **Fax:** 908/322-1738. **Contact:** Peter Gilbert, Managing Partner. **E-mail address:** peter_gilbert@notes.interliant.com. **World Wide Web address:** http://www.certifiedpersonnel.com. **Description:** An executive search firm operating on a contingency basis. Certified Personnel Corporation focuses on placing Lotus Notes developers and administrators with international banks and financial institutions, large insurance companies, consulting organizations, and various *Fortune* 500 companies. **Positions commonly filled include:** Computer Programmer; MIS Specialist; Systems Analyst. **Average salary range of placements:** More than $50,000.

**CHRISTENSON HUTCHISON & McDOWELL**
466 Southern Boulevard, Chatham NJ 07928. 973/966-1600. **Contact:** Manager. **Description:** An executive search firm.

## CHURCHILL & HARRIMAN, INC.
244 Wall Street, Princeton NJ 08540. 609/921-3551. **Fax:** 609/921-1061. **Contact:** Kenneth J. Peterson, Principal. **Description:** An executive search firm that also provides information technology consulting services on a per diem basis. **Specializes in the areas of:** Administration; Computer Science/Software. **Positions commonly filled include:** Computer Programmer; Systems Analyst. **Average salary range of placements:** More than $50,000. **Number of placements per year:** 50 - 99.

## COMPUTER EASE
1301 Monmouth Avenue, Lakewood NJ 08701. 732/370-7148. **Contact:** Manager. **Description:** An executive search firm. **Positions commonly filled include:** Computer Programmer; Systems Analyst.

## CORPORATE INFORMATION SYSTEMS INC.
71 Union Avenue, Rutherford NJ 07070. 201/896-0600. **Contact:** Manager. **Description:** An executive search firm. **Specializes in the areas of:** Information Technology.

## COX DARROW & OWENS, INC.
6 East Clementon Road, Suite E4, Gibbsboro NJ 08026-1199. 609/782-1300. **Fax:** 609/782-7277. **Contact:** Bob Darrow, Vice President/Partner. **Description:** An executive search firm operating on a contingency basis. **Specializes in the areas of:** Banking; Engineering; Industrial; Manufacturing; Mortgage; Personnel/Labor Relations; Sales; Technical. **Positions commonly filled include:** Chemical Engineer; Chemist; Electrical/Electronics Engineer; Human Resources Manager; Mechanical Engineer; Purchasing Agent/Manager; Quality Control Supervisor; Telecommunications Manager. **Other U.S. locations:** Nationwide. **Average salary range of placements:** $30,000 - $50,000. **Number of placements per year:** 50 - 99.

## D'ANDREA ASSOCIATES INC.
296 Amboy Avenue, Metuchen NJ 08840. 732/906-0110. **Fax:** 732/906-0116. **Contact:** Nick D'Andrea, President. **Description:** An executive search firm. **Specializes in the areas of:** Banking; General Management. **Positions commonly filled include:** Bank Officer/Manager; Financial Analyst; Fund Manager; General Manager; Human Resources Manager; Sales Executive; Sales Manager; Sales Rep.. **Average salary range of placements:** More than $50,000. **Number of placements per year:** 1 - 49.

## DATA HUNTERS, INC.
P.O. Box 884, Ramsey NJ 07446-0884. 201/825-1368. **Fax:** 201/327-4234. **Contact:** Bette Rosenfeld, President. **E-mail address:** datahunt@nis.net. **Description:** An executive search firm. **Specializes in the areas of:** Computer Science/Software; Data Processing. **Positions commonly filled include:** Computer Programmer; Internet Services Manager; MIS Specialist; Software Engineer; Systems Analyst; Telecommunications Manager.

## DATA SEARCH NETWORK
P.O. Box 305, Emerson NJ 07630. 201/967-8600. **Contact:** Manager. **Description:** An executive search firm. **Specializes in the areas of:** Information Systems.

## THE DATAFINDERS GROUP, INC.
25 East Spring Valley Avenue, Maywood NJ 07607. 201/845-7700. **Fax:** 201/845-7365. **Contact:** Thomas J. Credidio, Vice President. **E-mail address:** postmaster@data-finders.com. **World Wide Web address:** http://www.data-finders.com. **Description:** An executive search firm. **Specializes in the areas of:** Computer Science/Software; MIS/EDP; Sales. **Positions commonly filled include:** Computer Programmer; EDP Specialist; Manufacturer's/Wholesaler's Sales Rep.; Services Sales Representative; Software Engineer; Systems Analyst. **Number of placements per year:** 200 - 499.

## CLARK DAVIS ASSOCIATES
7 Century Drive, Parsippany NJ 07054. 973/267-5511. **Contact:** Manager. **Description:** An executive search firm. **Specializes in the areas of:** Accounting/Auditing; Engineering; Information Systems.

## DEAN-WHARTON ASSOCIATES
166 West End Avenue, Somerville NJ 08876. 908/231-1818. **Contact:** Manager. **Description:** An executive search firm. **Specializes in the areas of:** Human Resources.

## M.T. DONALDSON ASSOCIATES, INC.
4400 Route 9 South, Suite 1000, Freehold NJ 07728. 732/303-7890. **Fax:** 732/303-6440. **Contact:** Sol Premisler, President. **Description:** An executive search firm. **Specializes in the areas of:**

Engineering; Food; Health/Medical; Industrial; Manufacturing; Personnel/Labor Relations. **Positions commonly filled include:** Chemical Engineer; Chemist; Food Scientist/Technologist; Industrial Engineer; Industrial Production Manager; Mechanical Engineer; Pharmacist; Purchasing Agent/Manager; Quality Control Supervisor. **Average salary range of placements:** More than $50,000. **Number of placements per year:** 1 - 49.

**DOUGLAS ASSOCIATES INC.**
158 Linwood Plaza, Suite 214, Fort Lee NJ 07024. 201/363-6500. **Fax:** 201/363-6550. **Contact:** Ms. Tobey Klein, President. **Description:** An executive search firm. **Specializes in the areas of:** Retail. **Positions commonly filled include:** Buyer; Human Resources Specialist. **Average salary range of placements:** $30,000 - $50,000. **Number of placements per year:** 50 - 99.

**DOW-TECH**
1700 Route 23 North, Suite 100, Wayne NJ 07470. 973/696-8000. **Fax:** 973/696-1964. **Contact:** Chris Dowling, President. **Description:** An executive search firm. **Specializes in the areas of:** Electrical; Electronics; Sales. **Positions commonly filled include:** Electrical/Electronics Engineer; Marketing Manager; Marketing Specialist; Sales and Marketing Manager; Sales Engineer; Sales Manager; Sales Representative. **Number of placements per year:** 50 - 99.

**DREIER CONSULTING**
P.O. Box 356, Ramsey NJ 07446. 201/327-1113. **Fax:** 201/327-0816. **Contact:** Jennifer Hernandez, Administrative Assistant. **E-mail address:** dreiercslt@mindspring.com. **World Wide Web address:** http://www.dreierconsulting.com. **Description:** An executive search firm operating on a contingency basis. **Specializes in the areas of:** Computer Science/Software; Engineering; Manufacturing; Medical Technology; Sales; Telecommunications. **Positions commonly filled include:** Biomedical Engineer; Design Engineer; Electrical/Electronics Engineer; General Manager; Graphic Designer; Industrial Engineer; Manufacturing Engineer; Marketing Manager; Marketing Specialist; Mechanical Engineer; MIS Specialist; Operations Manager; Production Manager; Project Manager; Sales Engineer; Sales Executive; Software Engineer; Systems Analyst; Systems Manager; Telecommunications Manager; Vice President of Marketing; Vice President of Sales. **Corporate headquarters location:** This Location. **Average salary range of placements:** More than $50,000. **Number of placements per year:** 1 - 49.

**DUNHILL PERSONNEL OF CHERRY HILL, INC.**
1040 North Kings Highway, Suite 400, Cherry Hill NJ 08034. 609/667-9180. **Contact:** Bill Emerson, Owner. **Description:** An executive search firm operating on a contingency basis that also provides some temporary placements. **Specializes in the areas of:** Office Support. **Positions commonly filled include:** Administrative Assistant; Clerical Supervisor; Secretary.

**DUNHILL PROFESSIONAL SEARCH**
303 West Main Street, Freehold NJ 07728. 732/431-2700. **Fax:** 732/431-0329. **Contact:** Rich Hanson, President. **Description:** An executive search firm. **Specializes in the areas of:** Accounting/Auditing; Banking; Finance; Secretarial. **Positions commonly filled include:** Accountant/Auditor; Administrative Assistant; Bookkeeper; Budget Analyst; Economist; EDP Specialist; Executive Assistant; Financial Analyst; Legal Secretary; Receptionist; Secretary; Typist/Word Processor. **Number of placements per year:** 1 - 49.

**DUNHILL PROFESSIONAL SEARCH**
393 State Route 202, Oakland NJ 07436-2744. 201/337-2200. **Fax:** 201/337-3445. **Contact:** Roger Lippincott, President. **E-mail address:** dsramnj@dunhillstaff.com. **Description:** An executive search firm. **Specializes in the areas of:** Personnel/Labor Relations; Sales. **Positions commonly filled include:** Human Resources Specialist; Manufacturer's/Wholesaler's Sales Rep.; Sales Rep.; Training Manager. **Average salary range of placements:** More than $50,000.

**DYNAMIC RECRUITERS INC.**
59 East Mill Road, Box 16, Long Valley NJ 07853. 908/876-8420. **Contact:** Manager. **Description:** An executive search firm. **Specializes in the areas of:** Aerospace; Industrial; Pharmaceuticals; Plastics. **Benefits available to temporary workers:** Accident/Emergency Insurance.

**EAGLE RESEARCH INC.**
373-D Route 46 West, Fairfield NJ 07004. 973/244-0992. **Fax:** 973/244-1239. **Contact:** Annette S. Baron, PA, President. **E-mail address:** asbaron@aol.com. **Description:** An executive search firm operating on both retainer and contingency bases. **Specializes in the areas of:** Biotechnology; Pharmaceuticals. **Positions commonly filled include:** Physician. **Average salary range of placements:** More than $50,000. **Number of placements per year:** 1 - 49.

**ELECTRONIC SEARCH INC.**
P.O. Box 506, Bradley Beach NJ 07720. 732/775-5017. **Fax:** 732/775-5035. **Contact:** Tom Manni, Regional Manager. **E-mail address:** tmanni@electronicsearch.com. **World Wide Web address:** http://www.electronicsearch.com. **Description:** An executive search firm operating on both retainer and contingency bases. **Specializes in the areas of:** Engineering; Wireless Communications. **Positions commonly filled include:** Applications Engineer; Electrical/Electronics Engineer; Sales Engineer; Software Engineer; Telecommunications Manager. **Corporate headquarters location:** Rolling Meadows IL. **Other U.S. locations:** Solona Beach CA. **Average salary range of placements:** More than $50,000. **Number of placements per year:** 100 - 199.

**ELIAS ASSOCIATES**
P.O. Box 396, East Brunswick NJ 08816. 732/390-4600. **Contact:** Manager. **Description:** An executive search firm.

**ELLIS CAREER CONSULTANTS**
1090 Broadway, West Long Branch NJ 07764. 732/222-5333. **Fax:** 732/222-2332. **Contact:** Lisa Shapiro, President. **Description:** An executive search firm for the retail industry. **Specializes in the areas of:** Accounting/Auditing; Advertising; Distribution; Engineering; Finance; Food; General Management; Industrial; Manufacturing; Personnel/Labor Relations; Retail; Sales; Transportation. **Positions commonly filled include:** Accountant/Auditor; Branch Manager; Buyer; Computer Programmer; Credit Manager; Customer Service Rep.; Engineer; Financial Analyst; General Manager; Manufacturer's/Wholesaler's Sales Rep.; Restaurant/Food Service Manager; Retail Manager; Systems Analyst; Transportation/Traffic Specialist; Wholesale and Retail Buyer. **Number of placements per year:** 50 - 99.

**EXECUTIVE EXCHANGE CORPORATION**
2517 Highway 35, Suite G-103, Manasquan NJ 08736. 732/223-6655. **Fax:** 732/223-1162. **Contact:** Elizabeth B. Glosser, Owner. **Description:** An executive search firm that operates on a contingency basis and focuses on the placement of computer-related sales professionals. Executive Exchange Corporation is also a member of Nationwide Interchange, a national job search network of recruiters. **Specializes in the areas of:** Sales. **Positions commonly filled include:** Account Manager; Marketing Manager; Recruiter; Services Sales Representative. **Average salary range of placements:** $30,000 - $50,000. **Number of placements per year:** 100 - 199.

**EXECUTIVE RECRUITERS, INC.**
855 Valley Road, Clifton NJ 07013. 973/471-7878. **Contact:** Manager. **Description:** An executive search firm specializing in the placement of insurance personnel.

**EXECUTIVE REGISTRY INC.**
12 Route 17 North, Paramus NJ 07652. 201/587-1010. **Contact:** Manager. **Description:** An executive search firm. **Specializes in the areas of:** Information Systems; Retail.

**EXECUTIVE SEARCH, INC.**
48 Headquarters Plaza, Morristown NJ 07960. 973/538-2300. **Contact:** Recruitment Coordinator. **Description:** An executive search firm. **Specializes in the areas of:** Accounting/Auditing; Administration; Banking; Finance; General Management; Insurance; Legal; Personnel/Labor Relations; Sales; Secretarial. **Positions commonly filled include:** Accountant/Auditor; Administrative Manager; Attorney; Bank Officer/Manager; Branch Manager; Claim Rep.; Clerical Supervisor; Credit Manager; Customer Service Rep.; Editor; Financial Analyst; General Manager; Health Services Manager; Human Resources Manager; Insurance Agent/Broker; Management Analyst/Consultant; Management Trainee; Manufacturer's/Wholesaler's Sales Rep.; Operations/Production Manager; Paralegal; Property and Real Estate Manager; Psychologist; Public Relations Specialist; Purchasing Agent/Manager; Securities Sales Rep.; Services Sales Representative, Technical Writer/Editor; Underwriter/Assistant Underwriter; Wholesale and Retail Buyer.

**FOLEY PROCTOR YOSKOWITZ**
One Cattano Avenue, Morristown NJ 07960. 973/605-1000. **Fax:** 973/605-1020. **Contact:** Richard W. Proctor, Partner. **Description:** An executive search firm. **Specializes in the areas of:** Health/Medical; Physician Executive. **Positions commonly filled include:** Administrator; Chief Executive Officer; Physician; Physician Assistant. **Other U.S. locations:** New York NY. **Average salary range of placements:** More than $50,000. **Number of placements per year:** 50 - 99.

**F-O-R-T-U-N-E PERSONNEL CONSULTANTS**
350 West Passaic Street, Rochelle Park NJ 07662. 201/843-7621. **Fax:** 201/843-8189. **Contact:** Manager. **Description:** An executive search firm operating on both retainer and contingency bases. **Specializes in the areas of:** Biotechnology; General Management; Materials; Medical Technology;

Pharmaceuticals. **Corporate headquarters location:** New York NY. **Other U.S. locations:** Nationwide.

## F-O-R-T-U-N-E PERSONNEL CONSULTANTS OF MENLO PARK
16 Bridge Street, Metuchen NJ 08840. 732/494-6266. **Fax:** 732/494-5669. **Contact:** Peter Provda, President. **Description:** An executive search firm. **Specializes in the areas of:** Engineering; Food; Manufacturing; Personnel/Labor Relations; Technical. **Positions commonly filled include:** Biochemist; Biological Scientist; Biomedical Engineer; Buyer; Chemical Engineer; Chemist; Computer Programmer; Designer; Electrical/Electronics Engineer; Food Scientist/Technologist; Human Resources Manager; Industrial Engineer; Mechanical Engineer; Operations/Production Manager; Purchasing Agent/Manager; Quality Control Supervisor; Science Technologist; Software Engineer; Systems Analyst; Transportation/Traffic Specialist. **Corporate headquarters location:** New York NY. **Other U.S. locations:** Nationwide. **Number of placements per year:** 1 - 49.

## FOSTER ASSOCIATES
The Livery, 209 Cooper Avenue, Upper Montclair NJ 07043. 973/746-2800. **Contact:** Manager. **Description:** An executive search firm. **Specializes in the areas of:** Accounting/Auditing; Consulting; Finance; Legal.

## THE FOSTER McKAY GROUP
30 Vreeland Road, Florham Park NJ 07932. 973/966-0909. **Fax:** 973/966-6925. **Contact:** Allen Galorenzo, Partner. **World Wide Web address:** http://www.hrm-inc.com. **Description:** An executive search firm operating on both retainer and contingency bases. **Specializes in the areas of:** Accounting/Auditing; Finance. **Positions commonly filled include:** Accountant/Auditor; Budget Analyst; Chief Financial Officer; Controller; Finance Director; Financial Analyst. **Parent company:** Human Resource Management Inc. **Average salary range of placements:** More than $50,000. **Number of placements per year:** 100 - 199.

## FOX-MORRIS ASSOCIATES
1050 Wall Street West, Suite 310, Lyndhurst NJ 07071. 201/933-8900. **Contact:** Manager. **Description:** An executive search firm. **Specializes in the areas of:** Human Resources.

## GARRETT GROUP
342 Parsippany Road, Parsippany NJ 07054. 973/884-0711. **Fax:** 973/884-1307. **Contact:** Mr. Bernd Stecker, Recruiting. **Description:** An executive search firm. **Specializes in the areas of:** Electronics; Engineering; Marketing. **Average salary range of placements:** More than $50,000.

## GIBSON MARTIN CONSULTING
694 Route 15 South, Suite 207, Lake Hopatcong NJ 07849. 973/663-3300. **Fax:** 973/663-3316. **Contact:** Robert Lee, Principal. **E-mail address:** gmcboblee@careergoals.com. **World Wide Web address:** http://www.careergoals.com. **Description:** An executive search firm. **Specializes in the areas of:** Accounting/Auditing; Administration; Computer Science/Software; Finance. **Positions commonly filled include:** Accountant/Auditor; Architect; Budget Analyst; Chemist; Computer Programmer; Financial Analyst; Systems Analyst.

## GILBERT & VAN CAMPEN INTERNATIONAL
99 Lake Shore Drive, Belvidere NJ 07823. 908/475-2222. **Contact:** Manager. **Description:** An executive search firm that places high-level executives.

## GILBERT TWEED ASSOCIATES INC.
155 Prospect Avenue, Suite 101, West Orange NJ 07052. 973/731-3033. **Contact:** Manager. **Description:** An executive search firm.

## LAWRENCE GLASER ASSOCIATES INC.
505 South Lenola Road, Moorestown NJ 08057. 609/778-9500. **Fax:** 609/778-4390. **Contact:** Lawrence Glaser, President. **Description:** An executive search firm. **Specializes in the areas of:** Food; Sales. **Average salary range of placements:** More than $50,000. **Number of placements per year:** 50 - 99.

## L.J. GONZER ASSOCIATES
1225 Raymond Boulevard, Newark NJ 07102. 973/624-5600. **Contact:** Manager. **Description:** An executive search firm.

## GRANT FRANKS & ASSOCIATES
929 North Kings Highway, Cherry Hill NJ 08034. 609/779-9030. **Fax:** 609/779-0898. **Contact:** Lou Franks, Owner. **Description:** An executive search firm operating on a contingency basis.

**Specializes in the areas of:** Accounting/Auditing; Engineering; Manufacturing. **Positions commonly filled include:** Accountant/Auditor; Biomedical Engineer; Chemical Engineer; Chemist; Claim Rep.; Credit Manager; Customer Service Rep.; Electrical/Electronics Engineer; Financial Analyst; Food Scientist/Technologist; Human Resources Manager; Mechanical Engineer; Operations/Production Manager; Petroleum Engineer; Physical Therapist; Quality Control Supervisor; Underwriter/Assistant Underwriter.

**HADLEY ASSOCIATES**
147 Columbia Turnpike, Suite 104, Florham Park NJ 07932. 973/377-9177. **Fax:** 973/377-9223. **Contact:** Thomas Hadley, President. **Description:** An executive search firm operating on both retainer and contingency bases. **Specializes in the areas of:** Health/Medical. **Positions commonly filled include:** Biological Scientist; Biomedical Engineer; Chemical Engineer; Chemist; Clinical Lab Technician; Environmental Engineer; Pharmacist; Quality Control Supervisor; Radiological Technologist; Statistician. **Average salary range of placements:** More than $50,000. **Number of placements per year:** 1 - 49.

**ROBERT HALF INTERNATIONAL**
**ACCOUNTEMPS**
581 Main Street, Sixth Floor, Woodbridge NJ 07095. 732/634-7200. **Contact:** Manager. **Description:** An executive search firm. Accountemps (also at this location) provides temporary placements. **Specializes in the areas of:** Accounting/Auditing. **Corporate headquarters location:** Menlo Park CA. **Other U.S. locations:** Nationwide.

**ROBERT HALF INTERNATIONAL**
**ACCOUNTEMPS**
959 Route 46 East, 4th Floor, Parsippany NJ 07054. 973/455-7300. **Contact:** Al Saverino, Branch Manager. **Description:** An executive search firm. Accountemps (also at this location) provides temporary placements. **Specializes in the areas of:** Accounting/Auditing. **Corporate headquarters location:** Menlo Park CA. **Other U.S. locations:** Nationwide.

**HARRIS EXECUTIVE SEARCH**
1800 Fairlawn Avenue, Fairlawn NJ 07410. 201/703-1414. **Contact:** Manager. **Description:** An executive search firm. **Specializes in the areas of:** Engineering; Manufacturing.

**HEADHUNTERS EXECUTIVE SEARCH**
96 Princeton Street, Nutley NJ 07110. 973/667-2799. **Fax:** 973/667-3609. **Contact:** Elaine Jones, Vice President. **Description:** An executive search firm. **Specializes in the areas of:** Health/Medical; Sales. **Number of placements per year:** 200 - 499.

**HEALTHCARE RECRUITERS**
3 Eves Drive, Suite 303, Marlton NJ 08053. 609/596-7179. **Fax:** 609/596-6895. **Contact:** Diane Rosamelea, General Manager. **Description:** An executive search firm. **Specializes in the areas of:** Health/Medical. **Positions commonly filled include:** Biological Scientist; Biomedical Engineer; Marketing Manager; MIS Specialist; Recruiter; Software Engineer. **Other U.S. locations:** Dallas TX. **Average salary range of placements:** $30,000 - $50,000.

**HEALTHCARE RECRUITERS**
55 Harristown Road, Glen Rock NJ 07452. 201/670-9800. **Contact:** Manager. **Description:** An executive search firm. **Specializes in the areas of:** Health/Medical.

**HOLM PERSONNEL CONSULTANTS**
333-B Route 46 West, Suite 202, Fairfield NJ 07004. 973/808-1933. **Contact:** Manager. **Description:** An executive search firm. **Specializes in the areas of:** Accounting/Auditing; Administration; Computer Science/Software; Personnel/Labor Relations; Sales; Secretarial. **Positions commonly filled include:** Accountant/Auditor; Administrative Manager; Budget Analyst; Buyer; Computer Programmer; Credit Manager; Financial Analyst; Human Resources Specialist; Management Trainee; MIS Specialist; Purchasing Agent/Manager; Software Engineer; Systems Analyst; Telecommunications Manager; Transportation/Traffic Specialist. **Average salary range of placements:** $30,000 - $50,000. **Number of placements per year:** 50 - 99.

**HUFF ASSOCIATES**
95 Reef Drive, Ocean City NJ 08226. 609/399-2867. **Contact:** W.Z. Huff, President. **Description:** An executive search firm. **Specializes in the areas of:** Health/Medical; Manufacturing; Technical. **Positions commonly filled include:** Biomedical Engineer; Ceramics Engineer; Chemical Engineer; Chemist; Civil Engineer; Electrical/Electronics Engineer; Hotel Manager; Manufacturing Engineer;

Mechanical Engineer; Metallurgical Engineer; Nurse; Operations/Production Manager; Physician. **Number of placements per year:** 1 - 49.

### INSEARCH INC.
231 South White Horse Pike, Audubon NJ 08106. 609/546-6500. **Fax:** 609/546-6228. **Contact:** Charles Marcantonio, President. **Description:** An executive search firm operating on a contingency basis. **Specializes in the areas of:** Accounting; Administration; Computer Science/Software; Engineering; Finance; Insurance; MIS/EDP; Sales; Scientific; Technical. **Positions commonly filled include:** Account Manager; Account Rep.; Accountant; Adjuster; Administrative Assistant; Administrative Manager; Advertising Account Executive; Applications Engineer; Assistant Manager; Auditor; Biological Scientist; Chief Financial Officer; Claim Representative; Clerical Supervisor; Computer Programmer; Consultant; Controller; Customer Service Representative; Database Manager; Finance Director; Financial Analyst; Human Resources Manager; Insurance Agent/Broker; Market Research Analyst; Marketing Manager; Marketing Specialist; MIS Specialist; Operations Manager; Sales Executive; Sales Manager; Sales Rep.; Software Engineer; Statistician; Systems Analyst; Systems Manager; Underwriter/Assistant Underwriter; Vice President. **Other U.S. locations:** Nationwide. **Number of placements per year:** 200 - 499.

### INTER-REGIONAL EXECUTIVE SEARCH, INC.
191 Hamburg Turnpike, Pompton Lakes NJ 07442-2332. 973/616-8800. **Fax:** 973/616-8115. **Contact:** Frank Risalvato, Managing Partner. **E-mail address:** ires@erols.com. **Description:** An executive search firm operating on a contingency basis. **Specializes in the areas of:** Accounting/Auditing; Engineering; Finance; Insurance; Sales. **Positions commonly filled include:** Accountant/Auditor; Administrative Manager; Bank Officer/Manager; Biochemist; Biological Scientist; Biomedical Engineer; Budget Analyst; Chemical Engineer; Chemist; Claim Representative; Credit Manager; Customer Service Representative; Design Engineer; Designer; Economist; Financial Analyst; Industrial Engineer; Industrial Production Manager; Insurance Agent/Broker; Market Research Analyst; Mechanical Engineer; MIS Specialist; Nuclear Engineer; Pharmacist; Purchasing Agent/Manager; Telecommunications Manager; Underwriter/Assistant Underwriter. **Average salary range of placements:** More than $50,000. **Number of placements per year:** 100 - 199.

### J.M. JOSEPH ASSOCIATES
P.O. Box 104, High Bridge NJ 08829-0104. 908/638-6877. **Fax:** 908/638-8220. **Contact:** C. Russell Ditzel, Managing Director. **E-mail address:** cditzel@vcx.net. **Description:** An executive search firm. **Specializes in the areas of:** Administration; Computer Science/Software; Engineering; Food; Health/Medical; Manufacturing; Personnel/Labor Relations; Sales; Technical. **Positions commonly filled include:** Financial Analyst; Food Scientist/Technologist; Human Resources Specialist; Industrial Engineer; Industrial Production Manager; MIS Specialist; Operations/Production Manager; Strategic Relations Manager. **Average salary range of placements:** More than $50,000. **Number of placements per year:** 1 - 49.

### KANE ASSOCIATES
41 Vreeland Avenue, Totowa NJ 07512. 973/890-9110. **Contact:** Manager. **Description:** An executive search firm operating on a contingency basis.

### KARRAS PERSONNEL INC.
2 Central Avenue, Madison NJ 07940. 973/966-6800. **Contact:** Bill Karras, Recruiter. **Description:** An executive search firm. **Specializes in the areas of:** Human Resources. **Positions commonly filled include:** Human Resources Specialist. **Average salary range of placements:** More than $50,000.

### THE KELLER GROUP
### CAREERS INC.
P.O. Box 520, Wyckoff NJ 07481. 201/837-6612. **Fax:** 201/837-8783. **Contact:** Keith Eller, President. **E-mail address:** keller520@msn.com. **Description:** An executive search firm operating on a contingency basis. Careers Inc. (also at this location) specializes in marketing placements. **Specializes in the areas of:** Biology; Chemistry; Food; Information Systems; Pharmaceuticals; Technical. **Positions commonly filled include:** Information Specialist; Internet Services Manager; Library Technician; Management Analyst/Consultant; Market Research Analyst; MIS Specialist. **Average salary range of placements:** More than $50,000. **Number of placements per year:** 1 - 49.

### KEY EMPLOYMENT
1014 Livingston Avenue, North Brunswick NJ 08902. 732/249-2454. **Fax:** 732/249-2521. **Contact:** Gary Silberger, President. **Description:** An executive search firm. **Specializes in the**

areas of: Administration; Engineering; Marketing; Sales; Technical. **Positions commonly filled include:** Chemical Engineer; Chemist; Civil Engineer; Computer Programmer; Construction Contractor; Design Engineer; Designer; Electrical/Electronics Engineer; Environmental Engineer; Financial Analyst; General Manager; Industrial Engineer; Industrial Production Manager; Market Research Analyst; Mechanical Engineer; Metallurgical Engineer; MIS Specialist; Nuclear Engineer; Purchasing Agent/Manager; Software Engineer; Stationary Engineer; Structural Engineer; Systems Analyst; Telecommunications Manager. **Average salary range of placements:** More than $50,000. **Number of placements per year:** 1 - 49.

## T.J. KOELLHOFFER & ASSOCIATES
250 State Route 28, Suite 206, Bridgewater NJ 08807. 908/526-6880. **Fax:** 908/725-2653. **Contact:** Tom Koellhoffer, Principal. **E-mail address:** tomkoell@aol.com. **Description:** An executive search firm. **Specializes in the areas of:** Broadcasting; Computer Science/Software; Engineering; Manufacturing; Technical. **Positions commonly filled include:** Aerospace Engineer; Biochemist; Biological Scientist; Biomedical Engineer; Electrical/Electronics Engineer; Materials Engineer; Mechanical Engineer; Metallurgical Engineer; Multimedia Designer; Physicist; Software Engineer. **Average salary range of placements:** More than $50,000. **Number of placements per year:** 1 - 49.

## KORN/FERRY INTERNATIONAL
One Palmer Square, Suite 330, Princeton NJ 08542. 609/921-8811. **Contact:** Manager. **Description:** An executive search firm that places upper-level managers. **Corporate headquarters location:** Los Angeles CA. **International locations:** Worldwide. **Average salary range of placements:** More than $50,000.

## PAUL KULL & COMPANY
18 Meadowbrook Road, Randolph NJ 07869. 973/361-7440. **Contact:** Paul Kull, Owner. **Description:** An executive search firm. **Specializes in the areas of:** Computer Hardware/Software; Engineering; General Management; Manufacturing; Sales; Technical. **Positions commonly filled include:** Aerospace Engineer; Biochemist; Biomedical Engineer; Chemical Engineer; Computer Programmer; Electrical/Electronics Engineer; Industrial Engineer; Manufacturing Engineer; Marketing Specialist; Mechanical Engineer; Software Engineer. **Number of placements per year:** 1 - 49.

## L&K ASSOCIATES
P.O. Box 202, Salem NJ 08079-1328. 609/935-3070. **Contact:** Gene Lank, President. **Description:** An executive search firm operating on both retainer and contingency bases. **Specializes in the areas of:** Computer Science/Software; Legal; Technical; Telecommunications. **Positions commonly filled include:** Attorney; Computer Programmer; MIS Specialist; Systems Analyst; Telecommunications Manager. **Average salary range of placements:** More than $50,000. **Number of placements per year:** 1 - 49.

## LANCASTER ASSOCIATES
## THE SWAN GROUP
94 Grove Street, Somerville NJ 08876. 908/526-5440. **Fax:** 908/526-1992. **Contact:** Ray Lancaster, President. **Description:** An executive search firm operating on both retainer and contingency bases. **Specializes in the areas of:** Computer Science/Software; Technical. **Positions commonly filled include:** MIS Specialist; Telecommunications Manager. **Average salary range of placements:** More than $50,000. **Number of placements per year:** 1 - 49.

## LAW PROS LEGAL PLACEMENT SERVICES, INC.
511 Millburn Avenue, Short Hills NJ 07078. 973/912-8400. **Fax:** 973/912-8558. **Contact:** Beth Richmond, Principal. **Description:** An executive search firm. **Specializes in the areas of:** Legal. **Positions commonly filled include:** Attorney; Paralegal. **Average salary range of placements:** $30,000 - $50,000. **Number of placements per year:** 100 - 199.

## ALAN LERNER ASSOCIATES
400 Lakeview Commons, Gibbsboro NJ 08026. 609/435-1600. **Contact:** Manager. **Description:** An executive search firm.

## MIS SEARCH
450 Harmon Meadow Boulevard, 1st Floor, Secaucus NJ 07094. 201/330-0080. **Fax:** 201/330-8729. **Contact:** Maryanne McGuire, Technical Recruiter. **Description:** An executive search firm. **Specializes in the areas of:** Administration; Computer Science/Software. **Positions commonly filled include:** Computer Programmer; Systems Analyst.

**MJE RECRUITERS, INC.**
123 Columbia Turnpike, Suite 204A, Florham Park NJ 07932. 973/765-9400. **Fax:** 973/765-0881. **Contact:** Barry Emen, President. **E-mail address:** mjerecru@aol.com. **Description:** An executive search firm. **Specializes in the areas of:** Accounting/Auditing; Banking; Finance; Insurance; Investment. **Positions commonly filled include:** Accountant/Auditor; Bank Officer/Manager; Budget Analyst; Finance Director; Financial Analyst; Fund Manager. **Number of placements per year:** 50 - 99.

**MAJOR CONSULTANTS**
500 North Franklin Turnpike, Suite 17, Ramsey NJ 07446. 201/934-9666. **Fax:** 201/818-0339. **Contact:** Pam Ericson, Consultant. **E-mail address:** recruiter@majorinc.com. **World Wide Web address:** http://www.majorinc.com. **Description:** An executive search firm operating on both retainer and contingency bases. **Specializes in the areas of:** Banking; Computer Science/Software; Engineering; Finance; General Management; Insurance; Personnel/Labor Relations; Sales; Scientific; Technical. **Positions commonly filled include:** Account Manager; Accountant/Auditor; Bank Officer/Manager; Branch Manager; Credit Manager; Design Engineer; Electrical/Electronics Engineer; General Manager; Human Resources Specialist; Mechanical Engineer; Operations/Production Manager; Software Engineer; Systems Analyst; Telecommunications Manager.

**MANAGEMENT CATALYSTS**
P.O. Box 70, Ship Bottom NJ 08008. 609/597-0079. **Fax:** 609/597-2860. **Contact:** Dr. J.R. Stockton, Principal. **Description:** An executive search firm. **Specializes in the areas of:** Food; Research and Development; Technical. **Positions commonly filled include:** Agricultural Engineer; Agricultural Scientist; Biochemist; Biological Scientist; Biomedical Engineer; Chemical Engineer; Chemist; Clinical Lab Technician; Dietician/Nutritionist; Environmental Engineer; Food Scientist/Technologist; Quality Control Supervisor; Science Technologist. **Average salary range of placements:** More than $50,000. **Number of placements per year:** 1 - 49.

**MANAGEMENT GROUP OF AMERICA, INC.**
250 Passaic Avenue, Suite 210, Fairfield NJ 07004. 973/808-3300. **Fax:** 973/882-9284. **Contact:** James W. Byrne, President. **Description:** An executive search firm operating on a contingency basis. The firm also provides some temporary and contract placements. **Specializes in the areas of:** Insurance. **Positions commonly filled include:** Customer Service Rep.; Insurance Agent/Broker; Sales Rep. **Average salary range of placements:** $30,000 - $50,000. **Number of placements per year:** 100 - 199.

**MANAGEMENT RECRUITERS INTERNATIONAL**
19 Tanner Street, Haddonfield NJ 08033. 609/428-2233. **Contact:** Manager. **Description:** An executive search firm. **Specializes in the areas of:** High-Tech; Sales. **Corporate headquarters location:** Cleveland OH. **Other U.S. locations:** Nationwide.

**MANAGEMENT RECRUITERS INTERNATIONAL**
P.O. Box 211, Hope NJ 07844. 908/459-5798. **Contact:** Manager. **Description:** An executive search firm. **Specializes in the areas of:** Human Resources. **Corporate headquarters location:** Cleveland OH. **Other U.S. locations:** Nationwide.

**MANAGEMENT RECRUITERS INTERNATIONAL**
1104 Springfield Avenue, Mountainside NJ 07921. 908/789-9400. **Contact:** Manager. **Description:** An executive search firm. **Specializes in the areas of:** Office Support; Sales. **Corporate headquarters location:** Cleveland OH. **Other U.S. locations:** Nationwide.

**MANAGEMENT RECRUITERS INTERNATIONAL**
150 Floral Avenue, New Providence NJ 07974. 908/771-0600. **Contact:** Manager. **Description:** An executive search firm. **Specializes in the areas of:** Information Systems; Sales. **Corporate headquarters location:** Cleveland OH. **Other U.S. locations:** Nationwide.

**MANAGEMENT RECRUITERS INTERNATIONAL**
1040 North Kings Highway, Suite 705, Cherry Hill NJ 08034. 609/667-3381. **Contact:** Manager. **Description:** An executive search firm. **Corporate headquarters location:** Cleveland OH. **Other U.S. locations:** Nationwide.

**MANAGEMENT RECRUITERS INTERNATIONAL**
10 Anderson Road, Bernardsville NJ 07924. 908/204-0070. **Contact:** Manager. **Description:** An executive search firm. **Specializes in the areas of:** Computer Hardware/Software. **Corporate headquarters location:** Cleveland OH. **Other U.S. locations:** Nationwide.

**MANAGEMENT RECRUITERS INTERNATIONAL**
4 Waterloo Road, Stanhope NJ 07874. 973/691-2020. **Contact:** Manager. **Description:** An executive search firm. **Specializes in the areas of:** Computer Hardware/Software. **Corporate headquarters location:** Cleveland OH. **Other U.S. locations:** Nationwide.

**MANAGEMENT RECRUITERS INTERNATIONAL**
440 County Road 513, Califon NJ 07830. 908/832-6455. **Contact:** Manager. **Description:** An executive search firm. **Specializes in the areas of:** Insurance. **Corporate headquarters location:** Cleveland OH. **Other U.S. locations:** Nationwide.

**MANAGEMENT RECRUITERS INTERNATIONAL OF MORRIS COUNTY**
17 Hanover Road, Suite 450, Florham Park NJ 07932. 973/593-0400. **Contact:** Sue Young, General Manager. **Description:** An executive search firm. **Specializes in the areas of:** Data Communications; Sales; Telecommunications. **Corporate headquarters location:** Cleveland OH. **Other U.S. locations:** Nationwide.

**MANAGEMENT RECRUITERS OF BAY HEAD**
106 Bridge Avenue, Bay Head NJ 08742. 732/714-1300. **Fax:** 732/714-1311. **Contact:** Bob Ceresi, General Manager. **E-mail address:** bob@mrielectrical.com. **World Wide Web address:** http://www.mrielectrical.com. **Description:** An executive search firm operating on a contingency basis. **Specializes in the areas of:** Computer Science/Software; Engineering; Industrial; Light Industrial; Manufacturing; Marketing; Sales; Scientific; Technical. **Positions commonly filled include:** Account Manager; Account Rep.; Branch Manager; Computer Programmer; Design Engineer; Electrical/Electronics Engineer; General Manager; Industrial Engineer; Manufacturing Engineer; Market Research Analyst; Marketing Manager; Marketing Specialist; Mechanical Engineer; Operations Manager; Production Manager; Purchasing Agent/Manager; Quality Control Supervisor; Sales Engineer; Sales Executive; Sales Manager; Sales Rep.; Software Engineer. **Corporate headquarters location:** Cleveland OH. **Other U.S. locations:** Nationwide. **Average salary range of placements:** More than $50,000. **Number of placements per year:** 50 - 99.

**MANAGEMENT RECRUITERS OF BRIDGEWATER**
1170 U.S. Highway 22 East, Bridgewater NJ 08807. 908/725-2595. **Fax:** 908/725-0439. **Contact:** Jennifer Lebron, Account Executive. **Description:** An executive search firm operating on both retainer and contingency bases. **Specializes in the areas of:** Banking; Finance; Insurance; Sales; Transportation. **Positions commonly filled include:** Accountant/Auditor; Bank Officer/Manager; Buyer; Claim Representative; Credit Manager; Customer Service Representative; Financial Analyst; Health Services Manager; Insurance Agent/Broker; Manufacturer's/Wholesaler's Sales Rep.; Services Sales Representative; Transportation/Traffic Specialist; Underwriter/Assistant Underwriter. **Corporate headquarters location:** Cleveland OH. **Other U.S. locations:** Nationwide. **Average salary range of placements:** More than $50,000. **Number of placements per year:** 100 - 199.

**MANAGEMENT RECRUITERS OF MEDFORD**
30 Jackson Road, Suite C4, Medford NJ 08055. 609/654-9109. **Fax:** 609/654-9166. **Contact:** Norman Talbot, President. **E-mail address:** mrinet@recom.com. **World Wide Web address:** http://pages.recom.com/~mrinet. **Description:** An executive search firm. **Specializes in the areas of:** Architecture/Construction; Biotechnology; Chemicals; Electronics; Engineering; Food; General Management; Industrial; Manufacturing; Paper; Petrochemical; Pharmaceuticals; Sales; Technical. **Positions commonly filled include:** Aerospace Engineer; Biological Scientist; Biomedical Engineer; Chemical Engineer; Chemist; Civil Engineer; Draftsperson; Electrical/Electronics Engineer; Industrial Engineer; Industrial Hygienist; Manufacturing Engineer; Mechanical Engineer; Metallurgical Engineer; Quality Control Supervisor; Safety Engineer; Software Engineer; Systems Analyst. **Corporate headquarters location:** Cleveland OH. **Other U.S. locations:** Nationwide. **Number of placements per year:** 50 - 99

**MANAGEMENT RECRUITERS OF PASSAIC COUNTY**
750 Hamburg Turnpike, Pompton Lakes NJ 07442. 973/831-7778. **Contact:** David Zawicki, Manager. **Description:** An executive search firm. **Specializes in the areas of:** Accounting/Auditing; Administration; Advertising; Architecture/Construction; Banking; Communications; Computer Science/Software; Construction; Electrical; Engineering; Finance; Food; General Management; Health/Medical; Personnel/Labor Relations; Procurement; Publishing; Real Estate; Retail; Sales; Technical; Textiles; Transportation. **Corporate headquarters location:** Cleveland OH. **Other U.S. locations:** Nationwide.

**MANAGEMENT RECRUITERS OF SHORT HILLS**
24 Lackawanna Plaza, Millburn NJ 07041. 973/379-4020. **Contact:** Manager. **Description:** An executive search firm. **Specializes in the areas of:** Computer Hardware/Software; Computer

Programming; Engineering; Sales. **Corporate headquarters location:** Cleveland OH. **Other U.S. locations:** Nationwide.

## MANAGEMENT RECRUITERS OF SPARTA
191 Woodport Road, Suite 201, Sparta NJ 07871. 973/729-1888. **Toll-free phone:** 800/875-1896. **Fax:** 973/729-1620. **Contact:** Lance Incitti, President. **E-mail address:** recruiter@ retailplacement.com. **World Wide Web address:** http://www.retailplacement.com. **Description:** An executive search firm. **Specializes in the areas of:** Accounting/Auditing; Finance; Retail. **Positions commonly filled include:** Auditor; Buyer; Controller; Financial Analyst; Human Resources Manager; Management Analyst/Consultant; Operations Manager. **Corporate headquarters location:** Cleveland OH. **Other U.S. locations:** Nationwide. **Average salary range of placements:** $30,000 - $50,000. **Number of placements per year:** 50 - 99.

## McDERMOTT RESOURCES INC.
74 South Powder Mill Road, Morris Plains NJ 07950. 973/285-0066. **Fax:** 973/285-5463. **Contact:** Maureen McDermott, President. **Description:** An executive search firm operating on a contingency basis. **Specializes in the areas of:** Banking; Secretarial. **Positions commonly filled include:** Accountant/Auditor; Bank Officer/Manager; Credit Manager; Financial Analyst; Human Resources Specialist. **Number of placements per year:** 50 - 99.

## RICHARD MEYERS & ASSOCIATES, INC.
15 James Street, Florham Park NJ 07932. 973/765-9000. **Fax:** 973/765-9009. **Contact:** Richard Meyers, President. **Description:** An executive search firm. **Specializes in the areas of:** Insurance; Risk Management. **Positions commonly filled include:** Insurance Agent/Broker; Underwriter/ Assistant Underwriter. **Number of placements per year:** 100 - 199.

## MIDDLEBROOK ASSOCIATES
6 Commerce Drive, Cranford NJ 07016. 908/709-0707. **Fax:** 908/272-6297. **Contact:** Rita Richards, Manager of Scientific Recruiting. **Description:** An executive search firm. **Specializes in the areas of:** Biology; Engineering; Food; Technical. **Positions commonly filled include:** Biochemist; Biological Scientist; Biomedical Engineer; Chemical Engineer; Chemist; Design Engineer; Environmental Engineer; Food Scientist/Technologist; Industrial Engineer; Pharmacist; Science Technologist; Statistician. **Number of placements per year:** 1 - 49.

## NORMYLE/ERSTLING HEALTH SEARCH GROUP
350 West Passaic Street, Rochelle Park NJ 07662. 201/843-6009. **Fax:** 201/843-2060. **Contact:** Charles D. Kreps, Managing Partner. **Description:** An executive search firm operating on a contingency basis. **Specializes in the areas of:** Biology; General Management; Health/Medical; Insurance; Marketing; Sales; Technical. **Positions commonly filled include:** Account Manager; Account Rep.; Administrative Manager; Biochemist; Biomedical Engineer; Clinical Lab Technician; Marketing Manager; Marketing Specialist; Registered Nurse; Respiratory Therapist; Sales Engineer; Sales Executive; Sales Manager; Sales Rep.; Vice President of Marketing and Sales. **Corporate headquarters location:** This Location. **Other U.S. locations:** Nationwide. **Average salary range of placements:** More than $50,000. **Number of placements per year:** 100 - 199.

## ORION CONSULTING, INC.
115 Route 46 West, Building B, Suite 13, Mountain Lakes NJ 07046. 973/402-8866. **Fax:** 973/402-9258. **Contact:** James Dromsky, President. **E-mail address:** oci@planet.net. **Description:** An executive search firm. **Specializes in the areas of:** Accounting/Auditing; Administration; Advertising; Banking; Chemicals; Communications; Design; Engineering; Finance; Food; General Management; Health/Medical; Industrial; Insurance; Legal; Manufacturing; Military; Operations Management; Personnel/Labor Relations; Pharmaceuticals; Procurement; Sales; Technical; Transportation. **Number of placements per year:** 50 - 99.

## PR MANAGEMENT CONSULTANTS
601 Ewing Street, Suite C5, Princeton NJ 08540. 609/921-6565. **Contact:** Jerry Koenig, President. **Description:** An executive search firm. **Specializes in the areas of:** Engineering; General Management; Sales. **Positions commonly filled include:** Biochemist; Biomedical Engineer; Chemical Engineer; Design Engineer; Mechanical Engineer; Software Engineer; Statistician. **Average salary range of placements:** More than $50,000.

## FLORENCE PAPE LEGAL SEARCH, INC.
1208 Washington Street, Hoboken NJ 07030. 201/798-0200. **Toll-free phone:** 800/762-0096. **Fax:** 201/798-9088. **Contact:** Florence Pape, President. **Description:** An executive search firm operating on a contingency basis. **Specializes in the areas of:** Legal. **Positions commonly filled include:**

Attorney. **Average salary range of placements:** More than $50,000. **Number of placements per year:** 1 - 49.

## RICK PASCAL & ASSOCIATES INC.
P.O. Box 543, Fair Lawn NJ 07410. 201/791-9541. **Fax:** 201/791-1861. **Contact:** Rick Pascal, CPC, President. **Description:** An executive search firm. **Specializes in the areas of:** Packaging. **Positions commonly filled include:** Designer; Management; Packaging Engineer; Packaging/Processing Worker.

## PENNINGTON CONSULTING GROUP
65 South Main Street, Building B, Pennington NJ 08534. 609/737-8500. **Fax:** 609/737-8576. **Contact:** Robert B. White, President. **Description:** An executive search firm operating on a contingency basis. **Specializes in the areas of:** Wireless Communications. **Positions commonly filled include:** Technician. **Other U.S. locations:** Richmond VA. **Average salary range of placements:** More than $50,000. **Number of placements per year:** 1 - 49.

## THE PENNMOR GROUP
25 Chestnut Street, Suite 107, Haddonfield NJ 08033. 609/354-1414. **Fax:** 609/354-7660. **Contact:** Anthony Trasatti, President. **E-mail address:** ttrasatti@pennmor.com. **World Wide Web address:** http://www.pennmor.com. **Description:** An executive search firm. **Specializes in the areas of:** Accounting; Banking; Finance; Personnel/Labor Relations. **Positions commonly filled include:** Accountant; Auditor; Bank Officer/Manager; Chief Financial Officer; Controller; Finance Director; Financial Analyst; Human Resources Manager; Operations Manager; Securities Sales Representative. **Average salary range of placements:** $50,000 - $100,000. **Number of placements per year:** 1 - 49.

## PERSONNEL ASSOCIATES INC.
239 U.S. Highway 22, Green Brook NJ 08812-1916. 732/968-8866. **Fax:** 732/968-9437. **Contact:** Thomas C. Wood, President. **Description:** An executive search firm operating on a contingency basis. **Specializes in the areas of:** Administration; Computer Science/Software. **Positions commonly filled include:** Computer Programmer; Internet Services Manager; MIS Specialist; Project Manager; Systems Analyst. **Other U.S. locations:** Nationwide. **Number of placements per year:** 50 - 99.

## PETRUZZI ASSOCIATES
P.O. Box 141, Scotch Plains NJ 07076. 908/754-1940. **Contact:** Manager. **Description:** An executive search firm. **Specializes in the areas of:** Chemicals; Health/Medical.

## PHILADELPHIA SEARCH GROUP, INC.
One Cherry Hill, Suite 510, Cherry Hill NJ 08002. 609/667-2300. **Contact:** Manager. **Description:** An executive search firm operating on a contingency basis. **Specializes in the areas of:** Health/Medical; Sales. **Positions commonly filled include:** Sales Manager; Sales Representative. **Average salary range of placements:** More than $50,000. **Number of placements per year:** 50 - 99.

## PHOENIX BIOSEARCH, INC.
P.O. Box 6157, West Caldwell NJ 07007-6157. 973/812-2666. **Fax:** 973/812-2727. **Contact:** Lee Stephenson, President. **Description:** An executive search firm operating on both retainer and contingency bases. **Specializes in the areas of:** Biology. **Positions commonly filled include:** Biochemist; Biological Scientist; Marketing Manager. **Average salary range of placements:** More than $50,000. **Number of placements per year:** 1 - 49.

## PRINCETON EXECUTIVE SEARCH
2667 Nottingham Way, Hamilton NJ 08619. 609/584-1100. **Fax:** 609/584-1141. **Contact:** Andrew B. Barkocy, CPC, President. **Description:** An executive search firm. **Specializes in the areas of:** Accounting/Auditing; Administration; Banking; Computer Science/Software; Engineering; Film Production; Personnel/Labor Relations. **Positions commonly filled include:** Accountant/Auditor; Aerospace Engineer; Agricultural Engineer; Bank Officer/Manager; Biomedical Engineer; Budget Analyst; Chemical Engineer; Civil Engineer; Credit Manager; Electrical/Electronics Engineer; Financial Analyst; General Manager; Human Resources Manager; Industrial Engineer; Mechanical Engineer; Nuclear Engineer; Petroleum Engineer; Purchasing Agent/Manager; Software Engineer; Systems Analyst. **Number of placements per year:** 1 - 49.

## RAMMING & ASSOCIATES, INC.
3 Thackery Lane, Cherry Hill NJ 08003-1925. 609/428-7172. **Fax:** 609/428-7173. **Contact:** George Ramming, Owner. **E-mail address:** georger@dvnc.net. **Description:** An executive search firm.

Specializes in the areas of: Engineering; General Management; Health/Medical; Manufacturing. Positions commonly filled include: Chemical Engineer; Design Engineer; Electrical/Electronics Engineer; General Manager; Mechanical Engineer; Software Engineer; Telecommunications Manager. Average salary range of placements: More than $50,000. Number of placements per year: 1 - 49.

### RETAIL CONNECTION INC.
271 U.S. Highway 46 West, Suite D-105, Fairfield NJ 07004. 973/882-6662. Toll-free phone: 800/770-4945. Fax: 973/575-5858. Contact: Carole Thaller, President. Description: An executive search firm operating on a contingency basis. Specializes in the areas of: Retail. Positions commonly filled include: Chief Financial Officer; Sales Manager. Number of placements per year: 50 - 99.

### JEFF RICH ASSOCIATES
67 Walnut Avenue, Suite 303, Clark NJ 07066. 732/574-3888. Contact: Manager. Description: An executive search firm. Specializes in the areas of: Accounting/Auditing; Finance.

### JAMES F. ROBINSON PROFESSIONAL RECRUITER
231 South White Horse Pike, Audubon NJ 08106. 609/547-5800. Contact: James F. Robinson, Owner. Description: An executive search firm. Specializes in the areas of: Legal. Positions commonly filled include: Attorney.

### ROCHESTER SYSTEMS INC.
227 East Bergen Place, Red Bank NJ 07701. 732/747-7474. Fax: 732/747-7055. Contact: Manager. Description: An executive search firm. Specializes in the areas of: Accounting/Auditing; Computer Science/Software; Logistics; Manufacturing; MIS/EDP. Positions commonly filled include: Computer Programmer; Financial Analyst; Industrial Production Manager; Management Analyst/Consultant; Manager of Information Systems; Operations/Production Manager; Software Engineer; Systems Analyst. Number of placements per year: 50 - 99.

### KEN ROSE ASSOCIATES
218 Route 17 North, Rochelle Park NJ 07662. 201/587-9611. Fax: 201/587-8609. Contact: Ken Rose, President. Description: An executive search firm. Specializes in the areas of: Fashion. Average salary range of placements: More than $50,000.

### THE RUSSELL GROUP INC.
23 North Avenue East, Cranford NJ 07016. 908/709-1188. Fax: 908/709-0959. Contact: William Russell, President. Description: An executive search firm. Specializes in the areas of: Sales. Average salary range of placements: More than $50,000. Number of placements per year: 100 - 199.

### ANTHONY RYAN ASSOCIATES
140 Route 17 North, Suite 309, Paramus NJ 07652. 201/967-7000. Contact: Marnie Livak, Manager. Description: An executive search firm. Specializes in the areas of: Computer Hardware/Software.

### RYLAN FORBES CONSULTING GROUP
379 Thornall Street, 7th Floor, Edison NJ 08837. 732/205-1900. Fax: 732/205-1901. Contact: Joe Stauffer, Vice President. Description: An executive search firm that also provides some temporary placements. Specializes in the areas of: Accounting/Auditing; Finance; Manufacturing; Retail. Positions commonly filled include: Accountant/Auditor; Budget Analyst; Financial Analyst. Number of placements per year: 50 - 99.

### R.S. SADOW ASSOCIATES
24 Heather Drive, Somerset NJ 08873. 732/545-4550. Fax: 732/545-0797. Contact: Ray Sadow, President. Description: An executive search firm operating on a contingency basis. Specializes in the areas of: Accounting/Auditing; Administration; Banking; Computer Science/Software; Engineering; Finance; Industrial; Manufacturing; Publishing; Scientific; Technical. Positions commonly filled include: Accountant/Auditor; Aerospace Engineer; Agricultural Engineer; Bank Officer/Manager; Biological Scientist; Biomedical Engineer; Budget Analyst; Ceramics Engineer; Chemical Engineer; Chemist; Civil Engineer; Clerical Supervisor; Computer Programmer; Controller; Credit Manager; Customer Service Representative; Draftsperson; Editor; Electrical/Electronics Engineer; Financial Analyst; Industrial Engineer; Industrial Production Manager; Materials Engineer; Mechanical Engineer; Metallurgical Engineer; Mining Engineer; Nuclear Engineer; Petroleum Engineer; Purchasing Agent/Manager; Quality Control Supervisor;

Software Engineer; Stationary Engineer; Structural Engineer; Systems Analyst; Technical Writer/Editor. **Average salary range of placements:** More than $50,000. **Number of placements per year:** 1 - 49.

## SALES CONSULTANTS
2 Hudson Place, Hoboken NJ 07030. **Fax:** 201/659-5009. **Contact:** Rick Sinay, Manager. **Description:** An executive search firm that also provides some temporary placements. **Specializes in the areas of:** Advertising; Food; General Management; Manufacturing; Sales. **Positions commonly filled include:** Biochemist; Biological Scientist; Biomedical Engineer; Chemical Engineer; Chemist; Food Scientist/Technologist; Mechanical Engineer; Metallurgical Engineer. **Average salary range of placements:** More than $50,000. **Number of placements per year:** 100 - 199.

## SALES CONSULTANTS
800 Kings Highway North, Cherry Hill NJ 08034. 609/779-9100. **Fax:** 609/779-9193. **Contact:** General Manager. **Description:** An executive search firm. **Specializes in the areas of:** Food; General Management; Industrial; Information Technology; Manufacturing; Publishing; Retail; Sales. **Positions commonly filled include:** Buyer; Customer Service Representative; Financial Analyst; General Manager; Insurance Agent/Broker; Management Trainee; Market Research Analyst; Purchasing Agent/Manager; Restaurant/Food Service Manager; Telecommunications Manager; Travel Agent. **Number of placements per year:** 100 - 199.

## SALES CONSULTANTS OF MORRIS COUNTY
364 Parsippany Road, Parsippany NJ 07054. 973/887-3838. **Fax:** 973/887-2304. **Contact:** Ernest Bivona, Manager. **E-mail address:** sci.manager@mrinet.com. **Description:** An executive search firm operating on a contingency basis. **Specializes in the areas of:** Computer Science/Software; Engineering; Finance; Food; General Management; Health/Medical; Industrial; Insurance; Publishing; Sales; Technical. **Positions commonly filled include:** Bank Officer/Manager; Biological Scientist; Biomedical Engineer; Chemical Engineer; Civil Engineer; Mechanical Engineer; Metallurgical Engineer; Sales Representative; Software Engineer; Telecommunications Manager. **Other U.S. locations:** Nationwide. **Number of placements per year:** 50 - 99.

## SALES CONSULTANTS OF OCEAN, INC.
2516 Highway 35, Manasquan NJ 08736. 732/223-0300. **Fax:** 732/223-0450. **Contact:** Mark Daly, Manager. **Description:** An executive search firm. **Specializes in the areas of:** Electronics; Environmental; Marketing; Packaging; Publishing; Sales. **Positions commonly filled include:** Marketing Specialist; Sales Representative. **Average salary range of placements:** More than $50,000. **Number of placements per year:** 100 - 199.

## SALES CONSULTANTS OF SPARTA
376 Route 15, Suite 200, Sparta NJ 07871. 973/579-5555. **Fax:** 973/579-2220. **Contact:** Harvey Bass, Manager. **Description:** An executive search firm. **Specializes in the areas of:** Accounting/Auditing; Administration; Advertising; Architecture/Construction; Banking; Communications; Computer Science/Software; Design; Electrical; Engineering; Finance; Food; General Management; Health/Medical; Industrial; Insurance; Legal; Manufacturing; Operations Management; Procurement; Publishing; Real Estate; Retail; Sales; Technical; Textiles; Transportation.

## SANFORD ROSE ASSOCIATES
12 Minneakoning Road, Suite 4, Flemington NJ 08809. 908/788-1788. **Contact:** Gary Bertsch, Manager. **World Wide Web address:** http://www.sanfordrose.com. **Description:** An executive search firm. **Other U.S. locations:** Nationwide. **Specializes in the areas of:** Engineering; Manufacturing.

## ROBERT SCOTT ASSOCIATES
P.O. Box 486, Rancocas NJ 08073-0486. 609/835-2224. **Fax:** 609/835-1933. **Contact:** Bob Scott, President. **Description:** An executive search firm. **Specializes in the areas of:** Chemicals; Engineering; Industrial; Manufacturing; Paper; Personnel/Labor Relations; Scientific; Technical. **Positions commonly filled include:** Biological Scientist; Biomedical Engineer; Ceramics Engineer; Chemical Engineer; Chemist; Civil Engineer; Electrical/Electronics Engineer; Human Resources Manager; Industrial Engineer; Manufacturing Engineer; Mechanical Engineer; Metallurgical Engineer; Operations Manager. **Average salary range of placements:** More than $50,000.

## SEARCH CONSULTANTS, INC.
P.O. Box 402, Paramus NJ 07653-0402. 201/444-1770. **Contact:** Walter Perog, Executive Recruiter. **Description:** An executive search firm. **Specializes in the areas of:** Personnel/Labor

Relations. **Positions commonly filled include:** Human Resources Specialist. **Average salary range of placements:** More than $50,000. **Number of placements per year:** 1 - 49.

**SEARCH EDP INC.**
150 River Road, Building C, Suite 3, Montville NJ 07045. 973/335-6600. **Contact:** Manager. **Description:** An executive search firm. **Specializes in the areas of:** Data Processing.

**SKUPPSEARCH, INC.**
580 Sylvan Avenue, Englewood Cliffs NJ 07632. 201/894-1824. **Fax:** 201/894-1324. **Contact:** Holly Skupp, President. **Description:** An executive search firm. **Specializes in the areas of:** Banking; Communications; Computer Science/Software; Finance; Insurance; Technical. **Positions commonly filled include:** Editor; Multimedia Designer; Technical Writer/Editor; Training Specialist; Webmaster. **Average salary range of placements:** $30,000 - $50,000. **Number of placements per year:** 1 - 49.

**SNELLING PERSONNEL SERVICES**
142 Highway 35, Eatontown NJ 07724. 732/389-0300. **Fax:** 732/460-2582. **Contact:** Frank Wyckoff, Owner/President. **Description:** An executive search firm that also provides some temporary placements. **Positions commonly filled include:** Administrative Manager; Branch Manager; Claim Rep.; Clerical Supervisor; Computer Programmer; Design Engineer; Draftsperson; Financial Analyst; General Manager; Health Services Manager; Hotel Manager; Human Resources Manager; Industrial Engineer; Industrial Production Manager; Management Trainee; Paralegal; Pharmacist; Software Engineer; Systems Analyst; Telecommunications Manager; Typist/Word Processor. **Average salary range of placements:** $20,000 - $29,999. **Number of placements per year:** 1000+.

**PHYLLIS SOLOMON EXECUTIVE SEARCH**
120 Sylvan Avenue, Englewood Cliffs NJ 07632. 201/947-8600. **Contact:** Phyllis Solomon, President. **Description:** An executive search firm. **Specializes in the areas of:** Pharmaceuticals. **Positions commonly filled include:** Account Rep.; Marketing Manager; Product Manager.

**SOURCE SERVICES CORPORATION**
**A BUSINESS OF ROMAC INTERNATIONAL**
100 Woodbridge Center Drive, Suite 101, Woodbridge NJ 07095. 732/283-9510. **Fax:** 732/283-0704. **Contact:** Manager. **Description:** An executive search firm. Divisions at this location include Source Consulting, Source EDP, and Source Finance. **Specializes in the areas of:** Computer Hardware/Software; Finance; Information Technology.

**SOURCE SERVICES CORPORATION**
**A BUSINESS OF ROMAC INTERNATIONAL**
5 Independence Way, Princeton NJ 08540. 609/452-7277. **Fax:** 609/520-1742. **Contact:** Manager. **Description:** An executive search firm. **Specializes in the areas of:** Computer Hardware/Software; Information Technology.

**SOURCE SERVICES CORPORATION**
**A BUSINESS OF ROMAC INTERNATIONAL**
One Gatehall Drive, Floor 3, Parsippany NJ 07054. 973/267-3222. **Fax:** 973/267-2741. **Contact:** Manager. **Description:** An executive search firm. Divisions at this location include Source EDP and Accountant Source Temps. **Specializes in the areas of:** Accounting/Auditing; Computer Hardware/Software; Information Technology.

**STELTON GROUP INC.**
904 Oak Tree Road, Suite A, South Plainfield NJ 07080. 908/757-9888. **Contact:** Manager. **Description:** An executive search firm. **Specializes in the areas of:** Manufacturing; Telecommunications.

**SUMMIT GROUP, INC.**
64 Lambert Drive, Sparta NJ 07871. 973/726-0800. **Fax:** 973/726-9188. **Contact:** Gary Pezzuti, General Partner. **Description:** An executive search firm. **Specializes in the areas of:** Engineering; Food; Health/Medical; Industrial; Manufacturing; Materials; Transportation. **Positions commonly filled include:** Buyer; General Manager; Industrial Engineer; Industrial Production Manager; Manufacturing Engineer; Marketing Specialist; Mechanical Engineer; Metallurgical Engineer; Operations/Production Manager; Production Manager; Purchasing Agent/Manager; Quality Control Supervisor; Transportation/Traffic Specialist; Vice President. **Average salary range of placements:** More than $50,000. **Number of placements per year:** 50 - 99.

**TATE & ASSOCIATES**
1020 Springfield Avenue, Suite 201, Westfield NJ 07090. 908/232-2443. **Contact:** Manager. **Description:** An executive search firm.

**TECHNICAL NETWORK SOLUTIONS, INC.**
P.O. Box 273, Sparta NJ 07871-0273. 973/726-4474. **Contact:** Elissa Marcus, President. **Description:** An executive search firm. **Specializes in the areas of:** Accounting/Auditing; Administration; Computer Science/Software; Finance; Insurance; Personnel/Labor Relations; Retail; Sales; Secretarial; Technical. **Positions commonly filled include:** Accountant/Auditor; Administrative Manager; Advertising Clerk; Branch Manager; Budget Analyst; Claim Rep.; Clerical Supervisor; Computer Programmer; Customer Service Rep.; Financial Analyst; General Manager; Human Resources Specialist; Management Trainee; MIS Specialist; Purchasing Agent/Manager; Services Sales Rep.; Software Engineer; Systems Analyst; Underwriter/Assistant Underwriter. **Number of placements per year:** 50 - 99.

**TECHNOLOGY SYSTEMS, INC.**
27 East Main Street, Little Falls NJ 07424. 973/256-1772. **Fax:** 973/812-1761. **Contact:** John Beddes, President. **Description:** Technology Systems, Inc. is an executive search firm. **Specializes in the areas of:** Engineering. **Positions commonly filled include:** Design Engineer; Electrical/Electronics Engineer; Manufacturing Engineer; Mechanical Engineer; Sales Engineer; Software Engineer. **Corporate headquarters location:** This Location. **Average salary range of placements:** More than $50,000.

**ALLEN THOMAS ASSOCIATES**
518 Prospect Avenue, Little Silver NJ 07739. 732/219-5353. **Fax:** 732/219-5805. **Contact:** Tom Benoit, President. **E-mail address:** recruit@allenthomas.com. **World Wide Web address:** http://www.allenthomas.com. **Description:** An executive search firm operating on a contingency basis. **Specializes in the areas of:** Health/Medical. **Positions commonly filled include:** Pharmacist; Physician; Sales Manager. **Average salary range of placements:** More than $50,000.

**TOPAZ ATTORNEY SEARCH**
383 Northfield Avenue, West Orange NJ 07052. 973/669-7300. **Fax:** 973/669-9811. **Contact:** Stewart Michaels, Chairman. **E-mail address:** topazlegal@aol.com. **Description:** An executive search firm operating on both retainer and contingency bases. **Specializes in the areas of:** Legal. **Positions commonly filled include:** Attorney. **Average salary range of placements:** More than $50,000. **Number of placements per year:** 100 - 199.

**WORLCO COMPUTER RESOURCES, INC.**
901 Route 38, Cherry Hill NJ 08002. 609/665-4700. **Fax:** 609/665-8142. **Contact:** Bob Hughes, Managing Partner. **Description:** An executive search firm. **Specializes in the areas of:** Administration; Computer Hardware/Software; Sales. **Positions commonly filled include:** Computer Programmer; Internet Services Manager; Marketing Specialist; MIS Specialist; Sales Rep.; Systems Analyst; Technical Writer/Editor; Telecommunications Manager. **Number of placements per year:** 100 - 199.

**WORLD HEALTH RESOURCES, INC.**
7000 Boulevard East, Guttenberg NJ 07093. 973/881-1777. **Contact:** Manager. **Description:** An executive search firm. **Specializes in the areas of:** Health/Medical. **Positions commonly filled include:** Certified Nurses Aide; Nurse; Physical Therapist.

**ZWICKER ASSOCIATES**
579 Franklin Turnpike, Suite 9, Ridgewood NJ 07450. 201/251-8300. **Contact:** Manager. **Description:** Zwicker Associates is an executive search firm. **Specializes in the areas of:** Food; Market Research.

# CONTRACT SERVICES FIRMS

**BUTLER INTERNATIONAL, INC.**
110 Summit Avenue, Montvale NJ 07645. 201/573-8000. **Contact:** Manager. **World Wide Web address:** http://www.butlerintl.com. **Description:** A contract services firm. **Corporate headquarters location:** This Location.

## CDI CORPORATION
899 Mountain Avenue, Springfield NJ 07081. 973/379-9790. **Contact:** Manager. **World Wide Web address:** http://www.cdicorp.com. **Description:** A contract services firm. **Specializes in the areas of:** Technical. **Corporate headquarters location:** Philadelphia PA.

## INTERIM TECHNOLOGY
9 Polito Avenue, 9th Floor, Lyndhurst NJ 07071. 201/392-0800. **Contact:** Manager. **World Wide Web address:** http://www.interimtechnology.com. **Description:** A contract services firm.

## JOULE INDUSTRIAL CONTRACTORS
429 East Broad Street, Gibbstown NJ 08027. 609/423-7500. **Toll-free phone:** 800/445-6853. **Fax:** 609/423-3209. **Contact:** Ken Leipert, Recruiter. **Description:** A contract services firm. **Specializes in the areas of:** Food; Light Industrial. **Positions commonly filled include:** Millwright; Pipe Fitter; Welder. **Benefits available to temporary workers:** 401(k); Dental Insurance; Life Insurance; Medical Insurance. **Corporate headquarters location:** Edison NJ. **Average salary range of placements:** $20,000 - $29,999. **Number of placements per year:** 100 - 199.

## ROTATOR STAFFING SERVICES INC.
P.O. Box 366, 557 Cranberry Road, East Brunswick NJ 08816. 732/238-6050. **Fax:** 732/238-2152. **Contact:** Dan Klein, Senior Staffing Specialist. **Description:** A contract services firm. **Specializes in the areas of:** Administration; Architecture/Construction; Computer Science/Software; Engineering; Secretarial; Technical. **Positions commonly filled include:** Architect; Biochemist; Biological Scientist; Biomedical Engineer; Chemical Engineer; Chemist; Civil Engineer; Clinical Lab Technician; Computer Programmer; Cost Estimator; Design Engineer; Designer; Draftsperson; Electrical/Electronics Engineer; Environmental Engineer; Industrial Engineer; Landscape Architect; Mechanical Engineer; Mining Engineer; MIS Specialist; Nuclear Engineer; Pharmacist; Quality Control Supervisor; Structural Engineer; Systems Analyst; Technical Writer/Editor; Telecommunications Manager. **Benefits available to temporary workers:** 401(k); Medical Insurance. **Average salary range of placements:** $30,000 - $50,000. **Number of placements per year:** 500 - 999.

## SHARP TECHNICAL SERVICES, INC.
P.O. Box 323, Mount Royal NJ 08061. 609/853-5752. **Fax:** 609/853-0780. **Contact:** Manager. **E-mail address:** resume@sharptechnical.com. **Description:** A contract services firm. **Specializes in the areas of:** Design; Engineering. **Positions commonly filled include:** Biochemist; Buyer; Chemical Engineer; Civil Engineer; Computer Programmer; Construction and Building Inspector; Cost Estimator; Design Engineer; Designer; Draftsperson; Electrical/Electronics Engineer; Environmental Engineer; Industrial Engineer; Mechanical Engineer; MIS Specialist; Purchasing Agent/Manager; Software Engineer; Structural Engineer; Systems Analyst; Technical Writer/Editor; Telecommunications Manager. **Benefits available to temporary workers:** 401(k); Credit Union; Medical Insurance; Paid Holidays; Paid Vacation. **Other area locations:** Eatontown NJ. **Average salary range of placements:** $30,000 - $50,000. **Number of placements per year:** 200 - 499.

## YOH SCIENTIFIC
30 Columbia Turnpike, Florham Park NJ 07932. 973/377-8634. **Contact:** Manager. **Description:** A contract services firm. **Specializes in the areas of:** Chemicals; Pharmaceuticals.

## YOH SCIENTIFIC
5 Independence Way, 1st Floor, Princeton NJ 08540. 609/514-1210. **Contact:** Manager. **Description:** A contract services firm. **Specializes in the areas of:** Pharmaceuticals; Scientific.

# RESUME/CAREER COUNSELING SERVICES

## A PROFESSIONAL EDGE
248 Columbia Turnpike, Florham Park NJ 07932-1210. 973/966-6963x14. **Fax:** 973/966-6539. **Contact:** Martin P. Murphy, Executive Vice President. **Description:** A career/outplacement counseling firm. **Specializes in the areas of:** Accounting/Auditing; Administration; Advertising; Banking; Computer Science/Software; Economics; Fashion; Finance; General Management; Insurance; Personnel/Labor Relations; Retail; Sales; Secretarial; Technical. **Positions commonly filled include:** Accountant/Auditor; Administrative Manager; Bank Officer/Manager; Branch Manager; Brokerage Clerk; Computer Programmer; Counselor; Customer Service Representative; Financial Analyst; Human Resources Specialist; Insurance Agent/Broker; Management

Analyst/Consultant; Management Trainee; MIS Specialist; Operations/Production Manager; Public Relations Specialist; Securities Sales Representative; Services Sales Representative; Software Engineer; Systems Analyst; Telecommunications Manager; Typist/Word Processor. **Average salary range of placements:** $20,000 - $100,000. **Number of placements per year:** 200 - 499.

## AARON CAREER SERVICES
520 Main Street, Suite 302, Fort Lee NJ 07024. 201/592-0593. **Contact:** Manager. **E-mail address:** careerw@aol.com. **Description:** A full-service resume writing and preparation service that also offers executive recruiting and career counseling.

## CAREER RESUME ADVANTAGE INC.
959 Route 46 East, Suite 101, Parsippany NJ 07054. 973/402-8777. **Toll-free phone:** 800/RESUME911. **Fax:** 973/402-6434. **Contact:** John Thorn, President. **E-mail address:** john@resume911.com. **World Wide Web address:** http://www.resume911.com. **Description:** A resume writing and career counseling service. John Thorn is a Certified Professional Resume Writer and a founding member of the National Resume Writer's Association. **Other area locations:** Hackensack NJ.

## SANDRA GRUNDFEST, ED.D.
11 Clyde Road, Suite 103, Somerset NJ 08873. 732/873-1212. **Fax:** 732/873-2584. **Contact:** Sandra Grundfest. **Description:** Provides career management counseling services. **Corporate headquarters location:** Princeton NJ.

## SANDRA GRUNDFEST, ED.D.
## CAREER MANAGEMENT SERVICES
601 Ewing Street, Suite C-1, Princeton NJ 08540. 609/921-8401. **Fax:** 609/921-9430. **Contact:** Sandra Grundfest, Principal. **E-mail address:** grundfest@worldnet.att.net. **Description:** Provides career management counseling services. Founded in 1984. **Specializes in the areas of:** Art/Design; Business Services; Education; Finance; Health/Medical; Legal; Nonprofit; Scientific. **Corporate headquarters location:** This Location.

## METRO CAREER SERVICES
784 Morris Turnpike, Suite 203, Short Hills NJ 07078. 973/912-0106. **Fax:** 973/379-5489. **Contact:** Judy Scherer, President. **E-mail address:** metcareer@aol.com. **Description:** A career transition and coaching service that generates and evaluates work alternatives and helps clients market themselves.

## PERMIAN INTERNATIONAL, INC.
227 Route 206, Flanders NJ 07836-9114. 973/927-7373. **Fax:** 973/927-7172. **Contact:** Don Marletta, President. **Description:** A career/outplacement counseling service. **Number of placements per year:** 1 - 49.

# INDEX OF PRIMARY EMPLOYERS

**NOTE:** *Below is an alphabetical index of primary employer listings included in this book. Those employers in each industry that fall under the headings "Additional employers" are not indexed here.*

# M

M&M/MARS INC. • 182
MCT DAIRIES, INC. • 182
MDA SERVICES • 220
MDY ADVANCED TECHNOLOGIES • 136
MACNAUGHTON EINSON GRAPHICS • 257
MACROMEDIA, INC. • 257
MACY'S • 269
MADGE NETWORKS • 123
MAERSK INC. • 285
MAGLA PRODUCTS INC. • 232
MAIL-WELL ENVELOPE • 251
MAINTECH • 136
GREG MANNING AUCTIONS, INC. • 105
MANNINGTON MILLS INC. • 64, 251
MARATHON ENTERPRISES INC. • 182
MARCAL PAPER MILLS, INC. • 251
MARCAM SOLUTIONS • 136
MAROTTA SCIENTIFIC CONTROLS • 243
MARS GRAPHIC SERVICES INC. • 257
MARSAM PHARMACEUTICALS INC. • 95
MATHEMATICA POLICY RESEARCH, INC. • 105
THE MATHENY SCHOOL AND HOSPITAL • 201
MATTEL INC. • 232
McBEE SYSTEMS • 257
FRANK A. McBRIDE COMPANY • 70
McCARTER THEATRE • 78
THE McGRAW-HILL COMPANIES • 257
McMASTER-CARR SUPPLY CO. • 294
MEDAREX, INC. • 96
MEDICAL ECONOMICS COMPANY • 257
MEDICAL RESOURCES, INC. • 201
MEDIQ INC. • 201
MEGASOFT, L.L.C. • 136
MELARD MANUFACTURING CORP. • 71
MELCOR CORPORATION • 163
MERCEDES-BENZ OF NORTH AMERICA • 83
WILLIAM M. MERCER, INC. • 53
MERCK & CO., INC. • 96
MERCK MEDCO RX SERVICES • 269
MERCK-MEDCO MANAGED CARE • 220
MERRILL LYNCH ASSET MANAGEMENT • 177
MERRIMAC INDUSTRIES INC. • 163
METEX CORPORATION • 172
METLIFE • 221
M.H. MEYERSON & COMPANY, INC. • 177
MICRO METRICS INC. • 163
MICRO WAREHOUSE, INC. • 269
MICROSTAR COMPUTERS INC. • 136
MIKRON INSTRUMENT CO., INC. • 243
MIKROS SYSTEMS CORPORATION • 123
MILLENIUM CHEMICALS • 114
MINOLTA CORPORATION • 243

MINUTE MAID COMPANY • 182
MISCO • 136
MITA COPYSTAR AMERICA • 294
MOBIL OIL CORPORATION • 248
MOBILECOMM • 123
MODERN MEDICAL MODALITIES CORPORATION • 201
MOKRYNSKI & ASSOCIATES • 57
THE MONEY STORE INC. • 177
MONMOUTH PARK • 78
MONTCLAIR STATE UNIVERSITY • 147
MORETRENCH AMERICAN CORP. • 169
MOTOR CLUB OF AMERICA • 221
MOTOROLA INFORMATION SYSTEMS GROUP • 136
MOUNTAIN CREEK • 78
JOSEPH L. MUSCARELLE, INC. • 71
MYRON MANUFACTURING CORP. • 232

# N

NCR CORPORATION • 136
NSI SOFTWARE • 137
NABISCO FAIR LAWN BAKERY • 182
NABISCO INC. • 182, 183
NAPP TECHNOLOGIES • 96
NATIONAL STARCH AND CHEMICAL COMPANY • 114
NATIONAL TOOL & MANUFACTURING COMPANY • 115
NATIONS, INC. • 137
NAVAL AIR ENGINEERING STATION • 61
NETWORK SPECIALISTS INC. • 137
NEUMAN DISTRIBUTORS • 96
NEW JERSEY CITY UNIVERSITY • 147
NEW JERSEY DEPT. OF LABOR • 189
NEW JERSEY DIVISION OF MOTOR VEHICLES • 189
NEW JERSEY INSTITUTE OF TECHNOLOGY • 147
NEW JERSEY INTERNATIONAL BULK MAIL • 189
NEW JERSEY MANUFACTURERS INSURANCE COMPANY • 221
NEW JERSEY RESOURCES • 292
NEW JERSEY SHAKESPEARE FESTIVAL • 78
NEW JERSEY SPORTS & EXPOSITION AUTHORITY • 78
NEW JERSEY STATE POLICE HEADQUARTERS • 189
NEW JERSEY TURNPIKE AUTHORITY • 189
NEW LISBON DEVELOPMENTAL CENTER • 201
NEW YORK GOLD BROKERS • 295
NEWARK POST OFFICE • 189
NEWARK STAR-LEDGER • 258

## Other Adams Media Books

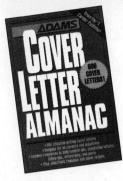

### The Adams Cover Letter Almanac

*The Adams Cover Letter Almanac* is the most detailed cover letter resource in print, containing 600 cover letters used by real people to win real jobs. It features complete information on all types of letters, including networking, "cold," broadcast, and follow-up. In addition to advice on how to avoid fatal cover letter mistakes, the book includes strategies for people changing careers, relocating, recovering from layoff, and more. $5\frac{1}{2}$" x $8\frac{1}{2}$", 736 pages, paperback, $12.95.

### The Adams Resume Almanac

This almanac features detailed information on resume development and layout, a review of the pros and cons of various formats, an exhaustive look at the strategies that will definitely get a resume noticed, and 600 sample resumes in dozens of career categories. *The Adams Resume Almanac* is the most comprehensive, thoroughly researched resume guide ever published. $5\frac{1}{2}$" x $8\frac{1}{2}$", 768 pages, paperback, $10.95.

### The Adams Job Interview Almanac

*The Adams Job Interview Almanac* includes answers and discussions for over 1,800 interview questions. There are 100 complete job interviews for all fields, industries, and career levels. Also included is valuable information on handling stress interviews, strategies for second and third interviews, and negotiating job offers to get what you want. $5\frac{1}{2}$" x $8\frac{1}{2}$", 840 pages, paperback, $12.95.

## Available Wherever Books Are Sold

If you cannot find these titles at your favorite retail outlet, you may order them directly from the publisher. BY PHONE: Call 1-800-872-5627 (in Massachusetts 781-767-8100). We accept Visa, Mastercard, and American Express. $4.95 will be added to your total order for shipping and handling. BY MAIL: Write out the full titles of the books you'd like to order and send payment, including $4.95 for shipping and handling, to: Adams Media Corporation, 260 Center Street, Holbrook, MA 02343. 30-day money-back guarantee.

**Visit our exciting job and career site at http://www.careercity.com**

From the publishers of the *JobBank* and *Knock'em Dead* books

# Visit our Web Site: www.careercity.com

...free access to tens of thousands of current job openings plus the most
comprehensive career info on the web today!

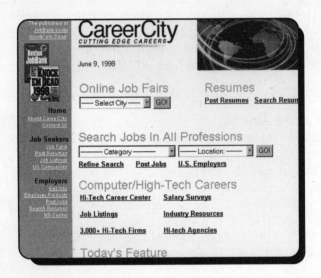

- Current job listings at top employers in all professions

- Descriptions and hot links to 27,000 major US employers

- Free resume posting gets noticed by top hiring companies

- Access to thousands of executive search firms and agencies

- Comprehensive salary surveys cover all fields

- Directories of associations and other industry resources

- Hundreds of articles on getting started, changing careers,
  job interviews, resumes, cover letters and more